Aemula Lauri

Aemula Lauri

The Royal Norwegian Society of Sciences and Letters, 1760-2010

HÅKON WITH ANDERSEN

BRITA BRENNA

MAGNE NJÅSTAD

ASTRID WALE

SCIENCE HISTORY PUBLICATIONS/USA
a division of
Watson Publishing International LLC
Sagamore Beach
2009

First published in the United States of America
by Science History Publications/USA
a division of
Watson Publishing International LLC
Post Office Box 1240, Sagamore Beach, MA 02562-1240, USA

www.shpusa.com

Library of Congress Cataloging-in-Publication Data

Aemula lauri : the Royal Norwegian Society of Sciences and Letters, 1760–2010 / Håkon With
Andersen . . . [et al.].
    p. cm.
  Includes bibliographical references and index.
  ISBN 978-0-88135-383-9
  1. Kongelige Norske videnskabers selskab—History.   I. Andersen, Håkon With.
  AS283.T9A33 2009
  020.6'22481—dc22   2009007173

Designed and manufactured in the U.S.A.

Contents

Preface

2010 marks the 250th anniversary of *Det Kongelige Norske Videnskabers Selskab*—The Royal Norwegian Society of Sciences and Letters. This book is a celebration of that event. And it is with our profound respect for and gratitude toward the society's founders, Bishop Gunnerus, Gerhard Schøning and Peter Suhm, that we present, for the first time in a language accessible to an international audience, a history of our Society, written by some of Norway's finest scholars.

It is no small accomplishment for a scientific society to reach such a venerable age. Nevertheless, we are aware that although we are on the verge of the second half of our third century, *The Royal Norwegian Society of Sciences and Letters* does not belong to that exclusive group of old and truly pioneering scientific societies of the scientific revolution of late Renaissance. Inevitably, in comparison with more prominent representatives of our kind, such as the illustrious Royal Society of London, ours will come across as a relatively modest society world. However, this does not belittle the feat of our predecessors who, despite the fact that they were situated in the periphery of academic Europe, have upheld, maintained and nurtured this scientific community through considerable historical changes and challenges. The history contained within the pages of this volume bears witness to the fact that our continuing existence is nothing short of a little miracle.

In 1760, the year of the founding of *The Royal Norwegian Society of Sciences and Letters*, Trondheim was a small town of some 7000 inhabitants who carved out an existence in an economy based on trading in fish, timber, and copper ore, and supplied raw materials to the larger and more developed proto-industrial economies of Europe. In this small town, without scholarly institutions beyond a cathedral school, three scientists—or in the terms of the period, natural historians and philosophers—met to practice and promote science. Bishop Gunnerus, Gerhard Schøning and Peter Suhm were the core members of what, due to the entrepreneurial spirit of the bishop, rapidly turned into an expanding society that obtained the right to the prefix "royal" in 1767, and that became one of the centers of the Scandinavian Enlightenment. These pioneering spirits took it upon themselves to introduce modern science to Norway, established a solid international network and the Society as a participant in the international scientific community of the day. First appearing in 1761, their journal, *Skrifter*, is today one of the oldest continuously running series of scientific publications.

This book addresses an international audience. Fifty years ago the first comprehensive history of the Society was written, in Norwegian, by professor Hans Midbøe. Due to the language barrier this publication has in reality remained inaccessible to scholars outside Scandinavia. For this reason, as well as for reasons of a more historiographical nature, the upcoming anniversary was seen as an opportunity to instigate the work on a new history of the Society, but this time to be published in English. This was not only out of desire to provide Midbøe's work with an international counterpart more in line with current concerns and interests. We chose to do so for primarily three reasons. We consider this volume a contribution to a common European history of knowledge and science of the past three centuries, and that hopefully offers fresh perspectives on well known topics. Moreover it is a central part of the history of science in Norway and thus of Scandinavia. It remains a fact that this society for more than fifty years was the only academic institution in Norway—a country without a university of its own up to 1811. Not until 1857 was a second academy of science founded, this time in Oslo, or Christiania as the capital was called at that time. Finally, we believe, although maybe not completely unbiased, that ours is a history with qualities that in themselves merit the interest of the avid reader. The shifts, changes and turning points our society has undergone and survived over the span of the last 250 years—at times through metamorphoses that at a first glance may appear to have transformed it completely—makes for entertaining reading; indeed even more so, when one also takes into account its anecdotes and episodes involving an interesting and occasionally colorful gallery of persons of learning who, their differences in temper and character notwithstanding, all share a yearning to promote science under most variable conditions.

Today the academy of *The Royal Norwegian Society of Sciences and Letters* has more than 600 members, the majority being Norwegian scholars, while others come from all over the world. We organize meetings, seminars, conferences, stimulate and finance research projects and award young promising researchers. We celebrate and honor our long history, but most of all we work to stimulate the academic world to work for a better future, to expand our knowledge and confront the problems and challenges of our day and age—a type of engagement more needed today than ever before and that carries on the Enlightenment stance that two and a half centuries ago drove the Society's founding fathers.

On a final note, we would like to extend our thanks and gratitude to those who made this tome come true: the authors, Håkon With Andersen, Brita Brenna, Magne Njåstad and Astrid Wale, as well as the editorial board that has worked closely with the authors throughout the entire process; led by professor Knut Ove Eliassen, the board has included the professors Ida Bull, Axel Christophersen, and Helge Holden. We also extend our gratitude to those who have given the economic support without which this book would not have happened: *Nordenfjelske Bykreditts Stiftelse, Adolf Øiens donasjonsfond, Det kongelige kunnskapsdepartement, I. K. Lykke, Statoil* and *Fokus bank.*

Steinar Supphellen
praeses

Introduction

KNUT OVE ELIASSEN

Tu Episcoporum omnium summus instar cometæ nova luce irradias et illuminas tenebri-cosa arctoa et de Te vere dici potest att det folk som i mörkret wandrar ser ett stort lius som uplyser hela werlden. Sero occidat Tua stella! The words are Carl von Linné's, from a let-ter to Bishop Gunnerus dated the 12th of March, 1762. An English rendering of this noteworthy passage—which begins in Latin, breaks off into the vernacular when the mode changes from direct to indirect speech, and then resumes the Latin—might be: "You the greatest of all Bishops, in the manner of a comet with new light illumine and enlighten the dark land of the North, and of You we can truly say, that the people that wanders in darkness see a great light that enlightens the whole world. May Your star go down late!"

Thus is Johan Ernst Gunnerus, the founder of *Det Kongelige Norske Videnskabers Selskab*, eulogized by the illustrious father of modern botany. Coming from a man who had been hailed by Rousseau as the greatest man living, such praise would certainly leave an impact, not merely on the addressee, but undoubtedly also on anyone else who would happen to read it (or heard it, as the 18th century's letter was, generally, a social event, read out loud to an audience, and often copied and circulated). Even if the pan-egyric also was the Swedish naturalist's way of encouraging his Norwegian counterpart and at the same time expressing his gratefulness for the samples he had received from him—and would be receiving in the following years—it still provides proof of his respect of Gunnerus, and an acknowledgment of his membership in the elite that is often referred to as "the republic of letters."

The Royal Norwegian Society of Sciences and Letters is a true born child of that broad European cultural, political and intellectual process called the Enlightenment. This his-torical phenomenon, that spanned more than a century and influenced the entire Western hemisphere, was in no way homogeneous. Hence the concerns of the French Enlightenment differed from that of its English equivalent. Marked by the political and cultural situation out of which they developed, the former was concerned with the power and ideology of the Catholic Church and the gangrenous social and political structures of feudal absolutism, while the latter—the revolution already behind it—faced religious and political problems of another kind. These differences were manifest in their respective views on the functions and value of science, as new truths and insights of the century's natural sciences were of considerable ideological consequence and more often than not considered to be at odds with those of theology—one time considered to be "the queen" of sciences.

Not surprisingly, the national accents were no less prominent in the less prestigious centers of Enlightenment: The Dutch Enlightenment differed from the Italian one, as the Scottish differed from the German, or, for that matter, the Russian from the Spanish, and so did their various understanding of religious issues. What further complicates this image is that the Enlightenment was not restricted to the capitals and centers. Enlightenment ideas were diffused and cultivated in smaller cities, in the many peripheries of Europe. Some of these places were more peripheral than others, Trondheim, a regional capital in the Lutheran Kingdom of Denmark-Norway merely a few hundred kilometers below the Arctic Circle, being an obvious case in point.

Thus, from the outset the identity and destiny of *The Royal Norwegian Society of Sciences and Letters* was marked by its geographical localization. Established in a small city, far from the dual monarchy's capital, Copenhagen, this society would become one of the centers of what one with some justification may call the "Northern Enlightenment." A particular trait of this Northern Enlightenment—and of its Norwegian version in particular—is that it was devoid of the anti-clericalism and latent atheism that fuelled its more prominent continental counterparts. Taking stock of the situation in Scandinavia, one could even be tempted to speak of a proper "Lutheran" or even "Pietistic" Enlightenment, and it has indeed occasionally been argued that the 18th century pietism of Northern Europe should be seen as an expression of an unusual and successful fusion between Enlightenment ideas, religious beliefs and political reformism. Accordingly, while the fact that one of the champions of the Enlightenment in Norway was a bishop might have appeared extraordinary from a continental perspective. From the point of view of the official State Pietism of Denmark-Norway, this was well within the order of the day.

Keeping the Northern Enlightenment's particular Lutheran and in some respects conservative character in mind the particularities of Linné's letter to Gunnerus become more explicit, and it indicates interesting aspects of the nature of the intellectual setting in which the two corresponded. The choice of language, Latin mixed with Swedish, is by itself worthy of some attention. Although most of the prominent Enlightenment figureheads were familiar with Latin, as most of them were products of Latin schools or colleges, where the classical languages still held sway as the highway to education, they generally preferred the vernacular both in correspondence and in scientific publications. Latin had become the language of an academic culture that at this time still was deeply marked by scholasticism and dogmatism. So, while Linné's choice of Latin might have to do with the fact that this was still early days in the correspondence of the two savants—they exchanged letters regularly from 1761 to 1772—it is tempting to see the botanist's use of Latin as an indication of a distinctive trait of the Scandinavian Enlightenment, that their most renowned protagonists, contrary to their continental counterparts, saw themselves not as an opposition to tradition and public authority but rather as their supporters.

Linné and Gunnerus were not adherents of "radical enlightenment;" in their world the distinction between the leaders and those led was crucial. This is curiously echoed by the shift in language; when the Swedish botanist changes perspective, and refers to the populace's judgment of Gunnerus, he switches to the vernacular. Rhetorically the passage thereby signals the parallel existence of two cultures, the Latin of the learned world, to which both Linné and Gunnerus belonged, and the vernacular of the people who "wanders in darkness." The impression is reinforced by Linné's use of elaborated panegyric metaphors and allegories borrowed from a classical, even religious register: Bishop Gunnerus is not merely a harbinger of light, but rather himself a source of enlightenment in what apparently else would have been left to an eternal darkness. And, a few years later, the good bishop *cum* natural historian would, on his return from one of his scientific excursions in the northern part of the country, be hailed by his secretary, Johan Nordahl Bruun—himself later to become bishop of Bergen—, as the new Adam, the man who for the first time bestowed upon the creatures and flowers of God's creation their true, scientific names.

Johan Ernst Gunnerus was no revolutionary. A staunch supporter of the Wolffian-Leibnizian philosophy and an adherent to its theological companion, "Physico-Theology" (or "natural theology" as it was also known as), he made his position clear in the pastoral letter that was issued to the clergy of the diocese upon his arrival in Trondheim in 1758 and printed and made public in Danish for the public benefit. Faith itself, according to Gunnerus, does not suffice for those who would like to penetrate into the deeper truths of Theology; mastery of philosophy and metaphysics is required for those would like to arrive at true insights into the laws of nature. Such profound philosophical knowledge is a necessity, and today more than ever, as the number of naturalists, deists, doubters and religious critics found within the church is increasing, Gunnerus notes. Philosophy is a requirement for the enlightened priest that would like to fulfill his public function as a servant of the church and the state in accordance with his faith.

Gunnerus was a genuine expression of that very particular Nordic phenomenon, the enlightened cleric; he was thereby also a representative of the country's administration, a civil servant for whom the interest of the state of and those of his office converged. His office was a part of the information system needed to run the conglomerate kingdom of Denmark-Norway; the clerical network of the diocese not only provided the church with the necessary channels of communication, but allowed Gunnerus, in the capacity of Bishop, to pursue and realize his mapping of Norway's natural resources by demanding of his subordinates to serve as his "scientific field assistants." As a natural historian, collecting and receiving information as well as objects, and passing these on, Gunnerus filled a double role. He served the interests of the state as those less worldly ones of science. This combination fitted well with the ideals of the period's prevalent economic theory in Denmark-Norway, the so-called *Kameralismus*, a German and Scandinavian version of mercantilism that Gunnerus was familiar with from his study days in Germany. Religion, science, enlightenment and public office thereby fused in a manner that characterizes the particularities of the Lutheran Enlightenment.

Two decades after the letter from Linné to Gunnerus, and ten years after Gunnerus' death, another, even more prestigious representative of the Lutheran Enlightenment, the citizen of Königsberg, Emmanuel Kant, famously defined enlightenment as "man's release from his self-imposed tutelage. Tutelage is the inability to make use of his understanding without guidance from another. This immaturity is self-imposed when its cause lies not in lack of understanding, but in lack of resolve and courage to use it without guidance from another. *Sapere Aude!* "Have courage to use your own understanding!"—that is the motto of enlightenment."

Kant's motto has been understood as an open defy to all forms of thought monopoly and nothing less than a call to arms challenging all individuals to assume the responsibility for their own intellectual and political freedom. However, those who have read beyond the first pages of his famous essay from 1784, "Antwortung an der Frage: Was ist Aufklärung?" will know that the introduction's apparent extensive individualism is tempered by the Prussian philosopher's distinction between public and private obligations. To be enlightened implies duties towards the state and to the community. Reasoning is an act that might be exercised individually but it finds its legitimacy when it is put in service for the common good. Thus there is little reason to be surprised that *Sapere Aude!*—originally a quote from Horace—also was the motto of a secret society of German civil servants that aimed at the propagation of Wolffian philosophy.

The society of the learned civil servant can be said to be one of the most typical expressions of the Lutheran Enlightenment. Here enlightenment is a process in which men participate collectively and where they act for the common good of the state, the nation and the people. Such was also the principle that seems to have been driving the founding fathers of *The Royal Norwegian Society of Sciences and Letters*, Gunnerus, the historians Gerhard Schøning and Peter Frederik Suhm. They might all fall in under the label of "gentleman savant" as none of them were professional scientists or scholars but they did not indulge in the learned sciences as merely a pleasurable pastime; their duties were to the common good.

Like his many German counterparts, one of Gunnerus' central concerns was the establishment of a new university, but the bishop was not driven by the desire to reform the old, but instead to establish for the first time a university in Norway. Gunnerus himself was a product of the old four faculty university. There is little reason to believe that what he had in mind was something like what was to become the Humboldt University, one of the proudest products of the German Enlightenment. However, his project stranded, and it was not until more than thirty years later that Norway was to have its first University. *Det Kongelige Frederiks Universitet* was indeed to be heavily influenced by the German university reforms, but it was placed in Christiania, the country's capital after the dissolution of the Danish-Norwegian monarchy in the aftermath of the Napoleonic wars. Trondheim was not to receive its university until the 20th century.

The legacy of Gunnerus would thus not be a Norwegian university, but a scientific society with an impressive collection of naturalia, the country's largest and most modern library, and quite considerable funds. And, last but not least, a reputation that went beyond the borders of the country. Thus befitting the values and practices of its founder, what Gunnerus bequeathed on his inheritors, was an institution for the propagation of useful knowledge, for diligence and public spirit, in other words a society charged with a mission: the spreading of light under the dark heavens of sub-arctic Europe.

Unlike most of its European counterparts, the destiny of *The Royal Norwegian Society of Sciences and Letters* was to remain in the periphery. Without any university in Trondheim that could provide a steady influx of new members, or serve as a tool for the implementation of new ideas and principles, the society had no direct interface with what was now the arena of science. Moreover, there was no court that could offer protection and money in the form of interested and enlightened benefactors. And there was no public sphere of importance, coffee houses, politicians etc. Five hundred kilometers from the country's capital, in itself quite insignificant in a European perspective, the Society had to cope with what little there was.

At the beginning of the 18th century, scientific societies were no longer the avantgarde of science; science and its institutions had changed, and the society in Trondheim along with it. The spread of knowledge and the Enlightenment of the general public rather than the practice of science, was now the main concern of the Society. And the founders of the society were long dead and gone. With them, and with the particular spirit of the Lutheran Enlightenment, and the bishop who had enrolled the organization of the diocese into the service of the society, the situation was of totally different nature. The lesson, which undoubtedly Gunnerus had already learned, was that to practice science in the periphery is to have to make do with that which is available.

For the whole of the 19th century this was also the case; turning weaknesses into strength, making use of what resources were available, the board turned the Society into a charitable institution for science and scholarship, or in modern parlance, a "research council", using its considerable fortune, bequeathed upon it through donations and gifts, to found, subsidize and finance science (thus continuing and refining a practice already begun under the aegis of Gunnerus). On the European arena the scientific societies of the century of Enlightenment had been replaced by the reformed universities as the agents of research, and the gentleman savant was gradually replaced by the salaried civil servant. While most other societies were found in cities with academic institutions, and adapted themselves to the situation by becoming forums for inter-disciplinary exchanges, social mingling and alliance building, *The Royal Norwegian Society of Sciences and Letters*, in a certain sense stuck to its original calling, the propagation of enlightenment. True to the spirit of Gunnerus prizes were handed out to skillful craftsmen and diligent farmers, and scholarships and stipends bestowed upon historians, naturalists and writers. But the Society was not any longer itself an arena for science and scholarly work; it had become an institution that saw to it that science was practiced and that knowledge was disseminated, and its central protagonists did not consider themselves scientists.

However, the Society's role as a research council was also to come to an end. Once more it was the relation to the university that became decisive, this time in the shape of two young scientists, arriving in Trondheim more or less straight out of the *Det Kongelige Frederiks Universitet*, and bent upon turning the resources of the DKNVS into a true scientific institution in line with what the times considered to be state of the art, namely a museum. With the avant-garde's disrespect for tradition and what was conceived as the dilettantism and amateurism of their forerunners, Wilhelm Storm and

Karl Rygh undertook the establishment of a museum that true to their respective train-
ings—as well as to the interests of the Society's erstwhile founder, the Bishop Gunnerus
—in that its focus was on natural history and antiquities and archeology, respectively.

Even though the two had little respect for their scientific contributions of the predecessors, including the efforts of the first generation, they nevertheless continued that
parallel perspective of natural history and history proper that had also been the main
interests at the time of Gunnerus. Nevertheless, this meant the end of the prize competitions and no more prize money were handed out to the diligent and ingenious farmer
who might have come up with a new way of tilling the earth, thatching the roof, or a
new way of setting up the loom. This did not mean, however, that this was the end to
the Society's civil responsibilities and its calling to educate the populace. The new
museum became extremely popular among the citizens of Trondheim who crowded
the site in numbers beyond those that any other regular attraction had managed.

The museum might have been the terminal station in the permanent metamorpho-
sis undergone by the Society since its inception, had it not been for the establishment
in Trondheim in 1910 of a polytechnic university, The Norwegian Institute of Technology, five years after the dissolution of Norway's personal union with Sweden. For the
first time in its history the Society would have to coexist with a university college. The
society had, however, changed character completely, all its resources over the last
decades having been invested in the establishment and running of a research museum.
The end result of several years of conflicting interests between the newly arrived scientists, eager to revive the Society as a forum for multidisciplinary exchange as well as a
social arena, and the champions of the museum bent on safeguarding and continuing
the research center they had succeeded in establishing, was a structure that was to
remain, although modified, throughout most of the century: The museum and the
library on the one hand and the Society on the other, all of them, however, rightful heirs
to the name, *Det Kongelige Norske Vitenskabers Selskab*. As a consequence of the process
of the reorganizing of the university in Trondheim in the 1970's and 1980's, when both
the museum and the library became separate institutions within the larger institutional
framework of the University of Trondheim, are the remaining parts from 2002 again
united under a common board as an academy and a foundation.

It might be a difficult task to identify the large patterns underpinning and remaining constant through the many shifts and changes in the history of *The Royal Norwegian Society of Sciences and Letters*. Various interpretations may present themselves.
Changes in structure as well as in the activities undertaken are considerable, and are
also behind the organization of this book into four parts: From enlightened scientific
society to research council and then museum before finally settling into the form of a
20th century academy. The different nature of the four quite distinct periods notwithstanding, a few constants might be discerned in the Society's history. First and foremost
of these is doubtlessly the Society's peripheral position. At the same time a resource and
a challenge, periphery on the one hand meant a privileged access to natural data and
objects that were considered both exotic and important by the rest of Europe. The pioneers of the Society were thus in possession of assets that made them attractive partners

for more centrally placed participants of the Enlightenment. On the other hand, periphery also meant limited resources both monetary and intellectually, not to mention slower and more limited access to the new insights of science. Moreover, the society has throughout its history, shown a remarkable reluctance to involve itself in explicit political issues; the civil servant, in both the usual and the literal sense, as the server of the public, has delivered the role model of the society's leading men (and occasionally women). Finally, and this might have to do with the last point, the levelheaded mentality of that particular Nordic Enlightenment might really be the trait that on the most profound level, links the Society's activities from the 18th century to the 21st. This book, taking the society's motto, *Æmula Lauri*, "The Rival of the Laurel Tree," as its title, recounts the story of this less than ordinary scientific society located three degrees below the Arctic circle.

Acknowledgments

The authors would like to thank and express their gratitude to a number of persons who have provided invaluable help in their work. To John Peter Collett, Kim Helsvig, Inge Jonsson and Kjetil Kvist who contributed with ideas and their knowledge at our first seminar. On our joint seminar with the authors of the history of the *Norwegian University of Science and Technology* in Trondheim we were joined by Harald Nissen, Thomas Brandt, Ola Nordal and the late Yngve Sandhei Jacobsen with whom we could discuss and exchange ideas on writing institutional history. We would furthermore like to express our debt to *The Royal Norwegian Society of Sciences and Letters* which gave us excellent work opportunities, and in particular praeses Steinar Supphellen and the general secretary Yngve Espmark who have followed the project closely on behalf of the Society. Turid Fredagsvik has been a constant support in arranging our meetings and sorting out all practical problems.

We have received great support from the employees at the Special Collection at the *Gunnerus Library*, Ellen Alm, Ove Wolden, and Stein Johansen who has also provided critical analysis of our work. The former librarian at the library, Monica Aase has given us valuable information, as well as reading through the whole manuscript.

In addition we would like to thank the following individuals for their generous sharing of sources and ideas, Mie Hidle, Jakob Maliks, Erling Sandmo and Elin Strøm. We would also like to thank Ernst Bjerke, who researched archives in Copenhagen for the project. The *Institut für Wissenschaftsgeschichte*, Göttingen provided a two week stay for one of the authors, to whom Wolfgang Böker proved invaluable in helping to find relevant material. Arild Stubhaug has also been a constant inspiration through our meetings.

Finally we would like to thank Unn Kristin Daling who has done an excellent job locating and organizing illustrations. Last but not least we extend our thanks to the book committee, Ida Bull, Axel Christophersen, Knut Ove Eliassen and Helge Holden, for their important work, support and critically helpful comments.

PART I

1760–1805

1

Light in the periphery

"Our fatherland was enveloped by darkness, its sight obliterated by haze," the historian Gerhard Schøning wrote in his obituary for Johan Ernst Gunnerus, whom he praised as the founding father of the Royal Norwegian Society of Science. Gunnerus, Schøning added, was the man who finally succeeded in bringing to Norway the light of science which had been ignited in most other European countries. This country with no university, no academy, no scientific society, no public library, no cabinets of naturals, medals, arts or antiquities should look upon herself in shame because she was surrounded by sister countries, albeit poor, who were endowed with these institutions.[1] In 1773 bishop Gunnerus died on one of his visitation journeys, after having strived to establish in Trondheim[2] precisely a library, a collection, a scientific society and a plan for a Norwegian university. He had brought the torch of science to the north, chasing the haze away. Hailed by Linnaeus as the Pliny of the North and by Johan Nordahl Brun, the poet, secretary of the Society of Science and later bishop of Bergen, as the rightful heir of Adam the name-giver, Gunnerus had succeeded in bringing to Norway what the country lacked: Enlightenment and knowledge.[3]

From the mid 18th century, scientific societies mushroomed throughout Europe, and even Trondheim, one of the northernmost towns on the continent could in 1760 witness the establishment of a scientific society of its own, a fact which has led the historian of scientific societies James McClellan III to state: "That an official learned society could arise just three degrees south of the Arctic Circle is eloquent testimony to the power of the learned society movement in the eighteenth century and to how much, again, the learned society was the model for the institutionalization of science and culture in the period."[4] McClellan situates the scientific society established in Trondheim within the broad "learned society movement" of the 18th century. His description of

---

[1] Schøning, "Tale over Johan Ernst Gunnerus."
[2] The name of the town was spelled in different ways during this period: Tronhjem, Tronhiem, Throndhjem, etc. For this reason we have chosen a uniform spelling, used today, Trondheim. In English the city was called Drontheim, in German Druntheim.
[3] Linnaeus cited in Amundsen, *Johan Ernst Gunnerus*, 29. ". . . Gunnerus, den største biskop jeg kjenner, den nordiske Plinius . . . ." Brun, *Naturens Navnedag*.
[4] McClellan, *Science Reorganized* 126–7.

this broad social and intellectual movement gives an important clue to why by the end of the 1750s members of a small elite in Trondheim should experience the *need* for a scientific society and take it upon themselves to establish one. They wanted a space for doing, disseminating and legitimizing science in the broad sense of *Wissenschaften*, and they managed to create this space. Why a scientific society was the solution to their heartfelt need will be a major topic in the pages to come. We will follow the main agents and acts establishing the Trondheim society, and we will at the same time ask how we can account for why these people, and especially Gunnerus, went through such extraordinary efforts to establish this modest meeting place. What ambitions could a scientific society satisfy?

The history of the establishment of the Trondheim society is saturated with the ambitions of intellectuals who had their education and aspiring professional life from Copenhagen and the continent. They were acculturated to ways of living a learned and social life which was acquired elsewhere, a way of living they tried to recreate in Trondheim. But it is also a history of the creation of a space of their own making, not only an import of a form of sociability and intellectuality from other cities, but of setting up an organization adapted to the particular topographical, societal, and intellectual makeup of Norway and the town of Trondheim.

Trondheim was a modestly sized city in the conglomerate state of Denmark-Norway, which consisted of several languages, political territories and dependencies and cultures. It contained small colonies in India, some islands in the West Indies, trading posts in Africa, the duchies of Schleswig and Holstein, as well as Greenland, Iceland, the Faeroe Islands,—and Norway. An absolute monarchy was introduced in 1660, but the landed gentry in Denmark, Schleswig and Holstein still held considerable power during most of the eighteenth century. Poor relief, schooling and jurisdiction were the responsibility of the gentry. Norway was seen as an independent demarcated territory with specific cultural traits most notably in jurisdiction and the tradition of free-holding farmers, and the kingdom was frequently labeled the twin kingdoms. The total population was about two million, of whom about 800,000 lived in Norway and a similar number in Denmark. The capital Copenhagen was the most important city in northern Europe with its 70,000 inhabitants. The second largest city was the trading city of Bergen on the west coast of Norway with about 14,000 inhabitants. Trondheim and its 7,500 inhabitants ranked in the third group of cities.[5] Up until Denmark lost Norway in 1814 in the aftermath of the Napoleonic Wars, Norway was the lesser part in the twin state, neither a colony nor a separate country, but something in between. The exact nature of this relationship is difficult to unravel. It also shifted over time, but one of the especially interesting features of the establishment of the scientific society in Trondheim and the science conducted there is how we can see it both as part of an internal colonization project within the conglomerate state and as an attempt at forging

---

[5] 1769 numbers. See for a more thorough discussion of the size of the different towns in Norway as well as their social composition Sætra, "Kristiansand som sentrum . . . ."

a distinctly Norwegian scientific enterprise—bringing the light of science to Norway and Norwegians.[6]

The north as a space for careers and adventures

Fortunate circumstances brought three of the most ambitious intellectuals in the Kingdom of Denmark-Norway to Trondheim at the same time, the historians Gerhard Schøning and Peter Friderich Suhm, and the theologian Johan Ernst Gunnerus. The historians arrived first. Benjamin Dass, the rector at *Katedralskolen* in Trondheim (the Cathedral School), was tired of teaching and of the constant quarrels with the bishop, who claimed authority over the school's affairs, so he offered his talented pupil Schøning his chair at the school on the condition that he be granted a pension.[7] Schøning came from a modest background in Lofoten in the north of Norway, had prepared for university at the cathedral school in Trondheim, before going to Copenhagen to study, and was awarded his Magister degree in theology at the University of Copenhagen in 1748. Dass supported him during his education and later when trying to make a career as a man of letters in Copenhagen. When Schøning accompanied Dass back to Trondheim in 1751, a young aspiring intellectual joined them, the 23-year-old Peter Friederich Suhm.

Suhm, a Danish-born man of good pedigree and gracious manners, had little money to pursue his interest, intellectual work. As an aristocrat, the law would be his gateway to the higher offices he was destined for, but by the time he came to Trondheim he had resigned from his post at the courts to devote himself fully to the study of history and languages. He had already published translations of Latin and French texts, and published his first work in history before venturing to Trondheim. He went to Trondheim to compete for the hand of the wealthiest known heiress in the kingdom, Karen Angell. His success was immediate; with the aid of good helpers they were allegedly engaged within one week of his arrival.

Benjamin Dass returned to Copenhagen and established himself in the intellectual elite of the town, as a broker of books and intellectual gossip for the Trondheim couple and others—leaving for posterity a treasure of letters which describe the "literary news" of the capital.[8] Dass was also an important link for Suhm and Schøning who through Dass had unique contacts in Copenhagen. In Trondheim these two men of very different origins, far apart both in birth and social standing, forged an intense working companionship. They met twice a week to study English and Italian, but foremost, as Suhm later wrote, "to reflect on the old History of the North, wherein we

---

[6] For discussions of science in the North as a form of colonial science, see Sörlin, "Ordering the World" and idem, "Rituals and Resources."

[7] DBL, Daae, *Tronhjems Stifts geistlige Historie.*

[8] The letters to Suhm are reprinted in Suhm, *Kammerherre og Kongelig.*

investigated the difficult and dark events."[9] They set themselves the task of enlightening the history of Denmark and Norway, their respective native countries and printed *Forbedringer til den gamle danske og norske Historie* (*Corrections in the Old Danish and Norwegian History*) in 1757. They were able to keep and uphold their position in the Danish kingdom of letters even as residents of the provincial city of Trondheim. Suhm was elected member of the Danish literary and historical society, and in 1758 both he and Schøning were elected members of the Society of Sciences in Copenhagen.

There are no signs that Suhm and Schøning were impeded in their careers and work in Trondheim—they produced scientific work, they worked on a collective scientific enterprise, and they had the means and materials to work. This is not least visible through the journal Suhm established in 1761. He founded one of the first Norwegian journals, *Tronhiemske Samlinger*, a one-man journal in the spectator genre.[10] A testimony to his wide interests and his ample access to literature is the sheer number of books he reviewed for this journal over a period of five years—833 works chiefly written in Latin and French—categorized under the telling titles, "On Good New Books" and "On Bad New Books."[11]

In working as intellectuals in Trondheim, Suhm and Schøning proved that not only could one conduct learned studies in Trondheim, it was also possible to author books which proved their worth in the learned Danish-Norwegian environment. Their work was a pretext to the establishment of the scientific society in 1760, but they would themselves only be active there for a few years. The marriage agreement and the conflicts Suhm had with his wife's uncle, Thomas Angell, who administered their estate, forced him to stay in Trondheim until 1765 when it became clear that the couple would inherit only half of the Angell estate. Suhm was to be the royal historian of Denmark, and when he passed away in 1798 he was considered one of the most famous intellectuals of the century. Schøning's interest was old Norse history, raising the Norwegian and Nordic antiquities and history to the height of Classical antiquity. He left Trondheim in 1765, the same year as Suhm, when he was offered the post of professor in Denmark at the noble academy of Sorø. When he passed away in 1780 he had not only been a professor in Sorø, but was working in the prestigious office as an archivarian of the king's ministry. He left an impressive contribution to Norwegian history in three volumes which ended in the year 1000 A.D. Only five years after the establishment of the Society, two of the three members had left town, a fact which was consequential for the fate of the Society.

---

[9] Suhm in Schøning, *Norges Riges historie*, bind III. Fortale. "Udi al den Tid vi vare sammen i Tronhiem saae jeg ham bestandig tvende Gange om Ugen hos mig, og vare vi da i det mindste sammen fire Timer. Denne Tid anvendte vi til at lære os indbyrdes det Engelske og Italienske Sprog, men i sær at overveie Nordens gamle Historie, hvor vi da undersøgte de vanskelige og mørke Begivenheder, som deri forekomme."

[10] The year before another journal had been started in Christiania, by a bishop's hand, it was a moral journal.

[11] Aase and Hård, "'Det norska Aten'," 45.

From centre to periphery?

In 1758 bishop Johan Ernst Gunnerus arrived in Trondheim. Suhm and Schøning were well aware of his qualifications and peculiarities, informed as they were through Dass' correspondence. Dass had been quite scornful in 1755 in his depictions of the self-affirming Gunnerus who had burst onto the Copenhagen intellectual scene, but three years later Gunnerus was warmly welcomed in Trondheim, especially by Schøning, who was happy to have a new bishop as his superior as rector (principal) at the cathedral school. Gunnerus was by Danish-Norwegian standards a great learned man. He was portrayed as "a profound philosopher, one that left others far behind."[12] To Trondheim he brought unquestionable academic credentials, administrative power and personal ambition. Full of energy dedicated to transforming the society to which he had come, he made it accommodate his own ambitions. Through his background and the way he directed his life in Trondheim, we can follow the directions of his actions— addressed to a public of the learned classes of Trondheim, to the elite in Copenhagen and finally to the community of scholars in Jena, where he had spent most of his professional life. His background accounts for these different public forums, but it is also important to keep in mind the role these publics played when his role in the establishment of the scientific society in Trondheim is to be understood.

When Gunnerus was appointed bishop, he had no previous personal experience in this position, not even as a priest for that matter.[13] Born in Christiania in 1718 into a family impoverished by the death of the father, the town physician, the brilliant young Gunnerus—according to his own account—was helped by patrons to obtain a degree at the Latin school, and later to pursue studies in theology in Copenhagen.[14] As was normal for students with little means, he did not rest for long in Copenhagen, even though his altogether two years in the city were more than many priests had spent at the university. After spending some time in his hometown Christiania, Gunnerus left for Halle in 1742 on a royal grant, where he studied broadly: philosophy, theology, Biblical philology, universal history, natural and Roman law, mathematics and physics.

Halle was the preferred university for the pietistic King Christian VI, and a rescript had been issued in 1741 stating that all theological students from Denmark-Norway should study with two distinctive professors, Francke and Lange, the first the son of the pietistic reformer and the latter responsible for expelling Christian Wolff from the university 20 years earlier. However, at the time Gunnerus arrived, Frederik II had ascended to the throne in Prussia, and the aging Wolff had recently returned to Halle with his systematic rationalistic philosophy of Leibnizian flavor. Gunnerus followed his

---

[12] Cited in Pontoppidan, *Natural History*, 249.

[13] The literature on Gunnerus is broad, but no substantially new information has appeared during the latter years. The best sources are thus his autobiographic notes in Worm, *Forsøg til et Lexicon*, DBL, NBL, Daae, *Throndjems Stifts*, Thrap, *Gunnerus*, Gunnerus, *Mindeblade*.

[14] The main and only sources for his earlier years are is his own autobiographical notes printed in Worm, *Forsøg til et Lexicon*.

lectures in physics and natural law, and was deeply influenced by Wolff and German metaphysics in his own work.

In 1744 Gunnerus moved on to Jena, together with two noblemen from Kurland for whom he served as private tutor (*hovmester*). Here he obtained his Magister degree in 1745 with economic support from his employers. This enabled him to start a career as a private lecturer, an occupation which also gave him time to author books on theology, philosophy, and natural law.[15] When Gunnerus visited the University of Jena it was far from the bustling intellectual centre it would later become. The period has been described as "calm," but we should also add that this is viewed in relation to the prominent status the university acquired in the late 18th century. Jena University was at the time one of the four major German Protestant Universities, along with Halle, Leipzig and Göttingen, which all had between 600 and 1000 students. Among these, Jena was considered the university of the paupers (*universitas pauperum*), due to the relative lack of nobles. The student group was dominated by the lower or middle classes. Still the city had a flourishing social intellectual life, judged by the number and varieties of civic societies. Six learned societies existed by the time Gunnerus left. In addition there was a Masonic lodge, "Zu den drei Rosen," established in 1744/45.[16] Gunnerus was among the founding members and the teacher who would inspire Gunnerus's most important work, Joachim Georg Darjes, became the master of the lodge and remained in this position all through Gunnerus's stay in Jena.[17] Gunnerus published widely in Jena, his main work being the eight-volume *Erklärung des Natur und Völker-Rechts nach dem Grundsätzen des hrn Darjes*. Gunnerus embraced Darjes' main tenets, especially hailing him for giving the true Christian useful philosophical help, but ended up in a dispute with him on the interpretation of will and freedom, but only on minor details.[18] Still, both the organizational life and not least Darjes himself must be seen as formative influences on Gunnerus. Darjes was a theoretical academician but also an important practical reformer in Jena. He was also important for the mid-century development of Cameralist economic theory in Germany, an important current of thought for the politics in Denmark-Norway and not least for Gunnerus. In 1770 Darjes would accept the invitation to become a member of the Trondheim society.

In Jena Gunnerus established a reputation as a lecturer, first as a *Magister legens* giving public lectures, and from 1753 as a member (*adjunctus*) of the philosophical faculty. He gave lectures in philosophy, mathematics and theology. Offered the position as rector (principal) of the cathedral school, he declined, insisting instead on a university

---

[15] As will be treated in Chapter four, Gunnerus's enlightened practices were a product of German Aufklärung, informed by the reconciliation of Pietism and Wolffianism. See Clarke: "The Death of Metaphysics."

[16] The names of the founding members are to be found in Bauer, "Freimaurerei, Geheimgesellschaften."

[17] For Darjes see Bauer and Müller, "Zwischen Theologie und praktischen Wissenschaften" and *Biographisch-Bibliographisches Kirchenlexicon*.

[18] Selmer, *Opplysningsmenn*, 23–28.

career. Whether Gunnerus was viewed as a profound philosopher or a lesser academic in the learned world of Germany is disputed. Notably there has been a tendency to downplay his role as an academic in Jena. He certainly left no lasting traces as a philosopher and theologian there, but he did leave as a respected member of the philosophical faculty. For his farewell ceremony a cantata and a poem were performed in his honor, hailing him especially for his abilities in teaching, "Er führt uns ohne Stoltz den graden Weg zur Wahrheit/ Er lieset uns, nicht Sich. In allzeit heller Klarheit."[19] However, his philosophical works were also praised as eternal memories of his wisdom in this program which was attested by more than one hundred students.[20] In 1754 he was summoned by the minister Johan Ludvig Holstein to serve as professor and pastor at Herlufsholm, the oldest and most prestigious boarding school in Denmark, and moved to Copenhagen in 1755. Wanting to stay close to the university, he managed to exchange his new parish with a position that would enable him to lecture at the university. For the next few years he gave an astonishingly high number of lectures, up to four a day. Importantly he also served as tutor to the sons of one of the powerful ministers, Adam Gottlob von Moltke.

In an audience with King Frederik V in 1758, Gunnerus received his calling as bishop of Trondheim. This came as a surprise, "contrary to all my thoughts and expectations," as he later recalled.[21] The calling has led to a number of theories as to why he was removed from Copenhagen, a question which has to be left to speculation due to a lack of sources.[22] Was the calling a reward or punishment, and did he leave voluntarily or reluctantly? The title of bishop meant that Gunnerus had acquired the position of one the most powerful men in Norway, a territory with only four bishops, and in this absolutist protestant monarchy a bishop's duties were wide-ranging, implying the leadership over school, church, and welfare. It was also a well-paid position. So it was a substantial promotion. But due to the rather distant location of Trondheim, a position here could also be regarded as more of a demotion, or banishment, rather than a promotion. Numerous writers have taken it for granted that Gunnerus left reluctantly and accordingly there must have been reasons for expelling him from the capital. Was he moved because he broke off an engagement and became the talk of the town? This happened late in 1755. Allegedly he excused his broken vow by referring to his impotence resulting from venereal disease.[23] This could be, of course, both a reason to get him out of town—breaking a marriage vow was a punishable offence—and a reason for

---

[19] Gunnerus, *Dem HochEhrwürdigen.*

[20] Gunnerus, *Dem HochEhrwürdigen.*

[21] Gunnerus, *Hans Opvækkelige Hyrde=Brev,* 4.

[22] New studies by historian Ernst Bjerke in the archives in Copenhagen have not brought additional information that can explain this.

[23] He thereby acquired the nicknames of "Professor Gonorhæus" and "Professor Impotent." *Slekten Holmboe fra 1944,* 256. In: O. Holmboes "Haand-Bog fra 1751–1773." November 1755: "Professor Gunerus opsloeg med Jomfrue Hagen under lidderlig Paaskud sc. at han selv var impotent og havde Fransoser, hvorfor han fik det Øgenavn Professor Gonorhæus."

him to aspire for a position elsewhere. But as this happened late in 1755, it hardly explains that he left almost three years later.[24]

It has also been claimed that he was unpopular with the other professors because of his modern, Wolffian and popular philosophy and theology. This is of course possible, but could at best be seen as a reason for not giving him a post as a regular professor at the university.[25] The appointment of Gunnerus as bishop could, after all, be seen as a promotion, and we do not have any indication that he actually went to Trondheim against his own will, except the way he phrased his calling as appearing "unexpected." Gunnerus was a man without an inheritance, and, moreover, was a big spender—he would probably gladly accept a higher salary. And as Gunnerus was of international fame, giving highly successful lectures and writing extensively on themes which were not at odds with the political system, there would have to have been a very good reason for wanting to expel him to Trondheim.

If we consider the north as a region of expectation and political ambition, rather than as a backward remote outpost, we could also argue that the administration had positive reasons for Gunnerus's work in Trondheim. Evidently Gunnerus was on good terms with the powerful chancellor Moltke, whose sons he tutored. At least two reasons can be suggested as to why he would be sent to Trondheim. Firstly, at this time the new bishops in Norway were Norwegians, and Gunnerus was a likely candidate who was free to enter into duty. Another reason could have been the wish to place a scientifically adept bishop in Trondheim. Perhaps Gunnerus's strong scientific ambitions would enable him to enlighten the dark north, and make the resources attainable for science and the economy? One important argument against this interpretation is that before going to Norway, Gunnerus had neither credentials as an empirical scientist, nor as a writer on economic matters. Nonetheless, he is quite explicit in his own *Flora Norvegica*, which was published in 1766, that he had a mission in Norway. He stated "that this duty and this task were given to me not only so that I should devote myself to science, but also so that I should enlighten in the greatest possible degree, and not even that being enough, I should inspire others to do their best to the benefit of science and the Fatherland."[26] We can deduce that Gunnerus had a mission; whether it was given

---

[24] See letters from Dass to Suhm in Suhm, *Kammerherre og Kongelig*, 227. Nov. 15th 1755. "Prof. Gunnerus er i disse Dage Byens Snak og Fabel, eftersom han har ophævet sin offentlige Forlovelse med Jomfru hagen, Fru Kratzensteins Søster. Paa Jomfruen skal han ej have Noget at udsætte, men han har tilskrevet Prof. Kratzenstein, at han selv var plaget af visse Svagheder. Endel vil mene, at man ved Proces vil tvinge ham til at erstatte Jomfruen hendes mange Omkostninger paa Møbler . . . , men andre sige, at man vil lade ham gaae for den han er. Han holder nu Collegia over Jus Natur., Logic og Metaphys. (for at vise, kan jeg troe, at han er større Theoreticus end Practicus), og skal have temmeligt Tilløb, særdeles af Regentsianer."

[25] His teachings were also followed widely up after he left Copenhagen, where lectures were given by no less than five different adjuncts over Gunnerus's various writings during autumn term 1759 and spring term 1760. See Nyerup, *Historisk-statistiske skildring*.

[26] Cited in Ramberghaug, *Biskop Gunnerus*, 58. Translated from Latin by Marek Thue Kretschmer. "Derfor mener jeg at denne plikt og dette arbeid var meg gitt ikke bare for at jeg skulle ofre meg for vitenskapen, men også for at jeg skulle opplyse så meget som mulig, og ikke nok med det; jeg skulle dessuten anspore andre til å gjøre sitt beste for vitenskapen og fedrelandet."

him by God or the king, or both, we do not know. And evidently, Gunnerus's actions in Trondheim and the diocese were very much in line with the contemporary practices and politics of the ministry in Copenhagen.

Chronicle of a Society foretold

Arriving in Trondheim in 1758, Gunnerus most probably brought with him plans for the establishment of a learned society, but his assignment was to be the spiritual head of a huge diocese stretching from Romsdalen to the Russian border. His duties were extensive: To supervise deans, ministers and parish clerks, churches, hospitals, schools, and poor-houses in the whole diocese. Bishops were religious superintendents in a monopoly system where only one religion was accepted, and deviants punished. They were first and foremost loyal civil servants to the king, and they controlled, administered, and judged according to the king's will. They were also cogs in the most powerful administrative organization of the kingdom, the Church. On the one hand, the king's decrees were brought out to the subjects as proclamations and propaganda; on the other hand, information traveled the opposite direction in the form of careful visitation reports and tabulations of living and dead. The bishop would report back to the central administration on numerous matters, including the knowledge of the Bible to be found in the parishes, the voices of the ministers, their ability to ignite their subjects and the moral and religious standards both of ministers and the population.[27]

Soon after his appointment, Gunnerus issued a pastoral letter to the clergy of the diocese expressing his theological philosophy and dogmas, but emphasis was elsewhere: He expressed how he expected the priests to cultivate knowledge, on a range from oratory and mathematics to metaphysics. "We are called Learned, Well and High Learned," he explained. "Therefore, it would be a great shame for us, my brothers, if we did not aim at well-founded knowledge."[28] Gunnerus encouraged the priests to produce learned papers, first by showing all that had been previously accomplished in this supposedly unlearned diocese, in the form of an intellectual bibliography of what learned men had produced when living in the diocese and what learned men the diocese had produced, listing all written works of merit. Here were examples to be followed. A compilation of what had already been achieved could encourage the ministers to see themselves as the learned men they were, according to Gunnerus. Insisting that his ministers were well and highly learned, he performed a rhetorical game in a country where most ministers would have only a rudimentary university education. But he continued by urging his priests to serve the Church and the Fatherland through their learned papers.

He also presented his ambition to establish a learned society, where the priests could present their texts, in "Oratory, poetry, natural and other history, physics, the

---

[27] See for the duties of a bishop Supphellen: *Den politiske bisp*; Horstbøl: "Pietism and the Politics."
[28] Gunnerus, *Hans Opvækkelige Hyrde=Brev*, 20. "Vi heder Lærde, Vel= og Højlærde. Det vilde derfor være en stoer Skam for os, mine Brødre, om vi ikke beflittede os paa grundig Lærdom."

intent and divine hallmarks of natural things, economy, *Psychologia Empirica* and other subjects that . . . can be treated in a beautiful and pleasurable way, and do not exceed the horizon of the reasonable but untrained."[29] A pastoral letter urging priests to pursue scientific studies, and at that even in the form of secular sciences, was totally unprecedented. Such a letter would normally contain theological explorations and practical advice, which this also would do, but it is the irregular tenets of the pastoral letter which interests us here. The additional twist is that he wanted the priests to "popularize," to work as enlighteners for the reasonable, but uneducated. It would please me, he writes, if those of you who were capable would present your insights, and so "serve the Public in one way or another."[30]

In the pastoral letter, the ministers were also told to set an example for their congregations. Teach them both through advice and example how to understand their houses and improve their circumstances, insisted the bishop, and "haul the peasant under his arms and show him [. . .] how he can take better advantage of his land and his other assets."[31] Thus the priest's efforts should be directed both to a wider community of learning in which they would take part, and to serving as models of practical farming, living examples of the rational tenure of the earth.

The priests in Norway were thinly spread out in a topographically challenging landscape. Around 1750, there were about 480 priests in the entire country.[32] Their income would often be meager, their contact with others than fishermen and farmers scarce. But they were the elite and there were not many others to apply to, if spreading enlightened ideas and practices to the population was the goal. In Gunnerus's "evocative" pastoral letter, historian Trygve Lysaker asserts, "Gunnerus stood forth as the spiritual authority which had something new and important to convey to the clergy. If the men of the church shall be able to counter the anti-clerical tendencies, a spiritual renewal and rearmament is necessary."[33]

However, when the pastoral letter created a stir, at least in Copenhagen, it was not because of the theological content. It was the news that a learned society was about to be formed that enticed the public in Denmark in 1759. Dass wrote to Suhm that they longed to get hold of the pastoral letter, both the German and the Danish version, and

---

[29] Gunnerus, *Hans Opvækkelige Hyrde=Brev*, 31. "Oratorie, Poesie, den naturlige og anden Historie, Physik, de naturlige Tings Hensigt og Guddommelige Øjemerke, Oeconomie, *Psychologica Empirica*, og andre ting, som, og for saa vidt, de lader sig afhandle paa en smuk og behagelig Maade, og ikke overstiger fornuftige Ustuderedes Horizont, bliver derudi vort Øjemerke."

[30] Gunnerus, *Hans Opvækkelige Hyrde=Brev*, 21. "Og paa det at og andre, som ere uden for, kunde see Eders Lærdom, saa vilde jeg ikke lidet fornøye mig, om De iblant Eder, som vare duelige dertil, lode undertiden nogle Prøver paa Deres indsigt komme for Lyset, hvorved de kunde tjene Publico paa een eller anden Maade."

[31] Gunnerus, *Hans Opvækkelige Hyrde=Brev*, 40. ". . . griber Bonden under Armene og viiser ham, fornemmelig ved deres eget Exempel, hvorledes han bedre kan benytte sig af sin Jord og andre Ejendeele."

[32] Mannsåker, *Det norske presteskapet*, 21.

[33] Lysaker, *Nidaros erkebispestol og bispesete*, 332.

they were eager to know the plans of the society. Was it true, Dass wondered, that the only members were Schøning, Gunnerus and Mr Abilgaard at Røraas? And were the rumors that the son of minister Moltke would become *præses*, the president, true?[34] We do not know what Suhm answered, but his description of what happened in Trondheim was printed in his much later *Characteristics of Schøning*. "Gunnerus, who wanted to make his native country Norway as famous and enlightened in sciences as are the most renowned countries in Europe, proposed immediately after his arrival in 1758 that Schøning and I establish a learned Society, so that the three of us would immediately start writing, and when some treatises were ready, allow a volume in print without waiting for more collaborators." Together with the pastoral letters and the letters from Dass, this is the clearest indication that these three men were to form the core of the Society, and that they started discussing it as soon as Gunnerus arrived in town, based on his initiative.[35] Apparently it also took some time before what they had formed could be called a "society." It was not decided to make it into a proper society before 1760, Suhm would later write.[36]

The Society was public before it was real, that is, the pastoral letter announced a learned society as a vision before there was any reality to it. The Society was used by Gunnerus as a motivating force in his relations with the priests. The rumor that the son of the most powerful minister could become *vice-præses* is an indication that the idea of the Society was conceived as a statement directed at the Copenhagen elite. Finally, the very swift translation of the pastoral letter into German could be a sign that Gunnerus wanted to relate to his old friends and colleagues in Jena—"I am still one of you," it is like he is saying, I am a missionary spreading light and science in the far north. In 1761 the first fruit of the work was issued as the *Tronhiemske Skrifter* (Writings from Trondheim) by *Tronhiemske Selskab*, the Society of Trondheim.

---

[34] Suhm, *Kammerherre og Kongelig Historiographus*, 1798, 279–80. Letter from Dass February 3rd 1759. "Men hvorvidt er det kommet med det ny oprettede lærde Selskab i Trondhjem? jeg har i kort Tid havt tvende Breve fra Rector Schøning, men han melder ej et Ord derom, og her have vi dog havt det Rygte, at den unge Grev Moltke er udvalgt til Præses, og sluttelig bliver Hans Højærværdighed Vice-præses. Af Membris har vi her ej hørt flere nævne end min Hr. Etatsraad, Rector Schøning, og Hr. Abildgaard paa Røraas. Vel siger man: *tres faciunt collegium;* men uden Tvivl ere der vel flere indlemmede i Selskabet, hvorom jeg ønsker nærmere Underretning, samt hvordan Indretningen er, og hvad der skal forhandles . . . Især længes vi her meget efter at see det udkomne Hyrdebrev saa vel paa tydsk som paa dansk, ligesaa en Gjenpart af det, som i Christiania er udkommet. Min herre maa bede Rector Schøning, at han ingenlunde glemmer med første Lejlighed at sende disse Rariteter."

[35] Suhm in Schøning, *Norges Riiges Historie bind III. Fortale*. "En Mand af utrættelig Iver for Videnskabernes Beste, en grundig Philosoph og Theolog, som gierne vilde gjøre sit Fødeland Norge ligesaa berømt og oplyst i Videnskaber, som de mest bekiendte Europæiske Lande ere det. Til den Ende foreslog han strax efter sin Ankomst 1758 Schøning og mig at oprette et lærd Selskab, saaledes at vi tre skulde strax begynde med at skrive, den ene meddele den anden det, og naar man havde nogle Afhandlinger færdige, da lade et Bind trykke, uden just at vente paa flere Medarbeidere."

[36] Suhm in Schøning, *Norges Riiges Historie bind III. Fortale*. ". . . dog blev det ei besluttet at gjøre det til et egentlig Selskab før 1760. Som en Frugt deraf udkom til Kiøbenhavn 1761 i 8vo den Iste Deel . . ."

A royal Society

In December 1766 members of *Trondhiemske Selskab*, which by then had existed for six years, met in the house of Bishop Johan Ernst Gunnerus. Three matters were deliberated. First, the host was appointed the perpetual *vice-præses* and director of the Society, and it was decided that a *patronus illustris* and *præses*, i.e. a patron, should be found. Second, a secretary, cashier, draughtsman, and inspector for the library and the natural-collection were elected. And third, it was decided to ask for a royal certification of the statutes and permission to be designated *Det Kongelige Norske Videnskabers Selskab* (The Royal Norwegian Society of Sciences), and two seals bearing the name were proposed for approval by the king.[37] This is the first recorded meeting in the Society's protocol. The protocol did not come into use before 1768, but it would start by referencing the meeting held in 1766. This could imply that this meeting was regarded as the true starting point of the *royal* Society. Here a public society had assembled and decided upon its leadership, the distribution of tasks and a royal title and official seals.

Nevertheless, the Society had already existed for six years. It had produced four volumes of the *Skrifter*. We know, however, very little of how the work was carried out, who took part, and not least what its members considered the Society to be. Before considering its further development we need to investigate what sort of society this was meant to be, and what sort of society the members saw themselves as members of. This touches on the question of what constituted a learned life in the mid 18th century. What was science? How were the sciences related? Where did the dividing lines between them go? What was the role of scientific societies vis-a-vis the old university system? And how did language, religion, and state-borders impinge on the different understandings of what were the proper names, practices, and purposes of both sciences and learned societies? These questions are of course too broad to answer here, but the issues they raise reside in almost every category we try to apply to the Society. The following pages will try to sort out the question provisionally by looking at the different names proposed for the Society and the different subject matter considered worthy.

A society for the *beautiful arts* was what Gunnerus had planned to establish, first as a resident of Copenhagen, later as bishop in Trondheim. "I had the ambition in Copenhagen, to establish a Danish Society, which would bear the name of the beautiful sciences," he noted in the pastoral letter, going on to say that he would attempt to establish the same in Trondheim with help from friends and patrons (*Velyndere*).[38] A person who wanted to join would be admitted when "he had published or conveyed to the

---

[37] DKNVS. *Protocol*, 1.

[38] Gunnerus, *Hans Opvækkelige Hyrde=Brev*, 30–31. "Jeg havde foresat mig i Kjøbenhavn, at oprette et Dansk Sælskab, som skulde føre Navn af de smukke Videnskaber. Dette vil jeg nu med nogle andre Velynderes og Venners Hjelp oprette her."

Society a proof of his good knowledge in one matter or another."[39] The society Gunnerus proposed in this new Norwegian setting had traditional book learning as its main focus even if it adhered to a wide definition of what would be considered suitable sciences—oratory, poetry, natural and other history, physics, the intent and divine hallmarks of natural things, economy, *Psychologia Empirica*, and other subjects. There were slight revisions in the German edition: Surprisingly enough, history had fallen out from the list, as had natural history, being replaced by *Natur-Lehre*, a term which would be equal to natural philosophy.[40] The German version of the pastoral letter also proposed a higher and a lower class, where theology and philosophy would make up the higher class, the rest of the sciences and literature, the lower class. Economy was also absent from the list of subjects in the German letter.

It is hard to decide what exactly Gunnerus meant by the designation "a society for the beautiful arts." There were a society of sciences and a society for history and literature in Copenhagen when Gunnerus resided there up to 1758, both of them stemming from the 1740s. In 1759 a society of the beautiful arts and useful sciences was established in Copenhagen with the aim of improving Danish language and literature, *Selskabet til de Skiønne og Nyttige Videnskabers Forfremmelse*. This society had important patrons in the king's ministry, it attracted royal funding and was to play an important role in publishing and announcing prizes.[41] We do not know whether Gunnerus had a competing project in mind, or if he was part of the negotiations for what was called, first derogatorily, and later as a nick-name, *Det Smagende Selskab* (The Tasting Society). But his list of what were the suitable subjects for the society is much more encompassing than the themes of the *Det Smagende Selskab*, which were principally concerned with poetry and literature.

When the Society was established in 1760, it was called a *learned* society. Since we have no records or other sources from meetings from that date, we do not know how often and where the Society assembled, who took part in the meetings, or what the activities were. We must assume that the production of the journal, *Tronhiemske Skrifter*, was the main task, as also Peter Friderich Suhm had asserted in retrospect. Gunnerus, Suhm and Schøning were responsible for a large portion of the journal published from 1761, which meant that theology and natural and civil history were the main themes of the journal. In the preface of the first issue we are again reminded about the subjects

---

[39] Gunnerus, *Hans Opvækkelige Hyrde=Brev*, 31. "Hvo som har Lyst til at træde derudi, skal gjerne antages, naar han har udgivet eller vil meddeele Sælskabet en Prøve på sin gode Indsigt i den eene eller anden Materie. De Skrifter, som Sælskabets Medlemmer forfærdiger, bliver da siden oplæste, og naar de synes at fortjene det, trykte."

[40] Gunnerus, *Johan Ernst Gunnerus erweckliched Hirten=Brief*, 79. "Die Rede= und Dichtkunst, die Natur=Lehre und der natürlichen Dinge Absicht und Göttlicher Zwek, die natürliche Gottesgelehrtheit und Sitten=Lehre, die erfahrende Seelen=Lehre und andere Dinge, die, und in soweit, sie sich auf eine schöne Art denken und abhandln lassen, und nicht den Horizont derer Vernünftigen nicht studierten übersteigen, sol darin unsere Beschäftigung sein."

[41] Even if later historians have made derogatory descriptions of their conservative stance, this is obviously not the whole history of how it functioned.

found suitable: History, first and foremost, the Fatherland's learned, civic, natural and church history; philosophy, especially mathematics, natural knowledge and its use within medicine, economy, morals, and the natural teachings on God and religion. On certain conditions religion, poetry, and civic and public law would also be welcomed. Apparently Gunnerus here proposed five categories: history, philosophy, theology, poetry, and law, but as we can see, the delineation as to what is within and what is outside the different categories is hard to grasp. All in all what he terms a society for the beautiful arts, a learned society, and later a scientific society seem to be much of the same thing, even though the emphasis in practice was shifting. There are two ways to interpret this—either that he carelessly employed the first term at hand, or that there were genuine ambivalences and difficult semantic negotiations involved. There are good reasons to propose that the second answer covers most ground: scientific practices and names were changing, as were teaching curricula and ways of organizing scientific work. Both scientific societies and scientific disciplines were in the making.[42]

Societies, academies and universities

"The Age of Academies" was what Bernard de Fontenelle, the powerful secretary of the French *Académie royal des sciences*, from 1697 to 1740, labeled his own time.[43] Academies and scientific societies had been instituted in major metropolises, in London (1660), Paris (1666), Berlin (1700), St. Petersburg (1725), and Stockholm (1739), and these were the ideals which were emulated by the new societies springing up by the mid-eighteenth century. Fontenelle's claim was also a prophecy which many historians have confirmed. Notably, James McClellan III corroborates Fontenelle's claim in *Science Reorganized: Scientific Societies in the 18th century*: The 18th century, so it goes, was the heyday of the general scientific society. He proceeds by arguing that "organised science in *all* its aspects was entirely recast under the dominion of the scientific societies in the eighteenth century."[44] In this period scientific societies were the prime carrying institutions for science, for scientific communication, for the role and profession of science, and for the science-society interface.[45] This claim, which has been forwarded by many different historians, is—and was—not uncontested. This was precisely the figure of speech used to legitimate the establishment of new scientific societies. When asserting scientific societies to be centers of scientific innovation, other institutions were constituted as the opposites, especially the universities. Historians and commentators have predominantly portrayed scientific societies as the places of innovation and research, universities as the conservative maintainers of traditional knowledge since the

---

[42] Cf. Latour, *Science in Action*, and Breidbach and Ziche, "Einführung. Naturwissen und Naturwissenschaften."

[43] McClellan, "Scientific Institutions," 90.

[44] McClellan, *Science Reorganized*, xix.

[45] McClellan, *Science Reorganized*, xix.

time of Fontenelle. Recent scholarship has attested to both the close cooperation between scientific societies and universities and forwarded more nuanced evaluations of the role of universities.[46] When addressing the society in Trondheim, it is important to keep in mind that not all societies were sites for carrying out scientific practices that were absent from the universities, but as the society encompassed other areas than the "new sciences," it differed from the elite societies.

Except from the *Königliche Preussischen Akademie der Wissenschaften*, all old elite societies and academies encompassed predominately the natural sciences. The oldest and most powerful of them, *The Royal Society for the Improvement of Natural Knowledge*, in England, and the *Académie des sciences*, in France, were tightly connected to propagation of the advancement of the natural sciences during the 17th century, and this had an important impact on the whole society movement in the 18th century. Scientific academies and societies practiced and were pictured as organizations for the pursuit of "the new sciences." The constitution of the specialized learned societies in the second half of the 17th century, Lorraine Daston claims, "made two things clear: the formation of a research ideal independent of tradition and produced in an academy, an institution apart from the university, and second the growing conviction that knowledge about nature is different from all other kinds of knowledge."[47] Thus, on the one hand, knowledge was pictured as produced under totally different conditions and aims than within the universities. The first president of the *Göttinger Societät der Wissenschaften*, Albrecht von Haller, insisted in the early 1750s that the university was "Akademie zum Belehren" while the academy of science was "eine Akademie zum Erfinden."[48] On the other hand, natural knowledge was promoted as a kind of knowledge which was different from other kinds of learning in most respects. When Robert Hook proposed statutes for the Royal Society in 1663 he contended: "The Business and Design of the Royal Society is: To improve the knoweledge of natural things, and all usefull Arts, Manufactures, Mecchanick practices, Engynes and Inventions by Experiments—(not meddling with Divinity, Metaphysics, Moralls, Politics, Grammar, Rhetorick, or Logick)."[49] Avoiding these themes was a way of avoiding scholastic disputes and religious quarrels. Empirical natural knowledge was free of dogma, scholasticism, just pure and simple matters of fact.[50]

In Trondheim they thought otherwise. The priests were encouraged by Gunnerus to develop and refine their arguments to be able to counter opposition to the state-ordained fate from naturalists, deists, doubters and those despising religion.[51] The first article of the first issue of the society's journal made it abundantly clear that theology had a prominent place in the Society; written by Gunnerus, it was titled "*Afhandling*

---

[46] See for example Hammerstein, "Innovation und Tradition."
[47] Daston, "Die Kultur der Wissenschaftlichen Objektivität," 12. Our translation from German.
[48] Voss, "Akademien und Gelehrte Gesellschaften," 20.
[49] Cited in Hammerstein, "Innovation und Tradition," 617.
[50] See for example Schapin and Schaffer, *Leviathan and the Air-Pump*.
[51] Gunnerus, *Hans Opvækkelige Hyrde=Brev*, 14.

om Sielens Udødelighed" (On the immortality of the soul). Metaphysics and theology were indeed welcome. These are clear indications that the fabric of the Society of Trondheim was weaved from other fibers than its English and French counterparts. From the inception in 1742, the *Videnskabernes Selskab* (The Society of the Sciences) in Copenhagen was first and foremost a society of anything but natural knowledge. It started with an emphasis on antiquarian and philological knowledge, and expanded from there to encompass a broad range of *Wissenschaften*, in the German sense of the term, and natural knowledge was to have a prominent place. The German societies which undoubtedly served as important inspirations for Gunnerus's plans also have a history of broader subject fields than the English and French societies. The Trondheim society in many ways resembled these, but what distinguishes the society in Trondheim is the active relationship to theology. The German societies would rarely encompass theology and jurisprudence.[52] Actually Gunnerus had not mentioned them on the list in his pastoral letter, except as natural theology, but they were explicitly mentioned later as subjects which would be welcomed in the journal of the Society. The single most important point in understanding the role and practices of this society is that different from most other scientific societies or academies worldwide, theology had a prominent place. The royal *scientific* society in Trondheim became a scientific society where theology reigned as queen of the sciences. In practice "pure" theology would seldom be a matter of discussion, but the role of religion was undisputed.

But how should we interpret the different notions of a society for the beautiful arts, a learned society and a scientific society which Gunnerus employed? And what relation do they have to "academy"? The beautiful arts seem to have implied language, history, and literature, and would thus be the translation of Class four in the reorganized Berlin Academy of 1744—*belles lettres*. We can quite simply say that what Gunnerus and his friends went about making was a society which encompassed the *belles lettres* but was much wider than that. Second, "a learned society" seems to have implied a broad society, a society for the learned, whatever subject they might proffer in. When the Society received royal confirmation in 1767, this was as a scientific society. Jürgen Voss makes a distinction between academies and learned societies—in Germany—by pointing out that "Akademie" was a designation for different kinds of secondary education. In German a notion of "Akademie" to designate a French style society was imported through the 18th century, but only as a designation for the governmentally approved, elite and scientifically active societies. The learned societies were typically more local, not officially approved, according to Voss.[53] And this may be the second peculiar trait of the Society in Trondheim, which was a scientific society launched to prepare the way for a teaching institution, variously called academy or university.

---

[52] Sontag, "Albrecht von Haller on Academies," 381.
[53] Voss, "Akademien und Gelehrte Gesellschaften," 617.

In his journal *Tronhiemske Samlinger*, Suhm had aired the idea of a Norwegian university at the beginning of the 1760s. On the first celebration of the king's birthday in the Society in 1768, this topic was raised again in Gunnerus's inaugural speech: There was no lack of "happy heads," no lack of talents in Norway, he stated. There was no lack of patriotism, eagerness or interest. But there was a lack of encouragement and guidance, Gunnerus claimed, and "there is no public library, no university, in the whole country."[54] The idea of a Norwegian university, and the idea of the Society in Trondheim as its midwife, was a key item on Gunnerus's agenda. In 1771, when the King's physician Struensee was the de facto ruler of the country, Gunnerus was called to the capital to prepare a new act for the Copenhagen University. During his stay he benefitted from the occasion to sketch a plan for a Norwegian university in Christiansand, at the southern tip of Norway. Gunnerus's visions for Copenhagen University and his grand idea to establish a Norwegian university would never be realized. Had Struensee remained in power, they might have been at least considered, but when the Struensee regime fell, the plans came to naught. This was perhaps just as well for the Society in Trondheim. Gunnerus had proposed that the Society should move to Christiansand to be connected to the university. This last fact can undoubtedly be interpreted as a sign that the Society was first and foremost conceived as a first step towards establishing a Norwegian university.

This is also elaborated on in a speech given by Gunnerus after his return from Copenhagen. On the occasion of a visit by the Prince and Princess of Hessen to the Society, Gunnerus seized the opportunity to further the university cause by recounting the place of universities in the development of the Danish kingdom: "To contemplate the improvement and diffusion of Sciences and Arts in a country, without at the same time considering the establishment of a real university, will never lead to a happy progress. The university is the place for cultivating the promising youth, the teachers and leaders of the youth, all important and high-ranking state officials, generals and statesmen, or at least the enlightened men who will prepare the youth, as also all the civilians who love and desire wit and excellent insights. It shall enliven the schools, gymnasiums, learned societies, arts, manufactures and factories, mines, agriculture, fisheries, trade and all other industries, and without it, there will never appear enlightenment in a country, whatever else one does to further it."[55]

---

[54] Gunnerus, "Fortale," in *Skrifter IV*, 21.

[55] Gunnerus, "Tale til prinsen og prinsessen av Hessen ved deres besøk i Trondheim," 4–5. "At tænke paa Videnskabers og Konsters Opkomst og Udbredelse i et land, uden tillige at være betænkt paa et ordentligt universitets oprettelse, vil aldrig have nogen lykkelig fremgang. Universitetet er det rette Plantested, hvor den haabefulde Ungdom, de unges lærere og ledere, alle vigtige og höie Embedsmænd, Generaler og Statsmænd, eller i det mindste de oplyste Mænd, som skal tilberede dem, tilligemed alle de borgere, som elske og har lyst til vittighed og udmerkede indsigter, bör dannes. Det skal oplive skoler, gymnasier, lærde selskaber, kunster, manufakturer og fabriker, bergværker, agerdyrkning, fiskerier, handelen og alle övrige nærgingsveie, og uden det bliver det aldrig ret lyst i et land, i hvad man endog ellers foretager sig til dets beste."

Conclusion

To be an enlightened country, according to Schøning, certain institutions were necessary, and none of these were present in his native country which he had abandoned to become a professor of oratory and history at the aristocratic academy of Sorø in Denmark. It was not undisputed that there was no university, nor an academy, a scientific society, a library or collections in his fatherland, as Norway was part of the conglomerate state of Denmark-Norway, and in the capital Copenhagen, all these institutions were of course present. But Schøning, Gunnerus and other men present in the Trondheim community were concerned about the backwardness of their country, which they defined as Norway—not the conglomerate state. Something was lacking in the country, and they were the men to start rectifying the problem.

The rhetoric accompanying the Society of Sciences which was set up in Trondheim in 1760 to become a royal society in 1767, radiated light. Gunnerus, the bishop father of the Society certainly brought science, but he also brought a Christian enlightenment, an ambition to enlighten hearts as well as minds, and this Christian enlightenment hovers in the rays. The rhetoric was used to legitimize the space and project of science in Norway, with addressees in the Danish government, as well as in the more humble minds encountered in Trondheim. It was also used to further a specific form of enlightenment thinking, a Christian and Cameralist enlightenment where science and religion were not at odds, but co-constitutive of what was regarded an enlightening mission. Gunnerus—and Schøning—entertained this familiar Enlightenment rhetoric and portrayed themselves, or more precisely each other, as the carriers of light to the city of Trondheim, and to the Fatherland. If the country was to rise to its true glory, natural resources would have to be surveyed by science, the history of the country recorded and told, and the people had to be enlightened in Christianity and Science. The Society was portrayed as the first brick in an edifice which could mould a new enlightened era; by surveying the country and educating the people, manufactures would be instituted, more metals found in the mines, forests cleared away, farms cultivated, and in this way—this history had proven—even the climate would become milder.

Science and sociability

In 1749 King Frederik V of Denmark-Norway ventured north from his capital of Copenhagen to oversee the vast Norwegian part of his kingdom. The plan was to visit various regions of the country, but the King and his company did not make it much further than Christiania, the seat of the vice-governor.[56] In Christiania the majesty wined and dined, was saluted by canons and cheered by enthusiastic Norwegians throughout the summer. Rather than going out to the people, the sovereign's loyal subjects came to him. They had to make the journey from various regions of the country to pay their tributes in Christiania. Military officers, clergymen, civil servants and laymen arrived to honor the king and do business with his ministers and each other. A king's visit was an extraordinary occasion, as there had only been two such visits over the previous 50 years. This made Christiania a thriving political, cultural and intellectual centre for the summer. The king brought theatre, opera, ministers and ambassadors with him. His visit also occasioned the first mention of a Norwegian society of sciences.[57] This never actually came about, but it was recorded by bishop Pontoppidan of Bergen who more or less willingly had traveled across the mountains from Bergen to entertain the king. While the scientific society came to naught, the summer of 1749 still saw the first civic society established in Norway, a Masonic lodge with the king as its most prominent member.[58]

The Danish kings visited four times during the century. This was a country for all practical reasons without any nobility, and there were no learned institutions beyond the cathedral schools. However, there were priests, merchants and military officials who had been educated elsewhere and they formed an internationally oriented constituency which was inspired by international trends. In 1749 they formed a Masonic lodge, during the 1750s several teaching institutions for higher education were established, and in 1760 a scientific society was set up. Learning and sociability were organized at the same time.

---

[56] The office of governor was not occupied for large parts of the 18th century. From 1750 a vice-governor, Jakob Benzon, was appointed. Prince Carl of Hessen, who was to play a role in the establishment of the Royal Society in Trondheim, was the titular governor from 1766 to 1770, without staying in Norway, and in 1770 Benzon was appointed governor. See Sprauten, *Byen ved festningen*.
[57] Pontoppidan, *Levnetsbeskrivelse*, 142–43.
[58] Sprauten, *Byen ved festningen*, 417.

When Frederik V visited Christiania in 1749, scientific and learned societies had already made their impression on the Copenhagen public scene with the establishment in 1742 of the *Videnskabernes Selskab* (Society of the Sciences), an elite society with tight connections to the king's administration. In 1745 the more modest, when it comes to the status of the members, *Det kongelige danske Selskab for Fædrelandets Historie* (The Royal Danish Society for the History of the Fatherland) was established. The activities of both these societies consisted of meetings and publications, on the one hand the *Skrifter* (Transactions) of the Society of the Sciences, on the other, the journal *Danske Magazin* (Danish Magazine).[59] These were important channels in the publishing arena in Copenhagen, where many new journals made their appearance in the 1750s and in the following decades. Most of them were short-lived. Both of these societies also soon received royal protection. A Masonic lodge was also founded in Copenhagen in 1743, as were also no less than four theatres after the pietist King Christian VI passed the throne on to his son Frederik the V in 1746. As most men in Norway with more than basic education would have had to visit the University of Copenhagen to acquire higher degrees, state officials in all ranks and offices as well as many of the upper-class gentlemen would have shared the experience of living in the cosmopolitan city of Copenhagen for shorter or longer periods of time. In addition, the capital was the uncontested publishing centre in the kingdom of Denmark-Norway. Hence, the learned, as well as the social and cultural life of Copenhagen was of great importance to the social life of the elite all over Norway.

Among the characteristics of the 18th century culture were the emergence of new forms of interaction and reasoning, a new sociability. As many historians have pointed out, this was an era of organized sociability: This was a century of the scientific and learned, reading and patriotic, public and clandestine societies. In recent decades the interest in the organizational forms of the new bourgeois culture has attracted a great deal of scholarly attention.[60] This has brought 18th century civic societies into focus. But many studies have treated *scientific* societies and academies as a phenomenon apart from other organizations, a tendency which has recently been criticized.[61] It has been claimed that what we now need are analyses of scientific societies and academies in their interrelationships with other cultural spheres than the "purely" scientific ones.[62] This is also how we will pursue our analysis of the scientific society in Trondheim, whose history will best be understood, as we see it, by looking at the local environment

---

[59] See Pedersen, *Lovers of Learning.*
[60] Habermas, *The Structural Transformation.*
[61] From the perspective of understanding the social and intellectual life in cities, where scientific societies are treated as a phenomenon among other societies and institutions of learning, there are many notable exceptions, and most relevant in this connection, since they explicitly examine Trondheim, are Bull, "Foreningsdannelse i norske byer" and Aase and Hård, "Det norska Aten."
[62] Zaunstöck, "Gelehrte Gesellschaften im Jahruhundert der Aufklärung," 8. The article includes a good introduction to *forschungsstand* 2000, and also draws attention to the new contributions which examine a broad range of societies.

and its intellectual and bourgeois culture, as well as the connections to other international transformative movements.[63]

The Trondheim society changed and developed in tandem with the town, but perhaps more succinctly we could argue that the Society played an important role as an intellectual arena and a catalyst for sociability in the 1760s and 1770s.[64] It was the first organized society in the city. Its role as both a social and scientific meeting place was gradually undermined after that, for various reasons we will come back to, but one important factor is the emerging importance of other civic institutions. The first newspaper in town was founded in 1767, the first civil school in the Nordic countries, i.e. *Trondhjem borgerlige realskole* (Realschule or secondary school), was established here in 1783, several journals began to publish in the last decades of the century, many clubs and societies were founded, for example *Borgerklubben* (The civic club, 1783), *Det forende borgerlige Selskab* (the United Civic Society, 1797), *Trondhjems Læseselskab* (a reading society, 1784), *Liebhaberselskabet* (a musical society, 1768) succeeded by *Trondhjemske musikalske Selskab* (1786) and a dramatic society in 1798.[65] These are, needless to say, competitors of the Scientific Society, and they point to a development in public life where the household-based activities as well as church institutions were gradually less important. The question is how a scientific society in Trondheim would navigate in this society of societies which was inaugurated by the king's visit. It became the first civic society in Trondheim and the country's first non-Masonic society. But contrary to the Masonic societies, this was an open society, and as such it helped pave the way for other civic societies in Norway. But the specialty it traded in—science— would prove a difficult occupation to maintain activity around.

Trondheim in the periphery

From Copenhagen, Norway was peripheral. But Norwegians were also concerned with this position, as Schøning and Gunnerus repeatedly alluded to the darkness and lack of means of their fatherland. The country had no university, as Schøning pointed out. It had a few specialized teaching academies, *Det Kongelige Norske Berg-Seminarium* in Kongsberg, the Mining Academy established in 1757, *Den frie Mathematiske Skole* in Christiania, that is the Military Academy from 1750, and *Seminarium Fredericanum* in Bergen, which was a small teachers' Academy established in 1752. Trondheim was host to *Seminarium Lapponicum*, the Sami Missionary Academy from 1752. All of them were established in the wake of king Frederik V's visit to Christiania in 1749. There were, moreover, four cathedral schools in Norway which prepared Norwegian students for university training. The puzzling question about the establishment of an enduring

---

[63] The study by Aase and Hård. "Det norska Aten" is an invaluable help in this regard.

[64] See Aase and Hård "Det norska Aten" for a thorough introduction to the knowledge culture in Trondheim.

[65] Bull, "Foreningsdannelse i norske byer."

scientific society in Norway by the mid-18th century is not necessarily that it was far removed from the centre of the state geographically, but that it was established in a country with so few people who could live off intellectual work and which had so few institutions of learning. Moreover, the city where the Society prospered, Trondheim, was neither the administrative centre (Christiania), nor the largest city (Bergen) in Norway. Still there are reasons why Trondheim would become the home of the Society: "A century ago Trondheim was perhaps the Norwegian town which for a man of science offered most comfort, allowed him to suffer the least hardships," Norwegian historian Ludvig Daae wrote in 1863.[66] Daae was trying to understand what environment could have fostered a scientific society in what could, especially from the vantage point of the mid-19th century, be considered a highly unlikely choice.

Daae and many of his successors have expanded upon the fact that Trondheim was a city of state activity, mercantile prosperity and intellectual activity in the mid-seventeenth century. The city was the centre of religious, civil and military government for the northernmost quarter of Norway. Orders from the king in Copenhagen were channeled through the city, and vice versa: tax money and information traveled from the districts through Trondheim on the way to Copenhagen. Commercially, the main trading goods, fish, timber and copper, arrived in Trondheim from the districts before being shipped off to North Sea ports. Fortunes were made, the contact networks were wide. The bourgeoisie were internationally oriented, many of them of foreign, notably Dutch, English but mostly German (predominantly Flensburg) descent.[67] As the centre of scientific advancement has been said to have moved to the North Sea region from the end of the 17th century, the commercial networks which the city traded in could also explain why the city had an intellectual activity of some repute.[68]

There was a proportionally large group of the bourgeoisie who would decorate their houses with books, and probably even read them.[69] One source for the fact that Trondheim was a germane city for intellectual endeavors in the 18th century is the most well-known Danish-Norwegian author and intellectual in the first half of the century, Ludvig Holberg, who claimed that Trondheim was *per capita* the best town in Denmark and Norway to buy books. That implied that his books would sell well here, whereas— as Holberg stated—people from Bergen, his own hometown, cared for nothing but commerce.[70] Trondheim is in fact the Norwegian city that can provide the most catalogues from book auctions in the 18th century, which at least proves that there was a market for books, whether to be read or used as status objects. Apart from the "secular" learned culture, the institutions of learning in the town were linked to religious

---

[66] Daae, *Tronhjems Stifts geistlige Historie*, 184. "For hundrede Aar siden var vel Throndhjem den af de norske Stæder, der for en Videnskabsmand frembød fleest Behageligheder, eller maaske rettere, lod ham føle de færreste Savn."
[67] Supphellen, *Innvandrernes by*, 104f.
[68] Supphellen, *Innvandrernes by* and Aase and Haard. "Det norska Aten."
[69] Dahl, *Questioning Religious Influence*.
[70] Aase and Haard, "Det norska Aten."

tasks. The cathedral school was established according to tradition, as Trondheim was a diocese, and the bishop had the formal role as superintendent of the school. The school prepared students from the northern part of Norway for studies in Copenhagen, and its teachers were an important intellectual resources of the city. The diocese and two parish churches also ensured a community of clergymen. The *Seminarum Lapponicum* educated teachers for the Sami population of Norway, with a pietistic missionary aim, which encouraged missionary activities for the Sami in their own language. A priest and specialist in Sami languages, Knud Leem, served as a professor for the seminar until it was dissolved in 1774.[71]

However, the most credible reason to explain why Trondheim was regarded as the scientific stronghold of Norway in the 18th century was the establishment of the learned society itself in 1760, and the intellectual activities emanating from it. One important reason for establishing the Trondheim society, as well as giving it a royal charter in 1767, and granting money for prizes from 1772 onwards, must have been the importance of the north generally and the Trondheim diocese particularly during some crucial years in the middle of the 18th century.

The priests and the riches of nature

From the 1740s on, several attempts were made at cataloging the resources of the kingdom systematically and gathering information about the economic state of affairs.[72] People were counted, nature was surveyed, the resources of the kingdom identified. One of several examples is the 43-question survey sent to all the *stiftsamtmenn* and *amtmenn* (heads of dioceses and departments) of the whole kingdom of Denmark-Norway. They were asked to answer questions on topics ranging from the number of people, the quality of the soil, the number and nature of antiquities and animals, and the most common women's and men's names.[73] The questions were sent down the hierarchies, to be answered by priests, deans and county officers.

The interest in knowing the resources of the state was coupled with an interest in strengthening the natural sciences at the university. The king wanted professionals who could help improve the economy. These were the ambitions of the state. The university was not convinced and declined cooperation, its main reason being reluctance to add to the number of professors. The alternative was to obtain foreign expertise, either by hiring extraordinary professors or by sending students abroad with scholarships to specialize in natural knowledge. The 1750s saw the building of a botanical garden in Copenhagen and a natural history collection financed directly by the king. These institutions were commissioned to discover what minerals and plants existed in the state, and what they could be used for. Moreover, they were to explore which plants could be

---

[71] For Leem see Hagland and Supphellen *Knud Leem og det samiske.*
[72] Herstad: "De 43 Spørsmål."
[73] Cf. Røgeberg, *De 43 spørsmål.*

imported and exploited commercially in the state, and the public was to be educated in the results. In connection with the institutions, two new posts for professors were established, in natural history, which consisted of mineralogy, chemistry and physics, and in economy, which mainly concerned botany.[74] The titles and the content show what nature was to the king, an economic resource, and that natural history was an activity aimed at contributing to the growth of the country.

While "the politics of science and culture" under Christian VI was aimed at an audience within the borders of the kingdom, this had changed under Frederik V, who reigned from 1746 to 1766. His policy was directed at Europe. Within the fine arts, literature and history, measures were taken to promote excellence and Europeanize the Copenhagen scene.[75] He aimed not only to lift Danish science and culture to the heights of the European level, his ambition was also to give specific Danish contributions to the enlightened cultures of Europe.[76] Behind the singular "he" in the above sentences was to a lesser degree than the weak and pleasure-seeking king his team of ministers, the real arbiters of power. This group of mainly foreign-born ministers (four from German states, one Danish born), with the *Oberhofmarschall*, Adam Gottlob Moltke, acting as the prime minister, led a policy geared to promoting and improving Danish science.[77] With respect to science, this group had two ambitions, first, they wanted to promote the status of the state abroad, and second, they wanted to enforce a new kind of economic policy.

The government's Cameralist policy drew its inspiration partly from Sweden. There Linnaeus had worked to improve the wealth of his nation through, for example, importing new plants that would make Sweden less dependent on imports. Cinnamon groves, tea plantations and rice fields were some of the ambitious projects which Linnaeus and his students tried to carry out.[78] Nature was economy. But first and foremost this was a German political and economic system developed from the 17th century in the courts of the princes, and made into a university discipline complete with curricula and professors some decades into the 18th century. The aforementioned teacher of Gunnerus, Joachim Georg Darjes, was later described as one of the most outstanding Cameralists of the period of Frederik II. He was appointed professor of Cameralist sciences at the University of Frankfurt an der Oder in 1763, but had published works in this tradition earlier, as the title of a 1754 publication tells us, *Von der Verbesserung der Landwirtschaft zum Nutzen der herrschaftlichen Cammer*. His main tenets were that the state should enable and support agriculture, industry, and the production of goods, and that there

---

[74] For a treatment with English summary, see Wagner, "Fra Kunstkammer til moderne museum."

[75] The examples of this politics are extensive—journals were issued in French and German, painters, architects, historians and poets were invited to stay and work in Copenhagen as a measure of mercantilist policy to promote self-sufficiency, also in the arts. See Feldbæk, *Fædreland og modersmål* and Feldbæk, "Aufklärung und Absolutismus."

[76] Feldbæk, "Aufklärung und Absolutismus."

[77] Feldbæk "Aufklärung und Absolutismus," 35–36.

[78] The broad treatment of Linnaeus the Cameralist is given in Koerner, *Nature and Nation*.

was a need to deploy and refine raw materials and resources within the territory.[79] These were thoughts that were discussed and disputed on the Copenhagen political scene in the 1750s, and they had also been strongly voiced in Jena, foremost by Gunnerus's intellectual tutor, Darjes.

But how could initiatives at improving science and making it useful for the welfare of the nation be transported out of the capital? One attempt was to make the priests the spearheads of science. The University of Copenhagen was basically a priest school where about 67 per cent of the students left university with a degree in theology, and about 30 per cent were educated in law.[80] Even though the university was economically self-reliant, the king exerted political influence on certain aspects of university life through the patron who was also one of his ministers. However, when one of the king's ministers wanted to install the German Georg Christian Oeder as a professor in economy, he was rejected by the university on the official grounds of lack of knowledge in Latin. He was instead offered a professorship at the king's new botanical garden.[81] With a keen eye on the development in Sweden, and especially informed by the rhetoric of Linnaeus, numerous voices expressed the advantage that could be gained from giving the theological students a broader scientific education.

A new position as pro-chancellor at the university was established, with the ambitious task of reforming the university. It was made for the bishop of Bergen, Erich Pontoppidan, who was a polyhistor under the patronage of Johan Ludvig Holstein, minister of the king and patron of the university in 1754. Pontoppidan was a powerful learned man, and had served as "the chief-ideologue of pietism" under the reign of Christian VI, but he was also a historian, antiquarian, and church historian.[82] In Bergen he had devoted himself to natural history and issued the first natural history of the kingdom, *Det første Forsøg paa Norges Naturlige Historie* in 1752–53 which also appeared in German and English translations.[83] He presented a tripartite motivation for studying nature which embraced science as a pleasurable endeavor that kept the priests away from idleness and supplied them with work to perform as good protestants, it would

---

[79] Bauer and Müller, "Zwischen Theologie und praktischen Wissenschaften," 146.

[80] Krag, *Natur, nytte og ånd*, 45.

[81] Wagner, "En disputatshandling" gives a detailed account of the process, and finds that the weaknesses were there, but also that competing schemes among the "modernising" Ministers was a reason for the rejection.

[82] For his intellectual role see Gilje and Rasmussen, *Tankeliv i den lutherske stat*, 316f.

[83] Pontoppidan: *Natural History* I, vii–viii (English edition). He argued that for priests who were called to attend a country parish, natural knowledge will "not only furnish them with many clear arguments, and edifying reflexions to themselves and their hearers, but it will besides prove a liberal amusement in their solitude; it will enable them, by much greater opportunities than the learned enjoy in towns, to make useful discoveries or improvements, from the products of nature, to the lasting benefit of their country, which it is their duty to promote." In Norway, skills in metallurgy would be of the greatest importance, that is knowing "the species of ores and minerals, to make little experiments by fusion, and thus to form a judgment of the intrinsic value of a mine, and how far it will answer the expense of opening."

also furnish them with intellectual stimulation as they moved to the barren peripheries, but not least, it would make them serve as useful servants of the state, helping to harness the treasures of the countryside. The bottom line was that science was useful, and even more useful in the provinces than in the capital; therefore, the ministers were the prime targets of reform.

Two years later, the university was directly challenged to address this theme. "It is the King's will," wrote Holstein, "that the mathematical and especially the physical Studia should be more prevalent and practiced with more enthusiasm," in making useful improvements and bettering the lot of the country. The means would be to encourage theological students to study physics.[84] There were also suggestions that priests who could document natural knowledge should be preferred for new positions. But these attempts at reforming the priest's education were all turned down, as one more instance of the inability of the king to impose his will on the university.

Even if these initiatives did not change the university, they were well-known and would provide strong motivation for priests with an interest in the study of nature, if they got the message. This was a message Gunnerus did his best to pass on, himself being hauled home from Jena by the same man responsible for many of these initiatives, Johan Ludvig Holstein, the leader of the general church inspection office, to whom all clerics would have to report.

Members

In Gunnerus's pastoral letters, the priests were urged to submit their writings to a Society where they would have the chance to publish and become members. Still only a precious few of the parish priests would be offered a place in the Society during its early period. However, the information we have regarding the membership during the first years of the Society's existence is rather ambiguous. People who are mentioned as members in 1763 and 1766 are up for election at later dates, as if they had not been members before. Judging from the earliest record, a letter from Gunnerus to the French Ambassador in Copenhagen, Ogier, there were 18 members in 1763. As many as five of these men were Gunnerus's famuli and young helpers: Daniel Hveding, Jacob Lund, Johan B. Eeg, Henrik Tonning and Cornelius Müller. Of more international notoriety was Carl Linné, who was an important correspondent for Gunnerus. Other notable members included Peder Ascanius, professor at the king's *Amphitheatrum oeconom-*

---

[84] Kragh, *Natur, nytte og ånd*, 47 ". . . de mathematiske og især physiske Studia skal være mere almindelige og excoleres med mere Iver i hans Majestæts Riger og Lande end hidtil er skeet, paa det derved kan gives Lejlighed til nyttige Opdagelser, som kunde geraade til Landets Bedste." Midlet ville være å sørge for at "en Del af dem der lægge sig efter Theologien, dels blev opmuntrede, dels imponerede til at lægge sig efter Physiken tillige, og deri lade sig examinere ligesaavel som i alt det der henhører til *Studium Theologicum.*"

icum and Georg Christian Oeder, professor in economy at the king's botanical garden. The two of them had both acquired their positions as professors outside of the university as part of the plan to institutionalize natural knowledge in the kingdom. Gunnerus, Suhm and Schøning were of course on the list, as was their friend and protector in Copenhagen, *magister* Benjamin Dass. Three practicing priests from the districts were also counted as members, although only one of them was from Gunnerus's own diocese, Eric Schytte, who was missionary, priest, and doctor. The priests Herman Ruge and Hans Strøm were the others, the first an eager collector of ghost stories and other supernatural phenomena, as well as author of moral tales, the latter on the road to becoming an esteemed natural historian and writer of topographical works. Only one local civil servant is mentioned in this letter, the Lithuanian Johan Daniel Berlin, town musician and inventor.[85] Except for the wealthy aristocrat Suhm, these members were of humble origin, of modest means, and they were predominantly theologians.

The local prominences were few, as is not wholly surprising given the outlook of the Society the first three years as a "working society" with active scientific practitioners. But other names we would have expected to find are lacking. Robert Stephan Henrici, the town physician is not on the list. Neither is the poet and playwright Niels Krogh Bredal, the vice-major of the town. Both he and Henrici were explicitly mentioned as learned in Gunnerus's pastoral letter in 1758. There can be various reasons for their absence—for example, simple forgetfulness. One indication of this was that Henrici was mentioned, together with Schøning and Suhm, in the first minutes of the protocol as one of the people who had worked together with Gunnerus for the benefit of science whilst the Society was still private. More remarkable is the absence of Professor Knud Leem, the only working professor in Norway who actually lived in Trondheim, and who in fact never became a member. Various reasons have been forwarded to explain this. One is his strong pietistic conviction, which has been proposed as offensive to Gunnerus. Another reason put forward is Leem's conviction that Sami people should be officiated (*forettet*) and taught in their own language. At the *Seminarium Lapponicum*, Leem would instruct young Sami boys to become teachers, and even missionaries and priests in Sami areas. This also implied that the Sami youth had to attend *Katedralskolen* where Gerhard Schøning was rector (principal). Schøning disapproved of their presence, and he was also of the conviction that Sami people should learn Danish, not their own language. That Gunnerus was loyal to his friend Schøning has thus been suggested as the most probable explanation for why Leem never became a member of the Society.[86] The precise motive is hard to find, but "the Leem case" is important for the simple reason that it shows that the Society was not for all—whether they themselves chose not to become members or they were intentionally excluded is harder to establish.

---

[85] See Michelsen, *Johan Daniel Berlin.*
[86] Grankvist, "Seminarium Lapponicum."

Others became members, but as seen, not very many before 1766. This is also the verdict of Gunnerus: "From the 1760s when I together with two thoroughly learned men and my very good friends, Mr. *Etats Raad* Peder Friderich Suhm and Mr. Professor, then Rector, Gerhard Schiöning [sic], the very first time started this Society in Trondheim, until the year of 1767, there have been only a few members and no real constitution. But after a multitude of the most considerable and learned men, especially in Norway, were elected last year, the Society has received specific statutes, unanimously decided in a considerable and numerous assembly here in Trondheim."[87] Only a few members and no real constitution is Gunnerus's conclusion regarding his own society, and as such it did not differ much from other societies. Closest at hand is the society of the sciences in Copenhagen which did not have proper statutes defining its purpose or structure, nor a Royal Charter or criteria for becoming members before 1774.[88]

From private to royal

As a part of the preparation for turning the Society into an official institution, a hectic correspondence which was to recast the social physiognomy of the Society took place in late 1766. Here was obviously the moment for using the political, economic and intellectual connections which were at hand. Invitations were sent off to the commanding general in Norway, to the commanding general in Trondheim, and other military men, but also to notable civil officers, diocesan governors (*stiftsamtmann*), mining officials (*oberberghauptmann, bergamts-assessor*) and leading theologians and priests around the country. Some of the wealthy merchants of the town were invited, as were also some priests from the diocese. Altogether 27 new members were added at this time, and the scene was now set for moving from a private society with "few members and no real constitution," as Gunnerus had put it, to a public and nationwide society with learned and honored members. At the meeting mentioned above, where the new organization was established, the local notable members were drawn into the deliberations to draft an application to the king, and to discuss the invitation of an honored person to be the protector of the Society. To make this an official society there was a need to have members with higher social standing than priests and intellectuals. Suhm and Schøning had both left for Denmark in 1765, and thus the most eager contributors

---

[87] Gunnerus, "Fortale," in *Skrifter IV*, "Fra Aaret 1760, da det af mig, i Selskab med de tvende grundlærde Mænd og mine meget gode Venner, Hr. Etats=Raad Peder Friderich Suhm og Hr. Professor, da værende Rector, Gerhard Schiöning [sic], allerførst her i Tronhiem blev begyndt, indtil aaret 1767, har det ikkun haft faa Medlemmer og ingen ordentlig Forfatning. Men, efter at en heel Mængde af de anseeligste og lærdeste Mænd, i sær af Norge, i sidstbemeldte Aar til Medlemmer vare blevne udvalte, har de bekommet sine faste Love, ganske samtydigen vedtagne i en anseelig og talrig Forsamling her i Tronhiem."

[88] Pedersen, *Lovers of Learning*, 38, 43.

to the Society's *Skrifter* (Transactions) had left town. Something had to be done to save the Society. We still do not have a decisive answer to explain why they chose to go to such lengths to make the Society more official. The departure of two central members could be one answer. Other reasons must also have been important: the general success the *Skrifter*, the enthusiastic support from Linnaeus, the general positive reaction from scholars in Copenhagen, but also more strategically, a more official society could be important for furthering the plans for a Norwegian university.

During the hectic meeting activity in 1766 it must also have been decided to ask Carl, prince of Hessen-Cassel, governor of Norway and brother-in-law to the king, to become the Society's patron, and a draft of the letter to him has survived. The letter, however, never reached its addressee. Luckily, one might add, as the prince later that year fell out of favor with the king and was expelled from the country for a period of time. The initative to choose the prince, who was in name the *Stattholder* (governor) of Norway as a patron, could be interpreted as a means of establishing the Society as a *Norwegian* enterprise. Even if the prince did not reside for long in Norway, he bore the official title of governor of the country. When the prince could not be elected, this question was left open in the statutes. A patron was not found until 1772, when the prince and half-brother to Fredrik, the king accepted the honorary position, which he kept until 1805.

We do not know if and how meetings were conducted before they started to record the minutes. The first meetings recorded from 1766 are also irregular, and in 1768 only two meetings were recorded. The first was to be the annual public meeting of the Society on the birthday of the king, on 29 January, which was established as the yearly festival day (*høytideligheds-fest*). All persons of quality (*stand*), officials (*kongelige betjente*) and other notable (*fornemme*) inhabitants in Trondheim were invited to the official program in 1768. Vocal and instrumental music written for the occasion by the town musician, fire-brigade officer and "inventor" Berlin was performed and Gunnerus and the secretary, Bredal, gave speeches. On this first celebration of the king's birthday another 17 members were elected, most of them from the diocese, and most of them with status but without scientific merit.

In the second meeting recorded this year, the ambition was clearly to expand the scope of the Society by reaching out to the foremost scientists of the day. No less than 34 new members were elected, ranging from Holck, a student in town, to captain Carsten Niebuhr, the only survivor of the grand state scientific expedition to Yemen, and Maximillian Hell, the Hungarian Jesuit who had measured the Venus passage in Vardø on commission from the Danish king, to d'Alembert, Haller, Bonnet, Reaumur (who had been dead for nine years), the Göttingen professor Michealis, and the English naturalists Ellis and Pennant. These were men who were widely recognized for their contributions to science—six of the men elected had proffered in the languages and history, but predominantly their reputations were made from their contributions to natural history and natural philosophy. The impact of Linnaeus was probably the reason, as Gunnerus had asked Linnaeus who should be invited. He received answers by way of his student Tonning who studied with Linnaeus in Uppsala for two years. In a letter to Gunnerus on 13 April 1767 Tonning regretted that Linnaeus was out of town, but in a helpful gesture he supplied the names he himself found suitable. Later he would supply names he had been given directly by Linnaeus, and in the end Linnaeus would also himself provide names of persons he saw as fit members.

For our purposes, the list supplied by Tonning is interesting, since it indicates who was not seen fit for election for the members of the Society. The names we have encountered so far are monosexual, women are simply absent from all accounts in the Society. However, in his letter to Gunnerus from Uppsala, Tonning would propose the election of several female natural philosophers. Mrs Laura Bassi of Italy, who according to Tonning read anatomy with the highest "celebrity" and had many important male students, was proposed, as was a certain Mme. Chetardie, a doctor of medicine in Paris. From England he proposed Mrs Miller and Mrs Mohnson (which is probably a misspelling).[89] The females he proposed were obviously seen as unacceptable, and no females were elected. Other Societies did have female members; the Society in Trondheim clearly did not see this as an alternative. In the local arena the question never seems to have occurred to the members, but as we can see, the idea of inviting women was indeed aired.

How to become a member?

From the official festival day on January 29 in 1769 (celebrating the king's birthday), the Society set a rhythm by arranging meetings every first Monday of the month in the home of *vice-præses* Gunnerus. Papers and letters were read, decisions made, new members invited, and an occasional guest would visit—as Maximillian Hell did on his way back from Vardø in the far North. On November 6, 1769, for example, d'Alembert's letter to the Society was read, as was Hans Strøm's meteorological observations for the years 1767 and 1768. He had also prepared a paper on two strange birds, while Schnitler read "a chorographic description of Grötten," and a treatise by *amtmann* Eiler Hagerup was read: "Undersøgning om den Politiske og Moralske Dyds Indflydelse paa Selskabet" (The influence of political and moral deeds on society). The authors were already members and in addition two new members were also elected.

The Society was working, the meetings were regular, scientific matters were discussed, important learned men from an international community were added and attracted. The Society's board consisted of a secretary, Niels Krog Bredal, a draftsman and inspector for the natural cabinet, Jacob von der Lippe Parelius, a cashier, M.F. Bang, and a vice-librarian, Ole Christopher Holck. It also had its royally confirmed statutes and official signets. But on the April 15, 1770, an important addition to the statutes was decided upon: "In the Society," we can read, "no member will be admitted unless he has delivered a specimen, whereby the Society can prove him worthy; unless all the members unanimously decide to admit someone as an honorable member." This is further emphasized by once more insisting that this also has to be a decision made in unison.

---

[89] Tonning to Gunnerus, April 13, 1767, Dahl letter. 667.

"Or if anybody renowned for his writing is proposed. Though votation is always required."[90] The numerous elections the years before this attest to the fact that many members were elected who were not contributing scientifically. These were predominantly local and Norwegian members who could secure status, political support and not least financial donations to the society.

The rules had been clear—this was to be a society for active learned people, but the practice had been different. Fifty years later the then *præses* of the Society would scornfully comment on the strategies of the three founding members, Suhm, Schøning and Gunnerus: "The three mentioned scientists found it necessary to let good people work with their pockets, whilst they worked with their heads. They therefore included anyone who lived at the place and had a fortune, and who were bad enough to feel flattered by being a member of a society they did not understand the aim of."[91] This verdict is harsh, not least against Suhm and Schøning who had left town long before the influx of local notables into the Society. But he was correct in his comment that anyone with a fortune was invited in—he could also have included those who had social status as state officials and were considered important political allies. Whether this strategy should be scorned is another question. It was precisely these people who were to become important for the Society's survival. First they provided members who could actually attend meetings, which was out of the question for the far-off learned priests or Parisian scholars. And second, they provided the Society with funds and books for the library.

But certain principles were held. Cecilie Christine von Schøller, who would later be awarded the title *Geheimrådinne* (a noble title invented especially for her) for her own substantial relations and money, donated the astonishing sum of 300 Rdlr to the Society in 1769. She was to be responsible for building the largest and most elegant house in town, running a business, collecting natural objects and keeping an elegant *Salon*. The money was destined to be used for buying the "most magnificent and useful work which was available."[92] To donate a substantial sum or make a gift to the Society would always lead to membership in the Society. Even this way of gaining admittance was

---

[90] DKNVS. Protocol, 9. "I Sælskabet bliver herefter ingen optagne til Medlem, uden han har indleveret et Specimen, hvorefter Sælskabet kunde erkiende ham værdig; Med mindre alle Medlemmer, eenstemmigen fandt forgodt at optage nogen til *membrum honorarium*. Men dertil maatte alle eenstemmigen samtykke. Eller og om een og anden, for sine Skrifter sær berömt Mand blev proponeret. Dog skal der altiid voteres."

[91] Letter from Bugge to Christian Frederik July 3, 1806, cited in Brøgger, "Christian Fredrik og Videnskabselskabet," 122. "De nevnte tre Videnskabsmænd fandt det altsaa nødvendigt at lade Got Folk arbeide med deres Lommer, medens de brugte Hovederne. De antog derfor til Medlemmer enhver, der paa Stedet havde Formue, og som var daarlige nok til at finde seg smigret ved at være Medlem af et Selskab hvis forma de ikke kunde fatte."

[92] DKNVS. Protocol, 6, June 20, 1769,"Samme Dag indlöb til Höyærværdige Hr: Vice=Præses, Frue Cammer=Herrinde Schöllers Skrivelse, hvorudi hun gunstigst giör Sælskabet en Offerte af 300 Rdl, for derfor at indkiöbe til Sælskabets Biblioteque det prægtigste og nyttigste Værk, som kunde være at overkomme. Sælskabet forbeholdt sig paa en offentlig Maade derfor at aflægge sin fyldgiste Taksigelse, ved den förste offentlige Tale, som i Sælskabet bliver holden."

closed to women. It was decided that Schøller would be thanked in a speech at a forth-coming meeting.

Giving gifts was one way in, if you were a man. Another way was to be rich and pow-erful, if you were from within the conglomerate state. From other countries, you needed a scientific reputation. Visiting was also a way of acquiring membership, whether you were a professor from Copenhagen or a Portuguese ambassador, a visit to the Society would be honored with membership. The less powerful in Denmark-Norway could also become members if they contributed scientifically. Gunnerus's priests were not forgot-ten. The text which tried to delineate admittance to those who could contribute stated that a specimen had to be delivered. A specimen could be either a written text or a con-tribution to the library or to the Society's collection. When the Society received a speci-men, the reward would be to offer the person in question membership.

Looking at this issue from another angle, how could a member be expelled? That, in fact, was much more difficult than getting into the Society, as only one case is known. It could be imagined that people who did not attend meetings, did not deliver specimens, or never paid the admittance fee would at least be threatened with expulsion, but there are no signs of this. However, writing and publishing a defaming letter to the *præses* was a possible way out. One Mister Fries was expelled by a unanimous assembly in Septem-ber 1794. What he actually wrote in the letter that was his undoing is not known.[93]

An institution without funds

From 1767 to 1772, the Society did not experience any pecuniary advantages from its official status. Rather the opposite, it had to pay 14 Rdlr of the total income of 40 Rdlr in 1768 for the confirmation letter from the king.[94] So, how was it to survive? The ad-mittance fee from new members was to be the only funds the Society had at its disposal. This did not amount to much, as given the choice between donating books or paying 10 Rdr to the society as an admittance fee, many members seem to have opted for the first option. But some of the priests donated their 10 Rdlr, whilst some of the more wealthy members would add to the sum, thus endowing the Society with some basic funds. From 1769 to 1771 the Society did receive payments from enrolled members which could have been used to build up a fund, but the members, or perhaps most notably Gunnerus, were quick spenders—and most of the money was immediately spent on books from book auctions. The book donations would also ensure that the library expanded quite rapidly, and in the years to come, only a very few members would pay the admittance fee.

This left the Society as a financially precarious construction and not least as a con-struction where no one could ever hope to earn money. None of the aforementioned

---

[93] DKNVS. Protocol, 128 and Schønheyder in a letter to Nyerup, in Daae. *Udvalg af Breve*, 15–17.
[94] DKNVS. Det lærde Selskabs Cassabog.

positions of secretary, librarian or keeper of the natural cabinet would be salaried, and few expenses would be covered. This was a scientific society of amateurs in the sense, people who did not have an income from scientific work. Few scientific societies in Europe could pay their members, but two particularities are evident in Trondheim: Firstly, there were no members in town who were employed in higher scientific institutions, and secondly, as a royal society it was particularly poor, as it had no income from commissions for the state or from almanac sales.[95] The only persons ever to earn money from their contributions were non-members, the printer of book catalogues, competition announcements and diplomas and the town musician who entertained during the annual celebration of the king's birthday (after the town musician Berlin died, the society had to start paying for music performances). The Society's reliance on personal engagement was thus apparent, everyone contributed according to ability, as the statutes from 1767 stated: "Everyone who is admitted as a member gives one or several good books to the library of the society, or the same value (which should not be less than 10 Rdlr), for which no foreign person can be obliged, nor poor persons, before their condition can allow it."[96] As we can see, a lack of funds was not to be a reason for not joining the Society, but if you had no money, it was imperative to perform by giving papers, whilst the rich could buy their way in. The drafts for the statutes prepared in 1767 clarify this point: There the question is raised as to whether it would be appropriate that those who did not work for the Society should give some addition to the funds of the Society on an annual basis. But this was not included in the statutes, perhaps because stating the issue thus clearly would be offensive to those who were invited to serve as political and pecuniary allies.[97]

During the first years of its existence, the annual income of the society was modest. Gunnerus had earlier complained that he delivered work and paid expenses for the Society without remuneration.[98] He used his own funds in his different initiatives to promote Norwegian science, and left a debt of 9000 Rdlr when he died. He even provided the society with the premises for their meetings; he was providing for the naturals cabinet, he housed the library, paid the draughtsman as well as the coppers for the *Skrifter*. While he was called to Copenhagen in the summer of 1771, to return in the summer of 1772, the meeting activity of the society stopped. His presence was necessary for the organization to function. However, upon returning from Copenhagen, he could serve the Society with a new mission and new money. The heir to the crown and half-brother of King Christian VII, Frederik, had agreed to become *præses* of the Society.

---

[95] The amateurs were pivotal in 18th century science and the "normal" state was not to be able to live from scientific work, see Clark, "The Pursuit of the Prosopography of Science."

[96] Paragraf 8 in *Skrifter*, 4 1768: "Enhver, som bliver antaget til Medlem, giver een eller flere gode Bøger til Selskabets Bibliothek, eller sammes Værdie (som ikke bør være under 10 Rigsdaler), til hvilken Udgift dog ingen Udenlandsk kan forpligtes, ikke heller fattige Personer, førend deres Omstændigheder det tillade."

[97] "Spørsmål om det ikke var billigst at de som intet arbejde, gave aarlig noget vist til Selskabets Kasse." Utkast til statutter 1767 in DKNVS, Saksarkiv, Statutter, IV:6:1, Spesialsamlingen.

[98] See the letters 61 and 69 in Dahl about Berg.

Even more importantly, he had offered 300 Rdlr as a yearly contribution for competition prizes for the Society. It was not exactly what Gunnerus had hoped for, but it was without doubt useful. This contribution to the financial situation would give the Society a new ground, it would make it into a giver rather than a receiver, and contribute to the possibilities it had to formulate and practice a politics of knowledge, but it would also transform the organization in the years to come.

By the year 1775, the Society elected its member number 200, but very few of them were local men who felt obliged to pay admittance fees. Only a handful of the newly elected members would see it as their duty to endow the Society with pecuniary means. However, some of them, mostly wealthy Norwegians, either in Copenhagen or dispersed throughout the country, would give substantial contributions. Suhm gave 100 Rdlr for an economic treatise, other notables would earmark their contributions for the purchase of books for the library. Accordingly, very little of the Society's funds would be for free use, most of the money was committed to prize money or earmarked for special purposes: for the library, for some scientific objects, or for outfitting their new premises when they needed furbishing in 1787, which will be explained in the next chapter. But the situation grew steadily more critical. In the early 1790s the Society would each year deal with a negative balance. The cashier had to pay the bills out of his own pocket, and only some extraordinary testamentary gifts from the self-made rich man Peter Andersen Dahl in Copenhagen enabled the Society to remedy the crises. The financial crises might be a result of overspending while they waited for Christopher Hammer's testamentary gift, where he promised to leave his entire estate to the Society. Unfortunately for the Society, he lived to an old age (see Chapter 5).[99]

A patriotic society?

Gunnerus returned from Denmark with the promise of an annual gift from the prince—300 Rdlr—which was to be used for the promotion of the sciences, the Norwegian economy, and for remunerating enterprising farmers. The prince stated that his wish was to promote science and loyal Norwegians. The Society decided that the prizes were to be awarded in three categories: 1) for scientific treatises, 2) for treatises dealing with Norwegian industry (*næringsveie*), and 3) for members of the farmer population.[100] Thus in 1772 the annual gift from the *præses* was regarded as a promotion devoted to developing Norwegian science, industry and industriousness. From now on, deciding what would be the subjects for the competitions, and publicizing and judging them would be the extensive tasks for the Society. Thousands of competition applications were processed by the Society, and the decision as to which competitions should be publicized, the judging of the winners and then finally announcement on the king's birthday would be a time-consuming task. Even if the prizes for the farmers, and thus

---

[99] In part two, dealing with the next time period, this will be treated more thoroughly.
[100] Protocol, p. 11.

the patriotic side of the society, were only one part of this work, it was by far the most extensive. However, in connection with these prizes it became clear that the prince was more than an honorary member. He and his advisor, Ove-Høegh Guldberg, who had been strongly involved in the *coup-d'etat* against Struensee in 1772, were the ones controlling how the Society used the money. The lists of proposed winners would have to be controlled by Guldberg before being allotted the winners. Thus the Society was, even more than a patriotic society, an agent used by the state to encourage and control farmers, hunters and working women and men all over Norway. In this sense, the Society was a tool for enforcing the state policy of the Cameralists in Copenhagen; it was also a tool for controlling by proxy.

In the 1770s it is clearly obvious that the Society was uncertain as to how free it was to make decisions on its own. When Gunnerus died in 1773, the Society asked the *præses*, Prince Frederik, to decide who should become the new *vice-præses*, and the new dean of the diocese, Ole Irgens, was installed as *vice-præses* (the new bishop, Bang, did not want to become *vice-præses*). In 1774 a letter from Guldberg proposed a new arrangement for the organization of the Society: To elect directors for different departments of the Society's work. This time the Society resisted and answered, after long deliberations, that this would be against the statutes.[101]

Was this now a patriotic society? The answer is both no and yes. Yes because it was partly a patriotic society, no because it continued to function as a scientific society. And it can be deduced from the protocol of the Society that it was a hard-working and efficient scientific society. Throughout the 1770s and 80s the regular meetings (almost) every first Monday of the month would include readings of papers, discussions and presentations of specimens, correspondence with foreign scientists and societies and the election of new members.

However, the Society might view itself as scientific, whilst in the eyes of others the patriotic side of its activities was much more apparent. Each year new placards would announce the year's prizes for the farming and working population. On the king's birthday, January 29, the prizes would be announced in Norwegian newspapers and in newspapers in Copenhagen. The public image of the Society was indeed patriotic. It has been argued that the most prevalent competitor of the Society would be the *Det Kongelige Danske Landhusholdningsselskab* (The Danish Patriotic Society) and not *Videnskabernes Selskab* (the Danish Society of the Sciences).[102] The Danish patriotic society, established in 1769, would announce competitions which received many Norwegian entrants, and at one point an agreement was established between the two societies that they would consult each other about the prizes to be announced, to avoid competition and the same individual being awarded prizes by both Societies. Looking at the competition subjects of *Videnskabernes Selskab* in Copenhagen does not necessarily confirm the claim that the Society in Trondheim had become a patriotic society. The turn to economy and industry was also part of the policy of *Videnskabernes Selskab*,

---

[101] See DKNVS. Protocol, meetings February 7 and May 2, 1774.
[102] Midbøe, *Det Kongelige Norske Videnskabers Selskabs Historie*, 124.

and making these subjects into main areas was in fact quite in line with the contemporary regime's definition of science.

It would thus be more important to relate the number of members of the different societies and who would be invited in. The Norwegian society had opted for a broad membership structure, with an unlimited and generous amount of members. This was also the case with the Danish patriotic society, which only one year after its establishment would have the astonishing number of 210 ordinary and 39 corresponding members.[103] The elitist character of *Videnskabernes Selskab* would leave the society with only 18 foreign and 36 ordinary members in 1784, whereas the Norwegian Society had elected 200 members already in 1775 (by 1784 the Norwegian society had 27 foreign and 145 ordinary members).[104] What made the *Det Kongelige Danske Landhushold-ningsselskab* and the Society in Trondheim competitors was thus their ambitions in reaching out to a broader constituency. The scientific society in Copenhagen did not need this broadness, as their income was secured by other means.

From 1782 on, notwithstanding its earlier reluctance to follow Gulberg's proposals, the Society organized a number of commissions to accommodate its mandate. From 1780, the new bishop Christian Fredrik Hagerup was *vice-præses* and during his leadership the Society organized its work in a more structured way. In 1782 the Society was divided into commissions for agriculture, economics and commerce, arts and manufacturers, and a literary commission for different sciences, "such as natural history, history, philosophy, mathematics, law, theology etc."[105] The commissions would both deliberate on the treatises to be printed in the *Skrifter* (Transactions), as well as on the subjects of new competitions and the evaluation of the contributors. And the reason was obvious: Deliberations on treatises and competitions required more and more of the time allotted to meetings, making the assemblies more into competition committees than discussion groups for scientific matters.

Again in 1791 when the new *vice-præses*, Bishop Johan Christian Schønheyder, had assumed his office, new commissions were proposed. The ambitions were grand, the total of nine commissions were set to work, for theology, law, philosophy, history, physics and natural history, mathematics, agriculture and husbandry, arts and manufactures, and lastly economy and trade.[106] At this point further measures were also

---

[103] Kragh, *Natur, nytte og ånd*, 79.

[104] Kragh, *Natur, nytte og ånd*, 58–59.

[105] DKNVS. Protocol, 72, October 7, 1782, "blev besluttet, ved plurima vota i næste Samling at bestemme af indenbyes Medlemmer visse Commisiones, nemlig en i Agrardyrkningen, en for Oekonomie og Handel, en for Kunster og Manufakturier; en literarisk Commision for de forskiellige Videnskaber, saasom Naturhistorien, Historien, Philosophien, Mathematiken, Lovkundighed, Theolgoie og s. Videre"

[106] DKNVS. Protocol. 116, December 7th 1791, "Da adskillige af de d 4 Nov 1782 til de forskjellige litterariske Comissioner valgte Lemer ved Døden vare afgangne saa blev i den Samling i de afdødes eller bortflyttede stæd valgt nye Lemer, saa at Comissionerne nu bestaaer af følgende:

1 Comissionen for Theologien—Hagerup og dr Jonas Angell.

proposed to make the Society more of a social meeting place and reach out to the public in Trondheim. The new *vice-præses* wanted to institute academies where once a week members of the public, both men and women, were invited to attend lectures in science. In Christiania and in Copenhagen, such public lectures had been instituted with considerable success by *Naturhistorie-Selskabet* (the society of natural history) in Copenhagen and by the notoriously rich gentleman Bernt Anker in Christiania. In Trondheim, the public did not show up. There were also initiatives from the Society to inaugurate the production of regular pamphlets which could capture the general public's interest and serve enlightenment. This was also abandoned.

Where are the members?

In 1796 an initiative was made to get the newly established musical Society to perform on the king's birthday, and to invite the female members of the higher classes to attend the occasion. Expectations were sky-high. They considered whether to print tickets in advance, as there was only capacity for 450 people in the Society's hall.[107] How many actually turned up? We do not know, but this effort to make public and festive annual meetings open to both sexes was not repeated. The meetings had been openly announced from the beginning, and evidently people turned up over the years, but in the 1790s the overriding problem was to get members to attend ordinary meetings.

The Society had enormous problems attracting members, over and over again only four members would show up at the meetings in the 1790s, until the absolute bottom was reached in August 1797 when only three members turned up, in addition to the *vice-præses* and secretary.[108] In 1798 the *vice-præses* proposed to renew the statutes, as there were not enough members present at meetings to makes decisions. One of the

---

2 Comissionen for Lovkyndigheden af Hr Etatsraad Dons og nu valgt Hr Bergraad Dons.
3 Comissionen for Philosophien af Hr Professor Monrad som nu belv valgt og Hr Mag Holst.
4 Comissionen for Historien, Hr Etatsraad Dons og H Mag Holst.
5 Comissionen for Physiken og Naturhistorien, Hr Berghauptmand Heltzen og Hr Doctor Friman, som begge nå bleve valgte.
6 Comissionen for Mathematiken Hr Krigskomissær Wiibe som nu blev valgt, og Hr Mathematicus Fester.
7 Comissionen for Agerdyrkningen og Landvæsenet ligesom forhen af Hr Oberste von Krogh, Hr Justitsraad Nissen, Hr Cancelliraad Must, og Hr Parelius.
8 Comissionen for Kunster og Manufakturer—Hr Capitain von Rosbach, Hr Assessor Willumsen, Hr Bergmester Bendeke og Hr Parelius hvoraf den første og 3de nu bleve valgte.
9 Comissionen for Oeconomien og Handelen, ligesom før Hr Generalconditeur Collin, Hr Major Bang, H Assesor Willumsen og Hr Henrich Meinecke.
107 DKNVS. Protocol, 134–35 "Byens damer—kan komme." On the next occasion the sentence reads "endeel av Byens indvaanere," 139.
108 DKNVS. Protocol. August 9, 1797, there were three members present.

proposals discussed for the new statutes was that the members residing in Trondheim either had to attend or give good reason for their absence.

Social activity in Trondheim in general was burgeoning. Cultural and political clubs drew the social elites into a beehive of social interaction. Numerous voices attest to how arriving as a foreigner in Trondheim you would be whirled into a social life that demanded a good constitution. Deciding upon which bear hunter or fence builder deserved prize money the most, or listening to new papers on the barometrical observations on the west-coast, seem to have appeared less attractive. At this point in time we are also faced with the central enigma of the Society, its ability to rise from the ashes like the phoenix. As we will discuss more thoroughly in the next chapter, the material basis of the Society, the collection, the library and the premises in *Katedralskolen* more or less forced it to carry on. Similarly, as will be discussed in a later chapter, the financial prosperity of the Society, after it had received the testamentary gifts at the end of the century, would give it a strong motivating factor to continue its work.

New organizational forms

The efforts to create new activity in the society and the work to establish new statutes resulted in the confirmation of new statutes in 1805. These did not focus on explicating what the role and function of the Society should be—first and foremost a new organization was being proposed. According to these statutes the Society would be divided into four classes, and each member would belong to one of them—the philosophical, the mathematical, the historical and the physical-economic; the last being the class including everything belonging to "Landindustrie, Kunstflid, Agerdyrkning og Næringsveie" (agricultural industry, handicrafts, agriculture and manufactures). All of these classes were supposed to advertise subjects for competitions and judge them. This made for a Society where the sciences were divided and the unity of science was decidedly passé, but it also made for more of a working cooperation than the common discussion of scientific matters. In addition, two commissions embracing the Society as a whole were proposed—one was to serve as a permanent commission for the Society's finances, the other was to serve as a committee which was to treat all subjects where there were proposals to change or improve the organization of the Society. Most notably these statutes imposed detailed restrictions on the secretary's duties, stressing how the secretary was responsible for keeping books and natural objects under tight control. The conclusion was that as soon as there were means, the secretary should be offered a salary.

These statutes were not in effect for long, and a new set of statutes were confirmed by King Frederik VI (the son of the former *præses*), with the stated aim of giving more attention to scientific work in them, as well as proposing a new organization. The main idea in the 1805 statutes, the king stated, had been to preserve the collections of the society. Now the aim was stated more clearly: The aim of the Society is, "to work for the promotion of science (*Videnskabelighed*), enlightenment and industriousness (*Vindskibelighed*)."[109]

Towards a conclusion

With its establishment as a learned society in 1760, as a German-inspired humanistic and natural-scientific society, it had few but some remarkably active members who managed to publish an ambitious scientific journal with the first issue in 1761. When the society was reorganized in 1766 to prepare for its application to become the Royal Norwegian Society of the Sciences, on the one hand the organizers forged links to the highest notables in Trondheim, and on the other hand to a long range of international scholars through honorary memberships. At the time of the death of its founding father, Johan Ernst Gunnerus, in 1773, it had also become a patriotic society which awarded prizes for patriotic activities, and this activity was to become the main focus of the Society's work in the years to come. Nevertheless, it also functioned as a reading society, subscribing to journals and works which would circulate with its local members. The death of Gunnerus—who had himself been responsible for more than half of the articles in its journal, and whose personal networks in the diocese, in the country and internationally were also the network of the Society—provoked a crisis that was largely overcome by the allowance for prizes offered by the protector of the Society, the Danish-Norwegian Prince Frederik. As the proclamation of prizes increasingly became the main task of the Society, as the attendance of the meetings dwindled, and the financial situation worsened by the end of the century, the Society seems to have survived largely because of the inheritances it received and the material obligations it carried, with its book collection (the largest in Norway), its museum (the first public collection in Norway) and its building (inaugurated in 1787).

But there are also other reasons why it could survive: First, in this period the Society had no real competitors as a nationwide scientific society. Second, it was a society which would speak to the patriotic sentiments of the inhabitants of the city, who could channel the interest in promoting the city and the state through their investment in

---

[109] (The means would be "a) Ved sine Sammenkomster, sin Bogsamling og øvrige lærde Apparater bidrage til at knytte et fortroligere Baand, og fremkalde en virksommere Meddelelses-Aand imellem Norges Videnskabsmænd og de, langt fra Litteraturens Hovedsæder, i Norges forskjellige Egne, adspredte Videnskabs-Dyrkere, samt aabne en nærmere Kilde, hvoraf disse, idetmindste i Norges nordlige Egne, med en større Lethed end ellers var muligt, kunne hente Kunskab om de i Videnskaberne gjorte Fremskridt.

b) Være et Opbevarings-Sted for Videnskabs-, Natur- og Konst-Mærkværdigheder.

c) Med de Midler, der staae i dets Magt, fremelske og udmærke Nationens gavnlige Bestræbelser i Videnskaber og Industrie.

d) Befordre til Trykken indsendte nyttige Afhandlinger, især saadanne, som uden dets Medvirkning ellers vanskeligen vare blevne bekjendtgjorte."

public activities. And third, it had from the very beginning been a church-friendly society, which for the first 50 years had a leading clergyman as its head. It was thus tied into the strongest and best organized part of the Danish-Norwegian state, the church administration.

Gunnerus was a bishop, a theologian, but he was also deeply interested in empirical science and became the most arduous writer on natural-history themes. Those who took over and carried on the tradition of the Society were also educated as theologians. First Ole Irgens, the dean of Trondheim was a *vice-præses* from 1773 to 1780. When he moved to Bergen to become a bishop there, he was succeeded by Dean Christian Frederik Hagerup, who was *vice-præses* from 1780 to 1791, when the next bishop of the diocese Johan Christian Schønheyder continued the tradition until 1803 before Bishop Peter Olivarius Bugge became the leader of the society and continued in this position until his resignation in 1815. Hence, over more than 50 years the Society was successively run by a leading theologian.

There was a strong political current which underscored the role of priests as the carriers of enlightenment and improvement in Norway. But during the decades after Gunnerus's death, the position of Christianity and the Church versus the new science was never as unproblematic as before. Even though the protestant countries of northern Europe were strongholds for a "moderate" Enlightenment, the anti-authoritarian enlightenment emanating from the continent would create strong currents in the North as well. The potential dangers of science were clear, as was the possible revolutionary uses of scientific ideas. With the bishop at the head, the Society would suffer no charges of anti-state and anti-church practices, but it would perhaps also fail to attract the more radical thinkers and scientists. Seen from Copenhagen there were also other threats to the scientific aspect of the society—the regime of Guldbergh would be more inclined towards practical than theoretical science. Fence building and weaving were preferred to mathematical proofs and new descriptions of unusable natural objects.

3

Scientific sites and specimens

Arriving in Trondheim in 1807, the German geologist Leopold von Buch admired the beauty of the city, the views and the streets, the mountains and the fjord. He scorned the elegantly adorned wooden palaces surrounding the main square because they were built in a material the geologist claimed could not stand the test of time. Looking east in *Munkegaden*, the mighty ruins of the cathedral *Nidarosdomen* still hovered despite repeated pillaging by the Swedes through the preceeding century. Even as a ruin, claimed von Buch, the cathedral was an eternal monument in *stone*. Tellingly, von Buch also praised the "large, simple and beautiful" stone building of the Society of the sciences and cathedral school which was located on the main street leading from the town square to the cathedral. In this recently erected edifice, the cathedral school had its classrooms on the first floor, the scientific society on the second floor, and the teacher's quarters in the loft. "The society is a good institute for the dissemination and nurture of science," von Buch stated, "it has a sound foundation and amongst the chaos in its cluttered rooms, it still has many good materials for excellent collections."[110]

von Buch was one of many Trondheim visitors who by the end of the 18th and the beginning of the 19th centuries commented on the Society, its building, and its collections. A gentleman traveler would here as elsewhere in Europe visit the scientific centre of town; even in Trondheim the Society, and its collections, was an obligatory item on the traveler's agenda.[111] However, many of these accounts were somewhat condescending. They would express astonishment at finding a scientific society this far north, and they would hail the glorious past of the Society when Gunnerus was still alive and the *Skrifter* of the Society "in reality [would] compete with the noblest societies of Europe."[112] The building located on the prestigious ground between the square and the

---

[110] von Buch, *Leopold von Buchs Resa*, 91. "Societeten är ett godt institut till vetenskapernas utbredande och förkofran under denna bredd, ty den har en god fond och ibland allt det chaos, som ligger hopadt i dessa rum, likeväl många goda materialier till förträffliga samlingar."

[111] Travelers to Trondheim will be cited later, cf. also Eliasson, *Platsens Blick* on the apodemic travel literature.

[112] von Buch, *Leopold von Buchs Resa*, 92. "och då hennes skrifter i sjelfva verket kunde täfla med de fornemsta societeter i Europa."

cathedral would attract attention, the book collection would deserve positive mention, but the collection of natural and artificial objects would be left to either ridicule or outright contempt.[113]

Why would the collection garner such disdain? One hypothesis is that the collection which was created by Gunnerus had been a site of action, of research, and it was connected to the personal ambition of Gunnerus. When his collection was transferred to the Society after his death in 1773, it continued to grow, but it was no longer a site for scientific activity and it could not be kept as an up-to-date instrument of science. Still, what we need to account for is the almost unanimous negative evaluation of the collection in the last decades of the 18th and the beginning of the 19th centuries. As will be argued in this chapter, the collection started by Gunnerus has a special genealogy, where national pride, the political economy of the priest-bishop relationship and the specific scientific interests of Gunnerus were intertwined. After the death of Gunnerus, the collection would serve new functions, and even if many visitors, like von Buch, deplored the lack of order, the collection should not be dismissed as uninteresting. The collection *was* cared for in the period after Gunnerus's death, it was classified and arranged, cupboards and tables were bought and there was a steady flow of donations from Society members, and the Society even spent money on new acquisitions. The history of the collection from 1760 to 1805 to be told here will thus be divided into two parts; once again, before and after the death of Gunnerus will be the dividing line.

As will become apparent from our history of the building process which finally gave the Society its own premises in 1787, the natural cabinet was not the single privileged site in the life of the Society. Far more space was projected for the library and the meeting hall, and even an observatory, which, however, was never realized, than for the natural chamber. The history of the material setting of the Society thus needs to assess the other sites furnished, the instruments used as well as the collection assembled by the Society. The building, the collection and the various other scientific instruments were all-important for the Society's work and development, and by looking at the ways in which the Society at various points ordered and managed its material we can gain an understanding of how people in the Society envisioned themselves and the institution they constituted. Was it as members of an organization dedicated to storing, producing, or disseminating knowledge?

In the previous chapter we saw how the Society tapped into different networks, and found its members and its public in different arenas. Or better said, the Society created an arena for differently located members and publics. In this chapter we will investigate how these networks were also traversed by books, instruments, antiquities, and naturals, and quite literally expanded the physical site of the Society to fields and fjords in Norway, to museums and offices of the learned scholars around Europe.

---

[113] See citations later in this chapter and Aase and Hård, "Det norska Aten," 63–65.

Collecting cultures

During the second half of the 18th century collecting objects became a worldwide practice. In metropolitan, and not so metropolitan, centers cupboards and cabinets were filled up with objects of all kinds—plants, minerals, shells, birds, and fish—but also medals, antiquities, art, stunning handiwork, and exotica. The market seemed insatiable, and the *commercial* activity connected a vast network of actors, a network where knowledge, power, and money found good outlets. *Scientifically*, collections were made to be the indispensable tools for teasing out the secrets of nature, systematic collection made for systematic knowledge, the favored epistemological stance within the community of learned men. The collections were also *meeting places*, for people as well as for the multifarious objects they contained.[114] Collections were nodes in economic, intellectual, and social networks. They were also at this point straddling the border between private and public. Collections were often situated in the most public quarters of private houses, and activities in the collections were as often portrayed as public as they were counted as private. Personal pleasures and public gain were intrinsically united in many collectors' activities—as Krystof Pomian has shown was the case in major European collecting communities in Italy and France. In the 18th century collectors and naturalists marveled at nature, not as curious facts, but as an orderly nature to be known, delighted in, and exploited—for public gain.[115]

Gunnerus set up what he called a *Natural Samling* (natural collection) and a botanical garden at his farm, Berg, just outside Trondheim.[116] He portrayed and legitimatized his collection and his botanical garden as public benefits—even though they were spatially located in his private house. Gunnerus was a man of his times, and his activities can be neatly situated within contemporary and worldwide practices. Still the historical particularities of Gunnerus's work seem of more interest than him acting in accordance with the trends of his day. Gunnerus was a particular collector, and the one particularity that looms over all others is how he collects *qva* bishop. As a state-official of a state-church, Bishop Gunnerus had great power over his subjects; his was the task to oversee, supervise, and control all the inhabitants of northern Norway. Through his activities he could extend the power of the king in Denmark to include the mineral, vegetable and animal kingdom in Norway; not only subjects, but also objects would move at the behest of the bishop.[117] Things big and small were under his command, or as his correspondence partner Linnaeus stated it: "In Your Fatherland, You will be able to achieve more than any other mortal. You, who have every minister in the district

---

[114] Cf. Findlen, *Possessing Nature* and Bennett, "Pedagogic Objects, Clean Eyes."

[115] Pomian, *Collectors and Curiosities*, 218–219.

[116] See letters 63, 64, 65, 68 in Dahl.

[117] This analysis is inspired by Actor-network theory in its early configurations by writers such as Michel Callon, Bruno Latour and John Law.

under Your command, use Your instruments with success!"[118] These instruments would quite literally make *things* move.

A visiting bishop and moving objects

The pastoral letter which Gunnerus issued on his arrival in Trondheim in 1758 urged the priests to be active as learned men, and most notably to publish. Soon a number of manuscripts arrived with promises and plans for literary activities. Given both the content of the pastoral letter and the learned background of the bishop, this was not surprising. But in a few months, the arts and historical narratives were far outnumbered by natural objects and observations.[119] The breakthrough came with the visitation journey which Gunnerus undertook to Vardø and Vadsø during the summer of 1759.[120]

A visitation journey was at the time a well-regulated and ritualized journey from parish to parish, where the priests, the schools, and the moral and intellectual condition of the inhabitants were inspected. Evaluating, controlling, and inspiring were the tasks to be fulfilled by the bishop on tour, he was the incarnate representative of the power of God and the king. The bishop would travel with his own comfortable boat along the coast, with one or two amanuenses to assist him, with someone to cater for him, and rowers for eight pairs of oars. And the bishop was, judging by the results, doing well in making his subjects work for him. After the first journey, which lasted from May to September, the priests began to deliver.

The meetings between Gunnerus, the priests, and the congregations might accurately be described as micro-rituals of official presence. This concept originating with Stephen Greenblatt has been used by the historian of northern science, Sverker Sörlin, to describe the encounters between priests and the local inhabitants in northern Scandinavia, where the most prominent aspect of official presence was the church and the clergy.[121] Gunnerus would soon learn that his eclesiastical position implied the power to make things move; not only his own written protocols, and the annual lists of deaths and births, but material objects and the territory would present itself at his doorstep.[122]

"Following orders, I send 12 stuffed birds packed in a half-barrel, small sticks are tied to their necks with numbers written on," wrote *sogneprest* (minister) Augustin

---

[118] The total correspondence is translated in Amundsen, *Johan Ernst Gunnerus*.

[119] Antiquities, exotica and other curious man-made artifacts were also sent in, but they were not as eagerly sought for, and they were far less in number than the natural objects. As will become clear later, observations were mostly connected to the delivery of objects.

[120] This is clearly observable from his correspondence.

[121] See Bravo and Sörlin. *Narrating the Arctic*, esp. pp. 83–85

[122] Knowing the exact human resource capital of the state was an increasingly important ambition by the mid-eighteenth century. The first scholarly attempt to exploit the existing knowledge and not least to make it publicly available came in a book-length study by Pontoppidan: *Oeconomiske Balance*.

Buschmann from Nesna.[123] He expressed doubts as to whether he could find a vessel which would carry the living eagle he wanted the bishop to have. The *sogneprest* Ole Ross in Orkdalen humbly asked the bishop to receive a couple of living hares.[124] The *personlig kapellan* (personal chaplain) at Inderøy, Ole Høyer, had made an appointment with the Sami people to bring Gunnerus a living reindeer. "I ask you humbly to receive this small and meager present which I hope will not be disagreeable with you."[125] The variety and volumes of the gifts are amazing, and so are the priests' struggles to fulfill the bishop's wishes. "Of Naturalibus I have not yet been fortunate enough to overcome anything, but, if God were to preserve my life and health until spring, I have fair hope of some achievement," wrote *sogneprest* Ole Molde.[126] "It shall be my devotional duty and proof of my loyalty to do my utmost to find and retrieve to give my merciful Master some elevated pleasure," replied *residerende pastor* Mathias Bruun from Øksnes.[127] "Your least command, then, should be enough to make me most active in procuring anything that I may be able to achieve. There is nothing that I would strive for with more *Empressement*, than your satisfaction . . . ," the missionary Eric Schytte from Lyngen stated.[128] Hundreds of letters and as many objects arrived at the

---

[123] Dahl, letter 334 August 31, 1759. "Efter Ordre sendes de 12 udstoppede Fugle i en halvtønde indpakkede, smaae Pinde ere bundne til Halsene paa eenhver med paategnede Numere, hvorefter Navnene paa indsluttede Fortegnelse ere anførte. Jeg veed icke om Jeg tør skrive: at den levende Ørn, som mig fra Hr. Dreyer er tilsendt, følger med, siden Jeg frygter: at Ingen af Tronhiems Borgere paa deres Jægter, som sædvnalig ere stærk tillastede, vil imodtage dette Dyr, som baade indtager noged Rum paa Fartøyed, saa og daglig kræver frisk Spise enten af Fisk eller Kiød . . ." Apparently the eagle landed. In a note in the margin of the letter Gunnerus has written, "The birds arrived. The eagle stuffed."

[124] Dahl, letter 340 October 10, 1759. "Et par levende unge harer, som hermed følger, beder jeg underdanig maatte antages. Finder Deres Højærværdighed behag i Dem, da troer jeg gierne de kand leve, naar et lidet Rum indrømmes dem til forvaring. Kaalblade, hafre og qvister er deres gode føde, naar de faaer Vand til."

[125] Dahl, letter 342 October 25, 1759. "Da Jeg nu hører at finnefolket har efterkommet min aftale med dem, i at tilbringe Deris Høyærværdighed et Reens-dyr Levende om det blev mueligt: Saa beeder Jeg ydmygst, at denne Ringe og Liiden present ey maatte mishage dem, men gunstigst være modtagen."

[126] Dahl, letter 330 July 31, 1759. "Af Naturalibus har jeg endnu ej været saa Lykkelig at kunde overkomme noget; Men har temelig Formodning, at kunde faae noget om Gud sparer Liv og Helbred til Foraaret. Om jeg da bruger den Frihed, at tilsende noget, som enten intet er værd, efterdi jeg, af saadane Ting er mere Elsker end Kiender, eller saadant som Deres Høyærværdighed havde nok tilforn, maatte det gunstigst holdes mig til Gode."

[127] Dahl, letter 332 August 16, 1759. "Frommeste Herre! Min underdanig Hiertens redebonhed frembær aldt hvad, ieg efter ringe Evne, kand frembyde til Høygundstigst Velbehag, og min høyst fortiente Hengivenheds ringe bevis, der i intet andet kand fremviise sin tilskyndelse; beder underdanigst, hvad som fremsendes, som dend mindste deel, af bædres skyldighed, maatte med vanlig Graite, ansees, i sand uskyldighed og hengivenhed. Det skal være mig en underdanig pligt, og skyldigheds beviis at bestræbe, hvad ieg, til høyst gundstigste Herres høye velbehag, kand opsøge og tilveiebringe."

[128] Dahl, letter 331 August 15, 1759. "For øfrigt skal Deres mindste Befalning være nok til at sette mig i den største Activité til hvad De forlanger, som er mig mueligt at præstére: Der er intet, jeg med større Empressememnt vil stræbe efter, end at kunde behage Dem, og fortiene saa goed en Skiønneres Bifald. Det er min Pligt, og tillige min største Ære, paa al optænkelig Maade at vise, at jeg er med all Soumission etc. Deres . . ."

bishop's home, and the tone of these letters was intensely submissive and written in a rhetoric fitting the subordinates writing to their bishop.

The traveling objects and animals can be seen as means of achieving personal favor with the bishop—and ultimately the king. As we have seen in the previous chapter, the king had signaled that the exploration of Norwegian nature would be met with the greatest benevolence. And it was indeed reasonable to seek to enjoy the bishop's favors: Many priests were isolated in extremely poor parishes, where promotion was the only path to a better income. "I offer myself to be enveloped in Your memoirs of promotion," wrote the personal chaplain to Tromsø, Fredrik A. Bødtker, in the last paragraph of a letter where he described a *runebomme*, a Sami ritual drum he tried to get hold of for the bishop. This was a normal phrase, but Bødtker was making more out of his case than many others, "Pious Father! Do something for the sake of my minor children!"[129] And Gunnerus never made it a secret that advancing science, especially by procuring objects for him or undertaking natural historical observations, would be a good career move: "I greatly thank you for the two very beautiful pieces," he wrote to missionary Mathias Birch in Snåsa, "and it will be my pleasure if I can return the favor, even in relation to Your promotion."[130] In short: Interest and participation in natural historical investigation would be beneficial for securing a better position. It was not among Gunnerus's prerogatives to hire priests, but his recommendations were important.[131] This is also obvious in the many letters from grateful priests who had obtained better positions.

Visitation journeys

Gunnerus managed and mapped his territory, but not only through correspondence— he eagerly fulfilled his duties as a bishop through visitations in his wide-ranging diocese. Due to the climate conditions, the bishops would prefer the summer seasons for visitations to the more distant parts of their dioceses. Gunnerus started planning his first long-distance visitation journey soon after arrival in Trondheim. The trip would take him to the most remote parts of the diocese, through a strenuous journey where he would experience extreme weather conditions and encounter foreign lands and people. Gunnerus was to go on visitation journeys nearly every year from 1759 to 1773— Vardø and Vadsø (1759), Nordmøre and Romsdalen (1761), Tromsø (1762), Dalerne (1764), Kjelvig, Magerøy (1767), Nordmøre and Romsdalen (1768), Innherred (1769), Tromsø (1770), Dalerne (1772), Nordmøre and Romsdalen (1773). Finally this was

---

[129] Dahl, letter 337 September 11, 1759: "Iøvrigt tilbeeder jeg mig at maatte være indesluttet i Deres naadige Erindring til Forfremmelse. Fromme Fader! giør dog noget for mine umyndige Børns Skyld, at de ikke med mig skal mangle det fornødne Livets ophold."

[130] Dahl, letter 49 March 30, 1763. "For de mig til min natural-Samling tilsendte 2de meget smukke Stykker takker jeg høylig, og skal det være mig kiert, om jeg kan være D. Ærværd. til nogen Gientjeneste, endogsaa i henseende til D. Forfremmelse . . ."

[131] See for example Johansen on Borgrevink in *vitenskap som springbrett*.

also how he was to end his life. Gerhard Schøning had been granted a substantial amount of money to undertake antiquarian journeys in Norway, and in 1773 he joined Gunnerus on his visitation on the west coast. Here Gunnerus fell ill at sea, and after a few days in bed he passed away with Schøning at his side in Christiansund.

Gunnerus's activity on his visitation journeys has been particularly well studied, as one might suspect the naturalist bishop of caring more for naturals than the moral state of his subjects, a charge that was in fact leveled against the bishop in his own lifetime. During the brief period of freedom of print from 1770, one cleric of the north used the opportunity to launch an attack on Gunnerus. Bishop Nicolous Christian Friis of Bodø (a titular bishop who had bought the title) was thereby taking his revenge on Gunnerus, who had reported how he used the missionary funds to fill his own pockets. Accordingly, the charges Friis leveled at Gunnerus did not have direct consequences. Nonetheless his accusations undoubtedly touched upon important features of Gunnerus's activities. In his pamphlet, Friis opened by explaining that visitation journeys were of great use when they were conducted in the right way and when the right duties were performed, such as the edification of priests, congregations, and churches, the enforcement of good Church conduct (*Kirke-Skik*), order and ecclesiastical-*politie*, in addition to looking after poor relief, the conditions of the schoolmasters, the education and upbringing of the youth. If these duties were observed, then the country would gain much in return for the costs of such a journey, but when they are not followed, the bishop could just as well stay at home, Friis contended. He also explained how he saw Gunnerus performing his duties:

> "When for example a bishop on a visitation journey shows himself more as a naturalist than an ecclesiastical and makes it his business to serve natural history rather than cultivate theology, by asking for herbs, stuffed birds, fish, stones and minerals, even medals, yes, on his visitations even expressing that he would never make journeys like this unless he could please his curiosity and collect naturals, what use does the public have from such visitations, and what does the country gain from the pains with conveyance and other troubles with this sort of journey, which is certainly not a small account?"[132]

Comparisons of Gunnerus to other bishops do not indicate that he was less eager in his church duties than other clerics.[133] However, he was obviously more than usually interested in naturals, and it is not difficult to see that his way of traveling could give

---

[132] An, *Illustration over Bispe=Visitatserne.* "Naar for Exempel en Bisp paa sine Visitats=Reiser viser sig mere som Naturalist en Ecclesiastiqve, og lader sin fornemste Ergon være Natural=Historien i stæden for Theologien at excolere, ved at spørge efter Urter, udstoppede Fugler, Fiske Steen=Arter og Mini-ralier [sic] lige til Medalier, ja paa sine Visitatser kan selv udlade sig med, han aldrig giorde slige Reiser, dersom det ikke var, for at fornøye sin Curiosité og samle Naturalier, hvad Nytte har Publikum af slige Visitatser, og hvad har Landet for sin Bemøielse med Skyts og videre Besværing ved slige Reiser, hvilket visselig ikke for saa lidt er at regne?"
[133] Cf Ramberghaug, *Biskop Gunnerus, geistlig embetsmann.*

rise to some vexations. One can easily imagine that a parish priest with small means could dread an announced visitation journey where he would have to cater for the bishop and his company. Looking at how he himself described his journeys, there is no doubt that he envisioned and planned his trips as a combination of research expedition and visitation journey.

In the spring of 1770, he planned his forthcoming visitation journey to the northern-most parts the diocese, towards the Russian border, a journey that would last four to six months.[134] This summer he wanted company. He invited successively the two newly appointed professors of natural history in Copenhagen to join him on the trip. In his letter to the professor of economy and natural history at the University of Copenhagen, Johan Christian Fabricius, Gunnerus described that most of the trip would be conducted by sea, where the bishop's boat would offer comfortable boarding, and "under these conditions the journey would surely prove agreeable, and the expenses would not be considerable, as in my company you will have free food and drink in the vicarages."[135] The professor post in natural history was poorly paid, hence Gunnerus emphasized that the expedition would cost Fabricius nothing.

The letter describes in detail the route they were to follow. When the party went ashore, they would be offered "handsome situations" and "attractive fields," Gunnerus assured, and "by all such occasions "Your Honorable" will have time to observe and collect a large amount of Naturals and to make important discoveries in Natural History and other things, which could deserve Your attention."[136] Along the route naturals of all kinds abounded, and this was the alluring bait Gunnerus could lay out for the young and poor professor of natural history in Copenhagen. He would also have additional bait—he was at this time one of the most renowned scholars of natural history in the kingdom, his visitation journeys to the north were reputed as expeditions of discovery, and his correspondents would enquire and congratulate him on the "treasures from his Northbound journey"[137] or the "beautiful collections of rarities from the Northern countries."[138] Gunnerus even mustered his own research assistants. As he particularly urged professor Fabricius to bring his own draftsman, he made it clear that he was himself traveling as a naturalist, emphasizing that the draftsman he brought along "will attempt to draw only half of what is collected for me on a voyage like this, and which need immediate drawing."[139]

---

[134] The most substantial treatment of the visitation journeys are to be found in Ramberghaug, *Biskop Gunnerus, geistlig embetsmann* and Hagland, "Vitskaplege visitasreiser i Nord-Noreg."

[135] Dahl, letter 1034, Gunnerus to Fabricius March 6, 1770.

[136] Dahl, letter 1034, Gunnerus to Fabricius, March 6, 1770.

[137] Dahl, letter 482. Letter from Torkel Klevenfeldt, København, October 15th 1762. ". . . haaber og, at min høyærværdige Ven betænker mig (skiønt u-forskyldt) med noget af den Nordlandske Reysis Skatter . . ."

[138] Dahl, letter 486. Letter from Cornelius Müller, København, October 20th 1762. "Ellers haver jeg den ære at gratulere med den Skjønne Samling av Rariteter, som mig av hr Amtmand Hammer er sagt skulle være forskaffet i dette Aar i Nordlandene."

[139] Dahl, letter 1034, Gunnerus to Fabricius, March 6, 1770.

The journey was thus portrayed as a scientific expedition, but how was it possible to organize this within the confines of the church? Gunnerus stressed the utility of collections and scientific observation, and he could address the priests as state employees and good Christians—both the State and God favored natural history. But Gunnerus also expressed another sentiment: a sense of mission, of scientific work as an honor to God, and not only to honor God by studying his work, but to enlighten others scientifically: "Therefore, it is my opinion that this duty and this task were given to me not only so that I should devote myself to science, but also so that I should enlighten in the greatest possible degree, and not even that being enough, I should inspire others to do their best to the benefit of science and the Fatherland. Two things have been of great use to my goal and my work: travels of exceeding length, both at sea and on land (on which I set out every year to attend church meetings), and the eagerness and enthusiasm of my countrymen in recounting anything that may seem remarkable in the realm of Nature."[140] Explicit in this statement printed in the first volume of the *Flora Norvegica* from 1766 is first, the importance of the visitation journeys as means to collect specimens that the bishop could convert into natural knowledge, and second, the importance of the priests' cooperation in the project. Thirdly, we notice how the Fatherland, science and God were weaved into the pattern that characterized northern natural science in this period. Bishop Gunnerus set up what has accurately been labeled a "church-scientific organization," and we might qualify it further by terming it a "state-church scientific organization."[141] This form of organized science was also the source of Gunnerus's multifaceted collection.

Learning to understand naturals

His countrymen enthusiastically conveyed to him what they found remarkable, Gunnerus claimed. That is something of an understatement when one looks at the extent to which they presented him with gifts. There was a steady flow of objects: Some living, but for the most part dead birds and fish, models, ritual Sami drums, old daggers and swords, flowers, seeds, trees and landed coconuts. How could the ministers know how and what to collect? Some of them did not. Gunnerus not only received scientific specimens, but barrels of butter, cloud berries and smoked salmon—objects suggesting that the understanding of the bishop's wish for "naturals" was broadly interpreted. "As there is a lack here of rarities to send, I humbly beg for Your Highness to accept 1 barrel of oysters and a small pot of sprat, which I send to You with the utmost devotion," wrote *sogneprest* Niels From.[142] The economy was based on natural wealth, and paying off honor and services in naturals was the common practice. The priests themselves received large parts of

---

[140] Ramberghaug, *Biskop Gunnerus, geistlig embetsmann.*
[141] Hagland, "Vitskaplege visitasreiser i Nord-Noreg."
[142] Dahl, letter 584, March 27, 1765.

their income in this way.[143] In this sense, the naturals traveling to the bishop's house continued a well-known tradition of giving the bishop natural gifts, and the way Gunnerus's subjects "misunderstood" his appeals to be provided with naturals shows how he tapped into a tradition of gift economy.[144] The bishop introduced a new definition of the good gift in an existing gift economy.

This also means that one of the achievements of Gunnerus was to install a new understanding of nature in his subjects. He instructed on how to make good nature finds and gave precise descriptions of what could be counted as *naturalia*. He was on the one hand interested in all things, "naturals . . . be they of any kind, also the ordinary."[145] "I happily receive everything You collect *ex 3bus regnis naturæ*."[146] On the other hand, his conception of "ordinary" was not easy to convey to uninformed collectors. He would be interested in everything that was ordinary in northern Norway, but things were of greater value if they were extraordinary within the learned community of scholars. The north contained treasures in the form of natural specimens which would be all too familiar to the people actually living there, but seldom and extraordinary for members of the scientific community: "There is nothing unusual about this Molluscum (an ink-fish), as it has been described and drawn by many authors, but it is very good that You do exercise by describing these sorts of things."[147]

He would encourage the use of systematic approaches, as he stated in the introduction to the first issue of *Skrifter* in 1761. The Society would especially wish for the countrymen to work within economy and natural history, ". . . but to ensure that one could work with more happiness, order and clarity, it would be most welcome, if one were to make a thorough acquaintance with *Linnæi floram*, as well as *Faunam Svecicam*, and in addition the newest or tenth edition of his *Systema Naturæ*."[148] Books, and most importantly Linnaeus' works, were the scientific tools that he most eagerly wanted his subjects to put into use. We see him ordering considerable numbers of books from Copenhagen and more remote booksellers, for himself, but also acting as a broker for

---

[143] Arne Bugge Amundsen, *Norsk religionshistorie*, and idem, "Prestesekken som aldri ble full."

[144] See for this Cook: "Global Economies and Local Knowledge" esp. pp. 116–117.

[145] Dahl, letter 186. April 20, 1762. "Det er mig meget kiært at fornemme, det D.V. haver samlet til mig nogle *naturalia*, og dersom de enda imidlertid kand overkomme nogle andre, være af hvad slags, ogsaa gemeene, som de være vil, saa skeede mig derved en meget stor fornøyelse."

[146] Dahl, letter 147, December 10, 1764. ". . . jeg tar med tak imod alt, vad de samler ex 3bus regnis naturæ."

[147] Dahl, letter 189, May 25, 1768. "Der er intet meere rart ved dette *Molluscum*, da det tilforn af mange auctoribus er bleven beskrevet og aftegnet, dog er det meget godt, at D.V. øver sig i at beskrive deslige Sager."

[148] Gunnerus: "Fortale" In *Skrifter* 1761. "Dog kunde vi ikke negte, at vi jo i Besynderlighed ønskede at vore Landsmænd vilde arbeide udi Oeconomien og den naturlige Historie og indsende til Selskabet deres Thermometriske og Barometriske Observationer, samt hvad de ellers kunde vide og erfare til Oplysning i Henseende til Naturens Rige: Men paa det at man herudi kunde være des lykkeligere, ordentligere og tydeli gere, saa var det meget ønskeligt, at man giorde sig vel bekiendt *Linnæi floram*, saa velsom og *Faunam Svecicam*, og fornemmelig hans *Systema Naturæ*, det nyeste eller tiende Oplag."

new publications, using the deans to send out subscription lists. In some instances he would order several copies, which he would sell on to various contacts, for example the important piece, given the make-up of his diocese, on *How to send naturals by way of the seas*.[149]

He also gave more explicit practical advice to those who wished to collect and send naturals. "If you should come upon some sea-products like small worms, insects, sea-trees or corals—and the insects always inhabiting these plants could be kept in spirit—in addition mountainous and other herbs with Norwegian names, it would give me great pleasure," he wrote.[150] He gave detailed descriptions of how to prepare flowers and insects, and increasingly asked for specific samples.

To others he posed questions, following a long tradition for collecting facts through surveys, which had been used with success since the early days of the Royal Society in London, and perhaps more directly relevant, addressed in the *Kungliga Svenska Vetenskaps Academiens Handlingar*.[151] He inquired about two types of capelin he had received: When were they fished? If any of them smelled bad? What time of the year did they come and depart from the fjord? Are the fish eaten? And so on.[152] Many of the priests' answers pointed to the great difficulties involved in obtaining the kind of information Gunnerus requested: From the wrecked, unhealthy, illness-infected and poor parish of Vardø, *sogneprest* Henning Kaurin wrote with resignation that he was unable to provide the Norwegian names of the flowers he sent. He had no tools—that is, books—to help him, and from the ignorant inhabitants there was no help to be had. They knew all the plants by "the well-known name flowers."[153] Kaurin's position also gives a good indication of how precarious the livelihood of the priests could be, and thus explains their ambitions of promotion and natural history. Kaurin and his family had first arrived in Vardø after six weeks of strenuous travel. On arrival they found that most of the inhabitants had died, only 20 *Rettighedsmænd* (property owners) were left, and even many of the soldiers had died, leaving only twelve. In addition, the fisheries had failed, and that left the last inhabitants without means to pay the priest.[154] Kaurin would stay in Vardø for several years, but he would strain himself to observe and procure natural knowledge for the bishop, acquiring better understanding of what natural history with an episcopal flavor was all about, working towards promotion.

Gunnerus was educating the priests by interrogating and explaining. He encouraged a certain kind of observation. Not pastoral poetry or grand eposes. He cultivated a certain kind of "factual sensibility," to use the words of Lorraine Daston.[155] A kind of observation and collecting that could be used to bring forth good natural objects. The

---

[149] The Danish translation of du Monceau: *Underretning om, hvorledes Træer*.

[150] Dahl, letter 86, Jan. 15, 1765.

[151] But see also the 43 questions, Røgeberg, *Norge i 1743*.

[152] Dahl, letter 161, March 29, 1765.

[153] Dahl, letter 562, Aug. 10, 1764. "thi Jeg Slipper at faa nogen underretning av disse dumme Indbyggere, Som kalder dem alle med det bekiendte Navn blomster."

[154] Dahl, letter 558, June 25, 1764.

[155] Daston, "The Factual Sensibility."

objects ought not to be improved upon by human ingenuity. When he encountered an especially well-made Basilisk, he admitted that a person without good knowledge about such things could easily be fooled. "Nevertheless it must be stated: The more natural, the better; because pure Nature . . . without human hand and art intervening is by far the best for honoring the Wisdom, Power and Goodness of God," he exclaimed.[156] The nature he preferred was one that honored God, that proved useful in all matters of improvement, but which could also deliver facts to the greater world of learning. What he promoted was to observe in and collect from nature what contemporary naturalists would deem scientifically interesting. Thus he directed the eyes of the priests towards a specific nature, which consisted of objects of "pure" nature, one that could be collected and described. Naming and describing the surface, and noting possible uses were all-important.[157] According to his eulogy the fruit of his work was that others were encouraged and enlightened: "A passion to wander about in the Kingdom of nature, to contemplate its riches, to observe its magnificence and graces with a more attentive eye, and to collect thereof, all unfolded everywhere."[158]

The exception was to be found in the gathering of names. Eighteenth-century natural history was at its core a naming sport. The visible should be provided with a nomenclature.[159] This indeed is the essence of Gunnerus's activity; he was naming the visible nature, and he trained an army of priests to look and identify with him. This does not mean that everything visible was important; one had to learn what to see, as Foucault underlines in his study on 18th-century natural history. One of the most striking traits of the natural historical research of Gunnerus, but also of the majority of works of natural historians in the period, was that one name was not enough. For Gunnerus, all the names of a plant or a fish were important—the Sami, the Finnish and the local Norwegian dialect. But this was highly dependent on the existence of one common denominator which, of course, was Latin. And so even the *Flora Norvegica* which Gunnerus collated, which was filled with important information for those who lived and worked on the soil in Norway, was published in Latin, and the vulgar edition which Gunnerus hoped to produce never appeared.[160] Thereby the politics of language in this natural historical enterprise made certain kinds of knowledge a precondition for participation.

The need for mastery of Latin put severe limits on who could participate in the realm of natural history. Priests and pupils who had graduated from the Latin schools

---

[156] Gunnerus: "Om Hav-Katten," 312. "Dog maa det her hede: Jo naturligere, jo bedre; thi den blotte Natur er i deslige Ting, førend menneskelig Haand og Kunst kommer dertil, allerbeqvemmest til at herliggiøre Guds uendelige Viisdom, Magt og Godhed."

[157] See for the same understanding of naturals, Eliasson, *Platsens blick*.

[158] Schøning, "Tale over Johan," 67. "En Lyst at vander omkring i naturens Rige, at betagte dens Rigdomme, med et mere opmærksomt Øue at beskue dens Pragt og Yndigheder, og at indsamle deraf, udbredte sig nu overalt."

[159] "Natural history is nothing more than the nomination of the visible," writes Foucault, *The Order of Things*, 144.

[160] Because of lack of money, accordingly.

could be taught to be good observers as well as collectors. In other countries physicians would make up a substantial part of the naturalists; in Norway their contributions were limited in number, as there were only about eight physicians in the whole country at the time.[161] Those with knowledge in Latin would in many instances be encouraged to write pieces and publish them in *Skrifter*, while those who had no such training were bound to be observers of another category. Most notably this is expressed by P. C. Buck, the head of the *Den Kongelige Handel* (The Royal Commerce), the privileged commerce company for the north, who became an important participant in Gunnerus's natural observation and collection network. Living in Hammerfest, which was to become the world's northernmost town when it acquired town status in 1789, he lived in an environment with few learned men. Or to put it more bluntly: Hammerfest became the allegedly smallest town in the world with its 77 inhabitants (1801).[162] But Buck, claiming to be an untutored lover of naturals, was a busy merchant and naturalist. He had ample contact with people who visited areas untouched by science—*ishavsfarere* (hunters in the Arctic sea region) who docked in the town, Russian traders from Siberia, and Sami hunters and herders. He saw natural history as a possibility of finding new resources for commercial activity in the north, but he also eagerly made descriptions of creatures and objects which were meant to support the scientific enterprise of the bishop. His letters also clearly expressed an aversion towards the new public sphere. Buck explained that he did not want to have his observations presented—"I am too weak to withstand the critique"—he claims, pointing to the way the newspapers criticize the learned and famous.[163] On the other hand, we can deduce from his humble letters an ambition to be counted among the members of the Society in Trondheim, an honor he would never attain, notwithstanding the drawings, relations, and observations he produced.

The collection as a site of action

For Gunnerus the whole diocese, the marshes and meadows, fields and fjords, mountains and mines were places where nature could be studied, where objects and knowledge could be obtained. He went botanizing, he prospected for stones and minerals, and he brought draftsmen with him on his visitation journeys to ensure that naturals were recorded. But first and foremost he established one privileged place for the study of this nature, the place where many of the objects from the priests ended up to be described, dissected, and observed: his own collection. Here, observations and natural objects were transformed into knowledge. What did the collection look like? How was it ordered? How did he arrange all the things? Where were the books and the instruments and the living animals? This is difficult to determine. Two sources mention a visit to

---

[161] See Cooper, *Inventing the Indigenous* for the importance of physicians in Germany.
[162] Nielsen, "Ishavet er vår åker," 51.
[163] Dahl, letter 764. Buck to Gunnerus. July 6, 1771.

the cabinet before Gunnerus died in 1773: In 1768 two Jesuits, Maximillian Hell and Johann Sainovics, passed through Trondheim on their way to Vardø where they would watch the passage of Venus the following summer. In Sanovics's travel journal the mention of the bishop's collection is indeed quite short. Between sentences telling about the Savoyarde musician with a monkey who entertained them in the bishop's house and the making of magnetic tools to help Hell carry out magnetic therapy on the sick in Trondheim, we learn: "The bishop showed us on the 17th his collection of fishes, birds, conches, and seeplants, and his really outstanding library."[164] There is not much more to learn from Peter Collett who wrote on a visit to the collection in his diary: "The morning we stayed at home until 11 o'clock when we viewed the natural cabinet of Mr Bishop Gunnerus. This mostly consists of national naturals and does in particular have a beautiful collection of conches and fishes."[165] We can scarcely envision what the collection looked like from these excerpts and the auction catalogue made after his death, but we do know how the bishop wanted to use it: It was going to be published in the *Skrifter*. And what we do know, by way of his own writing, is what he *did* with his collection.[166] And as we will see, his collection was established as a tool, not an entity to be viewed, but a tool to be utilized and made public.

His first natural historical article in the first volume of *Skrifter* opens with the following introductory remark: "On my visitation journeys, and especially in Nordland and Finnmark, I have collected some naturals of all kinds, and I have prepared myself to describe some of the pieces, those that seem to me to deserve it most."[167] In this first article about the Fulmar (*Havhest*) he established himself as a collector, and at the same time, the collection as the place for doing scientific work. He immediately stated that this strange bird was a worthy object of scientific study, not least because it "gives us sufficient proof of the Wisdom of God." This introduction establishes the collection as a place where Science and God are honored through the bishop's work.

After this initial framing there followed an extensive description of the bird, its color, size, the form of its eyes and head, the length of the throat, the form of the body, the length of feathers and wings, with special attention paid to feet and beak. Attentively he examines the bird, and all its visible and differential signs. Then he opens its insides, evaluates the intestines, nerves, blood vessels and muscles—it is a bird of strong nature and long life.[168] Gunnerus was not describing a general fulmar. He described this particular specimen found by the North Cape, transported for weeks or months on a boat, before arriving here, in the hand of Gunnerus. He compares, fetches books where sim-

---

[164] Sainovics in Littrow, *P. Hell's Reise nach Wardoe*. "Der Bishof zeigte uns am 17ten seine Sammlung von Fischen, Vögeln, Konchilien und Meerplanzen, und seine wahrhaft ausgezeichnete Bibliothek."
[165] 6te august, Collett: *Dagbok på en reise i Norge 1773*, "Foremiddagen vare vi hiemme til Kl: 11 da vi besaae Hr. Biskop Gunneri Natural Cabinet. Dette bestaar mest af nationale Naturalia og har en smuk Samling af Coquiller og Fiske i Besynderlighed."
[166] There is an auction catalogue from 1774.
[167] Gunnerus, "Om Havhesten," 184.
[168] Gunnerus, "Om Havhesten," 184–185.

ilar birds are described or illustrated, compares some more, and invites the reader to look at the bird and compare together with him. And then he cuts. On some occasions he must make do with birds already dead and preserved on arrival, and only compare their surfaces. Sometimes he dissects on his own; at other times he says, "I let the specimen be cut," implying mostly that the town-physician Henrici, educated by the famous Albrecht von Haller in Göttingen, did the cutting.

Thus the fact emerged as made in his collection. The dead animal was made into a scientific fact through his work in the collection and the writing of the article. Once established, the facts could be used by Gunnerus to counter descriptions made by others, Other naturalist's misperceptions and false descriptions were contradicted. Old-fashioned stories in classical works, or fable and folk tales are presented, evaluated, and corrected. The direct experience of the object in the enclosed space of the natural cabinet was the warrant of truth, as he sat there directly sensing it. In this he relies on a specific use of the senses. Establishing differences in species through sounds will not do. Plain observation out there in the field is also more or less reliable. But sitting there, object in hand, with the possibility of opening it up, caring for it, gives by far the most trustworthy information.

Historian of science Paula Findlen has asserted in her book, *Possessing Nature*, on the early natural historical collections in Italy, that the collectors saw the museum as a tool to making a more precise natural history where nature became uniquely proximate. And just as the telescope and the microscope did, the collection was an instrument that enhanced the senses.[169] Gunnerus's collection would serve this same function. The man who was among the first to investigate large parts of Norway scientifically, to observe and label Norwegian nature in its large variety, needed the collection as a tool to get close enough to nature to describe it. Authoritative and true knowledge about nature was hence best produced in a natural cabinet in Trondheim.

But the way his collection was configured as the privileged space for construction of natural facts was also a result of his pedagogic style of writing. ". . . Your works are so beautiful, so fulfilled and elegant that I have hardly ever read anything with greater pleasure," wrote Linnaeus from Uppsala. "You present the natural objects so visibly that I imagine seeing them with my own eyes and feeling them with my own hands."[170] Gunnerus's texts reveal his pedagogical ambitions. His papers on specific objects give exact information on how he goes about examining the objects, how objects should be treated, looked upon, examined. The stress is put on how to convey what essential and enduring qualities to look for, but he also wrote in a didactic genre that would make it possible for those who wanted to follow him to understand the method of a naturalist.

---

[169] Findlen, *Possessing Nature*, 200–201
[170] Linné to Gunnerus, March 12th 1764, in Amundsen: *Johan Ernst Gunnerus*, 29. "Deres verker er så vakre, så fullendte og elegante at jeg knapt noen sinne har lest noe med store glede; for De fremstiller naturgjenstandene så anskuelig at jeg synes å se dem selv med egne øyne og føle dem med hendene."

Instruction, institution, and patriotic pride

Gunnerus envisioned his own collection as part of an establishment promoting science for the public good. He moved to one of the farms which was part of the bishop's endowment, being just outside Trondheim, and started converting it into an institution of natural history. Here he laid out a botanical garden where he planted and cultivated seeds and trees he had received and ordered from his diocese or from foreign correspondents. Linnaeus was the example he wanted to emulate. Linnaeus' institution in Uppsala served as a model for several Danish projects at this point, and Gunnerus seems to have brought this model with him to Trondheim. During the 1760s he also developed a friendly and not least scientific correspondence with Linnaeus. The botanical garden laid out in Copenhagen the years Gunnerus lived there, which was paid for by the king, inspired by Linnaeus, and with professorships attached, was another source of inspiration.[171] Gunnerus was in constant need of money, and at one point he attempted to convince the authorities to lower the taxes on the farm, and to let him purchase it so that he would be able to cultivate it better. In these letters he portrayed his work as patriotic. He argued "that my botanical garden could as time passes, become an honor for Norway . . ."[172] And to another recipient he claimed that his projects at Berg aimed at "the encouragement of my compatriots and utility for the public."[173] The question of what patriotism meant and implied at this point in time is far too comprehensive a topic to delve into here, but one of the letters where the "honor of Norway" is emphasized is addressed to the mighty *Geheimraad* and chancellor to the king in Copenhagen, Otto Thott. We can thus deduce that promoting Norway was not opposed to promoting the conglomerate state and the king, but that quite the contrary, the Cameralist policy of the king's ministry in Copenhagen was promoted by Gunnerus in Trondheim. The context of these letters was that Gunnerus spent a fortune, according to himself, on building the farm into an institution for natural history. The project was abandoned sometime around 1766 when Gunnerus moved back to Trondheim. That he indeed must have used a fortune is indicated by his debt at the time of his death.

However, not only the botanical garden, but also the collection and not least the work *Flora Norvegica* were conceived of by Gunnerus as means of promoting the nation. Most importantly, the collection was not portrayed primarily as a physical site for public use; it was referred to as something that would "in our Tr.hjemske actis [be made] publicly known," that is, the intention of the collection was to be published.[174] Even though the first museums had at this time been established (the British Museum had opened in 1754), it is still particularly evident in these letters that Gunnerus never

---

[171] Wagner, "Fra Kunstkammer til moderne."

[172] Dahl, letter 64, September 17, 1763. "at min *botaniske have*, som med Tiden kunde blive en *Honeur* for Norge . . ."

[173] Dahl, letter 65, September 17, 1763. ". . . som ei lidet vilde opmuntre ig til at anvende alle mine kræfter og min ringe Formue til *publici nytte og nationens ære.*"

[174] Dahl, letter 65, September 17, 1763, to Geheime Raad Tott.

established a public museum. Museums in the parlance of the day could be many things. An older meaning of the word, as a study chamber of the learned man, was still in use. The modern public museum was yet in its early stages. This is even more obvious when the term museum is used in the statutes of the Society. Manuscripts, drawings, printed books, and naturals are part of the *Museum Societatis*. The museum contained the material objects of the Society, and no less important: these were the scientific objects. The museum was not open to the public in the sense that whoever wanted to would be let in, the bishop's collection and later the museum of the Society were public in the sense that they would be open for use for the benefit of the public.

Embodied scientists in the making

Scientific objects did not exist as such. They had to be configured and transformed into objects for scientific study. The same goes for the subjects of science, they needed to be equipped with the proper eye and hand for performing scientific activity. Gunnerus especially, but also other active members of the Society, would see it as preparation for the foundation of a Norwegian University. In the meantime, Gunnerus prepared students for a life devoted to science. He kept a number of *amanuenses* or *famuli* during the 1760s who managed his correspondence, made illustrations of naturals, and helped to dissect animals. Some of them would also produce their own articles for the *Skrifter* of the Society, and two of them would go to Uppsala to study with Linnaeus. Most of these helpers and students had finished or were on their way to finishing their theological studies, and worked with Gunnerus while they were waiting for the final exam or for a position in the Church. Being Gunnerus's helping hand in natural history was regarded as a good career move, in the same way as we have seen for the priests. His amanuensis for seven years, Jacob von der Lippe Parelius, received a letter of reference from Gunnerus stating all the merits that would make him a good priest—his Christian and respectable conduct was important, but so was his extensive knowledge of Norwegian agriculture, fisheries and natural history.[175] He was one among many to have his knowledge of natural history given as a good reason for being promoted to a position within the church. The group of students Gunnerus promoted ventured into different careers, but by far the most common was to become a priest, and none would end up living off their scientific work. Men of letters earning their living from civil or ecclesiastical positions were the normal state of affairs in European intellectual life in general, but in Norway the lack of institutions of higher teaching produced a glass ceiling against gaining merit by way of scientific proficiency.

Gunnerus also ensured that pupils of the cathedral school had the possibility to attend lessons in natural history and to receive mathematical training. Neither subjects had a prominent place in the school curricula. Town physician Robert Stephan Henrici, whom we have met as one of the first members of the Society, was paid to give the pupils

---

[175] Dahl, letter 39, May 15, 1773.

thorough teaching in the physical sciences, botany, mineralogy, and other parts of natural history from 1765, by way of excursions every Wednesday afternoon. When Didrik
Fester was employed as teacher of mathematics in Trondheim, through a donation
from Thomas Angell's testament, he was also to give the pupils the education they did
not acquire through the school. Henrici and Fester were both active members of the Society, reading papers, correcting and proofreading the papers of others, and basically
keeping the Society scientifically vigorous after the death of Gunnerus. Henrici did not
write himself, involved as he was in serving the community with a hospital service and
being a physician on meager pay. But he was apparently eager to promote natural history as a teacher. Henrici had a prominent education from Göttingen, Fester on his part
was an autodidact who had made his career solely from the love of mathematics. Ending up as a "public" teacher of mathematics without any university training was exceptional. He also contributed to the *Skrifter* of the Society, presented mathematical
problems in *Adressecontoiret*, the local newspaper, and authored texts on a range of topics.[176] The initiatives and foundation were built to promote natural knowledge and natural history in Trondheim by informing the young. Unfortunately, for both Fester and
Henrici, students were difficult to attract. Repeated attempts were made to have the
rector (principal) at the cathedral school persuade pupils to attend these lectures.[177]
Eventually in 1783 the first "Borgerskole," actually the first *Realschule* of Scandinavia,
was established in Trondheim.[178] The grounds for this could well be said to have been
laid by the activities connected to the Society and Gunnerus's ambitions, but this school
had a very different agenda than to produce researchers. The school was to teach the
pupils what they needed for private enterprise and capitalist expansion, or for *det reale
Liv* (the real life). Making the intellectually-minded student was a matter of concern for
the early establishment of the Society, but when Trondheim managed to get a school
which would teach modern languages and mathematics this was to be a school for serving the commercial needs of the bourgeoisie.

The right tools for collection

Apart from the naturals, what exactly was it Gunnerus wanted to have in his collection? On the curiosity side of it, we learn that he already had an interest in natural and
living things before he came to the region known as the *Nordenfjellske* (literarily: north
of the mountains) landscape. Right before leaving Copenhagen he ordered a parrot
from the West-Indies. Whether or not it arrived in Trondheim we do not know. But
there were other conspicuous objects: A Greenland kayak was ordered from Copenhagen, and from later inventories it is possible to confirm that Gunnerus had a collection from Greenland. Why? There were no Eskimos in Norway. We can think of

---

[176] On Fester see Brun, *Regnekunsten i Norge* and DBL and NBL.
[177] Dahl, letters 1–6.
[178] The foundation was laid in 1778, while it started delivering lectures in 1783.

two reasons why the kayak was shipped off from Copenhagen to Trondheim together with a microscope from London. First, a kayak was a standard object in a northern European, and especially Danish, natural chamber. The famous 17th century polymath Ole Worm, whose collection had become a fragmented part of the Danish king's *Kunstkammer*, would still be very well known from the widely distributed catalogue which contained an engraving from his collection, complete with kayak and Greenland gear. Collection conventions in northern Europe can explain the presence of the kayak in Gunnerus's house. Second, we might attribute the presence of the Greenland objects to an ambition to build a Norwegian research station for the north. Greenlanders were living in conditions that were sometimes depicted as equal to those in the far north of Norway. People and plants on the same latitude could be viewed as interchangeable, so to speak.[179] Perhaps the full meaning of the kayak was that it actually fulfilled both functions.

Getting hold of a microscope was essential for Gunnerus. However, this was a tool that required expertise, money, and patience. Gunnerus addressed professor Oeder in Copenhagen to receive help in ordering the right type. The microscope was ordered from John Cuff in Fleet Street and brought to Copenhagen before it could start the long journey to Trondheim. And obviously, on arrival, it was soon put to use, as the *Skrifter* (Transactions) repeatedly refer to observations and drawings made on the basis of the microscope—everything from bits of the basking shark's skin to close to invisible sea creatures. In terms of today's technology it was not really a microscope but rather an advanced magnifying glass. It was called an aquatic microscope, where the object was put in water, and it had obvious advantages for the traveling bishop as it could be folded together and kept in an easily carried box. For a man of Gunnerus's ambitions, this was a necessary instrument, and the frequent references to its use point to the status it was accorded. But even more fascinating as an instrument of science, and more remote from our perceptions of how to look the part of the scientist, was the solar microscope Gunnerus acquired some years later. This instrument had to be placed close to a window, where the sun could reach the object, making a magnified picture appear on the wall. A microscope is a machine for the lonely worker, whereas the solar microscope would allow for an audience. According to Gunnerus in his letters to Linnaeus, both instruments had been used to present the *rauåte* (Calanus, a kind of plankton) to the Society.[180]

The value of these instruments was immense, not only in scientific terms. They were objects of great sensation—seeing things in a magnified state was not only a way of enhancing the senses and making new treasures of nature appear but also demonstrating the power of science. Kaurin, the priest of Vardø, whom we met earlier depressed and deprived in Vardø, was delighted when the Jesuits Hell and Sanovics spent the winter there, not least because he was allowed to look at things through Hell's microscope.

---

[179] Environmental historian Karen Ousland has shown this through her work on the forced migration of Reindeer from Norway to Island. Ousland, "Nature in League with Man."
[180] The information stems from Ekblad, "Biskop Johan Ernst Gunnerus."

Objects of value

Gunnerus collected a capital of naturalia which was of interest to a wide European network of natural historians and collectors: The far north. This vast territory had few visitors, especially of the kind that could provide scientific knowledge and collectable
items; still it contained valuables in the form of extraordinary exhibition pieces with
an economic and social, as well as scientific value in the mid-eighteenth century collector's market. The examples are abundant: The pro-chancellor at the University of
Copenhagen, Erich Pontoppidan, wanted Gunnerus to provide the duchess of Portland with some living grouses, which he believed could be shipped to London by
freight boat by one of the local shipping magnates.[181] The historically and genealogi-
cally interested Torkel Klevenfeldt in Copenhagen, who claimed to be collecting on
behalf of the Viennese court, approached Gunnerus with the wish of obtaining "everything that Norwegian Nature brings forth, preferably the best pieces that could be fitting for a Cabinet that will become the best in the world [i.e. the Viennese]."[182] And
he received natural objects from Gunnerus, like many others. Even if Klevenfeldt was
only able to give some bottles of Tokayer in return, the objects from the north provided means by which Gunnerus could tap into a collector's market in Copenhagen
and Europe. He would gain social and scientific recognition by delivering natural objects to Danish noblemen, English noblewomen, world-renowned Swedish naturalists,
and to the *Kunstkammer* in Vienna. There is nothing to indicate that he was actually
paid for what he sent off, but the prestige, and not least the objects he would get in
return, proved valuable.

Through the various items which Gunnerus sent off he made himself a name as a
man of natural knowledge and he stabilized his identity as a learned man in an international network which understood the value of the scientific objects, economically, socially, and intellectually. The priests who submitted these specimens to Gunnerus in the
first place had fewer possibilities to tap into this network of valuable collecting pieces.
Gunnerus had his ministers under command, and could extract the value from these
exchanges and convert it into new currencies in Copenhagen and elsewhere. While his
informants and collectors would engage in a reciprocal economy with him, he himself
would be able to move into a space where values circulated, and gains and values could
be accumulated on quite a different scale.

From personal to institutional collection

When Gunnerus died, his collections, books, and other artifacts were auctioned, the standard way of realizing value after a death. He had no direct descendants, but the heirs, his

---

[181] Dahl, letter 414, Jan. 29, 1761. The Duchess of Portland built an immense private collection at this
time.
[182] Dahl, letter 416, Jan. 31, 1761.

sister and her family who were part of his household, needed to convert the *realia* into cash due to the debts the bishop had acquired. The Society deliberated that the artifacts should be bought by the Society, before Heinrich Meincke, a rich member, intervened and made a bid for the whole collection which he subsequently donated to the Society. The collection was termed a Natural cabinet, even though far from all the approximately 180 items were natural specimens. Gunnerus had abandoned the farm at Berg years before, because of the cost, and the realization that he would not be able to keep it for his family if he was to leave his office as bishop. But the collection and the library were obviously safely stored in the bishop's town house, close to the town square in *Dronningens gade* (street) 5.

The items listed in the auction catalogue are far less than what we could expect after the flood of objects which had passed over the doorstep of the Gunnerus house. What had happened to them? Some were sent off to the natural cabinets of learned men and aristocrats in Copenhagen, some were exchanged for specimens from other European naturalists, but very many objects must have been used up through the scientific investigations of Gunnerus and through general decay. Minerals and conches survived without constant care, but the biological material suffered. The auction catalogue tells us little about the way this collection was ordered or kept. It is a simple list. What it does tell us is thus first and foremost what survived, which undoubtedly can be termed a mixed bag. Herbs and flowers (Gunnerus's herbarium exists to this day), gold, silver, iron and other minerals make up the most considerable part of the collection, which might be because they can be listed separately. Conches were only one item, two turtles, and a collection of fish likewise. Teeth and heads of fishes as well as five stuffed seals were listed, as were two wooden models of the basking shark, five coconuts and a set of tea cups made from the same material. Various carved and adorned objects were listed, as well as the handle of a sword or dagger, excavated from a barrow possibly belonging to the renowned Viking chief *Egild Ulfserk*. Curiosities and oddities are mixed with the scientific and systematic, one could deduce, but the list does not indicate how and where these things had been exhibited.

Perhaps the most striking fact of many of the oddities is that they are representations in a format which strikes us as unscientific: The wooden models of fish, the centerpiece for a table representing the various crafts in Norway, two models of Sami tents, two stunted offspring of cows. This testifies to the pain experienced in trying to make representations and illustrations of scientific merit. Finding a *lanterna magica*, a looking glass, a perspective with 56 tables, and the above-mentioned microscopes testify to the various attempts at making exact representations, and as was the overall ambition of the scientists in Trondheim, as well as elsewhere, seeing and representing was the overall goal of science.

As pointed out above, we do not know how Gunnerus's collection was displayed, or what it looked like. What we do know is that he favored order and system in line with Linnaeus, that he was a systematic collector and that he demanded rigor from the collectors he cooperated with. As the list from the estate of Gunnerus does not really give us any clue to his system, the catalogue produced in 1779 is more instructive, even though we do not know whether the principles used for classification here were in accordance with the order before Gunnerus died.

This is a catalogue of the whole collection of the Society, which means that books were a substantial part of this.[183] The object part of the *Catalogus Librorum atqve Rerum naturalium et artificalium* is divided into two main parts: *Rerum naturalium* (objects from nature) and *Rerum artificalium* (artificial objects). The naturals are divided into *Regnum animale* (115 items), *Regnum vegetabile* (21 items) and *Regnum minerale* (50+ items). The artificial objects are divided into *Instrumenta et Artefacta* (31 items) and *Arma, Antiquitatis, exotica &c.* (32 items) and *Suppellex Grönlandica* (32 items). The main dividing lines are thus either natural or man-made; thereafter we find a division based on well-established categories within contemporary collecting practices. Why objects from Greenland should deserve a separate category is not clear, but we could easily imagine that there was a sense of these objects belonging together geographically and also that the pragmatic reason that there is enough of them to form a distinct group.

Within the group of artificial objects a second principle is at work: The material an object is made from forms the basis for ordering it inside the group. Vessels for drinking are for example divided into those made of metal and those made of wood. In other categories objects made of metals are grouped together and mentioned before those made of stone. This mode of classification can also be found in earlier collections in Europe—for example, within the Catalogue of Ole Worm from 1655.[184] What is different in the Society's collection is the very strict separation between natural and artificial objects. This is also the prevailing form of classification within the contemporary classification schemes in the 18th century, as is the lack of interest in chronological divisions. As archaeologist Axel Christophersen points out, there was neither a division between that which is found beneath or over the earth's surface nor was there a division of objects from different periods.[185] An arrowhead is an arrowhead. This again locates this collection in the mainstream of European collections.

In the community in Trondheim books based on and dealing with collections circulated, including the books written by Linnaeus based on the royal collections in Sweden, as well as the *Neues systematisches Conchylien-Cabinet geordnet und beschrieben* from 1769, based mainly on a large Danish collection, and donated to the Society by *Geheimraadinne* Schøller. What begs the question is of course what connections there were between the catalogue on the one side and the actual display and the store of objects on the other.

Looking after the collection

Visitors were not impressed by the order. Professor Fabricius of Copenhagen was less than pleased when he visited in 1778 while the museum was in secretary Wittrup's

---

[183] The description of the catalogue leans heavily on Christophersen: "Selskabets Cabinet."
[184] Mordhorst, *Genstandsfortællinger.*
[185] Christophersen: "Selskabets Cabinet."

house. He hailed the great Gunnerus as a man of great spirit, with knowledge of many sciences, with great energy and not least the ability to encourage others.[186] The description of the collection was less encouraging. Here were specimens from all three natural kingdoms, models and antiquities. "It is really a pity that it [the natural cabinet] is not kept in the order or the condition that it deserves. Many pieces seem to be on the verge of destruction."[187]

When the Society acquired new premises one could imagine or at least hope that this would ensure a better verdict of the Society's collection. Surgeon and member of the Swedish Academy Pehr Gustaf Lindroth visited the collection in 1797 in connection with a study trip along the coast. The secretary showed him "the Assembly hall of the Scientific Society, where we viewed the library and the naturals collection, which consisted of two badly stuffed animals, a leopard and a tiger, which had a quite beautiful skin. A small but badly conserved collection of birds were partly hanging inside a cupboard, partly lying in paper. A rather beautiful collection of conches and insects, the conches had many doublets but few species, not yet in order . . . Of fishes there were few, badly stuffed or dried . . . and all sort of Greenlandic costumes and house gear as well as boat tools were amassed."[188]

When Thomas Malthus and Edward Clarke visited Norway during the summer of 1799, they visited the collection and Clarke was enthusiastic about parts of the Museum: "At the end of the library is the Museum, a square chamber filled with antiquities, minerals, plants, animals, etc. Opposite to the entrance, in a glass case, is a human body in a remarkable state of preservation; the skin only being removed, and every muscle displayed to view in the greatest perfection. Below the case containing this body are preserved the bones and weapons of a Norwegian King, . . . Among the other curiosities, we saw the *Runic Tympanum*, or *magic-drum* of the Laplanders. . . . The Museum also contains other things which relate to the customs and history of the *Lapps*. From the ceiling are suspended the canoes, weapons, and utensils of the *Greenlanders*. . . . The collection of *Natural History* is very little worth notice. Two tigers, presented by an officer, but in a bad state of preservation, are placed on an eminence in the middle of the room. The body of a large birch is shown, which, when split by an axe, disclosed a horseshoe, unaltered as when it was made, in the very heart of the tree. There are, moreover, magnificent specimens of coral, from the *Norwegian* Seas; and we saw that curious animal the *Lemming*, or *Mountain-mouse*, as preserved in alcohol."[189]

---

[186] Fabricius: *Reise nach Norwegen*, 245–46.

[187] Fabricius, *Reise nach Norwegen*, 246. Es ist in der That Schade, dass es weder in der Ordnung noch in dem Stande erhalten wird, wie es wol verdiente. Viele Stücke scheinen ihrem Untergange nahe zu seyn.

[188] Aase og Hård, "Det norska Aten," 64. "Vetenskaps Societetens samlingsrum, hvaerst vi besågo Bibliotheket och Natural-Samlingen, som bestod av 2ne illa utstoppade Djur, en Leopard och en Tiger, hvilkas skinn voro ganska vackra. En liten men illa Conditionerad samling av foglar dels hängande tilsammans uti ett litet skåp och dels liggande uti Papper. En ganska vacker samling af Kräftor, och Insecter; snäckorna voro många doupletter, men få Species, ännu ej i ordning . . . af fiskar voro få, och illa upstoppaded eller torkade . . . och af alla sorter af Grönländarnas drägt och husgeråd samt båtredskaper voro här hopsamlade."

[189] Clarke, *Travels in Various Countries*, pp. 237–243.

The enthusiasm of Clarke was not connected to a vision of the Society's collection as a scientific collection, and the many critical descriptions leave us with the suspicion that the collection of objects was left to decay after the death of Gunnerus. But the minutes of the Society give another impression. During the last decades of the 18th century the collection was kept up and looked after by various means. New acquisitions were made, in particular a good collection of minerals arrived from Kongsberg, where the Society had active members, and where they could boast a mineral collection of great renown. From Røraas they had also received a good mineral collection. The male skeleton with prepared muscles was donated from Henrici along with a range of other objects. And already in the catalogue from 1779 we can see other donators than Gunnerus.[190] Still, the striking fact about that early catalogue is that it shows how large a portion of the Society's collection stemmed from Gunnerus's time. Even though a keeper of the natural cabinet is mentioned in the first statutes, it is doubtful whether there actually was a collection belonging to the Society aside from Gunnerus's collection before his death. After the donation by Heinrich Meincke, though, objects also flowed in from other members of the Society. Medals and old coins, antiquities and other naturals came into the collection, either through active acquisition or as donations. Several herbariums were donated, and a particularly fine collection of birds, even comprising a paradise bird, arrived from the Danish colony Tranquebar, where one of the Anker brothers was governor. A sea-captain, de Jong, would also donate what was called a substantial collection in 1795.

Thus we can infer that the collection was looked after collectively by the members of the Society. As a strategy for keeping up a collection this is demanding and has its obvious drawbacks. Things need repair, dusting, updating; pickled specimens need refill of alcohol, stuffed animals need to be refurbished, new items need to be put in place, and old ones rearranged. In a Society without any paid assistant this is the kind of work that demands a huge effort on the part of its members. One such member was the aforementioned Didrik Fester. In December 1777 the Society decided to update its *globus terrestris*. The occasion was the recent voyages of James Cook. Taking part in the second journey around the world, father and son Forster produced a lengthy book study which was printed in 1777.[191] The new information about the geographical conditions in the South Sea was read with great interest in Trondheim. Fester approached the meeting with his plan to redo the terrestrial globe to have all the new lands discov-

---

[190] *Catalogus Librorum arqve Rerum.* The material objects which were not donated by Henrik Meincke are marked on the list with the initials of the donators.

[191] Forster, *Observations made*; DKNVS. Protocol. "1777 den 11 December. var Selskabets ordentlige Samling hos Vice=Præses hvor da først

    1) blev tagne under betragtning en heel Deel allerede indkomne Anmeldelser fra bondestanden, men da endnu flere kunde ventes, blev besluttet nærmere ved næste Samling at bestemme de udleverede Priiser til de mest fortiente.

    2) besluttet Selskabet af de nyeste Opdagelserne i sær mod Sydpolen og som i Forsters Engelske beskrivelse over de nyeste Reiser, paa det i ham befindtlige Kort ere exprimerede at uddraget det vigtigste til forbedring paa Selskabets ringede Globus terrestris, hvilket Hr Fester paatog sig at ville besørge."

ered during Cook's voyage engraved on it. In the Society's archive we can find his meticulous list of new islands to be recorded on the globe, but how exactly he managed to engrave the new information is something we do not know. The globe has disappeared. However, what this information testifies to is first to what degree various instruments and other materials were looked after, and second, how unevenly information and scientific materials traveled. It took two years to get a microscope, letters could be on their way for months; on the other hand, news from around the South Pole could be engraved on the globe in Trondheim the same year that the book appeared on the market. Few globes, we gather, would be updated on such short notice as the globe in Trondheim was.

The site of the Society

One question remains: Where was the scientific society located? In the heads of the members, in the protocol or was there a physical site? Notwithstanding the banality of the question, this is harder to answer than it would first seem. Where the Society was situated before it acquired its statutes and a protocol in 1767 is a question which is not really possible to answer. But presumably the houses of Schøning, Suhm and Gunnerus would serve as the place where articles were discussed and prepared for printing. After this date, the Society's regular meetings were in the house of the "*vice-præsidis,*" i.e. Gunnerus's house, until his death. On the festival days and when an exceptionally important meeting was taking place, as in the case of reading eulogies for deceased members, the home of Johan Daniel Berlin served as "the public auditorium of the Society."[192] This house was located at the outskirts of the city, at the corner of what is now Erling Skakkes gate and Prinsens gate and where Trøndelag theater is now located. After this date the open meetings were held in the cathedral school while the regular meetings were held in the house of the *vice-præses.* But the *Museums Societatis,* the collection of books, naturals and antiquities, was elsewhere.

From the death of Gunnerus until the inauguration of the new premises in the cathedral school in 1787, the collection was kept in the house of the secretary. According to the statutes of 1767, the collection should be the responsibility of the librarian of the Society, "... his duty is to keep an inventory of the manuscripts, *naturalia,* drawings, printed books etc. of the Society, and accurately describe *Museum Societatis,* so that this can in time be rendered in print."[193] Thus the librarian was intended to have a broad responsibility; the problem was that there were no means to pay him for the work. Gunnerus had seen the necessity of having a paid secretary to make the Society function better: "With the next mail I will write hr *Etatsraad* Guldberg and ask him to

---

[192] This again is inferred from the fact that his name is mentioned sometimes, and that in 1774 he asks to be relieved from his responsibilities for holding the public auditorium of the Society.

[193] Statutes in *Skrifter IV*. "... hans Pligt er, at holde en Fortegnelse over Sælskabets haandskrifter, Naturalia, Teigninger, trykte Bøger etc; og ordentlig beskrive Museum Societatis, saa at det med tiiden kunde gives i Trykken."

secure 1000 Rigsdaler yearly for the Society, if it shall be able to accomplish something honorable, for the gain of the state and especially Norway."[194] In the same letter he proposed to offer the secretary who worked with him on the university reform in Copenhagen 1771–72, Johan Henrik Tauber, to come to Norway and become the real secretary of the Society—and this is most probably the reason why Lorentz Wittrup was designated vice-secretary for a period of time until it was resolved that he was indeed to be the real secretary of the Society.

During the first decade after Gunnerus's death, the *Museum Societatis* was kept in the house of the secretary—Wittrup (secretary from 1772 to 1784)—and the different care-taking tasks were fulfilled by him, serving both as secretary and librarian. This is important in several ways, but most notably because as one man was looking after the Society's collection, it was possible to keep it together. On the other hand, the Society did not meet in his premises, and thus the collection and the library were not "present" at the meeting of the Society. We will return to specific fates of the collections. The essential question here is where the Society went to.

New premises: the Harsdorff building

When returning from Copenhagen in 1771 Gunnerus brought with him the name of a new *vice præses* and funds for prizes. In addition there was a substantial allowance given for scientific instruments by count Thott in Copenhagen. The very same year work was begun on finding a permanent location for the Society, and not least to combine this with an observatory where Thott's instruments could be put to work. *Katedralskolen* was in a deplorable state. Built in 1706 it had been a disgrace ever since it was established by a corrupt bishop who used as little money as possible on the building. On the death of Thomas Angell in 1767, the uncle of Suhm's wife, the town received an inheritance of immense proportions. There were strict restrictions on the use of these funds, but attempts were made to get hold of some of the money to build a new cathedral school with premises attached for the Society.[195]

An application was sent from the *Stiftdireksjon* (the highest authority in the diocese consisting of the bishop and the diocesan governor) to the Chancellery in Copenhagen where financing the building was the main topic, and the co-location of the Society and the cathedral school was proffered as a good solution. The role of Prince Frederik as the patron of the Society was of course also referred to. Already in April the application was accepted, but the final appropriation of the plans and the building process would be seriously hampered during the next few years. One problem was the drawings for the building, which did not meet the continental standards of the court architect; another problem was the financing.

---

[194] Letter to Suhm, July 11, 1772. In Dahl 1891, 49. "Med næste post skriver jeg Hr. Etatsraad Guldberg til for at anmode ham om at forskaffe Selskabet aarlig 1000 Rdlr., om det skal rejse Hovedet i Vejret og præstere noget retskaffent, til Nytte for Staten og især Norge."
[195] For the history of the building, see Baustad, *Harfsdorffbygningen*.

In the meantime, efforts were being made to prepare a suitable building. Johan Daniel Berlin, the autodidact and multitalented member of the Society made the drawings. Berlin was one of the most active members of the Society; he was also an important contributor to the infrastructure of Trondheim, be it as town musician, fireworks inspector or waterworks superintendent.[196] He was also a contributor to the *Skrifter*, undertook metrological observations over a 20-year period and had a substantial collection of scientific instruments. He would never be asked to have any official task in the Society, a signal that his humble origins and lack of formal qualifications barred his way to the socially and intellectually higher classes.[197] Nevertheless, now Berlin became important. He produced a set of drawings of a grandiose brick building with an imposing observatory tower as the central feature. This was the occasion where the Society could really turn itself into both a landmark of the town, and a scientific society which could undertake scientific tasks. Observatories had been important working tools and symbolic features for scientific societies around Europe—for example in Stockholm, where the observatory played a prominent role. Berlin's drawings were sent to Copenhagen for appropriation. There they were rejected by the court builder and professor of architecture Caspar Frederik Harsdorff. Whereas Berlin's drawings suggested a town hall, Harsdorff's project was more in line with a military *caserne*, it has been stated.[198] But that was the end product. In the meantime Harsdorff had also presented a drawing of a building where the observatory was the main feature.

The lay out of the building was to present one big room for teaching pupils of the cathedral school, with an adjoining library. In the second floor the assembly hall of the Society would be flanked by a room for the collection and a library. The rest of the building would house teachers and the principal.

The responsible person of the Thomas Angell foundation protested that the plans were too extravagant and expensive. He thought it sufficient to erect a wooden building. However, the king intervened and decided that the building would be made of brick, but "constructed in such way that if possible it would have a mess hall but without an observation tower." Thus an observatory where the scientific instruments given from Thott could be put into use would never be erected, and this occasion for making a more scientifically active society was lost.[199]

On 5 February 1787, the Society was assembled in the house of the *vice-præses*. It was then stated that on 29 January, the birthday of the king would be celebrated with double pleasure. The Society would receive and inaugurate its new premises, the "huge and splendid assembly hall," the library and natural-objects cabinet. Additionally the portrait of the *præses*, Prince Frederik, was presented to the Society accompanied by "instrumental sound."[200]

---

[196] For more on Berlin, see Michelsen, *Johan Daniel Berlin.*
[197] According to Suphellen in Michelsen, *Johan Daniel Berlin.*
[198] Pedersen cited in Baustad, *Harsdorffbygningen*, 31.
[199] See Baustad, *Harfsdorffbygningen.*
[200] DKNVS. Protocol, 96.

But why would they meet in the house of the *vice præses* the week after they had opened a new building? The cabinet and library were still in the house of the former librarian, as there was a lack of tables and cupboards in the new building. Nor do we know whether or not the chairs, which each of the members had to buy personally, were ready at this point. Money was scarce, and for this and the following years it seems the rest of the small capital the Society had was used to furnish its new building. So it would still take time before the building could function as an assembly room; and in the winter, it did not. For regular meetings they would still assemble at the home of the *vice-præses*, heating the elegant premises was quite simply far too expensive.

Public and private library

On April 12, 1774 the new *vice-præses, stiftsprost* and *sogneprest*, Ole Irgens, greeted the members with a speech on "the societal industriousness for the maintenance and growth of science as an important duty." In a verbose prose where the exclamation marks were reserved for hailing the royal family, Irgens, who had the difficult task of shouldering the heritage of Gunnerus, stressed the need for book collections. "We should strive and desire to make our society famous and useful by way of important discoveries, but could we have the same progress as the Societies which possess in abundance those facilities we highly lack?" Irgens begs for forgiveness when he speaks his earnest and true meaning without hypocrisy. Even if most discoveries happen by way of chance, they never happen without necessary book collections, "and these are utterly and deplorably lacking in our poor Norway."[201]

Irgens saw the possibility that Norwegians could make discoveries within agricultural science (*Landhusholdnings=videnskab*), natural history and medicine. There were also possibilities within antiquarianism, even if Norway had few remnants from antiquity, "but if our societal diligence shall have the luck of making discoveries in any sciences, it should be our utmost concern to furnish our book collection with useful writings."[202]

The library of the Scientific Society was to be its first priority and its most important asset in the following decades, the biggest library and in theory at least, the first public library in Norway. The statutes of the Society from 1767 stated that the Society should elect a *Bibliothecarius* (librarian) whose duty was to keep an inventory of the manuscripts, naturals, drawings, printed books and so on that the Society had, and orderly describe the *Museum Societatis* and prepare it in due time to be printed. In these statutes the library was part of what was termed the museum, but it was not a public museum the statutes intended to make room for, but a public library: The librarian ought to keep the library open for students every Wednesday and Saturday from 2 to 4, and be responsible for what he lends out. Note that he "ought" to keep the library open.

---

[201] Irgens, *Den Sælskabelige Stræbsomhed*, 17.
[202] Irgens, *Den Sælskabelige Stræbsomhed*, 17.

No books though, could be lent out of town. This programme for a library serving both the public and the members is followed by a paragraph stating that the admittance fee for the Society would be one or more books for the library, but never less than 10 Rdlr. The idea of a public library was kept alive during the years to come, but in practice it seems that the members themselves were mostly the users, not least because the Society and the library lacked public premises.

At its inception, the library would be situated in the house of Bishop Gunnerus. We do not know how they distinguished between the bishop's own book collection and the library's collection, but on the bishop's death it was clear that there were some problems in keeping the two collections separate. The first librarian had been an amanuensis for Gunnerus, Peter Daniel Baade, who held the position as librarian until he left to serve as priest in Denmark in 1768. He was followed by the auditor at the cathedral school, Ole Christopher Holck, who was given the title of vice-librarian and lived for a period in the bishop's house. After Gunnerus's death a meeting was held in the presence of Holck, another of Gunnerus's amanuenses, Jacob von der Lippe Parelius, and the vice-secretary, Wittrup. Here Holck declared that he would not be held responsible for the loans given after he had moved out of the bishop's house, and that Parelius "probably had information about books the bishop had loaned." Parelius was prepared, and could deliver "the finds of manuscripts, naturals, drawings and printed books." It could be that members and others from the city had borrowed these objects from the Society's collection, but more probably some of these were also found among Gunnerus's assets.

But Gunnerus's death caused problems, not only for the Society as such, but also for its objects: Where were they to house the library and the collection? If tradition should rule, the premises of the *vice-præses* would be the logical candidate. But it seems this was never seriously contemplated, as already in December a memo from the above-mentioned meeting states that "Vice-secretary M.L. Wittrup was claimed in his house to receive the library." The awkwardness of this sentence is present in the original, so it is impossible to know if he asked for the collection and the library, or whether he was ordered to receive it as part of his duty as vice-secretary. Most certainly the collection was soon installed in his house. At the meeting of the Society on February 7, he invited his fellow members to inspect the collections in his premises, and the members agreed, according to the protocol, that "the book collection could not be better off, than if he would keep it in sight."[203] For his part, the secretary (by now he had again become

---

[203] DKNVS. Protocol, February 7, 1774. "At saasom Selskabets Bogsamling stod i den Afdöde Vice= Præsidis Huus uden Tilsyn inden lukte Dörre, fandt Selskabet sig vel fornöiet med at samme var af Mr Parelius mod rigtig Designation udleveret til Sekreterern og i hans Huus opsat, paa et beleiligt sted, som han indböd de tilstædeværende Hrr Medlemmer at tage i Øiesyn, hvilke da erklærede, at Bogsamlingen kunde for nærværende Tid ei være bedre faren, end naar han med samme vil have Indseende. Dernæst blev Selskabets Tanker indhentede, angaaende de Bogsmlingen tilhörende Boubletter, 8 Bind in 4to af Gabricii Biblioth: Græv: og nogle af Vossii Skrifter. som vare förhen destinerede til at sælges, kunde nu indsættes paa nogen af de forestaaende Bog=Auctioner, hvilket blev samtykket paalagt Sekretereren at Besörge. I övrigt önskede Sekretereren at Bogsamlingen kunde bringes mere og mere til Fuldkommend Nytte og Brug, at Publicum intet kunde tvilve paa dets bestandige Vedvarenhed."

secretary, not vice-secretary) claimed that "the book collection should be brought to higher and higher perfection and use so that the public in no way could doubt its unceasing continuity."[204]

Organizing knowledge

The librarians were essential for looking after the book collection, but as the books started to accumulate, the necessity of inventories and catalogues became apparent. From early on lists of the books in the Society's possession were published. This was imperative, as new members who wanted to donate books would have to know what the Society already had. In 1770 a list was produced, and then again in 1775. By the end of the 1770s efforts had been made to create a systematic catalogue, which appeared in 1779 as the afore-mentioned *Catalogus Librorum atqve Rerum naturalium & artificialium sub auspiciis serenissimi principis Regii fratris Friderici curâ et operâ Societatis Reg. Scientiar. Norvegicæ. Collectorum in publicum Patriæ usum.*[205]

In the first catalogue of new books, which were prepared from 1768, a system was employed which had 23 categories.[206] Among these, the first eight were all devoted to different kinds of theological literature; other fields of knowledge would only have one entry each. Where this system emanated from is unclear, but it was obviously a system that was not suited to what developed into the main interests of the Society. Still this system was used in the catalogues produced in 1770, 1779, and 1804. The system would also serve as the vehicle for making acquisition catalogues.[207]

The amount of books which belonged to the Society was manageable until the first major donation, which totally changed the institution of the library. Gerhard Schøning died in 1780 and donated his collection, which included Dass's library, to the Society. This meant that 12,000 volumes were shipped to Trondheim from Copenhagen, and all of a sudden the library had a treasure unparalleled elsewhere in Norway. This was not only a gift of newer books, but of old manuscripts and rare works from the 16th and 17th centuries. There were also around 4000 academic dissertations in this collection.

This book collection would not have a place to be displayed before the new building was completed, but then the organization of the library would also become problematic. Various attempts were made to settle on suitable organizational principles and catalogues which could provide overview and order. This was finally achieved at the beginning of the next century by turning the task over to Rasmus Nyerup, a pupil of Suhm and member of the Society, who was one of the foremost literary historians and librarians of Denmark. He had also helped to organize Suhm's enormous library as well as serve in the post as head librarian at the Royal Library in Copenhagen. The catalogue

---

[204] DKNVS. Protocol, February 7, 1774.
[205] Niderosiæ 1779. Typis Vindingianis.
[206] For more on the systematic systems see Tranaas, "Kataloger og klassifikasjonssystemer."
[207] Tranaas, "Kataloger og klassifikasjonssystemer," 1–3.

bearing his name was prepared in Copenhagen based on notes from Trondheim. In the celebratory introduction he wrote: "Of such extension, of such magnitude are the scientific treasures which are being kept and displayed for public use in the capital of Trøndelag, that this volume will only contain the list of the books . . ." Nyerup would only present the books in this first volume of the catalogue, leaving the naturals, the antiquities and pieces of art, coins and medals, instruments and models for a second volume (which would never appear). He nevertheless emphasized the great value of the whole Museum, implying in the use of the term both the library and the collection, and he stressed that it could be regarded as a separate institution apart from the Society.[203]

Conclusion

By 1805 Det Kongelige Norske Videnskabers Selskab had developed into an institution of learning with a solid material foundation. By this we mean that the Society had its own space for arranging meetings, it had an impressive library containing rare and precious books, and it had a collection of objects which made it into one of the most advanced institutions of learning in Norway. With the inheritance received from Christopher Hammer it also was an institution of means. What the Society lacked was a membership base that performed scientific work. Without this, one could easily imagine that the Society would be unable to survive, but the ensuing development, both in Trondheim and in Europe at large, seems to indicate that it was precisely because of its favorable material conditions it was able to uphold itself as a Society and continue as Det Kongelige Norske Videnskabers Selskab.

---

[208] Further treatment of Nyerup's catalogue will be given in Chapter 6.

Prizes, patriots and scientific texts

"What a founder of an establishment must keep in view," Gunnerus wrote in 1768, "is the common utility meandering towards the whole, promoting the happiness of the state and the citizens."[209] Gunnerus could, on the occasion of the first issue of *Skrifter* after the Society had gained its royal status, offer the reader a history of how the Society had been organized, and he closed his preface to the volume by stating that the organizers had for their part done what they could. "[T]he rest is left to God and the king, and the industriousness and zealousness of all honorable patriots."[210]

Through writings on this and numerous other occasions the Society promoted itself as a Society by and for patriots, linking itself to the king, God and the wellbeing of the fatherland. Working for the promotion of utility, the Society used different means to reach out to a broader constituency. The Society sought a public for its activities through its writings and through prize competitions for theoretical essays as well as for members of the lower classes who had done practical work for improvement. These activities gave the Society a public face as both a scientific and a patriotic-economic society. Through all these activities runs the notions of patriotism and utility. They formed the core of what the Society was up to, even though the means were various.

This chapter will discuss the two main activities which connected the Society to the public during the 18th century. On the one hand, we find the main activity and material entity which presented the science of the Society: the *Skrifter*. On the other hand, we find the competition prizes for theoretical and practical works which were to be a decisive part of the Society's activities. One depreciatory verdict of the Society's activities after the death of Gunnerus was that it became a mere patriotic society awarding prizes for stone fences, pieces of cloth, and the killing of bears.[211] This was in part an accurate judgment, but even these activities involved and demanded skilled judgments from the members of the Society. And other activities, such as awarding prizes for

---

[209] Gunnerus, "Første Tale," 3–4.
[210] Gunnerus, "Fortale," in *Skrifter IV*. "Resten overlades til Gud og kongen, samt alle rettskafne Patrioters Flid og Nidkiærhed." Fortale.
[211] For example Midbøe, *Det Kongelige Norske*.

academic treatises, publishing essays, speeches and eulogies, and arranging public lectures for the dissemination of knowledge, also kept the members busy. The aim of this chapter is to present the multifarious learned activities of the Society, as well as to investigate what the limits of these activities were. Thus a major concern will be to discuss what could be defined as the proper activities of the Society and who would be actively negotiating the terms. Of importance is also what the *Skrifter* of the Society tells us about who the person of learning could be. The relation between who could write, what could be written, and what the content of these texts was will help us ascertain who the scientific persona could be.[212] What were the preconditions for being allowed a voice in the enlightened discourse in Norway in the 18th century?

Historical works have presented the Society as a patriotic society from 1773 when it first started announcing competitions and prizes for farmers and practical activities. This chapter will maintain the thesis that this activity was as much a logical sequel in the work and activities promoted by the Society, as a *scientific* society, as it was a separate function. First the textual activities of the Societies will be considered before we look more closely into the competitions.

Audiences for science

"It is rare," Gunnerus reflected in his pastoral letter, "that one thinks through a case as carefully and properly, and ventures as deeply therein, as when one places one's thoughts in writing, particularly when one intends to convey them in public."[213] For Gunnerus writing was not only an important channel for dissemination, it was also the most important tool for thinking. Writing, as he stated its importance, was the technology of the learned. He advised his ministers to write all sermons, word for word, and read them out loud according to the written text. This was the only foolproof way of following the rules of oratory.

Writing, as Gunnerus promoted the activity, was the principal and decisive step in becoming a learned man, and a community of learned priests was also a prerequisite for forming a Norwegian (re)public of learned citizens. Thus writing would not only shape the individuals who did the writing, sharpening thoughts and disciplining minds, it would also be the principal means of constructing a public. The priests needed to pursue writing to be learned men, as the congregation they ought to serve was not only their parishoners, but a wider "imagined community."[214] The implication was that the

---

[212] As we will return to, the notion of scientific personae is particularly promising for identifying conditions and restraints, and enabling and disabling mechanisms with respect to the practitioners of science who were attached to the society.

[213] Gunnerus, *Hans Opvækkelige Hyrde=Brev*, 30. ". . . thi det er sielden, at man eftertænker en Sag saa nøje og ordentlig, og gaaer saa dybt ind deri, som naar man sætter sine Tanker skriftelig op, allerhelst naar man agter at meddeele dem Publico."

[214] Cf. Anderson, *Imagined Communities*.

priests were encouraged to put less emphasize on oral performance and instead devote themselves to a culture of writing. As we have already stated, the learned men in Norway were scattered across the country, and writing and reading would form the means for transmission of thoughts over fjord and mountain. Writing was essential for tying the learned citizens to each other, to the state and to a larger international community, but the writings could also serve the purpose of extending the number of scientifically adapt persons. The society Gunnerus advertised in his pastoral letter demanded contributions which were beautiful and agreeable, without "surpassing the horizons of the reasonable untutored."[215]

The ambition was to form a new public by issuing works which could enlighten even those outside the community of the learned. This was not meant to be a Society of futile abstractions, subtleties, and quibbling, Gunnerus stated in the speech he presented to the Society to celebrate its status as a royal society in 1768. The Society would apply theories to what was useful for human life and "in a language that could be understood by every person in the country."[216] By this means not only "the so-called learned, but also the warrior, the burgher, and the peasant could read with pleasure and advantage for himself and his order the *Skrifter* of the Society, take part in the Society's work, and take his share in educating his compatriots."[217] The rational mind was widely distributed in this enlightenment thought, and the vision and ambition was to help illuminate these minds.

The use of the vernacular was a clear sign of the ambition to reach out beyond the borders of the learned republic, or to redraw the borders on the basis of another language and other social groups. The choice of Danish as the language in the *Skrifter* was arguably a precondition for fulfilling these ambitions. The project was hardly new, as a tradition had been established for using the vernacular as the language of scientific communications from the second half of the 17th century, with the *Transactions* of the Royal Society in London setting the standard from 1665. The notable exceptions—for example, the Berlin and St. Petersburg societies' publishing in French and Latin—were exactly that, exceptions. The communication within the republic of letters—the group of scholars who would sense a belonging across boundaries—would therefore proceed through translations and abridgements, and thus the institutions that aimed at disseminating

---

[215] Gunnerus, *Hans Opvækkelige Hyrde=Brev*, 31. ". . . og ikke overstiger fornuftige Ustuderedes Horizont."

[216] Gunnerus, "Første Tale," 14, "tillige i et Sprog som af alle i Landet forstaaes."

[217] Gunnerus, "Første Tale," 14. "Ei at opholde sig ved unyttige Abstractioner, Subtiliteter og Haarkløverier, eller at blive staaende ved det blot theoretiske i Videnskaberne, men at anvende Theorien paa det, som er virkelig og meest nyttig i det menneskelige Liv, og det paa en Maade, og, naar Øiemerket i sin rette Fuldkommenhed skal erholdes, tillige i et Sprog, som af alle i Landet forstaaes; Saa at ikke alene de saa kaldede Lærde, men og Krigsmanden, Borgeren og Landmanden kune saavel med Fornøielse og Nytte for sig og sin Stand læse Selskabets Skrifter, som og tage Deel i dets Bemøielser, og bidrage sit med til at undervise sine andre Medborgere: Og dette vil ikke lidet hjelpe til, at Fædrene=Sproget bliver retskaffen forbedret og dyrket; Kundskab, Vittighed og god Smag meer udbredet."

new universal knowledge were paving the way for the diversification of the scientific languages and not least for the refinement of national languages.

In Trondheim, the playwright and vice-mayor, Nils Krog Bredal, underscored the role of the scientific societies in his speech celebrating the royal status of the Society in 1768: "Besides having spread a shining light onto all the strands of the sciences, these learned societies one and alone should be given the honor to have formed, multiplied, and adorned the language of their Fatherlands." According to Bredal, the refinement of the native language was a major effect of the establishment of scientific societies. He continued praising the societies for inaugurating a new epoch in the learned history, "namely that one did not refrain from issuing and teaching neither the beautiful (*smukke*) nor the most accurate sciences in the language which was spoken by the fair sex, the burgher, and the artist."[218] A scientific language based on the spoken tongue was a means for unification of the different strata of society, in Krog Bredal's view. But as this quote shows, women, artists, and burghers are addressed as speakers of the language, not as writers. This should not be read as an invitation to write learned treatises for these groups, but as an invitation to be readers—a public. As Gunnerus insisted in the quotation above, even peasants should be included in this public.

Politics of language

Following in the wake of the *Videnskabernes Selskab* (the Danish Society of the Sciences), which had published in Danish from the inception of its *Skrifter* in 1745, the Norwegian society seems to have had no doubt about giving privilege to Danish, the common written language of the two countries. Rather the use of Danish was forwarded as a positive program: "All treatises will be printed in Danish," the statutes of 1767 read, "therefore everything submitted in other languages will be translated into Danish by the Secretary. As among other things, the perfection of the language is a motivation for the society, a beautiful and fluent style must be observed, and a reasonable orthography . . ."[219] This program was totally on a par with the work of the two major learned societies in Copenhagen, which had the development of the Danish language as a main preoccupation.[220] The task was both to elevate Danish to a language that could

---

[218] Bredal, "Den anden Tale," 44–45, "Foruden at have udbredet et skinnende Lys over alle Videnskabernes vidt udstrakte Dele, tilkommer det deslige Lærde Selskaber ene og alene den Ære at have dannet, formeeret og pyntet, deres Fædrenelands sporg. Strax fremstod i den Lærde Historie en nye Epoke, nemlig, at man understod sig til at fremsætte og lære ei alene de smukke, men endogsaa de allergrundigste, Videnskaber i det Sprog, som det smukke Kiøn, Borgeren og Konstneren, talede."

[219] *Skrifter IV*, statutes, § 9. "Alle Avhandlinger trykkes paa Dansk, og bliver derfor alle, i et andet Sprog indsendte, først paa Dansk oversatte af Secretereren. Iblant andet, da Selskabet og har Sprogets Fuldkommenhed til Øiemærke, maa nøie sees paa en smuk og flydende Stiil, samt en fornuftig Orthographie, i Henseende til hvilken sidste i sær Selskabet bør forene sig, at ikke alt for stor Uoverensstemmelse i dets Skrifter skal bemærkes."

[220] See Feldbæk, "Fædreland og Jndfødsret," 120.

be used for such worthy activities as poetry and science, and to extract Latin and French expressions from the language. By the 1760s the goal seemed closer to realization than ever. An important step in this process was the performance of the first Danish *synge-spil* ("Singspiel"), *Gram og Signe, eller Kierligheds og Tapperheds Mesterstykker* in 1756.[221] Nils Krog Bredal, later the secretary of the Society in Trondheim, was the author, and the success of his libretto helped him to rise to the position of vice-mayor in his home-town of Trondheim.

But was the purification and elevation of Danish more important than reaching out to an international community of learned men? Latin was the preferred second language of the *Videnskabernes Selskab* in Copenhagen, which had its first volumes translated into Latin, while the Norwegian Society 15 years later would have its first four volumes translated into German. Both projects seem to have been initiated by the publisher, but without doubt the translations were encouraged by both societies.[222] That the Danish society opted for Latin, the Norwegian for German, probably has to do both with the dwindling status of Latin as a language for science after the middle of the eighteenth century, but also with the different international networks the leaders of the two societies were connected to through, respectively, the 1740s and 1760s. Gunnerus steered towards the German states.

Krog Bredal emphasized that the scientific societies had introduced publications that could be understood by women, burghers, and artists; Gunnerus mentioned the warrior, burgher, and peasant; and Danish was established as the language of the *Skrifter*. The language chosen should be a language understood by a broader constituency than the learned members of society. However, Danish was not the language *spoken* by most inhabitants in Norway, a fact which was hardly unknown to Bredal and Gunnerus.

In Norway most people spoke Norwegian, except for the Danes who occupied about half the higher civil servant and state official positions. But Danish was the *written* language understood by Norwegians, as it was the language of the Church and language taught in the primary school system. In Copenhagen and the German parts of the conglomerate state, the situation was even more complicated. As described in poetry at the beginning of the 19th century, the learned man at the beginning of the 18th century was portrayed as a writer of Latin, as conversing with women in French, speaking German with his dog, and Danish with his servants.[223] By the middle of the 18th century, German would still be a language with wide distribution, as it was the first tongue for about one third of the inhabitants of Copenhagen, and many of the leading state servants, professors, and ministers were of German descent. French was also in vogue with the elite. From the ascension of Christian VII to the throne in 1766 and during the following decades, not only Danization of the language but also Danization of the official posts

---

[221] See Feldbæk, "Fædreland og Jndfødsret," 122.

[222] *Der Drontheimischen Gesellschaft Schriften, aus dem Dänischen übersetzt.* Kopenhagen: 1765, Kopenhagen und Leipzig: 1765, 1767, 1770.

[223] Christian Wilster, Digtninger, 1827; cited in Feldbæk, "Fædreland og Jndfødsret," 119.

would lead to a new emphasis on national correctness in the state.[224] The choice of Danish as the language of the *Skrifter* was quite conventional seen in relation to the tradition of scientific societies, and a Norwegian language was non-existent and certainly was not an alternative: Danish was the language understood by Norwegians who could read; and many could. The exact numbers are contested but recent scholarship proposes that up to 90 percent of the adult populace could read.[225] Did those responsible for *Skrifter* envision such a broad group of readers? Probably not, but there was nothing awkward in proposing that "the reasonable untutored" would be able to read the transactions of the Society.

Seen from an international perspective, the price for using the vernacular in scientific communication was considerably higher for intellectuals and scientists from smaller states, within small scientific communities, than for those of larger language groups. As there was only one Danish-speaking university, the odds for acquiring a large readership were far from promising, hence many books were published in both Danish and German. When the Trondheim society addressed women, burghers, warriors, and peasants, it was part of an effort to enlighten, to disseminate knowledge in an enlightenment mode, but it can also be seen as a way of broadening the critical mass for intellectual activity and for publishers.

What was a suitable style and what was a reasonable orthography? The answers were not unanimous, as the Danish language was in a process of standardization and change. The establishment of the Society and its publications was one of the many initiatives for making a new Danish language, cleansed of Latin and German, and capable of being used in more than Church and "popular" publications.[226] In an article about the establishment of new forms of prose from the mid-18th century, historian Arne Apelseth writes: "In close connection with the development of scientific prose, stands patriotism. Maybe it will be more appropriate to say that patriotism framed the scientific activity."[227] Both agent and witness to this process was the Society in Trondheim, and the irony of the choice of language was in the way the Society and its members would become some of the most ardent spokespersons of a patriotism which was primarily based on Norwegian-ness.

Writings by the learned

In the preface of the first *Skrifter* (Transactions), the readers, "the lovers of the sciences,"[228] were invited by the Society to assist in the promotion and diffusion of its intentions. Everyone could freely choose the topic of their contribution, the preface

---

[224] Indfødsretsloven, the law proclaiming that only citizens born in the state could attain official positions, was instituted in 1776.

[225] Fet, *Lesande bønder*.

[226] In a letter in Dahl, 111, Gunnerus gives a description of his orthographic politics.

[227] Apelseth: "Lærdom, borgarleggjering og skriftkultur," 46.

[228] Gunnerus, "Fortale," in *Skrifter I*, "Videnskabers Elskere."

stated. The Society would appreciate treatises on history, i.e. learned, civil, natural, and church history. Furthermore, it would accept all parts of philosophy, in particular mathematics, natural knowledge, and its application within the art of medicine, but also economy, moral knowledge and the natural teachings on God and religion. Thorough treatises on the revealed God were also welcomed, as were poetry and the beautiful arts (*smukke Videnskaber*), as far as they deserved the name beautiful (*smukt*). Moreover, civil and public law was encouraged as long as the author was knowledgeable in natural law and the history of law. Thus, it was added, "our goal is very extensive."[229]

Indeed, this was a generous invitation worthy of a society with a broad conception of science and learned activities. Nevertheless, the *Skrifter*, issued in eight volumes during the eighteenth century, would predominantly become a forum for natural and civil history, with the occasional appearance from other areas of learning, most notably economy in its broad 18th-century conception. This was also as earlier recorded announced in the first volume: ". . . in particular [we] wished that our compatriots would work within economy and natural history, and submit to the society their thermometric and barometric observations, as well as what else they might know and experience for enlightenment regarding the kingdom of nature."[230] Minerals, herbs, fish, and birds were given special mention. While the preface emphasizes the broadness of the scholarly work the society desired to support, the exemplification delineates the space of possible contributions to two separate but related fields, natural history and economy. Why this was the case, what actually characterized the publications of the Society up until 1805, and who the authors were, will be the theme of the following pages.

The first Skrifter

Tronhiemske Skrifter was one of the first journals to be published in Norway. In 1760 Frederik Nannestad, Gunnerus's predecessor in the bishop's seat in Trondheim issued his *Ugentlige korte Afhandlinger* in Christiania, with its moral and theological essays, considered to be the first Norwegian journal. The second journal to appear was Peter

---

[229] Gunnerus, "Fortale," in *Skrifter I*, "Enhver har selv Frihed at vælge, hvad for en Materie, han vil; thi vi tager imod Afhandlinger af Historien, dog fornemmelig Fædernelandets Lærde, Borgerlige, Naturlige og Kirke=Historie: Ligeledes af Philosophien og alle dens Dele, dog i Særdeleshed Mathematiken, Naturlæren og dens Anvendelse paa Læge=Konsten, Oeconomien, Dyde=Læren og den naturlige Lære om Gud og Religionen. Grundige Afhandlinger af den aabenbarede Lære om Gud, skal og være os kierkommen . . . Vers, saavel med, som uden Rim og andre artige i de smukke Videnskaber løbende Afhandlinger see vi og gierne, men saadant maa og virkelig fortiene Navn af smukt, naar det skal bekomme Sted blant vort Selskabs Skrifter."

[230] Gunnerus, "Fortale," in *Skrifter I*, "Dog kunde vi ikke negte, at vi jo i Besynderlighed ønskede at vore Landsmænd vilde arbeide udi Oeconomien og den naturlige Historie og indsende til Selskabet deres Thermometriske og Barometriske Observationer, samt hvad de ellers kunde vide og erfare til Oplysning i Henseende til Naturens Rige."

Friderich Suhm's *Tronhiemske Samlinger*, which was published between 1761 and 1765. Printed in Trondheim, it was a one-man journal during its four years of existence. The first volume of the *Skrifter* of the scientific society was also issued in 1761, but it was printed in Copenhagen.[231] Hence, in the same year two new literary genres appeared in Norway, and Suhm was part of both of them. *Skrifter* was modelled on the journals of other learned societies. *Tronhiemske Samlinger* was a Spectator-journal accentuating a subjective style. *Skrifter* was to be the official publication of a society of science, with a content of learned treatises. But what role did *Skrifter* play in the life of the Society? In the preface to volume three of his friend Gerhard Schøning's history of Norway, posthumously published in 1781, Suhm recounted the beginning of the Society thus: Bishop Gunnerus "proposed immediately after his arrival in 1758 to establish a learned society, in the manner that the three of us should immediately start writing, the one conveying it to the other, and when we had some treatises ready, then let them be printed, without waiting for other collaborators . . ."[232] Here the establishment of the society was recorded 20 years later as a society of authors and as a site for the production of texts. On the basis of this statement and other sources, we can claim that the chief aim of the Society during its first years was to publish a scientific journal. This journal should not be one man's work, but the work of a society, where the texts could be discussed and improved upon through the relations between the members.

Reading the first volume—the "first fruit" of the Society's work—gives credence to the storytelling of Suhm, as the three men mentioned above were authors of nine out of ten pieces in this volume. In addition to this there were two lists, about marriages, births and deaths in the diocese and about taxation. Why these lists were printed we can only guess: To contribute to statistical description of the nation? Perhaps it was important to convey how many people actually lived in this northern diocese, what resources there were, both in the form of inhabitants and resources, to a Danish and international public? Apparently it was not the kind of information the Society wanted to keep disseminating, and in the following volumes these lists were substituted with thermometric and barometric observations.

Of the ten articles in the first volume, five were produced by Johan Ernst Gunnerus, two by Peter Friderich Suhm, two by Gerhard Schøning, and one by missionary Eric Gerhard Schytte. The predominance of Gunnerus as author was soon to become a tradition, as he was by far the most prolific writer in the first 50 years of the Society's history. The topics covered by this first volume would also to a large extent be echoed in the volumes to come. Gunnerus's two main areas of publication, theology and natural history, were announced: Theology through his articles "Treatise on the Immor-

---

[231] 'Skrifter' signifies quite simply 'writings', and the title was the same the Society of the Sciences in Copenhagen had chosen for their publications in 1745.

[232] Suhm in Schøning, *Norges Riges Historie III*, Fortale. ". . . foreslog strax efter sin Ankomst 1758 Schøning og mig at oprette et lærd Sælskab, saaledes at vi tre skulde strax begynde med at skrive, den ene meddele den anden det, og naar man havde nogle Afhandlinger færdige, da lade et Bind trykke, uden just at vente paa flere Medarbeidere . . ."

tality of the Soul" and "Meditation on Solomon's Third Sermon" and natural history in three articles, two on birds and one article entitled "Miscellaneous Considerations Particularly about Minerals in Nordland and Finmarken."[233]

The first article of the first volume is "*Betragtninger over Sielens Udødelighed*," "Treatise on the Immortality of the Soul," a philosophical investigation into what was at the time a highly popular topic. The investigation is a metaphysical discussion in which Gunnerus reveals his allegiance to German metaphysics in general and to the philosophy of Christian Wolff in particular. Basically this is not an argued proof for the immortality of the soul, but a confirmation of the fact that the soul must be immaterial. Since all material entities are subject to the laws of necessity, free will must be located in an immaterial soul. Furthermore, the soul must be immortal, since that is the only reasonable way of fulfilling God's intentions, and lastly, an immaterial and immortal soul is indispensable for the order of society, hence for the state and the church. Materialists, Epicureans and Free-thinkers were his contenders, Leibniz, Wolff, Darjes his chief protagonists.[234] What interests us is the placement of this text as the first piece in the *Skrifter*. It can be seen to serve several purposes. It anchors the scientific society, the journal and the various branches of the sciences securely within conformist Protestant state theology. Science is neither against religion nor against the order of the state, the article teaches us. The use of reason does not lead to disorder, rather reason and science are our allies against disorder. Second, it proves itself a "modern" journal, by presenting German Wolff-inspired theology as its opening piece. In Copenhagen, Gunnerus had been one of the first and most ardent defenders of Wolffianism, and could here prove to former pupils and colleagues that he was still one of the moderns.[235]

Third, it gives theology a prominent place in the conception of the Society. We do not know whether they ever discussed the role of theology between them as they inaugurated their meetings in Trondheim in 1760. Theology would seldom be accepted as one of the preoccupations of other scientific societies, as there was a strong conviction that theology led to disputes and would not be a suitable subject to be treated in such a forum. When in 1758 a new set of statutes was proposed for the *Videnskabernes Selskab* in Copenhagen, theology was proposed as a part of it. The former bishop Pontoppidan, an ardent natural theologian, made it clear in his remarks upon this proposal that theology was not considered as such in other societies, and that he could see no reason to include it.[236] The inclusion of theology in Trondheim could of course be a result of Gunnerus's own theological-metaphysical background at the University of Jena, but even the historian Suhm, who had not even studied theology, followed up on Gunnerus's articles. He started his series on "*Nærværende 18de Seculi Character*" (The Character of the Present

---

[233] Afhandling om (Betragtninger over) Sielenes Udødelighed, Betragtning over Salom. Prædik. III, Om Hav-Hesten, en Søe-Fugl, Om nogle Lom-artede Fugle, Adskillige Efterretninger, fornemmelig angaaende Mineralier i Nordland og Finmarken.

[234] See Selmer, *Opplysningsmenn i den norske kirke*, 13–34.

[235] See for "his modernism," Tauber cited in Nyerup, *Historisk-statistiske*.

[236] Cited in Lomholt, *Det Kongelige Danske*.

Century) with a history of the development of religion in different countries. In this article he traced how religion had developed up to the present, as he in later articles would present the development of art, commerce, and sciences. He insisted that Protestantism was the only religion which admitted a free consciousness, and underscored, as did Gunnerus, the close connection between religion and the state: "Religion cannot perish without at least undermining if not overthrowing the state."[237] Hence, even if Gunnerus was the one who would publish explicit theological texts, other texts with historical subject matter, and even more those which had natural historical content, would reinforce the message that the Society was supporting Protestant theology. And if disputes about religious matters were to be avoided, the role of the bishop as the leader of this society would mean that the risk of religious quarrels was minimal—to attack the bishop, especially on religious matters, was very risky business.

The fourth important effect of this article seen in connection with the rest of the volume is that metaphysics and empirical science are not only made compatible, but also indispensable to each other. "Metaphysics," Gunnerus stated in a later speech (printed in volume four), "this high and noble science, is devalued by many, but how dangerous do not the Newtons and Clarks stumble when they wander without this light? A light which covers and enlightens all sciences, all human knowledge, and could thus not without harm be dispensed with by any thorough-working man."[238] Gunnerus established firm links between economy, natural history and metaphysics. Still the bulk of his articles in the following issues would be empirical investigations of natural history. Birds, fish, and minerals were described in great quantities, following closely the Linnaean systematic natural history.

Suhm and Schøning had another agenda, their object being history—but even Suhm would claim in the same vein as Gunnerus that "philosophy alone enlightens our intellect; on the other hand, all other sciences make us only experienced and learned in certain things."[239] The contributions of Suhm and Schøning to the first volume were historical, but in different senses. Suhm commenced two series of articles which were to dominate the volumes to come: "On the Character of the Present Century" would be continued through three volumes while "Anmærkninger over Verdens Almindelig Historie" (Remarks on The Common History of the World) was to make up substantial parts of the following five volumes. "Remarks" are today quite hard to read and make sense of, as they consist of 570 pages of footnotes to the work "The Common History of the World." The four pieces on the character of the 18th century have the opposite scope, with sweeping historical brushes covering thousands of years, as well as more specific

---

[237] "Religionen kan ei forgaae uden at Staten med det samme aldeles i det mindste svækkes, om ei og tilligemed kuldkastes." Suhm, 18de Seculi Character, Skrifter Vol. 1, p. 103.
[238] Gunnerus. "Første Tale," "Metaphysiken, denne høie og ædle Videnskab, agtes vel ringe af mange, men hvor farligt snuble ikke Newtoner og Clarker, naar de vandre uden dette Lys? Et Lys der udbreder sig over og oplyser alle Videnskaber, al menneskelig Kundskab, og kan derfor ikke, uden Skade undværes af nogen grundig lærd Mand," pp. 6–7.
[239] "Philosophien alene oplyser vor Forstand, alle andre Videnskaber giøre os derimod ikkun erfarne og lærde i visse Ting." Suhm, "Nærværende 18de Seculi Character," 118.

characterizations of scientific and artistic developments, as well as characteristics of different nations. His article testifies to wide reading, and a great desire to characterize.

Of importance for understanding the topics that would be addressed in the *Skrifter*, Suhm's reading of Montesquieu and his twist on Montesquieu's climatic theories are worth a presentation. This is important for understanding the broad interest in improvement and patriotism in the circles of the Society, and the emphasis placed on practical farming, which was voiced by the Society. Not only did climates form people, people were also forming climates, according to Suhm. In Italy and Spain the climate had not changed during two millennia, Suhm claimed, "but in France, England, Germany, the North, [it is] quite transformed: Those countries were then completely covered with forests, full of swamps, thus far colder than today. Everywhere they gave a wild and bewildering view. They offered no other pleasures than hunting and fishing. The way of life of the inhabitants was of necessity hard and vagrant. Different air, different mores; why? Because the mores change the air, as this changes the mores. The farmer chops the forest down, thus making the air milder, and himself more steadfast."[240] Linking manners and matter in this way, the improvement of the soil could be connected directly to the advancement of civilization in the north. Schøning had also made the same claim in his *Velmeente Tanker om Agerdørkningens muelige Forbedring i Norge* (The Possible Improvement of Agriculture) from 1758, and this direct link also sets a standard and a frame within which to move.

Schøning's contributions were primarily concerned with historical-economic topics, "*Kort Beretning, om endeel Uaar og Misvæxt, særdeles i Trondhiems Stift i Norge*" (Short Narration on Some Bad Years and Crop Failures Especially in the Trondheim Diocese in Norway) as well as "*Betekning, om offentlige Forraads-Huses Opretning og Indretning i Norge*" (Considerations on the Establishment and Organization of Public Provision Houses in Norway).[241] The first of Schøning's articles was a historical investigation where all known sources of Norwegian history were searched for information on hunger, cold weather, and other signs of crop failures from the time of Tacitus to contemporary Trondheim. The other text was intimately connected to this story, being a reasoned argument about the need for public storehouses for grain and how one should go about establishing them. Both Suhm and Schøning were particularly eager to denounce hasty solutions, not to embrace the new because it was new, but expressing a cautious middle road between learning from the past and not encouraging *project mageri* (project-making). This denouncement of extremism and the insistence of learning from the past while contributing to improvement of the present, which we today would link to a kind of Burkian conservatism, was expressed again and again. That does not mean that they were totally uncritical to the prevailing political system. Suhm for example steadfastly argued the case for freedom of speech, at least in Latin,

---

[240] Suhm, "Nærværende 18de Seculi Character," 124.
[241] Nærværende 18de Seculi Character, Kort Beretning, om endeel Uaar og Misvæxt, særdeles i Trondhiems Stift i Norge, Betekning, om offentlige Forraads-Huses Opretning og Indretning i Norge, Anmærkninger, over Verdens Almmindelige Historie.

based on the argument that the evils of freethinking could only be fought through public contradiction.[242]

The only contributor who was not among the founding fathers of the society, Eric Gerhard Schytte, had his letter "*Adskillige Anmærkninger, indsendte til Biskopen i Trond-hiem*" ("Miscellaneous remarks, supplied to the bishop of Trondheim") published. This was an obvious invitation and encouragement to others to procure natural historical information for the bishop.[243] The letter was particularly free from any other considerations than the exact mention of specific cases, and was thus more in line with the contributions we know from the *Transactions* of the Royal Society in London.

The content of this first volume set the tone for a scientific society where theology was the queen of the sciences; economy, and civil and natural history her rightful daughters. As was later set down in the statutes of the Society, the volume presented the articles in the order of the faculties at the university—which meant that theology would come first. Although theological texts would be few and far between in the volumes to come, theology would have an important place in the *Skrifter*. Natural history was basically portrayed as a religious practice, not in every article, but in prefaces and from time to time in articles of natural historical content. Economic considerations were likewise well within this protestant theological horizon and as we pointed out in a previous chapter, the Cameralist ideology merged natural history, economy and state Protestantism into a remarkably flexible whole.

Natural and theological specimen

The *Skrifter* were filled with an impressive amount of strange species; birds, fish, stones, worms, and large sea mammals were described in painstaking detail. The practical, empirical, case-oriented study would become the normal format for an article, not metaphysical speculation. But as already mentioned, theology would have its role to play in the natural historical articles. Through *Skrifter* a specific version of God was inscribed into Norwegian nature. Perhaps the most important—and impressive—actor in the first five volumes of the Society's publication was the basking shark (*brugde*), a creature of the sea which appeared both for natural-historical and theological reasons.

In the summer of 1763, a basking shark was harpooned off the coast of Smøla outside Trondheim. Normally this enormous fish would be killed and the liver cut out while still at open sea. This time the fish was towed to shore, where four horses were needed to get it onto the beach. The skin was then removed, before being filled with grass and moss. The upholstered fish was thereafter sent by boat to Trondheim and transported by way of two horses to the Berg farm just outside the city. Here at the res-

---

[242] Cf Danish and Norwegian patriotism in the period as discussed by Engelhardt, "Patriotism, nationalism."

[243] See Gunnerus's letter to Linnaeus where he presents this paper and his encouragement for others to do the same. In Amundsen, *Johan Ernst Gunnerus.*

idence of Bishop Gunnerus, the enormous stuffed fish would be observed with the utmost care. Gunnerus had been waiting eagerly for this possibility of examining the basking shark, never before described, which he would now be able to name *squalus maximus*. The year before fishermen had been instructed to gather specific information about the fish, and they had provided Gunnerus with a drawing, a wooden model and testimonies. But now finally he could see for himself. All visible features were recorded: mouth, eyes, gills, the size and placement of the fins. Bits of the thorny skin were put under the microscope to be better seen. An article in *Skrifter* described the fish, accompanied by a drawing of the whole fish, and by parts of the skin and gills which had been studied under the microscope. This article also presents the entire process of getting hold of the species, and those who had helped him were mentioned.[244]

In the next volume, a new article on the basking shark was published in the *Skrifter*. This time Gunnerus had received a complete and fresh head of the shark—and especially by examining the teeth and mouth of the shark, Gunnerus was able to establish more facts about the creature. Again he provided information about the work involved in getting the head from the far-away ocean to his own collection. But this time he also established the fish within another scientific field. The article proves, according to Gunnerus, that the basking shark was the fish that swallowed the biblical figure of Jonas.[245] After considering all relevant sources, Gunnerus could show by way of a natural history examination that the shark was the only likely fish that could have swallowed Jonas without hurting him. The natural facts were thus situated within the field of theology as well as the field of natural history. The articles about the basking shark actually place it both as a physico-theological creature and as a figure within Biblical physics—two genres which were important for the practice of natural history as well as for the legitimization of natural history.[246]

The strategy implemented by physico-theologists was to use the new sciences in the service of God to strengthen belief. For the physico-theologists this link between the new science and religion was natural. Indeed, science was precisely the tool needed for the progression of Christianity. From all provinces of the Creation one could find ever new arguments about the power, wisdom, and existence of God. From the work of the intestines, the function of the eye, the movements of the planets, and the incredible life of moths one could gather ever-newer arguments that attested to God as the creator of all things. For those delving into Biblical physics, the main occupation was to ascertain the truth of the Bible through investigations of the species mentioned from the three kingdoms of nature in the Bible. Whereas physico-theology used the book of nature to establish independent proofs of God, biblical physicists would use natural history to establish the truth of the Bible.

Perhaps the basking shark was the ideal object for science in Trondheim. It was previously not described, and thus contributed to the scientific quest for new discoveries. It

---

244 Gunnerus, "Brugclen"
245 Gunnerus, "Videre Oplysning"
246 Cf. Brenna, "Fysikoteologi, bibelsk fysikk."

was an impressive and awe-inspiring example of nature, it threw light on biblical history, and it was indeed very useful. Descriptions of how to *use* the basking shark for nutrition as well as for its oil was an important part of Gunnerus's writings about this fish.

Volumes and authors

This preliminary description of *Skrifter* gives an indication of what the main topics were, but it provides few facts about the actual amount of articles and the nature of the authors. Through the eight volumes of proceedings which were published by the Society during the first 50 years of its existence, the number of authors grew rapidly, as did the number of "specimens," "pieces" or "treatises" which were the various names given to the texts. The first five volumes appeared up until 1774 (the year after the death of Gunnerus). The next two volumes in the series—*Nye Samlinger (New Collections)*—appeared in the 1780s. These were volumes with a wide range of authors and topics, which was also the case for the last series of *Skrifter* published in the 18th century, *Nyeste Samlinger (Newest Collections)* which appeared as only one volume 1798. This development undoubtedly mirrored the development of the Society and its activities, where the first 15 years saw a high level of scientific and textual activity by a small number of the Society's members. During the next decades, *Skrifter* served as a publishing arena for a handful of active members in Trondheim, but authors from other parts of the kingdom and some foreign authors also contributed. Quite a few of these texts stemmed from authors who submitted theses because they wanted to become, or just had become, members of the society. The volume from 1798 was the only volume between 1788 and 1817.

The following is the distribution of articles and authors for the first eight volumes of *Skrifter*:

Skrifter 1:	1761, four authors, 10 articles, 300 pages
Skrifter 2 :	1763, seven authors, 16 articles, 432 pages
Skrifter 3:	1765, six authors, 21 articles, 578 pages
Skrifter 4:	1768, seven authors, 21 articles, 479 pages
Skrifter 5:	1774, 11 authors, 17 articles, 600 pages
Nye Samling 1:	1784, 17 authors, 25 articles, 596 pages
Nye Samling 2:	1788, 12 authors, 28 articles, 642 pages
Nyeste Samling 1:	1798, nine authors, 18 articles, 352 pages

A relatively small number of authors produced the texts in the first four volumes. These were the founding fathers, Gunnerus, Schøning and Suhm, some clerics in the diocese and Gunnerus's amanuenses, Peter Daniel Baade, Jacob von der Lippe Parelius and Cornelius Müller. The most scientifically successful of the authors outside the triumvirate was the priest Hans Strøm, who would never play an important role in the organizational life of the society. Most likely the reason for this was that he never took up residence in Trondheim. Still he remains, as we can see, the second most prolific writer during the first fifty years of the Society's existence. He contributed to *Skrifter*, but he made a name for himself as one of the most renowned natural historians and topographers in Norway. This earned him a better position as a priest, but also the recognition as a member of numerous scientific societies around Europe. As we will point out, next to Gunnerus, he would come to embody the exemplary natural historian *cum* cleric in the kingdom.

Breaking with the trend of the priest-author altogether were two of the most important writers in the society, first, Johan Daniel Berlin, the afore-mentioned musician and autodidact jack-of-all-trades, who was neither priest, nor learned, but a man of the crafts who kept track of the weather through measurements through the seasons in Trondheim, in addition to publishing a piece on mathematical music theory and one piece on a new threshing machine of his own invention. Second, Didrik Fester, who was also an autodidact who earned recognition, which for him meant a position as a teacher at *Katedralskole*. He was mainly concerned with mathematical problems and as such was the odd man out in this group of civil and natural history, and agriculture interests.

All in all 156 articles were written by:

Gunnerus	38 articles
Strøm	20 articles
Suhm	15 articles
Fester	12 articles
Berlin	9 articles
Schøning	6 articles

Who are these personae?[247]

The society was a society of amateurs in our sense of the word. It was composed of persons who for the most part made a living from anything but the sciences they pursued or wrote about: Bishops, priests and missionaries, a principal at the cathedral school, a town physician, or a town musician. They came from different levels of society but none of them could make a living from their research. Thus they were amateurs in the sense of pursuing unpaid interests. But they were amateurs in another sense as well: Few had any education that could prepare them for the sciences they cultivated—a bishop dissected worms, a priest and a town musician made barometric observations, the missionary collected minerals, and so on. Thus they were amateurs if lack of education in the field of study is an indication of amateurism. They also cherished the notion of delight and pleasure in scientific activities, and thus they could be called amateurs in the sense that they expressed their love for the activity—the root of amateur is *amare*, love.

But the notion of amateur misses the point if we are to understand the character of the activities, the divisions and the borders that would allow for some activities and suppress others, invite some and exclude others. In the whole of Europe, scientific societies would consist of persons, mostly with no formal education, without a

---

[247] Daston and Sibum, "Introduction: Scientific Personae."

professional paid job, where they could pursue their scientific interests. Most scientists in the 18th century were precisely amateurs in this sense. Even in the French academy, with its salaried posts, where it was said that men of science could be able to make a professional career, most employees could not make a living on their salaries alone.[248] Furthermore, the lack of formal education of the members of the Society in Trondheim was a normal state of affairs, as most universities did not have posts or educational courses which were based on the new sciences. And finally, even if the rhetoric in the Society alluded to the pleasurable conduct of science, the main argument would be that one should pursue science for the sake of utility, not in the name of pleasure alone.

Looking at the members and authors in Trondheim, we will find some of the best-educated men in the kingdom, being in fact part of the academic elite in Denmark-Norway. And we will find men who stressed the importance of their activities for the common good, for the state, and God. The most striking attribute of the authors is that most of them were state officials, and most of them were educated as theologians. The connection between theology, science, and the state is perhaps the most striking characteristic of the group of members and authors of the Society in Trondheim.

In his journal, *Tronhiemske Samlinger*, Suhm described the nature of scientific personae in Norway. "It is rare," he wrote, "that others than those who have certain state-positions, ranks, or means can pursue sciences. The first group need them for their businesses, the second are regarded in the noble world as badly raised if they do not possess a certain knowledge in some sciences, and the third have, considering them all, the most time and possibility to pursue and improve the sciences, as they can devote themselves to them totally. Anyone can deduce from this why there is such a lack of sciences in our country, so that theology is almost alone known."[249]

Suhm contended that as Norway was a country without a university, but also a country where there were few notables or people with their own means, it was the men of office and first and foremost the theologians who could pursue scientific activities. He found himself among the few who actually had the means to follow his own intellectual path, but his understanding was that the most important persons for making a scientific culture in Norway were the theologians. We shall quickly pass over his recommendations for what a theologian should know to call himself a thorough *Theologus*—most probably none would ever reach the peaks Suhm was trying to make them aspire to. But his writings, along with Gunnerus's and the various writings of parson-priests, underscored the extent to which the priest was seen as the target of reform. The priests were also the men of hope; only through molding a new breed of priests could

---

[248] Clarke, "The Pursuit of the Prosopography."

[249] Suhm, *Tronhiemske samlinger*, "Det er siælden at andre end de, der have visse Embeder, Stand eller Midler kunne legge sig efter Videnskaber. De første behøve dem uomgiængeligen til deres Forretninger; De andre ansees gemeenligen i den slebne Verden for ei at have havt en god Opdragelse, dersom de i det mindste ei have en løslig Kundskab i visse Videnskaber, og de tredie have af alle best Tid og Leylighed til at legge sig efter og at forfremme Videnskaberne, da de gandske og aldeles kunne opofre sig til dem. Enhver seer heraf letteligen, hvi der er saa stor en Mangel paa Videnskaber i vort Land, saa at Theologien er fast eene nogenlunde bekiendt."

Norway become an enlightened and scientifically advanced nation. Patriotism, the honor of the king, and of God, were the most important figures of speech in the official statements. The common good and the king could be honored through economic treatises, while God could be venerated in nature. True pleasure was to be found in nature, where one could honor God by studying his creation, the king by finding things that could be economically useful, and the compatriots by writing about Norwegian nature. What one could argue after reading the different prefaces and speeches of the Society is that it is strange that anyone but the priests, and anything but Norwegian nature, was ever transacted in the *Skrifter*.

The materiality of writing

In a letter to the king in 1762, Gunnerus asked for permission to let the *Skrifter* be censored by the bishop (i.e. himself) in Trondheim. Due to the lack of publishers in Trondheim, *Skrifter* had to be printed in Copenhagen, he argued, and because of the large variety in the content, numerous faculties would be responsible for overlooking the material. This caused considerable delay in the publishing process, and Gunnerus promised that the bishop "would most humbly and earnestly assure you that nothing in the above-mentioned writings would introduce anything that might contravene the obligations and prohibitions normally observed when publishing books."[250] The reason for concern by the king was marginal as we have seen from the content of the first volume. Even if Suhm's plea to abandon censorship and promote free speech in his article on the "Character of the Present Century" was controversial, they were not forbidden ideas, and not surprisingly, the right to censorship was granted to the bishop. If this had any effect—other than speeding up the publishing process—is hard to tell, but no signs have been found to indicate an active censorship by the bishop. When the statutes were set down in 1767 to prepare for the operation of a more official royal society, paragraph eight stated that the Society "would not exclude any thorough, useful, or beautiful science," but neither translations nor "bad writing" would be tolerated in the *Skrifter*.[251] What was considered "bad" is not entirely clear. It was perhaps self-evident at the time, and most probably it had no exact limitation, but to argue against protestant religion, the state, or the king was probably well within the definition of bad. There was also strong control on what could be printed, at least in theory. The statutes stated that every submitted or deposited paper would be "tried" and "judged" in plenum; thereafter the paper would be delivered to one or more members for further "trial." Only after there were "found merits" would the paper be incorporated into *Skrifter*. How this process worked in practice is not easy to determine.

---

[250] Dahl, letter 228. Gunnerus to the King, June 5, 1762.
[251] *Skrifter IV*, Statutes, "Selskabet udelukker ikke nogen grundig, nyttig, eller smuk Videnskab; dog tager det ikke imod Oversættelser, for at indrykke samme i de sædvanlige Acta, ikke heller imod slette Skrifter . . ."

Before 1767 we do not know exactly who took part in the meetings, and what form they had. There is a letter from Gunnerus in which an article is refused, with the explanation that the historical class of the Society was not satisfied. This is probably only a sign that it was read by Suhm or Schøning, or both. After 1768 we can follow the deliberations of the Society in the protocol, and it contains many entries about manuscripts. However, sometimes it was stated that the paper was accepted for publication in *Skrifter*, but the article was never published. In other cases there is no mention of approval or disapproval, but the paper in question would later appear in the journal. Where and how the decision to print or not to print was mostly taken is thus not easy to decide, but the lack of mention of decisions is most probably due to the haste of the secretary, rather than a consequence of *Skrifter* being edited elsewhere. Through the 1770s and 1780s the articles submitted to the Society were read out loud at meetings, whether they were barometric observations or relations on life on Greenland, and the texts were put under closer scrutiny by one or several of the members.

The first five issues of *Skrifter* appeared regularly, but from 1774 and through the rest of the century *Skrifter* appeared sporadically—and slowly. This has been taken as a proof that the scientific activity of the Society was drastically reduced after the death of Gunnerus. It is certainly true that the bishop's seat no longer functioned as a scientific centre, but we argue that the difficulty in getting material printed was the chief reason why the activity was reduced, and further that the decline in the publication rate was one of the main reasons why the Society itself declined as an important scientific centre. The inability to get *Skrifter* published on a regular basis can be seen as a chief explanation as to why the reputation of the Society and the supply of good scientific articles was drastically reduced.

From 1774 onwards the delay in publication of *Skrifter* was an immense problem. In 17 November 1776, the Society received a letter from Hans Strøm, by now one of the most renowned natural historians in Denmark-Norway, asking the Society to return four manuscripts which had been accepted for publication. These manuscripts had already been sent to Copenhagen for printing in the forthcoming volume of *Skrifter*, according to the Society, and in the meeting the members agreed to compose a letter in which Strøm was offered to have the manuscripts back given that they were not already in print in Copenhagen (which they obviously hoped they would be) and if he would substitute them with other interesting articles.[252] Eight years later the articles appeared in print. The articles and the complete volume of *Skrifter* had been lying in Copenhagen for eight years, and they had been unable to get it printed from Trondheim. Strøm's article on leprosy could probably be read with care and curiosity in 1784. It is harder to see that his meteorological observations from Sundmøre in the years 1767 and 1768 would be read with much interest in 1784.[253]

---

[252] DKNVS. Protocol, 1776 den 4de Novembr, 34.
[253] Strøm, "Fortsættelse af Metorologiske Iagttagelser."

It is very difficult to ascertain why the delays occurred, why all discussions and proofreading by the Society and its members would end in total failure. As a matter of curiosity, one might be interested in knowing whether the decision taken in December 1772 to publish all texts from the Society in Latin rather than Gothic letters could have had any influence on the delays. During a meeting this decision was taken, with the explicit aim of getting rid of the Gothic letters, and of heightening the esteem of the Society.[254] In all events, in 1775, one year after the last volume of *Skrifter*, the protocol of the Society stated that there was material enough for a volume VI and a volume VII.[255] But they never appeared, as what appeared in 1784 was volume one of *Nye Samling af det Kongelige Norske Videnskabers Selskabs Skrifter*. Perhaps the members and former active participants in producing *Skrifter* were no longer eager to support the Society? From the first volume of *Skrifter* there were good helpers in Copenhagen who negotiated with the publisher, proofread the texts and ascertained that the illustrations were correctly reproduced. Professor Oeder, the natural historian who had started the work on *Flora Danica*, magister Dass, Schøning's predecessor as principal at the cathedral school, and some of Gunnerus's former amanuenses had been actively working to prepare the publications. In the 1770s many members of the Society lived and worked in Copenhagen, first and foremost Suhm and Schøning, but also the secretary, Nils Krog Bredal, had returned to Copenhagen to become director of the theatre, and Johan Nordal Bruun was now an active student in Copenhagen. One could expect them to pay their due to a society they were closely involved with. But nothing happened.

The Society itself put the blame on the lack of patriotic sentiments among the publishing houses in Copenhagen. When the Society decided to approach their old publisher, Pelt, in 1775 to ask whether he would pursue the work with *Skrifter*, they could not know that it would take another nine years before a new volume would appear. "To the Reader," we can read in 1784: "It is by no occasion the fault of the Society or lack of enterprise which have caused that nothing of the Society's work has been presented for the public for so long; . . . even more time could have passed, had not bookseller Prost found the right patriotism, which the Society, not without anxiety has sought and found lacking with others."[256] The preface stated that the lack of interest shown by the publishers was quite unforeseen in "this epoch of Literature and Publishing houses," and ended the lament with a consideration of the difficulties one had to conquer in a place which lacked almost all literary facilities and which was situated so remotely and inconveniently in relation to the rest of the learned world. Trondheim was indeed portrayed as ever more peripheral. But the question still remains as to why

---

254 DKNVS, Protocol, 1772 December 7th, 13.

255 DKNVS, Protocol, 1775 March 6th, 25.

256 An., "Til Læseren." "Det er aldeles ikke Selskabets Skyld, eller Mangel paa Driftighed, som har voldet, at i saa lang Tid intet af dets Arbeider er fremlagt for Publikum; men uformodentlige Tilfælde og Samvirkning af Omstændigheder, som man allermindst i denne Liutteratur=og Forlægger=Epoke skulde formode, have indtil nu tilbageholdt Selskabets Skrifter, og kunde end længer have tilbageholdt dem, dersom ikke Selskabet hos Hr. Boghandler Prost havde fundet den Patriotisme, som det, ikke uden Bekymring, maae tilstaae at have søgt og savnet hos andre."

the Society should have more difficulties with the printing houses from the 1770s onwards.

Why were the publishers so reluctant? Trondheim had had its printing press since 1739, and a great many books were printed in town—among them the journal of Suhm and the celebratory speeches held by the *vice-præses* of the Society on the occasion of the birthday of the King each year. But the Society needed a publisher, not only a printer. It needed an agency which could afford the expenses of printing without demanding payment, and which could take the whole responsibility of marketing and selling the volumes. This was also the reason why the Society was so reluctant to give volumes to members and others; it simply sold the rights to publish its volumes, and received only a small amount of issues itself. This was apparently decreasingly an interesting task for the publishers to take on. We can guess that the volumes sold less and less, or that other printing commissions gave more revenue. But we should also take into account that the loss of Gunnerus also implied the loss of a profiled intellectual and a name that sold. Perhaps the dwindling status of natural history within the leading circles of Copenhagen was also a factor detrimentally affecting sales. After the fall of Struensee in 1772, when the *Guldeberske* period set in—that is, when Ove Høegh-Guldberg would be the most powerful man in the state—the ambitions to strengthen the natural sciences seem to have waned.[257] Guldberg stated in a later letter that the natural historians of the country should not believe they were being useful just by incessantly discovering new species. A state would perhaps need two systematic natural historians who could augment the book of nature; the rest should "direct their industriousness, their investigations towards the useful."[258]

The gradually reduced frequency of the volumes, until the almost 20-year break between 1798 and 1817, would first and foremost, according to the sources, be a consequence of the lack of interest on the part of the publishers. When the *Skrifter* began to appear with less and less frequency, the authors would be discouraged from sending their contributions, and the stock of articles would gradually be reduced. As the number of scientifically active persons located in Trondheim also declined, the stock of articles would be further reduced. And both for the potential writers in Trondheim and for out-of-town members, the steady increase in other publishing channels would represent serious competition. Competition in the literary market intensified rapidly throughout the second half of the 18th century: Newspapers were established in numerous towns in the kingdom, and journals of different genres appeared. *Vice-Præses* Schøneyder expressed this clearly in his preface to the 1798 edition of *Skrifter*: He had been forced to print his yearly inauguration speeches in journals like *Hermoder* and *Minerva*. There were also other outlets: the topographical society in Christiania published its journal from 1792, the Danish patriotic society issued its journal *Det Kongelige Danske Landhuusholdnings-Selskabs Skrifter* from 1776, and the Natural History Soci-

---

[257] See for an interpretation of this Bjerke *Uavhengighet gjennom vitenskap*, 28.
[258] As cited in Bjerke, *Uavhengighet gjennom vitenskap*, 28.

ety in Copenhagen (1789) issued its Skrifter from 1790. In addition various patriotic journals could offer broader distribution and quicker editorial work than the peripheral society in Trondheim. In this sense Trondheim was being pushed further out on the periphery. The town grew, merchants accumulated fortunes, the *Borgerlige skole* was established, to name but a few signs, but Christiania grew faster, *Kongsberg Bergakademi* was more and more professionally operated, and it was difficult to uphold Trondheim as the scientific centre of Norway, even though the society carried the name of the *Royal* Norwegian Society of Science.

A patriotic society?

In September 1772 a long announcement could be read in the local newspaper, *Tronhiems Kongelige allene privilegerede Adresse=Contoirs Ugentlig Udgivende Efterretninger*. Prince Frederik, it was announced, had given a new proof of his gracious disposition towards the scientific society and the Norwegian populace by granting 300 *Rigsdaler* yearly for the announcement of rewards. Three groups of rewards would be given. 50 *Rigsdaler* for a treatise on a scientific matter, 100 *Rigsdaler* for two prizes for treatises about Norwegian occupations (*Næringsveye*), and 150 *Rigsdaler* divided into four prizes for native-born Norwegians of the peasant estate. These last would be rewarded for having shown particular industry in agriculture, fisheries, forestry, and in the administration of these fields. What kind of Society would announce these kinds of prizes? Or more to the point: Did this announcement contribute to transforming the Society from a scientific to a patriotic society?

In the widest meaning, a patriot in the vocabulary of the day was a man who loved his fatherland. In a more specific sense, a patriot referred to a person who was engaged in promoting the common weal. This was also the stated aim of the Society in Trondheim—science was a means of promoting the happiness and wellbeing of the fatherland, the state and its inhabitants. Was it then a patriotic society from the outset in 1760? It was a scientific society, which was a particular genre of society which could be recognized as such. Patriotic society was a name used for a different type of society. The name referred to the economical and agricultural societies, and generally societies working for public utility. These societies were spreading throughout Europe in the second half of the century, especially inspired by the Royal Society for Art, Manufactures, and Commerce in London (1754) and *Die Oekonomische Gesellschaft* in Bern (1759). These Societies were particularly working for practical improvements, giving prizes for inventions, new technologies, and agricultural practices as well as for theoretical treatises which were concerned with economical and agricultural subjects. In that sense the society in Trondheim was not inaugurated as a patriotic society, but it was to become one when it started issuing prizes for economical subjects and practical work in 1772. Still, what becomes obvious in the study of this particular society is that the patriotism expressed and cultivated was essential for both types of societies, and that furthering science and furthering practical improvement could be seen as two sides of the same coin.

It has been claimed about German patriotic societies that they were especially important as political and economical instruments of mobilization for the absolute monarchical state.[259] This is obviously also the case for the Trondheim Society, which was an instrument for mobilization both as a patriotic and a scientific society. However, also other perspectives have been applied to the patriotic societies—they have been seen as important for politicizing the consciousness of the bourgeoisie, and as an arena for exercising egalitarian middle-class communication forms.[260] Thus an emancipating function has been stressed. Following up on this, one could say that scientific societies were characterized more as elite organizations than the economical societies that would have a broader group of middle-class members. Again, referring to the Norwegian situation, and the Trondheim society in general, the middle classes in Norway had a heavy predominance of state officials. As a scientific society it had a particularly strong element of middle-class state officials, and as a patriotic society it had an especially small element of merchants and manufacturers. Maybe this also made the combination of the scientific and patriotic-economical function more natural.

One complexity in reading the texts emanating from the Society stems from the shifting value that was placed on Norway as the fatherland and the state as the Danish-Norwegian kingdom. This was an ambiguity which was widely discussed in the literature during the period we are dealing with, and the interpretation has been that a patriotism based on belonging to a native country was gradually becoming more important as opposed to a patriotism based on citizenship.[261] But in Trondheim the two were voiced simultaneously, and not before well into the 19th century can we see a predominance of the nativist argument. It is also important to stress that patriotism in Denmark-Norway from the 1760s on was not republican and as a patriotic society, *Videnskabsselskabet*, was definitely paying its tribute to the king and the absolute state.

In 1772 Gunnerus came home from Copenhagen with the money for the scientific society: 300 *Rigsdaler* yearly granted by the prince. This money was not intended for the free use of the Society, but for prizes. As the Society did not have any other substantial income, this donation forced the Society into the role of a patriotic society, even if, as we have shown before, it continued to function as a scientific society. From 1772 on, awarding prizes would become one of the main functions of the Trondheim Society, and in this way the government in Copenhagen managed the Society in Trondheim, directing the member's attention from useful science to useful work. The *Skrifter* of the Society were, as stated in earlier quotations, meant to be read even by the "reasonable but untutored." Norwegian farmers, soldiers, and women were seen as part of the public that could read the articles. From 1774 there were fewer publications and increasingly the peasant population would be a target for improvement and be put in a much more active role relating to the Society: They were rewarded for their own activities.

---

[259] Reinalter, "Einleitung," 10.
[260] Schlögl, "Die patriotisch-gemeinnützigen . . . ," 61.
[261] See Supphellen, "'Rational Norwegian Patriotism' . . . ," Storsveen, Norsk Patriotisme, Engelhart, "Patriotism, nationalsm . . ." and Damsholt, *Fædrelandskærlighed*.

This activity not only included the peasants, but also the whole chain of officials who were engaged in bringing the announcements of the prize assignments for the lower classes.

However, as is obvious from the announcement in 1772, the prize money from the prince was meant to be used for three kinds of prizes: scientific, theoretical about practical purposes and for practical work. Theoretical prizes implied awarding money for treatises that answered questions concerned with scientific issues applied usefully. Practical prizes would be awarded to farmers and others who had given proof of their *Vind-skibelighed* (industriousness).

Utility in theory

The first scientific prize announcement would be given for a treatise on the causes of leprosy and possible cures. For the treatises on theoretizations of good practices, the announcements were for best practices in herring fisheries and for the different advantages of Norwegian plows. But the essays were slow in appearing. When prizes were announced next time in February 1773, they were only announced for the peasants. In December that year three essays had appeared: One Latin treatise on the best way of salting herring, one Danish on the same matter, and one Danish treatise on Norwegian plows accompanied by two models and some iron. Two of the treatises were turned down on the argument that they brought up nothing new, while the decision on the Latin treatise on herring was postponed, as more trials were necessary. Thus the prize-money for these treatises was transferred to prize-money for Norwegian farmers. In 1774 again new themes were announced, on currents on the Norwegian coasts, on manure and soil types, and on how to find anthracite in Norway. This year two treatises on manure were handed in, but neither of them deserved prizes, according to the members. The trials of the treatises were thorough. The Latin treatise on herring was tested by putting the method proposed to use. On a meeting in December 5th 1775, a sample was opened, but the members did not find this sample better than others, thus the treatise did not receive the prize-money.

During the years, the problem with the theoretical prizes was low attendance and the low quality of the essays. The low attendance had one particular reason: No member of the Society living in Norway could compete for the money, and since the Society was generous in inviting new members in, there were few people left who could take part. During the years there were prizes awarded; The most important of these was the prize afforded to Morten Thrane Brünnich who in 1776 submitted *Forsøg til Mineralogie for Norge* (Attempt at mineralogy for Norway), which was to become a standard work in mineralogy for decades. But in 1777 the prince announced that since he in particular loved and liked the practical prizes, he wanted two-thirds of the prize money reserved for these. Attempts were made to receive further competitors. In 1784 it was decided to "encourage" also contributions in German for the theoretical prizes; this meant that Danish, Latin or German could be the language of a prize-essay. During a later meeting French and English were also included as possible languages. The same year, new types of prize assignments were given—for example, "a philological-juridical treatise on the best relation between crime and punishment," and for a treatment of whether and where there were petrifactions to be found in the Northern part of Norway. In 1791 again, the new *vice-præses* proposed that the members should be allowed to compete for the prize-money and this motion to the prince was supported, and the laws were then changed.[262] Without having the exact number of treatises delivered each year, there nevertheless is no sign that this actually helped. And once again, this was probably a result of less interest in the Society, in natural knowledge and in the competition from other societies. A thorough comparison with other societies would be needed to gain a better understanding of why the theoretical prizes in Trondheim would never be a great success in the 18th century.

Practical utility

The archives of Videnskabsselskabet contain a fascinating and enormous amount of material in all the applications for practical prizes received during the period prizes were awarded from 1772 to 1848. For the whole period there are 3300 applicants, from 1772 to 1806 there are approximately 1200 applications. Predominantly these were prizes awarded with the money from the prince, but in addition some members would give money to have special prizes proclaimed, among them Suhm. Another contributor was the copper work at Rørås.

Each year a placard would be made to spread the theme for the prizes of the year, along with an announcement in the newspapers. This placard was spread through different state officials in the whole of Norway, and the prizes of the Society were proclaimed from pulpits and on walls throughout the kingdom. The impressive amount of applications obscures the fact that there were only a few applicants for each prize. Monica Aase, who has researched this material thoroughly, has found that on average there were only 2.7 applications for each prize.[263] Concerning the agricultural prizes, her conclusion is that the farmers applied for prizes within areas they were already working in, while prizes that required the application of new methods, new crops, or animals, would received far less applicants.

What were the deeds that would be rewarded? Land reclamation, partition of farms, cultivation of new land, but also import of new races of sheep, cultivation of tobacco, hemp, flax, hops, cherries, vegetables generally, potatoes, as well as building different contrivances of stone, such as fences, barns, wells, etc. Different works with textiles received many applicants, and not least many female applicants, especially in weaving. Another large category was killing of carnivores—eagles, bears and wolves.

---

[262] DKNVS Protocol, April 11th, 1792, 120.
[263] Aase, *Patrioter og bønder*, 44.

The first years a single applicant could receive a huge sum; later the sums were mainly 10 *Rigsdaler* and in addition there were awarded medals instead of money for many of the applicants. For the farmers the money and honor could prove important; how important is difficult to tell. This is also beyond our scope here. For the Society the prizes meant that it had means for reaching out from its premises in Trondheim. The money would be an important way of making the Society known to others, both through the theoretical and the practical prizes. Furthermore, the prizes would ensure that the Society did work that could be regarded as patriotic. It did itself do practical work for augmenting the happiness of the state and its inhabitants. But the prizes also meant work, much and hard work, and that in an area which could not directly be considered scientific. Even so, as it has been claimed, the announcement of prizes did have a scientific program to it, backed by knowledge of agriculture in its widest sense, and economic doctrines. The prize-competitions were not haphazard.[264]

Conclusion

The society in Trondheim was very successful in its ability to attract members and it succeeded in bringing forth eight large volumes of scientific texts during the 18th century. As a society of small means and within a city without academic institutions or publishers, the achievement was remarkable. The strategy of reaching out to priests and other state officials, to collect forces for scientific work, did work. Especially important was the way it applied to the priests, and made a virtue of the role as priest, enlightener and naturalist. The Society was less successful in the attempt to attract theoretically advanced writers who could compete for prizes. One reason was that members could not take part in the competition until the 1790s. Another reason would be that the Society's fame was dwindling as the Skrifter was less frequently published, and the well known historians and naturalists of the earlier days disappeared.

We have argued that the economic-patriotic and scientific sides to the Society's activities were directed towards the same goal, the diffusion of enlightenment, practical improvement and patriotic sentiment. The practical prizes which the Society administrated with great zeal and success during the 18th century were means towards realizing the aims of the Society. They did reach a large public and they contributed to directing the attention towards the improvement of agriculture and other handicrafts. The problem would be that it demanded great effort, and it portrayed the Society as patriotic, not scientific, for the eyes of the public. In addition, as we will come back to, Trondheim and the Society would become more peripheral in the years to come, as population growth and building of teaching institutions would take place elsewhere.

---

[264] Midbøe, Det kongelige norske, 131.

PART II

1805–1870

A changing Society:
1805–1830

On 6 September 1811, *Videnskabsselskabet* gathered for a meeting. This was only the second meeting of the year, the first since late January.[265] Three matters were on the agenda. The first was the reading of a letter from Simon Barthelemémy-Joseph Noël de la Mortiniére. He was an inspector for a geographical survey for the French state and presented himself as a member of the Imperial Academy of Science of Turin.[266] De la Mortiniére was not a member of *Videnskabsselskabet*, although he was later to become one.[267] He was primarily interested in corresponding with the Society on the subject of the natural history of fishing, and generally on the classification of species of fish.

The second matter was the question of how to expand the library. A significant amount of money, 1500 *riksdaler*, was earmarked for this purpose. This was a considerable amount, given that the entire annual revenue of *Videnskabsselskabet* was perhaps approximately half this amount, and significantly larger than, for instance, the annual income of the head of the *Katedralskole*, who earned 1000 *riksdaler* a year.

But the by far most important issue at this meeting was the election of new members. While this was a regular event, what was unusual at this meeting was the scale of the elections—no less than 44 new members were elected.[268] This was more than had been elected during the previous 10 years (39 members elected in all from 1801 to 1810). In a meeting on April 2, 1812, an additional seven members were admitted.[269] These elections mark a change in the membership profile of *Videnskabsselskabet*, and they came about as a response to both long-term challenges and the extraordinary situation that arose around 1810. What kind of challenges were these, and how was the leadership of the Society to respond to them?

---

[265] *Generalsforsamlingsprotokoll 1768–1841* fol. 231–235. DKNVS archive II:1.

[266] This Society was founded in 1757, and was a Royal Society since 1783. During the French occupation of Piedmonte, the Society was given the new title "Imperial Society."

[267] De la Mortiniere visited Trondheim in 1821–22, working on a history of fishing and whaling, and was elected member of Videnskabsselskabet in December 1821. He died in Trondheim three months later. Schmidt, *Det Kongelige Norske Videnskabers Selskab matrikkel 1760–1960*: 80.

[268] A full list is presented in Schmidt 1960: 64–71.

[269] Schmidt, 1960: 71–72.

The generation shift

The election of 44 new members was a significant development. But not only is this high number a break with the policies of election in the previous decades; a closer look at who these newly elected members were also reveals that their election meant a change in the composition of *Videnskabsselskabet*.

During the first few of decades of its existence, the Society mainly elected Norwegian clergy (many of them residing in Gunnerus's diocese), scholars based in Copenhagen, primarily connected to the university, and foreign scholars, with Germans heavily represented. Over the years, this profile became more blurred, mainly due to mobility or death, and of course, not all members belonged in one of these groups.

What separates the members admitted in 1811 and 1812 from their predecessors is that they were to a large extent inhabitants of the city of Trondheim or its immediate neighbors. Clergymen from Trondheim's neighboring parishes were now admitted— for instance, the vicar of Frosta, Svend Brun Busch, who had been a student at *Katedralskole* (Cathedral School) in Trondheim. The same was the case for Johan Garman, vicar of Byneset. Both these parishes were close to the city and economically integrated with the city. Not only former students from the *Katedralskole*, but also members of the staff were among the new members. One example is Christian Møller, a former student who had since become a teacher at the school. The same applies to the staff at the *Borgerlige realskole*, the school for middle-class pupils. Moreover, several high-ranking officers and other civil servants in Trondheim or the neighboring districts were elected. One example is the *sorenskriver* (city recorder) Emanuel Balle in Strinda, and General Johannes Klingenberg Sejersted. What these men had in common was that they were all educated. Some of them had university degrees, others had passed an exam from a Latin School, or had a military-education background.

Another group now to become more influential was the local merchants. Prominent examples are Nicolay Lysholm, Otto Bejer and Hans Collin, all members of the economic elite that enjoyed its golden age from the 17th century to the early part of the 19th century. They were largely descendants of immigrants from the Danish-German border region and had to a large extent controlled the export of copper, timber and fish from the Trøndelag region, thus also controlling the economy and politics of the city for more than a century.

This group of merchants was by no means uninterested in science or literature. They usually had an international orientation through their business relations. Education in a wider sense from abroad was common. By the time he had turned twenty, for example, Nicolai Lysholm had spent more than half his life obtaining an education in Flensburg and Hamburg, both at a *gymnasium* (upper secondary education), and through practical work in trade. Back in Trondheim, he not only continued his family trade in fish and timber but also experimented in industrial production of herring oil and soap. This led to a general interest in chemical processes.[270]

---

[270] Schmidt, "Lysholm, Nicolay," NBL vol. VIII: 562–564, Oslo, 1938.

What motivated this shift in the pattern of elections from the previous 10 to 15 years? One possible factor is the need to recruit a new generation. While many members were elected during the first 25 years of *Videnskabsselskabet*'s existence, elections were scarce from the 1790s so that the members' median age was increasing and the number dwindling. Tellingly, only ten members were present at the meeting that elected the 44 new members. The elections in 1811 and 1812 can be seen as a reaction to this challenge.

But why were so many of the newly elected members local people? An immediate answer lies in the turbulent political situation. The Napoleonic wars made communication more cumbersome and the concept of a society of corresponding members an ideal hard to realize. For example, the last part of de la Mortiniére's letter was devoted to the problems of how to organize correspondence through the French embassy in Copenhagen, and this problem was also discussed by the members present. If *Videnskabsselskabet* was to continue to have a meaningful existence under these circumstances, it made sense to establish a more locally based society that would be able to draw on the intellectual resources of the city and its surroundings.

This was not an uncommon problem for the learned societies of the day. The French revolution and the Napoleonic wars seem to have been the cause of great problems in communication between the societies, and also a direct reason for the death of many of the 18th century societies.[271] A major setback in this regard was the decision in 1793 by the Convent in France to terminate all academies and learned societies. This was the starting point of the unraveling of the network of learned societies, a process that was speeded up by the constant warfare of the next two decades. Prominent societies, such as the academies in Brussels, Berlin and Bologna, were directly affected by war, either because they were plundered, as in Berlin, or because they closed their doors all together for a short or long period of time.

Thus, from the turn of the century, *Videnskabsselskabet* to a large degree was forced to base its activities on the educationally or financially privileged groups in a small town of fewer than 9000 inhabitants in the northern periphery of the Danish-Norwegian kingdom, occasionally cut off from effective communication with the rest of the continent by the constant hostilities of the period.

The long-term process

The elections can both be seen as part of the more long-term process of revitalizing *Videnskabsselskabet*, but also as an attempt to deal with the immediate challenges to the organization's position in the Norwegian intellectual society.

The election of the new members was not an isolated event, but came at the end of a long process of revising the statutes of the Society. It seems clear that the new *vice-praeses*,

---

[271] J.E. McClellan, *Science Reorganized. Scientific Societies in the Eighteenth Century*, New York, 1985: 253–259.

Peder Olivarius Bugge, who was elected in 1804, must have seen several problems threatening the organization when he took office.

Bugge (1764–1849) had studied theology in Copenhagen in the 1780s, and has been characterized as theologically somewhat schizophrenic.[272] On the one hand, he appeared in the early 1790s as an extreme anti-rationalist, partly pointing backward towards a very literal, Lutheran understanding of the Bible and partly inspired by the Herrnhut tendencies of his father, who was a vicar in southern Norway. On the other hand, his doctoral dissertation, accepted in Göttingen in 1796, meshed well with the theological rationalism of the times. The dissertation secured him membership in *Videnskabsselskabet*. In 1804, Bugge was appointed bishop of Trondheim in connection with the division of the diocese, which formerly had covered the whole of Norway north of the Dovre Mountains. Northern Norway north of Trøndelag was now to become a separate diocese. The partition of the diocese also meant that the *vice-praeses*, the former Bishop Shønheyder, now left the city and a new vice-president had to be chosen. Bugge was elected by a majority of the votes,[273] which led to a bitter conflict with *stiftsprost* (archdean) Hans Jacob Wille (1756–1808), who was the secretary of *Videnskabsselskabet* and obviously aspired to become *vice-praeses* himself.

Bugge was to become a politically important figure in the turbulent years of the Napoleonic wars, with the brief Norwegian independence in 1814 and the first years of the Norwegian-Swedish union. Establishing close contact with the *praeses* of the Society, Crown Prince and King Christian Frederik, Bugge became the prince's friend and adviser during the turbulent year of 1814. His positions were thus nationalistic and anti-Swedish. Bugge was elected to *Stortinget* (parliament) in 1815, and sided with the ultra-patriots. However, by 1818, he seems to have moved closer towards the political centre and established a realistic attitude towards the inevitable fact of the union. He also established good relations with King Carl Johan at his coronation in Trondheim in 1818, much to the chagrin of his former political compatriots. In the end, this also resulted in his retirement from public life, to the extent this is possible for a bishop. One effect of this was that he resigned as *praeses* in 1820.

The main problem *Videnskabsselskabet* had at the time of the election of Bugge as *vice-praeses* was the declining scientific activity of its members. Bugge started the process of revising the statutes of *Videnskabsselskabet* to meet this challenge. These revisions were a recurring theme in the meetings in the years leading up to 1811. The fall of 1810 was especially a period with intense activity; there were all together six meetings from the end of October to the end of December, and the revision of the statutes was their main subject.[274] The process of restructuring *Videnskabsselskabet* started with the revision of the statutes in 1805, and the new statutes of 1811, revised again in 1815, can be seen as a continuation of these, a process of revision which lasted for about ten

---

[272] Lysaker, *Fra embetskirke til folkekirke 1804–1953*, Trondheim, 1987: 7–72.
[273] *Generalforsamlingsprotokoll 1768–1841*, fol. 175–176, DKNVS Archive II:1.
[274] *Generalforsamlingsprotokoll 1768–1841*, fol. 225–230, DKNVS Archive II:1.

years. The main point of the 1805 revision of the statutes seems to have been the need to adjust to the new situation of scientific inactivity in *Videnskabsselskabet*, and also the new economic realities of a more wealthy Society.[275]

The statutes from 1805 differed from the 1767 statutes with respect to the administration of the economic means of the Society. The solution was to appoint a permanent commission consisting of the *vice-praeses* and four members who were responsible for the economic activity. On this occasion, the members were divided into four groups: the philosophical, mathematical, historical and physical-economic groups or classes. The responsibility for the advancement of practical arts was placed in the last group, thus in some ways promoting their role at the cost of the scientific activities of the Society. The increased importance given to the officials of *Videnskabsselskabet*, especially expressed through the detailed instructions and description of tasks for the librarian, indicates that looking after the collections was now to be an important part of *Videnskabsselskabet*'s work. The new statutes appeared to have some shortcomings, which prompted the process towards the 1811 statutes.[276] Some major changes were made, the most significant being the following three: The charges of the elected officials of *Videnskabsselskabet* were defined more precisely, the number of groups was reduced from four to three, and it became possible for persons who were not active in science to become extraordinary members.

This last point explains why so many members of the Trondheim bourgeoisie could join in 1811. The criteria for becoming an ordinary member were relatively strict, and would have excluded most of the merchants and officials who aspired to membership. Both in the 1805 and the 1811 statutes, ordinary membership was limited to persons who could attach evidence of scientific work with their application for membership. These works were to be read and discussed by the group of *Videnskabsselskabet* in which the work and its author would belong. This process was carried out anonymously; the members of *Videnskabsselskabet* assessing the quality of the work were not to know the identity of the author. This would effectively bar the speculative amateurs who basically would see membership to be of social rather than scientific value. The new statutes offered an effective back door for these aspiring members—they would become members, but they would have to pay a rather substantial fee to do so—at least 10 *riksdaler* per year, or 300 *riksdaler* for a lifelong membership. The benefit for *Videnskabsselskabet* was obvious. It would gain economically, it would have a solid local basis, and the new members would not be able to meddle in the scientific affairs of *Videnskabsselskabet*. The benefit for the new members was the social asset that membership represented. The results of these revisions were immediate—the election of the 44 new members in 1811, most of whom could not boast of any significant scientific production. The more specific tasks of the elected officials of *Videnskabsselskabet* probably reflect the growing economic importance of the organization. In his will, the prominent

---

[275] *Nye Statuter for det Kongelige Norske Videnskabers Selskab i Trondhjem*, Trondhjem, 1806.
[276] *Confirmation paa Statuter for Det Kongelige Norske Videnskabers-Selskab*, Christiania, 1811.

member Christopher Hammer, who had died in 1804, made the Society the sole beneficiary of his entire fortune, along with rather detailed instructions on how to use this
bequest.

The 1805 statutes can thus be seen as a consolidation of *Videnskabsselskabet's* policy of keeping the collections, especially the library, in good shape, and both the 1805
and 1811 statutes underlined the importance of awarding the industriousness and
skills of the common man. This interpretation was formulated explicitly, formally by
the *praeses*, Prince Christian Frederik, in a letter to the king, but of course on Bugge's
initiative.[277]

The competing institutions

Recruitment was not the only concern during these important years. While during the
period following its establishment *Videnskabsselskabet* had represented both the centre
of scientific activity and the promotion of industriousness in the Norwegian realm, it
now was faced with two competing institutions within these fields.

The most important was the establishment of a separate Norwegian university:
A royal grant for the establishment of a university in Christiania was given in the fall of
1811. The issue of a Norwegian university had been debated on several occasions from
the 1770s and onwards, most intensely in the early 1770s, with Bishop Gunnerus as one
of the prime movers on the Norwegian side.[278] The discussion at this time was halted.
Due to the collapse of the Struensee regime these initiatives came to naught and the
proposal was laid aside. Later, the issue continued to be discussed, but perhaps not with
the same intensity or realism as in the 1770s. In the 1780s, the political situation changed
when Crown Prince Frederik in effect took control of the kingdom from the mentally
incapacitated King Christian VII in 1784. The shift in power allowed more open political debates, and among the specific Norwegian topics discussed was the question of an
institution of higher learning. This question was highlighted in 1788, when the prince
visited Norway, and in July that summer arrived in Trondheim. As he was *praeses* of
Videnskabsselskabet, he naturally presided over an extraordinary meeting. The *vice-
praeses*, Christian Frederik Hagerup, gave a speech on the occasion, in which he very
clearly stated that the Norwegian kingdom lacked a university, to the great misfortune
of the country. Hagerup enthusiastically claimed that financing a university would not
be a problem; the Norwegians would gladly foot the bill so that such an establishment
would not put any strain on the finances of the kingdom. In the following months, the
matter was debated in the public sphere, but nothing came of it. The crown prince had

---

[277] "Tvende Skrivelser fra Selskabets Præses Hans Høihed prinds Christian Friderich af 14de og 17de
Dec. 1811 med et Kongebrev om en aarlig kongelig Gave til Selskabet," *Det Kongelige Norske Videnskabers Selskabs Skrifter i det 19de Aarhundrede*, vol. 1, Copenhagen, 1817: 27–32.

[278] K. Slettstrand, *"Trondheimsmiljøet" og tanken om et norsk universitet ca. 1760–1811. Ballade om et
nasjonalt symbol eller et ektefølt behov?* Master's thesis, Trondheim, 2005.

obviously not been persuaded by Hagerup's speech, and there was general skepticism towards his assumption that the financing of the university would be unproblematic. Moreover, the University of Copenhagen was reorganized at this time, which probably overshadowed the debate on a Norwegian university, and no conclusion was drawn.

The 1790s saw another round of debates on the university issue, also this time without immediate consequences. What was different was that *Videnskabsselskabet* in Trondheim was more or less absent from the debate. The initiatives in 1771 and 1788 both originated in Trondheim and also suggested Trondheim as a possible centre for a Norwegian university. In the early 1790s, the debate was dominated by persons from the region around Christiania, which was reflected in the arguments for the location of a university.[279] The outcome of the process was the announcement of a competition for the best essay on the question of "how a university in Norway can be established to the greatest benefit of the country in regard to the culture of the times and the condition of the sciences" to be held in 1794.[280] Fourteen essays were submitted. What they all had in common was their argument for the university to be placed in southern Norway, and furthermore the dismissal of *Videnskabsselskabet*'s role in a new university, if it was mentioned at all. Apparently the dwindling scientific status of the Society had marginalized its role in the public debate on the need for and location of a new university in Norway. The winning essay, by the independent man of letters Christen Pram (1756–1821), dismissed the idea of a university all together, instead arguing for a college which would prepare students for studies at the university in Copenhagen.

The whole debate of the early 1790s culminated in a negative reply from Copenhagen; in 1796 a royal resolution concluded that there was no need and no means for a separate Norwegian university. Instead, the four cathedral schools were given the right to award the degree *Examen Artium*, thus giving their pupils certification that they were ready for a university education. This agreed with the ideas of another dominant figure in the debate, the headmaster at the *Katedralskole* in Christiania, Niels Trewschow (1751–1833). Threscow, who had spent his formative years as a teacher in Trondheim in the 1770s, was later to become the first professor in philosophy in Christiania. He wanted a university that was primarily a scientific institution, not an educational one, and felt that the time was not ripe for such a university in Norway. With the resolution of 1796, the matter was laid to rest for a decade.

The new and extraordinary political situation resulting from the Danish-Norwegian entry into the Napoleonic wars on the French side again highlighted the need for separate Norwegian institutions. Danish-Norwegian neutrality had effectively been terminated by the British shelling of Copenhagen in the summer of 1807 and the subsequent theft of the Danish-Norwegian fleet. One side-effect of this was that communications between Denmark and Norway became more cumbersome, which quickly led to a critical situation in Norway. Even in normal times, Norway was dependent on imports

---

[279] J.P. Collet, *Historien om universitetet i Oslo*, Oslo, 1999: 16–21, Slettestrand, 2005: 84–130.
[280] "Hvorledes et Universitet i Norge kunde indrettes til størst Nytte for landet, med Hensyn til Tidenes Cultur og Videnskabernes Tilstand."

from Denmark, especially grain. The bad harvest in Norway in 1808 exacerbated the crisis. The situation in the following years was one of irregular communications, economic turmoil and a hunger crisis. In this situation, the role and position of Norway in the political construct of the "twin monarchy" became an issue, and the question of a separate Norwegian university resurfaced.

The debate was reopened in 1809, and immediately spawned another essay competition. The essays were to answer three questions: 1) Should Norway have its own university? 2) How could the establishment of a university be most efficiently organized? 3) Where could the financial means for the establishment of a university be found?

The ensuing debates were conducted in newspapers and magazines throughout the country; nonetheless, all the initiatives for a university were based in the Christiania region. In Copenhagen, the king and government clearly perceived the situation and the discussion as part of a nationalistic mood in Norway, and thus as something that had to be stopped or effectively contained. Frederik VI dismissed the idea of a university, but opened a dialogue with the heads of the University of Copenhagen on how to respond to the growing demand for a Norwegian university. One solution was to upgrade the four cathedral schools in Norway, in Christiania, Bergen, Christiansand and Trondheim, by appointing professors at these institutions. This suggestion was rejected by the university in April 1810. Instead, the leadership at the university proposed what can be called a lower institution for higher knowledge. The king approved of the idea, and suggested that such an institution could be located in the mining town of Kongsberg, in connection with the Academy of Mineralogy (*Bergakademiet*) which had been established in 1757. Kongsberg was at the time competing for the position of being the second most populous city in Norway—behind Bergen, but of the same magnitude as Trondheim, Christiania and the twin-city Bragernes-Strømsøe (present-day Drammen). The academy had its own staff of professors and teachers, teaching such subjects as mathematics, geology, mechanics and chemistry. In addition to this, a separate Latin school was established here to prepare the students for their studies.[281]

The debate and the historical events now proved to be somewhat beyond Copenhagen's control. The competition essays published in February 1811 were unanimously in favor of a separate Norwegian university, as well as quite patriotic in tone.[282] There was no consensus on the location of the university, but none of the essays argued in favor of Trondheim. Thus, it is clear that *Videnskabsselskabet* and its activities were not seen as an argument for the location of the university. Quite significantly, several of the authors had quite the opposite view: *Videnskabsselskabet* should be moved to wherever the university was eventually to be situated.

In the spring of 1811, one of the principal figures, not only in the university discussion, but also in the general public sphere of Norway, Count Herman Wedel Jarlsberg, was summoned to Copenhagen by the king. Count Wedel (1779–1840) was the

---

[281] B.I. Berg, "Bergseminaret på Kongsberg 1757–1814," A.K. Børresen & J.T. Kobberrød (eds.), *Bergingeniørutdanning i Norge gjennom 250 år*, Trondheim, 2007: 13–36.
[282] *Historisk-Philosophiske Samlinger*, Vol. 1–2, Christiania, 1811.

head of one of the three noble estates in Norway at the time. He was married to Karen Anker, the richest heiress in the kingdom, and through this marriage he also became one of the leading men in the important timber trade in the Christiania region. He held high positions in the war-time administration in Norway, but at the same time he worked clandestinely for a more independent role for the country, if necessary in union with Sweden. He and his compatriots were motivated in part by patriotism, but also by the need to reestablish good relations with England, which was Norway's most important trading partner.[283]

The exact reason why Wedel was summoned to Copenhagen is not known. There might have been some—well-founded—suspicion that he was nurturing contacts with Sweden with the aim of breaking up the union with Denmark. In that case, there was good reason to keep an eye on him, or even confront him with this suspicion. For his part, once in Copenhagen, Count Wedel was able to influence the decision on the university issue. In April, the heads of the university submitted their recommendation: A separate Norwegian university, to be situated in Kongsberg. In early September the same year, the king accepted the recommendation for a Norwegian university, but the decision on the location was still pending. In the following months, further steps were taken and a committee was established to shed light on the practical aspects relating to the establishment of the university. The committee had finished its work by March 1812, and among its recommendations was that the university should be located in Christiania. The king supported the conclusions of the committee, and the university was formally established by royal decree in April 1812.

Another competing institution that emerged during these years was *Selskabet for Norges Vel* (The Norwegian Society for Rural Development). Established by members of the Christiania elite in late December 1809, its aim was to work for the economic and spiritual improvement of the Norwegian society. It was partly based on already existing local organizations working with these aims, the so-called "parish societies" (*sogneselskap*). *Selskabet for Norges Vel* quickly became a prominent institution with local chapters in all the major towns and counties (*amt*). Its members were usually recruited from the educated classes, and *Selskabet for Norges Vel* was to become heavily involved in the improvement of agriculture, promoting new technologies, new crops and generally supporting industriousness and creativity. It thus emerged as a serious competitor of *Videnskabsselskabet* in this field. Furthermore, it was active in the efforts to establish a university in Norway, for instance by organizing the above-mentioned essay competition and publishing the results in its transactions. The establishment of both *Selskabet for Norges Vel* and the university within two years was a double threat to the very existence of *Videnskabsselskabet*. How did *Videnskabsselskabet* and its members react to this?

As we have seen, *Videnskabsselskabet* met infrequently in the crucial year 1811, as had been the case the preceding years. According to the protocol, the founding of *Selskabet for Norges Vel* a month earlier was not a topic of discussion in the Society's meeting on 28 January 1810. Instead, *vice-praes* Bugge gave a discourse on the topic

---

[283] Maurseth, P., "Wedel Jarlsberg, Johan Caspar Herman," NBL vol. XVIII: 339–373, Oslo, 1977.

"How lucky a nation is to be governed by a king such as Frederik VI."[284] This was of course self-evident, as it was the king's birthday which was ritually celebrated every year. But it seems that neither was the competing society discussed formally in the meetings of *Videnskabsselskabet*, nor were the efforts for the establishment of a university discussed. However, there is good reason to believe that these matters must have been discussed informally, even though we have no record of this.

There were different spheres of influence in Trondheim's public life at the beginning of the 19th century, of which *Videnskabsselskabet* was one. Equal, if not of more importance was *Det forenede borgerlige Selskab* (The United Civic Society), a club functioning as a meeting place for the well-to-do or educated groups in Trondheim.[285] The club had a more social aspect to it than *Videnskabsselskabet*; it had few pretensions beyond being a social setting and a common ground for relaxation and discussions, with good wine and food. As a more informal setting than *Videnskabsselskabet*, we must believe that a good deal of the challenges facing the organization might have been discussed here, both by *Videnskabsselskabet*'s members and other members of the Trondheim establishment.

To establish a national organization, *Selskabet for Norges Vel* also tried to set up a chapter in Trondheim. This was, needless to say, a touchy process. As mentioned above, this organization was based on local chapters, and Trondheim would naturally be a strong candidate. But the invitation to form a local chapter received a cool reception.[286] However, the existence of a competing institution may have been one of the reasons for some of the amendments to the statutes in 1811. The emphasis in the statutes of *Videnskabsselskabet*'s responsibility with respect to the advancement of industriousness and inventiveness was maintained, but formulated in such a way that made it clear that *Videnskabsselskabet* would primarily publish scientific works to achieve this, and to a lesser extent award prizes to particularly entrepreneurial individuals. Furthermore, the statutes of 1811 stressed that the extraordinary members could have their say in the awarding of prizes, as they were expected to contribute financially to *Videnskabsselskabet*. Thus, some of the responsibility for this was transferred to the less scientifically active parts of the Society. This seems to have made way for the establishment of local chapters in a regional organization of *Selskabet for Norges Vel*, with overlapping membership with *Videnskabsselskabet*. A Trondheim chapter was thus established in January 1813. Of the five leaders of the local chapter, three were members of *Videnskabsselskabet*, elected in the September 1811 meeting.[287] At the same time, all the leaders of the local regional organization were also members of *Videnskabsselskabet*.[288]

---

[284] *Generalforsamlingsprotokoll 1768–1841*, fol. 224–225: "Hvor lykkeligt et Folk er, som behærskes af en regent som Frederik den 6te." DKNVS Archive II:1.

[285] I. Bull, "Foreningsdannelse i norske byer. Borgerlig offentlighet, kjønn og politisk kultur," *Heimen* 2007:311–324.

[286] O.A. Øverland, *Det Kgl. Selskap for Norges vels Historie gjennem hundre Aar*, Kristiania, 1909: 91–94.

[287] C. Møller (teacher at *Katedralskole*), and the merchants C.L. Buck and P. Schmidt.

[288] Professor Chr. Krogh, Colonel Georg Frederik von Krogh, and the two priests Bendix Støren and Falch Widerøe. Støren was later to become a member of the leadership of *Videnskabsselskabet*, while Chr. Krogh would become its *praeses*.

The position of Trondheim as an important trading and military city in the 17th and 18th century is manifest in this prospect, *Throndhjem reconquered by the Norwegians, 1658*, from Samuel Pufendorf's history of Carl X Gustav from 1696. *Courtesy:* NTNU Library.

The Dane Peter Friderich Suhm (1728–1798) came to Trondheim to marry the wealthy Karen Angell and stayed in the town from 1751 to 1765. After taking part in establishing the Society he went back to Copenhagen to become one of the most important scholars of Denmark-Norway in the 18th century. Oil on canvas. Property of Willemoes-Suhm, Itzehoe, Holstein.
Photo: H. Mehlert. *Courtesy:* NTNU Library.

The historian Gerhard Schøning (1722–1780) from the north of Norway came to Trondheim to become principal at *Katedralskolen*. He took part in establishing the Society when he stayed here with his friend Suhm from 1751 to 1765. He later became Professor at Sorø. Lithography by I. W. Tegner.
Courtesy: NTNU Library.

The title page of the Pastoral Letter of Bishop Gunnerus from 1758, with Gerhard Schøning's signature. Here a program for a scientific society was announced.
Courtesy: NTNU Library.

The *Skrifter* (Writings) of the Society was issued with great eagerness in the 1760's. Here is the title page of *Selskabets Skrifter*, part 3, 1765.
Courtesy: NTNU Library.

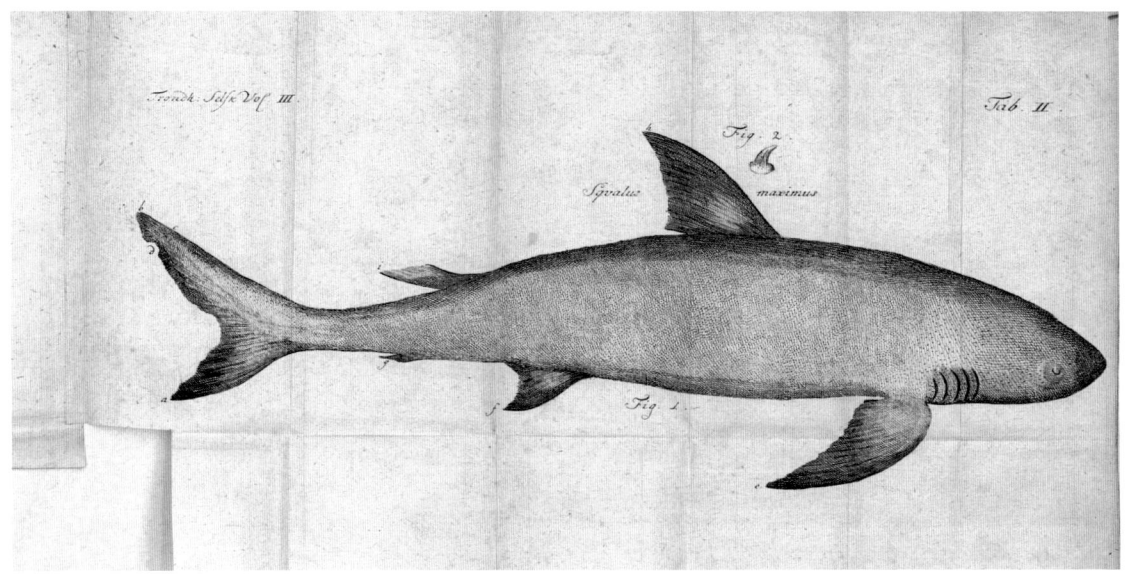

The Basking Shark was an important actor in the scientific work of bishop Gunnerus who first described the animal in 1765 and established it as a specimen of theology and natural knowledge. He named it *Sqvalus maximus*, a name which was later changed to *Cetorhinus maximus*. This illustration is from *Selskabets Skrifter*, part 3, 1765, tab. II. *Courtesy:* NTNU Library.

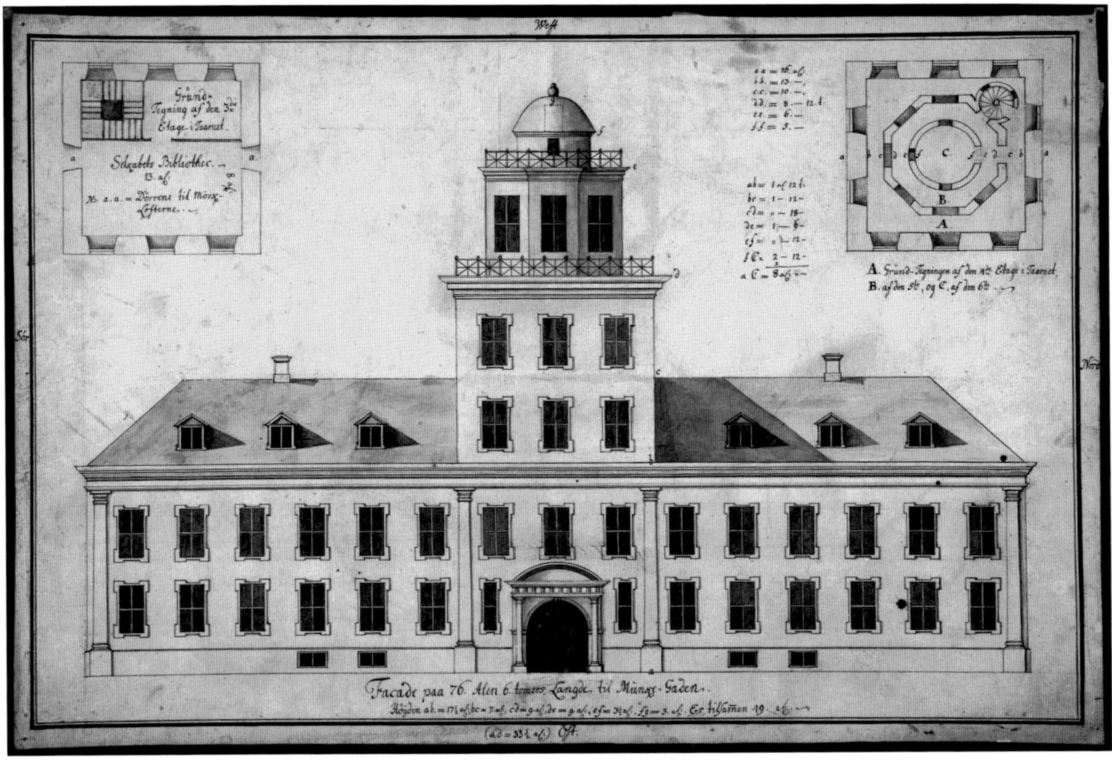

Johan Daniel Berlin's (1714–1787) project for a new building for *Katedralskolen* and the Royal Norwegian Society of Sciences from the 1770's. An astronomical observatory was projected as part of the edifice, but was never realized because of lack of money. A new building was finally inaugurated in 1787 in Munkegaten 8. *Courtesy:* Norwegian National Archives, Trondheim.

Johan Ernst Gunnerus (1718–1773) is depicted as a learned theologicus in front of his books in one of his many theological publications issued before he arrived in Trondheim.
Courtesy: University Library of Trondheim, Special Collection. *Courtesy:* NTNU Library.

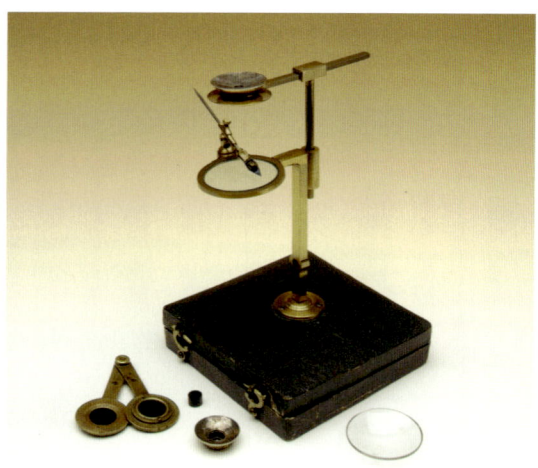

Gunnerus' microscope was bought from John Cuff in Fleet Street in London, via knowledgeable friends in Copenhagen and arrived after a year in Trondheim.
Photo: Per Fredriksen; 2002. *Courtesy:* Museum of Natural History and Archaeology.

This False Helleborine (Latin *Veratrum album*, Norw. *Nyserot*) is depicted in part two of Gunnerus' major work, *Flora Norvegica*, issued in two parts in 1766 and 1776. The plan was to prepare also a vernacular version, but only the first Latin volume arrived in Gunnerus lifetime. From Part II. Tab. I.
Courtesy: NTNU Library.

In Gunnerus' town house his books and collection were kept after he moved from the farm Berg outside the city. This was also the location for many of the meetings of the Society. Dronningens gate 5. *Prospect of Boreauchef A. L. Schult's mansion in Trondheim.* Painted by Mathias Ferslev Dalager, around 1830.
Courtesy: Museum of Natural History and Archaeology.

PROSPECT af STADEN TRONDHIM i NORGE.

Trondheim viewed from the east in 1817. To the far left the medieval cathedral. *Katedralskolen*, where the Society had its premises, can be seen rising above the surrounding buildings just to the north of the cathedral. Water colors. Prospect of Trondheim 8th of May 1817, Peter Fredrik Feilberg.
Photo: Kari Dahl, 2009. *Courtesy:* Museum of Natural History and Archaeology.

Frederik Moltke Bugge (1806–53), praeses 1838–49.
Courtesy: NTNU Library.

An example of the illustrations in Michael Sars' "Fauna littoralis Norvegica," vol. 3, Bergen 1877, TAB IX., written and published with support from the Society.
Courtesy: NTNU Library.

The new premises at Kalvskinnet ca. 1870. The building was at the edge of town, as can be seen from the plowed fields in the foreground. *Photo:* Marcus W. Noodt. *Courtesy:* NTNU Library.

Co-location of the university and Videnskabsselskabet?

The matter of a new university was not discussed in *Videnskabsselskabet* until early 1812, long after the decision to establish a university had been made. However, this does not mean that the members did not participate in the public debate, as several of the individuals involved in the debate in the newspapers and magazines were members. But they did not present and promote themselves as members, nor did they refer to the Society in their arguments.

One exception was Mathias Bonsach Krogh, the bishop of Nordland and Finnmark. A member of *Videnskabsselskabet* since 1787, he had submitted an essay for the competition in 1809. He did not mention his membership, but he was of the opinion that *Videnskabsselskabet* should be moved to the location of the new university, an argument based on the Society's present inactivity in the scientific fields.[289]

The same opinion was voiced by several of the contributors, most notably by the winner of the competition, Nicolai Wergeland, in his essay "*Mnemosyne.*"[290] Nicolai Wergeland (1780–1848) was at the time a teacher at the *Katedralskole* in Christiansand, and was later to become a vicar.[291] He was elected to the National Assembly, *Riksforsamlingen*, which in May 1814 declared Norway an independent kingdom, and drafted and agreed on a constitution and elected Crown Prince Christian Frederik as king. He was, however, of the opinion that Norway would not be able to survive as an independent state, and therefore advocated a close union with Sweden.

The thrust of Wergeland's argument with respect to *Videnskabsselskabet* was that it was imperative for the university to have access to the economic means of the Society. Wergeland specifically mentioned Christopher Hammer's foundation. He argued that if a Norwegian university had been established before Hammer died in 1804, he would surely have left his fortune to the university, not to *Videnskabsselskabet*. Hence, it was only reasonable that the university should have control over these means. Not surprisingly, a similar argument was employed with respect to another large foundation in Trondheim—"*De Angellske stiftelser*," a foundation established according to the will of the extremely rich merchant Thomas Angell, who had died in 1767. His testament instructed that the dividends from this foundation were to be earmarked for various purposes, mainly benefiting the poor in Trondheim. One third of the dividend income was to be added to the capital, but an argument was made that both the size of his fortune and the dividends from the foundation would make it very hard to find anything to invest in without the foundation becoming the sole owner of all tradable land in the diocese of Trondheim due to the exponential growth of the foundation that would

---

[289] M. Bonsach Krogh, "Forsøg til Besvarelse af de fremsatte Priis-Spørgsmaal om et Norsk Universitet," *Historisk-Philosophiske Samlinger*, vol. 2, part 2, Christiania, 1811: 75–76.

[290] N. Wergeland, "Mnemosyne. Et Forsøg paa at besvare den af det Kongl. Selskab for Norges Vel fremsatte Opgave om et Universitet i Norge," *Historisk-Philosophiske Samlinger*, vol. 1, part 1–2, Christiania, 1811.

[291] Amundsen, L., "Wergeland, Nicolai," NBL, Vol. XIX: 1–32, Oslo, 1983.

follow. This reasoning led to the foundation being used for the common good of the city of Trondheim, in such projects as a modern waterworks. It was this money Wergeland wanted to use for the establishment of a university. His argument rested on the one fact that in his will Angell had provided means to pay a teacher in arithmetic, and a student scholarship at the university in Copenhagen. This revealed an interest in higher learning of such a nature that it no doubt would be in Angell's spirit, according to Wergeland, if a part of his fortune was to be used for a university.[292] In fact, Wergeland was not the only one to publicly express this point of view. Mathias Bonsach Krogh had also pointed to Angell's foundation as a possible part of the economic foundation of a university.[293]

However, Wergeland was aware that the leading figures of *Videnskabsselskabet* might see things differently, and added that if *Videnskabsselskabet* was not willing to be co-located with the university, it should at least generously use its money to fund projects there and elect the professors of the university as members of the Society. Another contributor to the essay competition, the vicar of Våler near Christiania, Peder Schimmerup, had a more moderate approach. He was of the opinion that *Videnskabsselskabet* should donate liberally from its library to the establishment of a university library.[294]

The idea of a co-location of the university and *Videnskabsselskabet* was not new. Bishop Gunnerus had thought along similar lines when he wrote his report on a Norwegian university in 1771. At the time, his suggestion was to establish a university in the southern city of Christiansand, and it was clearly his intention that the Society should be located in the same place.[295] It is telling of the contemporary view of *Videnskabsselskabet* that Gunnerus's report on the subject from 1771 was now published in the transactions of the *Selskabet for Norges Vel*, along with the competition essays.

Thus, to the extent the role of *Videnskabsselskabet* was considered in the plans for a new university, the opinion was that it should be co-located with the university, or at least function as a sort of supporting institution in one way or another.

Consolidation

Denmark-Norway's involvement in the Napoleonic wars on the French side proved to be a disaster for the kingdom. Sweden, on the other hand, had chosen the winning side, and had Russia's and England's acceptance that it should be rewarded in one way or another, in part as compensation for the Russian occupation of Finland in 1809. In

---

[292] N. Wergeland, "Mnemosyne. Et Forsøg paa at besvare den af det Kongl. Selskab for Norges Vel fremsatte Opgave om et Universitet i Norge," *Historisk-Philosophiske Samlinger*, vol. 1, part 2, Christiania, 1811: 205–207.

[293] Bonsach Krogh, 1811: 110.

[294] P. Schinnerup, "Plan til et norsk Universitet," *Historisk-Philosophiske Samlinger*, vol. 2, part 1, Christiania, 1811: 149.

[295] Slettstrand, 2005: 52.

January 1814, after a victorious Swedish campaign in southern Denmark, Norway was ceded to the king of Sweden in the peace negotiations under English supervision in Kiel.

In Norway, the secession was met with intense activity from the politically dominant figures. Crown Prince Christian Frederik, who was *stattholder* (viceroy) since early 1813, laid the foundation for a Norwegian rebellion when he refused to follow the king's orders to bring the fleet home to Denmark and oversee the Swedish takeover of the Norwegian forts along the border. Instead, he consulted with groups of dominant persons in south-eastern Norway in late January and Trondheim in early February on how to proceed along a course towards Norwegian independence. This resulted in the election of a body, *riksforsamlingen*, with the defined task of giving the state a constitution. *Riksforsamlingen* drafted a constitution, which was accepted on 17 May, and subsequently elected Christian Frederik as king.

The establishment of Norway as an independent kingdom, with the heir to the Danish throne as king and probably one of the most democratic constitutions of its day, prompted a Swedish response. In the summer of 1814, Sweden invaded Norway, and after a short war, Norwegian defeat was a fact. However, during the course of events, the Swedish crown prince Carl Johan had come to accept the legitimacy of the Norwegian *riksforsamling* and its actions. Thus, the Norwegian defeat did not lead to the incorporation of Norway into the Swedish kingdom, but the union of two independent monarchies under a common king. This was accepted by both parties in the fall of 1814.

Since 1806, Crown Prince Christian Frederik had been *praeses* of *Videnskabsselskabet*, and developed close personal ties with *vice-praeses* Bugge during the turbulent period from his becoming *stattholder* in 1813 to his departure from Norway in the fall of 1814. This means that the leading figures of *Videnskabsselskabet* to a certain degree were involved in the political turmoil of 1814. But it seems that the Society as such took no stance on the political development or in any other way signaled any opinions on the matter. On the contrary, we can see that the board of directors met infrequently during these years; there were six meetings in 1813 and 1814 as compared to ten meetings in 1812 and 1815.[296] In the meetings that were held, the political situation was—judging from the minutes—never mentioned. In addition, no new members were elected in 1814.[297] But, as for the university, we must of course believe that the situation was debated in other settings, such as in *Den borgerlige Klub*.

The situation in the fall of 1814 was that the country became part of a new political entity, had a new king, and *Videnskabsselskabet* had to adapt to the situation. This seems to have caused no problems. *Videnskabsselskabet's* reluctance to participate in political events must have made the transition smooth, even though *vice-praeses* Bugge had been politically active on the side of the Norwegian patriots, and continued to be so for the next few years. When Crown Prince Carl Johan visited Trondheim in the

---

[296] *Det Kongelige Norske Videnskabers Selskabs Direksjonsprotokoll 1799–1826* DKNVS Archive II:3.
[297] Schmidt 1960: 73.

summer of 1815, he also paid *Videnskabsselskabet* a visit.[298] Carl Johan's visit in Trondheim was an attempt at reconciliation with some of the active ultra patriots of the spring and summer of 1814, with General von Krogh, who had been commander in chief in this region through the years of war, as the most prominent example. At the time, Bugge was in Christiania, attending a parliamentary session. He generally seems to have kept his relations to the Crown Prince and *protector* of *Videnskabsselskabet* cool until Carl Johan's coronation three years later. Nevertheless, he led the work on the new statutes, securing the continued support of the royal house.

Crown Prince Carl Johan had accepted the task as *protector* for *Videnskabsselskabet*. The title was new, and was part of yet another revision of the statutes, formally given in 1815.[299] The old position of *vice-praeses* was now elevated to *praeses*, while the old position of *praeses*, held by a member of the royal house, was now given the more neutral and modest title *protector*. The statutes thus, on the one hand, secured continued existence under royal protection, but, on the other hand, gave the leadership of *Videnskabsselskabet* a greater degree of independence.

Another change in the statutes was the even more detailed instructions for the officials of the Society, especially on the subject of how to manage the funds and how to deal with monetary rewards. The tasks of the librarian were also more specifically underlined, especially his role as the keeper and guardian of all the collections the Society had. *Videnskabsselskabet* thus also adapted quickly to the new political conditions following the turbulent months of 1814, and could continue its business more or less as usual in the post-war years.

The coronation of Carl Johan in 1818 also marked the end of a latent distrust of the new regime in another way. During the king's stay in Trondheim, a large number of his members of court were elected to *Videnskabsselskabet*. At the meeting held on this occasion, 18 new members were elected; of these, ten were members of the royal Swedish court or outstanding Swedish scholars. Examples of the first are Count Anders Frederik Skjöldebrand, Count Gustaf of Wettersted and Count Jacob Gustaf de la Gardie, while Professor Sven Caspersson Wijkman and Professor Nils Mårten of Tannström are examples of the latter.[300] This marks the beginning of a period during which election of Swedish members was to become more common, undermining the links to Copenhagen in the long run. In the following years *Videnskabsselskabet* thus developed close ties with the universities of Uppsala and Lund as well as the leading political circles in Sweden. This trend continued through the 1820s, with the election of such members as Erik Gustaf Gejer (professor in history at the University of Lund), Göran Wahlenberg (professor in medicine at the University of Uppsala), Count Adolf Göran Mörner (secretary of state and head of the Academy of Agriculture) and Esaias Tegnér (bishop,

---

[298] *Det Kongelige Norske Videnskabers Selskabs Direksjonsprotokoll 1799–1826:* Fol. 17–76 DKNVS Archive II:3.
[299] *Det Kongelige Norske Videnskabers-Selskabs af Hans Majeste naadigst sanctionerede Statuter givne i 1815,* Trondheim 1829.
[300] Schmidt, 1960: 75–77.

professor in Greek at the University of Lund, and a well-known poet). A number of engineers and practicing scientists from Sweden were elected through the 1820s, for instance the mining engineers Vilhelm Hisningerand, Gustaf Broling and Nils Gabriel Sefström, and the canal builder (and the king's *stattholder* in Norway), Count Baltzar von Platen.[301]

The early 1820s thus mark the end of a transitional period during which *Videnskabsselskabet* had to face a number of challenges, both of a political nature and in the form of competing or supplementing institutions. However, the idea of moving *Videnskabsselskabet* to Christiania as a supporting institution for the university was not quite dead. In 1823, the visiting Danish scholar Gustav Ludvig Baden wrote an article in the Christiania newspaper *Budstikken* on the subject of scientific societies.[302] His conclusion when it came to the Norwegian situation was clear: Christiania was the capital of the country politically, and should therefore strive to also become its scientific capital. One way to achieve this would be to move *Videnskabsselskabet* to Christiania, as the author could not see that Trondheim would lose anything, but Christiania—and the country—obviously had much to gain from such an arrangement. The article was applauded by the editor of *Budstikken*, J. Chr. Berg. He argued, in a footnote to Baden's article, that *Videnskabsselskabet* and *Selskabet for Norges Vel* should merge and the new entity should have its seat in Christiania.

The leadership of *Videnskabsselskabet* did not respond publicly to this article, but tried to recruit some of its prominent members in Christiania for a public defense of the Society's current mode of working. None of these members did so—but, on the other hand, they did not support the idea of a co-location publicly, which was probably as much as the leadership could hope for.

In the short run, Baden's article and Berg's approval of it did not lead to anything. But in the long run, it must have inspired the leadership of *Videnskabsselskabet* to co-operate with the scientific forces in Christiania in other ways than moving the infrastructure of *Videnskabsselskabet*. Nicolay Wergeland's suggestion from 1811—that the Society should elect members from the university, and use some of its economic means to support scientific activities at the university—must have seemed like a good alternative to the continuing pressure to move the whole Society. This was the course of action to be followed for the coming decades.

Stronger financial situation

The statutes of 1815 were detailed when it came to the management of the economic funds at *Videnskabsselskabet's* disposal, with good reasons. Major changes in the finances of the Society in the early 19th century followed the donation of Christopher Hammer.

---

[301] Schmidt, 1960: 78, 79, 88.
[302] H. Midbøe, *Det Kongelige Norske Videnskabers Selskabs historie 1760–1960*, Vol. 1, Trondheim, 1960: 247–248.

When Hammer died without heirs in 1804, he left his entire fortune to *Videnskabsselskabet*. This had in fact been anticipated; he had already made his will in the 1780s and had informed *Videnskabsselskabet* that it was to be his sole beneficiary. The dividends from the capital were to be used for various scientific purposes, while the capital itself was to be invested in land or loans.

Christopher Hammer (1720–1804) is a typical example of the 18th-century Danish-Norwegian civil servant. The son of a vicar in Hadeland, near Christiania, he had received his education in Denmark. After having completed education in theology and law, he held a series of administrative positions in Norway. From the late 1750s he was living on his estate in Gran near Christiania, dividing his time between a position as *generalkonduktør* (a senior surveyor) for Akershus *stift*, and his private scientific activities. His contact with members of *Videnskabsselskabet* on scientific matters stemmed from the 1760s, and he had been elected a member in 1772. Over the years, Hammer donated a good deal of books and manuscripts, both of antiquarian value or more recent titles.[303] He never published any works in the *Skrifter* of *Videnskabsselskabet;* instead he published works on his own account. Among his works was a treatise on the potato, with which he was so satisfied that he had it translated into French.[304] So even though Hammer did not participate actively in the scientific life of *Videnskabsselskabet*, he was not surprisingly flattered and courted by the leadership of the Society after his will was made public in 1781.

Hammer's will was not unconditional. Not only did Hammer leave a considerable fortune, but also a vast amount of unpublished manuscripts. But according to experts in the many fields Hammer had dabbled in, the scientific value of these manuscripts was uneven by most standards. However, in his will, Hammer made it explicit that a number of these manuscripts were to be published by *Videnskabsselskabet* in one way or another. Some of the funds were earmarked for trips to survey the natural history of Norway, but only after the publication of his manuscripts was complete. Likewise, other parts of his funds were to be used to expand the natural collection, but then again also on the condition of the publication of the manuscripts.[305] These restrictions were pointed out again by Hammer in 1798. As part of strengthening the natural collection, Hammer left his own collection to *Videnskabsselskabet*, but it was to be kept separate from the rest of the collection. This was to become a problem over the years, due to the expanding collection that belonged to *Videnskabsselskabet* and thus the diminishing space for organizing and keeping it. A literal interpretation of the will would also prove to be an obstacle to integrating Hammer's collection into the proper collection, rather than ending up with the irrational result of two separate collections.

---

[303] V. Elvestrand, *Generalkonduktør Christopher Hammer (1720–1804) og hans manuskriptsamling. Registratur, biografi, slektshistorie. Fra Københavns Universitet, Sorø Akademi og Ledreborg til Hadeland. Skråblikk på dansk-norsk opplysningstid og en selvsikker embetsmann, frimurer og odelsbonde*, Trondheim, 2004: 529–554.

[304] C. Hammer, *Afhandling om Potatos, med en Deel Tanker om Landhusholdningen*, Christiania, 1766, translated: *Traité boolaniques des batates accompagné des quelques reflexiones sur l'economie*, Copenhagen, 1788.

[305] Elvestrand, 2004: 546–547.

The conditions of the will were thus a challenge. Hammer had laid down no restrictions on *Videnskabsselskabet* with respect to revising his manuscripts to raise their quality. But when, in 1812, the collection of manuscripts was evaluated, the conclusion was that their shortcomings, both in terms of quality and their empirical basis, were so considerable that it might not be worth the effort to revise them to achieve a quality that could defend their publication. This evaluation was made by Professor Jens Rathke from the University of Copenhagen, and his verdict on most of the manuscripts was rather harsh: "Out of respect for the deceased, no doubt all persons of knowledge will wish that these manuscripts remain unpublished forever."[306] In fact, only two of Hammer's manuscripts were found by Rathke to be of a publishable quality, but only after thorough revisions.

This conclusion put *Videnskabsselskabet* in a tight situation: On the one hand, the will of the donator had to be respected, and on the other hand, there was the desire to uphold the standards of good science. The way out of the dilemma was to use a larger part of the dividends from the capital for trips. This could provide more empirical data that could be used to raise the quality of Hammer's manuscripts. But the wording of the testament was clear on this point, as Crown Prince Christian Frederik, *praeses* of *Videnskabsselskabet*, underlined.[307] The conclusion reached by the heads of *Videnskabsselskabet* was that one had to be careful with the dividends from the capital in the first place. The capital, on the other hand, was generously and ingeniously used to make loans to the general public in the Trøndelag region. One part of the will *Videnskabsselskabet* was able to fulfill in a relatively unproblematic way was the publication of Hammer's biography. This was done in *Skrifter* a few years later.[308]

A similar foundation was established by *amtsforvalter* Niels Poulsson, who had left his entire fortune to *Videnskabsselskabet* in 1798. Although amounting to only about one third of the capital of Hammer's foundation, Poulson's foundation was an important factor in the economy of the Society, and its importance was undiminished by the fact that fewer restrictions were placed on the use of these funds.

Both Hammer's and Poulssons's wills provided for the capital of their donations to be used for loans, and this avenue was pursued immediately. Loans were given at an annual interest rate of 4%, which was the maximum rate allowed. From 1814 this was raised to 5% for certain banks and other credit institutions, but not for *Videnskabsselskabet*.[309] It seems that the loans were not confined to a strictly limited group. Among the group of borrowers we find both distinguished members of *Videnskabsselskabet*, such as the *vice-praeses* himself, along with farmers from the entire Trøndelag region, and the staff of

---

[306] "Af agtelse for den Afdøde vil upaatvivlelig enhver Kyndig ønske at de for bestandig maa forblive utrykte." Elvestrand, 2004: 549.

[307] Elvestrand, 2004: 550–553.

[308] I. Mandix, "Biographiske Efterretninger om Justitsraasd og Generalconducteur Christopher Hammer," *Det Kongelige Norske Videnskabers Selskabs Skrifter i det 19de Aarhundrede*, Vol. 1, Copenhagen, 1817: 225–232.

[309] NHL: "Rentefot." The royal or otherwise political decision of a maximum interest rate on loans was not lifted until 1886.

the copper mines at Røros. However, the loans were granted against collateral in the form of a mortgage in properties, which means that they were restricted to persons owning land, or in the process of buying their own property. An interesting detail is that the members of *Videnskabsselskabet* seem to have had a lower interest rate: 3.75%. Within a few years, it seems that the Society could rely on an income from the interests of these loans of 3–400 *spesiedaler* per year, which means that the borrowers had approximately 10,000 *spesiedaler* in credit from *Videnskabsselskabet*. This alone was almost seven times the entire capital stock of the first real bank established in Trondheim, in 1823.[310]

Spesiedaler was the currency introduced by the new National Bank after the separation from Denmark, replacing the *riksdaler*, and had a silver value of roughly double that of the *riksdaler*. Generally, the lack of credit and credit-giving institutions was a problem in the 18th and early 19th centuries in Norway. For larger economic enterprises, such as the ironworks or copper mines, the royal chancery could be counted on for credit. For smaller enterprises, or private persons, foundations such as Hammer's were the norm. The banks established in the early 19th century were not aimed at offering credit, but primarily functioned as savings and insurance institutions for private persons.[311] Thus, the role of credit institutions was handled by private foundations and to a certain degree by the national bank until the mid-19th century. In effect, this means that *Videnskabsselskabet* was a major credit institution in the region along with other similar funds. And such institutions were sorely needed. In the wake of the Napoleonic Wars, an economic crisis hit the country and the city hard. The crisis was exacerbated by the strains the establishment of the new independent Norwegian state put on the economy. Both the funding for a new national bank and a series of extra taxes led to a shortage of cash. In such a situation, the funds from *Videnskabsselskabet* seem to have helped some of its more economically distinguished members through the crises. In the fall of 1816, the merchant Peter Schmidt took a loan of 5000 *spesiedaler*, and Jakob Melgaard took a loan of 4000 *spesiedaler*. All together, 12,000 *spesiedaler*, or almost the entire capital, were granted in credit that fall.[312] However, this was an extraordinary situation, and by the 1820s the normal situation would be a number of smaller loans. The management of the funds and the general economic activity of *Videnskabsselskabet* in the period up to the late 1820s thus bear the nature of a degree of caution and prudence. However, the foundation for a more ambitious economic activity was laid through the management of these funds. In part, some of the interest paid could be used immediately, and in the long run, the capital was increased by the addition of the rest of the interest paid on the loans.

---

[310] K. Mykland, *Trondheims historie 997–1997, Vol. 3. Fra Søgaden til Strandgaten 1800–1880*, Oslo, 1997: 77.

[311] S. Dyrvik et al., *Norsk økonomisk historie 1500–1970, vol. 1*, Bergen/Oslo/Tromsø, 1979: 224–227.

[312] *Kassadagbok 1812–55:* fol. 28, DKNVS Archives II: 13. Schmidt was also a figure of some political importance; he was one of the two representatives from Trondheim at the extraordinary national assembly that declared Norway independent and drafted the constitution in May 1814.

The activities: economic support and publications

There were two notable exceptions from *Videnskabsselskabet*'s cautious economic activity in the 1820s, mainly the liberal use of money to expand the library, and a continuation of the awarding of prizes or in other ways encouraging entrepreneurial activities.

The situation for the library will be presented more thoroughly in p. 146–151. What is important to mention here is that from 1818, *Videnskabsselskabet* was able to pay the librarian an annual wage of 70 *spesiedaler*, thus at last fulfilling the hopes and ambitions expressed in the statutes of 1805, 1811 and 1815 that such an arrangement should become possible.

As we have seen, awarding prizes to encourage industriousness and entrepreneurial activities among the common people had been an important part of *Videnskabsselskabet*'s activities since the 1770s.[313] But from 1808, this activity was organized in a slightly different manner. More limited geographical districts or specific problems and challenges were targeted more or less intentionally.[314] The prizes seem to be more or less limited to people in the Trøndelag region. A large number of people applied for awards in the form of prizes or medals; more than 2500 applications were received in the period from 1772 to 1848, when this part of *Videnskabsselskabet's* activities was terminated. Only a minority was awarded a prize, and then often in one of the targeted or limited fields. The prizes would usually range from 5 to 20 *spesiedaler*.

The activities promoted through the prizes would vary, although some remained constant through the entire period. From 1809 to 1813, for instance, several farmers in the Trøndelag region were awarded prizes ranging from 5 to 35 *spesiedaler* for draining wetlands.[315] Similarly, there seems to have been an interest both from *Videnskabsselskabet* and from farmers in the Selbu region in Trøndelag in how to make commercial use of resin around 1810.[316] The introduction of new crops also seems to have been rewarded, for instance rutabaga[317] and potatoes.[318] Handicraft in metals was encouraged throughout the period.[319] Moreover, extermination of predators that threatened farmers' livestock was a definite priority. *Videnskabsselskabet* thus amply rewarded the killing of bears, wolves, lynx and eagles.[320] The construction of edifices in stone was also

---

[313] M. Aase, "Premiesøknader i Det Kongelige Norske Videnskabers Selskabs arkiv," H.N. Nissen & M. Aase (eds.), *Til opplysning. Universitetsbibliotket i Trondheim 1768–1993*, Trondheim, 1993: 143–149.

[314] M. Aase, *Patrioter og bønder. Det kongelige Norske Videnskabers Selskabs arbeid med landbrukspremier 1772–1806*, Trondheim, 1997: 3.

[315] M. Aase, *Premiesøknader til Det Kongelige Norske Videnskabers Selskab 1772–1848*, Trondheim, 1988: 98–99.

[316] Aase, 1988: 100.

[317] Aase, 1988: 126.

[318] Aase, 1988: 138–139.

[319] Aase, 1988:,130–132.

[320] Aase, 1988: 143–146.

important.[321] This usually did not mean residential buildings, but mainly cowsheds and cellars of the barns. It also seems that servants or hired hands who had shown loyalty and diligence in their work could be rewarded at the suggestion of the heads of their households.[322]

The rewards and prizes were not confined to typical male activities. The production of knitwear, and especially knitted caps, was amply rewarded in the years around 1810.[323] Similarly, weaving was highly regarded throughout the whole period, and elevated to the importance of being rewarded with silver medals in the 1840s.[324] Sewing also received attention from *Videnskabsselskabet* for a period of time around 1830.[325]

The draining of marshlands and peat bogs was given extra focus from the late 1820s, mostly to farmers in Trøndelag. In these cases, *Videnskabsselskabet* was liberal, not only with its money, but also with silver medals.[326] No less then 31 farmers were awarded medals from 1834 to 1846 for this work. Similarly, the use of the waste products from this work, namely peat to be used for fuel or manure, was rewarded.[327]

This special interest in turning marshlands into farmland can also be seen in *Videnskabsselskabet's* own project of cultivating a large area of peat bogs approximately 10 kilometers south of Trondheim, at the Oustmyren property. The amount of money spent on this project in the 1820s is quite impressive; more than 1000 *spesiedaler* from 1826 to 1828.[328] The funds were used by the committee organizing and supervising the work and channeled into their rightful use, namely the buying of several properties. These properties mainly consisted of peat bogs, and in the long run two minor farms were established on these lands.[329] Later, *Videnskabsselskabet* borrowed an additional 1000 *spesiedaler* from *Opplysningsvesenets Fond*, a publicly owned fund based on the revenues from publicly owned church lands. This money was used for the running expenses on the project. This loan seems somewhat paradoxical, given that *Videnskabsselskabet* at the same time was a credit institution for the region. The explanation lies in the conditions attached to Hammer's foundation—the capital could not be used for such purposes.

The initiative for this experiment seems to have come from a royal source. The main road going northward towards Trondheim stretched over these bogs, and Carl Johan had traveled here, both in 1815 and after his coronation in Trondheim in 1818, and he was supposed to have verbally promoted the cultivation of these lands. The

---

[321] Aase, 1988: 161–167.

[322] Aase, 1988: 169–181. It is important to note that the average agrarian households would consist of an extended family and servants, the presence of servants not being a sign of wealth but a usual occupation in most households for both men and women in certain stages of life.

[323] Aase, 1988: 187–188.

[324] Aase, 1988: 190–196.

[325] Aase, 1988: 168.

[326] Aase, 1988: 133–136.

[327] Aase, 1988: 183–184.

[328] *Kassadagbok 1812–55*: Fol. 43, 45, 47, DKNVS Archives II: 13.

[329] E. Lauglo, *Leinstrand. Et lite stykke Norge*, vol. 1, Leinstrand, 1957: 276–286, 486–497.

background for the project was also an aborted attempt by *Selskabet for Norges Vel* to instigate such a project a few years earlier. *Videnskabsselskabet*, for its part, had given a prize in 1776 to a local farmer, Anders Kattem, for a similar project on a smaller scale in the same area. The enthusiasm for continuing this project on a larger scale must be attributed to the new *praeses* from 1820, Christian Krogh. Krogh (1777–1828) had been a prominent member of *Selskabet for Norges Vel* in its initial phase in Trondheim, and had a special interest in projects that could improve agriculture. In 1825 a committee was established for this project, which then organized the subsequent work.

This experiment in the draining of bogs and their subsequent cultivation does not seem to have been very successful. The digging of ditches was hard work, and inmates from the Trondheim prison provided some of the workforce. However, most of the labor on the project was performed by hired hands, partly from the neighboring Swedish province of Jämtland, as they were able to do the work even cheaper than the prisoners. The lands proved to be less suitable for farming, and the crops from the cultivated land were poor. *Videnskabsselskabet* sold the whole property to the local chapter of *Selskabet for Norges Vel* in 1835, which managed the project with moderate success until they sold the holdings to the farmers living on the two farms in 1855. The farms were seen at this point as being of poor quality both in soil and other resources, and also badly managed.[330] Even though the whole project was certainly no great triumph, it is still noteworthy as the first large-scale experiment in cultivation of boglands in Norway.

From the late 1830s, the encouragement of industriousness was less heeded. Medals and small sums of money would still be awarded, but the discussions on this theme have little place in the minutes from the meetings of the board of directors, and a skeptical attitude to this activity can be detected.[331]

As a part of the awarding of prizes, both for industriousness and essay competitions, *Videnskabsselskabet* was given the right to award medals in 1830. *Videnskabsselskabet* had the opportunity to award four different medals, large and small medals in gold or silver.[332] The gold medals were awarded in the essay competitions, while the silver medals were given as encouragement to industrious persons in varying fields. *Videnskabsselskabet* had also earlier occasionally awarded medals. After the resolution in 1830, the silver medals were awarded rather liberally, totaling between 80 and 90 medals all together. They were often awarded instead of money, which apparently deflated the interest in applying for awards.[333]

As the dangers and challenges of dwindling membership, failing finances, and competing institutions seemed to have been averted, *Videnskabsselskabet* could also

---

[330] *Matrikkelen 1865* as quoted in Lauglo, 1957: 285.

[331] C.N. Schwach, "Kort Udsigt over det kongelige norske Videnskabs-Selskabs Historie fra dets Oprindelse til Udgangen af 1844, *Det Kongelige Norske Videnskabers-Selskabs Skrifter i det 19de Aarhundrede*, Vol. IV, Trondheim, 1859: 1–28.

[332] K. Kvist, *DKNVS' medaljer—skisse av historie og problemstillinger*. Manuscript, Trondheim, 2006.

[333] Øverås, A., *Frederik Moltke Bugge. Kulturarbeid og kulturstrid i 1830–40-åra*, vol. 2, Oslo, 1949: 241–243, Schwach, 1844/59.

concentrate more on the task of publishing. Since 1798, no volume of *Skrifter* had been published, but in 1817, a new volume was presented, and the following volume appeared only ten years later, a short span of time compared to the preceding volumes.

The volume published in 1817 consisted of 14 articles, mainly in the topographical or historical genres. The board of directors explained this focus in the foreword to the volume, pointing to greater public interest in the topic, and illustrated this with examples, also mentioning the establishment of a topographical society a few years earlier.[334] Moreover, the volume contained a royal confirmation of the 1811 statutes (but not the 1815 statutes!), and a letter from Prince Christian Frederik promising a yearly pecuniary contribution to *Videnskabsselskabet*. In 1817, this was more of historical interest, as the statutes had been renewed and the prince no longer was prince (or king) of Norway. This shows that the period from submission to publication was still a long one—the essays submitted in the years around 1815 were not published until the 1827 volume (published in installments 1824–27). The dean Andreas Colban (1760–1828) in Lofoten, for instance, had to wait ten years for his "Attempt at a Description of Lofoten and Vesterålen, including a map," to be published.[335] The same Colban also saw his theological work on the books of Daniel and Job rejected as unfit for publication.[336] Later, however, Colban's translation of the Book of Job was published with financial aid from *Videnskabsselskabet*.

In spite of Colban's work on Lofoten and Vesterålen, the volume published in 1827 was of a quite different nature than the preceding one. It also contained three papers of a topographical or historical nature, but also three works on mathematical topics and one philosophical work. This philosophical work, along with two of the mathematical essays, was written by Fredrich Christian Holberg Arentz (1736–1825). Arentz had studied theology and philosophy in Copenhagen in the early 1750s, and later studied mathematics in Leyden, before he established himself as a teacher of mathematics and physics in Bergen. Later he was to become headmaster at the cathedral school there. He was a man of many interests, and it is typical both of this and of his vigor well into his late 80s that he was represented by these three articles in the 1827 volume of *Skrifter*; one on the concepts of time and space in Emanuel Kant's philosophy, and two mathematical works, on indeterminate algebraic equations and the nature of parallel lines, respectively.[337] Arentz had published on both philosophical and mathematical problems in earlier volumes of *Skrifter*. In many ways, he can be seen as the last member of the pioneer generation of *Videnskabsselskabet*. He had been elected to mem-

---

[334] "Fortale," *Det Kongelige Norske Videnskabers Sleskabs Skrifter i det 19. Aarhundrede*, vol. 1, Copenhagen, 1817: 1–VI.

[335] E.A. Colban, "Forsøg til en Beskrivelse over Lofodens og Vesteaalens Fogderie i Nordlands Amt, med et Situations-Cart," *Det Kongelige Norske Videnskabers Selskabs Skrifter i det 19. Aarhundrdee*, vol. 2, Trondhjem, 1827: 1–86.

[336] *Årsberetning*, 1816, 1817, DKNVS Archives IV:g:1.

[337] Arentz, F.C.H., "Om de ubestemte algebraiske Æqvationer," *Det Kongelige Norske Videnskabers Selskabs Skrifter i det 19. Aarhundrdee*, vol. 2, Trondhjem, 1827: 87–108, Arentz, F.C.H., "Forsøg til en med mathematisk Nøiagtighed fremsat Theorie om paralelle Linier og deres Egenskaber," *Det Kongelige Norske Videnskabers Selskabs Skrifter i det 19. Aarhundrdee*, vol. 2, Trondhjem, 1827: 109–130.

bership as early as 1774, and was marked by the enthusiastic—and perhaps at times amateurish—wandering into widely different fields of knowledge that was a typical trait of many of his generation, for whom science was an activity for gentlemen. Although little of his work has had any lasting importance, he was a pioneer in what we may label independent mathematical research in 18th-century Norway.[338]

Arentz was, however, not the only mathematician to be published in the 1827 volume of *Skrifter*. The volume also contained a paper written by the young mathematician Niels Henrik Abel (1802–29). Abel's essay was titled "A small contribution to the study of several transcendental functions," and he was elected as a member of *Videnskabsselskabet* at the same time.[339] Abel is arguably the most influential Scandinavian mathematician ever. He came from ordinary stock, but showed an exceptional talent for mathematics from an early age. By the time he attended the University of Christiania, it was clear that his abilities surpassed those of the professors there, and he embarked on a European journey in 1825 at the age of 23 to seek out the mathematical expertise in Berlin and Paris. Initially, his plan also included traveling to Göttingen to seek out Carl Friedrich Gauss, but this never materialized. Abel's travels had been partially paid for by the government, but on his return to Christiania in 1827 his financial situation was unstable. At this time he had a part-time teaching position at *Den militære høyskole* (The Military Academy), and also received a stipend from the government. His future plans seem to have included the possibility of employment at the University of Berlin. In 1828, however, he was stricken with tuberculosis, and died early in 1829.

It is interesting to note the differences in Arentz's and Abel's approach to their themes. In his essay on the nature of parallel lines, Arentz has a rather long introduction, debating the differences between pure geometry and the other sciences, underlining the eternal nature of the wisdom put forth by Euclid as opposed to the constant revision of other scientific fields, where new generations of scientists tear down and rebuild the work of their predecessors. Arentz clearly finds it problematic to discuss some aspects of the terminology concerning parallel lines which can be interpreted as a questioning of the clarity of Euclid, and needs to excuse himself. In sharp contrast, Abel wastes no time on an introduction, and goes directly to the mathematics. The paper was probably written just before Abel started on his trip to Germany in 1825. At this time Abel had started to make some of his fundamental discoveries regarding elliptic integrals, in particular how he could extend the French mathematician Legendre's results, and the paper can be considered an early attempt to communicate his results in this area. The paper was forwarded to the Society by Professor Hansteen, but only published in 1827.[340]

---

[338] Bull, F., "Arentz, Fredrich Christian Holberg," NBL, vol. 1: 223–226, Kristiania, 1923, V. Brun, *Regnekunsten i det gamle Norge: Fra Arilds tid til Abel*, Oslo, 1962: 77–83.

[339] N.H. Abel, "Et lidet Bidrag til Læren om adskillige transcendente Functioner," *Det Kongelige Norske Videnskabers Selskabs Skrifter i det 19. Aarhundrede*, vol. 2, Trondhjem, 1827: 177–207.

[340] Sylow, L, "Abels studier og hans oppdagelser," *Festskrift ved hundreaarsjubilæet for Niels Henrik Abels fødsel*, Kristiania, 1902.

The first decade after the consolidation of *Videnskabsselskabet* thus saw a return to publishing, both in *Skrifter* and the library catalogue published in 1808 (see p. 146–147). The 1830s would in addition see another type of publishing: the economic support of other publications.

Apart from the growth of the library, the awarding of industrious individuals, and contributions to the printing of scientific works, the main economic activity up to the late 1830s seems to have been the handling of *Videnskabsselskabet*'s funds as a credit-giving institution.

Conclusion

By the beginning of the 19th century, *Videnskabsselskabet* was clearly in decline. Membership was dwindling, the publishing of the transactions was slow and the international network was faltering, partly due to the unstable political situation on the continent. This decline was, if not reversed, at least slowed down by the radical change in *Videnskabsselskabet's* economic situation when it inherited a large fortune from Christopher Hammer in 1804. Even though Hammer's will put some very clear limitations on how the money could be used, it still meant that *Videnskabsselskabet* had the economic foundation for revitalization. This was clearly grasped by the newly elected *vice-praeses* Peder Olivarius Bugge, who instigated a process of modernizing *Videnskabsselskabet* to meet these new conditions.

However, the political situation turned events in an unexpected direction. The dramatic period from 1809 to 1812 provided new possibilities for the establishment of scientific institutions in Norway, and it forced the leadership of *Videnskabsselskabet* to make some difficult choices. *Videnskabsselskabet* had had two primary fields: supporting and encouraging industriousness and development in the rural society, and serving as a forum for scientific research and publications. But it was now being challenged in both these fields. The establishment in 1809 of a society for the advancement of the Norwegian economy (in a wide sense), operating on the national level, was a serious competitor of *Videnskabsselskabet* in this field. Moreover, the rather sudden establishment of a Norwegian university in 1811 was in many ways the realization of a vision which the founders of *Videnskabsselskabet* and many of their successors had worked and argued for. The events of a few hectic months had forced the leadership of *Videnskabsselskabet* to rethink the position of the Society drastically. In one way, its mission was accomplished, and one logical conclusion given the establishment of a Norwegian university would be to bring *Videnskabsselskabet* to an end in its current state and instead connect it closely to the new university in one way or another. This was clearly the prevailing sentiment outside *Videnskabsselskabet*. Another possible conclusion would have been to terminate the Society all together and leave its properties to the university and/or *Selskabet for Norges Vel*.

Why did Bugge and his companions not choose any of these options? Part of the explanation might relate to the fact that *Videnskabsselskabet* was an organization which had existed for nearly 50 years. There must have been a certain "strength of tradition" and a feeling that *Videnskabsselskabet* had carved a place for itself by surviving. Surviving the first generational transition, after the founding fathers had died or had left was a feat in itself. Even though the activities had declined, the structures were intact and could be filled with a higher degree of activity when the conditions were right. The economic blessings of Hammer's will must have made this choice of strategy an obvious course of action for the new *vice-praeses* and his board of directors. The statutes of 1805 point in a certain direction—*Videnskabsselskabet* was in the future not only going to be a society of scientists, but also a society that economically supported the scientific activities of others. This would give *Videnskabsselskabet* a more stable existence within the well-established frames of a scientific society on the periphery of the Danish-Norwegian monarchy.

The events of the following years sped up the process, and probably made the different options for the future of *Videnskabsselskabet* clearer. While the years around 1805 had seen a cautious consolidation of the Society with a more secure economic base and more updated statutes, the years around 1810 required a much more active attitude. Bugge and his companions must have felt that the structures and economy of *Videnskabsselskabet* had value in themselves, and that the original ideas and goals of a Norwegian university as put forth in the 1770s and 80s were less relevant now than then. The idea of a society that supported science, rather than a society of scientists, must have been formulated more clearly during these years, and the events of 1809–11 put this concept in the foreground when it came to arguing for the continued existence of *Videnskabsselskabet*. The intense work on another revision of the statutes in the years leading up to 1811 confirms this.

These ideas were not clearly formulated in the minutes of *Videnskabsselskabet*. It is also hard to tell whether there was a clear strategy from the leadership of *Videnskabsselskabet*, or if it was formulated in a more improvised manner along the way. But we can see from Nicolai Wergeland's competition essay that these ideas were known and accepted among the people who debated the future of scientific institutions in Norway during these years—even though they did not necessarily agree.

The idea of a society which independently of the university supported science in different ways—economically or by publishing scientific works—thus did make sense. But why still in Trondheim? Wergeland argued for the co-location of the university and *Videnskabsselskabet* in Christiania, and the publishing of Gunnerus's 40-year-old arguments for the same co-location certainly provides us with evidence that leading persons in the intellectual debate wanted this. This was also in line with what happened elsewhere in Europe. The reestablishment and reorganization of the scientific societies in other countries pointed in this direction. Especially in Germany, this seems to have been the case.

The amendments of the statutes of *Videnskabsselskabet* that opened it to non-scientists, and the subsequent election of several of the leading merchants in Trondheim as members contradicted this strategy. Again, the reason is probably found in this sense of "strength of tradition" and the existing infrastructure of the Society. A few years earlier, *Videnskabsselskabet* had moved into the second floor of the *Katedralskole*, in modern and spacious premises. The library was one of, if not *the* finest book-collection in Norway. Meetings were held, although not always well attended, at more or less regular intervals. The whole infrastructure of *Videnskabsselskabet* had become very physical in the sense that the Society no longer primarily was a network of persons, but a building, a library and other collections. The cooperation of a society and a university situated in the same city would have been unproblematic, but in the case of *Videnskabsselskabet*, the physical distance to the university was approximately 600 km and several days of traveling. A closer cooperation would in effect mean the termination of the Society in its present form.

The situation for *Videnskabsselskabet* as it emerges around 1820 falls into a European trend. The French revolution and the decades of war following it had dealt a serious blow to the learned societies of Europe. Many of these societies reemerged in the wake of the Napoleonic wars, but with different profiles and different tasks. Three major patterns can be seen. One, seen most clearly in France, was the emergence of the societies and academies as institutions of research, with a paid staff. Another, more common in Germany, was a closer cooperation of societies and universities, mainly in the wake of the "Humboldtian" university reforms of the first half of the 19th century. A third option, when the economic means were too scarce for the first option and no university was at hand for the second option, was for *Videnskabsselskabet* to become a more local elite association with small scientific ambitions. In addition to this, some of the important societies in the countries that were not directly ravaged by war or revolution continued more or less as before. This was the case, for instance, for the Royal Society in London and *Vitterhetsakademin* in Sweden.[341]

Det Kongelige Norske Videnskabers Selskab in Trondheim is closest to the last of these three options when we look at it in the wake of the Napoleonic Wars—an association for the local notables from the academic and economic fields, more based on social value than scientific activity. But several factors complicated this picture. First: *Videnskabsselskabet* did not have the wealth to aspire to become an independent institute of research. Nevertheless, it was, in a Norwegian context, a rather wealthy organization, which made it interesting to those with scientific ambitions who needed to finance them. Secondly: The newly established University of Christiania was not a modern university with research as its main goal, but still a provincial continuation of the higher school for public servants that the university in Copenhagen had been. And last: *Videnskabsselskabet* had an established infrastructure and fields of activity which it could continue or return to after the transitional period, mainly in the fields of encouraging industriousness in several ways, and in publishing scientific results in *Skrifter*. These factors gave *Videnskabsselskabet* an opportunity to play an important role in the intellectual life of the new state in the following decades.

---

[341] McClellan, 1985: 253–259.

6

The expanding Society, 1830–1850

The early 1830s were a period of change in *Videnskabsselskabet*. From a cautious use of the financial means of the Society, and an organization perhaps mainly occupied with the practical arts, *Videnskabsselskabet* was now to become a major player in Norwegian science through its liberal use of financial grants and support. The Society's financial position had been secured through the inheritance from Christopher Hammer, and was strengthened by both regular contributions from the state and king, and from more irregular contributions from its members. Hammer had placed several limitations on the use of his inheritance, mostly connected to the publishing of his works. This had initially led to a cautious use of *Videnskabsselskabet's* money, but by the 1830s the directors began spending more boldly. This was due in part to the fact that some of the obligations towards the benefactor's will were met in one way or another, but perhaps also that as time passed, the piety towards Hammer's wishes waned somewhat. Moreover, support from *Stortinget* and the royal family grew throughout the period. This paved the way for a period of increased activity for *Videnskabsselskabet*, a second golden age that was to last for two decades.

The architects

From the early 1820s, *Videnskabsselskabet's* financial situation can without question be described as both more stable and predictable due to the annual grants from both *Stortinget* (parliament) and the crown prince.

The parliament grants began from 1815, and amounted to 528 *spesiedaler* a year.[342] From the 1830s, the amount was paid quarterly, 132 *spesiedaler* for each quarter. At the same time, the tradition of a yearly grant from the crown prince seems to have been resumed, with a contribution of 100 *spesiedaler* a year from 1815. In 1837 he donated an additional 2400 *spesiedaler*, most likely a personal gift following his visit to Trondheim in 1835.[343]

---

[342] *Kassadagbok 1812–55:* Fol 62 DKNVS Archive II: 13.
[343] *Kassadagbok 1812–55:* Fol. 62 DKNVS Archive II: 13.

The grants from *Stortinget* and the king gave *Videnskabsselskabet* an income of approximately 600 *spesiedaler* a year, in addition to revenues from membership fees of approximately 100–150 *spesiedaler*, and the interest from the loans from Hammer's and Poulsen's foundations, amounting to approximately 3–400 *spesiedaler*. All in all, *Videnskabsselskabet* had approximately 1000–1500 *spesiedaler* at its free disposal on a yearly basis from the early 1820s. In addition to this, after 1835 capital was no longer tied up in the Oustmyren project, thus increasing the amount of money at the Society's disposal. Add to this the fact that as the directors began to see that the obligations to Christopher Hammer's will were fulfilled in many respects, they had a more liberal attitude towards the use of this capital. Thus, from the late 1830s, *Videnskabsselskabet* seriously began spending Hammer's money in a different fashion than in the preceding two decades, by not only using the dividends from the fortune, but also the capital itself. The main architect behind the increase in financial activity at *Videnskabsselskabet* must have been Frederik Moltke Bugge.

Bugge (1806–53) was the son of Bishop Peder Olivarius Bugge, who had been *praeses* until 1820, and who was still bishop in Trondheim at the time his son became *praeses*. Fredrik Bugge was educated in philology at Christiania, and after a short stint as headmaster at the *Katedralskole* in Stavanger, he became headmaster at the *Katedralskole* in Trondheim in 1834, and, of course, was promptly elected into *Videnskabsselskabet*.[344] He was elected *praeses* in 1838. Besides his work in the Society, Bugge's main interests were in pedagogical reforms and linguistics. Bugge used the *Katedralskole* as a laboratory for new pedagogical ideas, with smaller groups of pupils, a more varied menu of subjects to be taught, including physical education, and shorter days. Bugge's combination of being headmaster at the cathedral school and his ideas on how to organize a modern school made him an active participant in the public debate on the development of education in Norway in the 1830s and 40s. Bugge was a fierce defender of the role of the classical languages in the secondary schools, as opposed to the influential group of young civil servants and politicians, *Intelligentskretsen* ("the intelligentsia"), with the influential politician A.M. Schweigaard as the leading figure.[345] This group advocated a more modern school based on the technical sciences and living languages, such as German and English. Bugge was involved in debates on this topic for years, and also had a scholarship from the government to study the organization of education abroad, mainly in Germany, Italy, and France, from 1836 to 1837. This resulted in a work in three volumes on the state of education in contemporary Europe and suggestions as to how it should be organized in Norway.[346] This earned him a seat on a commission board established by the government to prepare a reform of the educational system in

---

[344] Øverås 1949.

[345] Keilhau, W., "Schweigaard, Anton Martin," NBL, Vol. XII, Oslo, 1958: 37–53.

[346] F.M. Bugge, *Det offentlige Skolevæsens Forfatning i adskillige tydske Stater, tilligemed Ideer til en Reorganisering af det offentlige Skolevæsen i Kongeriget Norge: en Indberætning afgiven til den Kgl. Norske regjerings Departement for Kirke- og Underviisningsvæsenet, ifølge Kgl. Naadigst Resolution af 23de Juni 1836*, Vol. 1–3, Christiania, 1839.

Norway in 1839, together with, among others, Schweigaard. This meant that for long periods of his leadership of *Videnskabsselskabet* Bugge was occupied in work outside Trondheim.

The first step in the increased financial activity during Bugge's period as *praeses* was to give the secretary a fixed salary. From 1837 he was given 70 *spesiedaler* a year, the same pay as the librarian.[347] The Society thus had doubled its paid staff. C.B. Bødtker, a local vicar, was the secretary at the time of this arrangement, but the most important secretary in this period was Conrad Nicolai Schwach (1793–1860).

As with most of his Norwegian contemporaries of learning, Schwach was educated in Copenhagen, but completed his education in law at the newly established University of Christiania in 1817.[348] He worked as a lawyer in Arendal in southern Norway until 1830, when he received the post as *andreassessor* (assisting judge) at the *stiftoverrett* (a regional higher court of justice) in Trondheim. The position was well paid, with an annual salary of 780 *spesiedaler*. Schwach was soon elected to membership in *Videnskabsselskabet*, as was not unusual for men of his educational background and position when they moved to Trondheim.

Among his contemporaries, however, Schwach was primarily known for his poetry, publishing extensively in the period leading up to the late 1830s. He was also an active translator, and all in all one of the leading men in the small Norwegian literary establishment. However, he more or less abandoned his literary ambitions after the hostile reception of his collected poems in two volumes (1837) by a leading figure of a younger generation of literary critics, J.P. Collett. Schwach's interest in literature and his friendship with several leading writers were, however, not abandoned, and he also initiated a literary association, *Den litteraire Forening*, in Trondheim in 1839.

Schwach struck up a friendship with Fredrik Moltke Bugge following Bugge's arrival in Trondheim in 1834. From the second half of the 1830s, Bugge and Schwach were the dominant figures in *Videnskabsselskabet* for more than a decade. Schwach was elected secretary in 1835 and Bugge *praeses* in 1838. Schwach, however, had to resign from his position for a couple of years from 1837 because he was held responsible for a letter containing money being delivered to the wrong person, with the subsequent loss of the money. The person to whom Schwach entrusted the letter as a courier turned out to be a swindler. Schwach had to cover the losses, and did this by handing over his collection of rare coins, valued at 500 *spesiedaler*, to *Videnskabsselskabet*, and thereafter resigning from his position as secretary for a period of five years.[349] Schwach was a passionate collector of coins, and also wrote the first history of Norwegian coins, which was published by *Videnskabsselskabet*.[350]

---

[347] *Kassadagbok 1812–55*: Fol. 58 DKNVS Archive II: 13.

[348] A. Stubhaug, *Helt skal jeg ikke dø. Conrad Nicolai Schwach, hans liv og erindringer*, Oslo, 2002, Svendsen, P., "Schwach, Conrad Nicolai," NBL, Vol. XIII, Oslo, 1958: 26–30.

[349] Stubhaug, 2002: 263–264.

[350] C.N. Schwach, *Udsigt over de tre nordiske Rigers Myntvæsen fra de ældste Tider til nuværende, samt Grundrids af Heraldikken*, Trondhjem, 1842.

Vice-praeses Fredrik Storm (1803–83) was the third of the leadership troika of the 1830s and 40s. Storm was priest at the hospital church in Trondheim from 1837, and seems to have been the binding force on the board of directors in Bugge's repeated absences, running the daily business during these periods and corresponding frequently with the *praeses*.

In the period leading up to Bugge resigning as *praeses* and leaving for Bergen in 1850 and Schwach leaving for a new position as *sorenskriver* in Skien in Southern Norway at the same time, these three men constituted the real leadership of *Videnskabsselskabet*. They were assisted in part by the various heads of the Society's classes, who must to some degree have influenced the decisions on financial support for projects in their fields. Their most important co-player, however, was the librarian, Johan Christian Tellefsen.

The grants–natural sciences

As mentioned above, one of the first signs of the more active economic activity of *Videnskabsselskabet* was a fixed salary for the secretary. Far more important than salaries for the librarian and secretary was, however, the use of money in the form of grants from the early 1840s. The finances of the Society were now of such a magnitude that it could afford in effect to pay wages to persons undertaking scientific projects, in addition to giving support for printing the finished works, as earlier. Bugge and Schwach seized this opportunity, and for a period of ten years liberally supported or instigated several projects in a number of fields.

The background for the increased financial activity from the late 1830s can be found around 1830 with the contributions to the printing of scientific works not published by *Videnskabsselskabet*. Although not very extensively at first, the Society started granting this kind of support in the 1820s, gaining momentum from around 1830. In the 1820s, money had been granted for the publication of Lorentz Diderick Klüwer's *Norske Mindersmærker* (Norwegian monuments), published in 1823, and the Danish linguist Rasmus Rask's edition of Knud Leem's Sami grammar, published in 1832.[351] The zoologist Michael Sars was promised such financial assistance in 1830 for his *Contribution to the History of Marine Animals* (Bidrag til Södyrenes Historie), which was published in 1835.[352] Similarly, funds for printing an edition of the medieval Norse laws were promised in 1830, although the work was not published until the mid 1840s. But the scale of this kind of support took on quite another dimension in the 1840s.

In 1841, the first grant amounting to 150 *spesiedaler* was given to Nicolay Lund (1814–47) to travel to northern Norway to undertake botanical surveys.[353] Lund was

---

[351] L.D. Klüwer, *Norske Mindesmærkeaftegnede paa en Reise igjennem den Deel af det Nordenfjeldske*, Trondhjem, 1823, R. Rask, *Ræsonneret lappisk Sproglære efter den Sprogart, som bruges af Fjældlapperne i Porsangerfjorden i Finmarken: en Omarbejdelse af Knud Leems Lappiske Grammatica*, Copenhagen, 1832.
[352] M. Sars, *Bidrag til Søedyrenes Naturhistorie*, Bergen, 1829–35.
[353] *Kassadagbok 1812–55*: Fol. 71 DKNVS Archive II: 13.

no stranger to *Videnskabsselskabet*. A few years earlier he had received a prize and a medal for his competition essay on the subject "Is every intelligent creature necessarily a free creature?" His trip to northern Norway led to his being employed by the University of Christiania in 1843 as a botanical researcher.[354] He published the results of his work for the Society in a personally flavored book.[355]

Another botanical scientist besides Nicolay Lund, Matthias N. Blytt, was also liberally supported by *Videnskabsselskabet*. Blytt (1789–1862) was the son of a vicar in Trondheim, and had studied law and natural history.[356] He was supported by funds from Hammer's foundation to publish a Norwegian Flora according to the Linnéan system, and at least in name based on Hammer's drafts for such a work. He had been engaged by *Videnskabsselskabet* as early as 1825 to do some preliminary work on this project.[357] However, it was not until the mid 1830s that this work was carried out in a more organized manner, and the first volume was not published until 1846.[358] The work was continued and completed by his son, Axel G. Blytt (1843–98) in the 1870s. Lund and Blytt's work was also to be used as a reason for liberating the funds in Hammer's foundation. Hammer's own botanical work could not be published—it was like most of his work lacking in quality and generally outdated already by the time of Hammer's death in 1804. But by supporting botanical work "in Hammer's spirit," the will of the benefactor could arguably said to have been fulfilled, and the funds be used more freely. A problem rose when Blytt initially refused to use Hammer's manuscript at all because he found it completely worthless.[359]

Michael Sars (1805–89) was, at the time he received his grants, a vicar in Manger near Bergen, but was already more known as a zoologist than a theologian. He had made a series of trips around Europe to research marine animals, and had published extensive results, both from these trips and from research on marine animals along the Norwegian coast. He was later to become professor of zoology in Christiania.[360] As mentioned above, he had already received funds from *Videnskabsselskabet* for the printing of his *Notes on the History of Marine Animals* (Bidrag til Södyrenes Historie), which was published in 1835.[361] The money in 1841 seems to have been earmarked for a major work on marine animals, finally published under the title *Fauna littoralis Norvegiae* in 1846.[362]

---

[354] Holmboe, J., "Lund, Nocolai," NBL, Vol. VIII, Oslo, 1938: 494–495.

[355] N. Lund, *Reise gjennem Nordlandene og Vest Finmarks Sommeren 1841*, Christiania, 1842.

[356] Wille, N., "Blytt, Matthias Numsen," NBL, Vol. II, Oslo, 1925: 51–52.

[357] *Årsmelding 1825* DKNVS Archive IV:g:1.

[358] *Årsmelding 1834* DKNVS Archive IV:g:1.

[359] Midbøe, 1960a: 333–339.

[360] Økland, F., "Michael Sars," NBL, Vol. XII, Oslo, 1954: 255–260.

[361] *Årsmelding 1830* DKNVS Archive IV:g:1.

[362] M. Sars, *Fauna littoralis Norvegia: oder Beschreibung und Abbildungen neuer oder wenig bakannten Seethiere, nebst Beobachtungen über die Organisation, Lebensweise u. Entwicklungen derselben*, Vol. 1–3, Christiania, 1846–77.

A couple of Sars's co-workers, Johan Koren (1809–85) and Daniel Danielssen (1815–1894), also received smaller grants to study marine animals.[363] One side effect of their studies and grants was that they supplied the collection of the Society with specimens of marine animals over a number of years.[364] Danielssen seems to have been given—or had assumed—the task of mapping marine life along the coast stretching from present-day Molde to the mouth of the Trondheim fjord.[365]

Danielssen's and Koren's work for *Videnskabsselskabet* was limited, but their scientific positions were indisputable. Danielssen was a pioneer in the scientific understanding of leprosy, publishing extensively on the subject. His pupil, Armauer Hansen (1841–1912), was later to continue this work in a most successful manner. In addition to this work and his work as a medical doctor, Danielssen had an interest in zoology, and started to cooperate extensively with Sars and Johan Koren when Koren was employed in the first scientific position as curator at Bergen Museum in 1846, after first having studied botany as the pupil of the above-mentioned Mathias Blytt. For his part, Danielssen became the leader of the Natural History section in this museum in 1852, and later became the director of the entire museum.

Bergen museum was to become important both as an ideal and contrast to the development of the collections at *Videnskabsselskabet* in the latter part of the century. The museum in Bergen had already been established in 1825. In its first years, it functioned more or less as an association with members who paid an annual fee which gave them the privilege of attending the exhibition, which was open one day a year. Initially, the museum rented the second floor of *Seminarium Fredericium*, a school affiliated with Bergen *Katedralskole*, which was responsible for educating teachers. The situation was thus not unlike the situation in Trondheim, where *Videnskabsselskabet* had a similar arrangement with the *Katedralskole* there. But Bergen Museum established its own premises as early as 1831, and laid the foundation for an expansion through new buildings in the following years.[366] It was in this situation that the librarian in Trondheim saw fit to donate around one hundred volumes of doublets to the museum. By the 1840s, Bergen museum was a professional institution with large premises, a decent financial position, and in the process of employing a scientific staff. The cooperation between this museum and *Videnskabsselskabet* on the personal level also shows the contrasts between a dynamic scientific institution based on research and with enthusiastic funding from leading figures of the local community, to a more sedate Society with a healthy economy, but where the main activity was to fund the scientific work of others. Interestingly enough, the Bergen museum had based its statutes on the statutes of *Videnskabsselskabet* in Trondheim, which shows that the differences between the two organizations were perhaps not so great, which later developments were to prove in the last quarter of the century.

---

[363] Øverås, 1949b: 247.
[364] *Årsmelding 1845, 1848* DKNVS Archive IV:g:1.
[365] *Årsmelding 1858, 1859* DKNVS Archive IV:g:1.
[366] A. Forland and A. Haaland, *Universitetet i Bergens historie*, Vol. 1, Bergen, 1996:12–70.

The grants awarded by *Videnskabsselskabet* through the 1840s, when this activity was at its most intense, were often channeled in the direction of the natural sciences. One example is professor in geology Baltazar Mathias Keilhau (1797–1858), who received grants amounting to 1225 *spesiedaler* in the period 1842–49.[367] Since the 1820s, Keilhau had been active in mapping the geology and the mineralogy of Norway, especially northern Norway and the Oslo fjord region. He had become a lecturer in mineralogy at the University of Christiania in 1826, and was later to become professor.[368] As a professor, he was also responsible for the mineralogical collections of the university. On a previous occasion he had also received funds from the Society. In 1834, the directors had found that his work merited a contribution from Hammer's foundation, in spite of the limitations on the expenditure of this money.[369] The work he undertook with the financial aid from *Videnskabsselskabet* resulted in his work *Gaea Norvegica*, published in three volumes from 1838 to 1850.[370]

The grants for natural sciences in many ways follow an established practice in the Society's history. Sars's, Koren's and Danielssen's work with marine animals resembles Gunnerus's interest in the same subject, and the general trend of mapping and cataloging the phenomena and resources of the north, as with Lund, is also in line with Gunnerus's strategy. What is new is that the work is professionalized and paid for. *Videnskabsselskabet* was not in a position to become an institution of research in itself, as the Bergen museum was becoming at the same time. Nevertheless, the relatively high funding points towards a professionalization of the Society.

The grants: language and history

Through the 1840s, *Videnskabsselskabet* was to expand its funding support to activities that had been more marginal in the earlier years of its existence: Linguistics and history. This was not a new activity. Both Gerhard Schøning and Peter Suhm, two of the three founding fathers, had been active historians. The first volumes of *Skrifter* had been a forum for the publication of some of their historical works. Likewise, the linguistic works of Marcus Schnabel in the 1770s and 1780s had not been unimportant.[371] But neither history nor linguistics had been a core activity or at the centre of attention in *Videnskabsselskabet*'s inner circle. This was to change in the 1840s.

---

[367] *Kassadagbok 1812–55:* Fol. 73, 76, 78, 92, 95 DKNVS Archive II:13.
[368] A.K. Børresen and A. Wale, *Kartleggerne. Norges geologiske undersøkelse 1858–2008*, Trondheim, 2008: 21–30.
[369] *Årsmelding 1834* DKNVS Archive IV:g:1.
[370] B.M. Keilhau (hgs), *Gaea Norveica*, Vol. 1–3, Christiania, 1838–50.
[371] For instance M. Schnabel, "Prøve paa hvorvidt de gamle Norske Sprog endnu er til udi det Hardangerske Bonde-Maal," *Nye Samling af det Kongelige Norske Videnskabers Selskabs Skrifter*, Vol. 1, Copenhagen, 1784: 297–322.

One of the more grand projects funded by *Videnskabsselskabet* in this field in the 1840s was the grants to Ivar Aasen from 1841 to 1850.[372] Ivar Aasen (1813–1896) was born into a rather poor peasant family in Sunnmøre in western Norway. He had made his living as a teacher in the primary school in his own region, a position which required no formal education. Later, he was a private tutor in several households of more well-to-do civil servants, and carried out more or less organized studies of the language and botany of his native region.

In 1841, Aasen was not yet an established linguist, but an autodidact of humble origins, working on a grammar of his native dialect. His work caught the attention of *praeses* Bugge on the occasion of some articles in a Bergen newspaper in 1841, where Aasen's work was praised. Bugge, himself a linguist, found Aasen's work interesting, and through the next ten years Aasen received annual grants varying from 120 to 200 *spesiedaler* per year. The first years were spent traveling to document dialects, while the later part of the 1840s were spent working on his manuscript of a grammar (1848) and dictionary (1850) of the popular language.[373]

The background of Aasen's work must be seen in the light of the romantic notions of nations and national languages as the binding force of the national collective. This idea was developed by Johan Gottfried Herder in the late 18th century in the context of a politically divided Germany. The notion of a cultural and national community independent of the political entities of the day was further developed through the early 19th century, partly in answer to the challenges of the Napoleonic wars and the revolutionary French army. The ideas of a national identity and a collective based on common language would in turn merge with ideas of the French revolution of democratic rights and participation in the public life by all citizens, leading to the liberal national movements that culminated in the revolutions of 1848.

The Norwegian population was in this respect so fortunate as to come out of the Napoleonic era with their own state and a liberal constitution giving political rights to what for the times was a large segment of the population. Achieving a distinct and binding Norwegian identity, culture, and language was another matter. A national language was an unsolved problem in the establishment of a new Norwegian state and a presumably Norwegian nation. The political events of 1814 had left Norway with Danish as the official written language, embedded in the revised constitution of November that year. This was a defensive measure against potential pressure to establish Swedish as the official language.[374] In a longer perspective, some felt this to be a half-way measure, and discussed the possible revising of the official Danish language, making a written language more in accordance with the spoken tongue in Norway, as practiced by, for instance, the poet Henrik Wergeland (see below). This was not an uncomplicated stance, as such a development would have to meet the challenges of social differences,

---

[372] *Kassadagbok 1812–55*: Fol. 73, 75, 77, 78, 81, 82, 87, 88, 90, 92, 96, 99 DKNVS Archive II:13.

[373] I. Aasen, *Det norske Folkesprogs Grammatikk*, Christiania, 1848; I. Aasen, *Ordbog over det norske Folkesprog*, Christiania, 1850.

[374] Ø. Sørensen, *Norsk idéhistorie III. Kampen om Norges sjel*, Oslo, 2001: 53–92.

the continued cultural ties to Copenhagen of the educated elites, and the extreme variation in Norwegian dialects.

The question of language also came to the foreground in the new historical research into medieval Norwegian history from the 1840s. The pioneering historians Rudolf Keyser and Peter A. Munch struggled with the concepts of an old common Norse language in the Scandinavian region, and how it had developed into the separate national languages sometime during the high middle ages. For this generation of historians, the existence of a separate national language in the middle ages was indisputable, but it was also seen as impossible to use this as a basis for a modern Norwegian language. Instead, the debate was whether to allow certain words and linguistic traits flavored by the dialects or commoner's language to be used, providing for a slow departure from the Danish written language. The dialects, on the other hand, were the subject of some interest, mostly in connection with the collection and publishing of fairy tales, popular legends, and folk music, all of which were phenomena gaining momentum in the 1840s.

This is where Ivar Aasen departed from the common view. In his work on cataloging the spoken dialects and establishing a common grammar for them, he deliberately chose to emphasize elements in them that pointed to the medieval Norse language, clearly making it a positive quality that such common elements could be found. He worked within the prevailing paradigm of the day of comparative linguistics, where common traits between languages were used to trace common roots, thus discovering linguistic evolution. In this respect, Aasen was a pioneer in using comparative linguistics on dialects, or comparative dialectology, treating each dialect as a separate language and then through this method uncovering common structures representing all dialects.[375] This gave the tools to catalog a common "folk language," as put forth in his grammar and dictionary.

Aasen's work was to have enormous impact on the political and cultural situation in Norway in the late 19th century. The grammar and dictionary were the foundations of a new language, *landsmål* (later *nynorsk*). But by constructing a language solely based on dialects and with a common set of grammatical rules with its roots in medieval Norse, Aasen had also constructed a language that was culturally opposed to the written language used by the educated elite. Aasen himself was aware of this, and actively took part in the growing "cultural war" of the second half of the 19th century. Thus, in the second half of the century, the use of this language and the campaign to have it accepted as an official one was an important part of the political and cultural struggles of the time. This particular struggle was both of a cultural and political nature, politically dealing with both the problematic relationship with Sweden and the emergence of a political system where the government would be under the control of the parliamentary majority, and culturally with the divide between an educated urban elite and the large population of farmers and the emergence of a new working class.

---

[375] E. Haugen, "Construction and reconstruction in language planning," *Word* 21 (1965): 188–207.

One of the reasons for *Videnskabsselskabet*'s interest in language is of course the personal disposition of *praeses* Bugge and secretary Schwach. Bugge was an educated linguist, and Schwach a practicing poet. Bugge was, for instance, personally interested in Ivar Aasen's project, and it has been suggested that he was the impetus behind the first phase of the work, in fact structuring Aasen's work.[376] One piece of evidence of this is that Bugge gave Aasen rather detailed instructions on how to proceed with his work. But in the course of the project, Bugge's influence became less evident, both due to Aasen's own ideas and Bugge's deteriorating health.

Another linguistic project supported by *Videnskabsselskabet* worth mentioning is Christopher Holmboe's comparative etymological work on Norwegian and Sanskrit.[377] Holmboe (1796–1882) had studied Arabian and Farsi in Paris in the early 1820s, and was later hired as the first professor in oriental languages at the University of Christiania. He was a man of many talents, applying his energy in many fields. His linguistic comparisons were heavily criticized, even by his contemporaries, while his work in numismatics has fared better.

The grants to Aasen and Holmboe show a new side of *Videnskabsselskabet*'s activities. History in general, and linguistic history specifically, was now to move closer to the center of the Society's field of interests. From 1843, Christian Lange was to receive annual grants to enable him to work on the study and publication of medieval Norwegian diplomas, in addition to a study of the medieval Norwegian monasteries.[378] Christian Lange (1810–61) had worked as a teacher at the naval college in Fredriksvern (present-day Stavern), and also ran a bookshop in this small town. From 1843, he worked on his history of the monasteries, published in 1847, and was appointed to head the National Archives (*Riksarkivet*) in 1846. Through this position, and through the grants from *Videnskabsselskabet*, he was able to start publishing the first volumes of a series of medieval diplomas, *Diplomatarium Norvegicum*, from 1847. The series contained private and public letters, legal settlements, ecclesiastic or royal decrees, cadastres and so on from the 10th to the 16th centuries. The following year, the financial responsibility for the publication was taken over by the government.

The scientific publication of medieval diplomas was not a specifically Norwegian undertaking in this period. The publication of sources was seen as an important task in several of the European countries at the time, and can be regarded as an important contribution to the (re)construction of national histories. In the understanding of "nations" as put forth by J.G. Herder, an important factor in the establishment of the true "spirit" or "essence" of the nation was to understand its history, to reconstruct it as meticulously and carefully as possible. German historians at the turn of the century

---

[376] S.J. Walton, *Ivar Aasens kropp*, Oslo, 1996: 62–129. See also A. Øverås, *Ivar Aasen og Frederik Molkte Bugge—Det Kgl. Norske Videnskabers Selskab. Ei minneskrift*, Oslo, 1950.

[377] *Kassadagbok 1812–55*: Fol. 94, 100. DKNVS Archive II:13. The work was published in 1852: C.L. Homboe, *Det norske Sprogsvæsentligste Ordforraad, sammenlignet med Sanskrit og andre Sprog af samme Æt. Bidrag til en norsk etymologisk Ordbog*, Wien, 1852.

[378] *Kassadagbok 1812–55*: Fol. 75, 78, 86 DKNVS Archive II:13.

uncovered the sources and developed the tools to investigate and construct the national histories. This meant a study of the written sources of the national history, and this again would lead to the publication of medieval sources as a part of this reconstruction.

What gave the publication of the *Diplomatarium Norvegicum* a specific Norwegian edge were the criteria for the sequence of publication. In the ongoing similar projects abroad, a strict chronological principle was followed. This meant that one should first obtain an overview of the collected masses of medieval diplomas, then date them, then publish them chronologically.

The Norwegian *diplomatarium* did not follow this principle. In his preface to the first volume, Lange explains that the main mission of the series is not only to make the diplomas accessible for the purposes of historians, but also to shed light on the development of the Norwegian language in the high and late middle ages.[379] In order to facilitate this work, each separate volume should consist of a number of diplomas from the whole period, chronologically presented, and also from all parts of the country. This would give the linguists something to work on right from the start.[380] Each volume should also consist of material that would shed light on different aspects of the medieval society that were of genealogical, juridical, political, and social importance. This principle of publication would speed up the publishing process since a strictly chronological principle could mean numerous delays while trying to obtain an overview of the collected corpus of diplomas and an exact dating of each diploma. This approach differs from the ones applied by similar projects in the neighboring countries, and can perhaps give us an insight into a specifically Norwegian approach to a general scientific trend of the time. Both the Swedish *diplomatarium* (starting in 1829) and the early attempts to publish a Danish *diplomatarium* (*Langbæk's diplomatarium*, started in 1772) were based on a chronological principle, while further Danish diplomataria consisted of separate collections and institutional (ecclesiastical or other) archives.

This was, however, not the first publication of Norwegian medieval texts *Videnskabsselskabet* had been involved in. As early as in 1830, 1250 *spesiedaler* had been promised in five annual terms to support the work of publishing the medieval laws, both provincial and national, and of both royal and ecclesiastical origin.[381] The project was to be co-funded by the government and *Videnskabsselskabet*, but was initially rejected by *Stortinget*. In 1833, however, the project was approved by *Stortinget*, and Rudolf Keyser and P.A. Munch could start compiling and editing the laws.[382] The first volume was published in 1846, and subsequent volumes appeared in the following decades.[383]

---

[379] Lange, Chr. & Unger, C.R., "Forord," *Diplomatarium Norvegicum*, Vol. I part, Christiania, 1847: V–XI.

[380] This was a correct assumption. At the present moment, (2008), the series is still under publication, with 22 volumes having been published so far.

[381] *Årsmelding 1830* DKNVS Archive IV:g:1.

[382] R. Keyser and P.A. Much, "Fortale," *Norges gamle Love indtil 1387. Første bind. Norges Love ældre end Kong Magnus Haakonssöns Regjerings-Tiltrædelse i 1263*, Christiania, 1846: II–XII.

[383] The project is still under publication, now covering the late middle ages. The last volume so far was published in 1992.

Both Keyser and Munch were members of *Videnskabsselskabet*, and were to receive grants for various projects over the years. Both were important figures in the establishment of history as a scientific discipline in Norway.[384] Rudolf Keyser (1803–64) was educated in theology at the University of Christiania, but was employed there to teach in history and statistics. Later he also came to lecture on the medieval Norse language; he had spent two years on Iceland in the 1820s to learn the Norse language in a suitable setting. Keyser was primarily a teacher and publisher of sources, but also published a two-volume history of the Catholic Church in Norway before the reformation, and several shorter studies on medieval topics.

Peter Andreas Munch (1810–63) was more of a researcher, and received grants from *Videnskabsselskabet* both for his major work *Det Norske Folks Historie* ("The History of the Norwegian People"), and for a translation of the ancient Norse *Orkneyinga saga*.[385] He was employed as a lecturer in history at the University of Christiania in 1837, and became professor in 1841. Both through his monumental multi-volume work on the history of Norway and through an extensive hunt for and publication of medieval sources, he was to become a huge influence on the development of history as a discipline for generations.

Both the support given to Ivar Aasen and to Rudolf Keyser and Peter A. Munch should be seen in the light of 19th-century nationalism and nation building. They were all involved in the process of establishing a distinct Norwegian identity through exploring the history and the language of the country. These attempts at finding and cataloging the distinct Norwegian nation and national identity clearly place the interests of the Society within the contemporary intellectual trends of the early 19th century.

The grants: literature and philosophy

Videnskabsselskabet's interest in language and literature is also evident from the grant given to the poet Henrik Wergeland in 1844. Wergeland was given 100 *spesiedaler* to publish a revised version of his main poetic work *Skabelsen Mennesket, og Messias* ("Creation, Man, and Messiah").[386] Henrik Wergeland (1808–45) is primarily remembered as a poet, but had in fact been elected to *Videnskabsselskabet* in 1843 due to his position as the head of the newly established *Riksarkiv* in Christiania, and his yearlong work for public enlightenment through popular science publications on a variety of topics. But the grant given in 1844, a few months before Wergeland's death, seems to indicate that the directors were more interested in his poetry than his science.

Wergeland was a public person to an unusual degree by the standards of the time. He had established himself as both a leading patriot and a leading man of letters, and

---

[384] Dahl, O. *Norsk hostorieforskning i det 19. og 20. århundre*, Oslo, 1990: 46–74.
[385] *Årsberetning 1851*, 1857 DKNVS Archive IV:g:1.
[386] *Kassadagbok 1812–55*: Fol. 100 DKNVS Archive II:13.

had to a large degree led his life in public.[387] His illness and subsequent death were in fact nothing less than a media event, whereby the public could follow his physical decline through the newspapers—on occasions reported by Wergeland himself in verse. A grant from *Videnskabsselskabet* in his last, terminal phase could thus be seen not only as a grant in itself, but also as support to a very public and highly controversial person.

Schwach was clearly behind the scenes when it comes to the Society's support of Wergeland. The reason for this was the extremely harsh criticism of his collected poems in 1837, written by J. P. Collett, a close associate of the poet Johan S. Welhaven (1807–73). Wergeland had made himself controversial in many respects, but one of the major public conflicts he was engaged in was with the contemporary poet Welhaven. Welhaven had established himself as a poet throughout the 1830s, partly by contrasting himself to Wergeland.[388] While Wergeland painted himself as a patriot, a man of the people and a romanticist, Welhaven set himself in the tradition of rationalism, belonging to the educated classes and with more than a nod to the common Danish-Norwegian elitist culture of the preceding century. He was also affiliated with "the intelligentsia." These contrasts came to dominate intellectual life in the 1830s, and Welhaven and Wergeland became the leaders and symbols of the two opposing groups. By electing Wergeland to membership and giving him the grant to edit his major work of poetry, *Videnskabsselskabet* made a clear stand in this conflict.

Welhaven probably had provoked this reaction through an unflattering metaphor describing *Videnskabsselskabet* in his major work *Norges Dæmring* ("The dawn of Norway"). The opening section of this cycle of poems lamented the sorry state of Norwegian society, describing the lack of vigor and intellectual life in the Norwegian cities. Describing Trondheim, Welhaven characterized *Videnskabsselskabet* as "an old cow that yet has to give milk."[389] The description was seen as an insult by the leadership of the Society and inhabitants of Trondheim, but also by wider intellectual circles, and probably contributed to Welhaven never being elected a member even though he became a professor of philosophy in Christiania in 1841.

In addition to this, *praeses* Bugge had his own conflict with the Welhaven-Schweigaard circles, based on his yearlong involvement in the public debate on educational reforms. He and Schweigaard had been fierce opponents when they worked together on a committee dealing with the reorganization of education in Norway. Here, they represented opposing views on the role of what we may loosely label a classical education, with Latin and philosophy as important subjects, versus a more modern education, giving more room for natural sciences and living world languages. Their cooperation had been unsuccessful; Bugge privately charged Schweigaard with deliberately sabotaging the work of the committee when things did not go his way. In this

---

[387] Amundsen, L., "Wergeland, Henrik Arnold," NBL, Vol. XVIII, Oslo, 1977: 476–562.
[388] A.L. Seip, *Demringstid. Johan Sebastian Welhaven og nasjonen*, Oslo, 2007; Andersen-Næss, R., "Welhaven, Johan Sebastian," NBL, Vol. XVIII, Oslo, 1977: 401–429.
[389] "en gammel Ko, der endnu ei har malket."

situation, Wergeland publicly supported some of Bugge's suggestions and views. Wergeland was, for instance, a supporter of systematically giving educational grants to financially disadvantaged but intellectually gifted youth to mobilize the full intellectual
resources of the country. In addition, Bugge and Wergeland had known each other as
students at the university in the 1820s.[390]

The animosity between Welhaven and Schwach, and Bugge and Schweigaard, led
to or marked a cultural divide between *Videnskabsselskabet* in Trondheim and the one
of the leading intellectual and political circles in Christiania, the so called "intelligentsia." It is symptomatic that few of the leading figures of this group were elected to
membership in the Society in the short run, although several of them, like Schweigaard
and minister of the interior, Frederik Stang, were to become members in the late 1840s,
when tempers perhaps had cooled somewhat.

Other than the support for Wergeland, *Videnskabsselskabet* did not venture deeply
into the world of arts and letters under Bugge's leadership. One other aspect of this interest in literature and art can, however, be seen in its yearly contribution to the local
art association and its gallery *Trondheim Kunstforening*, which was established in 1845.
The contribution was modest, a mere 10 *spesiedaler* a year.[391]

The inclinations of Bugge and Schwach were also reflected in a particular interest
in philosophical problems and trends which at times were expressed in the work of
Videnskabsselskabet. Bugge would at times touch upon these themes in his speeches at
the yearly public celebration of the king's birthday. Of more lasting interest than the
speeches by the *praeses* were the essay competition contests, which at times could be on
topics of a philosophical nature. As mentioned above, the botanist Nicolay Lund's first
encounter with *Videnskabsselskabet* was as the author of a winning essay on the topic "Is
every intelligent creature necessarily a free creature?" announced in 1835, and submitted in 1837. Lund's essay was found wanting in most respects, but nevertheless earned
him a gold medal and membership in 1838. The reasoning behind the decision to
award the prize in spite of the shortcomings of the submitted essay was simple: "One
has let oneself be led by a certain consideration of the importance of contributing to the
growth and tending of any trace of talent in the lamentable conditions for the development of science in our country."[392]

Bugge and the directors were not satisfied, even though Lund received the small
gold medal for his contribution, and the same year another contest on a related topic
was announced: "Is it possible to prove the freedom of the human will from evidence
of self-consciousness?"[393] Three essays were submitted by the deadline in 1838, and were
submitted for anonymous assessment by the members of the historical-philosophical

---

[390] Øverås, 1949a: 63.
[391] First time in 1846. *Kassadagbok 1812–55:* Fol. 82 DKNVS Archive II:13.
[392] "Saa har man ladet sig lede af et særdeles Hensyn til Vigtigheden af under vort Lands for det
videnskabelige Livs Udvikling mindre gunstige Forhold at bidrage alt Mulig til at enhver Spire af
Talent maatte omhyggeligen fredes og plejes." Quoted in Øverås, 1949b: 252.
[393] "Kan Menneskets frie Villie bevises af dets Selvbevidsthed?"

section of *Videnskabsselskabet*. The members found one of the essays worthy of the large gold medal; this was applauded by the directors of *Videnskabsselskabet* in January 1839. It was then revealed that the author of the essay was Arthur Schopenhauer from Frankfurt am Main.

Schopenhauer (1788–1860) was at this time not very known outside the philosophical circles of Germany. He had, however, been noticed a few years earlier by the leading Norwegian authority on contemporary philosophy, Niels Treschow (1751–1833), and Nicolay Lund also seems to have been acquainted with his work. Schopenhauer was also at this time on the verge of a breakthrough in Germany, where Hegel's influence had been somewhat waning after his death in 1831, and the time was more ripe for one of his fiercer critics.

To the question posed by *Videnskabsselskabet*, "Is it possible to prove the freedom of the human will from evidence of self-consciousness?" Schopenhauer's answer was "No," according to Christopher Janaway in his essay on Schopenhauer's concepts of Will and Nature.[394] But in the process of reaching this conclusion, Schopenhauer undertakes a thorough discussion on the concept of freedom and responsibility. The decision of the board was, even if unanimous, not met with outright enthusiasm by all the leading members. The content of both Lund's and Schopenhauer's essays touched on themes that could be seen as undermining established religion and values. For instance, Schopenhauer's discussion on the concepts of freedom and conscience left little room for common moral values.[395] This might have given some members of the board second thoughts. To avoid challenging the religious beliefs of a wider audience, *Videnskabsselskabet*'s directors decided to print the essay in German, not Norwegian as was the norm in *Skrifter*. Interestingly enough, the directors accepted that Schopenhauer published the essay in Germany in the same form, thus making it available to a potentially wide readership. The German public was obviously more mature and capable of handling the challenging thoughts of Schopenhauer, if we are to believe the directors of *Videnskabsselskabet*.[396]

The prize awarded to Schopenhauer went fairly unnoticed at the time. Apparently, it was the only academic award granted to him in his lifetime. Indeed, when Schopenhauer submitted an essay for competition on a similar theme arranged the following year by the Royal Society of Arts and Letters in Copenhagen, his essay was not found worthy of an award; instead, it earned him severe criticism from the jury judging the essays. Schopenhauer's response was to publish both of the essays in one volume, making a point on the title page of the fact that the one essay was awarded by the Royal Norwegian Society, the other one *not* awarded by the Royal Danish Society, and furthermore treating the Danish Society with deep contempt in the foreword to this

---

[394] C. Janaway, "Will and nature," in C. Janaway (ed.), *The Cambridge Companion to Schopenhauer*, New York, 1999: 138–170.

[395] J.F. Bjelke, "Kritisk introduksjon til prisskriftets problematikk," A. Schopenhauer, *Kan menneskets frie Villie bevises af dets Selvbevidsthed?*, Oslo, 1993: 19–47.

[396] Øverås, 1949b: 258–259.

volume. This was the cause of some amusement to the philosopher Søren Kierkegaard, who sarcastically noted that it was "unexplainable" that Schopenhauer, who "in such a talented way represented a misanthropic outlook," could be "so utterly happy when the Scientific Society in Trondheim (Good God! Trondheim!) awarded his dissertation" while "making a whole lot of noise in a serious manner" when the scientific society in Copenhagen decided not to.[397] Evidently, Kierkegaard was of the opinion that the, in Schopenhauer's opinion, unfair treatment by the Copenhagen Society and the award from the, in Kierkegaard's opinion, ridiculous concept of a scientific society in Trondheim, should be pleasing to Schopenhauer, as it confirmed his pessimistic view of the world.

In addition to these more philosophical topics, Bugge's interest in more mundane political problems were also to a certain degree reflected in the essay competitions. In 1839, for instance, a competition on the subject "Is Norway ready for the establishment of a polytechnic institute, or only for technical schools on a smaller scale, but with more special tasks? How should these be organized?"[398] No essays were submitted. This competition was probably part of Bugge's general work and thoughts on educational reform, which occupied him for much of his time during this period.

Journals and Skrifter

By the mid-1840s, *Videnskabsselskabet*'s policy of financially supporting publications was expanded from specific works to journals. In 1844, grants were given to the journals *Nor* and *Tidsskrift for Norsk Personalhistorie* (Norwegian Genealogical Journal).[399] The next year *Norsk Universitets- og Skoleannaler* (Norwegian University and School Journal) was to be added to the journals receiving support for their publication.[400] The support for journals was a response to a new trend in scientific publications both in Norway and elsewhere—specialization. Already in the 1830s there was a trend towards specialized journals in history or languages in Norway, and the middle of the century saw an acceleration in this development, as exemplified by the above-mentioned journals, and by journals such as *Historisk Tidsskrift* (Historical Journal) (1871). Moreover, there were the journals from the Bergen Museum, namely *Urda* in the 1830s and 40s, and later the yearbook of the museum. These were not single-discipline journals or publications, although *Urda* was basically a historical and archaeological journal, but were, on the other hand, based on the ongoing work in one institution, thus representing the collective work of one academic environment.

---

[397] J.Garff, *SAK. Søren Aabye Kierkegaard. En biografi*, Oslo, 2002: 713.

[398] *Årsmelding 1841* "Er Norge modent for Oprettelsen af et polyteknisk Institut, eller kun for tekniske Læreanstalter af mindre omfang og mer speciele Øjemed? Kunne disse forenes med Haandverksskoler, og hvorledes bør de i det hele taget være indrettet?" DKNVS Archive IV:g:1.

[399] *Årsmelding 1844* DKNVS Archive IV:g:1.

[400] *Årsmelding 1845* DKNVS Archive IV:g:1.

This development can be seen as a challenge to *Videnskabsselskabet*'s own publication series, *Skrifter*. As specialization was the trend, haphazard collections of dissertations on a broad variety of subjects were becoming a rather old-fashioned way of publication. *Skrifter* continued at uneven intervals; one volume appeared in 1843, the next one in 1859. Both were published in installments in the years leading up to the full volume being finished. These volumes continued the trend of the two preceding volumes: Collections of whatever had come into the hands of the board of directors, including their own papers, deemed to be sufficiently interesting for publication. The volume of 1843 was thus dominated by the two gold-medal dissertations of the late 1830s by Arthur Schopenhauer and Harald Wergeland (1811–1893). Harald Wergeland, Henrik Wergeland's younger brother, had written a somewhat more down-to-earth dissertation than Schopenhauer, with the title "Attempt at answering the question of what the still effective hindrances of a rational cultivation of the land in Norway are, and how these can be removed."[401] In addition to these, *praeses* Bugge decided to publish his speech on the constitutional government, which was held at the meeting celebrating the king's birthday in 1838.

The 1859 volume is somewhat different. To a certain degree it reflects the ongoing projects financed by *Videnskabsselskabet*. Ivar Aasen, for instance, gave a report on his work, including samples. Daniel Danielssen gave a report from one of his zoological travels. In addition to this, the secretary, Schwach, had two contributions, the most interesting one being the expanded version of his history of *Videnskabsselskabet*. Schwach's article, published as the first installment of the 1859 volume already in 1844, is part history, part apology, and part program. The history is a straightforward description of the great men and their work of the golden age, and of the lavish use of money on worthy projects in more recent years. However, this narrative is punctuated by jibes at "a certain young writer" who in "childlike ignorance" or "youthful flippancy" had described *Videnskabsselskabet* in a most degrading manner. Schwach obviously felt the need to make a point out of the financial activities of the organization, which certainly did not resemble J.S. Welhaven's old cow giving no milk metaphor. On the other hand, Schwach also concedes to the view that the use of money for projects like the cultivation of Oustmyren, in particular, and awarding prizes for inventiveness among the common people, in general, was perhaps not the wisest use of the money. Schwach explains this as a product of the situation in the 1760s: The founding fathers, careful as they were, had a suspicion that the king would not agree to the statutes of a purely scientific and literary society in Norway, as this would too much resemble an autonomous Norwegian institution of higher learning. But by including the prizes and the general tendency of supporting the practical arts and progress, it would be easier to obtain royal confirmation of the statutes. Moreover, still according to Schwach, this had been a good approach, in touch with the realities of the times. Much good work had been done

---

[401] H. Wergeland, "Forsøg til en Besvarelse af det Spørgsmaal: Hvilke ere de endnu virkende Hindringer for Jordens hensiktsmæssige Dyrkning i Norge, og hvorledes kunne disse hæves?, *Det kongelige Norske Videnskabers Selskabs Skrifter i det 19. Aarhundrede*, Vol. 3, Trondheim, 1843: 1–141.

in these fields in the first decades of *Videnskabsselskabet's* existence. But now, in independent Norway, with other ways of supporting these activities, it should no longer be the task of the Society. Especially the Oustmyren project had been a failure, according to Schwach. He is hesitant about predicting the future, but in the last pages of his history, he points to the library and the collections as the core of *Videnskabsselskabet*, on which its future activities must be built. This article was published at the same time that a committee had evaluated the state of the collections and library, and had come to the same conclusions.

The Library

An important part of *Videnskabsselskabet's* tasks, collections and self-understanding was to keep the library in as good order as possible. This had been the case from the 1770s, and was perhaps one of the main constant factors throughout the first hundred years of the Society's existence.

By the early 19th century, the size and quality of the library was quite impressive, although the order of the collection was perhaps wanting. The inheritance of Christopher Hammer's library had added a large number of books to the collection, and there was an immediate need to catalog what the library actually contained. Money could be taken from Hammer's foundation to finance this undertaking, as one of the obligations of *Videnskabsselskabet* under the will was to publish the contents of Hammer's gift, including the library. This initiated a cumbersome process which led to the publication of a library catalog in 1808.[402]

The library had also published catalogs of its contents at earlier stages, in 1770 and 1779. But these had a more modest collection to deal with: the 1770 catalog presented 600 volumes, while the 1779 catalogue consisted of approximately 2100 volumes. But in the 1780s, the library was greatly expanded by the inheritance of the libraries of Gerhard Schøning and Benjamin Dass, approximately 10,000 volumes all together. These gifts of course reflected the personal interests of the donors, which can explain the bias of the library in the decades to follow: An over-representation of theology, history, and philology. An attempt to catalogue these volumes in the 1780s was abandoned, but was resumed when Christopher Hammer's will provided the financial means to do so. This work was led by Professor Rasmus Nyerup in Copenhagen, assisted by the librarian in Trondheim, Christian E. Heltzen. The whole process took three years, and resulted in an impressive 652-page catalog. It was relatively systematic, divided according to 12 themes ranging from theology, philosophy, and morals, including politics, to economics, natural history, including physics and chemistry, and mathematics, including music. Each theme was organized into three sections according to the size of the books:

---

[402] *Catalog over Det Norske Videnskabersselskabs Samlinger. Første del. Bøger og haandskrifter*, Copenhagen, 1808.

Folio, quarto and octavo. All together, this gives 36 sections, but the order and method within each of these sections seems a bit hazier. Nevertheless, the catalog was a public statement, and a public guide to the treasures of the library, and Nyerup expressed the hope that they could introduce his proposed scheme of adding to the catalog by publishing the additions to the library every five years, and undertaking a critical review of the contents of the library every twenty years, not least with respect to the theological literature, of which one can sense he questioned the quality.[403] Nyerup also expressed satisfaction, both with his own and Heltzen's work, but also with the state and contents of the library. He labels the library as: "A national library, or perhaps the finest regional library in Norway."[404] Nyerup's hope for a continuous upgrading of the catalog was not to be fulfilled in the short run. Nevertheless, the catalog would be a guide for the order of the library for years to come.

The library contained approximately 20,000 volumes in 1808. Managing such a high number of books required the hand of an experienced librarian. In all the statutes from 1805 to 1815 the duties of the librarian were outlined in detail. Actually, he was responsible not only for the books, but the entire collection of *Videnskabsselskabet*. When it came to the library, he was to oversee the library loans. Books could be loaned for eight weeks at a time; overdue loans were fined a rather heavy sum of two *spesiedaler*. Books could be borrowed by any honest man in Trondheim, according to the 1805 statutes.[405] This was changed to any honest *person* living in Trondheim in 1811, formally opening the library to women.[406] All the books in the library were to be stamped with *Videnskabsselskabet*'s symbol. Any books found anywhere in the realm of the king—for instance, at book auctions or amongst the belongings of deceased persons—were to be returned to the library immediately. Not only books could be loaned, but also maps and models of agricultural tools that could be useful for the borrower. Schools, however, could not borrow books from the library, and more rare and valuable books or maps were not to be loaned. It was the responsibility of the librarian to acquire books and uphold subscriptions to the most important magazines and journals, within the economic limits set by the board of directors. Thus, he had to have an overview of the important developments within the scientific disciplines to be able to make the best decisions on what to purchase. Books were of course also added to the library as gifts. In addition to this, it was mandatory for all new members of *Videnskabsselskabet* to donate books worth at least 10 *spesiedaler* when elected.

These were all time-consuming tasks, and it was made explicit in all the statutes that the librarian should be given a decent salary as soon as the financial situation of *Videnskabsselskabet* allowed it. The annual public support granted by parliament from 1817 made this possible. From the following year, the librarian was the first paid

---

[403] R. Nyerup, "Fortale," *Catalog over Det Norske Videnskabersselskabs Samlinger. Første del. Bøger og haandskrifter*, Copenhagen, 1808: I–XXXII.
[404] "Nationalbibiliothek, eller om Man heller vil, Norges ypperste Stiftsbibliothek."
[405] *Nye Statuter for det Kongelige Norske Videnskabers Selskab i Trondhjem*, Trondhjem, 1806.
[406] Confirmation paa Statuter for Det Kongelige Norske Videnskabers-Selskab, Christiania, 1811.

member of the staff of the Society. The annual pay was modest, 70 *spesiedaler*, but then again it was not considered a full-time job. The library was to be open to borrowers one day a week.

The first paid librarian was Otto Fritzner (1779–1860), a teacher at *Katedralskole*, who was in the position for seven years, after which he had to quit due to poor eyesight. His successor was Johan Christian Tellefsen, who, even though he was 51 years old at the time of his employment, was to remain in the position for more than three decades. Tellefsen (1774–1857) had been elected to membership in 1812. He was the organist in the cathedral, and inspector of the municipal waterworks. These occupations gave him ample time to tend to his position as librarian, a task he pursued with great energy.

Tellefesen was no stranger to the library. As a student he had been employed to help organize Hammer's book collection in 1804 and was thus already well into the organization of the library. In his spare time he had also undertaken several tasks of organizing the collection of parchment manuscripts, and writing a catalog of these.[407] Enlarging the collection of manuscripts—medieval parchments and newer paper-manuscripts—was to be one of his main interests throughout his career. His first action as the paid librarian from 1825 was to awaken the more or less sleeping statute that new members should donate books valued to at least 10 *spesiedaler* to the library. He seems not only to have immediately followed up the new members, but also to have gone through the elections of the previous years and reminded the new members of this obligation. The result was an immediate increase in the number of donations.[408] In fact, he was so eager in this field that *vice-praeses* Storm half jokingly reported to *praeses* Bugge a few years later that postage to be paid for books arriving from foreign members threatened to become a strain on the finances of *Videnskabsselskabet*.[409]

During the first years of Tellefsens's work, information on the growth of the library was recorded in the protocols of the board of directors, to whom Tellefsen reported. But the number of books grew by such an extent that these lists filled up a major part of the proceedings of the board, and by the early 1830s it was decided to regularly publish lists of the books acquired by the library, thus fulfilling Nyerup's ambition from 1808. The board of directors offered Tellefsen a sum of 50 *spesiedaler* for the completion of this work, but this was out of the question for him. He was of the opinion that this task was a part of his work as librarian, and asked for the 50 *spesiedaler* to be added to the book budget instead.

This shows a side of Tellefsen's personality which was both a strength and a weakness for the library: He took his job so seriously he tended to regard the library as his own private property, and was not too happy to have people invading it, whether it was symbolically speaking by instructing him in his work, or literally in order to borrow books. Tellefsen might also have a blurred sense of what was his and what were the

---

[407] W. Støren, "Bibliotekets ledere," H. Nissen & M. Aase (eds.), *Til opplysning. Universitetsbiblioteket i Trondheim, 1768–1993*,Trondheim, 1993: 19–57.
[408] *Årsmelding 1825* DKNVS Archive IV:g:1.
[409] Ref. Øverås, 1949b: 223.

library's possessions. In recent years, medieval membrane fragments from the Society's library have resurfaced in the National Archives (*Riksarkivet*), where they had been deposited by Tellefsen's heirs.[410] Tellefsen thus emerges as a dilettante in the original sense of the word—uneducated, enthusiastic, and obsessive, and whose contribution to the maintenance and growth of the library was vast, but somewhat uncontrollable.

What were Tellefsen's priorities when it came to purchasing books? The catalogs of newly acquired books, published in 1833, 1848, 1853, and 1858 give us some clues. They cover the first five decades after the Nyerup catalog—the 1833 catalog also contains titles omitted from the Nyerup catalog. The main impression to be derived from the first catalog is that the acquisitions were mainly in three fields: theology, economics, and history. "Economics" covered the whole field of practical arts and economic theory. In the categories "Economics" and "History" there was a fairly large degree of recent literature—i.e., from the last 20 years—while the theological literature to a large degree was from the 17th and 18th centuries. When it came to other categories, such as mathematics, physics, and chemistry, the growth of the library was negligible in the short run. On the other hand, through the 1830s and 1840s, the subject of "legal literature" became more prominent. The category "literary history" was also to become prominent in the subsequent catalogs. Thus, it seems that Tellefsen, with the blessing of the board of directors, continued the 18th-century trend of the library, and expanded it mainly in the fields of theology, history, and "arts and letters." Of course, not all the additions to the library were under Tellefsen's control. There was, in part, the trading of publications with other Societies, and in part, there was the donation of books by new members, which might account for much of the antiquarian theological literature.

Another contribution to the growth of the library over which the librarian had little influence was the donation of whole collections. Several members made *Videnskabsselskabet* beneficiaries in their wills when it came to their private book collections. Some of these could be quite impressive, for instance the library of Broder Lysholm Knudzon (1788–1864), who dedicated most of his time to collecting books and keeping in touch with literary circles in England when not engaged in the family business.[411] He was also the treasurer of *Videnskabsseskabet* for a period of time. In his formative years, he had traveled extensively in Europe, and spent most of the years 1808–14 in England, where he struck up a friendship with, among others, Lord Byron. Later in life, he nourished a special interest in British literature, corresponding regularly with Byron and others, and building an impressive collection of both contemporary and antiquarian books. In addition to this, he was an ardent collector of art, and donated several works by the renowned Danish sculptor Bertel Thorvaldsen (1770–1844) to *Videnskabsselskabet* on

---

[410] E. Karlsen, "Liturgiske bøker i Norge inntil år 1300—import og egenproduksjon," S. Imsen (ed.), *Den kirkehistoriske utfordring*, Trondheim, 2005: 147–170. See especially footnote 17, p. 150.
[411] M. Aase, "En europeer i Trondheim—Broder Lysholm Knudtzon og hans bibliotek," H. Nissen & M. Aase (eds.), *Til opplysning. Universitetsbiblioteket i Trondheim 1768–1993*, Trondheim, 1993: 132–137.

his death. What was special about Knudtzon's gift was that he required his collection of books, art, and furniture (mainly specially fitted shelves) to be kept together in a separate room set aside for this purpose. Other testamentary gifts to the library were more modest, both in size and instructions for how to handle them.[412] Donations like the library of the Horneman family also would underline the 16th- and 17th-century bias of the library.[413]

Tellefsen also undertook a major reorganization of the library. One result of this clean-up was that in 1833 the Society was able to donate 142 volumes to the library of the University of Christiania, books that *Videnskabsselskabet* had more than one copy of.[414] The following year, a similar donation was made to the library at the Bergen Museum.[415] These donations were gifts, with no return expected. But in addition to this, the library expanded its collections by trading titles. The rather meager amount of publications by *Videnskabsselskabet* was to be the basis of a widespread exchange of books and journals from other learned societies in Europe. The Royal Society in London, for instance, provided the library with its publications on a yearly basis, getting a volume or an installment of *Videnskabsselskabet*'s *Skrifter* in return at irregular intervals. The learned societies in London, Berlin, Uppsala, Paris, Gothenburg, Stockholm, Copenhagen, Amsterdam, and Cherbourg are other examples of this trading network that figures in the catalogs or elsewhere.[416]

In the 1840s, space was becoming an acute problem for the library. With an annual growth of about 500 volumes, in the long run the library could not be contained in the rooms set aside for it 50 years earlier, and in 1844 this led to the drastic measure of taking a room occupied by the various objects left to *Videnskabsselskabet* by Christopher Hammer, which were co-located with the other collections.[417] This gave the library another room, and solved the problem for the time being. The pious attitude towards the great benefactor of *Videnskabsselskabet* was clearly waning at this point, both with respect to his donations to the Society's collections, and to the limitations put on the use of his foundation. Nonetheless, by 1850, the library contained approximately 40,000 volumes, and the assembly hall now had to be used as a storage space for books, in addition to the room set aside for the library, and the room formerly occupied by Hammer's collection. It became obvious that these solutions could only be temporary. In the long run the problem was still present. One thing was the sheer amount of books, another was that the weight of the books threatened to literally cause structural damage

---

[412] For instance the library of Colline Lassen, *Årsmelding 1856*, DKNVS Archive IV:g:1.

[413] *Continuations-catalog over Det Kongelige Norske Vidensabs-Selskabs Samlinger. Bøger og haandskrifter m.m. 1858–1862 No. 5*, Trondheim, 1863.

[414] *Årsmelding 1833* DKNVS Archive IV:g:1.

[415] *Årsmelding 1834* DKNVS Archive IV:g:1.

[416] *Continuations catalog over Det kongelige Norske Videnskabers Selskabs Samlinger. Bøger og Haandskrifter*, Trondheim, 1831. Ibid, Vol. 2, 1848, Vol. 3, 1853, Vol. 4, 1858, Vol. 5, 1863, *Årsmelding 1856* DKNVS Archive IV:g:1.

[417] *Årsmelding 1844* DKNVS Archive IV:g:1.

to the *Katedralskole*.[418] By the late 1840s, Tellefsen was in need of assistance, both due
to the amount of work and his advancing age. Carl P.P. Essendrop, a teacher at the *Katedralskole*, was assigned this task in 1845.[419]

Essendrop took upon himself the task of organizing the library according to filing
cards, not a catalog. This modernization made the organization of books by subject a
relatively easy task, and streamlined the incorporation of additions to the library. It also
made it easier to organize the library on other principles than themes and the size of
books. Alphabetical order could become more of an organizing principle under the different themes. All in all, this made the library more user-friendly, and Essendrop's
cards were the core of the library's catalog for more than a century.

When Essendrop had finished his work in 1849, he retired as Tellefsen's assistant,
but it was obvious that Tellefsen still needed help. Essendrop was therefore followed by
Hans H. Müller in 1850, and his main task was to prepare and publish the catalogs of
new additions to the library, published in 1853 and 1858. This expansion of the staff
also led to other fields of increased activity in the library. In 1847, the reading room was
opened. The reading room changed the nature of the library, from a mere storeroom of
books to a semi-public library. We can see an unmistakable pride in the annual reports
to the protector in the following years as to the frequent use of the room and the number of books now being loaned. In 1847, the suggestion to open the reading room to an
even wider public was made by *praeses* Bugge.

The organization—a crisis of identity?

As we can see, much of the activity of *Videnskabsselskabet* during these years was the result of the personal interests of a small handful of men. Nevertheless, they led a nominally large organization. This seems to have caused them few problems in the short
run. What we can see from the protocols of the board of directors is that the board actually met more infrequently in the 1840s when the financial activities were at their
peak.[420] This indicates a rather non-bureaucratic attitude towards the running of the
organization, and it actually appears that many of the decisions were made by *praeses*
Bugge and *vice-praeses* Storm corresponding privately when Bugge had his long stays
in Christiania.[421]

Through the 1830s and 1840s, the election of members to *Videnskabsselskabet* continued at a relatively high rate. All together 228 members were elected during these

---

[418] W.K. Støren, "'Ein heimstad for ånd'. Bibliotekets lokaler," H. Nissen & M. Aase (eds.), *Til
opplysning. Universitetsbiblioteket i Trondheim 1768–1993*, Trondheim, 1993: 64–92.
[419] *Årsmelding 1845* DKNVS Archive IV:g:1.
[420] The board would usually meet seven or eight times a year in the 1830s, but only two to four times
a year in the period 1843–47 and up to ten times a year in the late 1850s. *Direksjonsprotokoll 1826–55*
DKNVS Archive II:3; *Direktionsprookoll 1855–1891* DKNVS Archive II:4.
[421] Øverås, 1949b: 222–230.

twenty years. We can see a slight tendency towards members being either from Trondheim or from abroad during this period. The network of members in the two northern
dioceses seems to be less important. On the other hand, by the mid 1840s, more and
more of the educated elite in Christiania were elected. In one meeting in particular, in
November 1849, no less than 37 members were elected, of which 15 were either high-
ranking officers or professors or teachers at the University of Christiania. The foreign
members who were elected seem to have come under two main categories. One group
consisted of contacts made by *praeses* Bugge during his trips abroad in the late 1830s,
the other consisted of scientists or lecturers at the University of Uppsala. One particularly interesting group consisted of five persons from Calcutta, elected in 1844 and
1849. They were the leaders of the botanical gardens, the zoological museum and the
Asiatic Society of Calcutta, and were elected so they and their institutions could engage
in the trading of specimens. This shows that the concept of an international network
was still alive and activated at times. Another example of this is the election of the scientific staff of the French expedition to Spitsbergen in 1838. When the ship in the expedition, "La Recherche," briefly visited Trondheim in June of that year, the scientists
aboard were introduced to *Videnskabsselskabet* and some were elected as members,
while other expedition members were elected at a later stage. The expedition's members
consisted of scientists from several fields, both the natural sciences and social sciences,
and artists who were to make illustrations. The expedition can be seen as an early example of the purely scientific expedition, not primarily aimed at expanding the territory or glory of the nation, but rather aimed at collecting and processing knowledge.
The expedition was also reliant on cooperation with foreign scientific environments,
most notably the Swedish Academy and its influential secretary Jacob Berzelius, and the
University of Berlin and Alexander Humboldt. Thus it can be seen as an early example
of a multi-national research project doing work in several scientific disciplines.[422] Even
though the role of *Videnskabsselskabet* in this expedition was very modest, it can be seen
as a part of this international cooperation, and the election of expedition members into
the Society as a confirmation of the Society's international connections.

The local figures elected as members, on the other hand, were from the usual
groups of merchants or civil servants—teachers, priests, officers, judges and so on.[423]
By the end of the 1840s, these local members of the organization wanted to have their
say in important matters. A conflict ensued over a suggestion from Bugge in 1847 that
there should be easier access to membership for the general public. Bugge's reason
for wanting this was twofold: He wanted to strengthen the financial situation of
Videnskabsselskabet by increasing the number of paying members, and he wanted to use
the organization as a tool for enlightenment, inviting the brighter heads of the lower
strata of the city to join. How he wanted to organize this is not clear, but it seems he
wanted to facilitate access to extraordinary membership, or remove the criterion with

---

[422] Drivenes, E.-A., "'La Recherche'—Forskningseksedisjonen Frankrike glemte," *Historisk Tidskrift*,
1992: 11–35.
[423] Schmidt, 1960: 96–120.

respect to scientific publications for ordinary members. His main point was that as many people as possible should have access to the library, which had recently established a separate reading room, and thus turn it into a meeting place for the enlightened persons of all classes in the city, and also contribute to enlarging this group of enlightened persons.[424] But this suggestion opened up a gulf between the directors of *Videnskabsselskabet*, following the political fault lines of the times as they were manifested in Trondheim.

These political conflicts followed several patterns. One was between the local public servants and what was seen as nepotism and corruption within this elite, on the one hand, and the educated, but self-employed younger generation allied with an expanding middle class of small merchants and artisans, on the other. The conflicts between these adversarial groups would be played out in the newspapers or the elections to parliament or the city council. In addition, Trondheim was marked by a yearlong political conflict over the question of how to keep the harbor in the best condition. The harbor, at the mouth of the river *Nidelva*, was regularly filled with silt and had to be dredged. This was a costly affair, and the political opposition made it one of their main causes to move the entire harbor to the beach on the northern side of the peninsula on which Trondheim was situated, constructing a jetty to protect it from the ocean. This would destroy the livelihoods of the established merchant elite who had their warehouses and other properties along the river harbor. This elite, heavily represented among the members of *Videnskabsselskabet*, allied themselves with the higher civil servants in a "conservative" alliance which successfully stopped this project for decades.[425]

In this political climate, Bugge clearly sympathized with the radical side, and it seems that he used his position as *praeses* to advocate his stance. In 1847 he used the occasion of the *praeses*'s speech at the public meeting in celebration of the king's birthday to question whether the king's motto "Truth and Justice" was being followed by his government in Norway. There is reason to believe his answer was in part in the negative, and that this caused some distress among the more conservative members.[426] Bugge half-heartedly tried to brush over the implications of his speech, which seems to have been well received by the population of the city at large. But it probably added to the discontent among a section of the members of *Videnskabsselskabet*.

Bugge's main opponent on the board of directors in the library controversy and the recommendation to have a more democratic membership policy was *stiftamtmann* Karelius August Arntzen (1802–75), who was the head of the first class of *Videnskabsselskabet*. As *stiftamtmann*, Arntzen, educated in law in Christiania, was the king's and the government's most prominent representative in Trøndelag. He was a conservative man who was loyal to the prevailing order, and the democratic ideas of the day were foreign to him. Among Bugge's suggestions for new members was the lawyer Frederik Lerche,

---

[424] Øverås, 1949b: 232–239.
[425] K. Mykland, *Fra Søgaden til Stradgaten 1800–1880. Trondheims historie 997–1997, Vol. 3*, Oslo, 1997: 213–239.
[426] Øverås, 1949b: 393.

who was a leader of the political opposition, and a personal enemy of Arntzen due to his several not very flattering characterizations of him in public debates. Other suggestions for members from Bugge were the editors of the local radical newspapers, Anton Bang and Chr. Monsen. Frederik Storm tried to ease the tension by suggesting a low membership fee confining these members to the use of the library and reading room, but for Arntzen this was out of the question. Instead, he resigned from the board of directors *and* quit his membership in *Videnskabsselskabet*. In spite of this, the men in question were not elected. The conflict must have created an unpleasant atmosphere both amongst the board members and *Videnskabsselskabet* in Trondheim as a whole. In the wake of the membership discussion, some discontent with the lavish spending on grants and publications by the directors was also voiced.[427]

The following year, 1848, Bugge was not re-elected as *praeses*. Instead, Bishop Hans Riddervold (1795–1876) was elected. Riddervold was a rather conservative man in political, moral, and religious matters. The reason for his election as *praeses* was in part to be found in the discontent in the wake of the library dispute and Arntzen's resignation, but also in part due to the fact that Bugge was also under fire for his management of the *Katedralskole*. The main problem was that Bugge at times had a lifestyle which was considered by his peers in the Society as hard to combine with the respectability of his position, something the ephorship of the school pointed out both to Bugge and to the department of ecclesiastical affairs in Christiania on several occasions. Interestingly, the leading persons of the ephorship were his opponents on the board of directors of *Videnskabsselskabet*, namely Arntzen, and his elected successor as *praeses*, Bishop Riddervold. Their zeal in instructing Bugge on the dignity of his office as headmaster and in pointing out of his shortcomings in this respect bordered on harassment, and it is obvious that this must have led to personal hostility that in the long run had to affect the board of directors in *Videnskabsselskabet*. In the spring and summer of 1848, the controversy surrounding Bugge's leadership at the school peaked and Bugge had to mobilize his network in Christiania—for example, such members of the Society as Rudolf Keyser and Conrad Holmboe—to vouch for him and his abilities so he could maintain his position. He succeeded, but was placed on probation for two years.[428]

However, the move to replace Bugge was met with a set-back as Riddervold refused to accept his own election as *praeses* in 1848, due to having become secretary of ecclesiastical affairs in the government, and subsequently having no time for the task. Frederik Storm then had to lead the board as the acting *praeses* for a year until Bugge was re-elected in 1849.

But by this time, Bugge seems to have lost both stamina and interest when it came to *Videnskabsselskabet*. His high level of activity in several fields—politics, the *Katedralskole*, science—had put great strains on his health for a number of years, and his physical decline was probably furthered by what we might call the public debate on his

---

[427] Øverås, 1949b: 232–239.
[428] Øverås, 1949b: 418–467.

moral conduct, which must have been painful. In 1850, he resigned from the post as *praeses*. A few months later, in the spring of 1851, he also resigned as headmaster. Shortly thereafter he moved to Bergen to become headmaster at the cathedral school there. He died the following year.

The conflicts at the end of the 1840s seem to uncover a crisis of identity in *Videnskabsselskabet* that went beyond mere personal animosity and political conflicts: What were the main tasks of the organization to be, and how should they be organized?

Schwach had written his short history of *Videnskabsselskabet* in the early 1840s, and had concluded that the main tasks should be twofold: First, it should work for the advancement of literature and science, and second, it should base its activities on the collections of *Videnskabsselskabet*, both the natural-objects and antiquarian collections, along with the library.[429] These thoughts were discussed again in 1849, when a commission was established to make recommendations for new statutes. The committee consisted of C.P. Essendrop (the librarian's assistant), O. Vullum and Frederik Storm. In its report, the committee pointed to the dual purpose of the 18th-century Society, both as scientific society and an advocate of industriousness and inventiveness.[430] The committee saw this as problematic, and through a close reading of the statutes of 1767, 1805, 1811, and 1815 found that the latter function, promotion of industriousness and inventiveness, was and had been of secondary importance to *Videnskabsselskabet*. What it suggested in its drafts of new statutes was that this part of its activities should be removed all together: "Science and utility are two so different things and one Society cannot promote the advancement of both, but must choose one and ignore the other, or develop a half-hearted activity in both fields."[431] The point was made that there were other institutions that could address these activities, and it was also claimed that concentrating solely on the scientific side of *Videnskabsselskabet*'s activities would be a return to the original intentions of the founding fathers. From the introduction to the recommendations for the statutes we also learn that certain members advocated the idea of turning *Videnskabsselskabet* into a museum for the northern part of the country, *det nordenfjelske*. The committee does not subscribe to this view, but regards it as an expression of a lack of ambition. However, the recommendations themselves emphasize the importance of the collections. Apart from this, the recommendations are surprisingly vague as to the task of *Videnskabsselskabet* and its officials. The main point, as explicitly expressed by the committee, is to simplify the statutes, and to focus on the scientific side of the activities.

The recommendations for the new statutes were not implemented. They were presented as the turmoil around the leadership peaked, and it was probably not found to be the right time to alter the structure of the Society. On the other hand, the main change advocated by the committee, namely stopping the support for industriousness

---

[429] *Skillingsmagasinet* 1840; a longer version was published in *DKNVS Skrifter i det 19de Aarhundrede*, Vol. 4, Trondheim, 1859: 1–28.

[430] *Forslag* (til nye statuter), Trondhjem, 1849.

[431] Ibid: 2.

and inventiveness, was silently accepted, as the awarding of prizes and medals for these purposes ceased after 1848.

Conclusions

The period from the late 1820s to the 1850s was a period when *Videnskabsselskabet* played an increasingly important role in financing scientific research and publication in Norway. Throughout the period the emphasis was shifted from the awarding of industriousness and the advancement of new techniques in the agricultural field to promoting the publication of scientific works. The 1830s and 1840s were especially important decades for this activity.

The story of *Videnskabsselskabet* as a financial source for science is a story both of success and failure. The success lies in the scale of the activity and its importance in the long run. But on the other hand, the scientific ideals promoted by the Society during this period were partly on the losing side in the intellectual and political struggle in Norway in the middle of the 19th century.

One of the reasons why *Videnskabsselskabet* could play such a crucial role in the financing of research and publication for several decades lay in the relative wealth of the organization and the relative poverty of the newly established Norwegian state. This lack of means had consequences for the funding of the University of Christiania, even though much prestige was invested in the institution. But the primary task for the institution was to educate the public servants of the state, and even though the professors were handsomely paid and the buildings of the university were impressive, bearing in mind the state finances, research and publication of scientific findings were not the main priority in the first decades of its existence. The funds of the Society were to an increasing degree used to finance scientific activities which fell outside what was expected or financed through the university budgets, but carried out by university professors. The funding of the works of the geologist Keilhau and historians Keyser and Munch fall into this category.

But the financing policy reached further. The staff at the university was relatively small, but the scientific interest of the educated groups did not necessarily wane once they had finished their education. Often, valuable research would be carried out by the civil servants—vicars, teachers, judges and so on—in their spare time. *Videnskabsselskabet* could help these efforts by providing means both for the actual works and their subsequent publication. The funding of the works of vicar Sars, or Schwachs' own numismatic work falls into this category. Moreover, and more unusually, *Videnskabsselskabet* could detect talent outside the established educated groups and encourage and provide means for their scientific work or publish it. The autodidact linguist Ivar Aasen and the non-established *studiousus* Niels Henrik Abel are good examples of this.

Another interesting—and successful—aspect of the financial activity is the cooperation not only with university staff, but also with parliament and government. In the case of the publication of a Norwegian *diplomatarium*, or old Norse laws, we see that the initial financing from *Videnskabsselskabet* was in part passed on, after the projects were well established, becoming direct grants from *Stortinget* or the government, and the work was being done by people employed by the university or the head of the national archives, thus obtaining their salaries through their regular position. This triangle of financing and working could prove to be highly successful. The success of this system, if we can call it that, was partly based on personal relations within the educated and political elites of the period. For example, Michael Sars and Frederik M. Bugge were friends; they had both studied at the University of Christiania a few years earlier. This was only natural; the number of public servants in Norway, including priests, officers, judges, and so on would rarely exceed 2000 persons, and they had a high degree of mobility. To use the directors of *Videnskabsselskabet* as an example: Bugge, in his 20-year-long career, was headmaster of the cathedral schools in Stavanger, Trondheim and Bergen, was a teacher at the *Katedralskole* in Christiania, and spent several years in Christiania working for the government committee on educational reform, and traveled extensively abroad. Schwach, a more sedate person, also worked as a lawyer in Arendal, judge in Trondheim and *sorenskriver* (city recorder) in Skien during his career. These men are typical examples. What this network of civil servants had in common was that they all had studied in Christiania (or Copenhagen), had been socialized into an elite culture, and tied personal bonds to their fellow students. Furthermore, their subsequent movements from one position to another would contribute to keeping these contacts and friendships alive. This would in effect constitute a national network which would facilitate both the flow of information on interesting projects and the decisions on whether to support these projects. The process initiating Ivar Aasen's grants illustrates this. Aasen presented himself in Bergen and got the bishop there to write about his ideas in the local newspaper. Then the bishop and *praeses* Bugge started corresponding on Aasens's project, which he then introduced to the board of directors and gained their approval.

The years around 1840 saw a generational shift in the university circles in Christiania. A younger generation was establishing itself, questioning the role of the university in the Norwegian society and what the common intellectual horizon of the elite should be. This group, dubbed "the intelligentsia," promoted a modernization of Norway in which the public servant should be a crucial player. The group stressed that the common intellectual frame of thought and action should be one of the practical arts, economics and living languages. Philosophy and dead languages were seen as hindrances on the path towards modernization. The main ideologue of this group, Anton Martin Schweigaard, had his power base both in *Stortinget* and the university, and from there he led what has been characterized as "the first successful student revolt" in Norway. Schweigaard's generation and compatriots were to dominate public life in Norway for several decades, and laid the foundation for the modernization of the country through the politics of an active state.[432]

---

[432] R. Slagstad, *De nasjonale strateger*, Oslo, 1998: 11–54.

The policies of *Videnskabsselskabet* under the leadership of Frederik M. Bugge and his co-directors were in part contrary to Schweigaard's and "the intelligentsia's" views. Where "the intelligentsia" promoted the practical arts and at best saw philosophical speculation as a waste of time, *Videnskabsselskabet* arranged essay competitions on metaphysical subjects, awarding medals to semi-obscure German philosophers. Where "the intelligensia" promoted the establishment of a modern industry and infrastructure, *Videnskabsselskabet* collected old coins. Where "the intelligentsia's" ideal was the detached and neutral civil servant, making rational decisions on the basis of all available information, *Videnskabsselskabet* awarded loud-mouthed rabble-rousers like Henrik Wergeland. Where "the intelligentsia" promoted the study of living languages such as German and English, *Videnskabsselskabet* financed studies of the rural dialects or the common linguistic roots of Norse and Sanskrit.

Bugge and Schweigaard themselves clashed personally over these questions when they both were working in the committee planning the future of education in Norway in the years around 1840. Even though Bugge had rather good backing in the committee for his views, Schweigaard managed to bury them in the political process following the committee's work.[433]

It is no exaggeration to say that what we can call the proponents of "the neo-classics," counting Bugge among them, lost the struggle over education and the core values of the modernization project of mid-19th-century Norway. On the other hand, while the directors of *Videnskabsselskabet* may have been out of touch with the dominating political trends as they manifested themselves both in parliament and at the University of Christiania in the 1840s, their activities had more common ground with other contemporary trends. The emphasis on national history, as expressed in the support given to the publication of medieval sources and Munch's and Keyser's work, proved to be in line with what one may call the ideological nation-building project of the mid-19th century. The same can be said when it comes to the support of the study of rural dialects and their connection with medieval Norse.

When placed in a context where the "intelligentsia" is viewed on the one hand, and the national romanticism on the other hand as two not opposing but complementing modernization projects, the activities of *Videnskabsselskabet* fall more into place. What would happen over time was that these two trends—the modernization project of "the intelligentsia" and the nation-building of the national romanticists—would develop into a bitter political and cultural struggle. By the 1870s and 1880s this was a struggle over the political system of Norway, and the dispute over what was seen as an old-fashioned and elitist regime of bureaucrats and a popular democratic alliance of the rural population and the radical intelligentsia in the urban areas would end in victory for the latter group. Seen in hindsight at the turn of the century, the politics of *Videnskabsselskabet* in the 1830s and 40s could be seen as a forerunner for these trends—supporting the now national icon Henrik Wergeland instead of the now un-

---

[433] Øverås, 1949b: 7–69.

patriotic Johan S. Welhaven, supporting Aasen's work for a national language in opposition to the Danish language of the elite, and supporting the rediscovery of the heroic history of the nation through the publishing of medieval sources and historical texts. But, as we shall see in Part III, *Videnskabsselskabet* had taken quite another path in the meantime.

New directions, 1850–1870

With the departure of both secretary Schwach and *praeses* Bugge in 1849 and 1850, respectively, *Videnskabsselskabet* lost two of its main strategists. Both had left Trondheim on a bitter note. Bugge might have had reason to feel himself hounded out of the city by overzealous moral guardians who had robbed him of his job as a headmaster of the *Katedralskole* and furthermore taken control of *Videnskabsselskabet*. Schwach, for his part, openly characterized his 20 years in Trondheim as his "Borealian exile," and generally lambasted the city for being bourgeois and provincial-minded in an unpublished foreword to a collection of his poems from his period here, entitled *Farvel til Trondhjem* (Farewell to Trondheim).[434]

In addition to losing these two prime movers, the Society had ended its practice of awarding industriousness and skills of the common people. What was left for the organization was to decide the future course, based on the existing structures and members. The process at the turn of the century had turned *Videnskabsselskabet* into an organization located on the periphery but with ambitions to fill a role as an independent institution for funding and publication of scientific research on a national level. The Society had managed to do this in the 1830s and 1840s, but it was obvious that such a role required a strategy of concentrating on those fields where the local members of *Videnskabsselskabet* had more than average competence and the ability to detect talent, or had a national network of scientists to lean on whenever this competence was lacking. In the 1850s these conditions were not present to the same degree, which provided alternative modes of action for the organization.

In the long run, the course taken was one discussed in the 1840s, namely to develop *Videnskabsselskabet* further on the basis of the collections, to become a regional museum. One of the architects behind this policy was Frederik Storm. Storm, a man who did not get elected—or did not want to be elected—to the highest position in *Videnskabsselskabet*, nevertheless must have been an able administrator and had clear ideas about the future of the organization. He had been involved in outlining a future for the collections of the Society in the 1840s, and seems to have played an important

---

[434] Stubhaug, 2002: 288–289.

role in pursuing this strategy in the following decades. His aim seems to have been to transform *Videnskabsselskabet* into a scientific institution based on its collection, similar to what had happened in Bergen. However, around 1850 the collections varied a great deal in quality, and *Videnskabsselskabet* still prioritized a policy of financing research on a national level.

The collections

From the turn of the century to the 1840s, the expansion of the natural collections was unplanned and haphazard. The core of the collection was from the period of Gunnerus and his more or less systematic collection of specimens from his diocese. But after Gunnerus's death, the state of the collection had been deteriorating.

Through the first half of the century, *Videnskabsselskabet* would sometimes give smaller grants to persons who collected specimens for the natural collections, as when *studiosus medicinae* Mellerborg collected minerals for the mineralogical collection in 1817.[435] Another example is Peter V. Deinboll (1783–1874), who was a vicar in eastern Finnmark until the mid 1820s, and also represented Finnmark in *Stortinget*. He received modest financial support from *Videnskabsselskabet* to collect plants in this region—a continuation of the organization's special interest in natural phenomena and resources in the northern regions.[436] In part these works could be the foundation for further work, such as Deinboll's collections which M.N. Blytt used in his work on Norwegian Flora in the middle of the century.[437] The question of how to organize the collections was at times discussed, but no action seems to have been taken.[438]

In the 1840s, there was a change towards a more active policy regarding the natural collections. In his short history of the Society published in the early 1840s, Schwach had emphasized that the tending of the collections was an obvious task for the organization. The reason for this must have been the contemporary success of Bergen Museum. Even though this idea was in part wishful thinking, the matter was seriously discussed. A committee, led by *vicepraeses* Frederik Storm, was appointed to make recommendations as to how to work with and add to the natural collections in the most efficient way.[439] In the report to the board of directors in 1843, the committee identified the ornithological section as the part of the collection that was in the most critical stage, both due to the sorry state of its stuffed birds, but also to the many gaps and holes that needed to be filled if the intention to have as complete a collection of Norwegian birds as possible was to be realized. The committee also pointed to the need for a trained

---

[435] *Årsberetning 1817* DKNVS Archive IV:g:1.
[436] *Årsberetning 1820 m.fl.* DKNVS Archive IV:g:1.
[437] Midbøe, 1960a: 332–338.
[438] *Papirer vedkommende den paatænkte Forandring i Localet 1832–1843* DKNVS Archive IV:i:1.
[439] Midbøe, 1960b: 9–55.

taxidermist who could aid *Videnskabsselskabet* in its work with the animal and bird collections, and suggested that they either headhunt one from Bergen or Christiania, or
pay for the education and training of a student from Trøndelag, who could then later
be employed by the organization. Neither of these two proposals was acted on immediately, but eventually the second option was chosen. In general, the committee was of
the opinion that the main purpose of the collections should be to exhibit the natural
wonders and phenomena of the northern Norwegian region, or in other words: To aspire to become a regional museum. As a result of the committee's report, the collection
of animals and birds was reorganized in 1844.[440] The mineral collection was reorganized at the same time as the rest of the collection.

John H. S. Siebke, a young medical doctor with strong interests in entomology, was
hired for several months to weed out superfluous and spoilt specimens. He reorganized
the collections in two sections: The domestic and the exotic sections. This was the foundation for enlarging the collection in a more systematic manner. He also authored a
catalog of this part of the collection, citing name, place of origin and the name of the
donor. After the cleanup undertaken by Siebke, relatively immediately the field recommended by the committee, ornithology, was enlarged. Thus, *Videnskabsselskabet* began
investing heavily in birds, eggs, and nests. The very same year, 330 birds, 132 eggs, and
16 nests were added to the ornithological collection.[441] Other additions were made in
the following years, though not in the same magnitude.[442]

At the same time, the research into marine life was continued. Daniel Danielssen
and Johan Koren of the Bergen Museum did their main work for *Videnskabsselskabet* in
the 1850s. Their contribution to the collections was marine animals from the northern
part of the western coast, the coastal area adjacent to Trøndelag in the south. Their
work for the Society was a side-effect of their work for Bergen Museum, but the financing from Trondheim probably contributed to Bergen Museum being able to collect samples from a larger stretch of the western coast than would otherwise have been
possible. An aborted project in the same vein was the mapping of marine animals in the
Hardanger fjord south of Bergen, to be carried out by Peder Christian Asbjørnsen. Asbjørnsen (1812–1885) is mostly remembered as a folklorist and collector of folk-tales,
but also pursued an academic career within marine zoology in the 1850s. However, very
little came out of this research financially aided by *Videnskabsselskabet*.[443]

Frederik Storm and his committee had pointed out the need for a trained taxidermist to handle the collections of birds and other animals. In 1857, this ambition came
one step closer to realization as *Videnskabsselskabet* made room in its budget to pay for
the education and training of a young man to fill this position.[444] The taxidermist-to-
be was Wilhelm Storm, Frederik Storm's son. As soon as his training in Christiania was

---

[440] *Årsberetning* 1844 DKNVS Archive IV:g:1.
[441] *Årsberetning* 1844 DKNVS Archive IV:g:1.
[442] *Årsberetning* 1847, 1848, 1858, 1859, 1860, 1861, 1863 DKNVS Archive IV:g:1
[443] Midbøe, 1960a: 367–371.
[444] *Årsberetning* 1857 DKNVS Archive IV:g:1.

completed two years later, he was employed by the Society. His annual pay was 60 *spesiedaler*, half of that of the librarian. Eventually, Storm would become increasingly engaged in research and publications in a variety of fields. But he also took his work as conservator seriously, as we can see from the sharp increase in *Videnskabsselskabet*'s expenses when it came to glass cages, distilled alcohol, shelves and so on in the following years.[445] Storm's ambitions went beyond the tending of the collections—he wanted to do research, and one visible result of this inclination was that the Society equipped a modern laboratory. For instance, in 1862 a brand new microscope was purchased.[446] It was, however, not until the late 1870s that Storm was in a position where this ambition would be realized.

It is worth noting that by 1860 the proposals and recommendations made by the 1843 committee had more or less been met. The natural collections had the northern part of the country as their focal point, the ornithological collection was given close attention, and a taxidermist had been employed. Frederik Storm must have been pleased, both by the fact that the program set by the committee had been fulfilled, and that his son had been employed by *Videnskabsselskabet* as its first paid conservator and researcher. One feature of *Videnskabsselskabet*'s collections was the natural-objects collections. Of growing importance were also the antiquarian and numismatic collections, which had been given less attention in the 1843 committee's work.

The Society had become the owner of a large collection of coins and medals, in part through a set of coincidental circumstances. The secretary of the organization, Conrad N. Schwach, was a passionate collector of coins, and through a rather unfortunate incident in 1837, when he was held responsible for a financial loss for the organization, he donated this collection as compensation. By this time his collection had already been deposited in *Videnskabsselskabet*'s care for several years, so this transfer of ownership was more a mere formality than a penalty.[447] Now Schwach's collection was integrated into an existing one. We know that the existing collection was reorganized immediately after Schwach's arrival in Trondheim and his acceptance into the Society, and in the following years, money was spent on expanding the collection.[448] By 1832, the collection consisted of approximately 2000 coins.[449] Over the next 10 to 15 years, this would more than double. While this could be done by buying from private persons, the large expansions of the collection mainly came through buying or trading with the Universities of Christiania and Copenhagen.[450] The most intense interest in coins seems to have been limited to Schwach's period as the head of *Videnskabsselskabet*. Among his proposals was that there should be a separate numismatic section of the library.[451]

---

[445] *Årsberetning 1860* DKNVS Archive IV:g:1.

[446] *Årsmelding 1862* DKNVS Archive IV:g:1.

[447] *Direksjonsprotokoll 1826–55:* p. 125 DKNVS Archive II:3.

[448] *Årsmelding, 1831, 1832, 1833, 1834* DKNVS Archive IV:g:1.

[449] *Årsmelding 1832.* DKNVS Archive IV:g:1.

[450] In 1844 alone, it was expanded by more than 1800 coins through buying duplicates from the collection of the university in Christiania. *Årsmelding 1844.*

[451] *Direksjonsprotokoll 1826–55:* p. 365 DKNVS Archive II:3.

Schwach also contributed a history of Scandinavian coins, which was financed and published by *Videnskabsselskabet*.[452] After Schwach's departure from Trondheim, the numismatic collection still had a degree of importance, but additions were more infrequent and smaller than in the 1840s.

The antiquarian collection was to become a key part of both *Videnskabsselskabet*'s collection and the understanding of its tasks in the late 19th century. From the 1820s to the 1860s we can see a gradual change in the perception of antiquarian artifacts. In brief the interests went from collecting the extraordinary to collecting the representative. The reception of antiquarian findings, donated by the public, was a regular feature from the 1820s, duly noted in the yearly reports to the king. The early donations were often accompanied by attempts to connect them to famous persons from the Norse sagas. For instance, in 1833 one of the items received was a gold ring found close to Einar Tambarskjelve's estate.[453] Einar had been a famous local chieftain from the first half of the 11th century, and according to the 13th-century Icelandic historian Snorri Sturlusson, he was a central political player in the processes leading to the establishment of a Norwegian kingdom independent of Danish influence in this period. Possessing a gold ring which might have been on his finger was obviously a treat. At times, during the period up to the 1850s, *Videnskabsselskabet* would also give small funds in return for receiving reports and artifacts from amateur excavations of ancient burial mounds in the Trøndelag region.[454]

But by the 1840s, attitudes were changing. We now see an interest in preserving buildings which were more or less in a state of decline or at risk of deteriorating. For instance, in 1845 cand. theol. Haugen received 25 *spesiedaler* for his work to hinder the deterioration of the ruins of the medieval Cistercian monastery Tautra, located on the island of the same name in the Trondheim fjord, where he was a private tutor at the time.[455] Similarly, two years later *Videnskabsselskabet* funded the work to save an ancient dwelling house made of timber in Rennebu, some 70 km south of Trondheim.[456] The house in question was situated along the main road leading northwards to Trondheim, and had served as a lodging house for travelers for centuries. Drawings of this building were made at the same time, and copies of these were sent to the museum in Bergen. Also, an ancient drinking horn was purchased from the same farm. A point was made that several Norwegian kings, including the recently deceased Carl Johan, had visited the farm in question, and it was at least implied that they had drunk from the horn.

A monument of more grand proportions in the field of interest of the directors was the Trondheim cathedral, *Nidarosdomen*. This medieval structure was partly in ruins in the early 19th century, as the ravages of war and fire and rebuilding due to the demands of Lutheran liturgy had changed it far from its original shape. Schwach seems to have

---

[452] Schwach, 1842.
[453] *Årsberetning 1833* DKNVS Archive IV:g:1.
[454] Midbøe, 1960a: 286–292.
[455] *Årsberetning 1845* DKNVS Archive IV:g:1.
[456] *Årsberetning 1847* DKNVS Archive IV:g:1.

been particularly fond of the building. He published a brief description and history of the cathedral in 1838.[457] This was not the first description and history of the cathedral. Gerhard Schønning, one of the founding fathers of *Videnskabsselskabet*, had published an extensive history and description of the cathedral in 1762.[458] Compared to Schønning's 370 pages, Schwach's mere 40-page leaflet was more of a guidebook, and indeed Schwach had it as part of his repertoire to guide interested and educated travelers to the marvels of the cathedral. Ivar Aasen, for instance, notes in his diary that he went on a guided tour of *Nidarosdomen* with Schwach.[459] Schwach's book also contributed to a renewed interest in the cathedral, and throughout the 1850s and 60s this interest led to a grand project of reconstructing the cathedral to its original 14th-century style. Some of the main proponents of this were the bishops in Trondheim, Hans J. Darre and Andreas Grimelund, who both were also *praeses* in the 1850s and 1860s.

This interest in the preservation of ancient buildings and monuments was a trend of the times, both internationally and nationally. In Norway, this manifested itself in the establishment of an association for the preservation of buildings and monuments, *Foreningen til norske fortidsminnesmerkers bevaring*, in 1844. A local chapter of this association was established, and members of *Videnskabsselskabet* would naturally also be engaged in the association, donating liberally of their findings to the collections of the Society. There was a degree of latent distrust during the first decades. As more or less valuable treasures were unearthed, there was a considerable amount of pressure to donate these to the university museum in Christiania, which regarded itself as a national institution.[460] This was contrary to the ambitions of *Videnskabsselskabet*, as it had its own antiquarian collection, albeit in a semi-chaotic state. Not until the late 1860s was there a serious attempt at making an overview and catalog of the antiquarian collection.

By the mid 1850s the point was made that the Society should collect antiquarian specimens from the whole northern part of the country in a more systematic manner.[461] To ensure this, it should be willing to pay symbolically for the items received. As this strategy was followed, the antiquarian collection grew rapidly. In 1865, half of the yearly report to the king consisted of a list of antiquarian objects acquired in the preceding year, including a gold ring with inlaid precious stones, a dagger, a silver ring, iron rods and so on.[462] On the other hand, this posed a problem. The antiquarian collection was the responsibility of the librarian. However, the workload for the librarian just with books alone was getting to be more than enough for one person, and the antiquarian collection was therefore neglected to the point that no satisfying inventory of it was kept. This changed when the new headmaster of the *Katedralskole*, Karl Rygh

---

[457] C.N. Schwach, *Throndhjems Domkirkes Historie og Beskrivelse i kort Udtog*, Trondhjem, 1838.
[458] G. Schøning, *Beskrivelse over den tilforn meget prægtige og vidtberømte Dom-Kirke i Throndhjem, egentlig kaldet Christ-Kirken*, Trondhjem, 1762.
[459] Øverås, 1949b: 310–311.
[460] Midbøe 1960b: 56–70.
[461] *Årsberetning 1855* DKNVS Archive IV:g:1.
[462] *Årsberetning 1865* DKNVS Archive IV:g:1.

(1839–1915) was elected a member in 1866 and immediately started campaigning for the establishment of a position of conservator for the antiquarian collection along the same lines as the established position of conservator for the natural-objects collection. This meant transferring the responsibility for the antiquarian collection from the librarian, who at the time in addition to the books and the antiquarian collection also was responsible for the instruments and models, according to the statutes.

The library

The library had in many ways been the core of *Videnskabsselskabet*'s collections since the 1770s. By the 1840s the new reading room had opened, and the library was also open to a more general public. Usually, approximately 150 to 200 visitors would borrow approximately 2000 to 2500 volumes from the library in the course of a year. The popularity of the reading room was also so evident that it was decided to open it twice a week from 1851, and a third day was considered.[463] By 1860, the library was open five days a week; loans were confined to two days a week and the reading room was open the other three.[464] The increase in the number of borrowers through the 1860s was impressive—by the middle of the decade, the number had nearly doubled to around 300. But in 1862, the first public library in Trondheim opened, and this seems to have halted the increase in the number of borrowers in the Society's library somewhat, even though the public library was aimed at other social strata than the users of *Videnskabsselskabet*'s library. From the mid 1860s, the number of borrowers and borrowed books remained stable. The library loans were not restricted to people residing in Trondheim. Members from out of town would also borrow books—for instance, residents of Stavanger or Tromsø.[465] The most popular topics were history, philology, and fiction. History alone would account for more than half of the library loans in the years such statistics were kept.[466] This was of course in line with the policy of acquirements followed by Tellefsen, who had given historical literature high priority.

By the mid 1850s, it was clear that the current staffing of the library was not sufficient. Essendrop had seen it as his main task to organize the library through his system of filing cards, and had not continued as assistant to Tellefsen when this work was finished in 1848 (see p. 151). In 1856 the headmaster at the *Katedralskole*, Hans A. Müller, alerted the board of directors that manuscripts were missing from the collection, and that the procedures for library loans were far too lax.[467] At this time, Tellefsen was 82, and the board decided to let him go with a yearly pension of 50 *spesiedaler*, not much less than his salary of 70 *spesiedaler*. This was the first case of *Videnskabsselskabet* giving one

---

[463] *Årsmelding 1851, 1856* DKNVS Archive IV:g:1.
[464] *Årsmelding 1860, 1863* DKNVS Archive IV:g:1.
[465] *Årsmelding 1853* DKNVS Archive IV:g:1.
[466] *Årsmelding 1858* DKNVS Archive IV:g:1.
[467] *Direksjonsprotokollen 1855–98*: p. 23 DKNVS Archive II:4.

of its employees such a pension, and reflects the important role Tellefsen had played in the library for decades. Tellefsen died shortly after he left his job as librarian. Müller was now appointed librarian, with a yearly pay of 120 *spesiedaler*; an amount which probably reflected the workload of the position better than Tellefsen's modest salary had done.

Müller did not remain in his position, as he died after only two years. He was followed in 1859 by Sven T.W. Mosling (1818–1897). Mosling was a teacher at the *Borgerlige realskole* and chief editor of the most influential newspaper in Trondheim at the time, *Adresseavisen*. He was elected to membership in *Videnskabsselskabet* in 1852, was elected librarian in 1859 and secretary in 1866. Together with Frederik Storm, he was also a member of the building committee responsible for the construction of the Society's new building in the early 1860s (see below). It is not an exaggeration to say that he was a powerful man in the leadership of the organization during this period, and he would come to clash with other strong personalities on the future course of *Videnskabsselskabet* in the following decade.

Mosling's work as a librarian initially consisted of getting things in order after Tellefsen's long period in that position.[468] Tellefsen's main interests had been the books and the manuscripts. But part of the librarian's responsibilities was, according to the still-functioning 1815 statutes, to oversee *Videnskabsselskabet*'s collection of instruments, models, and antiquarian artifacts. The collection of instruments seems to have been in disarray by the 1850s. Mosling characterizes them as a heap of instruments "in bits and pieces thrown about and mostly completely defective," "no longer worth the name instruments" of types "which are unknown to me, and which I gather have gone out of use a long time ago."[469]

Another challenge Mosling faced was the responsibility for the antiquarian collection. This was not his main interest, but he aggressively tackled Karl Rygh's challenging suggestion of establishing a separate position of conservator for this part of the collection. Mosling's violent reactions to Rygh's suggestion probably had little to do with any specific interest in the antiquarian collection, as he seems to have neglected this part of his duties. One of the points the two men clashed over was the placing of a rune stone on the floor in the entrance to the library—visitors literally had to step on it when entering the library, which of course endangered the runic inscriptions. This did not show a very high level of concern for the artifacts by the librarian. What probably provoked him was the possibility of a "degradation" of the librarian's position through what could be described almost as a coup. Eventually, Mosling and Rygh recognized a common interest in transferring the responsibility for the antiquarian collection from the librarian to a conservator, which is what was done in 1869.

---

[468] W.K. Støren, "Bibliotekets ledere 1768–1993," H. Nissen & M. Aase (eds.), *Til opplysning. Universitetsbibiloteket i Trondheim 1768–1993*, Trondheim, 1993: 34–36.
[469] Midbøe, 1960a: 323.

The support, the public, and the publications

Throughout the 1850s and 1860s, *Videnskabsselskabet* continued to finance the cataloging of the resources in the northernmost part of the country. In Tromsø, the head forester Johannes Norman and the teacher Karl Petersen were regularly given money to support their collecting and cataloging of plants and minerals, respectively.[470]

Johannes Norman (1823–1903) studied the vegetation in eastern Finnmark on paid assignment for the Society. One interesting fact about Norman is that he was originally employed by the University of Christiania, but resigned his position in protest against what he felt was a too practical approach to botany—he wanted to do systematic research and cataloging, while the head of the botanical garden in Christiania, Frederik C. Schübeler, was more inclined to look at the practical benefits of the discipline. Norman's main opponent in this controversy, Schübeler, had applied for economic support for his research from *Videnskabsselskabet* a few years earlier, but had been turned down. Johannes Norman had Troms and Finnmark as his official district as head forester and could combine his trips there with work for the Society.[471]

Karl Pettersen (1826–1890) was also at odds with the established authorities at the University of Christiania in his position as a teacher and amateur geologist in Tromsø. The controversies were of a personal nature, where personal conflicts between professor B.M. Keilhau and his student and successor Theodor Kierulf involved younger geologists around them in an environment of mutual suspicion, envy, and hostility not unknown to academic institutions.[472] As in the case of Johan Norman, Pettersen's financial rescue came in the form of grants from *Videnskabsselskabet*, and the opportunity to publish in *Skrifter*. Pettersen is an interesting person in relation to *Videnskabsselskabet* also for another reason. He was to become a key player in the organization of a museum in Tromsø in 1872, and its first director. The establishment of a museum in Tromsø followed the same pattern as in Bergen 50 years earlier: a combination of personal interest and initiative from a few men with financial funding from the local authorities in the region and additional funding from the merchant elite and wealthier civil servants, combined with a promise of a yearly contribution from the royal house.[473] The museum was established in 1872, opened to the public in 1874, and employed its first conservator in 1876.

By the early 1870s, *Videnskabsselskabet* thus had given grants to the *praeses* of the highly successful Bergen Museum and the first director of the new museum in Tromsø, a city of a much more modest size than Trondheim, and with far less educational

---

[470] *Kassadagbok 1856–78*: 02.04.1862, 23.06.1868 DKNVS Archive II:14, *Årsberetning* 1863, 1865 DKNVS Archive IV:g:1, *Direksjonsprotokoll* 1855–97: 01.05.1865, 24.04.1866 DKNVS Archive II:4.

[471] Holmboe, J., "Norman, Johannes Musæus," NBL, Vol. X, Oslo, 1949: 222–225.

[472] Bugge, C., "Pettersen, Karl Johan," NBL, Vol. XI, Oslo, 1952: 90–91.

[473] N.A. Ytreberg, *Tromsø bys historie, vol. 1*, Oslo, 1946: 644–646, A. Andersen, *Handelsfolk og fiskerbønder 1794–1900. Tromsø gjennom 10000 år, vol. 2*, Tromsø, 1994: 403–404.

institutions, educated people and financial resources. This must have given the board of directors in Trondheim food for thought.

The interest in language and history of the 1830s and 1840s was still present in the following decades, although perhaps not as intensely. P.A. Munch continued to receive support until his death in 1863. *Videnskabsselskabet* also financed Andreas Erlandsen's work on Norwegian bishops after the reformation,[474] and the young historian Ludvig Daae (1834–1910) was given ample grants to undertake archival research in Copenhagen in order to shed light on Norwegian history during the period of unification with Denmark.[475] In addition to this, the bright young linguist Sophus Bugge (1833–1907) was given travel grants in the early 1860s.[476] Bugge was to become an important contributor to the studies of runic inscriptions, Norse language, and Norse mythology in the following decades.

One interesting project funded by *Videnskabsselskabet* in 1862 was a travel grant to the poet author and journalist Aasmund Olavsson Vinje to study the social and economic conditions in England and Scotland.[477] Vinje (1818–1870), of a modest peasant background, was a pioneer in the development of modern journalism in Norway, both through his work for a number of newspapers and journals, but mainly through his own journal *Dølen* in the 1860s. Vinje was also a pioneer in using Ivar Aasen's (re)constructed dialect-based Norwegian language *landsmål* as a literary language (see p. 136–138). Through his use of *landsmål* in his reportage, book-reviews, poetry, essays, debates, and polemics, he became a key figure in establishing *landsmål* as a literary language for all uses.

Vinje's at times radical political ideas might have been among the factors that made him an unlikely candidate for financial support from *Videnskabsselskabet*, but on the other hand, it might have been in the Society's interest to support the further development of the linguistic work initiated by Ivar Aasen. Thus he received combined grants from the government and the Society which enabled him to embark on a one-year journey in England and Scotland. He reported extensively from this journey in *Dølen*, and collected some of his impressions in a book published in English in 1863.[478] Although Vinje was a great admirer of British culture and the British legal system, his descriptions from his journey were rather harsh. He was a stark critic of the social and economic injustices he found on his journey, and his writings on these themes can be considered to be a pointed criticism of modern capitalism, as it manifested itself in contemporary

---

[474] *Årsmelding 1858* DKNVS Archive IV:g:1. Erlandsen, A., *Biographiske efterretninger om Geistligheden i Throndhjems Stift*, Christiania, 1844–55, Rygh, E., *Alfabetisk Register til A. Erlandsens Efterretninger over Throndhjems og Tromsø stifters Geistelighed*, Christiania, 1860.

[475] *Kassadagbok 1856–78*: 11.11.1861, 10.05. 1867. DKNVS Archive II:14, *Årsmelding 1861* DKNVS Archive IV:g:1.

[476] *Årsmelding 1861* DKNVS Archive IV:g:1.

[477] *Årsmelding 1862* DKNVS Archive IV:g:1, *Direksjonsprotokoll 1855–1898*: 30.05.1862 DKNVS Archive II:4.

[478] A.O. Vinje, *A Norseman's View of Britain and the British*, Edinburgh, 1863.

Britain. This might perhaps be one reason why his application for further grants to embark on a similar journey in America was rejected the following year.[479]

Videnskabsselskabet did not pursue its interest in art and literature in an organized manner after 1850. At times, some of the more nationally celebrated authors would receive travel grants, such as the Nobel laureate-to-be Bjørnstjerne Bjørnsson, who traveled to Rome at the Society's expense in the 1860s. Bjørnson also recommended that the directors give grants to the semi-established playwright Henrik Ibsen, also residing in Italy.[480] But the trend towards developing an identity as a society of arts and letters, which might have been nascent in the 1840s, seems to have been halted very early. Most likely the reason for this was the departure and retirement from the affairs of *Videnskabsselskabet* of the literary-minded Schwach and Bugge. On the other hand, the support of *Trondheim Kunstforening* continued undiminished until the early 1860s. Some discussion on the nature of science and art must also have taken place, as the board of directors decided to give a grant to a Mr. Udbye so that he could educate himself further in the art of lithography, while a similar request from J.P. Lange for a grant to study new techniques of photography was rejected on the grounds that this was not science, and obviously not art.[481]

In the 1840s the directors had at times contributed to the public debate on political and financial matters through essay contests and through speeches by the *praeses* at the public meeting on the king's birthday. This was an activity that was not on the agenda in the 1850s and 1860, although it would surface occasionally, as when *praeses* Grimelund elaborated on the topic "On science and its influence on practical life," followed by Ludvig Daae's reflections on "Truth in science is usefulness in life" on the king's birthday in 1866.[482] The grant to A.O. Vinje (see above) might also be seen as a contribution to the public debate on the political and socio-economic issues of the day.

Videnskabsselskabet had stopped its work for enlightenment through prizes and medals by the late 1840s. On the other hand, it went in another direction when it came to funding journals. From its initial support for scientific journals in the 1840s, it also started supporting the magazine *Folkevennen* (Friend of the people) in 1860, both directly and by buying a number of subscriptions for recently established public libraries in the Trøndelag region. *Folkevennen* was established in 1851 as a magazine aimed at enlightening the common people on various subjects of both a practical and spiritual nature. This can be seen as a sort of continuation of the enlightenment side of *Videnskabsselskabet*'s activities, although not a very strong one.

The 1860s were also a period of experiments in public lectures. The new librarian, Sven Mosling, held public lectures on astronomy and meteorology.[483] Furthermore,

---

[479] *Dirkesjonsprotokoll 1855–1898:* 20.08.1863 DKNVS Archive II:4.
[480] *Direksjonsprotokoll 1855–1897:* 28.10.1865 DKNVS Archive II:4.
[481] *Direksjonsprotokoll 1855–97:* 07.10.1859 DKNVS Archive II:4.
[482] *Direksjonsprotokoll 1855–1898:* 03.05.1866 "Om Videnskaben og dens Indflydelse pa det praktiske Liv," "Det sanne i Videnskaben er det nyttige for Livet." DKNVS Archive II:4.
[483] *Årsmelding 1858* DKNVS Archive IV:g:1.

the board of directors now began to regard the natural collection as something the public should have a share in. Mosling therefore regularly held what we may call guided tours of the collection, and by 1861 the collection was open to the public twice a week.[484] In addition to this, the mineral collection was used as a part of the curriculum at the *borgerlige realskole* from the 1850s.[485] By the late 1860s, *Videnskabsselskabet* tried to organize public lectures on a larger scale. The hope was that these would be so successful that the great hall of the newly established Gymnastic Society, *Trondheim Turnforening*, was rented for the purpose. Having to pay rent for this location, and nurturing a wish to be able to pay the lecturer a modest amount, the board of directors felt that they had to charge an admission fee—but, on the other hand, they donated free tickets lavishly to the workers' association, the artisans' association, the teachers' association and the association of lower-ranking officers.[486] However, these lectures do not seem to have become a regular feature.

The publication of *Videnskabsselskabet*'s *Skrifter* underwent a gradual change from the late 1860s. From 1817, a full volume had been presented every 10 to 12 years. But beginning with the volume published in 1868, nine years after the preceding one, the volumes began to appear with increased regularity: 1868, 1870, 1874, and more or less annually from 1878.

The content of the volumes also underwent a significant change. The three volumes from 1868 to 1874 almost solely consisted of publications based on research either financed by the Society, or based on its collections. The main contributors in these volumes were Karl Pettersen and Johannes Normann from Tromsø, who published their botanical and geological findings and results in nine articles all together. In addition to this, a catalogue of the antiquarian collection of *Videnskabsselskabet* by Karl Rygh was a major contribution to the 1874 volume, a first result of his new responsibility as conservator of the antiquarian collection. The remaining part of these three volumes consists of two historic sources—Knud Leem's "History of Finmark" from the late 18th century and count Schmettow's correspondence (1813–14), a report on chemical experiments at the Agrarian College (*Landbrukshøyskolen*) at Aas[487]—and an inventory of Broder Lysholm Knudtzon's gifts to *Videnskabsselskabet* on his death.

The preceding volumes had been a mixture of writings by members and contributions from outside *Videnskabsselskabet* on a variety of topics, seemingly with little planning or editorial work. The strategy seems to have been to publish the manuscripts as they arrived and were found fit for publication. From the 1868 volume onwards, the topics may still vary, but the core of the publication is the collection or the grants of the Society. The emerging profile of *Skrifter* from 1868 is comparable to what the yearbook of the Bergen Museum was to become somewhat later, and that *Videnskabsselskabet* also was to refine.

---

[484] *Årsmelding 1860, 1861* DKNVS Archive IV:g:1.
[485] *Årsmelding 1855* DKNVS Archive IV:g:1.
[486] *Direksjonsprotokoll 1855–1897*: 19.05.1869, 13.11.1869, 17.11.1869, 20.11.1869 DKNVS Archive II:4.
[487] Established in 1859 to educate agronomists and do research for the advancement of agriculture.

The museum in Tromsø followed the same path; from 1878 it published a yearbook based on research done at the museum or by scientists working in the polar region.[488]

The circulation of *Skrifter* was modest: 300 copies were printed. Of these, three were mandatory copies to be given to the ministry of ecclesiastical affairs and the University Library in Christiania. A further 18 copies were sent to learned societies or academies abroad as a part of an exchange network, and an additional approximately 30 copies were sent to subscribers in Norway, mainly in Christiania or as a part of a national network of exchange.[489] The intention was to sell the remaining 240 copies to members or other interested parties.

Towards a local society

Videnskabsselskabet was to take on a more parochial character in the 1850s and 1860s. One aspect of this was the membership profile. While in the 1830s and 1840s an average of 11 to 12 members had been elected annually, this was to be reduced to around eight members annually in the following two decades. Moreover, these members would to an increasing degree be inhabitants of Trondheim, mainly men from the merchant group or civil servants of different positions. The number of members outside *det nordenfjeldske* would be halved, and the election of foreign members would more or less cease—all together only eight members from outside Norway were elected between 1850 and 1869. This stands in strong contrast to the 1830s and 1840s. F.M. Bugge especially managed to get his international contacts elected to membership after his travels in Europe in the late 1830s. And although these foreign members hardly contributed to the work of *Videnskabsselskabet*, except through the books they donated to the library, it still gave some sort of proof that the Society belonged to an international scientific community. Attempts to revitalize a trading network of specimens and artifacts, by electing the members in Calcutta in the 1840s, and ambitions of participating in multi-national research projects by electing the members of the "Recherche" expedition in 1838, points in the same direction.

More significant than the loss of foreign members, however, were the looser ties to the academic and scientific environments in Sweden. A mere four Swedish members were elected for a 20-year period from 1850, compared to 23 in the preceding 20 years. One reason might be that the Royal Swedish Academy of Sciences also was in a transition phase at this time, from a society based primarily on publication and participating in international networks to a museum and a focus on polar exploration.[490] Nevertheless, this can hardly account for the disinterest in keeping up the ties to Swedish scientific communities at the time.

---

[488] Ytreberg, 1946: 645.

[489] *Direksjonsprotokoll 1855–1878:* 11.02.1860 DKNVS Archive II:4.

[490] T. Frängsmyr (ed.), *Science in Sweden. The royal Swedish academy of sciences 1739–1989*, Canton, Massachusetts, 1989.

The reason for this isolation from the international, and in part also the national, scientific community is hard to explain. Most likely, much of the answer again lies in the departure of Bugge and Schwach. The leadership in the 1850s might seem to have a more limited network and a more cautious public profile. In the 1850s and 1860s, the *praeses* would normally also be the bishop in Trondheim. Thus, Bugge's successor was Bishop Hans Jørgen Darre (1803–1874), who was *praeses* for five years (1850–55), and later, Bishop Andreas Grimelund (1812–1896) would occupy the same position. Both these men had a rather challenging task of upholding the religious unity of their diocese in a period of both external challenges in the form of competing religious societies, and aggressive lay movements within the established framework of the state church. It seems that this might have taken both a great deal of energy, and called for a cautious public profile in contrast to the more outspoken and slightly controversial style of the preceding leadership.

It seems that *Videnskabsselskabet* in this period had a more collective leadership, giving more influence to the other members of the board. It also seems that Frederik Storm continued to be an influential person, participating in such important committees as the committee for revising the statutes, and the building committee. Sven Mosling also became very influential through his position as librarian, secretary and member of the building committee. What these persons shared was a more local scope of action, not least Mosling, through his engagement as editor of the local newspaper *Adresseavisen* and a growing engagement in local politics. Mosling did not have a university education from Christiania, but was educated at the polytechnic college in Copenhagen, and was more peripheral to the networks of the educated civil servants, while Storm at this time had spent most of his life in the same position in the same town.

Perhaps the most important factor that both contributed to and which resulted in a shift in the scope of action from attempting to be a national institution with international contacts to a more local one was the establishment of an academy in Christiania, *Videnskabs-selskabet i Christiania*, later renamed *Det Norske Vitenskapsakademi*.

There had clearly been frustration among the university employees and the university-educated groups in the capital that there was no scientific society or academy in Christiania. When this frustration was aired, two conclusions were usually drawn: *Videnskabsselskabet* should move from Trondheim to Christiania, or an independent academy should be established in Christiania. The idea of moving *Videnskabsselskabet* to Christiania had been discussed in the early 1820s (see p. 117), and the idea resurfaced in the late 1830s.[491] The main problem, of course, was that there was no interest in Trondheim for these proposals, and on the latter occasion, its current existence was defended by supporting, among others, scientists at the University of Christiania.

A large portion of the potential members of a scientific academy in Christiania were, of course, already members of *Videnskabsselskabet* in Trondheim. This makes some of their rhetoric concerning the absence of an academy seem somewhat peculiar—the rhetoric exclaimed that Norway had no academy or scientific society, a dis-

---

[491] L. Amundsen, *Det norske videnskaps-Akademi i Oslo 1857–1957*, Oslo, 1957: 18–19.

grace to the nation in the international scientific community, "Norway" in this context obviously meaning "Christiania."[492] But rhetoric aside, the problem was real, as the majority of professional scientists had no opportunity to participate in the meetings of *Videnskabsselskabet* in Trondheim or in other ways influence the priorities of the leadership in any significant way. There was obviously a need for a forum where the scientific staff of the university and its intellectual hinterland could meet socially and exchange information and results outside the restraints of the established university structures and routines, and perhaps also establish channels for publication that could be more efficient than relying on the editorial whims of the leadership in the Trondheim Society.

The conclusion of these frustrations and discussions was the establishment of a scientific society in Christiania in the spring of 1857. This society had a rather modest financial basis for their first decades of its existence, and its activities were mostly restricted to meetings where new results would be presented and debated, and the publication of a series of *Skrifter* from 1858.

It is interesting to note that double membership between the societies in Trondheim and Christiana was a common trait for the first decades. Of the 29 constituting members in Christiania, 16 were already members of *Videnskabsselskabet* in Trondheim, six were to be elected to membership only three days after the establishment of the *Videnskabs-selskabet i Christiania*, and three more in the next few years. Only four of the founding members in Christiania were never members in Trondheim, most notably Johan S. Welhaven, whose sins from the 1830s obviously were neither forgotten nor forgiven (see p. 141).[493] Among those constituting *Vitenskabs-Selskabet i Christiania* were long-time members and recipients of funds from *Videnskabsselskabet*, such as Michael Sars, Christopher Holmboe, Balthazar M. Keilhau and Peter A. Munch. The trend continued in the following years; of the 94 members elected to the Christiania society from 1857 to 1871, 69 were already or would become members of *Videnskabsselskabet* in Trondheim.[494]

Interestingly, the leadership in Trondheim was not elected to membership in Christiania. Actually, none of *Videnskabsselskabet*'s members residing in Trondheim were elected to membership in Christiania. This can probably be explained by the membership profile and policy of election in the Christiania society. Even though their rallying cry had been the need of a national academy, as opposed to what was considered a regional Society in Trondheim, *Videnskabs-Selskabet i Christiania* was to become a very local organization, primarily focusing on the university. In 1877, only 13 of the 84 domestic members were living outside the capital.[495] Tellingly, of the few members of the Christiania society who were not members of *Videnskabsselskabet* in Trondheim, the majority were non-scientists, such as the teachers at the *Katedralskole* in Christiania.

---

[492] Amundsen, 1957: 1–29.
[493] Amundsen, 1957: 51–59, Schmidt, 1960.
[494] Amundsen, 1957: 51–163, Schmidt, 1960.
[495] Amundsen, 1957: 134.

What did the establishment of *Videnskabs-Selskabet i Christiania* mean for *Videnskabsselskabet* in the long run? There are two ways of looking at this: The Christiania Society as a competitor, or as a complementary institution. The competition with the Christiania Society was potentially mainly over public funding. There was reason to believe that funding for *Videnskabs-Selskabet i Christiania* could have a negative influence on the funding of *Videnskabsselskabet*, which was still receiving the annual 528 *spesiedaler* from the government as had been the case since 1815. The Christiania Society applied to the government for annual funding of 1000 *spesiedaler*, and with a parliament bent on as little public expenditure as possible, funding of such a magnitude could threaten the funding of the Society in Trondheim. But here events took an unexpected turn. The political life of the second half of the 19th century partly consisted of antagonism between a broad coalition of representatives of the rural society and radical urban groups, on the one hand, and the conservative urban middle and upper class in alliance with the nationwide network of civil servants on the other. The case of funding an academic elite institution in Christiania became a typical point of dispute in parliament, and the outcome of this political process was that the Christiania Society initially received no public funding at all, and later an annual funding of only 500 *spesiedaler*.[496]

With the establishment of *Videnskabs-Selskabet i Christiania* and its series of publications, on the other hand, the task of being one of the main publishing channels, or funders of publishing, was taken from *Videnskabsselskabet*. This meant that the Society's funds could to a larger extent be invested elsewhere. That posed no problem when *Videnskabsselskabet* entered into the process of establishing itself in new premises. Another, and perhaps more paradoxical, outcome of this relief was the increase in the frequency of publication of *Videnskabsselskabet's* own *Skrifter* from the late 1860s. Not needing to be concerned to the same degree about contributions from outside *Videnskabsselskabet's* immediate circles, and with more money to spend on the *Skrifter*, the time between reception and publication could, as we have seen, be shortened considerably. But one other condition also played a large role here, namely the focus on the Society's own collections and grants.

All in all, the establishment of *Videnskabs-Selskabet i Christiania* must have contributed to *Videnskabsselskabet's* further development towards a regional institution. Another great event of the 1860s would give more impetus to this development: The building of new and spacious premises in the early 1860s.

The premises

The 1840s had seen a series of reorganizations of the library, of the natural collection and of the mineral collection, partly at the expense of the integrity of Christopher Hammer's collection. But by the end of the 1840s, space was becoming so scarce that

---

[496] Amundsen, 1957: 65–67, 104–107.

the assembly hall in the *Katedralskole* was used for book storage in addition to two rooms set aside for the library. The natural collection was confined to shelves and cupboards along two walls in a relatively small room, Hammer's collection occupying the two others, and the antiquarian collection a fourth room. By this time, *Videnskabsselskabet* already had at its disposal more rooms than the original contract with the school had allowed for by using rooms originally designated as living quarters for teachers, and the use of even more of the school's premises was out of the question.

The process of cleaning up the collections and organizing the library did not alleviate the problem of space. In addition to this, the 1843 report on the state and the future of the natural collections had introduced a program for increasing the collections in a rational manner, a program which to some extent was being followed. And the books kept coming—the annual additions filled around 10–15 meters of shelves per year. Adding to this, a discussion was instigated on the library's shortcomings and what it lacked—where an extra effort was needed to become more up to date. Tellefsen had his interests and inclinations, and the other sections of the library were not given the same attention. By the 1850s one felt the need to make an extra effort to catch up to the natural sciences. This indicated an even larger need for storage space.

One matter which made the lack of space even more acute was the growing importance of *Videnskabsselskabet* as a semi-public institution. The reading room required space for the visiting readers, and the librarian needed a workplace to accommodate those who wanted to borrow books. Moreover, the pupils at the *Borgerlige realskole* regularly visited the mineral collection for educational purposes, and by the end of the 1850s, the natural, mineral and antiquarian collections were open to the public on a regular basis—under the strict eye of the librarian. On the other hand, requests to use the assembly hall for public concerts had to be turned down, as books that were kept there would have to be removed and stored elsewhere, for these occasional events.[497]

By the 1850s, the leadership of the *Katedralskole* was also alarmed. The sheer weight of the books stored on the second floor was now threatening the building—the walls were not constructed to carry the weight of approximately 40,000 volumes. It was becoming obvious that the only solution in the long run was to leave the school and move into premises built for this specific use.

The process towards the realization of the new building started in the mid 1850s. Initially, the idea was to construct the new building next to Bishop Riddervold's residence, less than a hundred meters from the school. Riddervold was willing to donate part of his property for the purpose, compensated by some minor repairs to own house to be paid for by *Videnskabsselskabet*. Drawings were made, but the plans were not realized. However, over the next few years more money was raised. Riddervold, also being secretary of ecclesiastical affairs (*kirkeminister*) in the government, had education in all

---

[497] W.K. Støren, "'Ein heimstad for ånd.' Bibliotekets lokaler," H. Nissen & M. Aase (eds.), *Til opplysning. Universitetsbiblioteket i Trondheim 1768–1993*, Trondheim, 1993: 64–92, *Direksjonsprotokoll 1855–1898*: 23 DKNVS Archive II:g:1.

its forms as part of his political responsibility. As such, he was able to broker a deal between the *Katedralskole* and *Videnskabsselskabet* that provided financial compensation to *Videnskabsselskabet* when the school moved into *Videnskabsselskabet*'s former premises. *Videnskabsselskabet* was to receive 4000 *spesiedaler* in three annual installments, and was to rent the assembly hall for a nominal fee for an indefinite period of time. In addition to this, the Society mustered approximately 6000 *spesiedaler* from its foundations and by cutting down on running expenses. This gave a building budget of 10,000 *spesiedaler*.[498]

In 1855, a committee was established to oversee the planning, financing and building of the new premises. The committee consisted of the headmaster at the *Katedralskole*, Hans H. Müller, who was to become librarian a couple of years later, the former *vice praeses*, Frederik Storm, and Colonel Nils Christian Collin. Müller died in 1859 and was replaced by the new librarian Sven Mosling, while Collin was replaced by postmaster Johannes M. Nissen. In the fall of 1863, the committee was informed by the board of directors that finances were in place and planning and building could be started.

By this time, plans had changed somewhat from the previous years. Instead of building on the premises of the bishop's residence, a new plot of land at Kalvskinnet had been purchased. This was at the edge of town, and was a wise choice, as it gave ample space for further enlargement of the buildings, and it was still in the vicinity of the old premises at the *Katedralskole*.

The process of drawing and erecting the building was surprisingly efficient. By early 1864, the drawings were complete, building started in the summer the same year, and by spring 1866 the building was complete. The library reopened in the new building in September of that year.[499]

The edifice built in 1864–66 resembled the drawings for the building planned in the mid 1850s, but deviated slightly from it on some important points. In the 1850s project more room had been set aside for an exhibition of the natural and antiquarian collection in the main entrance hall of the building. In the realized building, the collections were organized into separate rooms on each side of the entrance hall, which contained the staircase leading to the reading room and the library on the second floor. It is clear that the building primarily was a library—the rooms for the natural and antiquarian collections were full almost immediately, while the room for the books was planned to have room for another 100 years of additions at the current rate.[500] This seems to have caused a clash of interests in the building committee. In the specifications for the use of the building, to be sent to the architect, the role of the library was central, being specified in detail to the level where the expected growth of books was specified in the size of the volumes and thus size of the shelves. The needs of the natural collections were given far less detailed specifications and the antiquarian collection even less so.[501] The hand of Mosling

---

[498] Støren, 1993.
[499] Støren, 1993.
[500] Støren, 1993.
[501] *Byggekommiteens protokoll*, 28.10.1863, DKNVS Archive IV:i:1.

is visible here—he was the leader of the committee, and had had the needs of the library as his first priority. This seems not to have suited Frederik Storm, who left the committee shortly after, on the grounds of a "lack of competence" (*manglende Kyndighed*).[502] Storm had been mostly concerned with the development of the natural collections since the 1840s, and might have felt that the plans for the new building developed in a direction he was not comfortable with.

The whole building had cost just under 12,000 *spesiedaler*, and was completed in two years. Even if the process was one of the greatest undertakings of *Videnskabsselskabet* so far, it was modest compared to a parallel project in Bergen at the same time. As Bergen Museum had also become too small to accommodate the employees, collections and visitors, plans were laid for a new building. This process was instigated in 1853, and the budget was the same as in Trondheim a couple of years later: 10,000 *spesiedaler*. But whereas *Videnskabsselskabet* in Trondheim went a mere 2000 *spesiedaler* over budget, the final sum for Bergen Museum when it was completed in 1865 was 64,000 *spesiedaler*— 54,000 *spesiedaler* over the original budget.[503] What the leadership at Bergen Museum managed to do, was to expand the financial base piecemeal, involving the Museum itself, the general public in Bergen, Bergen local authority and the government in Christiania. By getting funding from some and guarantees for funding from others, the museum was able to expand the original budget from 10,000 to 40,000 *spesiedaler* and then overspend another 24,000 *spesiedaler* to have the arguably most impressive museum building in Norway.

Even if the process of drawing and construction of the building had been relatively painless, the board of directors had to make many sacrifices along the way and in the following years. By tying up so much of both the means from the foundations and of the other revenues (membership fees, the annual grant from the government) in the building, the board had to make some tough decisions on where to reduce other financial activities. This was a reoccurring theme at the meetings of the boards throughout the whole planning and building period, and also in the years to follow.

Several approaches were made. One was to raise the membership fee, which was done in 1859.[504] But this was not enough. After a generous round of stipends, given to Bjørnstjerne Bjørnson, H. Krefting (for making a map of Trøndelag) and Aasmund O. Vinje in 1862,[505] alarm bells were sounding at the size of these grants and the policy of grants all together. Vinje did not get his grant renewed the following year, and in 1864, applications for grants were in general turned down.[506] At the same time, the budgets for the library and the collections were reduced, both to save money and to avoid further large additions during the building period. There was a bit of a breathing space

---

[502] *Brev til byggekommiteeen* 04.05.1864—*bilag 23 Byggekommisjonens protokoll*, DKNVS Archive IV:i:1.

[503] Forland and Haaland, 1996: 50–52.

[504] *Direksjonsprotokoll 1855–1897*: 07.10.1859 DKNVS Archive II:4.

[505] *Direksjonsprotokoll 1855–1897*: 19.02.1862, 30.05.1862, 22.12.1862 DKNVS Archive II:4.

[506] *Direksjonsprotokoll 1855–1897*: 25.05.1864 DKNVS Archive II:4.

when the board of directors realized that the original budget of 10,000 *spesiedaler* could not be met, and expanded it with a 2160 *spesiedaler* loan from the national bank, *Norges Bank*, in 1865.[507] This enabled *Videnskabsselskabet* to continue to support Normann's and Pettersen's surveys in northern Norway in the summers of 1865 and 1866, and even support the playwright Henrik Ibsen with a grant of no less than 400 *spesiedaler* at the same time.[508]

More questionable is perhaps the board of directors' very generous fee of 900 *spesiedaler* to the building committee the following year.[509] This money, with the addition of a personal fee of 300 *spesiedaler* to the librarian Sven Mosling for his work in packing and unpacking the library, claimed more than half of the loan from *Norges Bank*.[510] All in all, Mosling received 600 *spesiedaler* for his work in the new building, in addition to his annual pay of 120 *spesiedaler*, during the building period.

The financial outlook was not good in the first few years after the completion of the new building. In 1869, all applications for grants were turned down with the exception of a small grant of 50 *spesiedaler* to Sophus Bugge to aid him in his work on runic inscriptions.[511] Thus established scientists such as the oceanographic researcher Georg Ossian Sars, the historians Ludvig Daae and Yngvar Nielsen and others applied in vain to *Videnskabsselskabet*.[512] The financial support for scientific journals, such as *Polyteknisk tidsskrift* and *Universitets- og skoleannaler*, was also drastically reduced or terminated.[513] Leaving no stone unturned, the annual 10 *spesiedaler* to the local art association and museum *Trondhjems Kunstforening* was cut from 10 to 9 *spesiedaler* in 1868.[514]

One project which was carried through, however, was the erection of a new monument in 1868 on Bishop Gunnerus's grave in commemoration of the centennial anniversary of the 1767 statutes.[515] The memory of Gunnerus had always been held high and contributed to *Videnskabsselskabet*'s self esteem. Although the centennial celebration in itself was fairly low key, this was to be a lasting monument and can perhaps be seen as an important step in the establishment of the historical self-image the Society wanted to convey. The celebration was held in May 1868.

Conclusions

In the 1830s and 1840s, *Videnskabsselskabet* had filled the role it had made for itself as an independent institution for funding and publishing scientific work. But by the

---

[507] *Direksjonsprotokoll 1855–1897*: 15.07.1865. DKNVS Archive II:4.

[508] *Direksjonsprotokoll1855–1897*: 01.05.1865, 28.10.1865, 15.01.1866, 24.04.1866 DKNVS Archive II:4.

[509] *Direksjonsprotokoll 1855–1897*: 09.04.1866 DKNVS Archive II:4.

[510] *Direksjonsprotokoll 1855–1897*: 23.04.1868 DKNVS Archive II:4.

[511] *Direksjonsprotokoll 1855–1897*: 05.04.1867 DKNVS Archive II:4.

[512] *Direksjonsprotokoll 1855–1897*: 17.04.1868, 01.05.1868, 26.04.1869 DKNVS Archive II:4.

[513] *Direksjonsprotokoll 1855–1897*: 22.07.1867 DKNVS Archive II:4.

[514] *Direksjonsprotokoll 1855–1867*: 23.04.1868 DKNVS Archive II:4.

[515] *Direksjonsprotokoll 1855–1897*: 20.09.1866, 14.01.1867 DKNVS Archive II:4.

middle of the century, this role was harder to fill. Being an institution of national importance had been an easier task at the beginning of the century. In 1801, Trondheim had around 8800 inhabitants, Christiania 9000. But by 1850, Trondheim had around 14,000 inhabitants compared to the 30,000 in Christiania, and by 1870, Trondheim's mere 20,000 pales in comparison to Christiania's 66,000 inhabitants. The development of the capital in the 19th century was enormous, in terms of size, population and concentration of public institutions. The concentration of human, scientific and cultural resources was becoming impossible to match. To uphold an independent institution of the kind envisioned and practiced in the second quarter of the century would demand a collection of local cultural or scientific resources that Trondheim in the long run was not able to muster. That would require a scientific institution or institutions of a higher level than the local *Katedralskole* or *Borgerlig realskole*. The competence of the local members, who would have to be able to decide on how to support different scientific undertakings, could only be found occasionally in specific fields among the educated group or enthusiastic amateurs which made up the local membership in Trondheim.

The challenges to *Videnskabsselskabet*'s role as a miniature research council were not clearly formulated, and perhaps not seen, in the 1850s or 1860s. Instead, one gets the impression of a half-hearted attempt to continue the policies of the 1840s by giving grants to various projects, and tending the collections as well as possible. But the leadership of this period does not seem to have the same stamina, competence in special fields or national and international network as in the preceding decades, and this gives an impression of a lack of direction in its policies. At the same time, the development of the university and other scientific institutions in Christiania made the need for a common forum for their employees evident. *Videnskabsselskabet* in Trondheim was in no position to fill this role, both because of its peripheral geographical situation and its lack of scientific competence. This resulted in the establishment of an academy in Christiania in 1857, which must have made it evident to the Trondheim leadership that the role of the independent, national Society or Academy was now occupied by someone else, at least in terms of an international context.

One area in which *Videnskabsselskabet* did become more professional in the 1850s and 1860s was in the tending of its natural collections. A policy of bringing these collections up to a higher standard and maintaining them in a modern way was instigated in the mid 1840s, and a program for developing the collections to become a full-fledged exhibition that could also be the basis of research was slowly being realized through this period. By the early 1860s, the natural collections were in a fairly decent state, and *Videnskabsselskabet* had also employed its first paid researcher, the conservator Wilhelm Storm, who undertook part-time research besides his task of tending the collections.

The library had been the most important part of *Videnskabsselskabet*'s collections throughout the entire first half of the 19th century, and continued to be so through the 1850s and 1860s. But its relative importance was now diminishing due to the growing importance of the natural collection. The librarian Johan Tellefsen's long reign also made the library mirror, to a certain degree, his fields of interests, and by the late 1850s the need to update the library in the newer scientific fields was obvious. The new librarian Sven Mosling took this task seriously in the 1860s.

Paradoxically, as *Videnskabsselskabet* became less relevant as a national institution and its scientific competence clearly less up to date, the development of the library and the natural and antiquarian collections at the same time demanded a higher degree of professionalism and more modern spacious premises. The cohabitation with *Katedralskole*, which had been harmonious for several decades, was clearly under strain due to the growth and popularity of the library and other collections, and the only solution to this problem was to end the partnership. The decision and process of moving out into a new building was one of the most important events for *Videnskabsselskabet* in this period, and the one with the most consequences. By the late 1860s, *Videnskabsselskabet* found itself in much the same position as it had occupied at the turn of the century. It was relatively wealthy, it was established in modern and spacious premises, it had a strong local membership base and the strength of tradition to lean on. What it lacked was scientific competence and a clear idea of what its mission was. In short, it had the infrastructure but was short on content. It was a scientific institution that lacked scientists. How to cope with this was going to be the main challenge over the coming years.

PART III

1870–1960

Fight over the Society,
1870–1874

The board meeting on 3 October 1870 arrived at an interesting decision: the board recommended a revision of the statutes of the Society. Eighteen days later the general assembly decided that a committee should review all the statutes and propose revisions. Rector C. A. Müller (1818–1893) from *Katedralskolen* (the Cathedral School), *justisråd* (judge) R. N. Horneman (1815–1889) and *prost* (dean) B. L. Essendrop (1812–1891) were elected to the committee. Interestingly, another Essendrop had also been a member of the 1849 committee, while Müller and Horneman were both directors on the board.[516] We can, of course, only speculate as to the reason for this intervention and interest in the statutes. However, this review would set its mark on the society for the next four years, and the process would result in a very different society, a society that had changed its course and identity and perhaps even relinquished its role as a scientific society, slowly transforming itself into a scientific museum. At least that was how some of the members saw it.

Why did this issue arise precisely in the fall of 1870? We have seen that in the earlier part of the 19th century the society had experienced very acute problems serving as a scientific society and, in particular, being the Norwegian scientific society. The establishment of *Christiania Videnskabsselskap* (Christiania Science Society) in Christiania (Oslo) in 1857 had been a success not the least due to its connection to the university in Christiania. Trondheim could not compete with this, neither with respect to the number of academics nor of population growth. While Christiana experienced a rapid increase in population, Trondheim grew at a slower pace. In 1875 there were around 22,000 inhabitants in Trondheim, representing almost a doubling of the population over the last 50 years.

There were other reasons as well. As we have seen, C. N. Schwach had proposed changes in the statutes in 1849, removing all sorts of practical goals from the statutes, for instance removing *vindskipelighet* (inventiveness and industriousness in an attempt to keep the Society more in line with the status of the 19th-century notion of what

---

[516] Protocol, board of directors 3/10 1870 (II.2); Protocol, general assembly 21/10 1870 (II.1).

science and letters was about, and moving away from the enlightenment period's emphasis on "useful knowledge."

Twenty years later, when the debate resurfaced and the rather antiquarian notions of inventiveness and industriousness still prevailed in the statutes, a slight modernization seemed appropriate to the board of directors, and more so now, as the society in Christiania (Oslo) had started to move and work towards being a society of "savants," of scientists and university professors working at the Royal Frederik's University in Christiania. Still, *Videnskabsselskabet* had at its disposal larger funds than the *Christiania Videnskabsselskab*, and it continued to support the work of the university professors. Perhaps this was one of the reasons why the statutes of the Society had begun to appear so antiquated and were felt to be much in need of an adjustment to what scientific activity was really like in the last third of the nineteenth century.

Only an adjustment?

The committee convened and set to work. It would be an exaggeration to say that it worked fast. However, it took its task seriously and delivered a report and recommendation that was to be the start of a complete makeover of the Society. This had not been the intention of the committee, but once the statutes were up for discussion, much more radical thoughts were promoted, and, as might be expected, these came from the younger section of the Society. Let us, however, start by looking at the rather conservative report made by the committee itself.

The main problem facing the committee was how to define and run a society that obviously had become less of a key player in academics and politics than it had been a hundred years earlier. Trondheim had moved more to the periphery of science, not only because of the reduced academic activity in the city, but even moreso due to the increase in activity in other places, and because scientific activities had become more professionalized and compartmentalized in new and previously unknown ways. In Christiania, the Royal Frederik's University had originally been established as the third university within the Danish-Norwegian kingdom and as the first in Norway (Copenhagen and Albrecht's University of Kiel were the other two). In 1870 there were almost 100 scientific employees at this university, making it by far the largest and some would say only active scientific community in Norway. Christiania's role as the main city for science became even more pronounced when the city became the capital of independent Norway in 1814.

However, apart from these rather obvious quantitative movements, there were two other matters so important that they threatened the continuation of the Society's identity: one was related to the aforementioned increased professionalization and compartmentalization of science, the other to the new era of empirical research—now it was the time of the museums rather than societies.

With this steadily increasing professionalization there also came differentiation. It became more and more difficult to be at the forefront of all sciences; specialization was the order of the day. Thus while the 18th century saw the educated gentleman as the ideal model for the scientist, the end of the 19th century was the time for the specialist, the focused researcher who wanted to contribute to a special and rather narrowly defined subfield or sub-discipline. For the Society in Trondheim this led to at least two challenges: one related to the scope of the Society, the other to the quality. Given these problems how could the Society contribute to the development and well-being of science in the future?

On these matters the Society was at odds with itself. Most of its leading members realized that something had to be done, but not necessarily what. The pressure for change had been building up since C. N. Schwach left for Oslo in 1850. What seems to be rather uncontroversial among all the members was a reduction in the scope of the Society. The problem was therefore to decide just how much the scope should be reduced. One answer was to do away with elements that now were considered to be outside of the proper field of the sciences and arts: the promotion of *vindskipelighet* (inventiveness) and the improvement of agriculture. The problem remained, however: should the Society continue as an all-encompassing Society supporting all disciplines or should it be more focused? Another question was whether it should support science through grants or if it should play a more active part in science itself.

We have already examined the proposed changes in the Society's statutes in 1849, but a short repetition might here be in order. The proposal of 1849 had at least two important changes that were not effectuated during the 1850s. First it wanted to remove the dual purpose of the Society. It would no longer be both a scientific society and a society promoting industrious work and inventiveness. With respect to the collections, the proposal was to strengthen the work relating to the *Nordenfjeldske* area (Central and Northern Norway, literally "north of the mountains").[517]

However, as we have seen, these proposed changes were not put into effect in the following years. But the basic reason for wanting to change the statutes had not changed, and for this reason, in 1870 the new committee was set to work. The three members were all in their 50s and, we must think, represented experience and tradition in the Society. It would probably be more a question of adjusting the statutes to the common practice as it had been established in recent years. Nothing very dramatic was expected, with the exception of some opposition from among the younger members of the Society.

In December 1872 the committee presented its report. It was almost a repetition of the report from the 1849 committee, but the wording was somewhat different.[518] The main idea was to change the statutes to terminate the prizes awarded for agricultural and industrial work and instead return to science and letters, which basically was a return to the ideas of the original 18th-century Society. But there were other and

---

[517] Printed proposal for changed statutes, without heading, dated 25 September 1849. In archive box marked *vedtekter*.
[518] "Indstilling fra den til Revision ad Det kgl.norske Videnskabers Selskabs Statutter nedsatte Komite." Dated December 10, 1872. (IV:b:1).

conflicting views. In 1849 the secretary of the Society, C. N. Schwach, had suggested that the Society should be turned into a museum for the northern part of Norway (*Nordenfjeldske*). He had, however, given up this idea, he said, because of the funds (both private and public) the Society probably would lose if such a change was made.[519] The 1870–1872 committee also said that they knew that these ideas were still present among some of the members (without giving names). The museum idea must have had its strong supporters because the committee started their argument by giving two reasons why the museum concept should be promoted, and then also propounding counterarguments.

The idea of a museum stemmed, of course, from the collections originating from the 18th century and, as we have seen, they had only haphazardly been increased in the 19th century. The exception was the library that had expanded continuously through the different exchange programs with other societies in Europe and the enthusiastic work of the librarian J. C. Tellefsen. A collection was, however, not a museum. In the second half of the 19th century a museum was much more; it was a systematic and sci-entific collection, preserved and used as a source for scientific research. The museum had become an important scientific tool in the sense that sciences in several disciplines depended on scientific collections, collections that had to be established, developed, and increased. Thus, if the ambition was to maintain its scientific identity, the only al-ternative for the wide-ranging Society was to transform itself into a museum. However, the committee emphasized, they were aware that similar thoughts of a total change of the Society were present among some of the members.[520] There were mainly two rea-sons why such thoughts came up, the same committee speculated: First was the feeling that Trondheim did not have sufficient scientific forces (*videnskabelige kræfter*) to up-hold DKNVS as a scientific society in the traditional sense. Second these members argued that a more concentrated effort on the collections might result in more attrac-tive and local (*nærtvirkende*) results.[521] These considerations, which were proposed by some of the members, were taken very seriously by the committee, as it used most of its recommendation to argue against these two main points of views: lack of scientific practitioners and a much more restricted field of work based on the collections.

The committee's counterarguments followed two lines of thought: First and fore-most there was the conservative argument. It might well be that the city did not have a sufficient number of active scientists to start a new scientific society. However, that was not the crucial point. More important was that as an obligation towards the inheritance from more glamorous days the present Society should protect the institution and keep it running as best they could in the hope that Trondheim would once more see glori-ous days with a vivid scientific community. And indeed, the new age dawned on Trond-heim. The committee was referring to the new polytechnic school that had just been established in Trondheim (1870), a school that could be the prime mover towards

---

[519] Ibid, 2.
[520] Ibid, 2.
[521] Ibid, 3.

modern times: *Trondhjem Tekniske Læreanstalt (TTL)*. The school provided a three-year education program to students based on an intermediate level (*realskole*). It was strongly inspired by the *Chalmers Tekniska Läroanstalt* in Gothenburg. Here, among the teachers and professors, there would surely be active scientists in the future. Thus, the argument went, as they were just on the brink of "modern" society, it would be a humiliating defeat to reduce the ambitions of the Society, not the least as it had survived worse times than the present situation.

An argument that was used by the proponents of a reduced program for the Society (more like a museum) was that if the only task left to the Society was to distribute money to the university professors and candidates, then the university might as well take over this duty. The committee's argument on this point was weaker, but consistently conservative: It would not be good to concentrate all support in just one institution. It would be better for science if some sort of diversity existed.

The other question conserning a more effective way of working through local collections was trickier. The committee had to admit that it would be an advantage for the city if the collections could be expanded more dramatically and perhaps also include the arts. However, the committee very quickly commented that if the Society wanted to change its main purpose (and become a museum), it would lose its funds and revenues. To make this even clearer they argued that the new scientific society in Christiania, *Christiania Videnskabsselskab*, would no doubt readily accept taking over the duties from the different funds, and willingly distribute the grants to scientists.[522] So instead of being able to use the funds for more local and concentrated museum activity, the Society might lose everything to the new society in Christiania and hence in the end nothing would be gained for the museum in Trondheim. In this regard one would have to start from scratch and go through the same hard struggle as Bergen Museum had done some years ago.

After this rather long and thorough reasoning as to why the Society should not "reduce its ambitions," the committee turned to what should change. As mentioned above, they wanted to do away with the misunderstandings about supporting inventiveness and industriousness and at the same time remove the clauses referring to agricultural prizes. The activities that these paragraphs provided for had not been practiced for many years, so this was in fact more an adjustment in line with practice than an actual change.

More revolutionary was the third proposal: It should no longer be the board of directors that decided who the lucky receivers of the Society's support should be; it should rather be left to the general assembly. It is interesting to speculate as to why this proposal was made precisely in 1872. If the distribution of funds were to be decided by the general assembly, it simply meant that the assembly had one more task to add to its responsibility for electing the board of directors. So instead of the indirect allocation of funds through elected candidates, this was to be done directly at the general assembly. This must have meant an increased level of activity among the members.

---

[522] Ibid, 5.

This development might be seen as a result of the "spirit of associations," the start of a society with more organizations and political parties than traditionally had been the case. Moreover, the 1870s were a time of great political tensions in Norway as the regime of the higher public servants was challenged by a more populist opposition. As mentioned, it was also a time for the establishment of national political parties. Hence, the controversies in the Society could be regarded as a symptom of a growing struggle for the Society's funds and different ways to interpret the Society's political functions: either as a more nationalistic move towards local collections and a museum or as a general supporter of science and the university professors. It might also simply have been a romantic attempt to activate members and pretend to be a "real society."

Support for the last interpretation can be found in the fourth proposal from the committee. Instead of restricting the field of work for the Society, they proposed what the opponents understood to be an expansion. The committee members argued that they simply wanted to make the statutes more readable and clear, and wanted to make explicit that in addition to science, the Society could also support the arts and literature.[523] Art was originally a part of what the first section of the Society could focus on, so the idea of increasing the support for art was not that far off the mark. However, one main argument in favor of the committee funding the arts was at least parallel to that of their opponents, who wanted to strengthen the scientific collections. The committee argued that supporting the arts could be a real benefit to the city if the collections were open to everybody. And, they added, this would especially be beneficial as long as Trondheim was considered to presently have little to offer in the arts.

As we can see, this argument is very close to what was argued for with regards to the scientific collection: concentrating support on scientific work in the region in a more or less museum perspective. The argument to allow support for the arts had much the same underpinning, although without the limitations: the Society was allowed to support art; it did not have to. But now, as they also proposed to transfer decision-making authority from the board of directors to the general assembly, it meant that members would have a more direct influence on what to support and in reality would be able to decide to support an art collection if they so wished.

What should we make of all this? On the one hand it appears that the committee wanted to get rid of everything practical and useful (the paragraphs on inventiveness and agricultural prizes), on the other, it wanted to add arts and literature as part of the Society's program. Compared to the first years of the Society's life, it is striking that the enthusiasm for all sorts of knowledge had been replaced by an interest in pure science (but not necessarily something the members themselves were actively involved with). In addition to this came the introduction of arts, of rather the "beautiful arts," not *Kunstkabinett* or "useful arts." Typically the two latter forms of art had been transformed and developed into the modern art museum and technology, respectively—both of which the committee did not see as parts of the work of the Society. The basic idea was to support general science, all sorts of science and then, from 1872 also arts,

---

[523] Ibid, 5.

understood as the beautiful arts, the arts taught at art academies and conservatories, and as literature.

It is tempting to characterize this change in attitude among some of the most important members of the Society as a transition from enlightenment values to values much more typical to the late romantic period. However, that would probably be both crude and superficial. Perhaps it was simply a consequence of two rather different impulses: the first to defend the honor and reputation of the Society by acting in a way that could ensure its national and hopefully international reputation by being serious and disinterested in anything else than supporting the best scientific endeavors. As for the city, the arts could be a good way of combining the local reputation with the national and international flavor of the Society. The solution also mirrors the problem of being a scientific society in a town with almost no scientific institutions, only institutions that used scientific knowledge, in schools, hospitals, administration or churches.

The unavoidable question is of course: who were the men on the committee that would consider such moves? A quick answer would simply be that this was the elite in Trondheim; those who were, in Ibsen's terms, the pillars of society. They were stuck in the rather provincial city of Trondheim while the center of academic and scientific activity was in the capital, in Christiania, or abroad in the international centers of learning. However, the national university was not yet a research university; its main task was to educate the higher civil servants, the *embetsmenn* that played such an important role in 19th-century Norwegian society. And the *embetsmenn* were precisely people like the three men behind the committee and its recommendations, men who had strong social links. C. A. Müller was important to the university as the principal of one of the few entrance ports to the university. It was in these years that the entrance exam to the university (*examen artium*) was transferred from the university to the *gymnasium* (*Katedralskolen* in Trondheim together with half a dozen other schools spread over the country).

The committee members all had their reputations and credibility linked to the same strata as the university professors and the *embetsmann* elite. Obviously, they did not want to destroy this by restructuring the Society into a local museum, even if this might contribute more to science. They were themselves not scientists but intellectual civil servants. Hence, supporting the arts was only a natural step for them, just as it had been to terminate the prizes awarded for agricultural work and the support of industriousness and inventiveness. The new modern Norway, whose servants they were, needed to build a solid scientific activity in Christiania or elsewhere to be taken seriously among the modern nations in Europe.

The Opposition

So, who were their opponents? They were active scientists, more or less. They were younger and did not have the same impressive social background as the committee members. On the other hand, they had the eagerness and impatience that marks the younger generation, not yet fully established and recognized. Two men brought the message forward—more often one than two actually—but usually they signed proposals together. They came to be the foremost spokesmen for the museum strategy and the abolition of the science society as understood by the revision committee.

The self-declared leader and spokesman was Karl Rygh. Born in 1839 in Verdal, north of Trondheim, Rygh was a student at *Katedralskolen* in Trondheim from 1853 to 1857. He then moved up to the university where he was an excellent student. He graduated with a top degree at the university in 1863, the *embetseksamen* in philology, no doubt under the influence of his older brother, Oluf Rygh, later professor at the same university in Christiania. In 1865 Karl Rygh was back in Trondheim, at Müller's school, this time as a young teacher (*adjunkt*).[524] In 1866 he was elected a member of the Society. Rygh's first scientific works were related to philology and history in general and the study of names of places and farms in particular. However, it was his brother, Oluf, who later was to excel in this. When he died in 1899, Karl was appointed to finish his brother's work "*Norske Gaardsnavne*" (Norwegian farm names) and he published the last five volumes of this gigantic effort (Vols. XIII to XVII).

It was not in philology but in archeology that Rygh made his greatest contribution, or, to be more correct, in his gathering of archeological material for the Society from the large district of central Norway. As a young teacher at *Katedralskole*, he eagerly pursued the study of the older history of Norway, its geography, names, and traces of ancient history. Already in 1868 he was elected member of the board of the local branch (*Trøndelagsavdelingen*) of the national association called *Fortidsminneforeningen*, which today is officially translated to the Society for Preservation of Norwegian Ancient Monuments (*Foreningen til norske Fortidsminnesmerkers Bevaring* and shortened to: *Fortidsminneforeningen*). The association had started 24 years earlier (in 1844) to protect the national heritage found in old monuments and later in excavations and by local farmers in the fields. The association started as a rather national romantic amateur interest, but because of people like Rygh, it became much more professional and introduced archeological excavations as a tool to collect and preserve antiquarian findings from field studies. From 1878 Rygh was elected chairman of the *Trøndelagsavdelingen*, a position he held almost until his death in 1915.[525] Rygh saw his work in *Fortidsminneforeningen* and in the Society as two complementary ways of working for the scientific analyses and collection of the ancient Norwegian past, and he made them work together in new ways.

As a member of the Society from 1866 and board member of *Fortidsminneforeningen* from 1868, Rygh volunteered to be an unsalaried conservator of the "antiquarian" collection that the Society had in its possession in 1870. As such he came to be a colleague of the only conservator that the Society had, the conservator for the natural history collections, Vilhelm Storm. Storm was four years older than Rygh, but, as we have seen in previous chapters, he lacked Rygh's academic status. Storm was elected member of the Society two years after Rygh, in 1868. Together they formed an odd pair. Both

---

[524] NBL, Vol. XII, 59.
[525] NBL, Vol. XII, 63.

were unmarried (and were to remain so for the rest of their lives) and both were dedicated to their tasks as conservators and collectors: one to natural history, the other to archaeology and reminiscences of ancient Norwegian culture.

Nevertheless, even if the two conservators acted as a pair, it was always clear who was in charge: Rygh. He was the aggressive one and the outspoken professional arguing against all sorts of what he termed "dilettantism."

It is hard to see it otherwise than that these two younger members, Rygh and Storm, led by Rygh, were a constant menace to the established board of directors. They were young, but they were also the two most active scientists among the local members of the Society; they were in reality the only local and active representatives of modern science as it was understood in the early 1870s. It was hence not an easy task to ignore their position, all things considered. Primarily Rygh, but also Storm, must have argued repeatedly while the committee responsible for revising the statutes was working. The only result of this appears to be the rather ambiguous notation "some of our members" that the committee in the end referred to.

As we have seen, on December 10, 1872, the committee presented its report and conclusions. Two days later, the board of directors decided to print the whole report and send it to all members in the Trondheim area. The following day the Society's general assembly convened. It basically supported the board and the committee and also stated that other opinions should be heard. Other opinions were then called for, to be presented in writing before March the following year, 1873.[526] Rygh's and Storm's views should have the opportunity of being presented at a meeting. Perhaps they were not as alone as one might think. Nevertheless, they had been invited to present their views, and this was an opportunity they made the most of.

On March 18, 1873, three months after the general assembly, Rygh and Storm delivered their alternative report, proposing a totally revised set of statutes as an alternative to the report of the senior committee. Their argument and the basic view that underpinned their proposal were twofold and related to what they referred to as the senior committee's misunderstandings. First, they said, the committee had underestimated (*miskjennelse*) the idea of the Society and the funds it had for its work. Second, the committee had misunderstood important aspects of modern science and, in particular, the collections' importance for scientific research. These were hash words coming from the two young, newly elected members; they were basically accusing the board of directors and the committee of not knowing what a scientific society was all about and for not understanding modern science. The criticism could not have been harsher. They argued strongly that the Society had to develop and implement a plan determining how its resources could be used to achieve the best possible scientific result. To do this, the Society needed quite other statutes than the ones proposed by the senior committee.

There were two main differences in Rygh and Storm's proposed statutes compared with the original committee's: first was the means the Society had to promote scientific activity. To Rygh and Storm the collections were the key element, and they named

---

[526] Protocol, board of directors 12/12 1872 (II.2); Protocol, general assembly 13/12 1872 (II.1).

them: the natural history collection, the antiquity collection (*oldsaksamlingen*) and the mint cabinet. The library, which had played such a dominant role earlier, was now to be focused on natural history, archaeology, and history. In other words, the library should be brought in line with the overall goal of building the collections and undertaking research related to them. The funds were to be used primarily for research and trips in the region (*det Nordenfjeldske*) that would be related to the goals set for the collections, that is, to collect the flora and fauna and antiquarian objects in the region. Second, the funds could be used to publish *Skrifter* (Transactions). In accordance with these basic changes in the goals of the Society there followed a series of changes related to a much more concise regulation of the collections. They proposed rules for conservators and managers of the collections, funds for their preservation, control institutions and so on.

The second item was a more radical change in the way members were elected and how the members of the Society were organized. Even the first committee wanted more or less to do away with the requirements regarding the member's personal scientific qualifications. Rygh and Storm not only argued against all such requirements but also against the organization of members into sections according to the science disciplines they felt they were connected to. And they wanted a larger annual membership fee, two *speciedaler* (later equivalent to eight *kroner*). They still wanted members to be elected by the general assembly, but the requirements were considerably lowered. It would be sufficient that a member informed the board of directors only eight days before the general assembly that he wanted to propose a new member who would then be eligible. Together with the rather high membership fee this started to look more like a supporting organization for a museum than a scientific society.

These two young conservators had given the more than 100-year-old scientific society quite a radical challenge. They basically wanted to turn the whole organization upside down. Their reason for doing so was argued intensely along the two above-mentioned lines: a misinterpretation of the Society and a misunderstanding of how modern science worked. It appeared that the two men were claiming that in Trondheim in the early 1870s the Society was close to becoming a façade, existing under false pretences, a bogus society. Something had to be done before this became too embarrassing and it had to be done quickly. Patience has never been the mark of youthful opposition. The fate of their counterproposal would obviously depend on how able they were to mobilize support and argue for a change, and what sorts of interests were connected with the old model.

And argue they did. They published their proposal in a 15-page, double-column leaflet. Even though the board of directors had promised to print their proposal, these young challengers did not trust this because the board held the door open for a postponement or tabling of the revisions. So the two eager conservators paid the printing costs themselves, and distributed the publication to all members.

The core of their argument rested on the Society's failure to understand and act on the important changes in 1811 and 1814. In 1811, the Danish king finally agreed to establish a university in Norway, in Christiania, and in 1814 Norway wrote its own constitution and was recognized as an independent nation even though it had to accept the close relationship with Sweden. In a rather speculative manner, the two conservators argued that the only explanation as to why the Society had such a broad and all-encompassing program from the start in the 18th century was that it hoped that this would be the foundation and instrument for the establishment of a separate Norwegian university, a university that did not become a reality until more than 50 years after the foundation of the Society. Norwegian independence in 1814 also meant that all the scientific forces of the rather poor, young nation had to be concentrated in one place, namely around the university. In this situation it would be contrary to all reason if *Videnskapbsselskabet* decided to broaden its program even more than before (thus including the fine arts, industry, agriculture and so on). The revision and ammended statutes of 1815 had been the final step away from the founders' intentions and a major step in the wrong direction. This was the real tragedy, the two argued, and the reason for the poor situation in the early 1870s. The Society had become only a façade.

What the 1815 revision should have done was to concentrat the efforts of the Society in areas where it really could contribute. That would have meant developing into a local and regional institution that would promote scientific material and scientific studies based on local and regional studies, excavations, and expeditions. This, of course, led to the conclusion that the only way to salvage the present situation was to become a decent and contributing scientific institution by becoming a museum with local collections as its core.

The second argument for this change was more focused on the sciences. Since the founders' time in the second half of the 18th century, science had changed and developed. First and foremost, however, it had expanded in all directions—theoretically, empirically, methodologically, socially, and culturally. This broadening of the scientific perspective and outlook also meant an increase in differentiation and professionalization. The all-encompassing ambition was no longer possible if one wanted to be a serious and contributing institution. The day of dilettantism had to come to an end and the Society should set up a program that was much more concentrated, realizable and contributive to modern science. Such a program, they maintained, could only be based on local and regional collections of material from nature and culture and the scientific work on these collections. This was the empirical way of modern science, they argued, and the only way to put an end to the present scam and get down to real scientific work. Work that would turn the Society into a museum would thus not mean the end of the scientific society, but rather the start of a society that really could contribute to scientific knowledge through its own activity.

It is interesting to note that the two conservators' arguments did not refer to the activities of other scientific societies in Europe. Usually these societies did not undertake work themselves, even though they may have contributed funds to support scientific projects. Most commonly, however, the members of these societies were active scientists themselves, as university professors or in another public or private capacity being able to do active research themselves. That was the real difference when it came to *Videnskabsselskabet*: the local members were not active scientists. They were teachers and higher officials, as we have seen in previous chapters, and there were also some wealthy merchants, but there were very few scientists. In a period when science differentiated into a number of disciplines and sub-disciplines, and scientists became specialists in increasingly narrow fields, this became a growing anomaly of the Society, one that became more and more visible, and that the two conservators wanted to remedy through rather dramatic means: If there were no active scientists in Trondheim, let the Society create them, they seem to argue.

It could not have been easy for the two men to present these arguments and support such a proposition. The consequences of the proposed changes would be that they themselves would get all the funds to develop their special interests in natural and cultural history. In a way they were arguing principally for something that everyone must have seen was obviously in their own interest, not only with regard to support for their work, but also for their salaries as conservators.

Hence it is hardly a big surprise that the board of directors opposed them and contra arguments were made. Their proposal document also described the story of their struggle as a minority in the Society over the previous three- to four-year period. While they argued for support to research into Norwegian natural history and Norwegian ancient history, the board of directors argued against them.

The arguments against them were invariably the ones used by the original committee reviewing the statutes:

- The Society would not accept a decision to relinquish the support given to the general sciences or to turn into a museum.
- The Society could lose its funds.
- They could lose the support of the king and the state.
- Awarding stipends was considered the most beneficial way of supporting science.

The most interesting part of the discussion was the way in which the board of directors and the conservators understood science and what science was and should be in the 1870s. This was the time when Darwinian theories were being discussed and evolution was the core of the European debate in science. At the same time, archaeology was established and developed, and the interest in serious research in antiquities was increasing. As for the universities, the acceptance of research as part of their program was seriously enhanced, and even the university in Christiania was slowly being transformed from an educational institution for the top civil servants to a much broader research-based institution. It was in the light of these developments that we must see the conflict in the scientific society in Trondheim. This was also why age mattered: the board of directors received their education in the 1840s, while Rygh was educated in quite another research tradition, in the 1860s—and he was still an active researcher.

The original committee's view of science was very much along the lines brought forward by Bugge and Schwach 20 years before. This angered the young conservators very much. They claimed that the old directors' model of science without solid empirical collections had long been "the stuff of the world of dreams (*henvist til drømmenes verden*)." This particularly seemed to anger them: the rejection of a science based on empirical findings and support of a more romantic understanding was not what science was about. Modern science as of the 1870s was empirically based on collections, it was specialized and professional. In this the Museum came to stand for the modern museum and research institution, while the old all-encompassing distribution of stipends was dilettantism and living in a dream world.

They were very precise when they argued that they did not want to turn the Society into a museum; to the contrary, they wanted to keep the Society as a scientific society but reduce its program to support collecting materials from the region's natural and cultural history. Only then would it in the eyes of the zealous young reformers be a real scientific society.

Economically, they had some interesting ideas which in fact provided for new possibilities. The model was the successful funding of the Bergen museum. This museum had never done anything else than collect and carry out research based on the collections. The conservators argued that Bergen Museum now received 2000 *speciedaler* while *Videnskapbsselskabet* never received more than 528 *speciedaler*. That is, the Bergen museum got four times as much for supporting a smaller number of sciences.[527] At the same time, the museum in Tromsø was opening and in a few years, they argued, Trondheim could perhaps fall behind both.[528] In Trondheim, no museum was started, and none was planned. The only real candidate was in fact the collections of the Society, as the two conservators argued.

At any rate, the two conservators presented the Society with a real dilemma: They could choose to continue as before, turning the Society slowly into a less credible institution, funding special research projects and supporting scientific publications according to their choice. However, the Society would then be turned into more of a social club for the local elite without any connections to science except to pretend to be benefactors. On the other hand, the proposal made by Rygh and Storm was that the Society actually should start to do science in an active way, concentrating and focusing on knowledge about the region, that is, as a museum.

The final showdown—1874

At the general assembly on October 13, 1873 these proposals were discussed. A new committee was established to see if Rygh and Storm's proposal was in accordance with the statutes and premises of the fund the Society had acquired over the years. The following men were elected to the committee: the lawyers and bank directors K.L.T. Bugge (26 votes) and C.W.S. Hirsch (21 votes), then K. Rygh (15 votes) and two from the old board, R.N. Hornemann (11 votes), and B.L. Essendrop (9 votes). Two other more peripheral candidates received fewer votes. It is interesting to see that the committee

---

[527] Rygh and Storm's proposal, p. 6. Box marked *Vedtekter . . .* (IV:b:1).
[528] Ibid, 7.

included two lawyers/bankers, Rygh and, with fewer votes, the old board members. In their first report, the two older members had already rejected the possibility of using the funds in the way Rygh and Storm proposed. In the new committee, however, Rygh received more votes than both of them together. The situation looked fairly positive for the opposition and the new line. Storm and Rygh's proposal was finally taken under consideration and the work of the committee could start.

Rygh was, however, not a patient man. He was upset about the actual situation, in particular due to the lack of space and what he saw as sabotage of the archaeological and antiquarian collection. This was one more source of conflict with the established board and its central officer, the secretary of the board, S. T. Mosling. In addition to the strife over the statutes, the conflict over the sharing of space and priority added fuel to the fire already burning. Mosling found no space for the archeological collections that Rygh had brought to the museum, mostly through his work as head of the *Fortidsminnesforeningen*. In frustration, Rygh quit his job as manager of the archeological collection. Rygh's main opponent, the secretary of the Society, Mosling, also notified the Society that he would be stepping down from his job by the end of the year. The conflict had escalated too much also for him and maybe his support was not as strong as he had thought.

In the meantime the committee that was to look into the feasibility of Storm and Rygh's proposal was split. The majority—Bugge, Hirsch and Rygh—was of the opinion that the proposal would be acceptable to the donors of funds to the scientific society. The main point in their argument was that the new proposed statutes did not turn the Society into a museum, but, on the other hand, only reduced the scope of the Society's activity and the means by which it worked: a society with a reduced program. The main objective of a museum, the majority of the committee emphasized, was to collect artifacts and objects to complete its original plan. Supporting research trips, scientific research and the publishing of scientific papers was a far cry from a museum's obligations. Hence, Storm and Rygh's proposal was just a temporary reduction in scope of a society that did not have the means and human resources to continue its broad activity covering all sciences in all geographical areas. This point was important in their argument because if the Society was turned into a museum, this would surely contradict the intentions of the donors. That was why it was so important to argue that it was not to be a museum but still to be a scientific society but with a "reduced program."

For two of the older members of the committee, the Senior Judge R. N. Horneman and Dean B. L. Essendrop, it was more a question of ethics—whether it was right to reduce the working program of the Society to natural history, archaeology, and history, even if the library continued as before and the Society in every other way continued as a learned society and not a museum. Their argument was mainly that it was morally wrong to reduce the working program even if it was legally acceptable. At around the same time as the committee did its work, another, self-organized group was also working on this issue and in January 1874 tabled a revised proposal based on Rygh and Storm's ideas. We find Bugge, Hirsch and Rygh as members of this committee as well, together with Storm, three of the staff from *Trondhjems Tekniske Læreanstalt* (TTL, the new technical college in Trondheim) (C. W. Carstens, L. Jenssen and A. Schøyen) as well as a pharmacologist (J. Brun).

Their modified proposal included a sentence stating that "as long as the means of the Society were rather limited . . . they should preferably be used to stimulate archaeological, natural historical and historical sciences."[529] They also had the same preference for the northern part of Norway (*det Nordenfjeldske*) as in Rygh and Storm's proposal. However, this more moderate committee also wanted to develop the library in other directions than just archeology and natural history. It is possible to see Bugge's moderating hand in this even if in substance it came very close to Rygh and Storm's original proposal.

The following general assembly on April 21, 1874, was full of intense negotiations. Initially the assembly voted in favor of putting the modified proposal for new statues from the above-mentioned self-appointed group (now called the Brun, Bugget et al. proposal) on the agenda. Thus the assembly had to choose between two different proposals, the independent one and the original revised proposal from the directors' committee. It must by then have been obvious that the Society was in for hard negotiations. At the end of the meeting a vote was held as to which of the two proposals should form the basis for further discussions. The assembley was split down the middle as 13 voted for each proposal. Then, according to the statutes in force, the *praeses*, the old and rather conservative Bishop A. Grimelund, was to cast the deciding vote. Nobody was very surprised when the old bishop voted in favor of the original committee's modest revision of the statutes.

However, with such a close race each section and paragraph was discussed intensely. The meeting on April 21 did not gain any further ground. A new meeting was called for April 28. At this point the *praeses*, Bishop Grimelund, had sent a note informing that he was stepping down as *praeses* of the Society with immediate effect. The assembly decided not to appoint a new *praeses* until new statutes were established. In the meantime the *vice-praeses* would act as *praeses*. With Grimelund out of the way, each section was discussed and voted on provisionally, and then to be decided at a final assembly meeting.

Already at the meeting on April 28 it became clear that the majority wanted to change the Society in the direction originally proposed by Rygh and Storm. The proposal of a restricted work plan was accepted almost like the Brun, Bugge, et al. committee had suggested in January with 12 to 11 votes (no *praeses* Grimelund this time). However, the library was to work on a broader scale (accepted by 13 to 10 votes). At this point the battle was in reality won by Rygh, Storm and their allies: archaeology, history

---

[529] "Forslag til Statuter for det kgl. norske Videnskabers Selskab i Thronhjem," dated January 1, 1874 and signed J. Brun, K.L. Bugge, C.W. Carstens, W. Hirsch, L. Jenssen, K. Rygh, A. Schøyen, V. Storm (IV:b:1). "*Saalænge de Midler, Selskabet kan raade over, ere saa begrændsede, at en methodisk og kraftig Virksomhed i en Flerhed av Retninger ikke er mulig, skulle Midlerne fortrinsvis anvendes til Fremme af de Naturhistoriske archæologiske og historiske Videnskabe, og Samlingerne som Følge deraf udvikles i disse Retninger.*"

and natural history in the northern part of Norway were to be the basis for the reduced scientific plan of the Society. A new meeting was called for May 4.

From then on things went more smoothly. The Brun, Bugge et al. proposal formed the basis of the revision and paragraph after paragraph was accepted unanimously in the following general assemblies of May 4, May 11, and June 10. The final statutes were then accepted in total against one vote on the meeting of June 10, 1874. Out of four years of discussion came a society that was still a scientific society with its funds, library, and collections, but now less ambitious and more focused on working in specific scientific disciplines within a specific geographical area: north of the Dovre Mountains. Members were still elected after they had been proposed to the board, but the rather latent requirement from the 18th century that new members also had to deliver a scientific thesis which was to be discussed, was now finally removed. There were to be no requirements that the members had to be active scientists.

It is difficult to see if the small Society in Trondheim had any choice as long as it did not want to merge with *Christiania Videnskabsselskab* (Christiania scientific society), which, incidentally, was never proposed. It was also clear to everyone that the reduction in ambitions—that is to work in only some sciences, i.e. in three carefully selected ones—was temporary until the city in the future once more had become a city of savants. There were optimistic signs marking the way: *Katedralskolen* (the cathedral school) expanded and the new *Trondhjems Tekniske Læreanstalt* (technical college) attracted new knowledgeable people to the city. Better to do something that might contribute to modern differentiated sciences than to continue randomly as they had done. During the process several senior members had been voted down and the *praeses* Bishop Grimelund had resigned. However, on July 29, 1874, the new statutes were confirmed by the protector of the Society, King Oscar II.

9

A new direction—away from a society of savants?

The events that started with the discussion of a revision of the statutes in 1870 and ended in the vote over the amendments in 1874 were more than a slight change in the life of the Society. They led to the establishment of something quite different from the eighteenth-century Society of Gunnerus. The year 1874 thus marks the beginning of a new era; this was a change that in time would prove irreversible. Fifty-two years later, the tension between the ambition of running a museum and a library on the one hand, and the desire to have a scientific society on the other, would result in two different institutions with different funding and different statutes. The only thing that would unite the two was the name: *Det Kongelige Norske Videnskabers Selskab*.

The events in 1870–1874 thus started the transformation of the Society into a museum. In this connection, several questions beg answers: why did they do it and what were the alternatives? Why did they build a museum while saying it was not a museum? What did it mean to be a museum in the 1870s? Who were the architects? Could the course of events have been changed during these years, and why did they not return to Gunnerus's idea when and if it became possible, as was argued in 1872–1874?

The answers to all these questions are not to be found only on Erling Skakkes gate where the new building of the Society was placed, or in Trondheim for that matter. We need to look at the Society in a much broader national and international perspective. Important, in this respect, is the question of how scientific activity changed, breaking into smaller fields and becoming specialized, and at the same time what the social activity of doing science came to be.

Let us start with what most of the members thought about the Society, at least those in the committee responsible for assessing compliance with the amendments to the statutes. Everyone, even the minority, Judge R. N. Horneman and Pastor B.L. Essendrop, agreed that something had to be done and that curtailing the Society's ambitions would be a realistic strategy. However, they disagreed on the need to amend the statutes. The minority in the committee felt that a permanent amendment to the statutes would be a betrayal of the funding patrons who had donated their money to a society that encompassed all sciences, arts and letters—and even technology.

This "betrayal" was clear enough—what made it after all acceptable was the way the sciences had changed over the last 50 years. As late as in the 1820s it was still possible to talk about the unity of sciences and scientific endeavors. By the 1870s it was obvious to most that science had started to break into smaller fields, new kinds of institutions had begun to take over research, and new forms of knowledge was being developed and established. First among these institutions were of course the universities. Thus it was a crucial point that the Society had not moved to Christiania and the university there, but had remained in Trondheim. In 1811–1813 it had not been obvious that the Society and its scientific activity would have to move. The new university was not conceived of as a center of research; it was to be a center for educating higher civil servants. By 1870 this had changed. The university professors had become the first salaried senior researchers; furthermore, they also stimulated aspiring students to undertake research. Over most of Europe this is a recurring pattern: university professors were now becoming the avant-garde of research. They were the first professional scientists, and they were steadily increasing in number. Traveling across Europe, they visited collections and laboratories and sent their students to the places with the best resources and where they had their contacts. It is important to note that also collections were important as goals for these trips. It could be argued that the collections were in fact, the most important goal and that laboratories only slowly gained equal importance, indeed not becoming dominant scientific institutions until well into the 20th century. By far, not all professors traveled like this, but the number that looked upon themselves as more than just teachers increased rapidly. The identity as researchers grew stronger whatever they conceived as most important, the collections or excellently equipped laboratories.[530]

Parallel to this, and, we might suspect, a consequence of this activity, the sciences and humanities also started to drift apart and differentiate. Gone were the days of the omniscient autodidact. The second half of the nineteenth century saw the birth of the specialized scientist, as the professional professor doing research and teaching, as well as guiding his students to and in his particular specialty. History had altered the role of the scientific societies of Europe; they were no longer centers of research and scientific organizations. Instead the societies took on a different function for this new class of research professor, as their chosen arena for scientific exchange within and across disciplines and fields of knowledge. This is, of course, a very general interpretation of the situation. The French model of academies continued to be important in many countries as both a funder of science and as an employer of scientists. In this case, the societies were turned into elite research centers while the universities were left to do the teaching. This was, however, not what happened with the Scandinavian societies.

Perhaps it was this process that made it the Achilles heel of the Society in Trondheim: all its members must have realized in their darkest hour that the only way to revitalize the Society as a center for research would be to move it closer to the university,

---

[530] See for example Hestmark, *Vitenskap og nasjon.*

to Christiania. Only then would it have active scientists as members and at the same time serve as a forum for the same members for debate on and distribution of the latest scientific findings. And most of all it would then be actively involved in funding, discussing, and establishing science among the leading scientists in Norway. Remaining in Trondheim meant that the university professors, even if elected, would at best be distant and rather passive members. Since they could not participate in meetings, their motivation for being members would primarily be reduced to their interest in gaining some economic support in the future.

There are no traces of a real discussion on this issue during the turbulent years in the early 1870s. A reasonable way to interpret this is to think that this was not a feasible solution for any of the parties. However, the rebellious young conservators, Rygh and Storm, suggested that the priority be on the area around Trondheim and northwards (*det Nordenfjeldske*). Those who would have the most interest in moving and re-establishing the Society would be the professors in Christiania who were members of the Society. And it should be noted—several of the university's professors were elected members. When there were no such proposals, we must conclude that the Christiania professors were not too interested in this issue and that it was not considered important.

A main reason for this was that the professors in Christiania already in 1857 had joined together in an attempt to form their own scientific society, *Christiania Videnskabs-selskap*, which they succeeded in doing.[531] It changed its name several times, to *Kristiania Videnskabsselskab* in 1878, when Christiania changed names to Kristiania, and to *Det Norske Vitenskabs-akademi i Oslo* in 1925 (when Kristiania changed its name to Oslo); later it was known only as *Det norske Vitenskabs-akademi*. This had become the central meeting place in Christiania for the premier scientists in Norway. Although in its infancy, its future prospects were bright. One could speculate that it suited the Christiania professors well to have a society in Trondheim that acted as a contributor to the university research funds as long as the means for research for both the Christiania Society and the university were limited. This would, however, change towards the turn of the century when the Christiania Society managed to accumulate a large amount of funds, thanks to the work of the important entrepreneur in Norwegian Science, Professor Waldemar C. Brøgger (1851–1940).[532] By the 1870s the function of *Videnskabs-selskabet* (DKNVS) was, from the Christiania professors' point of view, to be a somewhat erratic source of funds for the professors, and their assistants and students.

Thus, there seems to be no one who could or would propose the perhaps only realistic way to continue Gunnerus's ideas of a society of savants, namely to move the Society to where science was being performed, Christiania. The alternative was to lower the ambitions, reduce the scope of disciplines and areas, and fund those scientists whose work could guarantee the position of the Society. By doing this they were moving the Society in the direction of the French model, with salaried researchers employed

---

[531] Helsvik, *Elitisme på norsk*. Amundsen, Det Norske videnskaps-akademi.
[532] Hestmark, *Vitenskap og nasjon*.

by the academy. On the other hand, this would also mean that these scientists would constitute the core members of the academy; they would, in the French tradition, constitute the academy. In Trondheim, such a move would most likely, be a parody as the Society neither had the means nor the members with the necessary important qualities to make this a realistic option.

However, we must believe that the members in Trondheim, who knew the university and had been educated there, must have felt the pressure of international developments and the mere fact of the existence of the university in Christiania. These developments forced *Videnskabsselskabet* more and more to the side, separated from the main trends of science. Even if they did not appreciate Rygh's initiative, they must have seen this development as threatening and due to the lack of qualified scientists found it increasingly difficult to evaluate and grade applications from professors in Christiania. One way to deal with the university question was to elect the professors in Christiania as members. The most serious attempt to do this came at the meeting in October in 1870 when five professors were elected members. But this strategy was aborted and was tried only once. To summarize the situation, everyone wanted to keep the Society in Trondheim, but only Rygh and Storm had a strategy for how to accomplish this in a reasonable and justifiable way.

The question was not necessarily about whether to focus the efforts or not, but whether the statutes were to be amended. The latter position was favored by those who hoped that the situation for science in Trondheim would improve in time, not as far-fetched a hope as one might think. In 1870, with the help of Thomas Angell's fund, the local authority had managed to convince *Stortinget* (parliament) to fund a polytechnic college in Trondheim, *Trondhjems Tekniske Læreanstalt, TTL*, the first of its kind in Norway. As could be expected, all five members of the local authority committee were members of the Society.[533] They did not, however, participate very actively in the debate in the Society around 1873/1874. Parliament adapted the plan for the college, paring it down from four to three years for financial reasons, but it was nevertheless a positive sign for the future and gave the Society hope. Perhaps it was a matter of surviving until a new generation of teachers and scientists would move to Trondheim?

Storm and Rygh's first proposal was aggressive and divisive. As we have seen in the previous chapter, lawyer and member K.I. Bugge found some common ground between the opposing camps and established a compromise that was acceptable to most active members. Apart from removing the harsh criticism by Rygh and Storm, he introduced a very delicate balance between a scientific Society with concentrated efforts and a museum with a different focus. Nevertheless the initiative was very unclear as to what the Society actually would be turned into. The central question remains unexplained: how could everyone agree not to convert the scientific Society into a museum, and then end up with a museum and not, 30 years into the future, a scientific Society? This is even more remarkable as the statutes were only marginally amended between 1874 and 1903.

---

[533] Andersen, "Trondhjems tekniske læreanstalt 1870–1915," 18.

A possibility remains that the wording used by Bugge was only a way to camouflage his ambitions of a museum, and that he willingly deceived everyone in the way he did this. However, it is more likely that at least some of the opponents would have realized this, but there is no sign that the older distinguished members of Bugge's first committee, R. Horneman and Essendrop, had argued against such a view. Hence, there was probably more to this than meets the eye. In the same way as was true for the universities and the sciences, the museums were also undergoing dramatic changes in Europe in the last quarter of the 19th century.

Just as the central institutions of science were giving up the Enlightenment's focus on scientific societies by turning into the professional, research-oriented universities of the latter part of the nineteenth century, so did the museums. However, there were many coexistent opinions about what museums were about at the time, even moreso than what was the case for the sciences. Earlier in this book we discussed collections of all sorts that the Society was involved in, and noticed how the interest for the unique, the special and the extraordinary was the main principle. This was, in a way, in the tradition of the much older curiosity cabinet. The collection changed little in quality during the first two-thirds of the 19th century except for losing many items and making strange acquisitions. Still the exotic was much in demand. As a clear indication of the symbolic status of the collections, one might consider the new building from 1866, with almost two stories reserved for the library, but only a couple of rooms on the first floor for the other collections. The collections were accessible once or twice a week, but not without some difficulty.[534]

At the same time the museums changed. It was no longer the exotic that was in demand by the new group of scientists, but what might be scientific valid findings. Vilhelm Storm was trained at the university museums in Christiania as one of these men new to science (the natural history collection) and knew how a research museum functioned in the 1850s. However, it is unrealistic to see *Videnskapsselskabet* as a parallel to the university museums in Christiania. There were neither the resources for expansion nor competence for this in Trondheim. A much more realistic view of a possible future for the Society was to be seen in Bergen—the scientific museum, namely the Bergen Museum.

The Bergen Museum was established in 1825. A museum association had been created in 1833 complete with members and statutes. The statutes were based on the antiquarian museum in Copenhagen, Deichmann's Library in Christiana and, surprisingly, *Videnskapsselskabet* in Trondheim.[535] Hence, the leader of the museum's board had the title *praeses* conferred on him and the explicit objective of the museum was the promotion of science and scientific knowledge. However, right from its inception, the museum was far from a public institution in the sense of being open to the general

---

[534] Conflict between the general public's access to the collections versus the scientists' use of the same collections for research was well known also in Trondheim, as the conflict between the librarian and secretary Mosling and Karl Rygh showed in the late 1860s.

[535] Forland and Haaland, *Universitetet i Bergens historie*, 30.

public. On the contrary, if anybody wanted to see the fabulous and fantastic artifacts in the collection, they had to become a member and pay a fairly high annual fee. Tours for members were arranged on a yearly basis only.

Bergen Museum's collections and activity were growing fast. In the years between 1838 and 1840 the museum raised private funds and was able to build the first new and specialized museum building in Norway for more than four thousand *speciedaler*.[536] In 1846, the museum engaged its first academic curator or conservator, ten years prior to Trondheim. The museum was reorganized as a society of members with a general assembly and elected officers. Bergen had for a long time been known for its wealthy merchants but, among its members, the groups dominating *Videnskabsselskabet* also dominated in Bergen: higher officials, judges, clergymen, military officers and lecturers at higher educational institutions.[537] Towards the 1850s, Bergen Museum had one of the best, if not the best, natural-history and Norwegian-antiquity collections in Norway. Moreover, it had drawn up plans for collecting both high culture and folk culture. In comparison, only the book collection and the library in the Society in Trondheim were larger. Bergen focused on the museum while *Videnskabsselskabet*'s focus was on the library for a long time, the best research library in Norway until, eventually, the library at the Royal Fredrik University in Christiania surpassed it.

A major development for the museum in Bergen took place during the next 20 years, from 1853 onwards, when science and a new building were in focus. This focus on science and research represented a shift in interest from the antiquarian collections to natural history. Moreover, the museum began to hire academically trained researchers in these fields. This interest in science was not entirely new. The statutes of Bergen Museum were inspired in part by the purpose and organization of *Videnskabsselskabet*, and even before the 1850s, the museum leaned towards doing science, and even built a library that could support the collections and publish scientific papers.[538] However, it was not until the 1850s and 1860s that the museum really developed into a scientific institution. With the new focus on science, the center of gravity changed from antiquarianism to natural history and, in particular, zoology. In 1865 Bergen Museum also managed to raise an impressive museum building which remains to this day the symbol and central building of the more recent University of Bergen (it had two large side wings added in 1898). The historian Anders Haaland rates this building as one of the pioneer European museum buildings, a few decades before the larger cities in Europe built their museum buildings and before the large national museums were opened.[539] The price of the new building was 66,000 *speciedaler* in 1866. The government funded the museum's general activity with 4000 kroner (1000 *speciedaler*) in 1864, increasing this amount to 14,000 kroner in 1893. In 1892 they had total revenues of 28,000 kroner.[540]

---

[536] Forland and Haaland, *Universitetet i Bergens historie*, 38.

[537] Ibid, 41.

[538] Schetelig, *Norske museers historie*.

[539] Forland and Haaland, *Universitetet i Bergens historie*, 47.

[540] Forland and Haaland, *Universitetet i Bergens historie*, 67; 4 *kroner* equaled 1 *speciedaler* from 1874.

In Christiania, the university collections were off to a slow start. However, as we have seen, Vilhelm Storm was trained using the natural history collection, a collection which was probably the most advanced to begin with. Storm's training was mainly in preparing animals. Working closely with the conservators, he must, in spite of his specialty, have learned much about collections, species, and how to think about both of them in a systematic way.

Another part of the university collections, the antiquarian or as it later was called, archaeological collection, was also closely connected to the Society in Trondheim, but in a very different way: It was encouraged, developed, and expanded by Karl Rygh's six-year-older brother: Professor Oluf Rygh (1833–1899). In 1860 Oluf Rygh was appointed assistant for the antiquarian collection, and in 1862 he took over as director and manager after Professor Rudolf Keyser. He was also appointed Professor of History (following P.A. Munch) in 1866. In 1875 his position was transferred at his own request to a professorship in archaeology.[541] The careers of the two brothers were strikingly parallel: Both remained single throughout their lives, both were broadly interested in institutional and policy questions related to older history, be it philology in connection with farm and place names, or excavations and collections of artifacts. Both of them were strictly empirically oriented, and systematic lists of their findings were their main legacies. There was little time or room for overview, synthesis, or speculation. In this way both came to be close to the methods of natural history understood as taxonomy and the collection of varieties. This was the methodology of the old natural history in its new disguise in the form of collections from both nature and culture.

As we have seen, museums were gaining greater importance also internationally in the last half of the nineteenth century. There are many reasons for this, some scientific, some national, some related to a new and growing audience. We have so far primarily discussed the scientific part of this. The Rygh brothers were in line with the contemporary trends in science: the new scientific disciplines of archaeology and natural history demanded empirical research, exemplary items, typical artifacts, species, and hence collections, so that they could establish themselves as something different than the old all-encompassing natural history involving all sorts of curious findings.

At the same time, the collections and museums became a symbol of national wealth and a means to promote nationalism and national pride. The late part of the nineteenth century was the time of grandiose national museums all over Europe. In the intersection between nationalism, science, and the general public, smaller regional and local museums would thrive and expand. Museums were on the national agenda as never before.

A third element functioned the same way and increased the focus on the museums even more—the rise of a new audience. The new bourgeois societies established new norms and values, and new cultures. With the self-confidence of a new class growing in number and wealth by the day, museums became fashionable. This put the museums

---

[541] NNBL, Vol. 7, 456.

in a new light; they were no longer only a place for the new sciences and national sentiments but also had to cater to the new cultural interests of the rapidly growing new class of citizen. It was by no means obvious how this should be done. Karl Rygh was enthusiastic about both the new sciences and the national endeavors, but he was much more reserved when it came to the new audience.[542]

For the Rygh brothers, both philologists, the collected artifacts became the new text, the scientific sources from a past that had not found their way into the archives as the written sources had. The collections became the new archives—or—the extension of the archives. In this perspective the words of the committee were right: The Society was not turned into a "museum" but instead into an extended library and archive, this time with objects from both culture and nature. This was the new scientific museum.[543] Collections were the new and scientific way to comprehend both the very early history that did not leave any written sources and a natural world in need of reinterpretation. It was the time for the silent witnesses to a forgone past or to an unarticulated nature. However, these silent witnesses did not talk to everyone.

However, the other dimensions of the new museum, national sentiments and the new audience, were not necessarily dependent on this particular scientific view of the museum, even though they often were the reason for its funding, if not for its activities. In a way these two dimensions were linked: the audience and the nation. It has been noted by Tony Bennett that the museum in the latter part of the 19th century was closely connected to the modernizing efforts of the societies; it was part of the power relations in the new national states.[544] It was part of a strategy to, on the one hand, enlighten and educate the populace. On the other hand, it would also tell an organic story of progress in all fields: from the most primitive to the most advanced cultures (stone, bronze and iron age, and so on). This was paralleled with the stories it would tell about nature: from the most primitive to the most complex organisms and races. The thrust of these narratives was to show the development: from vulgar power relations to the much more sophisticated organized modern societies and their all-encompassing stately power. Even having such museums at all was a sign of high culture and a state that wanted to promote these learned institutions to the best of all citizens. And it worked: people from all classes went to see, learn, and accept.

Material culture, from natural history, archaeology and art was to be presented to the general public and not remain hidden in dusty scientific chambers or archives. For the museums the change was considerable: from these hidden locations to the interest in the classified, organized, pedagogical exhibitions of nature and culture, telling the visitor why we are here, where we come from, and what we are. This story told the natural history of man as the superb being, and then compared him with all sorts of lower animals and plants. Even stones and minerals were included in this

---

[542] NBL, "Karl Rygh" and Petersen, Karl Ditlev Rygh.
[543] Gustafson, "I Oluf Ryghs fotspor på Veien, Ringerike," 100 and Hagen, Gåten om Kong Raknes haug, 74.
[544] Bennett, The Birth of the Museum.

meta-history. At the same time, this was also the story of modern society's new organizational forms: the systematic displays mirrored the state bureaucracy, the military or the schooling system in fascinating ways without bringing these topics openly in touch with each other. The metatexts of the exhibitions were not necessarily outspokenly Darwinian, even if they were organic in some romantic sense. The message was on the other hand clear; humans were on top of the pyramid of organisms.

This was even more the case for the archaeological exhibitions. Here, however, it was not the story of nature and man as its ruler, but a parallel story of our forefathers and their struggle: from the most primitive to the advanced modern society that the spectator lived in. Since the findings were national, so were the exhibits. These exhibits came to display the growth and increasingly more advanced tools and expressions of the early Norwegians. At the Society it would have a strong flavor of what was known as the the greater region, the *Nordenfjeldske*, but as a part of the national experience this was probably no less national than the university museums in Christiania. Again a clear message was sent: the modern national state was at the top of cultural evolution.

Thus, the museums were not only scientific institutions; they served political puposes and they produced social distinctions as they appealed to the new cultural elite. In doing so they were also a new medium and as such represented a new media technology: the public exhibition as a means to communicate political ideas, cultural point of view, and scientific knowledge simultaneously. It was a great leap forward from the mid-19th century collection that was more of an overcrowded storage area than what came to be the modern display by the end of the century. As far as media technology goes, the museum displays all over Europe came close to another institution's public display: the new and multistoried department stores as seen along the boulevards of Paris. The scientific museum and the new consumer society started to share technology.

But of course, the message was different: Museums as advocates of nationalism, explicitly or implicitly, were different from the department stores' tempting offers. The means were, however, rather similar.

Life at the new museum

At the general assembly on September 21, 1874, *prost* Essendrop was elected by a great majority as the new *praeses*, while the pastor S. Skavland was elected as *vice praeses*. Two directors were elected. The lawyer, Bugge, *cand. miner.* C. W. Carstens and school director J. Aa. Bonnevie were also elected. Karl Rygh was not elected to the board. At the following meeting, also a general assembly, on December 4, 33 new members were elected as members of the Society: the new statutes had started to work and no scientific work was required from the new members. The newcomers represented a broad range of upper-class and upper-middle-class citizens. The new members were military officers, managing directors and merchants, lawyers, teachers in higher schools, higher public servants and lawyers. Typically, most of them lived and worked in Trondheim and its vicinities.

Within the framework of this new institution, Karl Rygh and Vilhelm Storm set to work. Both of them traveled in the summer, collecting items for the various collections. Rygh was eagerly trying to expand the archeological collection, and Storm continued to collect birds. However, in 1874 he also started to use a sediment scraper in Trondheim fjord. The attempt was not entirely successful to begin with due to bad weather and the lack of a crew, but it was considered promising and would be continued in the years to come with great success.

Turning a scientific all-encompassing society into a museum-oriented institution required physical changes of the society's premises. Already in the late 1860s, Rygh had argued strongly for more space, and the personal conflicts with the general secretary and librarian Sven Mosling were well known. With the triumph of Rygh in 1874, Mosling stepped down, together with most of the old leadership, and the road was open for a new physical layout of the Society's building, if it could be funded. In 1875, Mosling also asked to be relieved of his duties as librarian.[545] The building from 1866 can first and foremost be characterized as a library building, as the library occupied both the upper floor and the mezzanine floor. The collections shared the space on the first floor with the other activities of the Society. Rygh wanted to build an extension to this first building to give space for the collections, but also for working areas for the conservators, for a preparator and a taxidermist.

Rygh was elected to the board of the Society in 1875 as the replacement for C.W. Carstens. In late November 1875, the board sent a petition to the government, asking for an increase in the support for the Society's general activities (as activities had been increased due to the changes the year before) and a special grant for a new building to be erected adjacent to the old one. In March the following year, 1876, Parliament approved both requests. For the building, they followed a procedure that almost had been the rule: Parliament granted 4500 *speciedaler* if the Society could get an equal amount from other sources.[546] *Trondhjems Sparebank* (Trondheim Savings bank) made the money available in June 1876. The building was completed in the fall of 1878 at quite a higher price than the original estimate (67,400 kroner, which amounted to almost 17,000 *speciedaler*). Including the Society's own savings and a loan from Kongsberg Silverwork's fund, they still lacked 8300 kroner (equivalent to 2075 *speciedaler*). It was difficult to find funds for these extra expenses, but over the next few years they were able to acquire the necessary sums.[547] To put the situation in perspective, the total price of the new building in 1878 was only one quarter of the price for Bergen Museum's new building 12 years before, as we have seen earlier.

In the new building the archeological collection for the first time had sufficient space, as it was situated on the second floor of the new building. The zoological collec-

---

[545] In: *Skrifter*, Annual report 1875.
[546] In: *Skrifter*, Annual report 1876, p. 8.
[547] In: *Skrifter*, Annual report 1879 and following years.

tion occupied the first floor, while the first floor of the old building was in part an extension of the zoological collection and partly provided space for the coin and mineral collections. There were also a preparing room and rooms for the conservators and their respective collections. Most important: there was room for expansion of the collections. The Library still had their old space on the upper floor of the old building with its mezzanine. Finally the collections had come on par with the library, the direction and signals were clear: the collections now took the library's place as the Society's central activity.

The new building was originally conceived as an eastern wing off the old main building. It was not realized this way. Instead of a wing, it was built as a separate building in line with the old main building to the east along Erling Skakkes gate. It was connected to the old building on the ground floor by a small hallway. In this way two large exhibition halls were raised and competed with the façade of the old building. Today this building looks like the western façade of the new 1898–1904 building but it is in fact 20 years older.

From the start in 1874 there were four collections. The antiquarian, later called the *"oldsakssamlingen,"* which, for the sake of convenience, we will use an even later name: the archeological collection, and the natural history collection, which now mainly was a zoological collection, were the two major stocks. In addition there were two smaller ones: the coin collection and the mineral collection. The archeological collection had approximately 1200 items in 1874, a substantial part of them collected either by Rygh or during his time as manager of the collection. In 1875 this grew by 226 items, and the year after by 161.[548] In comparison, Rygh mentions that the archeological collection at the university in Christiania seldom reached more than 400 items in yearly acquisitions.[549] In the following years the collection increased at a fairly steady rate by between 100 and 200 items each year.

The way these findings were arranged was in line with what had internationally become the accepted way of sorting archeological findings, namely according to time period, based on the pioneer Danish archeologist C. J. Thomsen's method from the first part of the century.[550] It was actually a fairly simple approach: items were considered to come from the Stone Age, the Bronze Age or the Iron Age. Both the Stone Age and particularly the Iron Age were split into older and later stages. Around 1870 this distinction was split into even finer intervals.[551] The collections were concentrated on the later Iron Age, with the Stone Age and early Iron Age also well represented. The truly rare items were from the Bronze Age. There were also some miscellaneous items, mostly from the medieval age or more recent times.

The idea of three periods (Stone-, Bronze-, and Iron Age) was quite radical when Thomsen pioneered it in the 1820s and 30s. It implied an evolution of culture based on

---

[548] In: *Skrifter*, Annual report 1874, p. 7; 1875, p. 5.
[549] In: *Skrifter*, Annual report 1874, p. 7.
[550] Schnapp, *Discovery of the Past*, 300 ff. Svestad: Oldsakenes orden, 160 ff.
[551] Svestad, Oldsakenes orden, 193.

tools and status items that was at the time not obvious. However, by the 1870s this had become the basic way of undertaking archeology. Thomsen also introduced ways of attributing these time periods to real findings. Two key methods were introduced where earlier times simply had left the objects to pure speculation: comparisons and place of finding. The location of a find was important simply because one would assume that things found together actually were put down during the same period. Hence it would only be necessary to establish the right time for one item in a group of finds, and the rest could be assumed to be from the same period. Comparisons became important for understanding types of stone axes, bronze daggers or Iron Age swords. By systematizing finds from different places, one could see a development and variations of the same type of tool, weapon, or artistic object. Style, decoration, and method became important elements in dating.[552] In this way Rygh positioned the Society's archeological ambitions in a contemporary Scandinavian way of doing prehistory. As B. T. Trigger sees it: "The kind of history produced by Scandinavian archeologists made sense only in terms of the cultural-evolutionary perspective of the Enlightenment."[553] This was also Rygh's perspective: individuals and kings did not have priveliged places or functions in his history; history was about how culture developed from primitive to more advanced stages, with contemporary society as the most advanced.

Rygh's contribution was first and foremost the professional introduction of this way of ordering the collection and of insisting on detailed descriptions of the finds and what belonged together. Descriptions of how, when, where, and what were attributed to the items, which had never been done before. And, he was a master of the acquisition process. Here he had help. From 1873 and for some years, after a young student came to his assistance and traveled parts of Trøndelag to make finds in the summer. The young student was Ingvald Undset (1853–1893), who later rose to fame as an internationally famous archeologist with groundbreaking studies of northern and central European pre-history (he was also to become the father of the Nobel-prize winner in literature, Sigrid Undset). In his youth, he eagerly traveled Trøndelag in the summers with small grants from the Society. In his reports he wrote about the importance of such trips, both in terms of collecting items, but perhaps even more significantly, in terms of informing the local communities about the value of the prehistoric find for developing a national history. And what is more: informing the local population that it had important scientific, archeological knowledge without actually knowing it. We must assume that he was thinking of locations of burial grounds, articles found in the fields, strange landscape formations, old myths and the like.

Undset brought back finds from his trips, as did Rygh, who also went on such trips each summer. Gifts were for many years the main source of acquisitions, not only for the archeological collection, but also for the library and the three other collections. For archeology Rygh also commanded other resources. As we have seen, he was a

---

[552] Trigger, *A History of Archeological Thought*, 126 ff.
[553] Ibid, 135.

central member of the association that did voluntary work on preserving ancient buildings and sites in Norway, *Fortidsminnesforeningen*, or as the local branch was called in the 1870s: *Den Trondhjemske filial av Den Antikvariske Forening*.[554] This national organization was established in 1844 by the painter J.C. Dahl and his friends. Dahl brought with him strong impressions from Germany and wanted to preserve ancient buildings and places from a more national romantic perspective, as an important cultural heritage for the people who lived in the district and were to live there in the future.[555] In the 1860s a local division was established in Trondheim, and Rygh soon became the leader.

It was this association that was the most important donator to the Society's collections. In the summer *Fortidsminnesforeningen* would excavate burial grounds and the like and hand over all found items to the Society together with descriptions of place and other finds. In this way Rygh was able to both get excavations done and at the same time make sure that the result was handled professionally and properly registered and preserved without larger expenses for the Society in Erling Skakkes gate. It turned out to be a most successful arrangement.

Rygh reported on his findings and the gifts that he received. However, apart from a few of his smaller works he did not try to synthesize or establish a hypothesis of the prehistoric developments in central Norway to any large degree. In 1879 he published a thesis on prehistoric sites and archeological findings in Nord Trøndelag in the Society's *Skrifter* (Transactions). Otherwise he mostly gave his annual report as manager of the archeological collection and reported on acquisitions and gifts.

In the last part of the 1870s and the 1880s the Society quietly and persistently transformed itself into the museum that Rygh and Storm had planned. All the four collections (the archeological, the zoological, the mineral, and the numismatic collections), and the library grew at a steady pace without dramatic changes—either in staff, methods, or focus. A slow rate of change in the composition of the board only underlined and stabilized this new direction of the Society and the change of the persons in charge of the new scientific initiative. Gone were the theologians and merchants and in came ever more strongly the teachers at the old *Katedralskolen* (Cathedral School) and the new *Trondhjems Tekniske Læreanstalt* (Trondhjem Technical College). This also meant a stronger connection to the city of Trondheim. The local focus came to be not only a scientific focus but also an institutional and ideological one. Instead of a Norwegian Scientific Society, the ideology of a scientific museum for Trondheim came to replace the national ambition. It did not contradict it, as long as all parts of the kingdom were important to nationalism. However, the local identity grew much stronger as the empirical finds and most of the objects came from the local region. This way of seeing the national in the local was logical but the end result was nevertheless a rather strong feeling of it being Trondheim's museum.

---

[554] In: *Skrifter*, Annual report 1874, 9.
[555] Heiberg et al. (eds): *Fremtid for fortiden*.

Karl Rygh continued year after year as the leader and only salaried conservator (but not full-time as Storm was, as Rygh was still teaching) of the archeological collection. And steadily the collection grew in both scale and scope. In the last quarter of the 19th century, the archeological collection quadrupled in volume, from 1500 items in the mid 1870s to upwards of 6000 items by the turn of the century.[556] The scope of the collection also increased, in particular in the 1890s when the museum substantially increased its collections from the medieval ages and even from the last 400 years.[557] In fact, it increased to such a degree that in 1891 Rygh suggested that in the absence of other responsible museums the Society also had to take charge of these newer culturally very valuable items although they did not fall under Rygh's archeological approach.[558] The result was a broader and larger collection under Rygh's unquestioned leadership and authority.

Rygh was not alone, and he did not do this full-time. He was still an *overlærer* (headmaster) at the cathedral school. After 25 years, in the fall of 1898, he ended his career as a teacher and became a full-time manager and conservator of the archeological collection at the museum. He also engaged other promising young archeologists in his work, as the case was with Undset. However, his main collaborators in his work through all these 25 years came to be the society of which he also was the chairman for long periods: The Trondheim division of the "*Foreningen for fortidsminnesmerkers bevarelse,*" or the antiquarian society. All finds from this organization were handed over to the Society and were responsible for a substantial part of the growth of the collection. People (in many cases they must have been farmers) also sent items to the Society as gifts. From the middle of the 1880s gifts started to also come from the local authority, as digging in the city ground revealed increasingly larger finds from medieval times and later. The city engineer and his office thereby came to be an important source for the Society.

However, not everything was satisfactory. In the 1880s two new phenomena gave reason for concern both for Rygh and the Society. First of all, the Society faced competition. People had always been looking for gold and silver treasures in the ground. The new phenomenon from the 1880s was that agents and private collectors had started to buy antiquarian objects from farmers and others who had such things in their possession. For these reasons many items were lost to the museum simply because it could not pay for them. The interesting issue here is that it was now possible to sell these objects because a market for antiquarian goods had developed outside of the Christiania region—even if they were only made of iron, stone, or wood. This sign of increased awareness of history and prehistory is linked with the increased national sentiments that became increasingly stronger during the politically turbulent 1880s. At any rate, the innocent days of archeological trips and collecting had come to an end and in the

---

[556] In: *Skrifter*, Annual report 1875, 46 and 1899, 20.
[557] In: *Skrifter*, Annual report 1889, XIII.
[558] In: *Skrifter*, Annual report 1890, XXVI.

following years louder complaints were heard about these buyers. In the end the Society itself had to deal with them to buy particularly relevant objects. There was no law or other restrictions that could prevent trading in ancient goods and national heritage before 1905.

The second threat was the loss of items they already had collected and were actually in storage. Corrosion was the name of the source of concern. Particularly, all the iron objects that were excavated and thereby exposed to air started to rust. As the years went by, this became more and more of an open threat. The objects had to be conserved to halt the corrosion of the entire iron collection. The older methods proved to be no longer effective. By the mid 1880s Rygh started to experiment with a new German method based on treatment with lye. Rygh knew that this method had been practiced with success in Stockholm, and he wanted to use it in Trondheim. However, it was a time-consuming method and lacking an assistant to do the bulk of the work he was not very optimistic about its outcome.[559]

Rygh was without doubt the dominant person in building the archeological collection. Vilhelm Storm played the same role for the zoological department. As was the case for the archeological department, the zoological collection also grew steadily in the last quarter of the 19th century. There were, however, differences. First and foremost, Storm had been a full-time employee of the museum and manager of the zoological collection the whole period. Second, the focus of the zoological collection was not all that clear. The emphasis on local animals of all sizes always competed with extraordinary animals from much more exotic places. There was also a successful attempt to build a zootomic collection showing the anatomy of animals. Such exhibitions had proved very popular in Natural History museums in Europe.

The zoological collection did serve two rather different goals: one was to display animal life as it was, both in the local area and increasingly in exotic lands and in deep waters. The other goal was scientific exploration of new species connected with research on the objects. Storm was the man to keep these two rather different aims in one hand. He was, however, trained as a taxidermist and not as a scientist. Hence we would expect him to be more oriented towards the display of animals, in particular the vertebrates. Still, he managed to train himself to be a natural scientist. In his history of zoology in Norway professor Hjalmar Broch claims that Storm was very gifted, and he also speculates what Storm could have accomplished if he had been given a richer and broader environment to work in.[560]

In 1883 Storm reported that the museum had in its possession most of the vertebrates that lived in Norway, and in particular those that lived in the region were all present in different ages and plumages or coats. When it came to vertebrates, the museum now mostly exchanged objects, receiving gifts but also buying interesting items. In 1887, for instance, Storm communicated with the zoological museums in Trieste, Basel,

---

[559] In: *Skrifter*, Annual report 1886, 7.
[560] Broch: *Zoologiens historie i Norge*, 88.

and Berlin and received 25 foreign mammals and 60 birds. Apes, pouched mammals, armadillos, raccoons, and others were received.[561] In other years a lion, a tiger, and a zebra were acquired. No wonder that Storm complained of lack of space already in the early 1880s. Nevertheless, in spite of the scarcity of rooms the establishment of the vertebrate exhibition was a great success. Towards the end of the 1880s—that is, 15 years after the new exhibition had been established—it numbered 200 mammals, and the collection of skeletons had closer to 400 items. The collection of birds had increased from 500 to 1200. There was more: 1700 glasses of fish species and invertebrates from the sea and numerous insects and lepidopteron were also included in the collections.[562]

This exhibition was placed in a local community that never had seen anything like it. In the best of cases the well read had seen drawings in books or newspapers. There was enormous curiosity among Trondheim's population. Storm estimated that in one year the exhibition had been visited by at least 20,000 visitors. In a city with close to 25,000 inhabitants, that is an impressive figure. As he said: on average there had been 400 visitors each time the collection was open to the public. In addition, numerous school classes had visited it outside these hours.[563] The zoological collection really catered to the general audience of Trondheim and created what later came to be the strong link between the locals and the museum. The Society came to be *their* museum. However, not much science was involved, except for the idea of a system and for the curiosity and wonders of nature.

Storm's scientific contribution came in a different field—namely, unknown invertebrates living in the rich source that was Trondheim fjord, where he found forms of life that were new for a zoologist. Storm initiated the study of this very strange, deep, and rich fjord. By trawling and scraping the sediment and different parts of the fjord, he discovered an amazing richness of animal life to be classified and published. Storm thus started the exploration of the fjord, an exploration that would be followed up by many scientists in many disciplines in the years to come.[564]

The sediment scraping was mostly carried out as expeditions in the summer with an extra grant from the Society. The first years he started in the middle and inner fjord while later on he moved outwards and towards the mouth of the fjord. The results were published in a series of papers. He was interested in the smallest details and was a systematic researcher who worked under difficult conditions. His whole adult life was devoted to the Society, from 1856 until his death in 1913 at 77 years of age. In this he seemed to parallel Rygh—but there were great differences in their personalities. Storm did not like public life, and he avoided conflicts and public debates.[565] Rygh was to be the visible and controversial person, but Storm was the man who built the exhibitions that people came to see and admire. The last article he published before his

---

[561] In: *Skrifter*, Annual report 1887, 83.
[562] Ibid.
[563] Ibid.
[564] An excellent overview of this research is to be found in Sakshaug and Sneli, *Trondheimsfjorden*.
[565] NBL: Vilhelm Storm (written by H. Broch).

death was typical for this mild-mannered man: "Observations on the arrival of spring in Trondhjem."[566]

The mineral and coin collections lived a much more modest life compared with the two major museum collections. However, they should not be disregarded even if their conservators only did their jobs in their spare time with only a very modest compensation. As for the mineral collection, the Society asked *overlærer* (headmaster) C. W. Carstens (1841–1896), member of the new board of the Society, to lead the rebuilding of the collection. Carstens was considered very well suited for this, as he held a degree in mineralogy from the university in Christiania and because he was also in charge of the mineral collection at *Trondhjem Tekniske Læreanstalt* (the technical college, TTL). This was also the reason why he turned down the offer. He considered it might be a conflict of interest if he were to manage both the mineral collection of the *Trondhjem Tekniske Læreanstalt* and of the Society. Instead, Carstens agreed that he would assume the responsibility for the coin collection after Principal Müller left *Katedralskolen* and moved to Christiania.[567] Thus *adjunkt* (teacher) Kristian Getz was asked to take over the mineral collection, and accepted.

The coin and medal collection had approximately 5500 items when Carstens started in 1874. Immediately during the first year the collection was increased by 300 items, mostly through gifts from people all over the country, including the King himself.[568] Carstens continued as conservator of the coin and medal collection for 20 years until he stepped down in 1894. The collection had then expanded to more that 12,300 items when taken over by the teacher, later headmaster B. Hartmann as the new conservator.

The coin collection was more or less a hobby for Carstens. His main area of work would be in electricity, where he was in charge of all teaching in electrical engineering at *Trondhjems Tekniske Læreanstalt* (TTL) up until 1890. As such, he was one of the early pioneers of electricity use for industry and private homes in Norway. He was also a key figure in establishing the Polytechnic Society in Trondheim where over the years he held several positions.[569] The coin and medal collection was, in other words, not his field of expertise, even though he was a very dedicated amateur. In his opinion, the collection was not the basis for research, it was more a continuation of an old tradition mixed with the wish to display and show these items to the public. In this way the idea behind the collection was much the same as the way the numerous large mammals were displayed as opposed to the research Storm did on the animal life in Trondheim fjord.

The mineral collection also expanded steadily. By 1882 it had been taken over by *adjunkt* Carl Schulz (1851–1944), who continued as conservator for many years. As with Carstens, Schultz was also to be connected to the *Trondhjems Tekniske Læreanstalt* (TTL) and the teaching of electricity. In fact, he took over the job after Carstens had to step down in 1894. Schultz was first and foremost a teacher. He started his career after

---

[566] Ibid, "Iagttagelser over vaarens komme ved Trondhjem."
[567] In: *Skrifter*, Annual report 1874, 11.
[568] In: *Skrifter*, Annual report 1875, 42–43.
[569] Wale, Nyhet, nytte, framskritt, 111–112.

graduation from the university as teacher at *Katedralskolen* and moved across the street to *Trondhjems Tekniske Læreanstalt* (TTL) in 1893 and worked for the technical college for the rest of his life. When *Norges Tekniske Høyskole* (NTH, The Norwegian Institute of Technology) was established in Trondheim in 1910, he continued at the now-downscaled technical collage (*Trondhjems mellomtekniske skole*) as director of the school from 1917. In 1909 he published a textbook on electricity and was an eager politician advocating the establishment of a public electricity company. He came to be even more of a pioneer and advocate for electricity than Carstens, who died in 1896.[570] There was, however, a somewhat closer connection between Schultz and the mineral collection than between Carstens and the corresponding coin collection. When Schultz was employed by *Trondhjems Tekniske Læreanstalt*, he was engaged as a teacher in the subjects of electricity, physics, and metallurgy. An enthusiast for the region, he was also an avid mountaineer, published works on mountaineering and hiking, and is usually considered the founder of *Trondheim Turistforening* (*the Trondheim Trekking Association*). Today, one of the *Turistforeningen's* cabins is named after him (*Schulzhytta* in the mountain region of Sylane).

The collections grew in size. Some items were gifts, others had to be bought, and for the mineral collection, Schultz's excursions in the fields and in the mountains really paid off. He brought back a large number of samples to the collection. The mineral collection came in many ways to be his collection. So, as we have seen, both the older Carstens and the younger Scultz were pioneers in electricity, both were very active in organizational life and in politics, and both were very broadminded and typical "modern men" of the city of Trondheim. But they were probably not researchers in any contemporary sense of the word. This role was left to Rygh and Storm.

The library also continued to grow. It was still a key activity of the Society even if the expansion was not as spectacular as in the two main collections. During the last quarter of the 19th century, around 200 persons annually borrowed from the library. This number was amazingly steady, and as we have seen, also comparable with the first three quarters of the century. The growth in the number of volumes was also rather uniform, approximately 1200 books or prints (500 volumes) a year. Of these between 10 and 20 per cent were bought, the rest came as gifts or through exchanges. Typically, the two major fields that had the largest shares were natural history and history with archaeology. A bit surprisingly, in third place came journals and reports from foreign scientific societies. This was obviously a remnant of the days when there was exchange between societies. However, this tradition appeared to still be alive and continued to be one of the largest methods of acquisition.

It should be noted that even if the library was open and could be accessed by most people, it was the exhibitions that drew the large audiences. It was here people came to see the lion, tiger, and zebra. The books were still for the few, and, we would think, for the intelligentsia. As the number of loans usually was around one thousand a year, this

---

[570] Ibid, 114.

meant that each person borrowed four books or prints a year. That a total of 250 persons borrowed four books a year is a surprisingly stable figure and tells a tale of a city with a rather stable, but not very large population of intellectuals.

The 20-year period following the dramatic shift towards a scientific museum in 1874 was beyond doubt the period dominated by the two conservators and managers of each their collections: Karl Rygh in the archaeological section and Vilhelm Storm in the zoological section. There were others, many others who contributed and had a say, but through their dynamic and eager dedication these two men succeeded in building the collections and fulfilling the goal they had set in the early 1870s.

Rygh and Storm were very different persons: Rygh was a fighter, stubborn, inflexible, with an enormous capacity for work. He was really a working man in the garden of science. He was conservative, and active in the political battles in Norway around the mid 1880s on the losing side of the King and the established order. It was said that he considered the winner, the leader of the liberal opposition, Johan Sverdrup, to be a new Robespierre.[571] He was stubborn and at the same time modest on behalf of both his own need and the needs of the collections. This combination worked very well in getting the expansion of the museum started. Later on it became more problematic.

Storm, on the other hand, was Rygh's opposite when it came to stubbornness and aggressiveness. Storm was a hard worker, but no politician. He was, however, the one who had an interest in the audience, in reaching out to them, telling them about science and showing the population of Trondheim the marvels of nature. No wonder that Storm came to be the popular conservator.

Typically, Rygh was the one who stood for election to be a director in the Society, something that Storm was not very interested in (he was elected member of the board in 1893). Rygh was elected to the board quite early (already the year after the reform, in 1875) and later he was to be elected *praeses* of the society (from 1883). Since he kept his job as *overlærer* (headmaster) at *Katedralskolen* until he was 60, he could be an officer of the Society at the same time that it was his employer. Rygh saw no problem in this.

Both on the board and in other bodies of the Society there was a tendency in the 1880s and early 1890s for teachers at *Katedralskolen* and *Trondhjems Tekniske Læreanstalt* to have increasingly important roles in the Society. These two schools came to be the basis for much of the Museum's activities as well as for the board of the Society. They were not the only ones, of course, but with Carstens, Schultz, and Rygh as conservators (in addition to Storm who had his full-time position in the Society) and the majority of the board members, one could argue that these two institutions were the real foundation for the transition to a more museum-oriented society and a society that became a part of the city and modern city life. The museum became the city museum of Trondheim, more in practice than in name.

The two institutions also received goods and services from the Society. In 1884, for instance, the board decided that *Trondhjems Tekniske Læreanstalt* should be allowed to

---

[571] Petersen, "Karl Ditlev Rygh."

borrow all mathematical and physical instruments that were in the collection of the Society. The collection must have been in bad condition since the board decided to compensate the school for expenses they would incur from putting the instruments in working condition—if the Society wanted the collection back (which apparently was not that certain). So in 1884, 74 instruments were put in working condition and labeled as the property of the Society and displayed at the premises of *Trondhjems Tekniske Læreanstalt*.[572]

The last quarter of the 19th century saw great changes in the Society. As with many other scientific institutions in Europe, also in Trondheim, the museum movement took over as a key element in doing and exhibiting science. A museum came to be the perfect mix of both doing exclusive research and at the same time catering to a large audience, telling the people about the wonderful discoveries of science. In a time without cinema, radio, or television, the museum came to represent one of the strongest media experiences local people in Trondheim—and for that matter all over Europe and in the "colonies"—could experience. It was the lucky moment for the mix of science and museum. Here, in Trondheim, Karl Rygh and Vilhelm Storm came to be the architects behind this successful amalgamation, with good help from, among others, Schulz and Carstens.

---

[572] In: *Skrifter*, Annual report 1884, 48.

10

The golden age of museums

The years around the turn of the century came to be the great museum years in Norway as in many other countries. New museum buildings were erected in many cities all over the world, beautiful monumental buildings signifying the importance of the natural and cultural heritage. Let us just remind ourselves about some of them. It is reasonable to start with the beautiful new complex for the British Natural History Museum designed by Alfred Waterhouse in a very eclectic style, taking inspiration from both the gothic revival and the Romanesque styles. The building opened in 1881 and heralded a new age and way of catering to a larger audience with its emphasis on dioramas and new types of exhibitions. It was very symbolic that the exhibitions were transferred from the British Museum's main quarters to the Natural History Museum as if to underline the importance of also displaying the objects to a lay audience and not only to scientists.[573]

There were others, many others. In the capitals of Europe new and larger museum buildings were raised. In Stockholm, the Swedish national museum for natural history (*Naturhistoriska riksmuseet*) moved out of what had been an impressive building already in the 1870s to Frescati, in the outskirts of Stockholm, in 1904. The new building was even more impressive, as were the discussions over what the museum should actually do: science, education of the masses, or be a place for pleasant excursions outside the city on Sundays. In Vienna, the imperial nature of the museum was even more underlined with the two major buildings along the Ringstrasse: *The Naturhistorische Museum* and the *Kunsthistorische Museum*. Both palaces were erected and opened between 1871 and 1891. They were at the time also given the names of imperial museums and were opened, of course, by the emperor, Franz Joseph I. The museums had really become imperial and their buildings had to be palaces.

And so it went on all over Europe. In the Netherlands, Amsterdam Zoo's society, *Artis*, marked its 50th anniversary in 1888 with the opening of a new and large building for its Ethnographic museum which, of course, was augmented by the collection of the *Koloniale Veregeniging* (Colonial Society). The society had 6000 members, including many scientists. "Using zoology, music and exhibitions of a colonial nature, *Artis*

---

[573] Beckman, *Naturens Palats.*

emerged as a cultural centre that prominently displayed Dutch science and contributed to national pride," writes the historian Donna C. Mehos.[574]

The golden age of the museum came to represent a strange mix of two rather different values. First, the museums were the core institutions for doing science. The collections were, generally speaking, the main working tool for many scientific disciplines. At the same time, the museums also displayed great political value, both for national or imperial pride and unity. Science might not need the new palaces, but national or imperial dreams did.

What is a bit more surprising is that the extravagant building boom was not limited to the imperial states and their capitals. On the contrary, it seems as if it was necessary to reach all parts of the empires or nations with impressive museum buildings. So it was in the colonies of the empires, and so it was in the main cities of Norway, scattered as they were along a very long coastline.

The largest museum outside Kristiania was Bergen Museum. Two large wings were added to its already magnificent building in the years between 1893 and 1898.[575] The doubling of space made the museum into one of the most monumental buildings in Bergen. Also the new scientific museum in Tromsø (established in 1872) moved into its own new majestic building in 1894. Even more awe-inspiring was the new building that the museum in Stavanger erected in the years leading up to 1893. The museum was established in 1877, with the main emphasis on natural history and ethnography, while archaeology was added later. The building in the new Renaissance style underlined the importance of this rather new institution in the city.

The collections at the university in Kristiania also moved into new buildings. Through most of the nineteenth century they had been kept at the university's own premises in downtown Kristiania. In Kristiania the architecture of the new museum buildings was also spectacular: as was, for instance, the new historical museum built in 1897 to 1902 (housing archaeology, the coin cabinet and ethnological items). It was a grand building in the Jugend, or Art Nouveau style, both from the outside and, particularly inside. This invoked the response and criticism of such museum experts as Haakon Shetelig from the museum in Bergen: ". . . pilaster, decorative gilding, dominant shining chandeliers etc, totally reprehensible decorations in a museum that first and foremost should let its collections be displayed in tasteful and neutral rooms."[576] Being the central national museum of history had its price when it had to overshadow the museums in the other Norwegian towns (Stavanger, Bergen, Trondheim and Tromsø).

De naturhistoriske museene (The museums of natural history) needed more time to move to another area on the east side of Kristiania, to Tøyen. This was not due to a lack of interest but represented more disagreement over how they should be funded. Finally, in 1903 *Stortinget* made its first grant from the university's own "*Tøyen-fond*" to the

---

[574] Mehos, "Science displayed," 2.
[575] Shetelig, *Norske museers historie*, 69. Forland and Haaland, Universitetet i Bergens historie, 80–81.
[576] Shetelig, *Norske museers historie*, 42–43.

first of the natural history museums, the Zoological Museum. It was completed in 1910.[577] The Geological Museum was first opened t in 1920.[578] These museums were even more monumental, placed in a large botanical garden and made of the most typical Norwegian minerals, according to the rector of the university, W. C. Brøgger.

These national and local monuments marked the high prestige of the museums and thus of science. Neither before nor later was it possible to combine science and *wissenschaft* with popular culture as in these museums. It helped, of course, that the museums had few competitors as media for the general public. With no television, Internet or radio, and the cinema in its very infancy, only books and journals were available for distributing news about scientific findings. But what were these compared to a nose monkey, a tiger or a Viking sword? The aura of the real objects was extraordinary, even more so then than now.

It would, however, not be fair to say that it was the golden age only of the science museums. On the contrary: the popularity threatened the close connection between science, collections, and displays. New areas were emerging as popular fields for new museums, perhaps even more popular than the older scientific museums of the 1870s or earlier. If we want to oversimplify, there was a tendency to expand natural history and archaeology in the direction of more emphasis on arts and craft and on ethnology and cultural and folk history. However, the scientific or *wissenschaftliges* aspects of these collections were weaker than the old ones. The major museums in Bergen and Tromsø, as well as in Trondheim, as we have seen, and the university museums in Kristiania, all had a strong emphasis on research—and the way to do research was to have collections. The new museums of the 1890s were of another type—the collections and their displays were the central element, not science.

There are two types of museum that are of particular interest in our context. First, there are the museums for arts and craft or "*kunstindustri.*" Second, there are those that came to be known as "*folkemuseum*" or museums displaying national ethnographic objects, often in combination with outdoor displays of old houses with yards and so on. Or, if we want, a shift from styles of the upper classes to agrarian folk culture, a shift well in line with the national romantic ethos of the time. *Videnskabsselskabet* and its museum ended up outside this movement even though Karl Rygh already in 1882 had acquired the rather small Holtålen stave church on behalf of *Fortidsminnesforeningen* and had it temporarily erected on a plot owned by the Society. For Rygh this was an emergency, as the church would otherwise have been lost.[579]

The arts and crafts museums were inspired by the world exhibition in London in 1851 and the following international exhibitions. In 1876 a society for such a museum was established in Kristiania, and in 1887 in Bergen (*Vestlandske kunstindustrimuseum*). In Trondheim consul Klingenberg and a private society, *Utile cum dulci,* took the

---

[577] Collett, *Historien om Universitetet i Oslo*, 104 f.

[578] Ibid, 121.

[579] The church may today be seen at the *Trøndelag folkemuseum* at Sverresborg in Trondheim.

initiative in 1892 to do what had been accomplished in Bergen, namely to establish a museum for arts and crafts, *Nordenfjeldske kunstindustrimuseum* (1893). These museums also collected folk art objects, but only from an aesthetic point of view: what was considered particularly beautiful or representing genuine high quality craftsmanship.

The museum in Trondheim came to represent the link between the arts and crafts museums and the folk museums in a rather strange way. The first conservator of the museum, Hans Aall (1867–1946), was sent to buy old folk art in central Norway in 1894 on behalf of the museum. During this trip he came to recognize the problem of selecting only smaller objects and only based on esthetics and craftsmanship. He wanted to include all aspects of the old folk culture and transcend the borders of the arts and crafts museums.

In this he must have been inspired by Artur Hazelius (1833–1901), the Swede who started the largest project in this area: the *Nordiska museet* (the Nordic Museum) and *Skansen* in Stockholm in the years between 1873 and 1891. The new building of *Nordiska museet* at Djurgården was at last completed in 1907 and exceeded all other Nordic museum buildings in grandeur, decoration, and size. Built to resemble a Danish castle, it housed the largest hall in Sweden and probably in the Nordic countries for the next half century.

Hazelius was well known in Norway and was one of the many buyers who trawled the countryside looking for artifacts and items for his collection. Aall was on the same mission, as was the founder of the *Sandvikske samlinger* at Lillehammer, Anders Sandvig (1862–1950). Shetelig informs us that on his trip in 1894, Aall read a newspaper in which he saw a small piece on the opening of Hazelius' *Skansen* in Stockholm. He quit his job in Trondheim and went to Kristiana. He was no scientist so he aired his ideas to several university professors who became interested and helped him to form a society for *Norsk Folkemuseum* in December 1894.[580] In other words, none of the founders of the *Folkemuseums*—Hans Aall, Anders Hazelius or Andreas Sandvig—were scientists or ethnographers. They were collectors, focused on the goal of preserving the old culture found in the rural districts of Scandinavia. They came from the arts-and-crafts-museum tradition and developed it further in the direction of ethnography. Their main goal was not, however, to undertake science, but to collect and preserve.

Such was the golden age of the museums: the older types enhanced their status through new and magnificent buildings, while new ones were added in new and popular fields to underline the national romantic atmosphere already there.

The museum in Trondheim

Museums were expanding everywhere, and also in Trondheim. In 1890 the Society asked *Stortinget* most humbly if the contribution from the state could be raised from 6000 *kro-*

---

[580] Shetelig, *Norske museers historie*, 214.

ner to 8000 *kroner. Stortinget* accepted this increase on condition that other contributions to the Society were also raised by 2000 *kroner.*[581] So it was. *Trondhjems Brændevinssamlag* agreed some weeks later to raise their contribution from 2000 to 4000 *kroner.*[582] Very soon the board then decided to employ a second conservator in the natural history collection with a yearly salary of 2000 *kroner.* On December 17, 1891, the conservator at Tromsø Museum, Mikael Heggelund Foslie (1855–1909), was hired by the Society as the second full-time conservator, in addition to Storm, and was given the responsibility for the botany collection that Ove Dahl had put in order a year earlier.

With success came problems. The collection had expanded steadily through the 1880s and with the new conservator, space had really become scarce. Even at the time of the expansion in the 1870s the Society had drawings for additional wings and buildings. Now was the time to realize these plans. The economic climate and the prestige of the museums were now in such a state that it might be the best time to strike. The cost was estimated at 40,000 *kroner.* Knowing that the state would only agree to pay half the sum, the Society's first step was to apply for just half the sum offered by *Brændevinssamlaget*—however, without success this time.[583] Next year they tried again, with better luck, and they obtained 7800 *kroner* for a new building.[584] Several other attempts were made to increase the funds, but none of them succeeded the first time round. Slowly, however, a building fund was realized. In 1894 the situation changed when *Brændevinssamlaget* granted an additional 10,000 *kroner* to the building fund. The fund had then reached 22,000 *kroner,* more than half of what was needed and immediately the board submitted an application to *Stortinget* for the additional 20,000 *kroner.* The situation was by now critical, in particular for the zoological collection. When in 1893 it received good specimens of a tapir, a leopard, a boar, a couple of seals and other large mammals, it was obvious that they had to do what a decent zoological collection should not do: they would have to compromise the systematic exhibition, and even worse, they would have to put part of the collection of both mammals and birds into storage. The time of even more space-consuming media techniques had not yet reached the Society. No one even mentioned the new didactics of the dioramas as practiced recently at the Natural History Museum in London.

The response from *Stortinget* was not encouraging. No grant was given in 1894, nor in 1895, when the Society even cut its application down to 15,000 *kroner.* Once more *Brændevinssamlaget* lent a helping hand, also this time with an extraordinary grant. In 1896 *Stortinget* stated clearly that if it could not grant the funds needed immediately, the Society would be next in line after the Parliament had finished funding the two new

---

[581] St.f: Kgl. prop, beslutn 5/5 1891 and 6/6 1891. I: Annual report 1891, p. II.
[582] The *Trondhjems Brændevinssamlag* was a semi-public institution with a monopoly for the sales of liquor on the condition that the surplus should be used for social or cultural purposes. It functioned between 1883 and 1923. See Bratberg, *Trondheim byleksikon,* 572.
[583] I: *Annual report* 1892, p. XI.
[584] I: *Annual report* 1893, p. XI.

wings at Bergen Museum.[585] Bearing this in mind, and with an ever-increasing need for space, the board decided to change its plans. Instead of finishing according to the original drawings from the 1870s, they decided to have an east wing which could be paid for with the funds they already had collected and then expand more when *Stortinget* at last could grant funding. This solution was a way around the greatest problems and instead made it possible to continue to present the collections to the local community in Trondheim. It is an indication of priority that the board chose to build exhibition rooms instead of working space for the conservators. For the first time, exhibition trumped science even if it was an opportunistic action more than an ideological one. Hence, in 1897 drafts were reconsidered and an east wing was under construction to be opened in the summer of 1898 with new rooms for exhibition. The idea then was that the state later on would fund a southern wing with offices and work space for the scientists.

The Parliament was not too eager to fund the buildings. Several museums were under construction and the way *Stortinget* handled this was to increase the demand for local funding. In Trondheim, *Brændevinssamlaget* came to be the most important funder. This organization was based on a new and more restrictive law on the sale of liquor. It stated that there should be a publicly controlled sales monopoly and that the profit from this activity should be used to support the common good and cultural and social activity in the local district. It turned out that this attempt to curb the consumption of alcohol was the most important contributor to the new museum buildings. Without the support from this institution, the Parliament would probably not have provided their share of the funding.[586] Later, the funding of Trondheim biological station came to depend so much on the grants from *Brændevinssamlaget* that it was called the legitimate child of *Brændevinssamlaget*.

Whatever the source of funding, the idea of the museum's expansion was primarily to gain more space for exhibitions. The first wing of what was to be the new and large main building was already built by 1878. It was designed to hold two large exhibition halls—one on each floor. However, as the museum then also needed space for conservators and equipment, the halls were temporarily built with smaller rooms in anticipation of further expansion. This was what finally happened towards the middle and end of the 1890s. From being a rather strange appendix to the old main building, the wing from 1878 was transformed into a large main building in 1898, as what was called the east wing was added and the new central staircase was built somewhat later. The museum had thus acquired four great halls with beautiful cast-iron columns for exhibitions. The problem of housing services and offices was solved by adding what we above called the southern wing—which actually was a wing perpendicular to the main façade facing Erling Skakkes gate and the museum park. The new and impressive staircase linked the two façade wings, one from 1878 and the other built twenty years later,

---

[585] I: *Annual report* 1896, p. III.
[586] Bull, *Privatarkiv*, 75.

and the new more recessed office wing from 1903. Finally the link between the old 1866 building and the new exhibition area was extended to two floors in 1904 and completed the museum block facing Erling Skakkes gate.

All new buildings in the 20th century would be extensions to the south of the existing buildings, with the library as an addition to the old building in the west, and more office space for researchers and conservators behind the new 1904 office wing to the east. The main design of the museum and library was clear already around the turn of the century. The idea of having public service areas with exhibitions in front and storage, conservators and researchers in the back, was an international trend in museum buildings for the last 20 years of the nineteenth century.

The 1890s was a time of expansion of the staff and buildings, while the first decade of the 20th century became more or less a time of consolidation of what had been achieved. In 1904 the buildings were completed and the main façade facing Erling Skakkes gate remains the same today, more than a century later. The collections and the staff also reached a new plateau at the beginning of the new century. Most importantly, new and highly qualified personnel were recruited and employed by the museum. This underlined the impression of a *scientific* museum that preserved the Society's scientific ambitions at the same time as it rode the wave of the new museums. The Society built exhibition halls while the important activity as reported annually was research and development of the scientific collections. These collections did not necessarily coincide with the exhibitions.

The Society, now turned into a museum, had some advantages, as we have seen: it had an old collection, it equipped the men responsible for renewal, Storm and Rygh, with an institutional base to build the museum, and it had already some infrastructure, namely a building and funds. Combined with the enthusiasm of the conservators this made for a very good start of the museum period. However, it was not that obvious that things would continue to grow at the same speed. We have already looked at one or two problems concerning the expansion of the museum during the new-establishment phase. Funding for the new buildings was a problem, as the state could not guarantee an increase in investment in the long run. They were envious of Bergen, as Bergen had the rich merchants who were willing to invest more and more funds in the museum at the same time as the museum had the greater plan to become the core of a local scientific college, perhaps even a university in the not-too-distant future.

But it was not only funds that were lacking in Trondheim. Most of all, it was a lack of vision and entrepreneurship. This was internationally the time of the great museum masters, museum directors who went through fire and water to build their museums. The most well-known in Scandinavia was of course Arthur Hazelius who established *Nordiska Museet* and *Skansen* in Stockholm. In Norway, Anders Sandvig at Lillehammer tried something similar. At the museum in Bergen, Dr. Jørgen Brunchorst became the strong administrative leader, with the title of managing director from 1901, even if he had already actually functioned in that capacity for many years. Internationally this era is marked by the great museum masters: Henry Cole at the Victoria and Albert

Museum, George Brown Goode at the Smithsonian Museums, and Oskar von Miller at the Deutsches Museum and Wilhelm Bode at Berlin's Museum Island.[587]

The Society in Trondheim had Karl Rygh and Vilhelm Storm. Their main interest was science and not entrepreneurship. They had fought against the old dilettantism, but to go from that to becoming entrepreneurs for a new museum was a major step. Moreover, the way the museum was organized, as a society, without an executive leadership, might have been a problem. The board and its chairman, the *praeses*, had other positions. The closest we can come to an executive officer was the secretary, but in Trondheim the men who held that job never managed to rise to the position of director as Brunchorst did in Bergen in 1901.[588] The new museums had the advantage of being organized as museums from the start and not as membership organizations also involved in other matters. Hence, the seemingly democratic organization of savants in the Society did not work as well for a modern museum as for a scientific organization or perhaps a research institute. Already towards the end of the 1890s it must have been clear that the differentiation of institutions demanded an adequate organizational structure better adapted to the means and goals.

There is another line in this, however, and that is science. The museum expanded in the period but it expanded inside the original framework, which was as an organization that first and foremost was interested in pursuing science. This was the triumph of Rygh and Storm: as soon as possible, they tried to recruit new scientists to the organization. In the following we will look at some of them.

The new scientists

In 1892 the funds from the government combined with an increase in support from *Brændevinssamlaget* made it possible to increase the scientific staff by one person. It is interesting that it chose to do so. The funding could have been used for stipends or grants in connection with the work that Storm and Rygh already were doing. However, they chose to employ a full-time conservator. The choice fell on Mikael Heggelund Foslie (1855–1909), a 37-year-old conservator at the somewhat younger and smaller Tromsø Museum. Foslie was the second conservator to be employed full-time by the Society after Storm. Rygh only had a part-time position until he quit his job as teacher at *Katedralskolen* in 1898. The choice of Foslie obviously did not come out of the blue. The Society wanted Foslie and the way to get him was to offer a permanent position like the one he had in Tromsø where he had been working for more than six years.[589] Thus in the spring of 1892 the museum staff doubled, having now two conservators in the field of natural history and Rygh still alone part-time in the archaeology department.

---

[587] Alexander, *Museum Masters.*
[588] Forland and Haaland, *Universitetet i Bergens historie*, 73.
[589] Wille, "Mikael Heggelund Foslie," 7.

Foslie's scientific specialty was algae, especially salt-water algae. Throughout his lifetime his publications and scientific contributions in botany and, in particular, calcareous marine red algae (*corallinales*) became internationally famous. All in all he described 240 new species and almost as many new forms and sub-forms. However, later research has widened the definition of species so the number has been reduced; nevertheless, it was an important international contribution. In the beginning of the new century, Foslie had algae sent to him from all over the globe for description and categorization.[590] He collaborated with many algae specialists and professors all over the world, and became a good friend of the professor in botany at the university in Kristiania, Johan Nordal Fischer Wille (1858–1924). Wille, three years younger than Fosslie, outlived him by 15 years and wrote his obituary. Wille's specialty was also algae. He received his doctoral degree in 1885 for a thesis on their physiological anatomy. This was the first doctoral thesis at all in botany at the university in Kristiania. In 1886 Wille was called to a professorship at *Stockholm Högskola* and in 1893 he succeeded Fredrich Christian Schübeler (1815–1892) as professor in Kristiania.[591] Wille was a student of the famous Swedish specialist on algae, Professor Veit B. Wittrock (1839–1914) and it was Wittrock who opened the doors for Wille in Sweden. These three, the older Wittroch and the two younger, Wille and Foslie, became key figures in this new field of algae research in the Nordic countries.

The reason for discussing these researchers here is that many of them followed up the algae research that Foslie started in Trondheim. As we shall see later, Foslie was succeeded some years later by one of Wille's students, K. Henrik O. Printz (1888–1978).[592] Algae studies continued to be of importance to the natural history section at the museum, also after Foslie. Wille was also interesting as a researcher in botany because he offered a renewal of the old botanical tradition from Blytt's and Wille's predecessor, Professor Fredrik Chr. Schübeler (1815–1892). Wille insisted on laboratories as important elements in botany, emphasizing not only collecting, preserving and classifying, but also studying plant physiology in the laboratories.

Foslie became friends of all of these professors. However, he himself marked some sort of transition from the Enlightenment's amateur collector to the professional researcher with a PhD degree and a future, hopefully, as professor at a university. He was in a way closer to Storm than to Wille and Printz when it came to education and training. On the other hand, he shared Wille's interest in laboratory work. Foslie came to symbolize in a successful way the transition from the more or less self-educated collector to the professional scientist, and the way the Society was drawn between the two ideal types of institutions: on the one hand, the museum increasingly oriented toward the public, and on the other hand, the Society as a research institute with its laboratories and, of course, collections. The conservators following Foslie were all oriented

---

[590] Jørgensen, *Botanikkens historie i Norge*, 222. Wille, "Mikael Heggelund Foslie," 4–5.
[591] Jørgensen, *Botanikkens historie i Norge*, 70 and 219–221.
[592] Jørgensen, *Botanikkens historie i Norge*, 223.

towards PhDs and an academic career, while the earlier ones, Rygh and Storm, were either teachers in the high school or self-trained.

Foslie's personal history was extraordinary. He was born and raised at Borge in Lofoten. Here he was taught by the local pastor. Later he read mostly by himself and passed the upper secondary school exams as an external candidate in Tromsø. He continued to study after he had started working as a shop assistant and finally educated himself as a telegraph operator. There is a long anecdote about how he became interested in the beautiful marine algae through his girlfriend's interest, but in the end he started collecting and preparing what he found at hand. In the fall of 1879 he stayed for a while in Kristiania where he visited professor Schübeler, who shared his interest in algae. Foslie was given access to the university's collection of marine algae and the literature in the university library. Professor Wille wrote that Schübeler arranged for Foslie to obtain a position as telegraph operator in Kristiania so he could continue his studies of the algae and obviously help Schübeler with the collections, which he did from 1881 to 1885. In 1881 he published his first scientific work, which was followed by many more in the coming years. In 1885 he could finally quit the telegraph profession and enjoy a position as conservator at Tromsø Museum, and then he finally came to Trondheim and the Society as second conservator for the natural history collection in 1892. Here he stayed for 17 years, the remaining part of his rather short life.

During this time he wrote a great number of articles and identified many species of marine calcinated algae. He became an international specialist in this rather difficult field and samples were sent to him from all over the world for his expert opinion. Professor Wille tried to convince him to write the fundamental reference work on this kind of algae, but Foslie did not think he had the ability to do that. What he thought he particularly lacked was the training in the most modern microscopic methods. Finally Wille succeeded in persuading him to start this very ambitious work. The reference work should have photographs of all species in natural size and also microscopic photographs of their inner structure.

Foslie borrowed material from all the important museums in Europe and the USA. Together with the known literature, this was to be the basis for the new reference work. He managed to complete a great part of it, but as he told Wille, he would still need another two to three years of work to finish it. Foslie died rather suddenly in November 1909 in the middle of his work.[593]

Foslie was a friend of professors, in particular Wille in Kristiania and Wittrock in Uppsala. Wille describes him as hard working and modest, almost humble and without doubt the most knowledgeable researcher on calcinated algae in Europe. At the same time, Foslie was not a professor and could never be. A professorship required more than being a specialist on algae—even if you were the best specialist in Europe. In spite of his specialty and fame he only received a modest salary at the Society. A university professor would earn two to three times as much. Much the same could also be

---

[593] Wille, "Mikael Heggelund Foslie," 8–9.

said for Storm. Rygh was somewhat different, as he had a university degree already and also a position as lecturer and civil servant at the *gymnasium* (senior high school).

Another fascinating person connected to the Society was one of the most famous Norwegian researchers on moss, the medical doctor and bryologist Ingebrigt Hagen (1852–1917). He was approximately the same age as Mikael Foslie and substantially younger than Storm and Rygh. If Foslie and Storm represented the autodidacts without any university degrees, Hagen represented the university-educated professional, not in natural history, but in medicine. Per M. Jørgensen claims in his book on the history of botany in Norway that, in particular, the study of mosses came to be dominated by medical doctors in the later part of the 19th century and up to around 1920. Hagen was in a way the last of these doctors and in a way tried to sum up the works of these men in a large and partly unfinished work on Norwegian moss (*løvmoser*) published in several volumes from 1907 onwards.[594] Hagen became a member of the Society in 1888. In his youth he worked as amanuensis at the physiological laboratory at the university in Kristiana. Later he held several positions as district doctor in different parts of Norway, also in Oppdal where his family came from. Oppdal linked him both with the mountains (Dovre) and with other bryologists like the pastor (*sogneprest*) Christian Kaurin (1831–1906) and the pharmacist Elling Ryan (1849–1905). Hagen had met Ryan during his work in Fredrikstad, but Oppdal was Ryan's home district as it was Hagen's.[595] However, from 1887 until 1899 Hagen had worked as a doctor in Trondheim. When in 1899 he turned his interest towards Oppdal, it was the rich area for the study of moss in the Dovre Mountains that probably made him leave the city.[596]

Hagen published intensively internationally and in *Skrifter*, while his work as a doctor seemed less and less inspiring. In 1902 he wrote to professor N. Wille at the university in Kristiania, asking if he thought it would be possible to receive a grant from *Stortinget* to complete an all-encompassing study of Norwegian moss. However, Wille answered that this would be very difficult as a new professorship in botany would also be required. As Wille wrote, "[Hagen] also accepted this as reasonable."[597]

Hagen did not give up his attempt to quit the medical profession and work full time on the study of moss. In 1905 he offered the Society to take over all his funds (25,000 *kroner*), collections and library and in return give him an annual salary of 4000 *kroner* and a place to work. The board of the Society let a committee review the proposal and the majority found that it was not possible for the Society to accept the offer.[598]

Hagen never gave up; he was known to be a stubborn man.[599] In 1906, with help from his old friends as guarantors, he was able to strike a deal with the new fund in

---

[594] Jørgensen, *Botanikkens historie i Norge*, 208–213.
[595] Jørgensen, *Botanikkens historie i Norge*, 210–211.
[596] Wille, Ingebrigt Hagen.
[597] Wille, Ingebrigt Hagen, 5.
[598] I: *Annual report*, 1906, 4.
[599] Wille, Ingebrigt Hagen, repeats this several times.

Kristiania for the advancement of science: the Nansen fund. Well equipped with references from the most renown bryologists in the world, he was able to secure an annuity of 3000 *kroner*, while he in due time would transfer 30,000 *kroner* to the fund. All in all this was almost as good an agreement as his first attempt with the Society but this time it was split in two parts. The deal with the Nansen fund nevertheless guaranteed his income while he researched moss.

However, he still needed workspace and housing for his collections and books. To ensure that these would be taken adequate care of, he sought another deal with the Society in Trondheim.[600] He now tried to exchange all his herbaria, books, and laboratory equipment with the Society against an annuity of 1000 *kroner* and a working facility in the museum in Erling Skakkes gate. It turned out that this was easier to achieve, and the Society finally accepted giving him an annual payment of 800 *kroner* on these conditions. Hagen had got his way, and he stayed at the museum for the rest of his life. However, the magnificent work on Norwegian types of moss (*Bryophya*) was never completed, even if he continued steadily to publish it in parts.

Storm and Rygh never married, and the same destiny awaited Hagen. However, at the age of 58, in 1910, he married Magdalene D. Borgen whom he had come to know at the museum, where she worked as preparator and illustrator. He died seven years later.

Ingebrigt Hagen came to work at the museum, in the Society, without actually being on its payroll. His combined annuity from the Nansen fund and *Videnskapbsselskabet* was almost 4000 *kroner*, which was fifty percent higher than the other conservators. Hagen came in a way to represent the independent researcher who worked inside the framework of the Society cum Museum. This gave him both insight and independence. Combined with his uncompromising and stubborn character, this brought him into conflict with the board of the museum, and, we might guess, with another stubborn member and conservator, Karl Rygh.

Hagen felt that he was in the right position to criticize the Society and the museum. In the three years that he had been working at the museum he finally came to the conclusion that "something [was] rotten" in the Society, and, in particular, in the way that the Society was managed.[601] In a 46-page pamphlet he attacked the dilettantism of the board. The finances and the mix between the administration of some of the funds and the working budget was one issue. At the same time he pointed to the large need for more space for the library. Second, he was furious over the way the board had taken away the only conservator in the botany field after Foslie died in November 1909 and

---

[600] Wille, Ingebrigt Hagen, 8.

[601] I: Hagen: *Hvorledes Trondhjems museum styres. Optrykt av Videnskabsselskapets direktion til utdeling blant Selskapets medlemmer*. Trondhjem: Aktietrykkeriet, 1911. This was originally printed in 12 copies for the board only. Hagen demanded that the board tender its resignation at the general assembly in the fall of 1910; if not, he would have the whole pamphlet printed. The board did not resign and instead had it printed the following year with only small changes. All quotations here are from this latest edition.

transferred the position to a zoologist for further study of life in the Trondheim fjord. Third, and most interesting for us, he criticized the way the Society was governed. Since 1896 the provisions stated that the salaried conservators could not serve on the board. To facilitate the discussions and improve the quality of the decisions, it was decided in 1899 that all the conservators should be notified of the board meetings and given the opportunity to voice their opinion if they so wanted. Hagen's criticism was simply that this was never exercised. He was also very critical of the dominance of the teachers from *Katedralskolen* and from *Trondhjems Tekniske Læreanstalt* on the board. This, he thought, had simply been inherited from what he labeled the time of decay in the last century. The time had come, he thought, to put competence and scientific knowledge to work and to rid the Society of the dilettantism of the teachers.[602] Hagen's view on science was clear. He quoted Linné's saying: *Omnis vera cognitio cognitione specifica initatur*—all true knowledge must be based on specific knowledge.

Hagen was clear in his criticism and without acknowledging it, the board accepted some of his criticism. The conservators started to participate in the board meetings, and just a few years later a botanist (Printz) was engaged as conservator. Changes at the board level occurred more slowly, as we will see in the next chapter.

A new generation and a new institution

In the field of zoology, Storm continued his work. But from the early 1890s another institution in Trondheim came to play a vital role in the life of the museum cum society cum research institute. That was *Trondhjems biologiske stasjon* (Trondheim biological station). The early story of the Station appears to be a repetition of what happened with the Society and agriculture at the beginning of the 19th century. New knowledge and better techniques and means should be imparted to agriculture through the *Selskapet for Norges Vel*, and the Society participated in this, granting awards and money for best practices. Towards the end of the same century it was the fisheries' turn. Knowledge should be established and used for the practical purpose of increasing the catch, reducing failure and increasing safety. This also implied attempts to increase the fish population and to predict its location. A parallel to *Selskapet for Norges Vel* was established in 1879 and named *Selskabet for norske Fiskeriers Fremme*.[603] The idea was simple: Agriculture had been modernized, now the time had come for the fisheries, where enlightenment, science, and technology should be put to work to increase the output of this very important industry in Norway, second at the time only to agriculture. The main administration came to be in Bergen, which also became the research center.

In the last quarter of the 19th century, Trondheim had long been surpassed by Bergen and Kristiansund as the most important cities for fish trading and export.

---

[602] Ibid, 40.
[603] Schwach, *Havet, fisken og vitenskapen*, 45.

However, Trondheim held some importance as a fresh fish harbor and the fisheries in Trondheim fjord were far from negligible. Hence, during a meeting of *Selskabet for norske Fiskeriers Fremme* in 1891, a resolution was accepted that called for the establishment of a biological station in Trondheim that could do work of a scientific nature with practical goals for the fisheries in the district, or, in other words, a research institution for applied science in zoology with the goal of promoting the fisheries.[604] One of the main tasks was considered to be production of fry to stock the Trondheim fjord and thus increase the catch. In particular, fry of plaice was relevant and was the focus of much discussion. The idea was widely accepted and supported strongly by, among others, G. O. Sars.

Just as for the museum, it was difficult to find funding for such a research institution in Trondheim. Years went by, and several attempts were made. Finally, in 1900 *Trondhjems biologiske stasjon* was opened with its own house and hatchery in Heggdalen, just at the outskirts of Trondheim, thanks again to *Brændevinssamlaget*. With this station, the scientific community in Trondheim had an important addition, both in terms of researchers and research activity. The Society was very involved in the hatchery in different ways, with members on the board and as a funder of salaries and equipment. In 1897 the Society applied to the ministry for the funding of a researcher to undertake applied research on fisheries in Trondheim fjord. The ministry consented and from the beginning of 1898, Knut Dahl (1871–1960) was employed as *stipendiat* (research fellow) by the Society. In his first report, he described his tasks as research on the living conditions and reproduction of plaice and the migration of salmon fry.[605] Together with Knut Dahl this brought a new world to the Society. Dahl was only 27 years old when he was employed—and he was a university graduate. Not only that, he had worked in the laboratory of Johan Hjort (1869–1948) at the zootomic institute at the zoological museum in Kristiania. Johan Hjort, only a few years older than Dahl, would introduce modern marine biological techniques and means to the laboratories at the zoological museum at the university. Dahl was strongly influenced by Hjort and came to work together with him for many years. In the difficult years in the 1890s, when their ambitions were greater than their resources, for Dahl, the fellowship in Trondheim became part of the search for resources and the attempt to renew zoology that was based in the group of researchers in the circle around Hjort.[606]

The scientific ideal was changing in more than one way in this group (which, incidentally, also counted Kristin Bonnevie [1872–1948], later professor at the university). In a way Hjort and his followers tried to combine the most modern marine biology with the much older and applied field of fishing studies. Fundamental science and useful knowledge should be combined. This was not only a way to fund their scientific interest, but a true belief that basic science and usefulness could be combined. Hence

---

[604] Sakshaug and Sneli, *Trondheimsfjorden*, 298.
[605] I: *Annual report* 1898 "Fiskeriundersøgelsene."
[606] Schwach, *Havet, fisken og vitenskapen*. Broch, *Zoologiens historie i Norge*.

Knut Dahl's position in Trondheim was not an accident but part of a strategy. In 1900, Dahl was finally hired as manager of the biological station in Trondheim, a position he held until 1903, when he moved to Bergen to become scientific assistant for Johan Hjort, who had then been appointed executive scientific director for *Norges fiskeristyrelse* (the Norwegian Fisheries Board).[607] Dahl had published scientific works together with Hjort while he was in Trondheim, as well as more general and enlightening books as, for instance, *Fiskeforsøg i norske fjorde* (Fishing experiments in Norwegian fjords) from 1899. Dahl received his PhD in 1911 and was appointed professor in 1921 at the university.[608]

In Dahl's place, the Swedish zoologist Gustaf Schwenander (1874–1953) was hired in 1901, with both the study of the fisheries and as conservator for the bird collection as his areas of responsibility.[609] Schwenander took over Dahl's position as manager of the biological station in 1903. In 1906 he was called to *Svenska Riksmuseet* (the Swedish National Museum of Natural History). Later on he completed his PhD in Uppsala.[610]

Finally, in this overview of young professional researchers in marine zoology, we should mention Hjalmar Broch (1882–1969). He was a student of Kristine Bonnevie in Kristiania and later came to work with Johan Hjort and K. Dahl in Bergen. He obtained his PhD from the university in 1910, at the young age of 28. He was then given a conservator position at the Society to maintain the good connections between the biological station and the Society. Broch stayed on for 10 years until 1920, when he was hired as docent at the university in Kristiania. From 1937 he was professor at the same university.

Dahl, Schwenander and Broch represented the young professionals who were pursuing academic careers, linked to the new fields of marine biology and fishing research. In contrast to the older generation of Storm and Rygh, Foslie and Hagen, the young professionals represented another road taken for an academic career. The young group represented the first professionally trained researchers as opposed to the self-taught or amateur researchers from the 19th century. It was also a sign of how the times had changed and that it was now possible for young ambitious academics to fund their research and obtain a PhD. This process was not only visible in Trondheim, but also in Bergen, where at the Bergen Museum the same process took place around the turn of the century.[611] In other words, there were more possibilities for professional, scientific research for young people outside the university, and there were ways to return to the university and, in the end, obtain a permanent job as professor. Early in the 20th century the scientific museums were filled with two very different kinds of researchers: the older ones, self-taught individuals who had been working alone for many years and

---

[607] Schwach, *Havet, fisken og vitenskapen*, 89–92.
[608] Broch, *Zoologiens historie i Norge*, 131.
[609] 299.
[610] I: *Annual report* 1905 and Sakshaug and Sneli, *Trondheimsfjorden*, 199.
[611] Forland and Haaland, *Universitetet i Bergens historie*, 73.

the younger ones on a steady path, although with lots of ups and downs, on their way to PhDs and later permanent professorships.

The drawback of the younger members was of course that their calling was science and not a particular institution, be it a society or a museum. They would follow the opportunities in science wherever the funding was available. This was of course the opposite of the older generation, men who had secured their positions and their funding, and due to the funding provided by the Society they had the opportunity to follow science wherever they wanted for the rest of their lives. They could not and would not achieve any better agreements anywhere else. Professorships were out of the question for them and not a consideration on their part.

These strategic differences in interests might very well have been important in the years to follow when discussing the organization of the Society. We will return to this later on. At any rate, it is undoubtedly correct to characterize the first years of the 20th century as a transition phase for the museum, but it was in no way an easy transition. There must have been tensions between the old and young, between the loyal and disloyal, between those whose future (what was left of it) was at the museum in Trondheim and those to whom the world was open, with a professorship hovering tantalizingly in the distant horizon.

These differences must also have existed at other scientific museums and institutions in Europe. The particularities in Trondheim in this process were twofold. First, this occurred rather late due to under-funded institutions. Second, successful museums and institutions in Europe had strong administrations, witnessed by the name *museum masters* that had been coined as a key concept in these institutions. Even in Bergen, Brunchorst was appointed director, as we have seen. Not so in Trondheim. The board continued to consist of amateurs or teachers without any administrative management, except for the secretary of the board, and this position was only a minimum part-time job (approximately 20% of a full-time position).

There was one advantage with the self-taught, older researchers: they were rather inexpensive, and, as we have seen, did not have many other options, therefore they were loyal. The salaries of the older and the new young generation of professionals were on the same level, while the professors at the university could earn up to three times as much. Continuing to hire researchers without PhDs and with less academic qualifications would save the Society and museum a considerable amount of money and provide stability. However, it could also lead to an institution that would fall down to the second rank, one not very interesting to the international community. With people like Storm, Foslie, and Hagen, this was no danger, but it was unclear who would replace them when the time came. The Society had been very lucky with its recruitment so far.

Young academic researchers were also recruited to botany. After Foslie died in 1909 and following Hagen's criticism in 1910, the board appointed the 25-year-old Karl Henrik O. Printz (1888–1978) as conservator for the botanical collection. Printz was educated at the university in Kristiania as a student of Professor Johan N. F. Wille, specializing in marine botany. With Printz, the Society finally had a conservator with a degree under Wille's supervision. As we have seen, both Foslie and Hagen had worked with Wille, but without formally being his students. Printz had very broad botanical interests and, among other things, he continued Foslie's work. Printz was awarded his PhD in 1921 for his work on "The Vegetation of the Siberian–Mongolian Frontier." In 1914–1915 he had participated in a Norwegian Siberian expedition, and it was the results of this that were presented as his PhD thesis in 1921. Printz also became a professor in 1925 at *Norges Landbrukshøgskole* (Norwegian Agricultural University) outside Oslo.[612]

There where others. In 1906 there was once again a change in zoology. After Schwenander left for Stockholm, the combined position as conservator and manager for *Trondhjems biologiske stasjon* was open. The combination of the two positions most likely made it possible to attract a more senior researcher, since the salary came from two different sources. On April 8, 1906, the board decided to appoint the director of *Bergen biologiske stasjon* (Bergen biological station), Ole Nordgaard (1862–1931).[613] Nordgaard came to be a key person at the Society and museum for many years to come. Nordgaard was brought up close to Steinkjer, a city some 160 km northeast of Trondheim, at the end of the Trondheim fjord. He graduated with his *examen artium* and later finished his university studies with a Master's degree (*embetseksamen*) at Kristiania. From 1890 to 1895 he was a teacher at a senior high school in Bergen, but during the summer holidays he would participate in the sediment scraping of the Trondheim fjord as assistant to Storm.[614] In 1895 he was engaged as manager of the then quite new biological station in Bergen and held this position until he came to Trondheim in 1906.

Nordgaard has been characterized as one of the last polyhistors, a man with great interests in both marine life and humanistic perspectives. It is typical that he was recognized both as an international expert on the *Phylum Bryozoa* and the author of a large work on local history. Moreover, he was a keen writer of newspaper articles and journal notes that reached out to a larger audience with the findings from science. Hjalmar Broch describes his scientific style as similar to the older Sarsian tradition—that is, a systematic approach with emphasis on very thorough and solid facts.[615]

Broch's characterization of style also hints at the conflicts that were raised in Bergen in the late 1890s with Johan Hjort's insistence on doing research in marine zoology in a new way and on organizing it differently. This conflict and its solution might throw some light on the situation in Trondheim and how Trondheim came to be a safe haven for Nordgaard and the older way of doing marine zoology. The conflict involved from the start Fridtjof Nansen and Johan Hjort on the one side, and the secretary, later director of Bergen Museum, Jørgen Brunchorst on the other. Brunchorst had earlier argued for the importance of a broad development of the museum and the usefulness of having a biological station connected to it. As in Trondheim, the applied

---

[612] Jørgensen, *Botanikkens historie i Norge*, 343–345. Sakshaug and Sneli, *Trondheimsfjorden*, 303.
[613] I: *Annual report* 1906, 4.
[614] Sakshaug and Sneli, *Trondheimsfjorden*, 301.
[615] Broch, *Zoologiens historie i Norge*, 88–91. NBL (new). Sakshaug and Sneli, *Trondheimsfjorden*, 301.

study connected to fisheries was seen as an opportunity for research, funding and greater local influence. It was as part of this plan that Nordgaard was hired as manager of the station. At the museum in Bergen, almost the same discussions were raging as in Trondheim: should the museum be developed into a research institute, a museum, or a college? Brunchorst wanted a museum and a college for the west coast and in particular for Bergen. On the other hand, ambitious researchers with international links wanted to develop it into a high-ranking research institute.

The opportunity at hand was the governmental project for an international research center for oceanographic study and pelagic fishing, which was much more ambitious than the local biological stations. Behind this proposal we can see Fridtjof Nansen and Johan Hjort. Both insisted on having such a research center in Kristiania, while Brunchorst wanted it in Bergen to combine it with Nordgaard's biological station. Hjort and Nansen were very clear that this was not what they wanted, and Nordgaard was no match for Hjort, as Vera Schwach writes.[616] Hjort's argument is interesting to us: he said that an international research center should not be put under the administration of amateurs—that is, the board of the museum in Bergen museum. Could this be the same dispute that echoed some years later in Hagen's infamous pamphlet attacking the board of the Society in Trondheim? In the end, Hjort accepted a compromise: the research center was located in Bergen, but it was organized as a state institution outside Bergen museum. Brunchenhorst lost and in the end he left his position in 1906— exactly when Nordgaard went to Trondheim.

Trondheim was not engaged in this conflict, with the exception of hiring Nordgaard after the dispute ended. However, it would be wrong to think that the consequences of this conflict were not present in Trondheim as well: Should the Society be a research institute (and hence strive to become even more international and change its mode of research to a more modern approach), should it be a museum for a large part dedicated to enlightenment and local service, or should it embrace the attempts to bring higher education to Trondheim?

From the material we have presented so far, it is not easy to conclude. We have seen the young researchers who received funding while working on their PhDs, and we have seen the older members with permanent positions but without the possibility of obtaining a university professorship. So far we have also mostly dealt with natural history. We will therefore quickly look into what happened in archaeology and history before we return to the important question: in what direction did the Society decide to move in the beginning of the 20th century?

Archaeology was the responsibility of Karl Rygh, who turned 60 just before the turn of the century (1899). Rygh and Storm were still the seniors at the museum, and Rygh continued to work as he had always done. Relieved of his work as a teacher at *Katedralskolen* and not a member of the board, he had his work as conservator and, of course, continued as the leader of *Fortidsminnesforeningens* (The Heritage Associa-

---

[616] Schwach, *Havet, fisken og vitenskapen*, 84.

tion's) local chapter. The collection grew at a steady rate, mostly due to gifts but also excavations. Rygh worked alone as he always had, except for one of his students who became more and more interested in archaeology—Theodor Petersen (1875–1952).

Petersen had been Rygh's pupil at *Katedralskolen*. He was the son of the headmaster at the school and his grandfather had also been *praeses* of the society in the 1850s and 1860s. Petersen studied philology at the university in Kristiania and returned as a teacher at *Trondhjems Realskole* in 1900 and later at *Katedralskolen*. He was also hired as the librarian at the Society when he returned to the city. During the school's long summer holidays he participated as Rygh's assistant during the excavations and he joined the board of the local chapter of *Fortidsminneforeningen*. When Rygh died in 1915, Petersen took over both his position as conservator of the archaeological collection (until he retired in 1947) and as chairman of *Fortidsminneforeningen*, a position he held until 1933.[617]

With Nordgaard and Petersen taking over after Storm and Rygh, a new pair of local scientists was in charge. They were not the same as the previous pair, but they also differed from the rest of the young researchers who were connected with the Society in the first quarter of the 20th century. Neither Nordgaard nor Petersen had a PhD; they had both very broad interests and worked in several disciplines, as professionals as well as amateurs. They had firm connections to Trondheim or Trøndelag and stayed there for the rest of their lives. They came to shape the museum in the same way as Storm and Rygh had done a generation before, and it was formed as a museum, not a research institute. As opposed to Rygh, Petersen was eager to try to create better and more informative exhibits. He also eagerly established and designed a department for Trondheim's local history at the museum (*byavdeling*).[618]

In 1897 J. Brunchorst from Bergen Museum, who at the time was also a member of *Stortinget*, proposed together with other museum people, that Parliament as soon as possible should pass a law prohibiting the export of Norwegian antiquities. As we have seen, for several years buyers and traders had been looking for antiquities, as there was a growing market for such items. To prevent not the trade in but the removal of these artifacts from the country, Brunchorst wanted to outlaw exports. However, the ministry found it hard to formulate such an act of parliament and the whole matter was shelved for several years. In October 1903, the three museums in Bergen, Tromsø, and Trondheim joined forces on an initiative submitted to the ministry which ended in an emergency act accepted by *Stortinget* in 1904.[619]

This was, as the ministry probably suspected, only the hint of a solution. The antiquities from the medieval age and earlier had to be dealt with somehow. In a highly nationalistic age, these reminiscences of the old Norse country and state had to be handled seriously and be kept as national treasures. The step towards nationalizing all these

---

[617] Sakshaug and Sneli, *Trondheimsfjorden*, 308–309.
[618] Sakshaug and Sneli, *Trondheimsfjorden*, Sakshaug, 309.
[619] St.f. Indst. O. nr. 36 1903/1904, 85–86.

items was very short, and less than two years later a new act of parliament was passed that tried to make a full nationalized system of the preservation of antiquities. The act was passed on 13 July 1905, just as the union between Sweden and Norway was being dissolved with all the conflicts that involved, including the threat of war between the two countries. As a symbol of the new independent nation, an act regulating the nation's national heritage was most appropriate.

Karl Ditlev Rygh (1839–1915). DKNVS commemorative medallion for the 1944 gala meeting.
Photo: Per Fredriksen, 2008. *Courtesy:* Museum of Natural History and Archaeology.

Vilhelm Storm (1835–1913).
Courtesy: NTNU Library.

Exhibit of the museum's collection of stone axes.
Courtesy: Museum of Natural History and Archaeology.

Videnskab — Selskabet.

The new main building (the east wing and staircase from 1898–1903), the west wing (right, center) from 1878, and the old main building furthest right from 1866–1868. The office wing is hidden behind the façade. Postcard, 1905.
Courtesy: NTNU Library.

Trondhjem. Munkegaten.

View of Trondheim from the Cathedral looking north. To the right in front *Trondhjem Tekniske læreanstalt*, later the city hall. Further down the street, on the left, *Katedralskolen*. Postcard from Trondheim 1901.
Courtesy: NTNU Library.

The general secretary of the renewed organisation, Professor Sigval Schmidt-Nielsen (1877–1956). General secretary from 1926 to 1945. Oil on canvas, Oscar Sivertzén, 1937.
Photo: Karl-Erik Refsnæs.
Courtesy: NTNU Library.

Trondheim 1951 with the Cathedral, Munkegaten, the City hall (former TTL) and the *Katedralskolen* with the festive hall of the Society. Outside the picture frame to the right is the Museum.
Photo: Vilhelm Skappel, Widerøes Flyveselskap and Polarfly A/S, Oslo. *Courtesy:* NTNU Library.

Annual gala meeting 1951 in the festive hall of the *Katedralskole*.
Photo from the archive of DKNVS. *Courtesy:* NTNU Library.

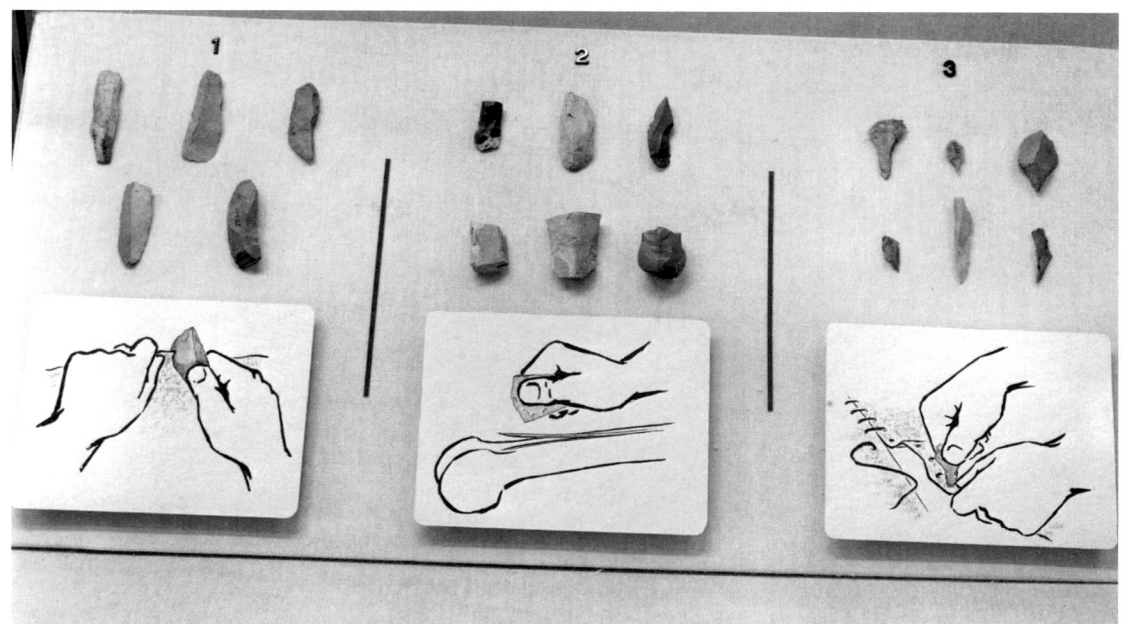

The Museum's exhibition of knives, sticks and gimlets from the Stone Age.
Courtesy: Museum of Natural History and Archaeology.

The Museum exhibition, samples of pottery and soapstone from archeological excavations in Trondheim.
Photo: Per Fredriksen, 1970. *Courtesy:* Museum of Natural History and Archaeology.

The Museum exhibition, avian diorama made 1960.
Photo: Otto Frengen 2006. *Courtesy:* Museum of Natural History and Archaeology.

The Museum exhibition, sea birds, avian diorama made 1960.
Photo: Otto Frengen 2006. *Courtesy:* Museum of Natural History and Archaeology.

The Museum exhibition, model of salmon in waterfall made ca. 1960.
Photo: Otto Frengen 2006. *Courtesy:* Museum of Natural History and Archaeology.

The Museum exhibition, samples of fish models made ca 1960.
Photo: Otto Frengen 2006. *Courtesy:* Museum of Natural History and Archaeology.

Praeses chain, donated to the Society in 1999.
Photo/courtesy: Studio Lasse Berre 1999.

The Society's meeting hall, Festsalen, Trondheim *Katedralskole*, after the redecoration in 1986.
Photo/courtesy: Thor Melhuus, 1986. *Source:* Stiftelsen Trondheim katedralskole 2009.

11

The Museum, the city, and the engineers

On 25 February 1903, a proposal was made to change the statutes of the Society. In brief, the proposal had three main points. First, it was proposed that an addition be made to the name of the Society, adding *Trondhjems Museum* (Trondheim Museum) in parenthesis.

Second, and perhaps even more significantly, it was suggested that the system of electing new members to the Society be abolished all together. As we have seen, the requirement that the members should have conducted their own research had already been removed in the 1874 reform. This time the suggestion would change the society to a regular membership organization where anyone who wanted could be a member by contributing the annual membership fee.

The third point would ensure that the board would have more power to decide about the budget at the general assembly. Two thirds of the votes would be needed to change the budget proposed by the board, while all other matters were to be decided by a simple majority.

In short, it was suggested to do away with the last reminders of a scientific society and replace it with a scientific museum with a supporting membership organization. The old all-encompassing society of savants was now to be turned into a locally based research institution in Trondheim, linked to the region's nature and culture, and governed by local members with employed conservators looking after collections, exhibitions, and research. This was the last step on the road from Gunnerus's international society in the spirit of European enlightenment to the local, scientific museum, the Trondheim Museum. It was an institution that could and would mobilize the local bourgeoisie for the museum as their museum.

The proposal was signed by a powerful and influential group of men. All three senior conservators were included, Karl Rygh, Vilhelm Storm and Mikael Foslie. They were joined by the rather new, and much younger, librarian, Th. Petersen. These four represented the Society's salaried staff. In addition, three of the five members of the board, including the *praes* and the *vice praes*, were among the signatories. The resolution was submitted to an appointed committee for review, as was stipulated by the statutes. Two people from the board, Rygh and the part-time conservator for the mineral collection, Carl Schultz, in addition to the former *praeses*, made some small adjustments, but in principle recommended the proposition. No wonder then that the new statutes were passed on November 6, 1903, and forwarded to the Ministry with the request that the proposal should be given to the Society's protector, the king, for acceptance. He gave it his stamp of approval on February 13, 1904. To put it bluntly: everyone with any power in the Society, whether the conservators or board members, accepted and wanted the change. This raises two important questions: why did they want it and why in 1903?

The proposing group presented arguments for the change. Rygh and Storm were the only ones left from the dispute over changing the statutes in 1874. Now they received support for their view that the changes in 1874 were not complete. The transformation was half done, it was a compromise. This time they wanted to do it properly. The aim of the proposal was to make the statutes fit the actual workings of the institution and to remove what might be seen as ambiguities relating to the objectives and position of the institution. One consequence of this could be to change the name of the institution to *Trondhjems Museum* all together, but the petitioner found this "not advisable, as such a change, among other things, might raise juridical questions."[620] This hints that the museum might be afraid that it would lose funding and donations if the name was changed from *Det Kongelige Norske Videnskabers Selskab* to *Trondhjems Museum*.

The group was quite clear in their proposal that it was the name, "*Det Kongelige Norske Videnskabers Selskab*," that made the situation difficult. Scientific societies and museums were very different institutions, they argued, as museums were financially supported by other institutions and that scientific societies were associations of scientists who received their salaries from other places.[621] The museum thus had to live with a name that did not suit it, but with the addition of *Trondhjems Museum* in parenthesis it was the best compromise they could arrive at. The membership question followed logically from the point of view of the museum. There was no point in electing members to a museum association. The idea was more or less to get the members to contribute financially to the museum and otherwise to elect the board of directors. They had no active part to play in the museum as such.

With this change in the statutes, Rygh found that what he started in the early 1870s now was complete, 30 years later. The Society had finally become a museum, also in name; a museum that insisted on undertaking research. In this way it was more of a research institute than a scientific society; it was a scientific museum, no more, no less. And there was across the board agreement on this question, with sixteen to five votes in favor of adding *Trondhjem museum* to the Society's name and fourteen to six votes in favor of changing the membership rules (open membership).[622] We might suspect

---

[620] In: *Annual report 1903*, 7.
[621] In: *Annual report 1903*, 6.
[622] II:1 General assembly, November 6, 1903.

that the opposing votes came from the qualified scientists who were not employed by the museum. They were not a strong group in numbers. However, the one member of the board who was not among the petitioners was the physician Halvdan Bryn, whom we will meet later. After the changes were approved, he did not seek re-election to the board. We can only speculate as to what were his reasons.

Another member we know something about, and who was present at the meeting in 1903 was the former librarian of the Society, by then *stiftarkivar* (the chief public archivist for the region), Kristian Koren (1863–1938). The later secretary general, S. Schmidt-Nielsen (1877–1956), remembered having asked Koren in the summer of 1902 why they wanted to do away with the membership criteria when the city had the potential to produce a number of natural scientists and its scientific community could grow. Koren had then answered that it was presumptuous to think that it ever would be possible to have a real and working scientific society in Trondheim. It might be just as well to do away with the long and misleading name and once and for all call it *Trond-hjems Museum*.[623] According to Koren, many of the members had a similar sentiment.

The reason for Schmidt-Nielsen's question, and the reason why he was somewhat taken aback by Koren's answer, was the fact that two years earlier, in May 1900, *Stortinget* had decided to establish the first Norwegian academic technical institute in Trondheim, *Norges Tekniske Høiskole*. The name alludes directly to the tradition in which the school was established, the German *Hochschules*. However, in English the official translation was American: The Norwegian Institute of Technology. In 1902/1903 it would have been common knowledge that in a few years time there would be several *bona fide* professors in the city and hence a substantial increase in scientific activity. *Norges Tekniske Høiskole* (NTH) was not built in a day or even a year. It took ten years before the institution opened its doors to professors and students in September 1910. Construction on the building at the Gløshaugen plateau started in 1905 using magnificent drawings by the architect Bredo Greve. He gave his design the title "*vis-à-vis*," which hinted at the location across the river from the ancient cathedral and gave the rather presumptuous expression of the cathedral of modern times: the Technological University, NTH. Already in 1900 it was obvious that the technical university was a national obligation whose goal it was to educate the elite of modern technological Norway.

While NTH was national, the museum became more and more regional. By and large, the museum was well-established and integrated in the city with the large and impressive buildings along Erling Skakkes gate, just completed in 1904, and a substantial number of visitors. The link to the city had been further strengthened through the way the fire security and maintenance of the new buildings had been structured. In the funding for the new buildings, the Society and the state had stipulated that Trondheim local authority had to accept the responsibility for these premises. In this way the museum became even more a part of Trondheim.

---

[623] Schmidt-Nielsen, "Karl Rygh, en merkesmann," 4*.

Nevertheless, once more we have to evaluate the Society's decision in 1903 to do away with as much as possible of the remaining scientific society in the transition to a scientific museum. They knew that scientists and technological professors would be coming to town. In 1874 Bugge's way of obtaining a compromise was to argue that for the time being the scientific community in Trondheim was too weak and too small to support a scientific society in the proper meaning of the word. Hence, the museum format, with reduced working programs, was chosen to carry on the scientific heritage from Gunnerus. Then, when the small scientific community in Trondheim finally saw that a real scientific community was on the horizon, what did they do? They consolidated the society in the form of a museum. The consolidation came in 1903, after the decision in *Stortinget* but before any concrete steps had been taken to bring the professors to Trondheim.

The most obvious explanation is that this was a consolidation against a perceived threat, precisely from a strong academic group, the coming professors of technology. This was a threat in many ways: to the board of directors, to the conservators, and to the city and its public. Let us first look at the board. As we have seen, the board was dominated by the teachers at *Katedralskolen* and *Trondhjems Tekniske Læreanstalt*. With a technical university in town, these two schools would no longer be the dominant intellectual institutions and the elected teachers on the board would either lose their positions or be marginalized, intellectually as well as formally. For the conservators, the real threat was linked to the museum and their status as researchers in a museum setting. The state funded only between a third and a half of the budget, the rest came from other funds and local support. Whoever controlled the funds would also control the conservator's future. Everyone was well acquainted with the workings of the *Videnskapsselskapet* in Kristiania (Oslo). There the professors dominated the board and used the new funds to finance their own research and that of their research students. If the new professors took over part of the Society in Trondheim, funding for the museum work would at best be reduced, at worst cut off all together. The museum was also dear to the local population of Trondheim and the local authority, which contributed to its funding. The technical university was, on the other hand, a national responsibility, funded not locally but by the government. A loss of or a reduction of the museum's activities would therefore be a loss for the city.

All these elements point to the possibility that the consolidation of the museum was paradoxically a defensive maneuver against the threat of being overtaken by a larger national scientific community that they must have expected would be coming to the city in the coming years. Rygh's dispute with one of the leading professors, J. H. L. Vogt, in 1912 indicates this, as did the negotiations that followed until a seemingly agreeable solution was found in 1926.

If the consolidation was only a defensive maneuver for the old power structure and for the status quo, why did Koren say that there would never be a scientific community of any size in Trondheim in 1902? This raises the question of the academic status of the technological profession. Perhaps Koren did not accept the technological professions as sufficiently academic to defend the position of a true scientific society. This is not as unreasonable as it might seem today. Around 1900, the technological professions were very young in the academic world. Most of the German *Hochschulen* did not gain the right to award doctoral degrees until 1899 to 1901.[624] The University of Kristiania, for example, did not want to establish an engineering education at all on their campus. Technology was considered part of the practical and economic world, removed from the ivory tower of academic science and philology, of *Wissenschaft*.

To Koren, science was mathematics, natural science, and the humanities disciplines connected to philology, history, and philosophy. There might be one or two professors in the established sciences at the new technical university in the city, but that would be all, he might have thought. Moreover, the size of the new institution seemed very small from the outset. Little did he know that NTH would double the size of the first class already in 1910 (from the proposed 50 to 100 students in the first year).

There may have been three related but rather independent reasons for the consolidation: fear of losing the museum and the associated funds, acceptance of the dim prospects for an increased number of true scientists in Trondheim, and a lack of acceptance of technology as a scientific discipline in its own right. From the perspective of these three reasons it is possible to understand why this consolidation took place in 1903 and not earlier. For the board and conservators 1903 was exactly the right timing if they were to establish a fortification defending the museum from the impending technical university and its professors. This decision was reached after Parliament had decided in 1900 and before any physical change (buildings) had put its mark on the city in the period between 1905 and 1910.

The decision in 1903 was not unanimous; there were other voices, but they were weak and perhaps their intention was simply to preserve the prestige involved in being an elected member of a scientific society, regardless of the museum. At any rate, they lost and from 1903 until the reform in 1926 everyone could be a member of the society by paying a rather high yearly membership fee of five *kroner*. The exclusivity issue was ensured through the membership fee. It was this local open-membership organization that now carried the rather strange name of *Det Kongelige Norske Videnskabers Selskab (Trondhjems Museum)*. A strange name was a small price to pay to keep the funds and use the dividends for museum purposes. It was now a museum and not an academy—the 1874 reform was complete and Rygh was satisfied. He was now 64 years old. In 1904 the last of the new museum wings was finally completed and the large main museum building with staircases and exhibition halls, workshops, and offices made a good impression on the public. We can see the same buildings today along Erling Skakkes gate and across the park, appropriately named *Museumsparken*, the museum park.

There were, however, some elements that did not quite fit the museum idea. In November 1895 the first "scientific meetings of the society's members" (*Videnskabelige Møder af Selskabets Medlemmer*) in many years were held. The first of these meetings

---

[624] The right to confer doctorates was granted to the German *Technische Hochschulen* between 1899 and 1901. König, "Technical education and industrial performance in Germany," 78.

had a lecture, given by Dr. med. L. Borten on scientific studies of leprosy, followed by a *"meddelelse"* (notification) by the *praeses* (K. Rygh) relating to a picture of St. Anna that had been donated to the antiquarian collection.[625] In 1896 there were three such meetings, and in 1897 five. Most of them had the same format: a lecture on a scientific topic and then a shorter notification, often about something related to the collections or the library. In the following years this activity continued with five meetings in 1898, three in 1899 and finally two in 1900. From 1901 on there were no more such meetings and, as we have seen in 1903, the idea of "scientific members" was left out all together. However, in the years between 1895 and 1900 there had been 19 such meetings with an impressive variety of topics: numismatics, the number pi, animal life in Western Australia, the tree of life in oriental and Christian art, meteorites and many more. There were no talks on Darwinism at all. In addition to these 19 meetings, there were always open lectures on the birthday of the Society's protector, the king, every year, as had been the tradition throughout most of the 19th century, but these meetings were not members' meetings. And finally, there were the general assemblies, held at least once a year, most often twice a year, to elect the board of directors and deal with all sorts of administrative and financial matters.

The years just before the turn of the century gave the impression of increased activity not only at the museum as a research institution (with the new buildings), but also as a membership organization with 19 meetings and scientific discussions. We can connect this to another of the Society's institutions, namely the increasing size and use of the library.

During the building period in the 1870s and around the turn of the century, the library had been, if not neglected, at least not given much priority. Rygh had had his dispute with the librarian Mosling. Mosling saw the library as a key department in the life of a scientific society, while to Rygh the library should in principle be a supporting institution for the museum and the researchers working there. In the 1874 reform a compromise was reached with respect to the library, not entirely in accordance with Rygh's wishes. Even if the research had been focused on archaeology, history, and natural history, the library, on the other hand, was to be developed in line with more general sciences and humanities disciplines; thus *"Derimot bliver Bibliotheket at udvikle i almenvidenskabelig Retning."*[626] This was not to Rygh's liking, so he rather quickly demanded his own budget to buy archaeological literature. Later on, in 1896, in his last act as *praeses*, he amended the statutes in a way that stated that at least half of the funds used by the library should be used for "historical literature."[627]

In 1869 there were 31,500 volumes in the library. This was at the time when the new building was being erected and the library had reasonable possibilities for expan-

---

[625] In: *Annual report 1895*, I.
[626] IV:b:1 *Statutes 1874*, paragraph 3.
[627] In: *Annual report 1896*, V.

sion on the top floors of the new building. Around the turn of the century the number of books had surprisingly more than tripled.[628] The library was not the top priority for the building period from the late 1890s until 1904. It was the last part to be expanded, and this expansion was achieved only by connecting the old and new buildings and the larger central exhibition halls. It was not completed until 1904.

One important reason for expansion at the end of the building period was a special gift the society received in 1899 and the following years. Caroline Jenssen, the widow of one of the richest merchants and landowners in Trondheim, Consul Anton Mathias Jenssen, contributed 50,000 *kroner* to establish a fund in memory of her husband. There was, however, one important condition. Half of the funds should be used to acquire one of the most important private libraries in Norway, the library of *Kgl. fuldmægtig* Thorvald Boeck.[629] Boeck had collected manuscripts, books, letters, and signatures for many years, and it was recognized as a treasure of Norwegian and Danish literary and intellectual history from the 18th and 19th centuries. It was also a very large collection, around 25,000 volumes, manuscripts, and other items. Negotiations with Boeck in Kristiania ended in an agreement whereby Boeck could keep his library as long as he wanted and that he annually would receive the interest on the sales sum. Thus the library only slowly arrived in Trondheim during the first decade of the 20th century. Mrs. Jenssen also had strong opinions as to how the other half of the fund should be used. She wanted it placed in secure obligations with the dividend going to the Society's library on the condition that other grants should not be reduced. This was not exactly a gift in line with Rygh's strategy for the Society; on the contrary it was a gift in the spirit of Gunnerus and of Schwach and Bugge 50 years before.

The library enjoyed success. Library loans increased steadily (doubling in the 1890s) and the lack of space was an acute problem. The loft above the library itself was put in order with shelves and panels on the walls, but still books were shelved in two layers in the reading room to save space. Using the small building connecting what was now called "the library building" (that is, the original building from 1866–1868) and "the main building" helped a little, but in 1904 the library already contained 162,000 volumes, five times as much as in 1869 when the "library" building was finished.[630]

It would take quite a long time before the library got its well-deserved new building and by then much had changed. It was not until 1939 that a new storage area (a book tower) and new reading hall and offices were inaugurated. The new building was situated exactly where Christie had proposed a new wing 73 years earlier, but this time it was larger and did not have Christie's elegant symmetry.[631] The building was expanded once more in 1975.

---

[628] Stang: "Samlingenes vekst," 131.
[629] In: *Annual report 1899*, pp. 4–5.
[630] Stang, "Samlingenes vekst," 131.
[631] Vedi: "Det Kongelige Norske Videnskabers Selskabs bibliotek i ny bygning," 44–48.

A new generation takes over the museum

As we have seen, the museum was consolidated as such in 1903. The old guard, the experienced and well-established conservators from the 1870s—Rygh, Storm and, somewhat later, Foslie—were the architects and catalysts of this change. They were not alone, however. The board supported the conservators. From 1902 to 1914 dr. philos Bjarne Lysholm (1861–1939) was *praeses*. Lysholm was educated in medicine and also worked for some years as a doctor. He took over the family firm for a couple of years but later sold out and used the money to finance his own entomological research.[632] This might be seen as a parallel career to I. Hagen who was also educated as a physician and came to fund his interests in natural science. In fact, Lysholm also signed an agreement giving him work space at the museum some years later, while in return he donated his collection and library to the museum at a later date. In other respects Hagen and Lyshom were very different: Hagen had a temper, was full of self-esteem and self-confidence. Lysholm is said to have been a very modest man, almost shy, and not willing to publish much of his material.

Together with Lysholm members of the board for the first 10–15 years of the 20th century included teachers from the large schools on the upper part of Munkegaten, close to the cathedral: *Trondhjems Tekniske Læreanstalt* (Trondheim Technical College) and *Trondhjems Katedralskole* (Trondheim Cathedral school). For many years (from approx. 1902 to 1915) the teachers Axel Sommerfelt, K. Schøyen and S. Wleügel joined Lysholm, together with another physician, Alexander Holst (1866–1949), chief physician at *Trondhjems kommunale sykehus* (the municipal hospital). Holst's interests went in other directions than the museum: he became director of the hospital and also chair of the national association of physicians. The secretary was another teacher, J. Richter, for much of the same period.

This regime, the three old conservators and the somewhat younger board dominated by teachers, was the one to move away from a scientific society towards a regional scientific museum and a museum association with open membership. In the ten years that followed the change in the statutes in 1903 this was a very stable regime with few changes, even though younger conservators were hired. It was during this regime that *Norges Tekniske Høyskole* came to the city in 1910 with its young professors and students. It is also under this regime that we see the first clash between the museum and the new scientific community in the city.

On average, with a couple of exceptions, as for example Professor Johan Herman Lie Vogt (1858–1932), the newly appointed professors were in their thirties. Vogt had a long international career as geologist and professor at the university in Kristiania when he came to Trondheim in 1912.[633] Parliament had decided to relocate *Bergseminaret* (the Mining Academy) from the university in Kristiania to the new technical uni-

---

[632] Forhandlinger XII, 16, 1929, 57–62.
[633] Amundsen, *Det norske videnskaps-akademi*, vol. II, 37.

versity in Trondheim, and so Vogt moved to Trondheim. In this way, right from the start the new *Hochschule* in Trondheim had a professor well acquainted with academic life and a member of several academies and societies. Vogt was familiar with the history of the Society and he must have seen it as important to try to establish some sort of academic environment for the young and new professors, also outside the teaching institution. Vogt was a prominent member of *Kristiania Videnskapsselskap* where he almost annually had given talks on his findings.[634] To Vogt it was quite obvious that the Society now could be revitalized as a real scientific society and that the interim period with a "reduced" program (as was argued in the 1874 reform) now could come to an end. If he was to stay in Trondheim he needed to establish a forum for science and a place where he could discuss broadly together with his equals in other scientific disciplines.

In the fall of 1912, just after having arrived in Trondheim, Vogt wrote the board of the Society. He found it reasonable that the Society had focused on archaeology and natural history and that it realized its program through working as a museum. This had to be respected. But, he argued, with the new situation, with so many new scientists in the city, higher goals needed to be set to be true to the traditions of the Society and to revitalize the meetings with discussions and talks. In the years to come Vogt saw it necessary to build strong connections and collaborations between the Society and the new technical university.[635]

The reaction from the Society to Vogt's letter was somewhat out of proportion. Karl Rygh put it in writing. He saw Vogt as an intruder who threatened to conquer the collections, particularly the mineral collection, and in the longer run to take over the Society and relegate the museum, his life's work, to obscurity. He saw Vogt's letter as the first of a series of attacks that no doubt would come from the new scientific community in the city, from the newcomers. He felt simply that the Society had to reject such a challenging and in reality insulting proposition. That would be in line with the tradition of the society, Rygh maintained.[636]

Rygh's response gives us reason to believe that the 1903 reform of the statutes was not an accident but a defensive move against the tide of the new and young professors flowing into Trondheim. In his answer we recognize the fierce fighter from the early 1870s and Rygh's battle for the museum. There is a consistent line here, from the establishment based on Bugge's compromise in 1874, through the consolidated reform in 1903 and now the start of the defensive maneuvers to preserve the museum. *Praeses* B. Lysholm supported Rygh, saying that the Society now worked exclusively through a museum and that it would not be possible to organize a real scientific society without putting the museum and its work at risk.[637]

---

[634] Amundsen, *Det norske videnskaps-akademi*, vol. II, 37.

[635] The original letter has not been found in the archive. The source for this discussion is the 200th anniversary book by Hans Midbøe, *Det Kongelige Norske Videnskabers Selskabs historie*, vol. II, 147–149.

[636] Also Rygh's answer is missing. The source here is once more Hans Midbøe: *Det Kongelige Norske Videnskabers Selskabs historie*, vol. II, 147–149.

[637] Ibid.

Rygh was in a way right. This was only the first of several attempts to reintroduce the basic idea of a scientific society. However, he would not experience nor be able to influence any more of the attacks and counterattacks. Rygh had succeeded in forming the Society the way he wanted, making it into a full-fledged scientific museum. He had been stubborn and persistent in doing this, and at the same time the situation in the sciences also came to his assistance. The transformation of the Society was supported by the golden age of museums throughout Europe. Rygh had been the young outsider, a real scientist attacking empty phrases and bad scientific judgments. Now he was old (73 years) and the new young scientists had laboratories, international experience, and recognition. Science and technology had taken the place of archaeology and natural history to some extent.

The 1903 rearrangement that did away with the elected members of the society and the 1912 dispute with Vogt marked the schism that Rygh had been more or less consciously preparing for. It was not a fruitful situation. On the contrary, it came to put its mark on the Society for the next 100 years. It was a conflict that would be buried for periods of time but would surface now and again over many years. The more than ten-year regime of the old conservators and the senior teachers firmly established the museum as the only reason for the existence of a scientific society in Trondheim. In this period very few new members were recruited to the Society. The same Society was now more or less an association for electing the board, a "friends-of-the-museum" association.

But nothing lasts forever, not the old conservators nor the regime of the board. Vogt's view gained ground and the number of young and ambitious scientists in Trondheim increased steadily. From the outside it looked like the museum was under siege. What really was happening had two sources: internal changes in the museum and important activity outside the Society.

Internally, the old conservators faded away. Foslie had already died in 1909, Vilhelm Storm died in May 1913 and finally Karl Rygh in June 1915. They were all in full activity as conservators even if they were in their seventies (except for Foslie who died when he was only 54). With all the three senior conservators gone, new and younger men took their place. We have already mentioned Hjalmar Broch, the zoologist who some years later was to become professor at the (by then renamed) University of Oslo. The other zoologist, O. Nordgaard, had come from Bergen in 1906. Henrik Prinz was employed as botanist in 1914 and finally, Th. Petersen filled Rygh's position as conservator in archeology. For the open position of librarian the board hired Dr. philos Johan Daniel Landmark (1876–1938). Landmark held a PhD in philosophy from the university in Kristiania and had continued his studies in Germany afterwards. For a couple of years he had been a trainee at the university's library in the capital before he was appointed librarian at the Society in Trondheim in 1915. These five men became the new core of scientists working at the museum and library. In 1915 they were between 27 (Printz) and 53 (Nordgaard) years of age, with the other three in their late thirties. Two held PhDs and a third (Prinz) was working on his. Nordgaard and Petersen were broadly trained and well published. First and foremost the new team represented modern sciences and the humanities as they were now practiced in Europe. Where Rygh had to fight and build understanding and acceptance for sciences in the 1870s, this group of men took all that for granted and in this way came to build on Rygh's impressive work from the last century.

The two remaining collections—the coin collection and the mineral collection—were much more modest and were administrated by two older curators as a smaller part-time activity: the teachers B. Hartmann and Carl Schultz. The more problematic side of Rygh's heritage was to be carried on by Carl Schulz.

The conservators were not the only ones to go through a generation shift in the 1910s; the board also changed. Not as dramatically, but significantly enough. The board broadened its recruitment base by taking on new members with other backgrounds than as teachers from the two schools in Munkegaten. The board was, moreover, expanded. Already from 1902 the Ministry of Church Affairs had demanded the right to appoint two members to the board due to the substantial public funding of the Society. However, the Ministry did not exercise this right until 1909 when they appointed the managing director of one of the largest banks in Trondheim, Andreas Berg, and later *stiftsarkivar* (chief regional public archivist) Kr. Koren to the board. When Koren was appointed national archivist, in 1913 the Ministry appointed the rector of NTH, Professor Sem Sæland (1874–1940), to the board.

In 1914 there were other changes. The earlier managing director of Røros Copper Works, Alfred Getz (1862–1922), became a member. Getz was born and raised in Trondheim and was in 1912 appointed professor of mining at NTH. He succeeded Sem Sæland as rector of NTH from 1914 to 1917. The same year Ole Nordgaard, the oldest conservator at the museum, also became a member, and in 1915 the internationally reputed judge in *overretten* (the highest court in the region) F. Beichmann, was voted in. In the end it was only the *praeses* from 1914, Axel Sommerfelt, who belonged to the old core of teachers from the two schools, together with the new secretary of the society, Carl Gundersen (from 1913).

All in all it was a substantial change: from 1914 two professors were members of the board, the rector and former rector of NTH, and in addition to them the oldest conservator, a bank manager and a judge. Neither to these men, nor to the new team of conservators did Rygh's response to Vogt's insulting proposition make much sense any more—and this was just a few years after it had been given. That said, they were all eager to preserve what had been achieved through the last 40 years' effort: the building of *Trondhjems museum*.

The new group of conservators and the new board was to be fairly stable from 1914/1915 onwards. Broch assumed his position at the University of Oslo in 1920 and was substituted by a conservator from Tromsø Museum, Carl F. L. Dons (1882–1949). Printz left for the agricultural university outside Oslo, where he became professor in 1926. In his place Ove Arbo Høeg (1898–1993) was appointed. There were other changes at the board; the most important was that the anthropologist and doctor H. Bryn substituted for Judge Beichman in 1920.

The two periods of the first quarter of the 20th century may be characterized in the following way. The first ten to fifteen years of the century were marked by an old generation of conservators and a board from the two schools close to the cathedral. The second phase was distinguished by a new generation of modern scientists as conservators and librarian, and a much broader and larger board with two rectors and a conservator as members. It appears that Vogt's proposal came some years too early to be taken seriously. A few years later the situation would change.

Trondhjems Videnskabelige Forening
(Trondheim Scientific Association)

Vogt wanted a place to meet other professional scientists, exchange views, and debate problems in science. This was what he missed most in Trondheim compared to his life as professor in Kristiania.[638] *Videnskabsselskabet* must have been an obvious choice for him if he was to create such a forum. As senior professor and one of the oldest and internationally most experienced, it was only reasonable that he took on the burden of creating such a forum and showed the younger professors what a scientific culture actually meant. Hence, when he was rejected by the Society he simply had to follow another path. He had to start a forum from scratch and build it up to become something similar to *Kristiania Videnskabsselskab*. *Trondhjems Videnskabelige Forening* (Trondheim Scientific Association) would be the answer. As the historian K. Lund Langlie argues, there are no archives left from this association, as it only lasted a few years. However, from Vogt's archive Lund Langlie was able to retrieve some facts, as well as from Midbøe's bicentennial history of the Society. Midbøe gives 1916 as the year of foundation of the *Trondhjems Videnskabelige Forening*. Vogt's closest collaborator in the *Forening* came to be the conservator Hjalmar Broch at the museum.[639]

Integrating the conservators in the *Trondhjems Videnskabelige Forening* was a very wise decision. On the other hand, this was exactly what had been done in the scientific society in Kristiania. Scientists were to be elected as members and the criterion for their election was their own independent scientific work. In Kristiania the number of members was restricted and the members were organized in sections according to their disciplines. To base such an organization only on scientists and technology specialist in the disciplines represented at the technical university would be too narrow and self-centered. It was, in other words, important for Vogt to broaden the base for recruitment of members. The obvious place to look was, of course, the conservators and scientists at the museum, as they represented the only other institution with several independent active scientists. And they became members: Th. Petersen, H. Broch

---

[638] The following is based on a Master's thesis in history by the historian Kristoffer Lund Langlie: "Lærde folk er irritable genus." I'm grateful for being allowed to use his work here. Vogt's motivation is taken from a letter from Vogt to his good friend W. C. Brøgger in Kristiania and is based on the work of the historian Anne K. Børresen and her forthcoming biography of Vogt. See Langlie, 30.

[639] Midbøe, *Det Kongelige Norske Videnskabers Selskabs historie*, vol. II, 150.

and O. Nordgaard. Printz and Landmark might also have been members, but we cannot be sure due to the lack of archive material. From the new technical university came Vogt, Sæland, Birkeland, Riiber, Lutz, Schmidt-Nielsen and Bragstad, and probably also others.[640]

Most of these members were rather young, not to be compared to members of the established academies later on. The average age must have been around 40 in 1915 for both the professors and the conservators. The activity of the association was membership meetings with lectures and discussions, a revitalized scientific public community, more or less as Gunnerus and his friends had practiced it 150 years earlier.

A paradoxical situation arose. The small and peripheral city of Trondheim had two scientific societies which both bore the name of such societies: *Videnskabsselskabet* and *Trondhjems Videnskabelige Forening*. As if this was not enough, the leaderships and memberships were mixed in both institutions with scientists from both scientific institutions. Professors (and rector) of the technical university were on the board and were members of the Society, while the conservators of the Society were on the board and members of *Trondhjems Videnskabelige Forening*. It was obvious to all that this could not last for very long; a solution had to be found to unite the two institutions so forces could be joined and better conditions could be established in the city of Trondheim.

In 1917 it seems to have been of particular interest among the professors at NTH to become members of the Society and museum. Almost a dozen professors joined as new members of the Society. We do not know the reason for this, but it is not unlikely that Vogt and his companions in *Trondhjems Videnskabelige Forening* wanted to have more influence over the museum. They also wanted influence the other way around so they elected the *praeses* of the Society, *overlærer* (headmaster, later principal) Axel Sommerfelt, as a member of *Trondhjems Videnskapelige Forening*. This was not without its own problems as Sommerfelt was not a particularly active scientist and did not publish research. He was educated in the classic languages and classic culture. As a teacher, he did not have research into the classical disciplines in mind. However, Nordgaard managed to convince Vogt of the political importance of having the *praeses* as a member, as it would build trust and facilitate amalgamation later on.[641]

Trondhjems Videnskapelige Forening was a tool created by Vogt to convince his colleagues of the need for a scientific forum, and, at the same time, to build a platform from which he could gain enough influence to change the course of the Society. A few years after the association was founded, and after several meetings, these gatherings and discussions proved to be fruitful for the participants from the museum and the technical university. Then, of course, the idea of having this old and prestigious scientific society in Trondheim and not being able to elect scientists as members and have meetings and publications seemed rather pointless. Most of those involved would probably have agreed on this issue by 1920.

---

[640] Langlie, "Lærde folk er irritable genus," 39.

[641] Langlie, "Lærde folk er irritable genus," 38

The reorganization

In December 1918, conservator Hjalmar Broch suggested changing the statutes relating to the board of the Society and how it was led. This was probably an attempt to open the Society to the new group of scientists in the city. Meetings and scientific discussions were already normal practice in the Society and museum. Not much came of the proposal, as "several of the board members were absent in the spring of 1919."[642] It was not until almost a year later, in October 1919, that the board tabled Broch's proposal for closer review. The board concluded, however, with a new postponement; something was happening between the members and some had argued, not surprisingly as we have seen, that the complete organization and hence all the statutes of the Society needed revision.[643] At the next meeting, more than a month later, Professor Sem Sæland accepted the task of writing a document outlining various solutions to the problem.[644]

What was happening among the members was first and foremost that Professor J.H.L. Vogt, together with several other members of the Society, had formulated a letter to the board of the Society, without actually sending it. Lund Langlie discussed this letter, arguing that when it came to deciding who wrote it, the members of *Trondhjems Videnskapelige Forening* were good candidates. On the other hand, he found it too harsh to the museum and would expect the conservators not to sign it.[645] However, the letter was never signed or delivered so we do not know who was involved. It was, however, the anticipation of such a letter that contributed to the decision to let Sem Sæland start working on a proposal. We know about the letter because Vogt used it as an introduction to his proposal for a reorganization of the Society one year later—where he explicitly told the Society that he had not delivered the original full proposal because the board had decided to start working on it by themselves. Vogt's final proposal for reorganization was dated December 9, 1920, while Sæland gave his report and recommendation in February the following year, 1921.[646]

Vogt's proposal, probably backed by the same group as mentioned above, was a reiteration of the 1912 letter, but now in a more moderate and polite form. The idea was to bring the Society back to its origins, its historical tradition, now that this was possible. There were three key requirements:

- The Society should have regular scientific meetings.
- To be elected a member candidates had to have scientific qualifications.
- There should be a maximum number of members.

---

[642] In: *Annual report 1919*, 6

[643] In: *Annual report 1919*, 6: "*Da der omtrent samtidig blev vakt motion om en helt ny organisation av selskapet, fandt direksjonen det hensiktsmæssig foreløpig at utsætte enhver statutændring indtil ogsaa det nye spørsmaal fuldt utredet.*"

[644] In: *Annual report 1919*, 6.

[645] Langlie, "Lærde folk er irritable genus," 53–54.

[646] The following proposals are printed in the annual report for 1922: Vogt's (pp. 70–73); Sæland's (pp. 74–100); Bryn's (p. 101); Beichmann's (pp. 102–108).

Moreover, it was important to manage the museum and library in the best possible way. A museum association (Trondhjems Museum) could be established that in one way or another could be closely connected to the Society. He then argued that the Society would be different from the scientific society in Kristiania as long as the scientists in Trondheim had an emphasis on science, mathematics, architecture, and technology.

The three first requirements seemed to have had general acceptance; the museum and library were the problem. In his own reworked proposal from 1920, Vogt discussed the museum in more detail. He thought that there should be a museum association with paying membership as a supporting institution to the museum. The museum and library should then be governed by a board with two members from the Society, two from the museum association, two appointed by the state, one from the conservators and perhaps from the Trondheim local authority—if they contributed considerably to the funding of the museum.[647]

Vogt's proposal was simply to say that the new scientists that came to the city in the 1910s (be they either professors from NTH or conservators at the museum) should take over the name of the scientific society, the museum should be reorganized as other scientific museums with an appropriate name and a supporting association, and the museum, library, and funds should be managed by a board with representation from all involved parties, including the Society. In this way the museum and library would continue to be the Society's museum and library but now in an orderly and clear way.

Sæland's proposal was larger and more thorough, with detailed proposals for statutes of all the proposed institutions and associations. He had really taken the mandate from the Society's board seriously and put a lot of effort into making his recommendations. He used the whole history of the Society and made evaluations of the different reforms. He found the 1874 arrangement (the concentration of the work and the museum idea) as a very good and necessary reform. On the other hand, he saw the abolition of electing members in 1903 as non-productive. The simplest solution, he said, was simply to reintroduce voting, but this would be very difficult with all the paying members. The abolition of elected members, whether real or not, reduced the scientific society to an association of friends of the museum. And that was something very different from a scientific society.

Sæland also gave several good reasons why it was so important to gather *all* scientific forces in the city; it was a confirmation of the scientific community, without which no science was possible. He differed from Vogt on this point. There was a definite imbalance in the city with regard to the disciplines, but Sæland simply proposed four

---

[647] In: *Annual report 1922*, 22. The funding from Trondhjem local authority was particularly important in these years as the Brændevissamlaget was closed down and the state limited their contribution to what local sources paid. The public (municipal) cinemas became the solution to this economic squeeze.

sections instead of the traditional two (as known from Kristiania): humanities; natural history and medicine; mathematics, physics and chemistry; and finally technology.

Like Vogt, Sæland also wanted to reorganize the museum. Sæland delivered a full set of statutes for the museum and library, now called *Trondhjems museum*. He also proposed a museum association and approximately the same solution for the governance of the museum as Vogt. However, Sæland used the statutes of the museum and its association from Bergen as his model. In this way he managed to put together statutes from two important scientific institutions in Norway: from *Kristiania Videnskabsselskap* and from *Bergen Museum*. He took the best from both and out of it he created his proposal for a united scientific organization in Trondheim. In the end he stated his two main intentions with the reorganization:

- To give the Society increased authority in all scientific matters
- To strengthen the museum and library with respect to scientific as well as local community interests[648]

Again, in a more polite and more elegantly argued form than Vogt's proposal, Sæland presented the case for a revitalized society with elected members and a museum connected to it with its own museum association. The scientific society kept the royal name while the museum changed its name to *Trondheim museum* and remained strongly affiliated with the Society. It should also be noted that Sæland wanted to join all scientific forces in Trondheim with no particular status for technology: technology was also a part of science, both to Sæland and to Vogt.

Thus the two professors wanted to re-establish the society of savants in Trondheim 150 years after the last successful period. The museum and library were important parts of this, but they had to either cooperate independently (as both Vogt and Sæland proposed) or be subsumed under the scientists' leadership as the Society's own research institutions (with no one daring to propose the latter or deeming it too unrealistic and therefore not viable).

Another model for an academy was just this: a highly selective membership organization that also boasted research centers with employed scientists. In the case of Trondheim, the museum could be the first research center under the guidance of the board of an exclusive scientific society with a long history. Vogt's and Sæland's proposals were to have two connected institutions with two independent membership organizations: the one as a scientific society, the other as a "friends-of-the-museum" association. The first was to be governed by an elected board, the second (the museum)

---

[648] In: *Annual report 1922*, p. 82: "*I det jeg hermed fremsender disse forslag, maa jeg til slutning faa lov at fremholde som et almindelig utgangspunkt for enhver diskussion av spørsmaalet om en omorganisastion, at selskapets interesser ikke kan være tjent med nogen annen ny-ordning enn én, som paa den ene side kan bidra til at give det øket autoritet i rent videnskabelig henseende og paa den anne side samle omkring museet og dets virksomhet saa sterkt som mulig saavel videnskabelige som lokale borgelige interesser. Begge disse krav har jeg søkt at imøtekomme.*"

by a representative board made up of the two organizations (the Society and museum associations) and the central and local authorities.

There was only one serious draw-back with Sæland's proposal: its fate was to be decided in the last instance by the general assembly of the Society, now an open membership organization with several hundred members. But first it had to pass the board. In the revised statutes from 1903 the board had to appoint their own committee to review Sæland's proposal. It was clear to everyone that if there were to be changes it would take time.

In accordance with the statutes, Sæland presented his proposal at the general assembly in March 1921.[649] The proposal was then submitted to the board, pursuant to the regulations, which in May the same year appointed the review committee, consisting of Sæland and the rector at NTH, Richard Birkeland, two of the most senior conservators, Nordgaard and Petersen, and lastly a person Sæland was allowed to appoint, bank manager Andreas Berg, who also was a board member.

More than a year later, in November 1922, after discussions at several board meetings, Sæland's proposal was finally presented to the general assembly for a decision. This time the attendance set new records. Usually around 10–15 members met at these assemblies. This time, however, 42 members had found their way to the meeting. No doubt the publicity in the press had led many to come. The future of the Society and the museum were at stake. Sæland presented his proposal and *praeses* Axel Sommerfeldt proposed that the general assembly should comply with Sæland's instructions and ask the board to continue to work along his lines. Two other proposals were also made. One proposal was made by Judge F. Beichmann, recommending that, in addition to the museum, the Society should revitalize the general meeting and asking the board to change the statutes in such a way to reflect this. A third proposal was submitted by Fritz Duus, the editor of one of the local newspapers, *Adresseavisen*. His proposal was quite simple: "The assembly asks the board to start work on transforming the Society into a scientific society in the modern meaning of the word. The museum activity continues unchanged."[650]

It is interesting to note that the Society board followed Sæland's proposal. They were obviously convinced that this was the right way to go. They had come a long way since Karl Rygh's day and Lysholm's answer to Vogt ten years earlier. This is also an acknowledgement of Sæland's abilities as a negotiator and leader. In 1923 Sæland was appointed professor at the university in Kristiania and very soon afterwards was appointed rector, one of the reasons again being his natural gift for negotiation and leadership.[651]

---

[649] II:1 General assembly protocol. In addition to the board and the secretary only seven members attended, two of whom were conservator Petersen and the librarian dr. Landmark. Professor Vogt was of course present.

[650] II:1 General assembly protocol 14/11 1922.

[651] NNBL, Sæland.

The other two proposals were much simpler, but with clear intentions: Beichmann's proposal was to preserve the status quo and reject a society with electing and scientific membership criteria. In fact it was a rejection of Sæland's proposal all together and the one that was most in line with Rygh's old intentions. Duus's proposal was on the other hand much more diffuse, and could be interpreted as very close to Sæland's, perhaps with less changes to the museum (to continue unchanged). Nonetheless, it accepted Sæland's objective for a modern scientific society with the necessary criteria.

One could argue that the natural way to vote would have been to start with the most extreme proposal, the proposal with the greatest changes and then vote for and against until a majority was reached. In this way the order of the voting would be to start with the *praeses*' proposal (Sæland), then move on to Duus's and finally to Beichmann's. However, the vote was held the other way around, starting with Beichmann's, as his was the proposal that deviated the most from the board's, then putting Duus's against Sæland's. The result was unsettling to say the least. Beichmann's proposal was voted down by a count of only 20 votes against to 18 for, with four probably abstaining. This close result provided the necessary impetus for the reestablishment of a real scientific society. How it was to be done was an area open to controversy, as Duus's proposal was accepted; it received 21, while the proposal of the *praeses* and Sæland received 13 votes, again with probably eight abstaining votes.[652]

Ten years after the Society's blunt rejection of Vogt's solution, it had now provided for exactly such a solution, in principle, and it had done so in an open meeting of members who were not elected for their scientific works, indeed quite the contrary. We have pointed to the shift in regime and persons on the board and among the conservators in this ten-year period, and now we can see that the opinion of the members had also changed, although it came close to a rejection of the whole idea (18 versus 20 votes for Beichmann's proposal).

Duus's accepted solution appeared to be a clever and decisive move. It was not. It was like asking for milk or honey and answering yes please, both. One key point was that the assembly at the same time rejected Sæland's proposal, since a vote for Duus was a vote against Sæland and the *praeses*. A simple *pro et con* voting order would perhaps have avoided this problem. Nevertheless, the assembly had said what they wanted, not how they wanted it done. It would take more than three years before new statutes and a new order finally were accepted and operational; in effect making a scientific society and at the same time continuing with the museum as if nothing had happened. The voting order probably reflected the fact that Sæland's proposal did not have a majority. Nevertheless, much fighting and rivalry would have been avoided in the following years if Sæland's carefully thought-out plan had been accepted. The plan still stands as a reminder of a gifted organizer, leader, and politician.

---

[652] II:1 General assembly protocol 14/11 1922.

Having your cake and eating it: 1923–1926

The board continued to discuss different solutions to the dilemma the assembly had placed them in. As the opposition now mainly came from outside the board, the general assembly in fact became the arena for decisions, not the board. In February 1923 there was a new meeting of the assembly at which Dr. H. Bryn, now also a member of the board, submitted a new and fairly short proposal stating that the Society should be organized into two independent departments, each with their independent boards. One of the departments should continue the current work and keep all the Society's properties and funds. It should be called *Det Kongelige Norske Videnskabers Selskabs Museum*. The other department should be organized as a modern scientific society to which core members should be appointed by the current board and the members, who are also elected members of *Kristianias Videnskapsselskap*. The name of this department would be *Det Kongelige Norske Videnskabers Selskab*. As an alternative, he suggested that the name of the scientific society could be *Trondhjems Videnskapselskap*. No decision was reached at the meeting as the board probably wanted to have a clear overview of the alternatives within the limits of the earlier decision (Duus's proposal).

Nevertheless, a final decision was approaching. The dual-department structure seemed to have broad acceptance; the question of independence for the two was another matter. One main problem was what to do with questions that affected them jointly. Beichmann's conservative proposal had been developed into accepting a dual-departmental structure, but with the established department (that is, the museum) as superior. Structuring the two the other way around was never raised as an option, but it might be seen as implicit in Vogt's approach.

The meeting of the general assembly in November 1923 was the one that finally laid the foundation for a dual-department society. This is easy to see with hindsight, but even the contemporaries felt the same way. It is typical that this was the only meeting of the general assembly where every speaker's contribution was recorded more or less in full in the minutes.[653] This meeting was also very well attended, with 37 members present at its peak. Given the very close result at the previous year's meeting, the board obviously wanted to move on and see what topics could be agreed upon. After the ordinary matters at the assembly (annual report, economy, elections), the last item of the day was the question of how to implement the reorganization process. Two weeks prior to the meeting the board had agreed on a proposal to the general assembly that had been presented by the *praeses*, Axel Sommerfelt, and was based on Halvdan Bryn's proposal. This called for two independent departments with the same name and different addendums: *Trondhjems museum* for the established activity and *Trondhjems akademi* for the new one. Both were to be independent and have their own independent board. This followed Bryn's proposal, also with respect to elections and funds, and

---

[653] II:1 General assembly protocol 6/11 1923.

then added a third point, a joint committee to deal with questions and problems of common interest to the two departments. This joint committee should consist of two members from each department with the respective leaders as *ex-officio* members. They would also have the chairmanship of the joint committee on alternating years.

Praeses Sommerfeldt proposed that the general assembly should accept this as the basis for the reorganization and petitioned the board to present revised statutes based on this proposal at a later assembly. The meeting accepted to a large degree Sommerfelt's (and Bryn's) proposal. By this time Sæland was gone; he had moved to Oslo to become professor and quite soon rector of the university there. This implied that Vogt could then expect more reception for his views, and he was not at all displeased with the proposal. On the contrary, apart from a discussion on how the basic core of members should be elected, he had only one important objection: the name. To call it a scientific society and then tack on "academy" did not make much sense to him. He would prefer the name without any addition for the Society even if that would be the same name as for both departments taken together. To add "academy" was, to Vogt, presumptuous; it was like adding the title of *keiser* to king.

The other objection came from Carl Schultz, now director of the (reduced) technical college and for many years part-time manager of the mining collection at the museum. Schultz voiced the sentiments of the deceased Rygh. He did not see any need for a new scientific society. If needed, they could continue the work of *Trondhjems Videnskabelige Forening*. In a way he looked upon himself as one of the last of the generation that had experienced Rygh's fight for a museum in 1874 as a very young man, and who had worked with him all the time afterwards. Schultz regarded the new professors as temporary intruders who should not be allowed to dismantle and change what Rygh had created back in 1874.[654]

Schultz proposed a postponement of the decision to split up the society so they could wait and see if he could obtain support. He did not, interestingly enough. So in the end he withdrew his proposal. Vogt also withdrew his when it became clear that the new departments would be allowed to develop their own statutes. Under such conditions the Society could revise the question of names once more. Thus ended the meeting in November 1923 with a unanimous acceptance of *praeses* Sommerfelt's and the board's proposal. What one year earlier was a very delicate balance between two almost equally large factions had now turned into an agreement on how to continue and develop the Society in the future.

It must be right to see the November 1923 meeting as the turning point and as the foundation for the new Society. It would still take more than two years before all the regulations and statutes were in place, but the foundation was now laid and a consensus had been reached. However, this did not mean that the new Society would be successful and there were obvious faults. In a way it was a federation by name only. And

---

[654] For a closer discussion of Schultz and his role in this process see Langlie, "Lærde folk er irritable genus," 67–72.

the names were more than confusing. It was an extremely decentralized organization, one could say, with the museum and the scientific society each going off in their own direction. It was not even clear what the name of the common body was or should be (*Fellesutvalget*—the joint committee) or what tasks it should have except to avoid anything that could be decided by the departments on their own.

Again, Sæland's proposal seems *ex post facto* as the best option for keeping the Society together, but that was not possible when he proposed it, but perhaps it would have been in 1924/1925? But, of course, then he had already left for Oslo. The lack of a closer connection in one way or another between the two parties which both had *Det Kongelige Norske Videnskabers Selskab* in their name has left its mark on the activity ever since and continues to do so today.

After the decisions in November 1923, the board appointed a committee of five members to propose new and revised statutes. The committee worked for more than a year on this. They were still not finished for the assembly in March 1925, but at this meeting they at least presented their proposal for names for the two departments: *Det Kongelige Norske Videnskabers Selskab* for the new department and *Det Kongelige Norske Videnskabers Selskab, Museet* (the Museum) for the old part. As we see, they had decided to drop "Academy." It was logical, but marked even a further step away from Rygh's old ideal. No name was proposed for the "federation," probably because it did not need a name, since for all practical and formal matters the two departments would be independent. The committee's and board's proposal was accepted by 15 to 4 votes.[655]

In October 1925 the proposed new statutes were presented to be decided about at a later meeting. The statutes for the joint society (the federation) were developed by the committee that the board had put together almost two years earlier. After a request from the committee, the statutes for the new department were put together by the eight members of *Kristiania Videnskapsselskap* who lived in the Trondheim region, while the statutes for the museum were simply the old statutes for the Society revised by the *praeses* and the secretary to accommodate the new situation.

Finally on 27 of January 1926 a new general assembly, this time with only 16 members present, could finally vote on the new statutes. There was only one dissenter—the old manager of the mineral collection, Carl Schultz, made it clear that he did not want to support the proposal and then left the meeting. The new set of statutes was accepted unanimously.[656] The society was now a loose federation of two strong and independent departments, the Society and the museum. The name of the federation, the joint committee and the two independent departments together was not a contentious issue. However, as the scientific society avoided the name "Academy" in any form, the joint federation could not have the same name. Thus the name *Det Kongelige Norske Videnskabers Selskab i Trondhjem* was introduced as a common name. It was never

---

[655] II:1 General assembly protocol 3/3 1925.
[656] II:1 General assembly protocol 27/1 1926.

used to any large degree, as the cooperation between the two departments never grew as strong as we might suspect the founding fathers had hoped or believed it would.

There is, however, a nice story connected to the addendum, *i Trondhjem* (in Trondheim). On January 1, 1925, Kristiania changed its name to Oslo. Thus in the fall of 1924, the *Kristiania Videnskapsselskap* discussed a change of name to *Det Norske Videnskaps-Akademi*. The board had decided to propose this name, but professor and former *praeses* W. C. Brøgger told his old colleague and friend in Trondheim, J.H.L. Vogt, about this. At the board meeting in Kristiania in late November 1924, Brøgger referred to a letter from Vogt saying that this name might provoke a protest from Trondheim. If they on the other hand called the academy in Kristiania *Det Norske Videnskaps-Akademi i Oslo* no one would object, and on December 5, 1924, the Academy in Oslo accepted precisely that name.[657] It is easy to think that this would in turn be a very good reason to call the joint society in Trondheim *Det Kongelige Norske Videnskabers Selskab i Trondheim*. However, no such addendum came and in Oslo the name "in Oslo" soon went out of use.

---

[657] Amundsen, *Det Norske Videnskaps-Akademi i Oslo 1857–1957*, vol. II, 317.

The new Society, 1926–1960

Trondheim in 1926 was quite a different city from the Trondheim of 1903, the last time the statutes were revised. Even the most optimistic view of the future had not come close to matching all the changes that had taken place. In the early 1920s there were two new, more or less scientific and national institutions in the city: *Norges Tekniske Høyskole* (the Norwegian Institute of Technology, NTH) opened in 1910, and the new, higher-education teaching training college, *Norges Lærerhøgskole* (NLHT) was established in 1922. Moreover, the other museums were expanding—for example, *Nordenfjelske kunstindustrimuseum* (the region's arts and crafts museum) under the dynamic leadership of Dr. philos Fredrik Wallem.

The two old, important schools on Munkegata (*Katedralskolen* and *Trondhjems Tekniske Læreanstalt*, TTL) fell more into the background with the new prominent institutions. They provided exactly what had been missing for establishing the academic and intellectual network and infrastructure necessary for the Society. The fate of the two old schools differed considerably. *Katedralskolen* continued to expand as the central upper secondary school (*gymnas* or high school) for the region and as a gateway to university. When the nation inaugurated the new institute of technology (NTH) in 1910, the role and function of *Trondhjems Tekniske Læreanstalt* changed. In Trondheim, Oslo, and Bergen these schools had become fairly advanced teaching institutions. With the establishment of the technical university, the national technical teaching system was expanded from two to three tiers. Until 1910 the education they provided had combined elementary drawing schools and the three technical colleges lasting three or four years (TTL). With a new top university-standard tier this model was found to be too much. The solution was that the technical colleges were to be downgraded to two-year intermediate technical schools. In the summer of 1915 the last students from *Trondhjems Tekniske Læreanstalt* (TTL) graduated along with the second group of students from the new intermediate institution, *Trondhjems Tekniske Mellomskole* (TTM). In 1930 the school (TTM) moved out of their old building in Munkegaten—it was to become the city hall building—and into new premises on the site of the old gas works.[658] Most of the teachers at the old *Læreanstalt* (TTL) stayed

---

[658] Andersen, "Trondhjems Tekniske læreanstalt," 28 and Odde, "Fra teknisk mellomskole til ingeniørhøyskole," 53.

with their old school, while some applied to the king for a professorship at the new *tekniske høyskole*, NTH. At *Norges Tekniske Høyskole* (NTH) things also changed rapidly during its first years of existence. When it opened, 50 students were expected on each level, but already during the first year the council of professors accepted 103 new candidates.[659] Into the 1920s more than 100 new students were accepted each year.[660] The number of teachers expanded correspondingly. From the modest start with under a dozen professors in 1910, the staff had more than doubled by 1920. The total number of scientific positions was closing in on 100, and in addition came other technicians and assistants which brought the number of salaried posts close to 150.[661] With ten years of growth at the Gløshaugen campus the future must have looked bright in 1920—there would surely be more professors, buildings and students in the years to come.

Another new, national institution came to Trondheim in 1922, without much warning ahead, but was welcomed with open arms by the city's scientific community. It represented the solution to an old problem. For many years there had been two ways to become a teacher—either through one of the many teacher's seminars (from 1902 renamed teacher's training schools), or through university studies. In general, the middle and secondary schools recruited from the university, while the primary schools (*folkeskolen*) took their teachers from the ranks of the teacher training schools. The way to the university was blocked for primary-school teachers as long as they lacked the higher exams from upper-secondary school (*gymnasium*). Thus there was a pressing need for continuing education for primary-school teachers and this was the main goal of the new institution, *Norges Lærerhøgskole* (The Norwegian higher teachers training college, NLHT). The Parliament had seen a heated debate over the location of this new institution, where the end result was Trondheim.[662] There were many reasons for this, but what we here will emphasize is the proposed collaboration with the other scientific institutions in Trondheim: NTH and the Society's museum.

The original initiative had come from *skoleinspektør* Karl Aas in Trondheim, who in a letter to the ministry in 1919 proposed Trondheim as the home of the new institution.[663] He also mobilized the city magistrate and, not surprisingly, the Society. The board decided to support the initiative and promised to open the library and the collections to the future students.[664] Similar requests were sent to NTH and also here the idea found support. The proposal was temporarily shelved, but a new initiative was made in 1920. Trondheim had strong arguments: Housing would be provided by the municipality, and teaching in biology, botany and zoology, physics, mathematics, and chemistry could be given by the local science institutions together with the fairly large scientific library and, not least, the already available laboratories for all these sci-

---

[659] Devik, NTH 50 år, 48.
[660] Hanisch and Lange, Vitenskap for industrien, 73.
[661] Hanisch and Lange, Vitenskap for industrien, 50; Devik, NTH 50 år, 327–335.
[662] See Kirkhusmo for further details on the discussion. Kirkhusmo, Akademi og seminar.
[663] Ibid, 41.
[664] Annual report 1919, 9.

ences. In 1922 conservator for botany, Karl Henrik O. Prinz argued for an extra person to be hired as assistant and preparer because of the teaching that would begin at *Lærerhøgskolen*.[665] The *Lærerhøgskolen*, it was argued, would profit from all this. When it was first opened, three professors were hired at the school: in pedagogy, history, and linguistics. The hope was that this small ensemble would expand considerably in a few years, as NTH had done. Not only *Lærerhøgskolen* profited from the academic environment already in place. An example is the librarian at the museum, Johan F. Landmark, who taught philosophy at NTH from 1920 until his death in 1938.[666]

However, the 1920s and 1930s were not like the first 20 years of the 20th century. The post-war crisis in 1920 was superseded by a local (national) currency crisis related to the gold standard. The world economic crisis in 1929 lasted for most of the 1930s, and the effect on the *Lærerhøgskolen*, as well as the rest of the scientific community in Trondheim, was financial disappointments and setbacks. Public funding for all institutions was reduced and the general level of unemployment and bankruptcies increased. It was not until after the Second World War that there was a new upturn in the funding of academic institutions, both for museums and colleges. In 1920 everything looked positive, but by the time the new Society was finally inaugurated in 1926, hard times were setting in, but, the members hoped, this would be short-lived. This did not, however, turn out to be the case, but for those involved, the only option was to look optimistically to the future.

In fact the museum probably had a more difficult situation than the renewed Society. Even if the museum kept all assets, funds and buildings, collections, and laboratories, while the Society started from scratch, the museum was in a more difficult position. The reason was quite simple: it had a high degree of expenses because of its activities. First and foremost the salaries for the conservators took up a large proportion of the budget. The museum's activities were dependent on the volume of the staff and hence a reduced grant from the public authorities meant a corresponding reduction in its activities. In this way the museum was in much the same position as the two higher teaching institutions, *Lærerhøgsholen* and NTH. The new Society, on the other hand, was not that dependent on an external budget (in fact it did not have one). The salaries for the members were all paid by other institutions; institutions where these members were formally employed. Funding for the Society was needed primarily for the activities, meetings and publications. The Society would have preferred being able to also remunerate the general secretary and treasurer but that would come.

The Society was of course also exposed to the economic downturn, but for the most part in an indirect way. In was harder to receive private funds and recruit donors in hard times. The members' home institutions, that is, their sources of income, were also experiencing hard times and faced staff reductions due to their poor financial situation. First and foremost the problem these difficult times brought to the Society was that it could not expand.

---

[665] Annual report 1922.
[666] Støren, "Bibliotekets ledere 1768–1993," 43.

In the following it will be necessary to be clear in our terminology so it will be easier to understand the discrepancies between the three institutions that made up the new scientific society in Trondheim. As we saw in the last chapter, the revitalization in 1926 created two totally independent departments: *Det Kongelige Norske Videnskabers Selskab, Museet* and *Det Kongelige Norske Videnskabers Selskab*. These names will hereinafter be abbreviated to "the museum" and "the Society," each with their own statutes, including their own right to amend them. An overriding institution was also created to deal with and solve joint problems: *Fellesutvalget* (the joint committee). The name of the entire institution was given in the statues for *Fellesutvalget* as *Det Kongelige Norske Videnskabers Selskab i Trondhjem*. This last name was seldom used and confusingly the institution as a whole was often called the same as the Society: *Det Kongelige Norske Videnskabers Selskab*. However, the creators of the new anarchistic federation had given the federation a name, even if the members did not use it.

Members and culture

To revitalize the Society two important problems had to be solved: what was to be recreated and who should be responsible for this? Let us start with the latter question. Who should the members be? There seems, from the start, to have reigned a consensus on at least one point: that a scientific, membership-based society be required to have a careful process of proposal, evaluation, and election of its members. It was thus seen as important to acknowledge and promote high standards in research activity. One way of doing this was to limit the number of members, at least the members who lived and worked locally who would make up the core membership group. It was relatively easy to describe the election process once established, but how should this start and how should the core group be selected? This was a fairly controversial question in the years leading up to 1926. In the end one opted for a two-step process: first to appoint an electoral college and then let this body nominate the core membership group who would then constitute the foundation of the new Society. The electoral college was made up of the board of the old institution, supplemented by the old members who were also members of what was now called *Det norske videnskapsakademi i Oslo* (The Norwegian academy of sciences in Oslo, before 1925: *Kristiania Videnskapsselskap*).[667] This decision was contentious, as the historian Kristoffer Lund Langlie has shown in his work. To Vogt, for instance, this would give the old board of the museum too much influence and as a consequence it might risk losing some of its credibility as a scientific society.[668]

The electoral college, however, settled on a core group of members that was given the responsibility of establishing the revitalized Society. According to the new statutes,

---

[667] *Forhandlinger*, Vol. I, 1926–1928, p. 10* (the star designates the report section as opposed to the short paper section that is numbered).

[668] Langlie, Lærde folk er irritable genus.

they were split into two divisions: the humanities and the mathematics-scientific divisions, with respectively 14 and 25 invited members. Their positions in their working life outside the Society varied, moreso in the humanities. In the science division, 15 of the 25 members were connected to NTH, and 13 of these were professors. Sem Seland and Richard Birkeland, in 1926 professors in Oslo, but both formerly rectors at NTH, were also appointed. From the old museum, only conservator Nordgaard and the former *praeses* Bjarne Lysholm were elected to this division from the start. A characteristic feature of the professors appointed was their connection to scientific technology or pure science—mathematics, physics, chemistry, metallurgy, and electro-technology.[669] The more practical fields—machine-building, civil engineering, and shipbuilding—were not well represented, with one exception, architecture. But architecture was difficult, as it represented a combination of science and art. Professor Sverre Pedersen was appointed member of the science division, while another architect, Professor Johan J. Meyer, joined the humanities division.

The members in the humanities division had a much more varied background. All three professors at the new *Norges Lærerhøyskole, NLHT*, were appointed, but among the members were also conservator Th. Petersen and the librarian J. D. Landmark from the museum, as well as the bishop and Judge F. V. Beichman. The director of the regional arts and crafts museum, F.B. Wallem and the *praeses* of the museum, A. Sommerfelt, were also appointed, along with four foreign members.

With these members in place, very close to half the maximum number of members in each division had been found and the revived Society could start its work. Two days after the electoral college had made their decision, the new appointees received an invitation to a constitutional meeting, to be held ten days later. On April 29 in 1926, the first meeting of the new Society was held. Twenty-four of the 39 members attended. The records note that "After some discussion the meeting decided to constitute the reorganized society according to the new statutes . . . ."[670] Thus the revived scientific Society was established on its own terms, in accordance with the negotiated new statutes.

The old organization still had to accept the partition. The new statutes also were passed by the general assembly of what was now to be the museum association. The old organization had reached compromises that were acceptable to everyone and thus this new meeting accepted the statutes and the work done so far. With the foundation and broad outlines supplied by Sem Sæland's substantial preparation and work, the end result was unavoidably variations on his recommendations.

After accepting the statutes, the next reasonable step for the new and revived scientific Society was to hold an election. Halvdan Bryn was elected as *praeses*. Together with Sæland (now in Oslo) and Vogt (who did not approve of the way the core group was elected), Bryn was the member who had been most active in the making of the new

---

[669] Langlie, Lærde folk er irritable genus, 88; Moe, "Historien bak etableringen av NTVA," 51–53.
[670] *Forhandlinger*, Vol. I, 1926–1928, 11*.

Society. It was his modifications on Seland's proposals that were finally accepted. Professor S. Schmidt-Nielsen (NTH) was elected to the important role of general secretary and the bishop, Dr. J. Gleditsch, was elected *vice-praeses*. In the science division, Professor C. N. Riiber (NTH) was elected chairman, while two other professors, also from NTH, were elected as vice chairman and secretary. In the humanities division, Professor R. Iversen (NLHT) became the chairman, with the conservator and the librarian at the museum filling the other positions.

The result was a fairly good blend of interests and backgrounds with no institution dominating, except for the science division, where NTH was very strong. But proportionally and as a reflection of the situation in Trondheim the result was impeccable. Nonetheless, the unsolved task was to satisfy the intention of the statutes with a viable solution—what should the identity and soul of the Socity be? Was it true, as Vogt had claimed back in 1912, that there really was a need for such an exclusive Society?

It was perhaps obvious, but the way to build a new identity for the Society was a return to the foundation from the 18th century and the founder, Bishop J. E. Gunnerus, while at the same time also looking forward with the future situation of science in mind. *Praeses* H. Bryn did just this in the opening address at the first meeting in October 1926. He chose to talk about J.E. Gunnerus and *Videnskabsselskabet* (DKNVS), claiming that the revival now was a revival in his spirit. Gunnerus was, the *praeses* claimed, the most versatile, creative, and resourceful of the 18th-century pioneers in Norwegian science and culture. When he came to Trondheim, he created a culture for science from scratch. Of all the things he had done, nothing had had as much vitality and impact as the Society that we today reactivate, the *praeses* claimed.[671]

With this speech, the foundation was laid for the Society's new identity. It was a revival of a glorious past; they had survived the dark ages and now the scientific community and culture in Trondheim would experience a new Golden Age. The continuity from the 18th century with the versatile Gunnerus that brought this city not far from the polar circle in touch with the larger streams of European knowledge and culture was revived. But this time the modern sciences, the applied sciences, and the technical sciences played a much more prominent role than before, and added to this were the pedagogical dimensions from NLHT.

This narrative led to various ways of focusing on Gunnerus. The old society and museum's gala meeting had always been held on the royal protector's birthday, but the new Society decided to use Gunnerus's birthday as the day for its annual gala meeting on February 26.[672] In the early autumn of 1926, the board also received an anonymous gift of 1000 *kroner* to start a medal fund with the aim of making a medallion in honor of the bishop that would be awarded as a prize for those who had contributed to the Society or to science in remarkable ways. The fund was also to be used to make smaller

---

[671] Bryn, "J.E. Gunnerus og Videnskapsselskapet," 47*.

[672] Board meeting May 6, 1926, *Forhandlinger*, Vol. I, p. 34*, later confirmed at the first meeting October 4, 1926. Ibid, 12*.

medallions to be given as gifts to the members who were present at the annual gala meeting. The board approved this and established the prize, the Gunnerus medal, and made it the Society's highest award. At the same board meeting they decided that the first Gunnerus gold medal should be awarded to Professor Waldemar C. Brøgger in Oslo for his major contributions to Norwegian sciences. Having found someone who was Gunnerus's equal in terms of versatility and dedicated input, this was an obvious choice. Brøgger was the senior figure of Norwegian science as organizer, founder, and scientist himself.[673]

This story of and identification with Gunnerus was important in many ways. The same board meeting that decided to award Brøgger the Gunnerus medal, also decided that all members should be addressed in correspondence, print, and other communication without titles, using simply Mr or Mrs; there was in fact one woman in the appointed core group—Dr. philos Signe Schmidt-Nielsen (1878–1959). She was born Signe Torborg Sturzen-Becker and was one of the first women in Sweden to receive her doctoral degree. As her name suggests, she was married to the secretary of the Society, Sigvald Schmidt-Nielsen. Together they published and co-authored several works in the Society's transactions and in other periodicals. But other than her, this was a male-dominated society, even when the election in 1928 of a professor in Oslo, Dr. Kristine Bonnevie, doubled the number of women.

The idea of avoiding the use of titles was, as would be expected, a way to show that everyone in the Society was equal. What was important was that they had all qualified for membership. There was thus quite the atmosphere of the 18th-century enlightenment within the revived society. History was used to create a cultural image of what the Society's core values reflected. Of course it was elitist, but it also had an egalitarian side to it. If you were one of the elected few, then you were equal to all the others. This was quite in contrast to the old Society and museum that had used titles most of the time, and where, we might expect, social status was as important as academic status. This was what Rygh had rebelled against, but the museum had never refrained from using titles. Now once again the new brotherhood of scientists was a reminder of the enlightenment's community of free spirits seeking the truth. Since 1926 the gala meeting has always commemorated Gunnerus and his Society, and titles have been abandoned by all members ever since.

The new Society at work

Narrating the past to create an identity and collective was one thing; to fill the future with meaningful activities was quite another. Before we look closer at the activities, it is important to keep in mind that the difference between the museum and the Society followed many different lines. The museum focused on regional pre-history and history,

---

[673] *Forhandlinger*, 1926, p. 35*. See also Hestmark, Vitenskap og nasjon, about W. C. Brøgger.

or on the natural history of the district. By now, it had become a local or regional institution, well known to the inhabitants of the region from their childhood and onwards. The Society, on the other hand, was a closed organization with members who had at least one thing in common: most of them were new to the district. They had been educated in Oslo or on the continent and now found themselves as newcomers in this small and somewhat remote city of Trondheim. That gave the Society a flying start, a feeling of community, building the reputation of science and living a life as scientists where other options were few and the networks and social circles of the local inhabitants were difficult to penetrate. Of course this also worked the other way: the Society also probably isolated newcomers from the local society.

Two important forces that linked the old Society, the museum, the city and its elite to the new one were the first *praeses* and the secretary general. *Praeses* Halvdan Bryn (1864–1933) was born and raised in Trondheim, earned his medical degree from the university in Kristiania in 1889 and returned to Trondheim in 1891. Through his work as a military doctor he turned his interest to physical anthropology and became a pioneer in this field. He was recognized both nationally and internationally as a researcher and was appointed honorary professor at the University of Uppsala in Sweden in 1927. His affiliation with the city and the Society went a long way back. He was part of the committee that established *Trondhjems biologiske stasjon* in the years before the turn of the century. He had been a member of the board of the Society from 1900 to 1903 and again from 1921 to 1926 when he played the role of arbiter between the various interests in the negotiations that led to the reorganization. He was also a member of the city council in Trondheim from 1898 to 1914, representing the Norwegian liberal party (*Venstre*).[674] We can only guess at the conflicts he must have had with the older and rather conservative Karl Rygh. Bryn was the perfect candidate for the first *praeses*, representing the old tradition of doctors who turned into researchers in other fields. However, he had all the bridge-building qualities that another doctor in the society, I. Hagen, had lacked. But Bryn also quit his doctoral duties when he passed 60 so he could work full time on his research projects.

The other important link was the secretary of the Society, Professor Sigval Schmidt-Nielsen (1877–1956). He was 13 years younger than Bryn, but his background was not that different. Schmidt-Nielsen was born in Røros, but grew up in Trondheim, where his father (an engineer) became *fiskeriintendent* (fishery inspector for the municipality), and in this position he was involved with the establishment of *Trondheim biologiske stasjon* together with Halvdan Bryn. Sigvald wanted to be an engineer and attended *Trondhjems Tekniske Læreanstalt* (TTL) in Munkegaten and after four years of higher-education studies in Germany, Belgium, and Switzerland he completed his doctoral theses in Basel in 1901. In 1904 he became docent at *Stockholm Högskola* (where many young Norwegian scientists before him had held positions, Vogt and Brøgger among them). In 1907 he moved to Kristiania to lecture in physiology at the university. However, he first had to

---

[674] NNBL for Bryn; S. Schmidt-Nielsen: "Halvdan Bryn," 56–65.

pass the required entrance, the *examen artium*. In 1913 he was appointed professor in technical organic and food chemistry, and he and his Swedish colleague and wife, Dr. Signe Schmidt-Nielsen, moved to Trondheim 16 years after he graduated from TTL.[675] Although important in reorganizing the old Society, Schmidt-Nielsen's major contribution was first and foremost his work during the first 20 years of the reorganized Society, when he served as general secretary. He represented the continuity of the reorganized Society through these crucial initial years, and firmly put the Society on its path with the identity, celebrations, and customs which are still alive and well today.

The Society regarded itself, as we have seen, as a close community of equals, all qualified as scientists and practitioners of sciences and the arts/humanities. It was taken for granted that all members would be interested in progress within any field of the sciences. It was understood that as practitioners they would all recognize and appreciate advances in other disciplines than their own. Perhaps the years before the Second World War represented the last time that such an ambition and way of thinking about the activities of the sciences could be seen in this way. The value of this collective approach was at least appreciated for many years. The lack of such a collective spirit was exactly what C. P. Snow criticized when he wrote his famous essay on the two cultures in 1957.[676] The society has always kept the dream of such a collective ideal alive and this is still mirrored to a great extent in the Society's program.

One of the most interesting aspects of this broad interest was the acceptance and integration, not only of the older sciences and arts, but also of the new ones: the applied sciences and the technological sciences. Particularly in comparison to the post World War II conflicts over technology, this seemingly peaceful coexistence in the interwar years was a striking contrast.

The Society encompassed all sciences with none privileged, old or new, applied or basic. However, it was the technology as science that was presented, not as design and constructions in its more traditional forms. Here was an unstable element that later proved disruptive: not all the professors at the *Høyskolen (NTH)* were considered sufficiently competent in the technological sciences to become members. They were considered to be practical-oriented constructors and designers more that scientists, practitioners rather than publishers of papers or experimentalists providing new insights into nature. With the professors at NTH so dominant in the science division, this reflected a hierarchy within NTH itself. Perhaps we could call the groups "the scientists" and "the practitioners"—and the scientists were the ones who were members of the Society.

This split between the technological disciplines was a clear sign of different values within the professorial group. Over time, all the technological disciplines became more and more science-based with experiments and reports, tests, and laboratories. Many of these disciplines were in fact rather new. Doctoral degrees in technology were not

---

[675] NNBL.
[676] Snow, *The Two Cultures.*

common before well into the 20th century, even on a European level.[677] The Second World War and the new status of science and technology probably became important catalysts for the changes whereby all technical disciplines were accepted as science, even if they were applied science.

Apart from the social and cultural events there were just two items on the Society's usual meeting agenda. There were meetings with presentations and lectures on scientific findings, followed by discussions and a presentation of coming publications. There were around six or seven such meetings each year. Usually there was a joint meeting for the two divisions followed immediately by separate meetings when needed for internal matters, that is, most often for the nomination of new members. The joint meetings had several lectures and shorter reports presented by members. No topic was too exotic to be accepted, be it "On the Flow and Extensibility of Concrete" by Fr. Vogt in 1935, or "On typologies of people and mental illness on the West Coast," by K. A. Andresen in 1932. Or another: Iversen' s lecture in 1931 on Henrik Ibsen's revisions of his language in "Kejser og Galilæer" (Emperor and Galilean) and Nordgaard's demonstration of bryozoans (sea mats) from Lopphavet (ocean area off the west coast of Finnmark) at the same meeting.[678] There is a truly romantic mix of short and long lectures and reports at the meetings, a scientific culture built in this small northern city. Twenty to thirty members would generally attend, which appears to be a little less than half the members. If we then accept that people traveled and some members were from outside Trondheim, we must consider this to be a substantial response from the members; they were active members, indeed.

The activity of the members was also displayed in another way, in the form of publications in the two series that the society had: *Skrifter* (Transactions) and *Forhandlinger* (Proceedings). The latter series, *Forhandlinger*, was new and had a more informal approach. Schmidt-Nielsen had restricted reports and articles to no more than four pages under any circumstances. Here short reports and summaries of lectures were published in addition to the minutes of all joint meetings and board meetings. Larger works were published in *Skrifter* (Transactions). The Transactions were a continuation of the old transactions of the Society dating back to the 1760s. Any major scientific contribution, essay or article, had to be presented to the members at meetings before it would be accepted for publication in *Skrifter* (Transactions). In this way the publishing was a major part of the Society's activities and internal life. In 1946 the general secretary looked back on the first 20 years of publishing (1926–1946), remembering the problems during the war and the first years afterwards. Overall, *Skrifter* (Transactions) had published 135 large articles by 110 authors, totaling 6448 pages. The *Forhandlinger* series was somewhat smaller—4621 pages with an impressive 917 reports by 211 authors.[679]

---

[677] The right to confer doctorates was granted to the German *Technische Hochschulen* between 1899 and 1901. König, "Technical education and industrial performance in Germany," 78.

[678] From *Forhandlinger* for the given years.

[679] *Forhandlinger*, 1946, 10*.

To maintain this activity the Society needed funds. Such an extensive publishing activity was a major expense. In 1936, for instance, the Society had revenues of slightly more than 17,000 *kroner*, and more than half of this was used for the publication of *Skrifter* that year and a little less than a quarter was used on *Forhandlinger*. The rest went to cover other costs (office equipment, meeting expenses, treasurer, insurance, medallions and so on). In other words, three quarters of the income was spent on the publications. The proportions varied a bit over the years, but on average three quarters of the revenues went to the publications.

Where did the revenues come from? We must remember that the museum kept all properties and all funds. The annual income from public sources was primarily used on the museum's activities. It was an enormous task for the board and general secretary to build a solid economic base for the reorganized society. Again, this work had to be done mainly by the general secretary, Schmidt-Nielsen. At the outset, simply to be able to start the Society, funds were collected from the members. At the end of the first year what was left from these resources went into a fund, *Medlemmenes Fond*. The general secretary also managed to convince Parliament to donate NOK 25,000 from the state lottery (*Pengelotteriet*) surplus to be made into a fund for the Society.[680] And money did come in. On November 3, the Society received 5000 Swedish *kroner* from managing director Johan Sande in Stockholm. The board immediately appointed Sande the first "donating member" in the society. The following year two more donating members were elected, each giving NOK 10,000. The engineer and director Yngvar Knudtzon established a fund for printing expenses in the name of *Ritmester C.A. Knutdtzons Fond*, the other was Consul Lars Christensen, who contributed the same amount to the medallion fund and thus secured the future of the Gunnerus medallion and the other medallions. He himself had received the Gunnerus medallion, in silver, together with W. C. Brøgger (who received it in gold) the previous year due to his efforts in the Norwegian sciences. Christensen was one of the whaling pioneers in Antarctica which had several companies and financed several scientific expeditions to the region.

We might percive the hand of the general secretary behind both the funds from Stockholm (Sande) and from Christensen. Schmidt-Nielsen lived in Stockholm for many years and a key scientific interest that he and his wife had was fat from whales and the development of the margarine industry, and other ways to make use of whale fat in food. In the following years he and the board managed to convince other wealthy people to establish funds, many of them becoming donating members.

Nevertheless, the most substantial contributors to the economy were the public or semi-public institutions. There were two of them: The Norwegian state lottery (*Pengelotteriet*) increased their contribution so that in 1939 one third of the value of the funds came from this source. The second was a gift from another semi-public fund: *A/S Varekrigsforsikringen*, providing a little less than one third of the value. The rest came from private donations to funds as we have seen. All in all the funds amounted to 380,000

---

[680] Parliamentary decision of July 9, 1926. *Forhandlinger*, Vol. 1, 1926–1928, 34*.

kroner in 1939. Moreover, the Society had managed to obtain a small annual amount from the central government budget and also an annual contribution from *Trondhjem Sparebank* (Trondhjem Savings Bank). But on average 80 percent of the annual revenues came from the dividends from the funds.[681] The size of the annual operating budgets by the end of the 1930s was in the range of just under 20,000 *kroner*.

The general secretary Schmidt-Nielsen was not altogether happy with the situation, but on the other hand, he was not too worried by it either. The Society had managed to secure its activities during the crucial first years. In particular it had made it possible to publish a large number of scientific articles and publications in the two series, *Skrifter* and *Forhandlinger*. These publications were the main external objective of the Society and crucial for the recognition of the Society as a scientific society. The contributions to the publications mainly came from the members. As they were mostly stationed at the three scientific institutions in Trondheim—NTH, NLHT and the museum—the writings mirrored their location and duties. It was only reasonable that a majority of the articles came from the technical university and discussed problems relating to the technological sciences. But the museum was also well represented with its more regional focus, still on natural history and archaeology.

The first 15 years of the Society were, as observed above, to a large extent a product of Professor Sigvald Schmidt-Nielsen's ideas and initiatives. However, he was not alone in this. The election of officers and representatives shows clearly a limited number of persons that over many years were active as the core of the Society. In addition to Schmidt-Nielsen, who held the office for the 20 first years, there was Professor R. Iversen, a linguist. He started as chair of the humanities division from 1926 and then he substituted for H. Bryn as *praeses* in 1933 when Bryn died. As *praeses* for the Society he then was in office for the same period as the general secretary, until 1946. If we regard Bryn as the bearer of tradition, then Schmidt-Nielsen from NTH and R. Iversen from NLHT represented the two new academic institutions in the city, on equal terms. But there were, of course, others.

Two professors from NTH deserve mention among the pioneers of the reorganized society, the two mathematicians, Viggo Bruun (1885–1978) and R. Tambs Lyche (1890–1991). Brun was secretary of the science division from 1926 to 1929 when Tambs-Lyche took over and held this position until 1945, except for the three years during the war when he was in German captivity. Brun was vice-chairman of the same group from 1934 to 1937 when he succeeded the former NTH rector, Harald Pedersen (1888–1945), as *vice-praeses*. He then switched positions with Professor R. Iversen, and became *praeses* of the society from 1946. Not for long, however, as he was granted a professor's chair in Oslo in 1946 and left the city. Thambs-Lyche stayed on, however, and took over as general secretary after Schmidt-Nielsen in 1946.

The humanities division was also remarkably stable. Two years after R. Iversen became *praeses* (and thus no longer chair of the humanities division) it was taken over

---

[681] *Forhandlinger*, Vol. XII, 16*–20*.

by A. Bergsgaard in 1936, and he remained in this position until 1949. The record in continuity was held by the vice-chairman of the humanities division, Th. Petersen, who held it from the start in 1926 until after the war. The third representative position in this division, the secretary, was held by the librarian at the museum: first J. D. Landmark (1876–1938) until his death, and then the librarian at the central library at NTH, J. Arsteinson (1893–1961).

How did the museum develop during these years? These were hard times financially. However, the museum had succeeded in securing both state and municipal funding in addition to a substantial contribution from *Trondhjem Sparebank*. With an operating budget at the end of the thirties of around 100,000 *kroner*, less than one-third came from funds. Nevertheless, the size of the budget was five times that of the Society. But then, of course, the Society did not have employees or exhibitions to maintain. Otherwise the museum continued almost exactly as it had done before the Society had been revived, with almost the same number of staff and the same fields of interest. Occasionally a professor would appear on the board, but mainly it remained composed of bank managers, directors, and teachers, just as had been the case before the split. The most important change was probably that the state gradually took over more of the annual funding even though the economic crisis made these hard times for everyone. The increase in public funding took the museum further away from the idea of a scientific community and toward a publicly funded and owned museum institution. This process had started before 1926, but as the scientific-society functions with particular requirements for membership were removed, both the identity and the tasks became truly that of a scientific museum and library.[682]

The Second World War and its aftermath

The Society met on April 8, 1940. Twenty-five members were present, including Professor Dehn. The meeting held few surprises. Mr. Bjørlykke and Mr. Høeg held lectures on respectively "The Alluvial Gold Areas in Finnmark" and "The Devonian and Upper Silurian Flora of Spitsbergen." The general secretary, S. Schmidt-Nielsen gave a short report on "The Organic Reminiscence of a Fossil Greenland whale." Two new papers were presented for publication. Little did the 26 persons gathered in the old festival hall of the Cathedral School know that it would take six long years before they once more could meet in the same hall. And, of course, they had no idea that during the evening and following night German warships would enter Norwegian fjords on their way to the occupation of Norway. The paradox of being invaded by the country whose language and scientific culture they knew so well must have been a shock to most. Many of the members had some or all of their education from Germany. The German Hochschules had always been a model and an ideal for the engineers and professors at NTH.

---

[682] Protocol for the general assemblies, Trondheim Museum, 1919–1951.

Not for very long, however. The German occupation of Norway was not as brutal as in most other countries, particularly in the east. The Society was allowed to continue their meetings as a closed society. And they chose to do so. But the occupation forces needed buildings and space. Both Lade gård (estate), the location of NLHT, and the festival hall at *Katedralskolen* were occupied. NLHT closed during the war, while NTH continued, even after the University of Oslo was closed. As mentioned, the meetings of the Society continued as before. The gala meeting was first moved to "Harmonien," but when that building was lost to a fire the library at the museum was used as a meeting room. Printing continued up to 1942 when problems with paper seemed to have slowed down the publications to some degree. For the gala meetings in February 1944 and 1945, the remembrance medallion for participants was made of zinc, not bronze, due to the situation. The annual number of meetings was reduced from seven to six due to the lack of heating fuel.

Five days after the German capitulation, on May 14, 1945, a meeting was held in the Society with only 12 members present. The *vice-praeses*, V. Brun, gave the opening speech, expressing the immense joy and gratitude that everyone was feeling. One of the members, Professor Leif Tronstad, had been killed in battle towards the end of the war. Tronstad was a key member of the allied squad that raided the heavy water plant at Rjukan and continued in the service of Great Britain almost to the end of the war. Five of the local members were imprisoned by the Germans and nine had to escape the city to go abroad. Members from other Norwegian cities had also been captured and imprisoned.

Brun asked whether the Society had experienced serious problems during the war. He answered his own question: "Apparently, perhaps not."[683] The Society survived and soon after the war even the printing of the two series was back on track, and in February 1946 it was possible to return to the festival hall at the Cathedral school.

Two actions were taken to remedy the wounds that the war had caused the Society and its members. On October 8, 1945, the meeting decided to establish an investigation commission to look into the members' actions and deeds during the war and evaluate if the Society needed to take action against any member who might have acted traitorously to king and country.[684] At the same meeting it was agreed to exclude those members who had remained members of the national Nazi party, *Nasjonal Samling*, after the attack on Norway, or who had not ended their membership as soon as possible afterwards.[685]

On the brighter side, the availability of funds that could not be used during the war had stimulated the financial situation and many new smaller funds had been set up during the war. Schmidt-Nielsen never tired of encouraging the brave and rich citizens and companies of Trondheim and other districts to establish funds in memory of per-

---

[683] *Forhandlinger*, Vol. XVIII, 1945, 11*.
[684] Ibid, 14*.
[685] Ibid, 14*.

sons who deserved to be remembered. All things considered, the financial situation was thus quite good. The funds had reached a value of almost half a million Norwegian *kroner* (462,721 *kroner*).[686] However, peacetime brought a new set of problems: a legally regulated, very low interest rate was one of them. Nevertheless, the future looked bright for the little Society.

The triumph of science

News of the more or less fantastic triumphs of science and technology reached the Society and its members quickly. Several members were quite up-to-date on the nuclear research that had resulted in the nuclear bomb. Niels Bohr was a member of the Society, and some members had worked with both him and other well-known physicists before the war. But also in many other areas organized state efforts and resources put into scientific and technological developments now showed triumph after triumph and were associated with the final victory. The national and international climate had created a belief in publicly funded science and technology as never before.

The war did not only have great impact on science and technology, but also on the way science and research was organized. Before the Second World War, many academies had relatively generous funds for financing research at their disposal. *Det norske Vitenskapsakademi* in Oslo controlled the Nansen funds, a most important source for Norwegian science, even if it was modest compared with what followed. The war led to a considerable change in the role the academies played as distributors of funds for science. In most Western countries, governments wanted to have a more direct influence on the priorities and strategies of research. Most countries increased the volume of research and at the same time also wanted to give priority to areas in research that might stimulate growth and development of the national economy or the national defense.

Norway was no exception to this trend. The volume of funding for research increased, but so did also the political interventions in the administration of the funds. This was of course contradictory to the central tenet of the academic societies, where it was thought that the quality of the research and not the area of research should be the basic criteria for funding. The republic of the learned were not to take this sort of policy criterion into consideration. Hence, while the war made the value of science clear to everyone, it also brought an end to the old ideal of equality and the ideal of quality as the sole criterion for obtaining funding.

In the Norwegian context, this had some particular consequences. During the war the Ministry of Defense, at the time in exile in London, had started to plan a research initiative as soon as they could return to Norway. This would keep all Norwegian scientists working for the allies in service for the newly liberated nation. Hence the Norwegian Defense Research Establishment (FFI) was organized as soon as the free

---

[686] *Forhandlinger*, Vol. XIX, 21*.

Norwegian forces returned to Norway.[687] Of greater importance to the Trondheim research community was the establishment of a government-funded research council for science and technology. It was given a rather ambitious title in its official English translation: The Royal Norwegian Research Council for Science and Technology or *Norges Teknisk Naturvitenskapelige Forskningsråd (NTNF)* in Norwegian. It was to fund research projects that could stimulate growth and development of Norwegian industry and society together with private funds. After much discussion it was decided that a particular body should grant funds to various projects. This body should consist of state representatives, industry stakeholders, and senior researchers, and its budget should be set by Parliament. The tricky question remained: could the Government still refrain from deciding which projects to support and would this new arrangement change the balance of power (between Parliament and Government) and the responsibility of the Government? In the end, with the addition of some private funds, the government handed the decision-making over to the council, and the Parliament followed suit.

The Society was not directly involved in the negotiations themselves. However, members of the Society were important contributors. The war had rocketed NTH to the forefront of the nation's knowledge policy. A clear sign of this is that the Government chose Fredrik Vogt as the chairman of the committee that was to prepare the new research council. He was professor and rector at NTH, son of the older Johan H. L. Vogt and brother of the *vice-praeses* of the Society, Thorolf Vogt. The committee worked quickly and in the summer of 1946 the new research council was established by a parliamentary bill. Fredrik Vogt became vice chairman, second only to the senior industrialist Alf Ihlen. In the early spring of 1946 the social democratic minister of finance, Erik Brofoss, stated that "the government, in recognition of the importance of scientific research for the economic situation" had proposed substantial increases in funding and new items on the state's budget.[688] Finally, scientific and technical research had obtained its status as a means for economic development.

However, this came at a price: "science" did not include all sciences. The humanities were among those left out. As a means to economic development, some disciplines became more important than others. This is not to say that only useful technology was funded; on the contrary, in his "Science, the endless frontier—Report to the President on a Program for Postwar Scientific Research," Vanevar Bush had argued against being too focused on "useful research." The war effort and the possibility to harvest earlier research in physics, chemistry and medicine was the perfect example of this. Radar, sonar, electronic computing and not to forget the atomic bomb were good examples. Just by following the search for new knowledge before the war, science had proven to be most useful.[689] Fredrik Vogt used Vanevar Bush's small pamphlet for whatever it was worth in the committee planning the research council, and the consequence was

---

[687] Njølstad and Wicken, *Kunnskap som våpen.*
[688] Kvaal, *Janus med tre ansikter,* 396–397.
[689] Bush, Science, the endless frontier; Kvaal, *Janus med tre ansikter.*

the name: *teknisk-naturvitenskaplig* (technological and scientific; officially translated to Science and Industry) and the choice of a council, more or less independent of the bureaucrats in the ministries. So, while being fairly broad, it was not all-encompassing—and while not being totally constrained by the higher officials in the ministries, it was not only in the hand of the researchers—the council had industrialists as well as some bureaucrats.

It is important to be aware of this particular structure of the new and comparably well-funded research council. It was to be an arena for balancing different interests in the process of funding new research. In this it was a great change from the years before the war when rather different bodies were responsible for the funding. The ministry of trade paid for smaller and well-restricted applied technical research projects while the academies in Oslo and Trondheim distributed their small sums on equal terms between all sciences and humanities disciplines. In brief, at the same time that science and research were raised in the political circles to become means for promoting the well-being of the society, the old way of assigning grants was becoming obsolete. The reason was that the results obtained during the war were seen as a consequence of substantial state-funded mission-oriented research projects and programs.

It is perhaps easy to underestimate the importance of the academies and scientific societies as sources of funds before the war. While it was true that the sum of money was not large, at least not in Trondheim, the whole logic of a scientific society was based on being the chosen ones, of being the scientific elite, of the ones able in an impartial way to see quality and only quality as the criterion for making funding decisions. Being elected to the Society meant that a new member now was recognized in such a way that he or she was capable, on equal terms, to decide the fate of an application for a research project. The new research council after the Second World War with its representative board undermined this function of the older academies, and this had consequences for them from which they never quite recovered. In the big picture, this was a price that had to be paid for the substantial increase in funding that followed the Second World War and for now being taken serious as a means for reaching political goals.

In dollars and cents, the academies before the war were not big spenders per se. In a system, however, where the salaries for the professors were state funded, these smaller grants were in a way one of the few available sources of research grants for trips and assistance, for printing and publishing (so important in Trondheim). The decision as to what to print and what to fund was in principle to be made by all the members. It is important to understand this when we now turn to a question that haunted the Society for many years: the limitation on the number of members. The important reason for limiting the number of members was precisely this: to have an elite deciding over limited resources, and who could tell the difference between very good and only good science. After the research councils were established it was no longer as obvious that the number of members needed to be so restricted. Perhaps the exchange of information should be more prominent and this did not need such a restricted election practice.

However, exclusivity is not easy to eliminate. Membership gave credibility and recognition, even without the power to distribute funds. When science and scientists became more popular and received recognition both from the political leaders and the general public, it became even more attractive to become a member. In Norway this manifested itself in many ways after the war, some of them particular to Trondheim.

First of all, there was the steady pressure from established members, particularly those working in the technical sciences, to increase the number of members. Second, other institutions, such as the museum, wanted a part in the increasing success of the Society. Third, several other academies or academy-like organizations were established or changed formats in the first half of the 1950s.

A technical academy?

The pressure to increase the upper limit on the number of members was linked to the question of a technical academy. There were several proposals in this regard. They can be broadly put into three categories: to increase the upper limit on members, to split the science division into two departments—one for the natural sciences and mathematics and the other for the technical sciences—and third, to make a separate third division for the technical sciences. Already from the start, the number of members in the science division was double that of the humanities division. This seemed reasonable in a city with a technical university and nobody wanted to change that.

During the war, the general secretary, Schmidt-Nielsen, had argued that the time might come when the Society had to take initiatives to raise the research question to promote the industries of the country and contribute to the self-reliance situation. However, as he argued, the Society's funds were at the present time all too small to achieve this. In the future, however, things might be different.[690] It was here that the peacetime government chose not to use the academies but instead establish the research council for science and technology (NTNF).

The pressure for increased representation of engineers, and particularly engineering professors from NTH, continued after the war. Rector Fredrik Vogt raised the question of a new technological division in 1946. His brother, the *vice-praeses* Thoralf Vogt, asked to have a committee evaluate a change in the statutes to accommodate a larger upper limit on members in December 1946.[691] A committee was appointed according to the statues and then another committee to evaluate the results of the first committee. Both of these had a majority of NTH researchers. At last, two year later, in 1948, the proposals were put to vote at the December meeting. The result of the voting guided the direction of future work. There was almost no support for a new division for the technical sciences, there being twenty-seven votes against and only three in favor of a new division. However, the vote resulted in a 19 to 11 result for an expansion of the upper limit on members, but most of the participants wanted a slow change, with the number laid

---

[690] *Forhandlinger*, 1944, 8*.
[691] Board meeting October 7 and December 9, 1946. *Forhandlinger*, 1946.

down in the statutes and not only by a decision in a meeting (23 against 6). The board received a clear signal from a well-attended meeting with almost 40 percent of all members present. None wanted to turn the society into a technical academy and only three of the 30 members present wanted a separate division for the technical sciences.

Finally, in November 1950 the new statutes were put to a vote and unanimously accepted. The limit on the number of members under 70 years of age was raised from 25 and 50 to 30 and 60 in the humanities and science divisions, respectively. In addition, up to 30 (10+20) foreign members could be elected. The limitations could not be easily changed, as they were laid down in the statutes and a new and long process was demanded to increase them.

From 1950 till his death in 1958, Thorolf Vogt was *praeses* of the Society. He had followed his father, J. H. L. Vogt, in the same professorship in geology and mining and had been one of the supporters for a broader representation from the technical sciences (as also his father and brother had been). In 1954 Thorolf Vogt again raised the question of an expansion of the technical sciences. This time, however, as one of two departments in the science division, one for the natural sciences and mathematics and one for the technical sciences. Once more the proposal had to go through the procedure of committees and finally in the spring of 1955 it was put to a vote at a general meeting. The *praeses* proposed that before they started to vote on the different parts of the proposal they should vote principally on whether the maximum number of members should be raised or not. The result was disappointing for Vogt: 14 were against change and just three voted in favor of an expansion.[692]

The decision in 1955 was important because members at NTH were about to lose patience. With no expansion in sight, many NTH professors felt that they needed a forum for the elite of the technical disciplines. However, there was more. The engineering disciplines lacked an advanced institution that could unite the most distinguished designers, engineers, industrialists, and researchers across the country. This would not be a community of scientists and academics as represented in the two academies in Oslo and Trondheim, but another type of community with much stronger links to industry and infrastructure. Here technology was to be the common ground, be it in design, construction, research, or economics. Towards the mid-fifties Thorolf Vogt, in his role as *praeses*, had come to see that the Society could never fully represent such a community, even if the number of possible members doubled. It was simply a very different community with a different ethos and ways of thinking about its role in society. Of course, for the researchers—many of the NTH professors—it made sense to be a member both of the research community, represented by the *Videnskabsselskabet*, and the engineering community, represented by the new academy.

The new academy had modeled itself on similar academies abroad. Most important was probably IVA, *Kungliga Ingeniörsvetenskapsakademien*, the Royal Academy for Engineering Sciences in Sweden, established by the Swedish Parliament (*Riksdagen*) in

---

[692] *Forhandlinger* 1954, Joint meeting April 5 and *Forhandlinger* 1955, joint meeting April 25.

1919. An important reason for establishing IVA in 1919 was to counteract the establishment of other academic institutions that would compete for funding for the technical sciences. IVA came to be a strong force in Swedish economic life, with acceptance and trust both from researchers and industrial stakeholders. Again, this was a special research community that placed most importance on industrial goals and engineering values.[693] Another inspiration was the Danish ATV, *Academiet for Tekniske Videnskaber* (the Academy for Technical Sciences) established in 1937. There were other reasons as well.[694] A major dilemma for the Trondheim professors at NTH was the fact that the share volume of industrial research and development was in the process of moving south to Oslo. NTNF (the new technical research council) had its administration in Oslo. Also the new military research establishment was mainly located in the outskirts of the capital. When the research council (NTNF) in 1949 also established a large research facility for industrial research close to the University of Oslo at Blindern (*Sentralinstituttet for industriell forskning*, SI), the Trondheim professors became quite worried.[695] Due to this, an academy for the technical sciences might very well be established in Oslo and not in Trondheim and hence outside the control of the professors in the technical sciences. However, it was also clear to them that a new technical academy had to be a national academy, even if the head office was to be in Trondheim.

On September 9, 1955, the new technical academy constituted itself under the name *Norges Tekniske Vitenskapsakademi* (NTVA) and on the following first annual meeting in December the same year, Professor Inge Lyse was elected the first president. The first meeting in Oslo was held in March 1957.[696] The academy (NTVA) started with a requirement for membership that a candidate had to have made an independent scientific contribution in technology or connected sciences. However, already the following year, in 1956, this was changed with the addendum: "... or whose work had been of particular importance for promotion of technology and the technological sciences." The upper limit for members below 70 years of age was set at 150.[697]

The Society in Trondheim could never have filled the role of such an academy without a total change of its objective, history, and members. An increase in the number of members or a new division could have satisfied the local professors, but it would very soon run into problems nationally. There is very good reason to believe that even if the Vogts and their allies had their way with the old *Videnskabsselskabet*, a new society would have been established in Oslo rather quickly. The solution now was one national academy for the technical sciences with rather broad criteria for membership, and with meetings and, after a while, with chapters in Oslo, Bergen and other places. Still there were two main academies in the traditional sense of the word that had local

---

[693] Moe, "Historien bak etableringen av Norges Tekniske Vitenskapsakademi," 69–70.
[694] Ibid.
[695] Gullowsen, *Bro mellom vitenskap og teknologi*.
[696] Moe, "Historien bak etableringen av Norges Tekniske Vitenskapsakademi," 65–66.
[697] Ibid, pp. 65–67.

focuses on Oslo and Trondheim, respectively, even though both had "Norwegian" in their name.

The local focus followed naturally from how these academies were supposed to work. If meetings and collegial interaction were important, they simply had to have a local focus. And as long as neither the Trondheim Society nor the academy in Oslo wanted to have sub-chapters, they had to stay put. But that of course raised the problem of what would happen in other centers with academic ambitions, such as Bergen and perhaps in due time also Stavanger. Bergen was particularly interesting on this point, as Bergen Museum was probably the strongest academic center outside the Oslo region before NTH was established in 1910. After the Second World War, Parliament was quick to decide that Bergen Museum should be developed into a full-fledged university (the second in Norway after Oslo). This was part of the same "package" to support science and economic development, of which NTNF (the research council) was another.

Since 1927 there had been a society for the promotion of the sciences in Bergen (*Selskapet til Vitenskapenes fremme*). This society was open for everyone who wanted to be a member and its main objective was to contribute to enlightenment and the promotion of science. When the University of Bergen and a business school were established together with a couple of large research institutions the society felt that it needed to cater more to the professors and researchers. They decided to set up a particular division of the society as an academic unit with elections and a limited number of members, just like the ones in Oslo and Trondheim. Even the number of members was exactly the same as in Trondheim: 60 in the science division and 30 in the humanities. Hence, from 1952 on there was also an academy in Bergen, even though it was not as independent as those in Oslo and Trondheim. Its success was limited; it seldom had meetings and issued no publications. In Bergen the society remained a subgroup under the Bergen Museum without the independence that J.H.L. Vogt and the others had insisted on in Trondheim.[698]

Stavanger also established an academy, *Rogaland Akademi*, in 1955. This was an open society, even if membership was only granted to graduates from universities or scientific colleges (with some exceptions).[699] In general it seemed that the interest in the academies was strong, but perhaps more in the direction of enlightenment and interest in science and technology than actually the collegial socialization and distribution of research papers and funds, as was the objective of the academies in Oslo and Trondheim.

However, as science after the war became more prestigious, the prestige of the scientists and the real scientists' academies also rose, even if the power of the academies was relatively reduced. In 1949 another research council was established in Norway, this time for the general sciences and humanities: NAVF, *Norges Almenvitenskapelige*

---

[698] Forland, *Forskningsformidling gjennom 75 år*, 48–51.
[699] Clausen, Med Sokrates i Rogaland, 13.

forskningsråd or the Norwegian Research Council for Science and the Humanities. While NTNF was important to the government policy of economic development and growth following the war, NAVF was an idea suggested as one way of distributing the surplus from the public football betting pools to the "spiritual and physical sports."[700] The aim was to support basic sciences and the humanities. The Society had here found a new source for funds and throughout the 1950s NAVF contributed substantially to the publication of the Society's two series: *Forhandlinger* and *Skrifter*.

The Museum, the Society, and a new university?

While the Society grew in size, finances, and activity, the museum also underwent changes. *Trondheim biologiske stasjon* (Trondheim biological station) had lived a more or less independent life but in close cooperation with the Society, first, and later with the museum. In 1948 the board of the station asked the ministry to formally become part of the museum. In the summer of 1949 the ministry accepted this and hence the museum increased its activities substantially. But there were other changes. During all the years the museum had existed it had never had a permanent management. Eventually, in 1949 they hired a "museum master," an executive director for the entire museum complex, including the library, Dr. philos Erling Sivertsen. Sivertsen was employed as a zoologist and conservator in 1936 and was to be the director for many years to come. It might well have been the ministry's wish that the museum be run by an administrative leader and not merely the board. The government budget had begun to finance more and more of the activities, both at the museum and the library. In 1950 the annual budget was 362,000 *kroner*, of which 215,000 came from the state and 66,000 from Trondheim local authority, while almost 80 percent of the expenses, including salaries, and books and journals for the library, were paid for by various public funds.[701]

This situation not only called for an executive director, but also for a reorganization of the whole museum. Towards the end of 1948 a committee had been convened to revise the statutes of the museum after discussions by the board of the museum (but not the board of the Society). New statutes were accepted at a general assembly in November 1950 and finally approved by the ministry in the late winter of 1951. The new statutes confirmed the institution as a museum and a library. This step was anticipated in the discussions in 1926, but was seen as a too-dramatic move back then. Now the membership of the museum was transferred to a separate museum association with its own statutes. The idea behind this move was that this association should help the museum and contribute to its economy. The museum as a membership organization was thus liquidated. In such an institution the way the board was appointed was the crucial element. In the new institution the museum association was to elect three rep-

---

[700] Skoie, Norsk forskningspolitikk i etterkrigstiden, 100 ff.
[701] *Årbok for museet*, 1949 and 1950 (Yearbook for the Museum).

resentatives to the board. The ministry should appoint two members and the local authority one. In addition, counties that contributed regularly could appoint one representative.

As an executive body the director was the unquestionable leader, while the heads of each department, together with the director, were now to be a senate that prepared items for the board. Finally the museum had a structure that was closer to that of other museums and the split away from the society became clearer. This differentiation process was not trouble-free. Particularly the museum's *praeses*, R. Brekke, expressed bitterness at the loss of the old tradition. Even if the museum still bore the name of DKNVS, it referred to two entities, the museum and the Society as two distinct and different institutions. He tried, therefore, on several occasions to re-introduce the idea from 1926 that the Society should have "academy" after its name as a parallel to the museum and then that the united organization should be called *Det Kongelige Norske Vienskabers Selskab* and not as now, *Det Kongelige Norske Vienskabers Selskab i Trondhjem*. The problem was that no one used a joint name for the two institutions that now were so different and had their own separate lives. Even the joint committee, *Fellesutvalget*, had not convened for many years. So it was with little dramatic effect that the board of the Society shelved and rejected Brekke's proposal.

However, it was another development in the 1950s that changed the mutual relationship of the museum and the Society. It also had considerable impact on their relations with the two most important scientific institutions of the city, NTH and NLHT. One needed only to look to Bergen and its brand new Bergen University based on Bergen Museum and one could easily anticipate a development in Trondheim that would call for a united university in the region, a *Universitas Nidarosiensis*. The name was based on the old medieval name for Trondheim, Nidaros. Under such a structure the museum would participate with its specialty in natural history and archaeology together with its large library that easily could be the basis for a university library together with the technical library at NTH. With a real university in place, the Society would really be the academic meeting place for all parts of such a future university: NTH, NLHT and the museum.

PART IV

1960–2010

13

Tradition and transformation

All in all, the activities of the Society continue to satisfy the purposes that have always been the aim of all the old academies from the 18th century. Otherwise, as far as I know, today only the St. Petersburg Academy (now the USSR Academy of Sciences) could claim to be wearing "true colors." The others—even the Paris Academy of Sciences and the Royal Society of London—have been reduced to the type of meeting and publication activities that are only half of what we do in our Society. Thus the Royal Norwegian Society of Sciences and Letters—if we consider it as a whole—is one of the very few old academies that continue to have their own research institutions with permanently employed scientists.[702]

This was part of a speech delivered by Harald Wergeland (1912–1987) when he retired as praeses of the Society in 1965, after serving as praeses since 1959. Even if "*DKNVS i Trondhjem*" (the Royal Norwegian Society of Sciences and Letters in Trondheim) was far away from the venerable old European academies, literally on the periphery, it was, according to Wergeland, possible to boast of being both an academy of sciences and a research institution, with its cultural and natural history museum. This fact, that *DKNVS i Trondhjem* consisted of both the *Society of Sciences and Letters* and the *Museum*, was not only a positive feature of DKNVS. It was also, as we will see, quite problematic, and much moreso than what might be gleaned from Wergeland's celebratory rhetoric. This two-part division had been the source of dispute and conflict since it was established in 1926, and it would be no less disruptive when the institution was to celebrate its bicentennial anniversary in 1960 and in the decades that followed.

The bicentennial anniversary

The bicentennial anniversary was duly celebrated, internally and with displays for the general public and citizens of Trondheim. On the formal day of celebration, the 26th of

---

[702] DKNVS *Forhandlinger* vol. 38, 1965:11–12.

February, the Society was honored with two Norwegians stamps: One with the face value of 45 øre and the other 90 øre, respectively, showing the Society's old seal in red and blue. The museum displayed an anniversary exhibition as well as a new permanent exhibition. The exhibition focused on the Society's history and research efforts through two centuries. It was in four parts, the first (1760–1773) covered the first steps and the three founding fathers Gunnerus, Suhm, and Schøning. The second part (1773–1874) informed about the so-called "intermediate" period, while the third part (1874–1926) was dedicated to the establishment of the museum. The fourth part detailed DKNVS's two departments, the Society (the academy) and the museum.

However, the exhibition could only show selected highlights of the Society's history. A more exhaustive history was presented in a book. Hans Midbøe (1915–1999) had been given the task of writing a bicentennial history. Midbøe was professor of Nordic Literature and literary history at *Norges lærerhøgskole* (the Norwegian College of Teacher Education), and was elected member of the Society in 1955. He wrote a two-volume treatise of more than 700 pages, both comprehensive and detailed. Midbøe's work was the most substantial result of the anniversary and has remained a reference on the history of DKNVS since then.

A wreath was laid on the tomb of Bishop Gunnerus to start the anniversary celebrations that would continue for three days. The Society's protector, HM the King of Norway, and HRH Princess Astrid attended as guests of honor during the celebrations. The first anniversary meeting took place in Trondheim's *Frimurerloge* (the Free Mason's Lodge) on Friday, 6 May, attended by 600 guests. In addition to the Society's Norwegian and foreign members, a number of invited guests from various scientific institutions attended, including representatives of the scientific societies in Norway, Denmark, Sweden, and Finland, representatives of the universities of Oslo and Bergen, from *Norges tekniske høgskole* (The Norwegian Institute of Technology), *Norges lærerhøgskole* (teacher's college) and *Norges geologiske undersøkelse* (Geological Survey of Norway), as well as representatives of a number of museums, primarily natural history museums and museum organizations in Norway. The *Zoological Museum* at the University of Copenhagen was also represented, the only museum outside Norway to attend. The guests included official representatives of the Norwegian Government[703] and state and local authorities. The press covered the event. Several banks were represented, having contributed financially to the anniversary. In the evening the local authority in Trondheim and the city's mayor, Professor Olav Gjærevoll, also a member of the Society, hosted a gala dinner. The printed report from the anniversary celebrations states that the dinner was arranged for "anniversary celebration participants and their female companions," illustrating the fact that with one exception the Society's members in 1960 and the invited representatives were all men.[704]

---

[703] Ministers Helge Sivertsen and Gunnar Bøe.

[704] Arvesen, Ole Peder and Olav Gjærevoll (eds.). *DKNVS Beretning om tohundreårsjubileet 6te til 8de mai 1960.* Trondheim, 1961.

Needless to say, a number of speeches and addresses were delivered by representatives of the celebrating institution and the many guests. The first speaker was *præses* Harald Wergeland, professor of physics at the Norwegian Institute of Technology. The second speaker was the *præses* of the museum, Director Reidar Brekke. Then the Society's protector, His Majesty the King, delivered a speech, followed by the host of the evening, Olav Gjærevoll, mayor of Trondheim. A long succession of greetings and gifts to the Society then followed. *Præses* Wergeland opened his speech in accordance with protocol by extending a warm welcome to the Society's protector, HM King Olav and HRH Princess Astrid. Wergeland also observed that "Royal" was not merely an embellishment of the venerable Society's name, it also had a deeper meaning: that ever since the time the successor to the throne, Fredrik (later Fredrik VI) became *præses* of the Society in 1767, the Society had enjoyed royal patronage. Wergeland devoted most of his speech to the university issue, an old matter that had gained new relevance.

There were plans in 1960 to establish a university in Trondheim, a matter that quite naturally attracted a lot of attention in the scientific community in the city. In a historical perspective, the founding of a university in Trondheim meant a final realization of the close ties Gunnerus had envisioned between the university as an institution and the *Videnskapsselskapet*. After more than 200 years, the Society would finally be able to work as a scientific society in a scientific university environment. Expectations for the university were universally positive, but Wergeland made no attempt at speculating on what a university would or might mean to the Society. Instead he used the opportunity to remind his listeners that the Society would not only be older than the new university, but also that the Society was far older than Norway's first university. He did this by quoting the former *præses* Prince Christian Fredrik, who at the founding of the University of Christiania (now Oslo) had on behalf of DKNVS greeted Norway's new university as its younger sister. In his speech *præses* Brekke also briefly mentioned the university issue, and the plan that the museum could join forces with other institutions in Trondheim to form the future University of Trondheim. But for the most part, Brekke devoted his speech to the Society's founder, Bishop Gunnerus, giving a detailed account of his scientific efforts and his work as founder of the Society.

The celebration of DKNVS was just as much a tribute to the founder of the Society, Bishop Gunnerus, as to the Society itself. Through the presentation of wreaths, lectures, and many speeches, Gunnerus and the heritage he left behind were praised. The fact that the founder of the Society was acclaimed during the bicentennial celebration was neither unexpected nor out of place. Without Gunnerus there would hardly have been an anniversary to celebrate. But there was also good cause to honor him from a science-history perspective, and highlighting the scientific importance of Gunnerus was also a way of underlining the importance of the Society. The Society's heritage and tradition were shown as important assets for DKNVS. In many ways the heritage and tradition had gained their own significance and value. Carrying forward the venerable Society had in itself become important. Therefore the anniversary did not spend much time reflecting on the contemporary and future functions of the Society. The university issue was mentioned, but there were few reflections on the opportunities and challenges that the building of a university in Trondheim would present. However, building the University of Trondheim, as part of the general expansion in the field of science during the last half of the twentieth century would indeed come to have a great impact on the institutional development of DKNVS, and would also raise fundamental questions about the functions and legitimacy of the Society and the museum. Before examining the changes and challenges DKNVS would be facing, we will examine in more detail the relationship between the two divisions of DKNVS, the Society and the museum.

A divided Society

The development within the Society in the years preceding the anniversary gave good reason for putting Gunnerus at the centre for the bicentennial festivities. In the decade prior to the celebration there had been an internecine dispute within DKNVS over the heritage after Gunnerus, and about the right to inherit the science society Gunnerus founded. The celebration of the bicentennial was arranged jointly by the two divisions of DKNVS in Trondheim: the Society and the museum. This was by no means a smooth process, as during the years before the anniversary the division in 1926 had again been the source of conflict.

The division in 1926 had not been a smooth process. The resurrection of the academy came at a cost; there had been conflicts and disputes that were not easy to forget. The solution in 1926 had been to establish two autonomous entities within the Royal Norwegian Society of Sciences and Letters: a museum and an academy. The museum kept all the properties, buildings, collections, legacies, and funds, while the new academic division received nothing but an honorable name and heritage. According to the statutes of 1926, the society as whole was to be called *Det Kongelige Norske Videnskabers Selskab i Trondhjem*, the museum was to be called *Det Kongelige Norske Videnskabers Selskab, Museet*, and the academy was to be called *Det Kongelige Norske Videnskabers Selskab*. This turned out to be quite confusing, especially when the full names most often were not used, but rather the shorter terms *Museet*, on the one hand, and *Selskabet* or *Videnskabsselskabet* for the academy on the other. In 1926 the division and names were at the centre of a dispute over how the statutes were to be interpreted and the status to be assigned to the common statutes for the total Society, *Det Kongelige Norske Videnskabers Selskab i Trondhjem*. Not unexpectedly the Society and the museum had diametrically opposed ideas about this. While ostensibly the dispute was about names, what was really at stake was the right to inherit Gunnerus's science society.

According to the Society, the division in 1926 meant that the original "Det Kongelige Norske Videnskabers Selskab" was re-established as a scientific society, and thus also acquired the right to the old traditional name. The name *Det Kongelige Norske Videnskabers Selskab*, without any suffix, for the academy division would have to be interpreted to mean that it was the academy division, or the *Society*, which was the true *Det Kongelige Norske Videnskabers Selskab*, and hence also the inheritor of Gunnerus's Society. The primary exponent of such an interpretation was Sigval Schmidt-Nielsen

(1878–1956), for many years the Society's general secretary. Schmidt-Nielsen, a professor of technical organic chemistry at NTH, had been one of the central figures in 1926 and became the Society's first general secretary, an office he held until 1946. According to Schmidt-Nielsen the joint statutes from 1926, which laid down that DKNVS consisted of two divisions, must be considered a pure formality required at the time to undertake the division and establish two autonomous institutions.[705]

DKNVS Museet had argued on several occasions against such an interpretation of the division and the joint statutes from 1926. The museum argued that the joint statutes, which were determined by Royal Resolution and thus legally binding, laid down that *DKNVS i Trondhjem* consisted of two equal divisions, a museum (*Museet*) and an academy (*Selskabet*), and that both divisions thus were the rightful inheritors of Gunnerus's society. The problem was that the names of the two divisions did not reflect this symmetry. In 1948, in connection with the Society's revision of the statutes, the museum had proposed that the academy division should also add a suffix to its name, so that the academy division would be designated as *DKNVS, Akademiet*. The naming issue was examined by a committee consisting of the Society's *præses*, Ragnvald Iversen, and the former general secretary, Schmidt-Nilsen, in addition to the director of the museum, Erling Sivertsen, also a member of the Society (voted in as a member in 1937). Not unexpectedly the proposal was vehemently rejected by the Society's *præses* and the former general secretary, while the director of the museum supported it fully. The final result was that the proposal was rejected. The name of the academy division from 1926, *Det Kongelige Norske Videnskabers Selskab*, or the Society, for short, remained in place until 2001. In connection with a more comprehensive restructuring of DKNVS in 2001, (see pages 371–372) the academy division of the Society was called *Det Kongelige Norske Videnskabers Selskabs Akademi*, or the Academy, for short.[706]

Thus the museum lost the name dispute at the end of the 1940s, and as the time of the bicentennial anniversary was also approaching, the conflict about the interpretation of the statutes from 1926 continued unabated. To be able to celebrate the anniversary together the museum felt it was important to establish a joint understanding of the idea of two equal institutions, and that both institutions had the right to the old institution's history, traditions, and name.[707]

---

[705] UBIT, Special collections. DKNVS IV:v:3. Statutes 1950. "Navnesaken 1948–1950" (The naming conflict 1948–1950). Memo by Schmidt-Nielsen, 25 February 1950.

[706] DKNVS *Forhandlinger* 2001. Statutes for *Det Kongelige Norske Videnskabers Selskabs Akademi* passed in a joint meeting on 11 December 2000 and confirmed by Royal Resolution 30 November 2001. This presentation will in general follow choice of name picked by contemporaries and the institution itself for the academy division, so that the name *Selskabet* (the Society) refers to the academy division until 2001. For the time after 2001 the designation *Selskabet* (the Society) will refer to all of DKNVS. To simplify matters, the abbreviation DKNVS used alone will be restricted to the total society.

[707] Memo 27 October 1955, "Ad forholdet til det kgl. Norske Videnskabers Selskab" (Re the relation to the Royal Norwegian Society of Sciences and Letters) by Erling Sivertsen.

The museum managed to gain acceptance for this interpretation. Through negotiations in *Fellesutvalget*, a committee with representatives from both divisions and which was authorized by the statutes of *DKNVS i Trondhjem* (section A: Joint statutes), a joint platform was established.[708] The honor for achieving this belongs to the *præses* of the museum, Reidar Brekke (1888–1971), who was elected a member of the Society in 1946. It was also Brekke who led the work with the anniversary celebration, and who secured the financial basis. One requirement for the celebration was that it could receive funding from outside the Society. The most important external contributions came from the Ministry of Education and Church Affairs and from the local business community. The fact that new people joining the Society had not participated in the conflicts in 1926 also helped to tone down the dispute.

The anniversary therefore became an important event for *DKNVS i Trondhjem* as an institution. The anniversary celebrations demonstrated that *DKNVS i Trondhjem* consisted of two equal divisions: the Society and the museum. Both were legal inheritors of the original Society from 1760, and of the name and heritage from Gunnerus. The joint statutes from 1926 were not only of a formal nature, they were also real. The anniversary celebrations thus helped to close the book on the 1950s controversy over the interpretation of the 1926 statutes, for the time being. The confirmation through the anniversary celebration of the fact that *DKNVS i Trondhjem* consisted of two equal institutions, the museum and the Society, could not, however, hide the latent tension between the two institutions. Contact between the two divisions in the years to come dwindled to the virtually non-existent. The Joint Committee did not meet after the bicentennial celebration until the middle of the 1990s, and, for example, the 225-year anniversary in 1985 was celebrated separately by the two divisions. The museum and the Society continued to exist side by side as two autonomous institutions with different purposes and functions, separate boards and separate *præses*, and with separate financing. The two institutions were also asymmetrical in size and finances, and as the 1960s progressed, this asymmetry would be further strengthened. Instead of a rapprochement between the two divisions the institutional division was further amplified, emphasizing that the superstructure *DKNVS i Trondhjem* was an institution that existed on paper only.

Changes and challenges

DKNVS i Trondhjem celebrated its 200th anniversary at a time when science was gaining an increasingly important position in society, and expanding institutionally, financially, and culturally. In Norway, as in the rest of the industrialized world after World War II, science was believed to be a major catalyst for growth and development. The thesis of American scientist and research administrator Vannevar Bush that science is

---

[708] UBIT, Special collections. DKNVS II:4. Board minutes. Summary from the meeting of the Museum Board, 22 April 1955 and 21 December 1955.

"the endless frontier," based on the successes of scientific research during World War II, was warmly embraced by the dominant policymakers who designed Norwegian research policy in the decades immediately following World War II.[709] Several of them had also stayed in Britain during the war and were strongly inspired by the research policy ideas prevailing in Anglo-American circles. This inspiration notwithstanding, the frontier thesis was modified to fit Norwegian conditions. Long-term independent basic research was given little priority. Instead the focus in Norway came to be on more practical and utility-oriented research. Independent basic research had far lower political acceptance. There were both pragmatic and political-ideological reasons for the emphasis on targeted technical-industrial research. As there were scarce state resources, earmarking too much funding for long-term basic research was deemed a luxury beyond the means of the Norwegian state, particularly when the country had a high degree of reconstruction to undertake after the war. This type of research would have to be left to richer and larger countries. The Norwegian Labor Party, which held power without interruption from 1945 to 1963, was dominated by a technical-instrumental view of scientific research. The primary task of research was to contribute to the establishment of industry and to the modernization and rationalization of the traditional industries in Norway, such as fishing and farming. The state focus on technical-industrial research was also an indication of a new ideology of cooperation when it came to the relation between the state authorities and private business and industry. Privately funded industrial research had a weak position in Norway, as did the tradition of the private donor. Therefore the state authorities were the dominant actor in Norwegian research, and this was the main characteristic feature of Norwegian research compared to the other trend-setting Western countries.

The increase in the state's focus on research resulted in institutional innovation on two fronts. First, several technical-industrial research institutes were established, whereof the two first and largest were a military research institute, the Norwegian Defense Research Establishment (FFI) in the spring of 1946, followed by a research institute for nuclear energy (then abbreviated IFA, now IFE—the Institute for Energy Technology) in 1948. In 1950 a technical-industrial research institute was established in Trondheim as an offshoot from the Norwegian Institute of Technology (NTH), *Selskabet for industriell og teknisk forskning ved Norges tekniske høgskole* (SINTEF). Second, a new state research council system was established and patterned on the model of similar councils in other OECD countries, such as Great Britain, but the Norwegian system was more sector-oriented.[710] The first research council was founded in the autumn of 1946, a council for technical-natural science research under the Ministry of Industry: *Norges teknisk-naturvitenskapelige forskningsråd* (NTNF). Several sector-oriented research institutes were established under the council. In 1949 a special

---

[709] Bush, Vannevar. *Science—The Endless Frontier*. Report to the President on a Program for Postwar Scientific Research. Washington: United States Government Printing Office, 1945.

[710] Skoie, Hans. *Norsk forskningspolitikk i etterkrigstiden*. Oslo: Cappelen Akademisk Forlag AS, 2005.

research council was established for agricultural research, *Norges landbruksvitenskapelige forskningssråd* (NLVF), which came under the Ministry of Agriculture.

In 1949 a special research council was also founded for general science research, *Norges allmennvitenskapelige forskningsråd* (NAVF), which came under the Ministry of Education and Church Affairs. In contrast to the other two councils, NAVF focused on the university and college sector, and right from the start was to all intents and purposes a researcher-controlled council. NAVF became a support for university research, and the research tasks that were funded were generally of such a nature that they coincided with academic career patterns. NAVF's activities came to reflect the independent position university research traditionally had enjoyed in Norway. NAVF also set up special groups for the humanities and social sciences right from the start, which had not been the case with the establishment of similar research councils in Britain, the USA, or Sweden.[711] Thus NAVF became a funding source for basic research in natural science, the humanities, and the social sciences. However, NAVF was not only a basic research council, nor was this its intended role. Even if the Ministry emphasized the idea that the council would play a particularly important role for advancing Norway's scientific and cultural heritage, the utility aspect was also emphasized. Thus the statutes stated that the council should encourage basic research to advance national business and industry and cultural development. Thus the seeds of two conflicting dimensions were embedded in NAVF from its inception: NAVF's relation to applied research, particularly in the field of the social sciences, and the division of work between NAVF and NTNF in the natural sciences.[712]

In the initial years NAVF was fully funded outside the normal national budget. The funding was assured through the establishment of a state-owned lottery, *Norsk Tipping AS*, in 1946, where the surplus was to be shared between sports and science, the "spiritual sports." NTNF also received funding from the state-owned lottery, and thus enjoyed a special position among the research councils, with funding contributions from the national budget, industry, and the lotterys surplus. Throughout the 1950s the surplus from the Norsk Tipping had risen far more than anticipated, which gave academic basic research far better conditions than ever before. Until 1961 the council's budget increased annually, but as the 1960s progressed the real value of the lotterys surplus allocated to NAVF declined. While the unique funding model through the lotterys surplus had placed Norway in an advantageous position in the 1950s compared to other countries where basic research was funded through the national budget, this was turned around in the 1960s. In the 1960s NAVF also came under the national budget, but the allocations were quite modest compared to the corresponding funding granted to NTNF.[713]

The two science academies in Norway, *Det Kongelige Norske Videnskabers Selskab* in Trondheim and *Det Norske Videnskaps-Akademi* in Oslo, both were to play marginal

---

[711] Helsvig, Kim Gunnar. *Elitisme på norsk. Det Norske Videnskaps-Akademi 1945–2007*. Oslo: Novus forlag, 2007.
[712] Skoie, *Norsk forskningspolitikk i etterkrigstiden*.
[713] Helsvig, *Elitisme på norsk. Det Norske Videnskaps-Akademi 1945–2007*.

roles in the state-controlled research system that was developed in Norway after 1945. Placed on the periphery in relation to the research-policy environment in the capital, the Society in Trondheim had not displayed strong ambitions to become a national research-policy actor. The academy in Oslo, on the other hand, had done precisely this, and had been the most important instigator for the establishment of NAVF, and had also tried to have the lotterys surplus allocated to NAVF only, and not be shared between all the research councils, which was the final outcome. The academy in Oslo had also aimed to ensure that they had the majority of the representatives on the council, but did not succeed on that point either. The academy in Oslo obtained four of the total of 32 places on the council, while the Society in Trondheim was awarded one seat. However, the majority of the appointed members, who were in part appointed by the Ministry and in part by the University of Oslo and other scientific institutions, were actually members of the academy in Oslo. The marginalization of the academy in Oslo as an institution was, however, an expression of the fact that exclusive institutions such as the science academies had little room in the social-democratic political regime that had come into power in post-war Norway.

The state research council system that developed at the end of the 1940s would remain virtually unchanged until 1993. At that time the various research councils were merged into one large research council, *Norges Forskningsråd* (NFR). The establishment of research councils and the development of research institutes constituted one of the two main pillars in the development of scientific institutions in Norway after 1945. The enlargement of the university sector in Norway, and the later extension of the college sector, constituted the second. This also meant the establishment of a university in Trondheim, and therefore the development of the university sector had far more direct consequences for DKNVS.

On March 26, 1968, *Stortinget* (Norwegian Parliament) voted to establish a university in Trondheim. The foundation of *Universitetet i Trondheim* (UNIT) (the University of Trondheim) was part of a major reform process in the Norwegian educational system, a reform process started in the 1950s. As in most other Western countries after World War II, education was to an increasing degree considered a condition for economic growth and development. To develop a modern industrialized society, heavily dependent on science and technology, it was of special importance to have a well-educated workforce. An official prognosis made in 1961 estimated a need for a capacity of about 18,500 students at the university level in 1970.[714] Compared to the 9200 university students attending in 1960 this meant a doubling within less than a decade. Economic reasons, though of great importance, were not the only motives. Firstly, expanding the study capacity at university level was also a response to an increasing demand for education at this level. Secondly, education was also seen as a means for developing a more social egalitarian society. This view was followed by an ideology that all citizens should have access to higher education independent of socioeconomic

---

[714] St. meld. nr. 91, 1961–62, 24–25.

background and geography. Both quantitative expansion and geographical decentralization of higher education therefore became one of the government's goals.

To attain these goals *Stortinget* decided to expand the two existing universities in Oslo and Bergen and establish two new universities, one in Trondheim and another in Tromsø, the largest town in northern Norway, and in the spring of 1968 the Universities of Trondheim and Tromsø were founded. There was strong political consensus among the political parties represented at *Stortinget* regarding this education policy, even though their more-ideological foundations varied. Hence the first plans for the university expansion were made under the government of the Labor Party, which was in power without interruption between 1945 and 1963. The rest of the 1960s, however, was a more turbulent period in Norwegian politics, and the final decision to establish the universities was made by a government coalition of *Høyre* (Conservative Party), *Senterpartiet* (Regional Party),[715] *Kristelig Folkeparti* (Christian Democrats) and *Venstre* (Liberal Party).

The new University of Trondheim was far from a brand new institution. It was based on the already existing scientific institutions in Trondheim: *DKNVS Museet*, *Norges tekniske høgskole* (NTH) and *Norges lærerhøgskole* (NLHT). This made the University of Trondheim special in relation to the other universities in Norway, and the issue of the structure of the University of Trondheim has thus been a bone of contention for many years, both in the years preceding the establishment and in the years immediately after. The Parliamentary decision called for a merger of the three institutions on establishment of the university to make the new University of Trondheim appear as a unified institution. Merging the three well-established institutions proved, however, to be far more complex than first assumed. We shall not go into detail about this process here, but only observe that the three old institutions were to remain relatively autonomous within the university structure until 1996.

Even if *DKNVS Museet* was made a part of the university, it continued to be part of *DKNVS i Trondhjem* until 1984. The inclusion of the museum in the university had decisive importance for the development of the museum itself—for example, the restructuring into a university institution resulted in substantial financial and institutional growth. At the same time, the inclusion in the university also had major long-term consequences for *DKNVS i Trondhjem*. In spite of the growth at the museum, it remained a minor entity within the *University of Trondheim* (UNIT). The largest parts of UNIT were the two educational colleges NTH and NLHT, and with the expansion of the university as a whole, it was here the largest growth came. However, the consequences of the inclusion in UNIT were very different for the two colleges, and this also applied to the institutions' attitudes to becoming university institutions.

Within NLHT (the Norwegian Teacher's College) comprehensive structural and organizational changes took place in connection with its inclusion in the university. NLHT was established in 1922 as a further education institution for primary school

---

[715] Former *Bondepartiet* (the Agrarian party).

teachers. The most important subjects were education science, Norwegian studies, and history, where from its inception three chairs for professors were established. From 1938 English studies were also included, while right from the start teaching in natural science subjects was given by teachers employed by NTH and the museum.

During the late 1950s, NLHT was completely reorganized, primarily in response to fundamental reforms in the primary and secondary schools. Compulsory schooling was extended from seven to nine years. Implemented gradually between 1955 and 1971, the reform created the need for more educated teachers in the secondary schools. NLHT was assigned a key role in educating the new group of teachers. As part of this, and also to prepare for a future as a university, the curriculum was reorganized in accordance with the curriculum at the University of Oslo. Thus NLHT acquired a university structure before becoming a university. In 1963 NLHT was granted the right to offer examinations on the Bachelor's level. Teaching was also given on the Master's level, but the right to offer examinations on this higher level was not granted until NLHT formally became part of the university.[716]

From being a small *teacher's college* with around 300 students in 1960, NLHT developed into a university institution with three university faculties—a faculty of the humanities, a faculty of social sciences and a faculty of natural science—with a total of around 9500 students in 1995. After the university plans had been launched, there was a continuous expansion of the academic fields and departments within the three faculties with the aim of having the broadest possible academic scope for the three faculties to be seen as fully-fledged university faculties equalling those at the University of Oslo. In 1960 the institution had 22 scientific positions, including nine professorships, while in 1995, the final year the three faculties were organized as separate institutional units within the university, the institution had around 260 permanent and close to 90 temporary scientific positions. The establishment of the university also led to changes in institutional identity. During the first years there was still a strong wish to maintain an identity that reflected the teacher's college tradition, but as the three university faculties developed, their identity was increasingly linked to the university. The university name, the University of Trondheim (UNIT), was primarily used externally, not *Norges lærerhøgskole* or *Den allmennvitenskapelige høgskolen* (AVH) which was the name of the institution after 1984.

The development of NTH—*Norges tekniske høgskole*—was a sharp contrast to the development of NLHT—*Norges lærerhøgskole*. The establishment of UNIT had little direct impact on internal development at NTH, where the studies structure and organization remained more or less unchanged until 1996. NTH, established in 1910, was based on the German model of *technishe Hochschulen*, turning out graduates, *sivilingeniører* (engineers), at the university level; and these graduates would become the

---

[716] For the history of *Norges lærerhøgskole*, from 1984 called *Den allmennviteskapelige høgskolen*, see: Kirkhusmo, Anders. *Akademi og seminar. Norges Lærehøgskole 1922–1982*. Trondheim, 1983, and Wale, Astrid. *Universitet og høgskole. Den allmennvitenskaplige høgskolen 1984–1996*. Trondheim, 1997.

technical elite in Norway. The identity of the institution was therefore not linked to the University of Trondheim, but precisely to this national technical college tradition, with a national education responsibility it alone bore in Norway. After the establishment of UNIT, NTH fought a hard battle to maintain its position as an independent institution within the university structure and to keep the original name of the institution. NTH's battle for independence was also the most important reason why there was such a long-term controversy over the organization of UNIT. NTH also saw substantial growth in the number of students, even if not as steep as at *Norges lærerhøgskole*. From around 1500 students in 1960 the number had increased to around 7900 in 1995.[717]

In 1974 a faculty of medicine was also established at the University of Trondheim. During the initial years, only clinical training was given at the faculty, while the pre-clinical training was undertaken at the University of Bergen. Eventually the study of medicine also became a complete course of studies at UNIT, with the regional hospital in Trondheim functioning as a university hospital.[718] Thus until 1996 the University of Trondheim consisted of a number of technical and partly natural science faculties organized as a technical college, three faculties of the humanities, social sciences, and natural sciences, organized as a separate college, a medical faculty, and a museum of national and cultural history.

In 1996 the name of the university was changed from the *University of Trondheim (UNIT)* to the *Norwegian University of Science and Technology* (Norges teknisk-naturvitenskapelige universitet—NTNU). The change of name was implemented in connection with comprehensive changes in the university structure. The two colleges, *Norges tekniske høgskole* and *Den allmennvitenskapelige høgskolen* (formerly *Norges lærerhøgskole*), which until then had existed as relatively autonomous institutions in the university structure, were discontinued. Other radical changes in the faculty and department structure were also introduced, including merging parallel subject departments.[719] Such a restructuring had been desired by the authorities for quite a time, but had not been carried out due to massive resistance from *NTH*, which wanted to retain its status as a technical *hochschule*, and to retain the NTH name which was well entrenched both nationally and internationally. The University of Trondheim therefore had a quite special organizational structure, different from all other universities in Norway. However, in connection with the introduction of a common Act for all universi-

---

[717] For the history of *Norges tekniske høgskole*, see: Hanisch, Tore Jørgen and Even Lange. *Vitenskap for industrien. NTH—En høyskole i utvikling gjennom 75 år*. Oslo, Bergen, Stavanger, Trondheim: Universitetsforlaget AS, 1985, and Hård, Mikael et al. (eds.). *Teknologi for samfunnet. NTH i en brytningstid 1985–1995*. Trondheim, 1997.

[718] In 2002 the Regional Hospital in Trondheim changed its name to St. Olavs University Hospital after St. Olav who was buried in Trondheim in 1030. This change of name was implemented in connection with the state takeover of the hospital from Sør-Trøndelag county authority.

[719] Both the colleges had had their own departments covering such subjects as mathematics, physics, chemistry and informatics. Thus the University of Trondheim had a double set of departments in several academic fields, primarily in the field of mathematics and natural science.

ties and colleges in Norway in the spring of 1995, the authorities took the bold step of restructuring the institutions in spite of the massive resistance. The change of the name from UNIT to NTNU was the result of a political compromise among the political parties in Parliament which enabled the Act to be passed, and this also introduced the reorganization of the university in Trondheim. NTH had conducted a successful campaign strategy and ensured the necessary political support for remaining an independent college and if necessary secede from the entire university structure. With the name the "Norwegian University of Science and Technology" (*NTNU*), which signaled that the university had and would continue to have as its primary focus the technical and natural-science subjects, a political majority could agree to the reorganization of the University of Trondheim.

In 2005 NTNU had a total of 2871 scientific positions, including 548 professors.[720] There were also a large number of administrative and technical positions. NTNU was the second-largest university in Norway after the University of Oslo. NTNU had also become the second-largest employer in Trondheim after the municipality.

Even if the university was the decidedly largest and most important scientific institution in Trondheim, UNIT/NTNU was not the only new establishment that was important for DKNVS. In 1961 NGU (Geological Survey of Norway) was moved from Oslo to Trondheim. NGU had been established in 1858 as a national institution with responsibility for geological surveys of Norway. The move to Trondheim came about because Parliament wanted to merge NGU with other geological institutions which were already in Trondheim. The aim was to strengthen the geological exploration of Norway, particularly the prospecting for ore. One institution was *Statens råstofflaboratorium* (the State Raw Materials Laboratory), originally founded as a temporary research program during World War I. The aim had been to develop alternative Norwegian raw materials for Norwegian industry and agriculture to replace imported raw materials which were difficult to get hold of during wartime. Led by Victor Moritz Goldschmidt (1888–1947), the temporary research program was expanded into a permanent geo-chemical research laboratory. In 1954 the institution moved to Trondheim. The second institution was *Geofysisk malmleting* (Geo-physical ore prospecting). This institution was established in the 1930s, initially loosely connected to the Department of Physics at NTH, to use and develop geo-physical prospecting methods to find ore. These three were merged into a new and larger NGU which undertook geological, geo-physical and geo-chemical surveys.[721] Together with the geology subjects at NTH (mining engineering and from the 1970s also petroleum geology) this made for an expert geological environment in Trondheim. The scientists at NGU, together with the geologists at NTH (UNIT, later NTNU) laid the fundament for establishing geo-science as a subject group within the Society.

---

[720] The R&D statistics bank, NIFU STEP. Both permanent and temporary positions, including scholars and post-doc positions were included.

[721] Børresen, Anne Kristine and Astrid Wale. *Kartleggerne. Norges geologiske undersøkelse 1858–2008.* Trondheim: Tapir Akademisk Forlag, 2008.

When DKNVS celebrated its 200th anniversary, the city was facing an enormous growth of science institutions. Through the expansion of the university and other scientific institutions the number of scientists in the city multiplied, and the number of scientific fields expanded dramatically. The expansion would also leave its mark on the city. This became particularly noticeable from the end of the 1980s, when the university grew dramatically while the city's traditional industries declined. At the end of the twentieth century NTNU, together with other knowledge institutions, was a dominant feature in the city, and the designation "Trondheim the knowledge city" was often used to promote the city's identity.

Having a retrospective anniversary celebration at a time when the local and national scientific field was going through comprehensive and radical changes now appears as quite a paradox. The expansion in the field of science would raise new but widely different challenges for the Society and the museum, which in turn created challenges for the joint institution *DKNVS i Trondhjem*. In which ways did DKNVS as the administrator of the two-centuries-old traditions manage to fill a meaningful and legitimate function in the new scientific context? The next two chapters will examine the consequences of the expansion of the scientific institution, particularly the University of Trondheim, on *DKNVS i Trondhjem*, and how the Society and the museum dealt with these new challenges.

14

The Museum becomes part of the University of Trondheim

The foundation of a university in Trondheim in 1968 was a fundamental change for both divisions of the *DKNVS*: the Society and the museum. In this chapter the focus will be on the museum, while the consequences of the university foundation for the Society will be examined in the next chapter. The museum became part of the new university while continuing to be a division of the Royal Society of Sciences and Letters in Trondheim. This dual structure lasted until 1984 when the museum and its properties were handed over to the Norwegian state, which meant a final separation of the museum and DKNVS. The museum was no longer a part of DKNVS, and DKNVS no longer owned a museum. However, this did not mean that the museum division was dissolved. Still possessing several funds and legacies, and some smaller properties, the museum division continued in a reorganized form. Thus the Royal Society of Sciences and Letters in Trondheim continued as two divisions, even after 1984.

In this chapter we will discuss the museum's incorporation into the newly established University of Trondheim as well as the separation of the museum from DKNVS later on. The question of incorporating the museum became inevitably entangled in the controversy regarding how to organize a university based on three well-established institutions. As part of this we will look at the internal development of the museum in this period and analyze it in a broader national context.

University controversy

Organizing the new university in Trondheim was far from easy. As it was founded on three existing institutions, *Norges tekniske høgskole* (NTH), *Norges lærerhøgskole* (NLHT) and *DKNVS Museet*, each with specific responsibilities and traditions, the University of Trondheim was different from the other Norwegian universities. In Bergen and Tromsø, only the museums existed prior to the creation of the universities, while in Trondheim all the faculties, with the exception of a Faculty of Medicine from 1974, already existed within the three old institutions. Thus, how this special university should be organized was controversial right from the beginning.

Two in principle opposite organizational models can be outlined: A university based on the continuing existence of the old institutions, or a radical reorganization of the existing institutions into a totally new university structure. In the first model the university foundation could be seen as a means for developing the existing institutions, in the second these institutions were the means for developing a new university.

Kirke- og Undervisningsdepartementet (the Ministry of Church and Education) favored the second model, the so-called integration model, primarily because it was thought that this model utilized the total resources in Trondheim in the most rational way. Through its director Erling Sivertsen, the museum also supported the integration model when the idea of a university in Trondheim first was launched.[722] The motives for this will be discussed later in this chapter. However, the rectors of the two other institutions, *Norges tekniske høgskole* and *Norges lærerhøgskole*, strongly favored a university model based on the continuing existence of their respective institutions. The reluctance to agree to radical institutional changes was particularly intense and motivated at NTH. Since 1910 NTH had been the sole national institution educating *sivilingeniører* (engineers), was well respected in Norwegian society, and was internationally recognized as providing excellent education in engineering.

As the university process proceeded, it became evident that no agreement on the question of an organizational model could be reached. Thus a radical reorganization of the three old institutions could not be implemented at the time of the founding of the university in 1968. However, *Stortinget* did state that the new university should be based on an integration of the three old institutions, which meant that these institutions had to be dissolved and replaced by a new university structure in one way or another. But this was a resolution only in principle. How the model was to be implemented in practice was not decided. The creation of organizational and administrative structures was left to the provisional university board to outline. Meanwhile the three old institutions were to be run much as before, and they continued as almost autonomous institutions inside the new university structure. Thus the DKNVS museum was made part of the university, while still continuing to be a division of the Royal Society of Sciences and Letters.

This organizational issue was then the root of a long-standing controversy within the University of Trondheim, and no agreement in accordance with the integration principle was achieved among the heads of the three institutions. Due to this conflict, the University of Trondheim was governed only by preliminary directives and regulations until 1984. Then the first permanent Act for the University of Trondheim was introduced.[723] This Act formalized to a great extent what had been the practice since

---

[722] *Innstilling om opprettelse av et universitet i Trondheim.* KUD 1964, 82–84. The committee was appointed on April 6, 1962, and gave its report January 15, 1964. *Ekspedisjonssjef* Leif J. Wilhelmsen from *Kirke- og Undervisningsdepartementet* (the Ministry of Education and Church Affairs) chaired the committee, also called the Wilhelmsen committee.

[723] The universities in Norway were governed by separate Acts for each university until 1989.

the foundation of the university. The *DKNVS Museum* as well as *Norges tekniske høgskole* and *Norges lærerhøgskole* remained autonomous institutions in almost every aspect. In some areas the institutions even gained more autonomy than they had had during the interim period. On the other hand, the Act also strengthened the overriding administrative level by expanding its budget and resources.

During the years when the Act relating to the University of Trondheim was being formulated, negotiations were being held between the board of the DKNVS museum and the Norwegian government relating to the transfer of the museum to the Norwegian state.[724] An agreement was signed on May 27, 1983, stating that the museum with its various divisions, including the library, was to be transferred to *Kultur- og vitenskaps-departementet* (the Ministry of Arts and Science).[725] The dual structure of the museum, being part of both the Society and the University of Trondheim, thus came to an end.[726] A quarter of a century passed from the start of the discussions on the incorporation of the museum into the university until the museum was no longer a part of DKNVS. Throughout this process the museum was positive about becoming part of the university, but the view of how the museum was to be incorporated into the university changed during the process. Early in the process the museum supported the so-called integration model which would mean relatively radical changes to the museum's organizational culture. During the process the museum administration became more concerned about preserving the museum as a completely autonomous entity within the university as far as possible. Before we consider the process which took the museum out of DKNVS, it is necessary to look at the development of the museum in the years before it became part of the university.

Organizational reforms and growth in state grants

Between 1948 and 1951 the internal organizational structure of the museum was radically changed. The first step was to strengthen the management of the museum, making its head the managing director. Erling Sivertsen, Doctor of Philosophy, the leader of the museum from 1937, was made managing director in 1948, a position he held until 1974. This reform was followed by a change in the museum's statutes to give it a more professional board and more formalized legal structures. These changes were important preconditions for further growth in the state grants, which were increasing regularly after World War II. The reform was thus not only a result of an internal process, but also a response to governmental policy.[727]

---

[724] UBIT, Spesialsamlingene. DKNVS arkiv, II:4. Direksjonsprotokoller.

[725] Formerly the Ministry of Education and Church Affairs.

[726] St. prp. nr 126, 1982–83. *Om inkorporering av Det Kongelige Norske Videnskabers Selskab, Museet i Universitetet i Trondheim.* "Avtale om overføring av Det Kgl. Norske Videnskabers Selskab, Museets eiendeler til staten ved Kultur- og Vitenskapsdepartementet."

[727] DKNVS Museet. Yearbooks 1948–50.

Until 1951 the museum was governed by the *Museumsforening* (Museum Association), which was open to everyone paying the annual membership fee. In 1951 the legal status of the museum was amended. The museum, *DKNVS Museet*, was turned into a foundation, which meant that it had to comply with Norwegian laws governing foundations. The *Museumsforening* was turned into a support association. The reform of the DKNVS museum did not directly affect the relationship between the two divisions of the Society. The Society's general statutes (part A) were not changed, neither were the statutes for the academy (part C). The reform was treated as an internal affair of the museum division of the Society, which reflected the fact that its two divisions acted as two autonomous institutions in accordance with the statutes. However, in the long term the amendments to the statutes were very important for DKNVS as a whole. The foundation was a new institutional link between *DKNVS i Trondhjem* and the museum, which was to serve as a management tool for the museum. The foundation and its board negotiated the transfer of the museum to the state, reaching an agreement that meant the foundation of the museum would remain as a division of *DKNVS i Trondhjem* after the transfer of the museum. However, with the later transfer of the museum to the state authorities the role of the foundation would change.

As a foundation, the election of the board was regulated by Norwegian law. The board consisted of the managing director and six appointed members: two members appointed by *Kirke- og undervisningsdepartementet* (the Ministry of Education and Church Affairs), one member appointed by the local authority, and three members appointed by the museum association. Moreover, each of the three counties[728] that regularly supported the museum financially could appoint a member to the board. The elected leader of the board was called *praeses*, the same title as the leader of the academy. A *kollegium* (senate), consisting of the managing director and the departments heads was also established to deal with internal affairs at the museum. The new statutes for the *DKNVS Museumsstiftelsen* were passed in the general assembly of the *Museumsforening* on November 20, 1950, and were approved by Royal Decree on February 23, 1951.[729]

After World War II the state grants to the museum increased considerably, from approximately NOK 50,000 to approximately NOK 240,000 in 1951, when the statutes were reformed. When the university plans were launched a decade later the grant exceeded NOK 0.6 million, and counted for approximately three quarters of the museum's budget.[730] In a long-term perspective the increasing state grants after World War II were a radical break with the tradition, a break which could be compared with the reform of 1872 and the division of 1926. According to Midbøe, the increasing state grants meant that the old independent institution was only nominally maintained.[731]

---

[728] Møre og Romsdal, Nord-Trøndelag and Sør-Trøndelag.

[729] Hjelm-Hansen, Paul. "En utredning om Det kongelige Norske Videnskabers Selskab, Museumsstiftelsen." *DKNVS Forhandlinger*, 1985, 9.

[730] St. prp. nr. 1, 1945–46; St. prp. nr. 1, 1950–51; St. prp. nr. 1, 1960–61.

[731] Midbøe, Hans. *Det Kongelige Norske Videnskabers Selskabs historie 1760–1960, Bind II*. Trondheim, 1960, 234.

The museum came more and more under the control of the government's educational and research policy—for example, in questions relating to the establishment of new positions or investments of any magnitude. The rise in the state grants was, however, part of a new general pattern in Norway. Most of the scientific research within both the universities and research institutes was and still is financed by the state.

To prepare the museum, including the library, to be part of the new university, the grants were expanded. When the museum was incorporated in the university in 1968, the annual grant passed NOK 1.9 million.[732] The result was a substantial rise in the number of employees. In 1946 the museum and library had around 6 or 7 full-time employees. In 1968 there was a staff of 13 in the library section and a staff of 18 in the other museum departments.[733]

From being the institutional framework around the large collections of scientific artifacts and books that were the responsibility of a handful of scientists and scholars, the museum, including the library, became an organization, still moderate in size, but with several employees, different departments and hierarchical organizational structures. After becoming part of the university, the grants continued to increase, but far more rapidly. During the first three years the grants were tripled. The financial dimension was thus an important part of the university issue. Being part of a university would secure future financial support and provide for institutional development through considerable growth in the state grants.

The departments inside the Museum

Containing 340,000 books and 65,000 other types of publications, the DKNVS museum's library was the third largest library in Norway, and it was therefore meant to play a key role in the university library that was to be established. As it was not to only serve as the library for the disciplines within the museum, it was necessary to broaden the range of disciplines covered by the book collections. Preparing for a future role as university library, the DKNVS library especially benefited from the growth during these years, and due to this, the library became a much stronger institution within the DKNVS museum.

This was not the first time the functions of the library were extended. As one of three libraries in Norway, the DKNVS library had been ordered already in 1941 to preserve copies of all publicly printed publications for future generations.[734] From 1946/47 the library had received special funding through the national budget for this purpose.

During the first decade after the establishment of the university in 1968, the library underwent major changes. Firstly, a so-called joint library was established, combining

---

[732] St. prp. nr. 1, 1968–69. Kap. 331.
[733] DKNVS Museet. Yearbook 1946; St. prp. nr. 1, 1968–69. Kap. 331.
[734] Act of 9 June 1939 relating to the Obligation to Submit Printed Matter to Public Libraries.

the DKNVS and NLHT libraries. The DKNVS library constituted the core of this joint library, while the teaching college library contained only approximately 9000 volumes in 1960. Secondly, the expansion to a university library was more space-demanding, and a new building was completed early in 1974, adjacent to the old library building at Kalvskinnet. In addition to a book tower the new building had a large reading room for students, workplaces for researchers, and administration premises. Third, comprehensive pioneer work was initiated to develop a computer-based cataloguing and registration system, called BIBSYS. The system was developed through cooperation between the DKNVS library, the NTH library and RUNIT (*Regnesenteret ved Universitetet i Trondheim*, an affiliate of SINTEF.) Over time BIBSYS was developed into a national automation system for all Norwegian universities.[735]

In the same way as the library, the antiquarian department had also public administration responsibilities within the region. Historical monuments were part of the museum's responsibility from the early 1900s, and with the Act relating to Historical Monuments from 1951 these administrative tasks increased. The museum was under obligation to handle and store old relics and artifacts, and take care of all historical monuments, such as burial mounds, stone monuments, and rock carvings within the region. This gave the DKNVS museum a public responsibility as the main archaeological museum for central Norway, i.e. from Nordmøre to Saltfjellet. The new Historical Monuments Act also meant an increase in archaeological excavations in connection with road or other construction activities. The dramatic increase in hydroelectric construction in the 1950s and 1960s, which led to the flooding of many cultural landscapes, was a main contributor to this rise in the number of excavations that the museum was responsible for. Archaeological and cultural-history research at the museum was to a large extent a result of the museum's administrative responsibility for cultural artifacts in central Norway. The antiquarian department was also responsible for teaching archaeology to history students at the teachers' college and later at the University of Trondheim, and later came to play a major role in the establishment of an archaeological department and studies at UNIT.

Since the end of the 1800s exhibiting the region's cultural history to the city's population through the museum's cultural-history collections had been an important part of the museum's activities. In 1956 the exhibition *Midt-Norges forhistorie* (The prehistory of central Norway) was opened, as a typical exhibition of its time. It was organized according to linear chronological principles, going from the old to the new. Spectators were guided through a cycle of the older Stone age, the Younger Stone age, the bronze age, the old iron age and the Viking period. A number of showcases displayed old artifacts arranged in chronological order with sub-groupings into functional categories. Arrowheads were displayed with their arrows pointing upwards, knives and swords with their points down, while axes were displayed with blades pointing to one side.

---

[735] Nissen, Harald and Monica Aase (eds.). *Til opplysning. Universitetsbiblioteket i Trondheim 1768–1993*. DKNVS *Skrifter* 1, 1993, 83, 229–31, 237.

In general, well-preserved artifacts were displayed, good specimens exemplifying the archeological types. Rare, imported and special specimens were also displayed and highlighted. Artifacts made from precious metals were, for example, presented on a background of red or green velvet, while ordinary and common artifacts were shown on a white canvas background. Waste products, such as piles of flint rubble and iron slag, were not displayed. Pedagogically and esthetically the archeological objects, the artifacts themselves, were in focus. Explanatory texts and drawings of the artifacts being used were placed separately, referring only to small numbered labels placed beside the artifact in question, so that the spectator's impression of the artifacts would not be tainted.[736]

The museum also offered other cultural-history exhibitions, such as a small but valuable ethnographical collection from Eskimo and Sami culture, archeological finds from medieval Trondheim, and more recent artifacts, a collection of religious art from northern Norway from the oldest Christian period until around 1700, and a numismatic collection. While the second floor of the museum was devoted to cultural history, the ground floor was dedicated to natural history with exhibitions of mammals, birds, and fish, primarily from Norway and the Nordic countries. An example of museum exhibitions was the new avian exhibition, which was created for the 1960 anniversary.

The exhibition was a diorama showing the birds of Trøndelag from the coast to the mountains. The diorama, 14 meters long and displaying 52 different species of birds, offered tape recordings of birdsong and accompanying commentary. The audio program also offered the transition from day to night and to a new day. Most of the audio recordings had been made by one of the museum curators and ornithologists, Svein Haftorn. Spotlights automatically highlighted the bird whose song was being played, placed it in a landscape with soil, stones, ground vegetation, trees and bushes, and against the backdrop of a painstakingly painted sky. By placing the birds in their natural habitat (admittedly artificially made), we can see an ecological approach to the presentation of knowledge. The exhibition not only presented knowledge about individual birds—for example, enabling viewers to recognize a species by its song and appearance—but also presented knowledge about the birds' relation to the surrounding natural environment. The element of perception was also important. The purpose was to create an illusion of being out in nature, in the natural bird habitat. Audio and light would give the viewer the "changing moods of nature."[737] The diorama was to contribute to knowledge about and make the locals familiar with the regional and local countryside. The bird diorama was typical of exhibitions prepared at the museum in the 1900s, which included a number of dioramas from Norwegian marine and terrestrial fauna, in contrast to the exhibition of exotic animals from foreign lands at the end of the 1800s.

---

[736] Bjerck, Hein B. "På museum i museet—et streiftog i Vitenskapsmuseets kulturlandskap." Spor 1, 2002, 30–32.
[737] DKNVS Museet. Yearbook 1960.

The technical aspects of the diorama exhibition represented something quite new. The sound and light system had been designed and assembled by a newly founded electronics company in Trondheim, Autronica. This company was one of the pioneers in Norway in the electronics industry, an industry that never really took off in Norway. There is reason to assume that the museum administration was right when claiming that the diorama featured some of the most modern electronic equipment of the time for recording and lighting effects. Measured by contemporary standards, and seen in relation to the museum's annual budgets, the exhibition was expensive, and would not have been possible without substantial funding from the city's private business sector.[738]

The exhibitions of the archeological artifacts and the birds, and some of the other exhibitions, would remain on view without changes right up to our contemporary times. During these decades the permanent exhibitions were seen by class after class of Trondheim's pupils. From 1965 the teaching activities focusing on the school sector were given higher priority. These activities were organized in a special school department, and a new position was established with special responsibility for preparing guided tours of the collections and appropriate tasks related to them, and to organize excursions in the city area.[739] In exchange for presenting knowledge to the city's general population, and particularly to school pupils, the city provided substantial funding to the museum.

While the library and the antiquarian departments both had been assigned public administration responsibilities, thus being more and more involved in the state knowledge and cultural policy field, the natural-science activities at the museum continued to be in a free position as late as the 1960s. The natural-sciences, primarily biology, zoology, and marine biology, was the dominant field. It had the highest number of scientific and technical positions. Natural science was also the most research-oriented, and it was also from this field that the museum directors were recruited. All the three directors after the director position was established in 1947 and until the museum was transferred to the state were biologists. They were employed as curators, but saw themselves primarily as natural scientists with biological research as their primary duty. This would also dominate the museum's attitude in the university issue.

The biological field was organized into three sections, *Botanisk avdeling*, *Zoologisk avdeling* and *Trondhjems biologiske stasjon*. In 1960 there were two scientists in zoology, one in botany, and one in marine biology. Some assistants and technicians were also on staff, most of them working within zoology, with the preparation of animals as one of their main tasks. By the middle of the 1960s two new positions, respectively in zoology and botany, were established.

During the first half of the 20th century the focus in botany had shifted from saltwater and the fjords to the inland and mountain areas. In 1950 the *botanical depart-*

---

[738] DKNVS Museet. Yearbook 1960.
[739] DKNVS Museet. Yearbook 1965.

ment had established a mountain research station in Trollheimen, a mountain area in the south-west part of central Norway. The research station was financed by *Norges allmennvitenskapelige forskningsråd*. It was nothing more than a small wooden hut, but this shelter enabled the scientists to do field research for long stretches of time. In 1975 a much larger research station, *Kongsvoll høgfjellsstasjon*, was built in the Dovre mountain area.

In zoology, however, the marine area was still an important field of research, not least due to the work carried out by the managing director himself, Erling Sivertsen. However, zoology in the inland and mountain areas also grew in importance. Freshwater fisheries and the consequences of the variations in water level due to the extensive development of water power plants became a new research field. In addition, with a new position established in the 1950s, the fauna of the inland areas and mountains were also incorporated in the museum's research field.

While the research in the botany and zoology departments was mainly focused on the mountain areas, the research in marine biology was carried out by *Trondheim biologiske stasjon*, established in 1891 as a research institution for applied science with the aim of supporting the fisheries in the Trondheim fjord. It was formally an autonomous institution outside the museum, receiving local financial assistance as well as state grants. In 1950 *Trondhjems biologiske stasjon* was incorporated in the museum, but this was more a formality than any real change. Although autonomous, the connection to the museum had been tight from the very beginning. The research conditions during the first years after the incorporation were difficult, as the station did not have a research ship. The very first research vessel "Gunnerus" had been confiscated during World War II. Thanks to private donations, a new research vessel, the "Harry Borthen," was acquired in 1962, replaced by another research vessel named "Gunnerus" in 2006.

The museum also had a large collection of rocks and mineralogical samples, but mineralogy had not been a priority field. The *Mineralogisk avdeling* employed no scientist or other staff, and was run by one person alone, whose main employment was outside the museum. Mineralogy at the museum existed in the shadow of *Bergavdelingen* (the Department of Mining, Geology and Mineralogy) at NTH, and would continue to do so within the proposed university. Moreover, from 1961 Trondheim was the host of the national geological survey, *Norges geologiske undersøkelse*.

Research within the natural sciences was thus limited to biology within the subdisciplines of botany, zoology, and marine biology. It was natural science in a very direct sense; it was indeed nature, primarily nature within the museum's region, which was the object of scientific research. This had also been the basis for the museums in Bergen and Tromsø, established during the 19th century. Cataloging the natural phenomena of each region had been one main objective, and also legitimized their existence. In the early 1950s nature was still a pivotal subject of research at all three institutions.

First developed into modern research institutions in the late 19th century, the museums of Bergen, Trondheim, and Tromsø were all transformed into university institutions in the three decades between 1946 and 1976. In 1946 Bergen Museum was the foundation of the second university in Norway, the University of Bergen. The success of this research institution in transforming itself into a university served as a strong model for the DKNVS Museum in Trondheim. Having had university ambitions long before Bergen Museum came into existence, the success in Bergen breathed new life into the old dreams in Trondheim.

During the 20th century Bergen Museum, established in 1825, had developed a broader range of disciplines compared to the DKNVS Museum, not least due to a much better financial base. Bergen Museum was also organized as a foundation and had far greater funds and legacies at its disposal, but the museum also had succeeded in obtaining substantial state grants.[740] Botany and Zoology had also been central subjects at the museum in Bergen right from the beginning. But in addition to scientific studies of flora and fauna in the Bergen region, biochemical and botanical laboratories were established at the museum in Bergen in the 1920s. In this way Bergen Museum was adopting the experimental sciences involving the new link between biology and chemistry. Geology also became an important research field, also incorporating seismology through the establishment of an earthquake station, *Jordskjelvstasjonen*, in 1904. Although mediating scientific and cultural knowledge to the general public was also an important part of this museum's tasks and legitimacy, scientific research was very much in the center. The idea of transforming this museum into a university had first evolved in the second half of the 19th century, and just after World War II the University of Bergen was founded with Bergen Museum as an integral part.[741]

Welcoming the university plans

The directors at the DKNVS museum warmly welcomed the plans for a university in Trondheim with the museum as an integral part of it. To integrate into the new university was also in accordance with the museum's own ambitions, as already indicated in the statutes from 1951, in which the original paragraph from 1926, stating that the museum's goal was to promote science, was extended. The new paragraph stated that the museum should strive to become a regional *vitenskapelig høgskole*[742] (scientific postgraduate college/university) within the academic disciplines represented at the museum—in other words, biology and archaeology.[743] Becoming part of the university was seen as an opportunity for the DKNVS museum and library to extend their activities, in particular the research activities which were considered the core activity of the

---

[740] Forland, Astrid and Anders Haaland. *Universitetet i Bergens historie, Bind I*, Bergen, 1996, 186.

[741] Forland and Haaland. *Universitetet i Bergens historie, Bind I*.

[742] In Norway *vitenskapelig høgskole* means a postgraduate college at the university level; the teachers are professors and both research and teaching are part of their professional duties. They differ from the universities in that they have a more limited range of disciplines.

[743] Hjelm-Hansen, Paul. "En utredning om Det kongelige Norske Videnskabers Selskab, Museumsstiftelsen." *DKNVS Forhandlinger*, 1985, 9.

museum. In his speech at the bicentennial anniversary in 1960, the *praeses* of the museum, Reidar Brekke, pointed out that in its capacity as a research institute, it was to become part of a new university in Trondheim, just as had been the case some years earlier for the museum in Bergen.[744]

The warm acceptance of the university plans was thus rooted in the museum's scientific and scholarly ambitions, reflecting that the university had become the key scientific and scholarly institution in Norway. The attitude towards the university question also reflected that little attention was given to the question of whether the aims and objectives of the museum's institutions differed from those of the university departments. Putting the research activities in the foreground, the aims and objectives were found to be very much the same. But as we will see, this was about to change after the museum had become part of the university.

From the perspective of the scientific disciplines, in 1960 the three institutions that formed the University of Trondheim were still complementary. The museum covered the biological disciplines as well as archeology, *Norges tekniske høgskole* (the Norwegian Institute of Technology) covered architecture and engineering subjects, as well as mathematics, physics, and chemistry, and *Norges lærerhøgskole* covered history, education science, and language studies. However, the science disciplines were also taught at *Norges lærerhøgskole*, but by the other academic institutions in Trondheim. While the museum taught studies in biology at the teachers' college, NTH taught mathematics, physics, and chemistry at the college. This way of organizing the teaching was done for purely financial reasons, as it made it possible for the government to establish and run a new education institution while spending limited resources. In 1958 the museum's teaching at *Norges lærerhøgskole* was formalized to a much higher degree when the chief curators in zoology and botany were promoted to *professor II* (adjunct professor) positions at *the teachers' college.*

From the museum's point of view, it seemed obvious that its biological disciplines should form a central part of a department of natural sciences at the new university. These ambitions and hopes were the foundation of the museum's standpoint when the university plans were launched. Erling Sivertsen (1904–89), who was the managing director of the museum from 1948 until 1974, had been appointed conservator in zoology in 1937. As a marine zoologist, Erling Sivertsen had been studying fish (both saltwater and freshwater), seals, and crawfish.[745] He was born in Tromsø, and some years before he came to Trondheim he had worked at *Tromsø Museum*, parallel with his studies at the University of Oslo. He had also worked some years at *Flødevigens utklekningsanstalt*, a hatchery for saltwater fish in the very south of Norway (in the vicinity of Arendal). Sivertsen participated in several marine science expeditions, both in the southern Atlantic and the very north, in the White Sea. His many expeditions in

---

[744] Arvesen, Ole Peder and Olav Gjærevoll (eds.). *DKNVS Beretning om tohundreårsjubileet 6te til 8de mai 1960.* Trondheim, 1961, 15–16.
[745] Norsk biografisk leksikon; DKNVS *Forhandlinger* 1990, 35–38.

the White Sea formed the basis for his doctoral thesis "On the Biology of the Harp Seal, Pchoca grøenlandia Erxl. (eben)," published in 1941. When he was elected a member of the Society in 1939, he was the youngest member ever elected, and in 1954 he was also elected as a member of *Det Norske Videnskabs-Akademi i Oslo* (the Norwegian Academy of Science and Letters in Oslo.)

Sivertsen's concern was first of all scientific research and how to create organizational structures that could reinforce the current research within the museum. Implicit in this was the expectation that the University of Trondheim should be based on some sort of integration of the three institutions forming the new university. The motives for this will be discussed later in this chapter. This was the view advocated by Sivertsen when he was appointed by the Government to advise on the formation of the University of Trondheim by sitting on the Wilhelmsen committee.[746]

However, institutional development within *Norges lærerhøgskole* did in fact change the foundation for the university before it was established. In 1965 *Norges lærerhøgskole* obtained its own professorships in biology and zoology, as well as in mathematics, physics, and chemistry, thereby establishing the foundation for an autonomous department of natural science within NLHT.[747] The government's decision to create a department of natural science at *Norges lærerhøgskole* was primarily due to a short-term need to educate teachers for these disciplines, and situating these disciplines within the well-established NLHT was seen as the most adequate solution to this problem.

This also meant that the previous complementary disciplines between the three institutions were replaced by parallel disciplines. What distinguished the three institutions was no longer which scientific disciplines each had, but first and foremost their functions: educating teachers as opposed to engineers on the one side, and museological functions on the other. From the museum's point of view this development was a radical break from what had seemed to be the basic premise for the forthcoming university. The result was a change in the attitude within the board.[748] Although still in principle supporting a model of integration, Sivertsen, the director, and the rest of the board, showed a greater willingness to protect the unity and autonomy of the museum, and to secure the museum an equal status with the other two institutions. This also meant avoiding the museum becoming a department within *Norges lærerhøgskole*, a model suggested by the majority on the Wilhelmsen committee.[749] Due to this, a new determination to emphasize the huge assets owned by the museum arose. It was still a

---

[746] *Innstilling om opprettelse av et universitet i Trondheim.* KUD 1964. Erling Siversten had replaced Olav Gjærevoll as the Museum's representative in the Wilhelmsen committee after Gjærevoll was appointed member of the Government on February 3, 1963.

[747] The *realfagsvdeling* (Faculty of natural science and mathematics) was established as an organizational unit to administer the teaching in 1962 when the Museum and NTH still had the scientific responsibility and positions.

[748] UBIT, Spesialsamlingene. DKNVS II.4. Direksjonsprotokoller. Protokoll 1897–1969. Board meetings 6.6.1967 and 15.6.1968.

[749] *Innstilling om opprettelse av et universitet i Trondheim.* KUD 1964, 78.

foundation, and from the board's point of view there was every reason to underscore that the museum's library was the third largest library in Norway.

A new strategy for autonomy

After the museum had become part of the University of Trondheim, the ambition to ensure the museum a greater level of autonomy within the university structure grew in strength. Several matters contributed to this. At the start of the 1970s the question of the role of the cultural-history and natural-history museums within the universities was a matter of debate. This issue was discussed at a conference in Tromsø when Tromsø Museum celebrated its 100-year anniversary in 1972. While the old museums in Bergen and Trondheim both had been unequivocally positive to becoming university institutions, Tromsø Museum was more skeptical and therefore it was not until 1976 that it was incorporated within the University of Tromsø (which was established in 1968).

Representatives of the museum at the University of Bergen stated quite clearly that being incorporated in a university was not an exclusively positive experience. Admittedly it had led to a dramatic increase in appropriations, including more employees, but the large increase in the number of students had put enormous teaching pressure on the staff. The specific museum functions had benefited little from the increase in funding. This first concerned all the functions connected to the collections, and second the teaching and presentations at the museum.[750] DKNVS *Museet* had experienced more or less the same. Here the heavy influx of students had pushed the specific museum duties into the background.[751]

When Bergen Museum was transformed into a university and the plans were launched to incorporate DKNVS Museet into the university, these museums had primarily defined themselves as research institutions where the objectives and duties of the museums coincided to a very large degree with those of the universities. But during the 1960s two things occurred that changed this perception. First, the emergence of the highly populated university, where the educational function increased at the cost of the research function. Second, there was a new awareness of the special functions of museums. Early in the 1970s the museums emphasized that their functions were different than those of the universities. The duties of the museums primarily focused on preserving and systematizing natural-history and cultural-history collections and on facilitating various uses of the collections, including teaching and research. The museums pointed out that when their specific functions had been

---

[750] Falck, Kjell. "Bergens Museum og Universitetet i Bergen." In *Museum og universitet. Jubileumsskrift til Tromsø Museum 1872–1972*, edited by Ørnulf Vorren. Tromsø, 1972.

[751] Lønne, Hans Jørgen. "Det Kgl. Norske Videnskabers Selskab, Museet og Universitetet i Trondheim." In *Museum og universitet. Jubileumsskrift til Tromsø Museum 1872–1972*, edited by Ørnulf Vorren. Tromsø, 1972.

inadequately understood and dealt with by the universities, this was generally due to the fact that the museums had been unable to clarify and define their special duties.

As was the case for the other cultural-history and natural-history museums, the DKNVS museum was based on the collections. Museums and their collections had been the vital institutions for both archaeology (cultural history) and natural science (natural history) in the 1800s. This would change in the 1900s. While museums continued to be the core of archaeological work, the role of museums in natural science became more marginal. The universities, research institutes, and also industry, became the new centers for natural-science research. The biological sciences split during the 1900s into natural-history and museum activities, on the one hand, and experimental biology on the other. Internationally, experimental biology grew at the expense of natural-history disciplines, stimulated by the prestige it garnered from its contributions to technological development. The 1960s were in some ways the golden age of experimental biology.[752]

However, towards the end of this decade the natural-history subjects strengthened their position, due in part to the growing interest in ecology, and the appearance of new state nature and resource management policies during the 1960s. In Norway this resulted in the establishment of a Nature Conservation Act in 1970, and the establishment of the Ministry of the Environment in 1972. Preparation of resource management and conservation plans became crucial instruments for this new nature and resource management, where natural-history collections and their documentation constituted a vital knowledge base. The new resource and environmental management thus gave a new function to natural-history studies and a new legitimacy, which was absolutely decisive for the development of new awareness of the special museum functions.

The new director of the Museum from 1974 and until 1980, Olav Gjærevoll, had been one of the central actors in the development of the new national resource and environment conservation policy, and played a prominent role in the design of the new understanding of the role of the museums in this area of management. Olav Gjærevoll (1916–94) had been appointed *konservator* in 1947. His field of interest was especially the mountainous areas and the mountains of central Norway. He had undertaken several studies of the alpine snow-beds (*snøleievegetasjon*), culminating in his doctoral thesis "The Plant Communities of the Scandinavian Alpine Snow-Beds" (1956). Gjærevoll's interests reached far beyond the scientific field of botany. He was also a politician, serving as mayor in Trondheim, and as a member of Parliament and the Norwegian Labor Party Government. But first of all he was a key proponent for establishing a national environmental policy, advocating nature conservation and establishing protected areas. He was also one of the founders of *Miljøverndepartementet* (Ministry of the Environment) in 1972, and was appointed the first head of this ministry.

As the director of DKNVS Museet, Gjærevoll was also the main architect of a much more active policy aimed at ensuring the museum as much autonomy as possible

---

[752] Roll-Hansen, Nils et al. *Universitetet i Bergens historie, Bind II*. Bergen, 1996.

within the university. During this process, Gjærevoll also sat on the interim board for the University of Trondheim, first as a board member (1973–75) and then as chairman (1976–79), and through this position had a great opportunity to influence development within the university organization. The change in policy at the museum was linked both to the local development within the University of Trondheim and to the more general shift in the attitudes regarding the functions of the museums within the universities. However, as the definitely oldest institution amongst the university candidates, with an honorable tradition dating back to 1760, we cannot completely ignore the latent desire of its members to keep the museum as a semi-autonomous institution.

The final negotiations

The negotiations between the board of DKNVS Museum, and the Norwegian government, regarding the transfer of the museum to the Norwegian state took place at the same time that the Act governing the University of Trondheim was being written.[753] The transfer required a change in the statutes of the DKNVS Museet, as the original paragraph stated that the museum could not be sold or given away. To remove this impediment, this paragraph was replaced by a new paragraph stating that the museum, with all its books, artifacts and possessions, could be transferred to the Norwegian state so that it could become part of the University of Trondheim, which then assumed the responsibility for achieving the scientific and museological objectives of the museum.

The board was not only concerned about the museum's future, but also the future of the museum foundation after the incorporation into the university. The museum foundation had to be maintained and keep its legacies and funds. However, the board also argued that although the Norwegian state was going to take full responsibility for the museum and it was to be at the university's full disposal, the buildings and properties, as well as the collections of artifacts and books, should continue to be owned by *DKNVS Museumsstiftelsen* (the DKNVS Museum Foundation.)[754] The desire to keep the museum foundation and its funds and legacies intact gained the support of the government, but the idea that the foundation should continue to own the museum's buildings and collections was categorically rejected. Due to the unresolved university controversy, the solution in 1968 was only temporary.

The determination to guard the interests of the museum and the museum foundation was very evident in these negotiations, and the result can be seen in the final transfer agreement. The final negotiation was lead by Gunnar Sundnes, who succeeded Olav Gjærevoll as director in 1980. Sundnes's aims were explicit: first to keep the museum as one entity, and second to secure a solid foundation for the future of the museum foundation. For example, the agreement contained a clause stating that the DKNVS library

---

[753] UBIT, Spesialsamlingene. DKNVS arkiv, II:4. Direksjonsprotokoller.
[754] St. pr. nr. 79, 1966–67, 54–55. *Om opprettelsen av et universitet i Trondheim.*

should be kept as an entity within the museum, and that the museum and collections should not be moved from Kalvskinnet, the location where DKNVS had resided since the first building was completed in 1866.[755]

A Society with no Museum

The museum foundation was not dissolved; rather, it was left with 34 funds and legacies with a total capital of around NOK 3 million. Some smaller properties also remained under its control.[756] Neither were the old honorable name, *Det Kongelige Norske Videnskabers Selskab*, nor the emblem and seal transferred. The name of the museum from 1984 was then *Universitet i Trondheim, Museet* (The University of Trondheim, The Museum), later changed to *Vitenskapsmuseet* (Museum of Natural History and Archaeology).[757] The name of the museum division of DKNVS, which since 1926 had been the *DKNVS Museet*, was changed to *DKNVS Museumsstiftelsen* (DKNVS Museum Foundation).[758]

Thus from April 1984 *Det Kongelige Norske Videnskabers Selskab* (the Royal Society of Sciences and Letters) neither owned a museum nor a library. This was a fundamental change, both for *DKNVS Museumsstiftelsen* and for *Det Kongelige Norske Videnskabers Selskab* as whole. The integration of the museum into the University of Trondheim and finally the transfer of the museum raised fundamental questions relating to functions and identity and to the organizational structure of *Det Kongelige Norske Videnskabers Selskab*.

What were the consequences of the museum's incorporation into the university in 1968 for the museum division of the society? And what were the consequences of the final transfer?

Until 1984 the old institutions that made up the university remained nearly autonomous institutions within the university structure, and formally the museum was still managed by the board of the museum foundation. As a consequence of both increasing and more specified state grants, the role of the state had become more and more crucial, a process started long before the museum actually was incorporated into the university structure. The museum director and the board dealt with internal affairs, including making the budget proposal which was formally approved by the board but where the real approval was made by the government and finally *Stortinget*.

---

[755] St. prp. nr 126, 1982–83. *Om inkorporering av Det Kongelige Norske Videnskabers Selskab, Museet i Universitetet i Trondheim.* "Avtale om overføring av Det Kgl. Norske Videnskabers Selskab, Museets eiendeler til staten ved Kultur- og Vitenskapsdepartementet."

[756] Hjelm-Hansen, "En utredning om Det kongelige Norske Videnskabers Selskab, Museumsstiftelsen."

[757] St. prp. nr. 1, 1983–84. Kap. 312 og 3312.

[758] From 1990 the DKNVS Museum Foundation was given the shorter name: the DKNVS Foundation (*DKNVS Stiftelsen*).

The administration of the legacies and fund, including revenues from some of the properties, was, however, still controlled by the board. Thus if we consider the final transfer of the museum and library in 1984 from a management perspective, it was as *Kultur- og vitenskapsdepartementet* (the Ministry of Arts and Science) stated, more a formality than a real change.[759] The incorporation and final transfer were part of a long-term process where the changes in institutional status did not mean any drastic changes.

However, if we look at this from an identity perspective, ownership of the museum was of major significance. Running the museum had been the main objective for the museum division ever since the reform in 1874, an objective not altered by the reforms in 1926 and 1951. The legacies and funds had first of all been means to support scientific activities within the museum, even though as the state grants increased considerably, the financial importance of the legacies and funds decreased dramatically. Although the board's management role had become less influential during the 1960s, and even moreso after the museum was incorporated into the university, the symbolic value of owning the museum had not diminished. On the contrary, it can be argued that as the university museum grew, the symbolic value of being the institution that owned the museum increased. The *DKNVS Museumsstiftelsen* did not only own a museum but a museum within a university. In this perspective the final transfer to the Norwegian state in 1984 was a highly significant event which highlighted the question of both the function and identity of the museum foundation. What was to be the function of the museum foundation when it no longer owned a museum? Before we return to this question we will have a look at the academy division of DKNVS in Trondheim.

---

[759] St. prp. nr 126, 1982–83. *Om inkorporering av Det Kongelige Norske Videnskabers Selskab, Museet i Universitetet i Trondheim.*

15

The Society—members and meetings

Two hundred years after the Society's foundation, universities, research institutes, and an increasingly science-based industry had become the new centers for scientific practice and communication. The role of science academies in general was becoming even more marginalized, and the Society also found itself on the periphery, both in relation to the scientific center of Norway and in relation to the center's power where research-policy decisions were made. Furthermore, the financial situation was weak. The lack of financial capital was in sharp contrast to the high symbolic cultural capital that the Society had acquired through its history and heritage. The mood at the bicentennial anniversary was nevertheless dominated by optimism and bright expectations. The planned university expansion would extend and vitalize the scientific environment in the city, and thus also expand the scientific environment in the Society. Finally the Society was to be active in a university environment! While the development of the university did indeed have a positive impact on the Society in many ways, it also introduced new and far greater challenges than expected. Building a university in the transition from the epoch of elite universities to the epoch of open-studies universities led to changes within academia and in society in general, and these contributed to undermining the function and legitimacy of the Society. What place did the Society occupy as the administrator of 200 years of scientific heritage within the scientific institutional structure that grew in Norway and in Trondheim during the final half of the twentieth century?

The members

The establishment of the University of Trondheim expanded the academic community in Trondheim, both in terms of the number of scientists and the number of academic disciplines. Hence the local recruitment base for the Society also became much larger. As the local academic environment expanded, together with a more general growth in the number of scholars and scientists in Norway, the question of increasing the number of members in the Society was raised, and in the years after 1960 the Society was indeed expanded. By 1960 the Society had 157 elected members with academic qualifications. In 2005 this had risen to 579 members. This means that over the last 45 years membership had nearly quadrupled.

Growth was relatively modest until around 1980. At that time the Society counted 198 ordinary members. From then on membership increased exponentially, with a more than 50 per cent increase each decade. The growth in membership occurred parallel to comprehensive growth in all types of academic positions in Norway, including professorships. One interesting question is whether the Society grew more or less exclusively. Scientific societies and academies based on election are by definition exclusive, but compared to a large number of academies abroad, the Norwegian ones have not been very exclusive. Both the Society in Trondheim and the academy in Oslo have been forums for a relatively large proportion of the Norwegian professors.

A comparison of the growth in the Society's membership with the growth of the number of professorships in Norway from 1960 to 2005 will indicate whether the Society grew more or less exclusively. Around 28 per cent of the total of 257 professors at the University of Oslo and the University of Bergen, NTH and NLHT in 1960 were elected members of the Society.[760] In 2005 less than 20 per cent of the total of 1989 professors at the universities of Oslo, Bergen, Trondheim and Tromsø had been elected members.[761] The growth of the Society was thus slightly lower than the growth in the number of professorships. The members were, however, not evenly distributed across the Norwegian universities. If we consider the Society's members outside Trondheim, we find that they were generally connected to the University of Oslo. This applied to both divisions, but to varying degrees. For the natural-science division Oslo was represented almost alone, while the University of Bergen was relatively well represented in the humanities division. Conversely both divisions only had a few members from the University of Tromsø.

If we consider the local conditions we find the same declining trend. In 1960 approximately 60 per cent of professors at NTH and slightly more than 70 per cent of professors at NLHT were members of the Society. In 2005 just under half of the professors at NTNU were members. The figures thus show that in spite of its growth the Society became slightly more exclusive. These figures must nevertheless be seen in light of the fact that the Norwegian professor title during the 1990s itself became less exclusive. In 1993 a scheme was introduced whereby staff members in lower academic positions (associate professor positions) were allowed to apply for promotion to the level of professor based on academic qualifications. This meant that the growth in the number of professors was stronger than the growth in institutional professorships. In such a context the impression that the Society became more exclusive must be moderated.

---

[760] *Statistics Norway*. Table 347.
[761] The R&D statistics bank, NIFU STEP. R&D staff, UoH sector, 2005. The figure applies to professor I positions at UiO, UiB, NTNU and UiTø. Counting all the institutions there were a total of 2666 professor I positions in 2005.

Throughout this period the local members formed the bulk of the Society and were the basis for its work and development. The expansion of the university and other institutions in Trondheim expanded and changed the composition of the local membership in both the natural-science and humanities divisions. In the natural-science division it was particularly the position of technologist that changed. Electing professors belonging to the more practical engineering subjects at NTH had already led to strife at the time of the establishment of the Society in 1926. The members who laid the premises for electing new members, thus forming the scientific profile of the Society, did not want to have an academy dominated by the far more numerous professors from the practical engineering subjects at NTH. Therefore the Society had not become a forum for the professors at NTH.

In 1947 this bone of contention was again placed on the agenda when a proposal was made by Karl Martin Faye-Hansen, professor of electrical machine building at NTH, and Thoralf Vogt, professor of mineralogy and geology at NTH, to introduce a technical-scientific division. Faye-Hansen belonged to the group of members elected in 1926, while Vogt had been elected to the Society in 1929. Vogt was also its *praeses* from 1950 to 1959. The proposal for a new division also meant substantially expanding the number of members. The rationale for the proposal was to also make the Society an academy for NTH professors.

The proposal was, however, quite firmly rejected by the board, as it rejected the idea that a person who had been deemed qualified for a professorship at NTH would automatically be qualified for membership of the Society. The arguments did not focus on the technical sciences per se. Instead it was asserted that many of the NTH professors did not have adequate scientific qualifications to be elected to the Society. The comprehensive teaching requirements, especially in the more practical engineering subjects, would lead to a professor at NTH not necessarily satisfying the scientific requirements posed for membership.[762] Even if the board did not explicitly state that this applied to professors in the technical subjects, it is a very reasonable interpretation to find that the board's statement was directed against this group of professors. Beyond this there was also a general wish to demonstrate moderation when it came to any increase in the number of members. The members of the Society supported the board's thinking. The rejection of a special technical section in the Society encouraged the professors at NTH to form their own technical academy in 1955, *Norges tekniske vitenskapsakademi* (NTVA—the Norwegian Technical Science Academy). However, as we have discusses earlier, their motivation for forming an academy of their own can probably not be traced only to their failure of forming a technical section in the Society.

The board did, however, provide for an expansion of the number of members in both divisions when they amended the statutes in 1950. For the natural-science division it was decided to increase the ceiling for the number of members from Norway from 50

---

[762] UBIT, Special collections. DKNVS IV:6:3. Statutes 1950. The Name Issue 1948–1950. Undated memo from the board.

to 60. The expansion in the number of members when combined with regular attrition still amounted to a considerable number of new recruits to the division in the 1950s. As many as 21 professors from NTH were elected, and if we consider the distribution according to academic fields, more than half, almost two-thirds, were professors from the technical-practical fields. The elections during this decade thus gave the practical-technical subjects a far more prominent place in the Society.

The expansion in membership meant that in 1960, the natural-science division had a total of 46 members who were resident in Trondheim. Apart from a handful of curators at *DKNVS Museet*, a few doctors working at *Sentralsykehuset i Trondheim* and two members operating their own businesses, the division generally consisted of professors at *Norges tekniske høgskole*, a total of 37. Bearing in mind that NTH was the decidedly largest academic institution in Trondheim, the dominance of NTH professors is not particularly surprising. In 1960 NTH had 67 professors, while the museum only had four curators in natural-science fields. At NLHT there were no professorships in the natural-science subjects before 1965.[763]

If we consider the academic background of NTH professors who were members of the Society in 1960, we find a relatively even distribution among the more general subjects of physics, chemistry, and mathematics, on the one hand, and engineering subjects such as metallurgy, ore processing, marine architecture, port construction, and wood processing to mention a few fields, on the other hand. All in all the natural-science division, "comprising the technical sciences," was more dominated by the technical sciences than by the natural sciences. There is little to suggest that the intention was to give the technical sciences a more representative position; this was rather the result of the general dominance of technologists in the technical-science academic community in Trondheim. If we consider that the majority of professors at NTH represented the more practical engineering subjects, this group was under-represented in the Society compared to professors in the more theoretical academic fields.

The splitting into two divisions with somewhat different identities, as in technologists or engineers versus natural scientists, produced some tension. Only with the establishment and gradually expansion of a natural-science faculty and a faculty of medicine within UNIT, together with the establishment and further expansion of *Norges geologiske undersøkelse* (NGU), did this tension abate. Technologists then became a smaller group, and the Society was no longer dominated by NTH professors. A far broader range of natural-science academic fields was represented. This move towards an increasingly broader range of disciplines led in 1967 to the establishment of a number of subject groups. Four groups were established: Medicine and biology; chemistry and geology; physics, mathematics and mechanics; and technology.[764] With further growth the number of subject groups was further expanded, and in 2005 the natural-science division consisted of eight subject groups: Mathematics; physics; chemistry; general

---

[763] *Statistics Norway yearbook 1962*. Table 347.
[764] UBIT, Special collections. DKNVS III:b:5. Circulars 1965–70.

biology; biochemistry, biophysics and molecular medicine; medicine; geo sciences; technology. This division into subject groups resulted in an explicit discussion on the principles of the distribution of subjects according to these classifications. The result was that the representation principle was no longer restricted to the relation between the natural sciences and the humanities. The subject groups also became the first hurdle for new members to clear, as the initial proposal for election would be dealt with in these groups. Beyond this function, the subject groups did not have many responsibilities. Of the 205 members in the natural-science division who in 2005 resided in Trondheim, around 85 per cent were professors at NTNU (formerly NTH). The others were primarily geologists at *Norges geologiske undersøkelse* or doctors at *St. Olavs University Hospital* (formerly *Regionsykehuset i Trondheim*).

Development in the humanities division was quite similar to the development in the natural-science division, but the point of departure was different. In 1960 there were 23 members in the humanities division who were resident in Trondheim. The humanities division was thus substantially smaller than the natural-science division, but it had more varied professions and institutional ties. Professors at *Norges lærerhøgskole* and *Norges tekniske høgskole*, and curators at the museum were the largest group, with a total of ten members, but they were still a minority in the division. Five clerics were members, and comprised the second-largest professional group after the professors. This division also had some heads of schools, senior teachers, archivists and librarians who were connected with various institutions in Trondheim.

With the expansion of the University of Trondheim and the increase in the number of members elected to the Society, member professions and institutional ties would change significantly. The local members in the humanities division would almost exclusively comprise professors employed at UNIT, from the faculties of the humanities and social sciences. From including a relatively broad range of a trained academic elite connected to a number of institutions in Trondheim, members were now almost exclusively recruited from the city's new academic ivory tower. Of the 86 members in the humanities division who in 2005 were resident in Trondheim, only two were not connected to the university.

The range of academic fields also increased. At the end of the 1960s, in the same way as the natural-science division, the humanities division also split into groups: Philosophy and religion; linguistic science; history and social science; archaeology and the arts. The number of groups was also expanded here. In 2005 the division consisted of six groups: Philosophy, history of ideas and religion science; psychology and pedagogy; linguistic science; social science; history and archaeology; and literary science and aesthetic subjects.

A Society of men?

Up to 1960 the Society was beyond doubt a community of men. Prior to 1960 only three women had been elected as members in the Society. By 1960 all but one of the 157 elected members were men. The one female member was dr. philos Hanna Munck af

Rosenschöld Rydh (1891–1964), from Stockholm. She was elected a member in 1934. This reflects the gender structure in the academic community in Norway, and of course the general gender situation at this time. By 1960 there were only six female professors in Norway, and none of them resided in Trondheim.[765] During the next fifty years the gender structure in academia would slowly change, in Norway as a whole and in Trondheim. Of the 2564 professors in Norway in 2005, 434 were female.[766] To what degree was the slowly increasing proportion of female professors being reflected in the election of members to the Society? Did the Society continue to be a community of men, or was this changing?

In 1961 professor Eva Sivertsen and *dosent* Gerd Høst Heyerdahl were elected as members.[767] They were the very first women to have positions in an academic institution in Trondheim. Sivertsen had been appointed professor in English language studies and Heyerdahl had been appointed *dosent* in German language studies, both at *Norges lærerhøgskole*, the same year they were elected members. The first woman in the *naturvitenskapelige klasse* (natural science division), after the two elections in 1926 and 1928, was elected in 1972. That year Barbro Gullvåg became a member. She had been appointed *første amanuensis* (assistant professor) at *Norges lærerhøgskole* in 1969. The very first female professor at *Norges tekniske høgskole*, dr. techn. Synnøve Liaaen Jensen, was elected as a member in 1974. She had been appointed professor in *organisk kjemi* (organic chemistry) in 1970.

Within the two first decades after 1960 a handful of women were elected members. All resided in Trondheim, and all but one held academic positions at *Norges lærerhøgskole*. There is no doubt that the Society welcomed the new small group of female professors in the city. Of a total of ten women appointed to a professorship, in one case *dosent* (associate professor), at NLHT between 1961 and 1980, nine were elected member within a few years after their appointment. By including the new female *dosents* and professors at NLHT they also followed a well-established tradition. Almost all of the male *dosents* and professors at NLHT, from its foundation in 1922, had been elected members. Not including the new female professors would have indeed been shocking, so the number of women increased after 1960, though very slowly the first three decades. At the end of the century, the number of female members rose more quickly. The result was that by 2005, female membership was around 12 per cent. However, if we only look at the members under the age of 70, the proportion of female members rose up to almost 15 per cent, or 45 female members. There were nevertheless significant differences between the two divisions. The age group below 70 years of

---

[765] *Statistics Norway yearbook 1962.* Table 347; Kirkhusmo. *Akademi og seminar. Norges Lærehøgskole 1922–1982.*

[766] R&D statistics bank, NIFU STEP. R&D staff, UoH sector, 2005.

[767] For a brief history of female membership, see Supphellen, Steinar: "Frå Johan Ernst Gunnerus til Grethe Authén Blom. Kvinners tilgjenge til Det Kongelige Norske Videskabers Selskab." In *Kongsmenn og Krossmenn. Festskrift til Grethe Authén Blom.* DKNVS Skrifter 1, 1992. Edited by Steinar Supphellen. Trondheim: Tapir Forlag, 1992.

age had approximately 21 per cent women in the humanities division, while only 10 per cent were women in the natural-science division. If we consider when women really began to be elected to the academy, we find that more than half of the female members were elected after 2000.[768]

Even if women became members of the Society/Academy, men continued to be the clear majority. This gender structure was nevertheless a fairly accurate reflection of the slanted gender structure in academia in general. The proportion of women in the academy corresponds well to the proportion of female professors in the respective academic fields at the Universities of Bergen, Oslo, Trondheim and Tromsø.[769] Thus if we only consider members under 70 years of age, the gender distribution in the academy reflected the generally slanted gender distribution of Norwegian professors.

The question of equal rights for men and women in academia was voiced as part of the political radicalization of the 1970s, a time when the universities became more open. The increasing number of female students was one of the most striking features of the emergence of the open-studies university in Norway. The study year 1992/93 was the first time more women than men passed university examinations for higher degrees.[770] Among scientific employees, the female proportion also rose, but far more slowly. In 2005, 17 per cent of all the professors in Norway were women.[771] During the 1970s under-representation of women in scientific positions led to a strong commitment at the universities in Norway, which resulted in the establishment of equal-rights boards, and at some universities the practice of moderate gender affirmative-action programs when hiring people for scientific positions. No similar movement was introduced in the Society. The practice of affirmative action, even in moderate forms, was a highly volatile topic within academia, an area of disagreement that was not always argued according to one's gender. The Society felt that including the gender aspect when assessing potential candidates for membership was in conflict with the prevailing opinion that ideal members should exclusively be elected on the basis of scientific criteria. The Society's first female *praeses*, professor Grethe Authén Blom, looked upon any form of gender quotas with great skepticism. This would not only violate the principle of scientific criteria as the only criterion, it could also feed doubts as to the scientific qualifications of female professors.

When we look at the election of foreign members, a gender bias becomes more evident. Remarkably few women outside Norway were elected as members. In 1984

---

[768] *DKNVS Yearbook 2005*. Membership list as of January 1, 2006.

[769] FoU-statistikkbanken, NIFU STEP. FoU-personale, UoH-sektor (The R&D statistics bank, NIFU STEP. R&D staff, UoH sector), 2005. In 2005 around 22 per cent of professors at the Universities of Bergen, Oslo, Trondheim and Tromsø in the humanities and social-science subjects were women (24 per cent in the humanities and 19 per cent in the social sciences). The corresponding figures for natural-science subjects were 10 per cent, for medicine 21 per cent, and for technology 6 per cent.

[770] NOS Education statistics. Universities and colleges October 1, 1993. Table 22.

[771] FoU-statistikkbanken, NIFU STEP. FoU-personale, UoH-sektor (The R&D statistics bank, NIFU STEP. R&D staff, UoH sector), 2005.

Eva Österberg, professor at Uppsala University (Sweden), was elected as a member in the *Humanistiske klasse* (humanities division), but she was only followed by a small handful of women. Not until 2004 was the first foreign woman in the natural-science division elected: professor in psychology and neurology Carol A. Barnes from the University of Arizona, USA. Why so few women amongst the foreign members? One reason may be that to be elected as a foreign member the person in question had to be considered one of the internationally most outstanding scientists in their academic field, and few females were considered to belong to this upper echelon of academia. An alternative or additional explanation may be found in the network amongst the male members in the Society. Perhaps the election of virtually only male foreign members reflected a male academic network. A third aspect addresses the difference in mobility between men and women. Many of the foreign members had been elected after being visiting professors at the University of Trondheim for some time, and because female professors, as other women, often were more tied to place by their families, they were not as able as their male colleagues to serve as a visiting professor in Trondheim.

Forum for scientific education

The member meetings were the Society's main activity. The Society functioned as an important forum for education in science in the scientific community. A fundamental principle was the idea of multidisciplinary thinking. The meetings with lectures were open to both divisions, and the topics alternated between the natural sciences, including technology, the humanities and social sciences. These meetings enabled members to stay abreast of scientific research in a wide field. In an increasingly differentiated and specialized world of science, not only between the disciplines but also within each discipline, the Society contributed to general scientific education, "Bildung," for each researcher. Precisely this function was a strong contributor to the Society's legitimacy.

The Society's annual agenda of meetings followed a set cycle with six or seven regular membership meetings each year and a gala meeting in February. The program for the meetings was also permanent: Lectures, in memoriam speeches for deceased members, internal matters and election of new members. The lectures, often given by Society members, were the permanent feature on the program. Attendance was quite stable. Almost half of the members resident in the Trondheim region in the 1960s would regularly participate in the Society's meetings. A very high number of the same members would attend each lecture, and in this way the Society functioned as a regular and prioritized meeting-place for large parts of the local scientific community. In the 1960s and early 1970s the number of members was still so small that that everyone basically knew everyone, which meant that the Society undoubtedly had the feel of being a gentlemen's social club.

The regular participants primarily came from the institutions that would constitute the University of Trondheim. The Society was an arena that gave participants the opportunity to have informal discussions across the boundaries of academic fields and institutions. However much it functioned as a university-policy network, it was completely informal. Many of the Society's members were strongly involved in the university issue, by virtue of their positions, but on the institutional level the Society avoided participating in the disputes on university policy. Needless to say, the Society fully supported the establishment of a university, but it did not take any standpoint on how it should be organized.

The Society had an insignificant function in the community, both in relation to the general public and more formal political arenas. In contrast to *Det Norske Videnskaps-Akademi* in Oslo, the Society in Trondheim had no ambitions of becoming an agenda-setter for research policy in Norway. This was evident when we look at the different roles the two institutions had when *Norges Allmennvitenskapelige Forskningsråd* was established in 1949. In contrast to *Akademiet* in Oslo, the Society had not been active in the establishment of the NAVF, nor had the institution attempted to obtain a central position on the council. Nonetheless, the Society had been given the right to nominate a representative to the council, but there is little to suggest that the Society as an institution was in any way involved in how the Society's representative exercised his function as a council member. When the NAVF reorganized in 1970, the Society also lost its one representative, as this seat was transferred to the University of Trondheim. The academy in Oslo also lost its right to nominate four representatives to the council, but as the University of Oslo was to nominate four members from this academy, it was ensured a form of representation.

Inspired by new research policy trends in the OECD, the restructuring of the NAVF was an expression of the increasing demand that research should be focused on satisfying national political objectives. This shift reflected the emergence of the social sciences as an instrument of political governance. Even if basic research continued to be defined as an important duty for the NAVF, more importance was attached to focusing general scientific research on satisfying defined social needs. Due to this requirement, program-based research increased dramatically in the NAVF from the early 1970s, and the government Ministries assigned research projects to an increasing degree.

The Society's board protested the loss of its representative, because, it argued, the Society could field "the most independent council members," and because the Society represented "pure science to a higher degree than the university with its less homogenous staff."[772] The protest fell on deaf ears, and was more symbolic than a genuine attempt to defend a position in the Norwegian research council system. The fact that the Society in Trondheim, and also the academy in Oslo, lost their rights to nominate representatives to the NAVF did not necessarily have immediate major consequences for the NAVF. Their exclusion was nevertheless a symptom that the traditional liberal science ideal the Society had advocated was under pressure, and it was above all a symptom that exclusive science institutions based on elected membership were now seeing

---

[772] UBIT, Special collections. DKNVS II:2. P1966–1988 (650). Minutes from board meeting, September 11, 1969.

the loss of their political legitimacy. Through their lack of representation they also lacked legitimacy when it came to the allocation of research resources.

When the Society lost its place on the NAVF council to the university, this could also be seen as a warning that the expansion of the University in Trondheim might not necessarily mean that the Society's position would be strengthened, as the expectations had been at the anniversary in 1960. Instead, the expansion of UNIT initially marginalized the Society.

The absence of research-policy ambitions on the national level was in many ways a very understandable strategy for the Society. Geographically, it was not in a central location in relation to all those involved in state and national research policy, and with very limited financial resources, this was a rational choice. More surprising, perhaps, was its lack of involvement in the local university-policy landscape. Through their positions at the institutions constituting the University of Trondheim, many of the Society members were deeply involved in university politics. But the Society itself kept out of this area, as part of what appears to have been a deliberate strategy. The Society was a free zone where the university-political disputes and interests were not present. This strategy may admittedly in part have been an attempt to prevent the university controversy from becoming a central part of the Society's life. The conflict over the organization of UNIT was intense and long-lasting, and members differed in their views on this issue. This may, however, also have been even more of an expression of a particular ideal of the Society as an arena for interest-free scientific discussion. During the 1970s, however, such an ideal would become more and more problematic and out of date. As we have seen, the science academies as institutions were increasingly marginalized in the national research policy regime, on the one hand, and, on the other hand, there was new pressure due to the growth of the open-studies university, and the emergence of new radical political movements in its wake.

Controversy over the scientific oath

In October 1968 the board approved a statement of support for the Czech Science Academy prepared by *Det Norske Videnskaps-Akademi i Oslo*. The statement expressed "deep sympathy with the academy's struggle for free speech and the right to unrestrained scientific research and international cooperation."[773] This statement is actually the only case where the Society chose to express a form of political support. The fact that the request came from the academy in Oslo, meaning that the two academies in Norway stood together behind this statement, was an important factor. There was also little doubt that the Society had its members' support in this case, even if the Society had not asked for their opinion. The invasion of Czechoslovakia by the Soviets in August 1968 shook all of Norway, and also sent shock waves deep into the leftist polit-

---

[773] DKNVS *Forhandlinger* vol. 41, 1968:17, minutes from board meeting, October, 10 1968.

ical environment, which during the Cold War had displayed at least some sympathy for the Soviet Union and the socialist project. This shared national condemnation, anger and—for some—disappointment was the one time when the Society departed from its traditional stance of not making any statements on national or international issues of a science-policy nature, including cases that involved the free practice of science.

The reluctance to become involved in these types of issues, which in many cases did not enjoy a wide consensus, became clear a few years later when the question of the individual researcher's responsibility for the use of his or her research results was raised in the Society. Which responsibility did each scientist have for the application and consequences of his or her scientific work? The participation of scientists in the mass extinction of Jews and other groups of people during World War II, and the explosion of the atom bomb by the allied powers over Nagasaki and Hiroshima at the end of the war, made this an extremely important and relevant question, primarily in the medicine and physics branches of science. One of the results was the Helsinki declaration from 1964, which stipulated ethical guidelines for biomedical research involving individuals.[774] But was this a question the Society as a science academy should have a responsibility for becoming involved in? At the start of the 1970s this was a highly controversial issue in the Society.

The controversy was triggered when in the autumn of 1971 the Society received a proposal that it should invite its members to sign a binding oath for scientists and engineers, similar to the Hippocratic oath for doctors, that they would not willingly and knowingly participate in scientific work that might be detrimental to the well-being of others. The Society was also urged that the oath be forwarded to other science associations and academies. The oath was worded as follows:

> An oath for Scientists and Engineers: I vow to strive to apply my professional skills to projects which, after conscientious examination, I believe to contribute to the goal of co-existence of all human beings in peace, human dignity and self-fulfilment. I will not use my scientific training for any purpose which I believe will be used to the harm of any human being. I vow to struggle through my work to minimize danger, noise, strain or invasion of privacy of any individual, pollution of earth, air and water, destruction of natural beauty, mineral resources and wildlife.[775]

Below the oath, which each scientist was supposed to sign, was the following addition:

> It is suggested that this goal requires the provision of an adequate supply of necessities of life (good food, air, water, clothing and housing, access to natural

---

[774] *Declaration of Helsinki* (1964). Recommendations guiding physicians in biomedical research involving human subjects. Adopted by the 18th World Medical Assembly, Helsinki, Finland, June 1964.
[775] *UBIT, Special collections.* DKNVS III:b:6. 1972:49.

and man-made beauty), education and opportunities to enable each person to work out for himself—with due regard to the rights of other people—his life objectives, and to develop creativeness and skill in the use of the hands as well as the head.[776]

This oath had recently been adopted at an international conference arranged in Trondheim in August the same year. A total of 100 scientists from across the world had joined the conference, where the topic was environmental protection and international control of pollution. The conference was arranged by the Society for Social Responsibility in Science (SSRS). SSRS had three members in Trondheim, and all three were members of the Society: Harald Wergeland, Haakon Olsen, a professor of physics at the University of Trondheim, and Per Christian Hemmer, professor of theoretical physics at the University of Trondheim.[777] Through the endowment fund "*Direktør Cyrus S. Eaton's legat,*" DKNVS had contributed funding to the conference. The opening address was given by philosopher Arne Næss, also a member of SSRS.

Victor Paschkis (1898–1991), founder of this organization, was also a participant at the conference. Paschkis, originally from Austria, came to the USA in 1938 and became a professor of *mechanical engineering* at Columbia University in 1948. A Quaker and pacifist, he was one of the foremost pioneers in the endeavors to establish the principle that scientists and engineers had a personal responsibility for the social consequences of their professional activities.

The proposal submitted to the Society was signed by an international group of scientists, most of whom had participated at the SSRS conference in Trondheim. They included Karl Bechert, professor emeritus at the University of Mainz, Kodi Husimi, professor at the University of Nagoya, Victor Paschkis, professor emeritus at Columbia University, Meredith W. Thring, professor at the University of London and Harald Wergeland, professor at the University of Trondheim, NTH. The proposal was later signed by Director Cyrus S. Eaton and Linus Carl Pauling, professor emeritus at the California Institute of Technology.[778] In 1954 Pauling (1901–1994) received the Nobel prize in chemistry, and in 1962 he was awarded the Nobel Peace Prize for his campaign against above-ground nuclear testing. Most of the petitioners were also members of the Society. In addition to Wergeland, the only member of the group from Norway, Bechert (elected in 1963), Pauling (elected in 1958) and Eaton (donating member from 1963) were members of the Society. Thring was not a member when the proposal was made, but was elected in 1974.

The proposal was raised through the Society's Norwegian member Harald Wergeland (1912–1987), who was a professor of theoretical physics at the University of Trondheim. He had been a member of the Society since 1946, and had participated actively in the Society's business, serving as *praeses* from 1959 to 1965. In 1970 he was

---

[776] *UBIT, Special collections.* DKNVS III:b:6. 1972:49.
[777] *Arbeider-Avisa*, August 19, 1971.
[778] *UBIT, Special collections.* DKNVS III:b: 6. 1972:49.

awarded the Gunnerus medal, the Society's highest honor. For many years Wergeland had been deeply involved in international scientific cooperation, such as CERN, NORDITA (the Nordic Institute for Theoretical Physics) and the IUPAP (the International Union of Pure and Applied Physics), and had a broad international contact network. He was also very concerned with the responsibilities that researchers and users of scientific results had. As a pacifist he was actively involved in activities to create peace, founding the Norwegian section of the Pugwash Conferences.[779] For many years Wergeland had participated in an international network of researchers who were deeply concerned about the social and ethical responsibility of researchers. Wergeland and the other petitioners had for years formed an informal committee which had collected information on the perceptions of scientists in relation to the many abuses of scientific methods and results. At an earlier stage, Nobel Prize winners Howard Florey and Cecil Frank Powell had also been members of the group.[780]

The proposal was initially discussed at a board meeting where Wergeland was allowed to present the issue. It appears that initially the Society board, primarily represented by *praeses* Tord Godal, who was the Bishop of Nidaros diocese, saw the initiative in a positive light.[781] Wergeland was invited to present the proposal to members at a meeting of the academy on 31 January 1972. A very small majority of the participants at the meeting supported the proposal: 15 for and 13 against the Society inviting members to sign the oath, and forwarding the oath to other scientific academies and societies.[782] In spite of this small majority support, resistance was intense, much more severe than Wergeland, and also the board, had expected. Bearing the small size of the majority and the intense resistance in mind, the board hesitated to take the matter further and present it to the members. Instead the board asked *Det Norske Videnskaps-Akademi* in Oslo about their view on this matter.[783] This academy was unambiguously negative when it came to promoting such an oath. In the view of the board this was not a "natural" matter for their involvement. First, such an oath was a "completely private and personal matter for each individual." Second, the oath was more relevant for a relatively small group of members. The members this directly touched on, "scientists and engineers," would probably deal with the oath in another way.[784]

Based on the response from *Det Norske Videnskaps-Akademi*, the Society's board found that the case should be put to the members, and invited Wergeland to present the

---

[779] The Pugwash Conferences on Science and World Affairs were founded in 1957 by Joseph Rotblat and Bertrand Russell in Pugwash, Nova Scotia, Canada, as a result of the Russell-Einstein Manifesto (1955) to prevent the use of nuclear weapons. See: Rotblat, Joseph. *Scientists in the Quest for Peace. A History of the Pugwash Conference.* Cambridge, Massachusetts, London: The MIT Press, 1972.

[780] *UBIT, Special collections.* DKNVS III:b:6. 1972:103. Wergeland: "Autoreferat av redegjørelse i fellesmøtet 29.1.73."

[781] *UBIT, Special collections.* DKNVS III:b:6. 1972:103. Letter from Wergeland January 1972.

[782] *DKNVS Forhandlinger* 1972, 5.

[783] *UBIT, Special collections.* DKNVS III:b:6. 1972:49. Letter June 12, 1973.

[784] *UBIT, Special collections.* DKNVS III:b:6: Letter October 20, 1972.

case at another academy meeting. In the meantime the wording in the oath had been significantly abbreviated, and the title had been changed so that it no longer was restricted to scientists and engineers:

> Declaration: Appealing for endorsement from all colleagues in the academic professions we submit the following pledge: I shall not use my scientific training for any purpose which I believe is intended to harm human beings.[785]

At this meeting, on 29 January 1973, this issue stirred emotions that led to a heated debate, with many divergent viewpoints among the 26 attending members. The meeting therefore decided to put the case to all members from Norway. The members were asked to take a standpoint as to whether the Society should invite members to sign the oath, file the received responses and distribute a list of names of those who had signed to academies and scientific societies the Society had exchange connections with. This invitation was accompanied by the board's recommendation. As the process moved along, the board had become far more negative to the proposal, and now had strong doubts as to whether the Society should stand behind the proposal. A total of 48 members responded to the invitation. Fourteen were positive to the proposal, while 34 were negative. Based on the overwhelming negative majority, a unanimous board decided that this issue would not be carried forward.[786]

In his correspondence with the other petitioners, Wergeland asserted that the strong resistance primarily came from the engineering professors at NTH. The result of the submitted votes shows that this is generally correct.[787] Among the members of the natural-science division, which had the largest number of votes, primarily professors in typical engineering subjects at NTH had voted against the proposal, while those who supported the proposal were primarily professors in more theoretical subjects at either NTH or NLHT. Needless to say, there were exceptions, and this does not paint the complete picture. Also among the humanities professors we find a clear majority that had voted against the proposal. By per centage the number of nay votes was larger in the humanities division than in the natural-science division. If we consider age and the year of membership, there is a weak tendency showing that younger and less senior members were more positive than those who were older and had more years as members. We thus notice a certain generation gap, but this should not be over-emphasized. Perhaps the most striking fact about the vote was the small proportion, actually only ten per cent, of the members who wanted the Society to promote the principle of a scientific oath.

It appears that the resistance took two main paths. First, there was disagreement or uncertainty as to whether this declaration presupposed an endorsement of pacifism. Wergeland, himself a pacifist, believed this was not the case. There was, for example,

---

[785] *UBIT, Special collections.* DKNVS III:b:6: Letter November 3, 1973.
[786] *UBIT, Special collections.* DKNVS *Forhandlinger* 1973:20. Minutes from board meeting, October 10, 1973.
[787] *UBIT, Special collections.* DKNVS III:b:6. 1972:103.

nothing about the proposal that would prevent those who signed from performing general military service. It was, on the other hand, open to interpretation as to whether the development of defensive weapons, which in principle would only be used when under attack, but which still had obviously been developed with the intention of injuring others, would be in violation of the declaration.

Second, the opponents rejected the idea that a scientific oath was a matter for scientific societies in general. The board of DNVA had asserted that an endorsement of a scientific oath was exclusively a private matter. This cut right to the heart of the matter, showing that fundamentally different views existed when it comes to what was a common cause for the scientific community. For the petitioners, preventing the use of science for purposes that would harm humanity and individuals was indeed a collective responsibility. The obligation of each individual researcher to assume an ethical responsibility was based on an understanding of the science community's collective responsibility in this area.

The issue of a scientific oath went far beyond local and national interests. If the Society had endorsed the proposal, this would have attracted attention in the international scientific community. Thus the Society would have fronted an issue that was highly controversial on the international level as well. It may be that such considerations, and also reluctance to lead the way in such a controversial matter, also contributed to the unwillingness to sign the oath. When Wergeland submitted the proposal of a scientific oath to the Society, the issue had only just begun to draw attention in the academic community and the research-policy establishment in Norway. This changed during the 1970s. An important expression of this change was the establishment of the commission for "Research and ethics" in 1979.[788] This commission had been convened by the *Hovedkomiteen for norsk forskning* (Main Committee for Norwegian Research), which had been established in 1965 as an advisory body for the Government on research-policy issues. Professor Grethe Authén Blom, then deputy *praeses* of the Society, was also on this commission. However, she had not been appointed as a representative of the Society, but rather through her position as professor of history at the University of Trondheim. This was also a problem field she was deeply involved in, and Blom had been among the few who had voted that the Society should become involved in the question of signing a scientific oath.

The commission's report represented the first time ethical issues in research were fully discussed by the research establishment in Norway. The report showed that there had been a noticeable shift in the way this issue was understood and handled. From starting with a strong individual orientation (an oath signed by individual researchers), the approach had become far more institutional. The commission argued that scientific

---

[788] Hovedkomiteen for norsk forskning (Main Committee for Norwegian Research). *Forskning og etiske ansvar. En rapport fra utvalget for "Forskning og etikk" nedsatt av Hovedkomiteen for norsk forskning* (Research and ethical responsibilities. A report from the commission for "Research and ethics" convened by the Main Committee for Norwegian Research). Oslo, 1981.

institutions, such as universities and scientific professional organizations, were responsible for raising awareness on issues relating to ethics in research, and for establishing ethical guidelines for all types of research activities that would bind institutions and individual researchers.

This case does not only have something to say about the Society's view on the issue of a scientific oath, as the manner in which the proposal was handled, with first two member meetings followed by a general vote, also demonstrates some of the basic features of the Society as an institution. It reveals an organization that was very democratic and not controlled from the top down. There was virtually no tradition that the elected board would on behalf of the institution take initiatives, have standpoints or make decisions in cases that in any way might be the object of controversy. The board basically had an administrative function, not a leadership function. As an institution, the Society was a membership academy, where this collective was the core of the Society. How this collective developed was, therefore, of vital significance for the Society as an institution.

Legitimacy crisis

We have already suggested that the establishment of the University of Trondheim did not necessarily mean that the Society's position was strengthened, but rather contributed to its marginalization. The immediate consequences of an increase in the number of members that were elected due to the development of UNIT support this impression. Electing an increasing number of new members did not lead to a corresponding increase in participation at the Society's meetings, which had been and continued to be the heart of the Society's activities. The attendance of members was almost strikingly stable for many years. In the 1950s attendance had hovered around 25 members. From 1960 up to 2005 attendance was around 30 members, rarely under 25 or over 35. The tendency where more and more of the recently elected members rarely or perhaps never participated in the Society's activities was noticed already in the 1970s, but did not really become a factor until the steep rise in the number of members around 1980. The stable level of attendance combined with the increase in the number of new members meant that in statistical terms only about 10 per cent of the members were participating in ordinary meetings in 2005.

The large majority of the many newly employed and newly elected professors at the University of Trondheim chose not to participate in the Society's activities for a number of reasons, where several and complex structural and political-cultural reasons contributed. The formation of the university also meant the formation of other and competing academic and scientific arenas. Other university and research-policy arenas were also established. The general trend in academia to differentiate and specialize also contributed to this. Combining scientific general education while spearheading one's research field became more and more difficult for the individual researcher. Thus the Society's ambition to be a forum for scientific education within the scientific community was facing increasingly difficult conditions. Another reason may also be found in the Society's tradition and culture. Some of the new members felt that the meetings were stiff and formal and that they had little relevance.

The declining participation by Society members undermined the Society's function as a meeting place for its members and as a forum for internal scientific education. When this function lost significance, the legitimacy of the Society itself was also undermined. Initially the Society countered the legitimacy crisis with an internal strategy. This was implemented in the 1970s, and was an attempt at making more members, particularly those who were recently elected, participate in the Society's meetings. The idea was to recreate the Society as a general science forum for members in Trondheim. To this end, in 1974 the board took the initiative to change the member election procedure.[789] The board urged those who proposed new members to consider whether it was probable that the candidate would contribute to the Society's activities. All sponsors should therefore contact their candidate after the proposal had been recommended by the division to ascertain whether the candidate was interested in becoming a member and in contributing positively to the Society, such as by attending meetings. In its argumentation the board stated that it was sadly the case that a number of members did not feel any obligation to actively participate in the Society's activities, and also at the same time blocked admittance for others who might be more positive members.

The members were also urged to show restraint when it came to proposing persons who had not put down roots in the scientific community in Trondheim, and to consider whether they would remain in Trondheim in the future. On moving, the person in question would be transferred to the category outside the territory and would thus lose the possibility of being elected again for years to come.[790] *Det Norske Videnskaps-Akademi i Oslo* saw this last recommendation to consider whether candidates had put down roots in Trondheim as a sign that the Society in Trondheim was a local academy, in contrast to the academy in Oslo, which at precisely the same time removed the appendix "in Oslo" from its official name, the purpose being to appear more clearly as a national academy.[791] However, if we consider the composition of members in the two academies, a striking common feature emerges: both had the bulk of their members from their "local" academic community, respectively Oslo and Trondheim. There was, however, one important difference. The academy in Oslo, located in Norway's capital, had a far stronger ambition of being a national academy, while the Society in Trondheim, on the periphery of the national centers of power, had never hidden the fact that its strong basis was in the region, in "local affairs." This was also expressed in the statutes, which laid down that when electing new members, importance should be attached to whether the candidate had undertaken research that was connected to the region.[792] If we consider

---

[789] *DKNVS Forhandlinger* 1974, 12. Minutes joint meeting, April 1, 1974.
[790] *DKNVS Forhandlinger* 1974, 22. Minutes board meeting, March 23, 1974.
[791] Helsvig, *Elitisme på norsk* (Elitism in Norwegian). *Det Norske Videnskaps-Akademi 1945–2007*, 126.
[792] Frostating or Hålogaland regions. This criterion was removed when the statutes were changed in 1989.

the figures for membership attendance, which remained stable, this indicates that the strategy for increased member participation had little effect.

At the start of the 1980s the practice of holding joint meetings with lectures was also debated. Separate lectures for each division might be a way of making meetings more interesting for members. It was difficult to present a scientific work in such a way that it would be interesting both for other researchers in the same field and for colleagues without competence in the field. However, this proposal, which was made by the board in 1981, was rejected.[793] Giving separate lectures for each division would break with the scientific education ideal that had been and continued to be a fundamental principle of the Society. Changing this would be a rejection of the heritage from the learned society. There was also no guarantee that this scheme would lead to bigger audiences. Differentiation and subject specialization were not only prevalent between natural science and technology, on the one hand, and the social sciences on the other, but also within all subject disciplines. Thus the joint multidisciplinary lecture and meeting was maintained, and the Society maintained the tradition of the internal science-education project.

A far more radical proposal was submitted by one of the relatively new members of the Society, Ulf Hafsten (1922–1992). Hafsten was one of the growing group of newly hired professors at UNIT to become a member of the Society. He was employed as a professor of botany at *Norges lærerhøgskole* in 1967, and was elected as a member of the Society in 1970. Hafsten questioned whether the Society's statutes and composition were still appropriate and whether the current organizational structure was the best way to strengthen the position of science in Trondheim and the surrounding region. He therefore proposed that a committee should look into reorganizing the Society.[794]

The background for the proposal was the strict admission criteria and the restricted number of places the Society had, limitations which excluded a substantial category of colleagues in the scientific community in Trondheim. According to Hafsten, there was undoubtedly any number of interested persons who would like to become members of the Society, if this option existed. Even if the lecture meetings in principle were open to all, experience showed that very few non-members attended. This particularly applied to active young researchers in the university environment. Hafsten therefore proposed to open the Society to anyone who was interested after submitting a written application. The time was now ripe to moderate some of the long and venerable traditions of the Society. It would benefit the expanding scientific life in the city and the region, and would probably help the general public to gain a better understanding of the importance of science in society.[795]

The idea of opening the Society for all interested persons who satisfied particular scientific qualifications had also been discussed before, but no specific proposal in this

---

[793] DKNVS *Forhandlinger* 1981, 13. Minutes from the joint meeting, October 12, 1981.
[794] *UBIT, Special collections.* DKNVS III:a:1–90. Minutes attachment 1975–76. Letter September 19, 1975.
[795] *UBIT, Special collections.* DKNVS III:a:1–90. Minutes attachment 1975–76.

direction had been submitted. In 1969 a committee had been convened to revise the Society's statutes with the membership numbers and the proportion of members in each division in mind. The background for this was the quantitative expansion of UNIT which brought an increasing number of qualified persons into the region, persons who could not be accepted because of the ceiling on the number of members. The committee, which consisted of the Society's *praeses*, bishop Tord Godal, Edvard Bull, professor of history, and Helge Larsen, professor of technical biochemistry, stated in its report that:

> The society should in principle be a center and meeting-place for all independent scientists who are working in the local community, and who have documented a certain level in their work. One consequence of this might be the elimination of the restriction on the number of members, instead basing election to the society only on documentation of a scientific level.[796]

The committee, however, did not make such a recommendation, reasoning that even if this might be an appropriate solution in the long term, it would not be advisable at the time due to the "very strong bias our local community has towards the natural-science and technical-science sector." Thus an opening of the Society was not rejected on principle, but rather due to the concern that the Society would be completely dominated by technologists and natural scientists. The split into divisions and the restriction on the number of members represented the only way to ensure a reasonable and desirable distribution of members. To make it easier to regulate and expand the number of places in the Society to keep pace with the expansion of the scientific environment in Trondheim, the committee proposed that the provisions relating to membership should be removed from the statutes and placed in a separate set of rules. When the statutes were amended in 1974 this was in fact done. The committee's views on the principle for the Society, to open it to persons with "high scientific qualifications" (the committee suggested that this might be placed at the *dosent*—associate professor—level), was not formally addressed. It was, however, likely that this was discussed in the Society as the proposal to amend the statutes was discussed at a number of meetings.

Hafsten's proposal was, as we can see, in accordance with the principles the statutes committee had recommended, even if they may have had slightly divergent views as to where the boundary should be drawn to define adequate scientific qualifications for election. The basis for these viewpoints was the concern that the Society would no longer be a forum for the entire scientific community in Trondheim, that it no longer represented the scientific community in Trondheim, but was on its way to crystallizing into a closed institution for a small local scientific elite.

---

[796] *UBIT, Special collections.* DKNVS III:b:5. Circulars 1971–77. Recommendation dated November 16, 1970.

The proposal must be seen in relation to the ongoing movement for greater democracy in the controlling bodies at the Norwegian universities. The emergence of open-studies universities led to a major expansion in the number of scientific employees at the universities, but the growth had primarily come in lower-level scientific positions, such as assistant professors and pure teaching positions. Professors continued to rule in the controlling bodies. The demand for greater democracy and representativeness was accompanied by comprehensive criticism of the study programs from a radicalized student body. The common factor was that the dominant position of the professors at universities was being fundamentally challenged. The era of the old professorial rule of universities was coming to an end. In 1975 the amended Act relating to the University of Oslo introduced the principle that all groups at the university, including students, should be equally represented on the controlling bodies.[797] At the University of Trondheim this principle did not come into force until 1984, when the first Act relating to the University of Trondheim entered into force. Until then the three institutions which made up the university had different practices. While a form of representativeness had been introduced at *Norges lærerhøgskole*, the rule of professors was very strong at NTH. Until 1984 NTH was controlled by a professor council and a professor committee. "The struggle against the rule of professors" was thus one of the slogans for the radical and activist students in Trondheim in the 1970s. The proposal of opening the Society must be considered in relation to the fundamental anti-elitism these political trends represented. As a *science society* the Society could of course not be open to all, but it should be open to all who had adequate scientific qualifications, and it should be representative of the scientific community in Trondheim. A more representative Society would increase the institution's legitimacy in the scientific community and in society in general.

All this notwithstanding, the proposal was firmly rejected by the board, which found Hafsten's outline for a proposal for reorganization so comprehensive that it would change the Society's character completely, and in reality mean that it would cease being a scientific academy. The board therefore totally rejected the idea of convening a committee.[798] It did not provide any further rationale, as it was suggested that it was self-evident that the proposal meant that the Society would cease to be a scientific academy. An opening of the Society as called for by the proposal would represent a clear break with the traditional organizational structure of science academies, and the Society would thus have divorced itself from its European sister academies. The board's attitude implicitly held the idea that exclusivity was a sustaining principle for the Society as an institution. The question of exclusivity was also discussed in *Det Norske Videnskaps-Akademiet* in Oslo during the same period of time, albeit in a less radical form. A proposal to expand the number of members of the academy, aiming to obtain a broader

---

[797] Collett, John Peter. *Historien om Universitetet i Oslo* (The history of the University of Oslo). Universitetsforlaget, 1999, 231.
[798] *UBIT, Special collections.* DKNVS III:a:1–90. Minutes attachment 1975–76.

national representation, was rejected because such an expansion would erode its exclusivity. Compared to other Nordic science academies, *Akademiet i Oslo*, with a total of 304 members in 1971, was large and thus not that exclusive. *Det Kgl. Danske Videnskabers Selskab* had at the same time 124 members, *Finska Vetenskaps-societeten* had 131 members, while the two Swedish academies, *Kungl. Vetenskapsakademien* and *Kungl. Vitterhets-, historie- och antikvitetsakademien*, together had 257 members.[799] In comparison the Society in Trondheim had 172 members that year.

The way the proposal to open the Society was dealt with strongly contrasts with the way the proposal for a scientific oath was approached. As the board rejected the proposal so out of hand, this is a strong indication that it was reasonably confident it enjoyed the support of the majority of the members on this issue.

An anniversary in a self-reflective mood

The bright expectations that had dominated in the Society at the anniversary in 1960 were replaced by concern about the Society's future on the 225th anniversary in 1985, and while tributes to heritage and tradition characterized the anniversary in 1960, the 1985 anniversary celebrations were marked by a self-reflective mood. The 225th anniversary was also celebrated in a more austere fashion than the anniversary in 1960, and the two divisions of DKNVS (*Selskabet* and *Museet*) conducted their celebrations separately. The *praeses*, professor Grethe Authén Blom (1922–2004), used her speech to reflect upon the history, function, and legitimacy of the Society. Blom had been employed as a professor of history at the University of Trondheim (*Norges Lærerhøgskole*) in 1969 and was elected a member of the Society the year after. She was elected *praeses* in 1982, the first female *praeses* in the history of the Society, a post she held until 1989. Before she assumed this position she had been the deputy *praeses* from 1978 to 1981, and before that she was the head of the humanities division from 1975 to 1977. For her many years of dedication to the Society and her scientific contributions in the subject of history, she was awarded the Gunnerus medal in 1992. In her speech Blom asked the question: Did the Society have legitimacy?

> For almost 60 years we have followed the track we were shunted on to in 1926, with various repairs along the way. However, it is no secret that some of those who are in our midst have suggested that now is the time to replace the whole train with more modern carriages that can seat more people. Many outside the Society are even of the opinion that the old narrow-gauge railway with plush-upholstered furniture should be packed away for ever. Does the Society still have a function?[800]

---

[799] Helsvig, *Elitisme på norsk. Det Norske Videnskaps-Akademi 1945–2007*, 127.
[800] *DKNVS Forhandlinger* 1985, 86.

Was the *Det Kongelige Norske Videnskabers Selskab* a "relic of the past," or could it continue to fill a meaningful and legitimate specialist function in the science community and in society in general? Blom felt the answer was yes. Of course as *praeses* it would be hard for her to suggest anything else, so her question was for the most part rhetorical. In her answer, Blom explained the most important characteristics of the Society. As a general forum the Society was a place where the humanities and the technical-natural sciences could exchange information and ideas. The Society preserved valuable traditions such as reading biographies at the gala meeting (*Høytidsdagen*), and awarding the noblest prize the Society had, the Gunnerus medal. The *Transactions* (*Skrifter*) were particularly important. *Skrifter* had ensured that many important events, ideas, and innovations in Norwegian science history had been recorded in writing, and as one of the oldest scientific series of writings still being published it served as the Society's face to the world. As we see, Blom emphasized the internal science function within the scientific community in the Society and through this the scientific environment in Trondheim, and then internally in the scientific community in general through the scientific periodical *Skrifter*. According to Blom, the internal science function was far more important than what many contemporaries, including many of the Society's own members, thought.

It can be said that Blom stood out as *praeses* because she so explicitly and clearly articulated a view of what was and should be the most important function of the Society, and in that we find its legitimacy. As a historian, it was part of Blom's profession to analyze the role and functions of institutions. Her discussion and arguments also revealed, however, a need to defend the fact that the Society actually exercised an important function. On celebrating 225 years of existence, the legitimacy of the Society was being fundamentally challenged. Tradition in itself was no longer adequate to legitimize the Society. The internal science function had eroded to a great extent, and could no longer supply the appropriate legitimacy. This function needed to be defended and justified. The emphasis on the internal science function was not necessarily in conflict with a more active external function. Blom had been among the few who had voted in favor of the Society promoting a scientific oath. As we shall see, it was during Blom's time as *praeses* that the Society began to open to the general society. Blom maintained the strong teaching tradition from Norwegian history research, and wrote a number of articles and chronicles in the newspaper on DKNVS. During Blom's time as *praeses* the first attempts were made to hammer out a new strategy to promote a public science.

Promoting Science

The 1980s were a critical period for all of DKNVS in Trondheim, and a period dominated by reforms and new orientations, both for the Society and the museum foundation. The foundation had been established in 1951, primarily as an instrument for the management of the museum, and with the transfer of the museum to the state in 1984, there was good reason to ask what the purpose and duties of the foundation should now be. For the Society, the 1980s were a time to clean up the internal organization of the academy. The financial situation and the statutes underwent comprehensive reforms. The results of the reform processes were not immediately visible, but they formed a decisive underpinning for further revitalization of the Society. The 1980s were thus a crucial decade for the Society. This decade also saw the design of a new strategy for promoting a scientific public arena for the academic community in Trondheim, and also for the general public.

From museum foundation to research foundation

The foundation had been established as a management tool for the museum. The legitimacy and identity of the foundation were based on this management function. Now what would become of the foundation after this management function was transferred elsewhere? What function could provide the foundation with its legitimacy and identity? The person to stake out a new strategy for the foundation after 1984 was Gunnar Sundnes (b. 1926). Sundnes was employed as a professor of marine biology at UNIT in 1972 with responsibility for *Trondhjems biologiske stasjon*, which was under the museum. Before this he had worked at the Institute of Marine Research (*Havforskningsinstituttet*) in Bergen. From 1980 to 1983 Sundnes was employed as the director of the museum, which also put him on the foundation board, in practice serving as the manager of the foundation. With the new arrangement the museum director was no longer a part of the foundation, and on Sundnes's initiative a general secretary position was established for the foundation.[801] Sundnes was employed in this position, which he held until the

---

[801] Interview with Gunnar Sundnes.

end of 1995. Thus Sundnes in effect continued to function as the general manager of the foundation. He also continued as the director of the museum, but as the elected director.[802]

Sundnes's ambition was to transform the old museum foundation into a research foundation, thus carrying forward the research tradition from *DKNVS Museet* in *DKNVS Stiftelse*. An almost unbroken research tradition in DKNVS from the days of Gunnerus had been continued through *Museet*, so it was indeed the oldest research institution in Norway. Now when the museum was no longer part of DKNVS, the tradition would need to be continued by *DKNVS Stiftelse*. Even when managing the museum, the foundation had supported research projects from funds and endowments, primarily research projects under the auspices of the museum. After 1984 this became the primary task of the foundation, and thus it became important to fund a minimum of one foundation-initiated research project of long duration. The research project was initiated and led by the foundation's general secretary, so it was also within the general secretary's own research field. The first project for the foundation, the *Beistadfjord* project, was one Sundnes had launched back in 1976, and it would continue until 1997. The objective of this project was to gain insight into the dynamics of a complex fjord system. Special emphasis was placed on studying hydrodynamic circulatory systems, population genetics in fish, physiology of fish parasites and physiological mechanisms and functions related to the fish heart and swimming bladder. Smolt production was initiated in connection with a hydroelectric scheme in the area. In addition to the field studies in Beitstadfjord, field work and experimental studies were also carried out in the Baltic States, the Mediterranean and the USA.[803]

In 1998 a new project, the Svalbard project, was launched and led by Yngve Espmark, who took over as general secretary in 1996. Espmark became professor of zoology at the University of Trondheim in 1976 with behavioral biology as his special field. He was elected to the Society in 1983, and was the general secretary for the foundation until 2002. From then and until 2008 he was the general secretary for all of DKNVS. The main objective of the Svalbard project was to investigate the relationships between environmental constraints in the Arctic and behavioral adaptations in snow buntings (*plectrophenax nivalis*), the only passerine species breeding regularly and in large numbers on the Svalbard archipelago. Variations in song features, plumage characteristics, mating strategies, the number of extra-pair offspring (EPO), paternal care, diurnal activity in relation to temperature, light and other ambient factors were variables that were analyzed in relation to, for instance, choice of mate, onset and duration of breeding time and breeding success. In addition, data on site fidelity, philopatry, reproduction and survival were collected and analyzed in relation to population dynamics and environmental monitoring. The field work was carried out in Adventdalen, near Longyearbyen, in Svalbard.[804]

---

[802] According to the Act relating to the University of Trondheim, which was passed in 1983, the museum director and other heads of institutions were to be elected.
[803] http://www.dknvs.no/research.htm
[804] http://www.dknvs.no/research.htm

The foundation's other main area of activity was the organization of an international interdisciplinary scientific research seminar, the Kongsvoll symposium. The first international Kongsvoll symposium was arranged in 1985, and also served as the foundation's celebration of DKNVS's 225th anniversary. The idea behind the Kongvoll symposium was to bring chosen researchers from various academic disciplines together to discuss a pre-determined thesis question. Researchers with related thesis areas, but with no tradition for communicating their research with each other, were linked in new and unaccustomed ways. The topic for the first symposium, "Diving in animals and man," was indicative. From an interdisciplinary-science perspective the seminars were innovative and can be rated as successful. The foundation arranged a total of six Kongsvoll symposiums with varying intervals.[805]

The symposiums were held at *Kongsvold fjeldstue*, located on the northern end of the Dovrefjell mountain range 886 meters above sea level, on the old road between Oslo and Trondheim. *Kongsvold fjellstue* had been an inn for travelers since 1670, and the oldest preserved buildings were from 1720. When *Dovrebanen*, the main railway line between Oslo and Trondheim, was opened in 1921, the mountain hotel would primarily function as a hotel for tourists, and later also as a hotel for courses and conferences. The Dovrefjell mountain range is a high-altitude mountain plateau with special fauna and flora, and was declared a national park in 1974. The adjoining mountain areas Drivdalen, Kongsvoll and Hjerkinn were at the same time given the status of protected landscapes. In 1975 *DKNVS Museet* built a biological station at Kongsvoll, which also included a botanical mountain garden that had been started in 1923.[806] The enormous Dovrefjell area also has great symbolic importance, and is a key location in the narrative on Norwegian independence. At the national assembly in 1814, Dovre was used as a metaphor for Norwegian concord and unity. After the Norwegian Constitution had been adopted, and the national assembly had been formally dissolved, the 112 elected representatives clasped hands in a long chain while making the pledge "United and faithful until Dovre falls!"[807] Thus this mountain created a special framework around the symposiums, an atmosphere the many participants from abroad might have experienced as quite exotic.

However, the financial situation placed clear restrictions on the opportunities the foundation had to initiate and operate its own research projects and seminars. After

---

[805] 1988: "Gas super-saturation and bubble formation in fluids and organisms."

1993: "Human impact on self-recruiting populations."

1994: "Biomedical and psychosocial consequences of radiation from man-made radionuclides in the biosphere."

1998: "Adaptive significance of signaling and signal design in animal communication."

2002: "Arctic Life. Conditions, Constraints and Adaptations."

[806] The mountain garden was established by Thekla R. Resvoll in cooperation with NSB (the Norwegian State Railways).

[807] Dyrvik, Ståle and Ole Feldbæk. *Mellom brødre* (Between brothers). *1780–1830. Aschehougs Norgeshistorie, bind 7*. Oslo: H. Aschehoug & Co., 1996, 155.

the museum and the library had been handed over to the state, the foundation was left with little else to work with. The foundation kept all the funds and endowments, as well as some property outside the city that gave some revenues, but the foundation did not receive any compensation from the state for the transfer of the museum. However, the foundation did reach a good agreement on its day-to-day operations, as it was granted free rental of office space for an unlimited time in the museum buildings, and the museum agreed to cover its secretariat function.[808] When the museum was transferred to the state, the foundation managed a fund capital amounting to around NOK 2.9 million. In the following years, the fund capital increased significantly, primarily through fund management and not through the addition of new funds. In 2001 the fund capital had increased to approximately NOK 12.3 million. Compared to inflation during this period, this represented real growth. Strengthening the foundation's financial situation had also been one of the priority tasks for Sundnes when he became the institution's first general secretary, and he was fairly successful in this. However, modern research was expensive, so it was clear that the opportunities the foundation had to function as a research foundation were limited.

Even if the foundation donated the museum to the state, it did not relinquish its grip on the museum, nor would it have been an easy process to cut ties completely. During the negotiations on handing the museum over to the state, after it had become part of UNIT, the foundation attempted to maintain a form of management responsibility, albeit in a very limited form. In the first proposal for new statues for the foundation, to enter into force after the transfer, the board proposed that the foundation should serve as the liaison between the museum and its geographical area of activities with special responsibility for stimulating the museum's external activities in the community. Its job was to ensure that the museum activities had the best possible development conditions within the university.[809] However, any continuation of the foundation's managerial responsibility was rejected by the state authorities. The final transfer of the museum to the state meant a complete split between *DKNVS Stiftelsen* and *Museet*.

The foundation still succeeded in having some conditions placed on the transfer which involved some clauses relating to the future management of the museum within the university. One requirement was that the museum would be maintained as a joint unit within UNIT, and that the museum activities would primarily be based at the cur-

---

[808] "Avtale om overføring av Det Kgl. Norske Videnskabers Selskab, Museets eiendeler til staten ved Kultur- og Vitenskapsdepartementet." (Agreement relating to the transfer of DKNVS, the Museum assets to the state represented by the Ministry of Culture and Science) St. prp. no 126, 1982–83. *Om inkorporering av Det Kongelige Norske Videnskabers Selskab, Museet i Universitetet i Trondheim* (On incorporating the Museum of DKNVS into the University of Trondheim).

"Vederlagsfritt få utført regnskapsføring og skrivearbeid ved Museets kontorpersonale og disponere telefon i samme utstrekning som i dag." (To have carried out accounting and writing tasks by the office staff of the Museum and to be able to use the telephone to the same extent as today.)
[809] DKNVS Museet. The board's annual report 1976.

rent premises at Kalvskinnet. Moreover, the library was to continue to be an organizational department under the museum.[810] This agreement, which was made between
DKNVS Stiftelsen and the state, represented by the Ministry of Culture and Science,
decided how the museum with the library was to be organized, and the university
administration would have to comply with this. This would be the source of disputes,
primarily with respect to the organization of the university library. In practice the
agreement meant that the large and very valuable book collections that were transferred, and which constituted a substantial portion of the university library, would still
have to be kept together at the Kalvskinnet building, which of course meant that it
would be quite some distance away from the other UNIT campuses which were located
up to four miles away. The academic community furthest away was the faculty of arts,
and their departments were the most frequent users of the book collections. The foundation took on the role of custodian of the agreement, and resisted any attempt to make
changes that did not agree with the intent of the agreement. This was also the case when
the university underwent major reorganizations towards the end of the 1990s and after
it became NTNU in 1996.[811] Thus the foundation did not fully relinquish its grip on the
museum, even after the transfer to the state.

A scientific public arena

During the 1980s a new ambition surfaced to make the Society more socially relevant,
both internally in the academy and in society in general. This ambition was expressed
in a two-pronged strategic approach. First, an attempt was made to revitalize the Society as an internal forum for scientific discussion, primarily choosing thesis questions in
science that had more social relevance. This strategy can be seen as a revision of the
internal strategy of the 1970s, so that instead, or rather in addition to encouraging
members to participate, it became more important to make it interesting to participate.
One step in this approach was to call for lectures on more relevant topics, such as the
conditions for science in society, examinations of important social challenges, problems or conflicts, or presentations of scientific research which raised crucial ethical or
political issues. To stimulate debate, more than one lecturer would be invited so that
the topic or issue could be illuminated from different angles, perhaps also with very
clear and divergent points of view.

---

[810] "Avtale om overføring av Det Kgl. Norske Videnskabers Selskab, Museets eiendeler til staten ved
Kultur- og Vitenskapsdepartementet." (Agreement relating to the transfer of DKNVS, the Museum
assets to the state represented by the Ministry of Culture and Science) St. prp. nr 126, 1982–83. *Om
inkorporering av Det Kongelige Norske Videnskabers Selskab, Museet i Universitetet i Trondheim.* (On
incorporating the Museum of DKNVS into the University of Trondheim).
[811] DKNVS *Forhandlinger* 1995, 244; 1996, 221; 2001, 277; Interview with Kjell Eimhjellen.

Second, the new internal strategy was supplemented with a strategy focusing on a public function. The Society would need to have a function beyond being a forum for its members. It would need to be open to society and the general public. This was a strategy whose aim was to promote a scientific public arena. It represented an entirely new trend in the history of the Society since 1926. The academy division was established to function as a science forum for the academic elite, the new NTH professors, and that had been the most important function of the Society since then. The orientation towards society, the city and the general public had been the task of *DKNVS Museet*. In the 1980s, however, the Society decided to address this tradition which the museum had administered alone. One step in this strategy was for the Society to arrange some open meetings in addition to the academy meetings. This was discontinued after a brief period. Instead the Society opted to open the academy meetings, in other words the lectures, to the general public, and the general public came, even if in varying numbers. In contrast to the membership's attendance, the attendance of the general public depended a great deal on the topic and its social relevance and general interest. As an expression of a new ambition to play a role in the public arena, the open academy meetings marked an important turning point. One of the meetings that attracted the largest audience, in 1986, featured several lecturers who talked about the exploration of geological resources on Svalbard and in the Barents Sea in connection with the political and military development in this region. Another meeting, also with three lecturers, looked at NMR (Nuclear Magnetic Resonance), a new aid for medical diagnostics and medical and technical research. Other topics that were on the agenda included international politics, such as the conflict in the Middle East.

Grethe Authen Blom, the *praeses* from 1982 to 1989, played an important role in the process of change and opening the Society to the public. She was a leader with strong opinions and points of view, never afraid of discussion and disagreement. This strategy for creating more interesting meetings that were relevant to the times must be characterized as comparatively successful. Even if the attendance of Society members changed little, the Society to some extent succeeded in reaching the public arena and the general public.

The ambitions of strengthening the scientific public arena also had consequences for the Society's gala meeting. In 1926 the new Society had reintroduced the custom of a gala meeting, but instead of celebrating the birthday of the king, the Society's protector, the gala was held on Gunnerus's birthday, February 26. The program was the same from one year to the next with music, reading the biographies of former members, lectures, reading the general secretary's annual report and awarding medals and prizes. The meeting would then be brought to an end with a formal dinner.

In 1986 the gala was expanded with a special lecture night on the evening before the meeting itself, called *Gunnerusforelesningene* (the Gunnerus lectures). The ambition was to present lectures of high quality given by prominent persons, whether researchers or others, and the intention was that the topics would be socially relevant. The first of these lectures was held in 1986 where the topics were biology and gene technology.[812] These lectures were part of the strategy of finding a scientific public arena, of making the Society more highly visible in the public arena, and of demonstrating that the Society was concerned with contemporary issues. The *Gunnerus lectures* preceding the gala were thus also the most important program celebration of the Society's founder.[813] Gunnerus was therefore also used to build the identity of the Society. To borrow a term from the economists, "Gunnerus" became a brand name for the Society.

Scientific prizes to young researchers

Awarding prizes as a token of gratitude for scientific achievement or for more practical and cultural contributions was an old Society tradition. After 1926 the Society had awarded two prizes, the Gunnerus medal for outstanding effort for science and the Society, and a memorial gold coin awarded to local non-professional contributors to culture. Both prizes were awarded for many years of dedicated work, and were therefore awarded to persons who were often well advanced in years and with long careers in their respective fields.

In the 1980s the Society established a new prize to be awarded to promising young researchers. The purpose was to encourage and inspire young researcher talents to pursue a career in science. The prize was first awarded at the gala meeting in 1984, and the recipients were the engineer Terje Espevik, for outstanding scientific work in biophysics and cellular biology, and Ph.D. Linda R. White, for outstanding scientific work on cellular biology and membrane physics.[814] In 1986 the foundation also established a similar prize, and the two prizes were awarded jointly at the gala meeting. Both prizes consisted of a diploma and a lithograph. The financial situation precluded the awarding of a monetary prize. As with the old prizes, their value was symbolic—awarding honor and conferring respect. Managing tradition, respect, and exclusivity, and also the power to award respect and honor of others was one of the Society's foremost assets. For younger researchers with ambitions of a scientific career such a symbolic prize might also have some financial value, as it could boost their careers and make them more attractive to funding institutions.

The prize for younger researchers was part of the strategy to make the Society more open and innovative. The prize pointed beyond the Society itself, as it was a specific,

---

[812] "Den biologiske revolusjon—de første 30 år" (The biological revolution—the first 30 years) by Harald Skjervold and "Genspleising—en ny teknologi som gir vide perspektiver for biologisk forskning" (Gene splicing—a new technology that gives wide perspectives for biological research) by Kaare Gautvik. A total of 70 persons attended.

[813] In 2006 this was made even clearer. The Gala Meeting was then for practical reasons moved from Gunnerus's birthday to a fixed weekday (Friday) in March.

[814] DKNVS *Forhandlinger* 1984, 17.

though modest, way of promoting work in science. This then also helped to strengthen the Society's legitimacy and relevance, being typical of the change and opening process that took place in the Society in the 1980s, and appears as symbolically important for DKNVS.

Statutes for a Society with a more outward focus

The statutes from 1974 strongly reflected an academy focused on local matters and internal affairs. During the second half of the 1980s, the statutes were again revised, and this revision went a long way toward reflecting the new ambition to shift the Society's focus outward. This was manifested in many ways: first in the sense of less emphasis on members' local ties, with new openness and social orientation, and a dawning wish for an international orientation. The meticulous work to revise the statutes was led by Sverre Westin, who just a few years earlier had headed comprehensive activities to put the finances of the Society in order. The statutes were simplified to a very extensive degree. A number of sections regulating the day-to-day activities of the Society (meetings, election of members, publication of *Skrifter*, awarding of prizes, and so on) were removed and placed in a separate set of rules.[815] Such simplification was also a Ministerial requirement if the Society was to continue to have its statutes confirmed by Royal Resolution.[816]

The statutes were not only simplified but also amended on important points of principle. A section from 1974 stipulating the importance of the regional ties of the candidate for election (Frostating and Hålogaland districts) was removed. The new rules also eliminated the regulation of the number of members inside and outside the districts. Only the proportional relation between members from Norway and abroad was retained. Other detailed provisions giving the impression that the Society was a local association of and for its members, such as members having the preferential right to have their scientific works printed in Society publications, were also removed. Maintaining relations with academies abroad and participation in international cooperation were introduced as a new item in the Society's objectives clause. The immediate practical consequences of these changes were not large, but the symbolic impact was important for the Society. Even if the Society continued to have its base and activities in the region, the new statutes signaled an ambition to be a national scientific society with an international orientation.

The regional dimension was also strengthened, but not in the direction of the local scientific community or the members, but rather towards society in general. Sharing scientific knowledge with the general public was included as a new item in the objectives clause. The provision limiting the admission of non-members to the Society's public meetings, the lectures at the academy meetings, was removed. This meant that

---

[815] UBIT, Spesialsamlingene. DKNVS supplement (Dora). Box 10. Revision of statutes 1984–1989.
[816] Letter dated 27 January 1989 from the Ministry of Culture and Science.

the statutes were now more in accordance with the practice of opening the academy meetings that had been established in the 1980s. The new statutes therefore also signaled the new ambition of promoting a scientific public arena.

DKNVS's publications

1976 was a milestone year in the publication history of DKNVS. That year the Society published a complete edition of the correspondence between Johan Ernst Gunnerus (1718–1773) and Carl von Linné (1707–1778).[817] Their exchange of letters commenced in 1761/62 and continued until Gunnerus's death. The exchange of letters between these two men has been almost completely preserved. The letters from Linné belong to DKNVS, and were initially published by Ove Dahl in his large work on Gunnerus, Volume 3, 1897, and Volume 4, 1903. The original letters from Gunnerus are kept at the *Linnean Society of London*, which was established in 1778. When writing the history of DKNVS for the anniversary in 1960, Hans Midbøe also took the initiative of having a complete edition of the correspondence published. This would prove not only to be a powerful contribution to the history of the Society, but it also shed light on a vital aspect of the history of Nordic scholars. The demanding work of copying the letters and translating the ones written in Latin (approximately one third) commenced early in the 1960s. Leiv Amundsen (1898–1987), professor of classical philology at the University of Oslo, was in charge of this work, while professors Rolf Nordhagen and Erling Sivertsen provided academic assistance when it came to botanical and zoological terms. The work was started and for the most part completed before funding for the publication was in place. The poor financial situation of the Society and financial problems connected to its publication series, *Skrifter*, made publication within the regular framework impossible. In 1970 the Society succeeded in obtaining external funding from the Swedish fund "Clara Lachmanns fond."[818] *Brevveksling 1761–1772. Johan Ernst Gunnerus og Carl von Linné* (Letters between Johan Ernst Gunnerus and Carl von Linné 1761–1772) was a major and unique effort for the Society, and made vital cultural and natural history source material available for research.

DKNVS's ordinary publications since 1926 were DKNVS *Forhandlinger* and DKNVS *Skrifter*. *Forhandlinger* (Proceedings) was the Society yearbook, but also included scientific articles. Starting in 2004 the name was changed to *DKNVS Årbok* (Yearbook). The name *Skrifter* (Transactions) was, however, maintained. *DKNVS Skrifter* was the oldest continuous scientific publication series in Norway, and also one of the oldest in the world. Through an extensive exchange network, *Skrifter* was distributed to a

---

[817] Amundsen, Leif. *Johan Ernst Gunnerus og Carl von Linné. Brevveksling 1761–1772* (Letters between Johan Ernst Gunnerus and Carl von Linné 1761–1772). Trondheim, Oslo, Bergen, Tromsø: Universitetsforlaget, 1976.
[818] UBIT, Spesialsamlingene. DKNVS III:a:1–90. Minutes attachment 1760–1987. Correspondence relating to publication of letters between Gunnerus and Linné.

number of libraries abroad, thus also found a wide international readership. *Skrifter* was the pride of the Society. Since the first issue was published in 1761, a number of recognized scientists in and out of Norway have published in *Skrifter*. Managing and continuing the traditional publication was considered to be of vital importance for the Society. In addition to the academy meetings, publishing *Skrifter* had been the primary task of the Society since 1926, and DKNVS's identity as a science society was strongly linked to this series.

The academic profile of *Skrifter* changed slightly during the second half of the 1900s. Even if it covered both the humanities and the natural sciences, natural-science articles dominated, and mathematics enjoyed a special position in the natural sciences. Driven by mathematicians at NTH, and some physicists, *Skrifter* continued to function in the 1970s as a modest medium for mathematics research, and was the only mathematics research publication produced in Norway.[819] In a global subject such as mathematics, however, this never had major significance. After 1960 *Skrifter* and *Forhandlinger* have published contributions from prominent Norwegian mathematicians, such as Atle Selberg (work published in 1942), Ernst Selmer, Thoralf A. Skolem and Viggo Brun. One important work was published by Werner Romberg (1909–2003), a German who was a professor at NTH. In 1955 he published a paper in the Society's *Forhandlinger* in which he introduced what later has been called Romberg integration, which is now a part of all numerical-analysis textbooks.[820] A number of foreign mathematicians have also contributed, even if these articles were never of a groundbreaking nature.

In addition to mathematics, articles were generally published on physics, chemistry, geology, and biology. The scope was nevertheless much less than for mathematics, and *Skrifter* did not here have the same internal discipline function. Contributions from these disciplines would eventually disappear from *Skrifter*. The last geology article was printed in 1960. The last articles in chemistry and physics were printed in 1982 and 1986, respectively. Only one article in the field of botany has been published after 1988. *Skrifter*'s mathematics tradition continued until recently, but contributions have diminished, and the position of *DKNVS Skrifter* and *Forhandlinger* as a medium in the mathematics discipline has gradually been diminished.

Even if *Skrifter* continued to have its main focus on the natural sciences, especially mathematics, this was not as pronounced from the end of the 1970s. Instead the number of humanities articles, primarily history and linguistics, grew. These academic fields, in addition to philosophy, had also earlier dominated the humanities. The social sciences were also represented, primarily pedagogy. Even though pedagogy was a subject with long traditions in Trondheim, dating back to the establishment of NLHT in 1922, it was not until the end of the 1980s that this discipline was represented in *Skrifter*. The shift

---

[819] UBIT, Spesialsamlingene. DKNVS III:a:1–90. Attachment to minutes 1973–74. Letter dated 6 March 1974 from Sigmund Selberg to NAVF.
[820] DKNVS *Forhandlinger*, Vol. XXVIII 7, 1955.

from natural science to the humanities also meant a certain linguistic shift from English to Norwegian, as articles in the humanities disciplines were published in Norwegian, in contrast to the natural sciences. Regardless of the language of publication, the number of contributions from foreign researchers also dropped, and this weakened the international profile of *Skrifter*. The change also meant that *Skrifter* took on more of the nature of a medium for presenting scientific topics focusing *beyond* the respective disciplines, instead of being a medium for development and debate *within* the respective disciplines, as it had been for mathematics. The works in this series had primarily been intended for the scientific community rather than the general public.

One important and challenging question for the Society is whether there is room for such a broad academic series dealing with natural science, the humanities, and social science in an increasingly specialized and fragmented science culture. Will *Skrifter* continue to be an attractive publication medium for researchers, and will it reach the relevant groups of readers? One benefit (as seen by researchers) of *Skrifter* compared to most other series of publications has been the possibility of being able to publish relatively large manuscripts such as treatises and monographs. Because of exchange agreements, *Skrifter* also reaches a number of recognized international libraries.

After 2000 a completely new national system was established for research documentation in Norway which has had and will have consequences for scientific publications. This research documentation system was introduced for two reasons. First, the intention was to establish better systematic knowledge about Norwegian research by making data about scientific publishing in Norway available. Second, the aim was to develop a data base for reporting statistics to the funding scheme for universities and colleges. The research documentation system was thus part of a comprehensive control and financing reform in academia. This documentation system divided scientific publications into two levels scoring different points. *Skrifter* was ranked on the lower level (level 1), where the minimum requirement was assessment by peer researchers and national authors. The question is how this type of quantification of scientific publications will affect *DKNVS Skrifter*.

Financial limitations

Printing *Skrifter* and *Forhandlinger* was the largest expense in the Society's operating budget. The surplus from revenues from funds, which pursuant to the statutes could be used to cover printing costs, was not large enough for this purpose. External funding was needed. Until the start of the 1970s the Society received printing subsidies from *Norges allmennvitenskapelige forskningsråd* (NAVF). The restructuring of NAVF's policy in this field led to the elimination of the printing subsidy. To some extent this was compensated for through increased state subsidies to the society, but these were not sufficient to cover the costs. Through the 1970s and 1980s the board made several attempts to improve the finances of *Skrifter* in both the earnings and expense columns in the budget. The board had some measure of success with this, such as some funding for publishing from external institutions, and the decision was also made to accept advertising in *Skrifter*.[821]

The financial difficulties for the series were a symptom of the generally poor financial situation of the Society. The 1960s and 70s had not been good from a financial perspective. State and other public agency subsidies, primarily from the City of Trondheim and the two Trøndelag county authorities, covered approximately half of the Society's operating expenses until the middle of the 1980s. The rest had to be covered by the Society's dividends from the fund. The operating expenses were generally connected to publishing *Skrifter*, and then to administration expenses (payroll and office costs). Beyond this the Society's revenues did not allow for much financial activity. As mentioned above, no money was awarded with the Society's prizes, and expenses from the academy meetings were also kept to a minimum. In spite of its modest operating budgets, the Society found it difficult to adequately cover expenses in the long term.

After a hefty increase in the fund capital in the 1950s, this gradually diminished after 1960. From 1950 to 1960 the fund capital had been doubled from NOK 500,000 to NOK 1 million, which was relatively substantial growth when considered in relation to inflation during this period.[822] The largest single contribution was made in 1959 by Harry Borthen (1884–1963), a ship owner who made an endowment "to promote scientific research of importance for shipping and ship technology, including marine biology."[823] For a number of years grants were allocated from the fund to Trondheim biological station. The endowment, which amounted to NOK 100,000, was the largest donation from any individual after the reestablishment of the academy in 1926, and Borthen was elected as an honorary member because of this donation.[824] The research vessel for *Trondhjems biologiske stasjon*, which was launched in 1962, was also named the "Harry Borthen." This ship was launched in 1962 and was financed by funds from NAVF. The financial situation therefore appeared quite bright when the Society celebrated its 200th anniversary, but developments during the next two decades did not in any way satisfy the positive expectations. In 1980 the fund capital amounted to only NOK 1.3 million. Compared to an inflation rate of 247 per cent during the same period, this meant a heavy depletion of the real value of the fund capital, and there were several reasons for this. First, the Society did not receive any new fund capital of significance during this period. Second, it appears that the management of the fund was not only very careful but also very passive. Third, little of the dividends from the fund were used to increase the fund capital. Instead most of it was transferred to the operating account. The negative financial development corresponds well with the Society's general development during this period, which was dominated by stagnation and a loss of legitimacy.

---

[821] UBIT, Spesialsamlingene. DKNVS II:2. Board meetings. Minutes board minutes 2 June 1983.

[822] Price growth (the consumer price index) was 56.8 per cent from 1950 to 1960. The Society's fund capital increased by around 100 percent.

[823] Minutes joint meeting 13 May 1963 in DKNVS *Forhandlinger*, Vol. 36, 1963, 9.

[824] DKNVS *Forhandlinger*, Vol. 33, 1960, 7.

At the start of the 1980s it was becoming increasingly obvious that not only was the Society's financial situation weak, but also that the accounting and budgeting practices were inadequate. In reality the Society had been under-budgeting for years. Printing costs, the largest individual cost item, had run over budget for several consecutive years. The under-budgeting had depleted the Society's disposable funds.[825] Nor were these always used in accordance with the individual fund statutes. In 1982 these matters came under strong criticism from the auditors.[826] Bearing this in mind, the accounting practice was thoroughly reviewed and revised. Between 1983 and 1985 clear lines were drawn between the Society's operating accounts on the one hand and the fund accounts on the other. Furthermore, the management of the funds was changed in accordance with the regulations in the Foundation Act, and the management of the approximately forty Society funds was rationalized.[827]

The change in the accounting system was a decisive factor for a long-term improvement of the Society's financial situation. At the same time the board was also actively endeavoring to strengthen the Society's fund capital. For the first time since 1959 it received some new funds, including some earmarked for scientific publications. Together with the restructured and more active management of the fund capital this led to a total increase in the fund capital, not only in nominal value, but also in real value.[828] The man who was the principal actor behind righting the Society's financial situation was Sverre Westin (1909–1992), professor of technical physics at NTH (UNIT) and elected to the Society in 1950. In 1983 he was awarded the Gunnerus medal.[829] The positive development continued into the 1990s. The result was that the fixed fund capital in 2000 amounted to more than NOK 5.8 million, which meant there was real growth since 1980.[830]

A modernization of the so-called "donating members" scheme was an important stage in the financial recovery. This type of membership, which derived from the 1926 statutes, was granted when a substantial donation had been made to the Society. The

---

[825] The touchable fund money includes earnings on funds that may be freely used by the Society in accordance with the statutes. The untouchable fund money includes the original legates/funds in addition to a portion of the annual earnings bound by the statutes to be added to the original fund/legate.

[826] DKNVS *Forhandlinger* 1983, 20–21. Declaration dated 5 April 1983. Haakon Olsen and H.J.A. Keyberg.

[827] DKNVS *Forhandlinger* 1986, 18–19; DKNVS *Forhandlinger* 1987, 16.

[828] The fund capital increased from 1980 to 1990 by almost NOK 2.6 million, due to the comprehensive sale of shares in 1985, yielding a profit of NOK 942 635.55. DKNVS *Forhandlinger* 1986: 20.

[829] For biography see: DKNVS *Forhandlinger* 1993, 53–56.

[830] Statistics Norway. Consumer price index and wage statistics. (08. Prices, price indexes and state of the market indicators. 06.05. Wages, labor costs. Table wages per normal work year 1946–2007.) The growth of the fund capital was 338 per cent, while the consumer price index increased by 162.4 per cent. The Society's costs nevertheless increased by more than the consumer price index because wage development in the period was higher than the consumer price index, but even when corrected for this factor there was a real growth of the fund capital.

last donating member had been elected in 1964, at which time the Society had a total of nine donating members. This number declined as these members passed away, and in 1984 the last donating member of the Society, consul Harald Setsaas, died. In the 1989 statutes the category of "donating member" was changed to "associated member," and the criteria for this type of membership were somewhat more liberal. A person who was interested in science and contributed to the purposes of the Society could be elected as a member.[831] This made it possible to have members who may not have been personally wealthy, but who through their positions in society, business, and industry were able to promote the Society and its purposes financially and in other ways. In 1997 it became possible for institutions to be associated members.[832] The first associated members were elected in the 1990s.[833] 1998 became a milestone year when a number of personal associated members and institutions were elected.[834] The Society's *praeses* from 1996 to 1999, Peder Borgen, professor of religious science, was a major recruiter of new associated members. Borgen was also the first to receive the Society's first *praeses* chain, donated by some of the new members at the gala meeting in 1999.[835] The chain consisted of 32 slightly oval silver plates that were linked together. The motif engraved on the plates alternated between the Society's small seal (the letter seal) and the motto from the Society's large seal: SIC NOS NOS NOBIS, which may be rendered as "Thus we work but not for ourselves." The central motif on the breast plate was an enlarged gilded version of the small seal.

Far greater financial benefit was found in cooperation agreements and donations. A few years later, the Society received two substantial fund donations from one of the Society's new associated members, Trond Lykke. At the gala meeting in 1999, Lykke presented a gift of NOK one million for a fund to award scientific prizes to young researchers.[836] The year after, the Society received another NOK million from Trond Lykke to establish a fund to grant scholarships to promising Master's degree students

---

[831] Statutes for DKNVS passed on March 14, 1989, confirmed by Royal Resolution on August 25, 1989.

[832] Adopted at a joint meeting on December 8, 1997.

[833] Trondheim Katedralskole's principal Gunnar Paulen was elected in 1995.

[834] Odd Arntzen, Director at the College of Sør-Trøndelag, Sverre Dragsten, senior judge at Frostating Court, Terje Herrem, Supreme Court lawyer, Trond Lykke, merchant, Trondheim, Jarle Malvik, Director of Thomas Angells Stiftelser, Kjell Okkenhaug, director, Vigdis Moe Skarstein, university director at NTNU and Erik Kristoffer Solberg, director. Institutions that became members in 1998: FOKUS BANK ASA represented by Bjarne Borgersen, General Director in Trondheim; SINTEF, represented by Roar Arntzen, General Director in Trondheim; STATOIL Forskningssenter represented by Roar Arntzen, Director of Research; Trondheim Katedralskole represented by Anne Lise Drege, principal.

[835] The chain was designed by Øistein Rønæss together with general secretary of the Society Harald Nissen. The chain was donated by Odd Arntzen, Sverre Dragsten, Terje Herrem, Trond Lykke, Jarle Malvik, Erik Kristoffer Solberg and Kjell Okkenhaug. See: DKNVS *Forhandlinger* 1999, 65–66 for a closer description of the chain.

[836] "Kjøpmann Trond Lykkes fond for vitenskapelig pris til unge forskere." (Merchant Trond Lykke's fund for scientific prizes to be given to young researchers).

and very young researchers not receiving any significant scholarships from other sources.[837] As we have seen, in the middle of the 1980s the Society and the foundation had established separate prizes for young researchers consisting of a diploma and a lithograph. The donation from Lykke made it possible to grant not only honor to young researchers, but also financial backing.[838]

In 1998 the Society entered into a completely new type of cooperation agreement with one of the new associated members, Fokus Bank.[839] This agreement made the bank the principal sponsor of the Society from 1998 through 2002, and the bank donated substantial annual amounts to projects operated under the aegis of the Society. The majority of this went to the presentation project *Byen, bygdene og kunnskapen* (The city, the districts and knowledge) which was launched in 1997 as DKNVS's gift to Trondheim on the occasion of the city's millennium anniversary. Similar agreements were later made with other associated institution members. The Society also succeeded in obtaining funding for specific projects from various public and private institutions. These enabled DKNVS to have more freedom to launch various schemes and projects under the auspices of the Society and also in cooperation with other institutions.

Thus the very critical financial position the Society had been in early in the 1980s was overcome, and the Society succeeded in gaining greater flexibility. However, the financial situation was still not ideal, and it continued to put restraints on what the Society was able to do for science.

---

[837] "I.K. Lykkes fond for priser til studenter og forskere." (I.K. Lykke's fund for prizes for students and researchers). DKNVSa, DKNVS press release 31 August 2000. In 2003 the two funds were merged into one which covered the purposes of the previous two separate funds.

[838] Initially each prize amounted to NOK 25,000, but in 2008 it was decided that the amount would be doubled starting in 2009.

[839] Fokus Bank was a regional commercial bank headquartered in Trondheim, originally a merger of seven smaller regional commercial banks.

One Society

The efforts from the 1980s to strengthen the legitimacy and social relevance of the Society, which was particularly focused on giving it a stronger presence in the local scientific public sphere, had positive results. Through this new orientation, the Society succeeded in changing the unilateral impression of a closed society of and for its members into a picture of a Society with legitimacy within the scientific community and within the scientific public sphere. Throughout the 1990s and into the new century, this ambition to strengthen this more public approach was continued. This new orientation in the 1980s did not, however, change the Society's non-interventionist stance in research-policy issues, an attitude that we saw expressed in the controversy over the scientific oath in the 1970s. However, a new century also brought changes in this field, and the Society developed a completely new approach to the research-policy field based on the ambition to influence and set policy. This shift was generally due to the comprehensive changes in the societal organization of scientific research, where greater importance was attached to program-based research, and to the introduction of new forms and instruments of governance at the universities in Norway. These changes gave the traditionally independent science academies more opportunities to have influence and be heard. The Society's opportunity to play a more active role in the scientific public sphere was, however, impeded by the fact that to the outside world DKNVS appeared to be a divided institution, with the Society (the academy) on the one side and the foundation on the other. If DKNVS was to be taken as a serious voice in the public sphere, it would have to stand united, and after a complicated negotiation process, from 2002 DKNVS stood as a united Society.

A united scientific society

The split from 1926 had dominated *DKNVS i Trondhjem* ever since, and created an asymmetrical and divided institution without substantial unity. The two institutions had different purposes and functions. While the museum managed large collections, performed research, instructed the general public, and taught on the university level, the Society was a membership institution with three types of activities: meetings for members with lectures, publication of scientific papers, and awarding of symbolic prizes for efforts in fields of science and culture. The scope of the activities and the size of the budgets could not be compared, and qualitatively resulted in completely different institutions. As a university institution the museum experienced strong institutional growth, while the Society struggled with a poor financial situation and legitimacy issues, so the differences between the two institutions only grew. The institutional level of independence was also different. The museum had become completely dependent on state funding, and as a museum and university it was controlled by state culture and knowledge policy. The Society, on the other hand, was an independent scientific institution, even if it received some public funding. But it had quite restricted financial resources with which to exercise its choice of activities. After the anniversary the gap between the two continued to grow. DKNVS's asymmetry was getting bigger and bigger, and there was no end in sight as long as *DKNVS Stiftelsen* managed the museum. A more united or coordinated DKNVS was a practical impossibility.

The transfer of the museum by the foundation created a completely new symmetry between DKNVS's two divisions. Financially they were relatively equal, even if the foundation continued to have a somewhat better situation than the Society. The finances of both institutions were primarily based on the management of funds. Neither of them was a practicing research institution anymore, but their purpose was to initiate and support scientific activity, and to promote scientific knowledge in the science community and in society in general. From such a perspective the transfer of the museum by *DKNVS Stiftelsen* was liberating, an event that provided for a reorganization and reunification of DKNVS. The existence of two institutions, both called *Det Kongelige Norske Videnskabers Selskab*, whereof one had added the soubriquet *Stiftelsen*, each with their own *praeses* and separate boards, was both confusing and meaningless to the outside world. This undermined the importance and legitimacy of DKNVS, and eroded the opportunity to work efficiently in the science community and in society in general.

The transfer of the museum thus allowed for closer connections and organizational ties between the two divisions of *DKNVS i Trondhjem*, and therefore the question of some sort of coordination was discussed after the transfer. Through an agreement between the general secretaries of *Stiftelsen* and *Akademiet*, Professor Gunnar Sundnes and Professor Olaf I. Rønning, it was decided that the academy and the foundation would be permitted to use administration premises in the museum buildings. Eventually financial cooperation was also established to cover administrative expenses.[840] As we saw in the previous chapter, cooperation was also established on other specific matters, but any closer form of coordination between the two divisions was not achieved. The old conflicts had not disappeared, and the situation was too dominated by a mutual lack of trust. The administrations of both institutions were, moreover, concerned about their own institutional problems and challenges. The foundation needed to find a new function and legitimacy after the loss of the library, while the Society was facing large financial, organizational, and legitimacy challenges.

---

[840] Conversation with Turid Fredagsvik.

In the middle of the 1990s new initiatives were made to create a united DKNVS. After the middle of the 1980s both institutions had strengthened their positions. The foundation had established a new function and identity as a research foundation. The Society had undertaken an internal reform process, and had strengthened its activities and legitimacy as a science society by adopting a far more active role within the science community and for the general public.

In the course of the 1990s the legitimacy of the science academies as social institutions had also been strengthened. This could be seen in several ways. *Det Norske Videnskaps-Akademi* had managed to assume a far more central role in the Norwegian research policy landscape, for example by establishing *Senter for høyere studier* (the Centre for Advanced Studies), where prominent researchers in three selected fields in the humanities, social science/law, and theoretical natural science were invited for a one-year stay, and the award of two new international prizes, *Abelprisen* (the Abel Prize), for excellent scientific work in mathematics, and *Kavliprisen* (the Kavli Prize), for excellent research in the fields of nanoscience, neuroscience, and astrophysics.[841] A new regional science academy had also been established in Norway when *Agder Akademi*, originally established in 1962 as a folk academy in 2002, was reestablished as *Agder Vitenskapsakademi* (Agder Science Academy).[842] After being marginalized in the 1970s, the science academies now experienced a renaissance. The new keener focus on quality and elite research, generally a response to the quantitative expansion of research in recent decades, helped reinforce the status and legitimacy of the science academies, and contributed to giving the academies greater political and cultural flexibility. The traditional defense of science academies for free basic research gained new relevance due to the increasingly program-controlled nature of research. Linked to the new rhetoric dealing with quality and elite research, a view of science that had previously been defined as conservative and outdated now gained new relevance. The traditionally independent position of the science academies, independent of state authorities and university and research institutions, was now seen as a particularly valuable asset. In such a new context, the fact that DKNVS was locked in old conflicts, lacking unity, appeared as petty and myopic and lacking in the innovative pioneer spirit.

In 1995 Gunnar Sundnes, who was still the foundation secretary but also a member of the Society, addressed the issue of this lack of unity within DKNVS. First, he reestablished DKNVS's joint committee, which had not been in action since 1960. Second, he addressed the old issue about names, and re-introduced the old proposal that the academy division should add the name "academy" after DKNVS. Sundnes also

---

[841] The Abel Award is named after the Norwegian mathematician Niels Henrik Abel (1802–1829). The Kavli Award was initiated and funded by the Kavli Foundation, established by the Norwegian-American engineer and businessman Fred Kavli (b. 1927).

[842] *Agder Akademi* was reestablished in 2002, but changed its name to *Agder Vitenskapsakademi* (Agder Science Academy) only in 2003. Agder Akademi Årbok 2002; Agder Vitenskapsakademi Årbok 2002.

argued that to strengthen DKNVS the existing but dormant joint statutes would have to be complied with—for example, by allowing the chairman of the joint committee to represent all parts of DKNVS outside its walls. Sundnes did not have the complete reorganization or unification of DKNVS as a goal; his intention was to strengthen the face DKNVS showed to the outside world, and to place the two institutions on equal footing internally under the existing statutes.[843]

The Society's board rejected both proposals out of hand.[844] Any confusion arising from the names was the foundation's problem, not the Society's, and was thus an irrelevant issue for the Society. Behind the board's irreconcilable attitude to the foundation there was the long-simmering irritation that the Society had not been consulted about transferring the museum to the state in 1984. Based on the statues, the foundation was fully authorized to negotiate such an agreement alone, as the joint statutes established that both entities were autonomous within their respective fields. The joint statutes also contained a section stating that cases that concerned both institutions should be dealt with by the joint committee. But the joint committee had not been active since the anniversary in 1960, and no initiative was taken to address the issue of the transfer of the museum. The fact that such a fundamental issue was not formally discussed at all in DKNVS truly reveals the depth of the institutional divide. In reality there was no DKNVS with two divisions, rather there were two parallel and independent DKNVS institutions. The Society's total disinterest in DKNVS as a whole was in many ways a reflection of this situation. There is little to indicate that the board at this point in time saw the existing division into two as a serious problem. The Society's strategy document from 1997 did not devote much attention to a united DKNVS.[845]

Several academy members with trusted positions in the foundation attempted to encourage greater coordination, but there was no breakthrough on this issue until the election of Karsten Jakobsen as the *praeses* of the Society in 2000. Karsten Jakobsen (b. 1928) was a professor emeritus of engineering design at NTNU, and was elected to the academy in 1991. Jacobsen was the rector at NTH from 1990 to 1993, and rector at UNIT from 1993 to 1996, and thus he had first-hand knowledge of the controversial restructuring of UNIT into NTNU. Jakobsen thus had very solid experience as a leader, and he had a broad contact network in the university environment in Trondheim. He was also resolute and pragmatic, qualities necessary to resolve the deeply entrenched tensions and animosities. Jacobsen cooperated well with the then-*praeses* of the foundation, Jon Ofstad Lamvik (b. 1929), who was the *praeses* from 1997 to 2001. Lamvik, a medical director at the hematological department of the Regional Hospital in Trondheim (now the University Hospital of Trondheim), and professor emeritus of hematology and clinical immunology at NTNU, had been a member of the academy since 1973.

---

[843] Letter September 13, 1995 and December 7, 1995 from Gunnar Sundnes to the board of DKNVS.
[844] Board decision DKNVS October 26, 1995; Letter October 31, 1995 and December 10, 1995 from DKNVS to Gunnar Sundnes.
[845] DKNVSa. Memo "DKNVS i framtida" (DKNVS in the future), adopted at the board meeting on August 15, 1997.

Both Jacobsen and Lamvik wanted to unite DKNVS, but they initially did not see eye to eye on how to bring this about. Negotiating organizational solutions proved to be very demanding, not least because any form of unification that implied that one of the institutions would be incorporated within the other was politically impossible. The process was democratic and any final decision and solution would need consent and legitimacy from both institutions. The coordination would also need to allow for the fact that the two institutions, in spite of coinciding purposes, had different cultures. The academy was an independent and exclusive scientific membership institution, in which its function as a scientific forum for members was absolutely essential. The foundation had to comply with the rules and regulations of the public authorities, which stated clearly how the foundation fund was to be administered, how elections were to be held and what composition the joint board was to have. The latter issue posed some legal complications that needed resolution before coordination could take place.

The new statutes which entered into force on January 1, 2002, therefore reflected compromise. The two units were maintained, but with new symmetrical names: *Det Kongelige Norske Videnskabers Selskabs Akademi* (the Academy of the Royal Norwegian Society of Sciences and Letters) and *Det Kongelige Norske Videnskabers Selskabs Stiftelse* (the Foundation of the Royal Norwegian Society of Sciences and Letters). In abbreviated form, the two divisions were called *Akademiet* (the academy) and *Stiftelsen* (the foundation). While the latter retained its former name, the academy was given a new name.[846]

From then on DKNVS was the name of the united society, and the two divisions would be led by a joint board and a joint administration for all of DKNVS. This was absolutely fundamental, as now DKNVS had one board which functioned as the administration of the institution within and outside its walls. The board had control over all the finances, including the funds that had been managed by the foundation and the funds that were managed by the academy. To preserve the academy's function as a membership institution, it was given the majority on the board, four of a total of seven members of the board, including the *praeses* and *vice-praeses*, who were both elected by the academy members and the two heads of division. To comply with the Act relating to Foundations, the remaining three members of the board were publicly nominated by, respectively, the Ministry of Education, Research and Church Affairs, NTNU, by the senate, and *NTNU Vitenskapsmuseet*, represented by the board.[847] The new statutes received approbation by the protector on November 30, 2001. The protector was then HM King Harald V who had taken over as the protector of DKNVS after the death of HM King Olav V on January 17, 1991. When HM King Harald took over as regent, Norway also had its first Queen since 1938, HM Queen Sonja, who was elected as royal honorary member of the Society in 1995.

---

[846] For clarity this chapter will use the names *Akademiet* (the academy) and *Stiftelsen* (the foundation) when specifically referring to one of the two divisions, regardless of whether the time before or after 2002 is being referred to, while DKNVS, *Videnskabsselskabet* (Science Society) and *Selskabet* (Society) are used about the institution as such.

[847] Statutes for DKNVS in force from 1 January 2002.

Popular scientific focus—tradition and renewal

In 1997 Trondheim celebrated its millennium anniversary. Through its participation in the anniversary celebrations, DKNVS managed to make the institution visible to the general population, and to make the institution far more active in the cultural-political field in the city. Based on Bishop Gunnerus's pastoral letter from 1758, and the DKNVS objectives paragraph, teaching and the imparting of knowledge to the general population were selected as the Society's contribution to the city anniversary. Presenting knowledge to "the reasonable, but uneducated" had been Gunnerus's encouragement to the clergy in his diocese. Even if the general population in AD 2000 was a long way from "uneducated", in the way Bishop Gunnerus had used the term, his encouragement also had meaning 250 years later. By placing the imparting of knowledge in focus, the Society managed to combine tradition and heritage with relevance to our time and our society.

"Byen—elven—kunnskapen" (The city—the river—knowledge) was selected as the overriding theme, and was also indicative of the geographical area of activity, which is the catchment areas of the Nea and Nidelv rivers, reaching all the way from the border to Sweden in the east to the Trondheim fjord in the west, where the final section of the water course meanders through the city of Trondheim. The topics embraced a number of subjects, including history, archeology, botany, zoology, geology, technology, and environmental protection. This idea was an extension of the ambitions from the 1980s to create a new scientific public stage, but it also represented something completely new. The form of presentation was far more varied, ranging from traditional lectures to guided trips and urban walks, and also longer excursions. Another new idea was that DKNVS drew on resource persons outside the ranks of the Society for planning the project. The idea for the project originally came from outside, from persons connected with the Museum of Natural History and Archaeology and the NTNU Library.[848] The Museum of Natural History and Archaeology, DKNVS's old museum, thus also became an important partner in the project. Financial contributions from external institutions were another requirement, and the heaviest contributors were the County Governor of Sør-Trøndelag County and NTNU. The anniversary project was initiated while the Society (the academy) and the foundation still continued as autonomous institutions, but the project was a joint project right from the start, toward which the foundation, especially, made a financial contribution. Thus the project came to have a positive impact internally in DKNVS as well.

During the anniversary year, a total of 80 events were arranged with generally very good attendance. In addition, "Byen—elven—kunnskapen" received very good cover-

---

[848] The originator of the idea was the senior librarian at the NTNU Library, Kari Christensen, who with Astrid Langvatn, the administrative head of the Museum of Natural History and Archaeology, produced the project concept.

age in the media, in spite of strong competition for attention during the city's anniversary celebrations. DKNVS was able to profile itself in a new and positive way through the project. It was a success, and showed that there was definitely general interest in this type of presentation of popular science. Bearing this in mind, it was decided to continue the project, and DKNVS succeeded in obtaining funding from various external institutions, a necessity for continued operations. NTNU, Trondheim local authority and for periods of time private sponsors were particularly important.[849] NTNU was also a crucial partner. In 2003, for example, the university established a permanent position to deal with the project.[850] But the owner of the project continued to be DKNVS.

Some minor but nevertheless important revisions were put into effect this way. The name was changed to "Byen, bygdene og kunnskapen" (The city, the districts and knowledge), to demonstrate that the target group was the entire regional population and not only Trondheim, and that several of the events were arranged in the districts. A sub-project focusing on children, "Children and nature," was also introduced. The program leaflet was also renewed. Under the heading "Kunnskapskalenderen" (the knowledge calendar), DKNVS invited other organizations offering popular science presentations to announce their events in the program leaflet. The response was positive—in the autumn of 2008, for example, some forty organizations and institutions were represented in the calendar. A searchable web version of the calendar was also prepared which was operated by NTNU. DKNVS's role as coordinator thus enabled the events of many other organizations to reach an audience, and the coordinator role was also important for the establishment and testing of new presentation forms, such as through cooperation between the university and Trøndelag Theater.

A decade after the project had been started, the around 150,000 inhabitants in the city of Trondheim, and quite a few of the remaining 250,000 inhabitants of the two Trøndelag counties, had been offered an uncommonly broad selection of popular science events, which showed the general population and the scientific community that the Society was an institution with social relevance and legitimacy. Through the new coordinator role for popular science presentations and teaching, the Society had found a need that so far had not been satisfied, a scientific niche between the large and weighty scientific and research organizations. Through the coordinator role, the Society, laboring under heavy tradition, also managed to incorporate the contemporary new organization trend, networking. With the project "Byen, bygdene og kunnskapen," DKNVS in many ways took the opposite road compared to general trends in academia, where scientific presentations to the general public had less and less benefit for individual researchers and for research institutions.

---

[849] Fokus Bank, which gave funding for a five-year period from 1998 to 2002, was the largest private sponsor.

[850] NTNU agreed to cover two-thirds of the wage payroll and parts of the operating expenses. Bjørn Sæther, who had led the project since its inception, was employed in this position.

Research projects under the aegis of the united DKNVS

The foundation's tradition of granting funding to research projects was continued in the united DKNVS. In 2003 the board decided to grant annual funding for a period of five years to a new interdisciplinary research project, "Minting at the Archbishop's palace in medieval Trondheim, Norway." This was an interdisciplinary project with participating scientists from materials technology, archaeology, cultural history, and numismatics. The objective of the project was to bring about a broad scientific documentation of the Archbishop's activities in the minting factories, and to put this documentation into an economic and power-political context.[851] In 2005 the project for studying the language history of the Trøndelag region received funding for a three-year period. The local dialect spoken in the two Trøndelag counties (Nord-Trøndelag and Sør-Trøndelag) plays an important role in making them a separate Norwegian region, and this spoken dialect also has an important identity-forming function for those who are "*trønder*"—persons from Trøndelag. The aim of the project was to both clarify how the current spoken language helps define Trøndelag as a special Norwegian area, and to study how the dialects of Trøndelag can be characterized and defined as far back in time as there are sources, i.e. to the first rock carvings with Runic inscriptions from around the 500s–600s.[852] The final research project "Koding og læring av luktinformasjon hos et skadeinsekt" (Coding and learning of odor information in a pest) was initiated in 2007, with funding for three years.[853] The project's aim is to identify the neural network involved in appetitive and aversive learning in *Heliothis virescens*, a night-flying moth. The major part of the project involves intracellular registrations from nerve cells in the smelling system by characterizing these physiologically and morphologically. The aim is also to find the connections with the smell and taste paths involved in associative learning and memory. The nerve cells that are characterized will then be placed in a standard brain atlas, i.e. a reconstructed average model of the brain, together with identified brain cells in the taste path.[854]

More attention was paid to funding both natural science and humanities research projects. The Society's financial situation sadly inhibited regular announcements of research funds, as any project funding needed to be undertaken in an ongoing way for brief periods of time. The selection of projects therefore primarily occurred on the basis of submitted applications from researchers initiated by the researchers. This applied to the two latter projects, both the result of self-initiated applications from the researchers in question. On the other hand, the first project (the language history of

---

[851] The research project was led by Otto Lohne at NTNU.

[852] *DKNVS Årbok 2005*, 50. The research project was led by Arnold Dalen, Ragnar Hagland and Ola Stemshaug; Department of Scandinavian Studies and Comparative Literature, NTNU.

[853] This project was led by Hanna Mustaparta, Department of Biology, NTNU. DKNVS contributes to the project funding with up to NOK 600,000 per year for three years.

[854] *DKNVS Årbok*, 2007, 50–51.

the Trøndelag region) was selected from applications submitted in connection with interdisciplinary research funding that had been announced by NTNU. An important point for the Society when funding good basic research projects was that due to their independent position they were able to grant funding to good projects that fell outside the program areas defined by the Research Council of Norway and outside NTNU's strategic focal areas of research.

A society without material structures

We have stated this before, but I am now stating it again. The important social aspect between us is not functioning as long as we are an academy without permanent premises, and with no means to acquire something better.

This was a statement made by *praeses* Grete Authén Blom in her speech at the 1985 anniversary celebration. At the start of a new millennium, the housing situation remained the same. In spite of its venerable old age DKNVS did not have its own building or adequate premises in Trondheim. All the library and museum buildings constructed throughout the time of DKNVS were transferred to the state together with the museum. In the negotiations with the state authorities on the transfer of the museum, the foundation managed to put in a stipulation that DKNVS would have the right to use office premises in the museum buildings, and as mentioned previously, the academy also was allowed to use office premises and a small meeting room for board meetings and the like, which at the time ensured that the day-to-day operations had much better working conditions.

Member meetings continued to be arranged in the 200-year-old Harsdorff building belonging to *Trondheim Katedralskole*. However, its splendid large hall, called *Festsalen*, was not suitable for informal socializing after the meetings, and at the start of the 1990s initiatives were made to obtain more appropriate premises for the social aspect. Through contributions from both the academy and the foundation, two large rooms adjacent to *Festsalen* were redecorated so they were appropriate for social events and the serving of light refreshments after the academy meetings. *Festsalen* was decorated with paintings of DKNVS's founders Gunnerus, Suhm and Schøning, and their earlier protectors, King Haakon VII and King Olav V. At the gala meeting in 1997, in connection with Trondheim's millennium celebrations, a new portrait of the protector of the Royal Norwegian Society of Sciences and Letters, HM King Harald V, was unveiled in *Festsalen*. The portrait was painted by Kari Grasmo. *Selskabet for Trondhjems Bys Vel* had contributed to the funding together with DKNVS. The long-established connection with *Katedralskolen* was further strengthened in 1998 when *Katedralskolen* was elected as an associate member.[855]

---

[855] DKNVS *Forhandlinger* 1998, 274.

In 2003 the celebrations for the gala meeting were moved from Hotel Britannia, the oldest hotel in the city, to the Archbishop's Palace. The Archbishop's seat in Trondheim dates back to the 1000s, and the large hall of the Archbishop's Palace was constructed in the middle of the 12th century. The hall, which had been restored to the style it was during the 1600s, with tiled floors, green wall drapes and the remains of frescos, was one of the Norwegian State's foremost residences for entertaining guests, creating a completely different and grand ambience around the events on the day of the gala meeting.

These improvements were not, however, an expression that the dream of owning their own premises had faded away, but how the thinking around what functions such a building should satisfy had changed. In accordance with the ambition of the Society to assume a more prominent and active role in general society, other needs had become more prominent. A general increase in activities, linked to the preparations for the 250th anniversary celebrations in 2010, created the need for more space for the administration and larger and more distinguished premises for arranging seminars and various events. To make it possible to invite members and other researchers to stay for a short period of time for the cause of research, there was also a strong wish to have more space for researcher workplaces. In the search for a suitable building, the old County Governor's house (*Fylkesmannsbolig*) at Kalvskinnet was found to be appropriate. It was situated on a small rise by the river *Nidelven*, inside a small park and just a stone's throw from the old buildings housing the Museum of Natural History and Archaeology and the library. This house was being used by NTNU, but was owned by the state. Negotiations for permission to use the building were still continuing in 2008.[856] Both the state authorities and NTNU had a positive response to the Society's wish to use the building, but a takeover would require the start of a large new building adjacent to the Museum of Natural History and Archaeology, NTNU. Financing of such a building was still unresolved in 2008.

DKNVS's efforts in the new millennium to acquire its own building indicate a far more assertive institution than the case was when *praeses* Blom summarized the status in 1985. The fact that DKNVS now appeared as a single institution to the surrounding world was vital. The change in the premises project also reflects the shift that had taken place in DKNVS during this period. From unilaterally thinking about a building for the internal collective of the Society, now the building was seen as necessary for external activities.

Challenges and ambitions—towards 250 years

The internal unification of DKNVS in combination with the regained legitimacy and status of the science academies formed the important underpinning for the Society to adopt a more assertive role in the science community, locally as well as nationally. At the start of the 1990s the Norwegian research council system underwent a radical reorganization. In 1992 Parliament decided to merge NAVF, NTNF and the other research

---

[856] DKNVSa. Recommendation from DKNVS's building committee May 9, 2008.

councils into one large research council, *Norges Forskningsråd*, NFR (the Research Council of Norway). NFR was divided into six academic fields, and as no distinction was made between basic research and applied research, basic research did not have any special anchor in the new research council. The model was also radical in the sense that it deviated from corresponding research councils in other Western countries. In spite of this, the reform had a great degree of support from the Norwegian research communities. *Det Norske Videnskaps-Akademi* represented one of the few exceptions. However, DKNVS did not involve itself in this issue. In 2002 the NFR model was revised so that basic research received a clearer institutional basis. The council was divided into three functionally based units, where one department was responsible for basic research and subject-discipline development (the science department).[857]

As we have suggested earlier, DKNVS had no tradition for getting involved in research-policy issues, and the reorganization of the research council system was therefore not formally discussed and commented on by the Society. Nor did this change have any direct impact on the Society as an institution, as it had already lost its representative in NAVF in 1970. However, from 2003 there was a clear change in the Society's practice in this field. For the first time the Society submitted commentary on a proposed public report, a report relating to a new Act for universities and colleges.[858] DKNVS had not been appointed by the ministry as one of the bodies for official comments, but took the initiative to comment on the report. This means that the Society was put on the list of bodies that were requested to make official comments in other cases also relating to university and research policy.[859]

The proposed amendment primarily concerned changes in the governance structure of universities and colleges and their relationship to the state authorities. The Society was critical of the majority recommendation on a number of matters, such as the proposal to have an external majority on the board and external chairman of the board, and the proposal of a foundation-like model where universities and colleges would be reorganized into separate legal bodies in the form of self-owning institutions. The Society concluded that the majority's proposal for an organization form would mean that the institutions of higher education would develop in the direction of service institutions where the administration and the management would have full control of the total work capacity of the teaching staff, and where financial-utility criteria would govern academic activities. The Society therefore recommended that the minority proposal, which proposed a strong element of continued academic autonomy, should be used as the basis for the new Act relating to universities and colleges.[860]

---

[857] Skoie, *Norsk forskningspolitikk i etterkrigstiden* (Norwegian research policy after WW II), 118–19, 127, 161.

[858] NOU 2003:25. *Ny lov om universiteter og høyskoler* (New Act relating to universities and colleges).

[859] Conversation with Karsten Jacobsen.

[860] DKNVSa. DKNVS. Høringsuttalelse om Ryssdalsutvalgets innstilling om *Ny lov om universiteter og høyskoler* (NOU 2003:25) (Hearing statement on the Ryssdal Committee's recommendation relating to New act concerning universities and colleges) 20 January 2004.

The Society was far from the only body critical of the recommendation; the universities and colleges also objected to many of the proposals. The final amendments to the Act were consequently modified on a number of points, one being that state universities and colleges would continue to have the status of administrative bodies with special authorization. An external majority on the board was also rejected, while the proposal for an external chairman of the board was retained.[861] All in all, the reformed Act was a clear expression of the growing influence of management thinking in university and college policy. The changes were in accordance with the general international trend, as voiced by the OECD and the EU, in the direction of "entrepreneurial universities", in response to the fundamental changes in the role of universities in a global knowledge society. This led to fundamental changes in the social legitimacy conditions for scientific research and universities, where the purpose of universities is more strongly defined as contributing to the national competitive power in a globalized world.[862] The Society's decision to enter the national research-policy arena was a new element in the history of the Society—unless we look all the way back to Gunnerus and his endeavor to create a university in Norway. The Society's entrance into this arena also demonstrates another aspect of the institution; through the board, management was now much more prepared to get involved in general society on behalf of the members.

The Society also became involved in other specific research-policy areas, such as cooperating long-term with *Norges Tekniske Vitenskapsakademi* to promote fish farming as a national priority area. The NTVA and DKNVS published two strategy documents, "Norway's opportunities for added value in the biomarine industry" in 1999 and "Exploitation of Marine Living Resources—Global Opportunities for Norwegian Expertise" in 2006.[863] The cooperation between DKNVS and NTVA, which also involved other institutions in the Norwegian aquaculture industry and research, was also an example of the Society increasingly establishing cooperative relations with other scientific institutions, regionally, nationally, and also internationally.

Several international prizes were established in Norway after 2000. As previously mentioned, the Abel Prize and the Kavli prize were awarded by DNVA in Oslo, and the Holberg International Memorial prize was awarded in Bergen to researchers for outstanding scholarly work in the humanities, social sciences, law, and theology. Thus Oslo and Bergen awarded respected international prizes, but not Trondheim. This was a contributing factor behind DKNVS's initiative to establish an international prize

---

[861] Proposition to Stortinget no. 79 (2003–2004). *Om lov om universiteter og høyskole* (On the Act relating to universities and colleges).

[862] Kristensen, *Ideer om et universitet. Det moderne universitets idehistorie fra 1800 til i dag* (Ideas about a university. The history of ideas of the modern university from 1800 to the present), 14–15.

[863] *Norges muligheter for verdiskaping innen havbruk.* Utredning fra Arbeidsgruppen for havbruk oppnevnt av Det Kongelige Norske Videnskabers Selskab og Norges Tekniske Vitenskapsakademi. Trondheim, October 1999; *Exploitation of Marine Living Resources—Global Opportunities for Norwegian Expertise.* Report from a working group appointed by The Royal Norwegian Society of Sciences and Letters (DKNVS) and Norwegian Academy of Technological Sciences (NTVA), 2006.

based in Trondheim. In the summer of 2007 the Society, in conjunction with the NTVA, which had been headquartered in Trondheim since its founding in 1955, proposed to the Norwegian Government that an international technology prize for sustainable development should be established. There were several reasons for choosing this focus for the prize. First, it is obvious that contributions to sustainable development are globally important, and that innovative technological development is vital to achieve this, in addition to efforts and innovation in the fields of international relations, politics, organizations, education, and ethical awareness. Second, the prize might be an important contribution from Norway, whose Prime Minister and the head of UN's World Commission on Environment and Development, Gro Harlem Brundtland, placed sustainable development on the international political agenda with the report *Vår felles framtid* (Our Common Future) in the spring of 1987. Therefore it was also proposed that the prize should be called the *Gro Harlem Brundtlands pris for bærekraftig teknologi* (the Gro Harlem Brundtland Prize for Sustainable Technology).[864] With NTNU, Trondheim was a national center for technological education and research and appeared as the obvious choice of location for awarding such a prize.[865]

The reorganization of *Universitetet i Trondheim* (UNIT—the University of Trondheim) in 1996 into *Norges teknisk-naturvitenskapelige universitet* (NTNU—the Norwegian University of Science and Technology*)* was a turbulent and chaotic process. As mentioned above, the name was changed in connection with a comprehensive reorganization of the university, giving it the same organizational structure as the other universities in Norway, which meant closing down NTH and AVH (which from 1984 had been the name of NLHT) as institutional units in the university structure. The faculty and department structure also underwent major changes, while the structure of the subjects largely remained the same.

Discontinuing the special college level was in itself a heavily debated topic at NTH, while the rest of the university generally considered this in a very positive light. The name change, on the other hand, gave rise to strong reactions. The new name was decided by the Norwegian Parliament during some hectic weeks in the spring of 1995 to bring the university reform to a successful end, and to keep the united university in Trondheim. NTH had conducted an assertive campaign to withdraw from the established university, and had obtained substantial support from the important business and industry organizations in Norway, as well as from a number of the political parties represented in Parliament. A new name signaling technology and natural science as the main profile at the University of Trondheim would, however, still ensure a political majority in Parliament for continuing with the united university.

There were many strong feelings about the name change at the university, and also at NTH. The strongest reactions were perhaps from students and employees at the

---

[864] DKNVSa. "Forslag om opprettelse av en internasjonal teknologipris for bærekraftig utvikling" (Proposal for the establishment of an international technology prize for sustainable development), DKNVS and NTNVA, Trondheim 4 June 2007.

[865] No final resolution had yet been made in this case in the autumn of 2008.

Faculty of Arts and the Faculty of Social Sciences and Technology Management. However, the administrators at the same institutions applauded the name change because
splitting up the University of Trondheim was seen as a much worse alternative. The
question of how this change of name was to be interpreted, including which implications and meanings were embedded in the new name, was also the source of dispute.
Parliament stated that the name "NTNU" only expressed that technology and natural
science would be the university's main profile, which in itself only reiterated the fact
that these academic fields made up the bulk of the total activities, while the "university"
in the name ensured that NTNU would offer a broad range of subjects in the humanities, social sciences, and medicine. The dispute over the NTNU name increased the gap
between the natural sciences and technology, on the one hand, and the humanities and
social sciences on the other, or in the words of C. P. Snow from 1959, a gap and tension
that had emerged in the West between "the two cultures" in the natural sciences and
humanities fields.[866] As a multi-field science society which embraced all the academic
fields at NTNU, the Society had the possibility of building bridges between the two cultures, building bridges between the natural scientists, technologists, humanities
researchers, social scientists, and doctors.

Snow's analysis of the difference between the two cultures continued to have a
high degree of relevance, but also overshadowed new tensions and trends in the university in general, the trends towards specialization, fragmentation, and relativization
of knowledge, where the university was developing in the direction of a multiversity. In
this context the tradition of *Videnskabsselskabet* as a forum for general scientific education could be mobilized as a tool for new forms of bridge building.[867] On its way to the
celebration of its 250th anniversary, the Society's vital signs bode well for the future,
because its tradition was actively employed as a resource for promoting science in a
continually changing scientific landscape.

---

[866] Snow, C. P. *The two cultures.* Cambridge: Cambridge University Press, 1998.
[867] Jakobsen. "Akademiene—Utvikling og oppgaver i fortid og nåtid." (The academies—development
and duties in the past and the present).

Notes on contributors

BRITA BRENNA (1963) is Associate Professor at Institute for Culture Studies and Oriental Languages at the University of Oslo. Her many publications deal with a wide range of topics: the history of international exhibitions and World's Fairs in the 19th century, the cultural history of natural history in the 18th century, consumption history and feminist science and technology studies. Among her English publications is the co-edited, *Technoscience. The Politics of Interventions* with Kristin Asdal and Ingunn Moser, Oslo University Press 2007. She has contributed Part I, 1760–1805, to this volume.

MAGNE NJÅSTAD (1962) is Associate professor at the Department of history and classical studies at NTNU (Norwegian University of Science and Technology), Trondheim. He has mainly worked with local history and political and social history in the late medieval and early modern period. His main works are *Grenser for makt. Konflikter og konfliktløsning mellom øvrighet og lokalsamfunnn ca. 1300–1540* (2003) and *Stord frå steinalder til oljealder. Band 1: Den eldste tida fram til 1720* (2005). Publications in English include: "Resistance in the name of the law. Peasant politics in medieval and early modern Norway" in Kimmo Katajla (ed.): *Northern Revolts. Medieval and Early Modern Peasant Unrest in the Nordic Countries* (2004). He is co-editor of the *Scandinavian Journal of History*. Magne Njåstad has provided Part II, 1805–1870, to this volume.

HÅKON WITH ANDERSEN (1949) is full professor at the Department of history and classical studies at the Norwegian University of Science and Technology. His particular interests include history of science and technology and cultural history and history of ideas. He has published several books and many articles in these fields including a textbook on technology, environment and values (*Frankensteins dilemma*, together with Knut H. Sørensen). His latest book is a co-edited volume, *Fabrikken* ("The Factory"). He has also been responsible for several national and international exhibitions and museum projects. He has served as dean of humanities as well as many other organisational roles. He is responsible for Part III, 1870–1960, of this publication.

ASTRID WALE (1958), dr. art. 2005. Independent scholar, affiliated with the Department of history and classical studies at the Norwegian University of Science and Technology. She has published on various topics within several fields: the history of technology (the introduction of electricity in Norway in the 19th century), 20th century industrial history, history of knowledge. She has published several books, written partly independently, partly in cooperation with others. She has contributed Part IV, 1960–2010, to this publication.

Source materials

Abbreviations

DBL: Dansk biografisk leksikon
DKNVS: Det kongelige Norske Videnskabers Selskab
NBL: Norsk biografisk leksikon
NHL: Norsk hisorisk leksikon
NOU: Norske offentlige utredninger
St.f: Stortingsforhandlinger

Literature and Printed Sources

Aase, M., *Patrioter og Bønder. Det Kongelige Norske Videnskabers Selskabs arbeid med land-brukspremier 1772–1806*, Master's thesis, University of Trondheim, 1987.

Aase, M., *Premiesøknader til Det Kongelige Norske Videnskabers Selskab 1772–1848*, Trondheim 1988.

Aase, M., *Patrioter og bønder. Det Kongelige Norske Videnskabers Selskabs arbeid med land-brukspremier 1772–1806*, Trondheim 1993.

Aase, M., "En europeer i Trondheim—Broder Lysholm Knudtzon og hans bibliotek," H. Nissen & M. Aase (eds.), *Til opplysning. Universitetsbiblioteket i Trondheim 1768–1993*, Trondheim 1993: 132–137.

Aase, M., "Premiesøknader i Det Kongelige Norske Videnskabers Selskab og Arkiv," H. Nissen & M. Aase (eds.), *Til opplysning. Universitetsbiblioteket i Trondheim 1768–1993*, Trondheim 1997: 143–149.

Aasen, I., *Det Norske Folkesprogs gramatikk*, Christiania 1848.

Aasen, I., *Ordbog over det norske Folkesprog*, Christiania 1850.

Abel, N.H., "Et lidet bidrag til Læren om adskillige transcendente Functioner," *Det Kongelige Norske Videnskabers Selskabs Skrifter i det 19de Aarhundrede* vol. 2, Trondhjem 1827: 177–207.

Alexander, E. P., *Museum Masters. Their Museums and Their Influence*, Nashville 1983.

Amundsen, A. Bugge, "'Prestesekken som aldri ble full . . .' Folkelige reaksjoner på sportler som del av prestens inntekt i efterreformatorisk tid." *Tidsskrift for Teologi og Kirke* no 4 1987: 253–271.

Amundsen, A. Bugge, *Norsk religionshistorie*, Oslo 2005.

Amundsen, L. *Det Norske videnskaps-akademi i Oslo 1857–1957*. Vol. I. Oslo 1957.

Amundsen, L. *Det Norske Videnskaps-Akademi i Oslo 1857–1957*. Vol. II. Oslo 1960.

Amundsen, L. (ed.), *Johan Ernst Gunnerus og Carl von Linné. Brevveksling 1761–1772*. Trondheim 1976.

Amundsen, L., "Wergeland, Henrik Arnold," NBL vol. XVIII, Oslo 1977: 476–562.

Amundsen, L., "Wergeland, Nicolai," NBL vol. XIX, Oslo 1983: 1–32.

An. *Illustration over Bispe=Visitatserne i Norge. Tilskrevet Hans Kongelige Majestet*, Kiøbenhavn, 1771.

An. "Til Læseren." *Nyere Samling af det Kongelige Norske Selskabs Skrifter*. Kiøbenhavn 1784: VII–XII.

Andersen, A., *Handelsfolk og fiskerbønder 1794–1900. Tromsø gjennom 10,000 år*, Tromsø 1994.

Andersen, H. W., "Trondhjems tekniske læreanstalt 1870–1915" in Hovde, P. (ed): *Trondheim ingeniørhøgskole 1912–1987*, Trondheim1987: 11–32.

Andersen-Næss, R., "Welhaven, Johan Sebastian," NBL vol. XVIII, Oslo 1977: 401–429.

Anderson, B., *Imagined communities: Reflections on the origin and spread of nationalism*. London 1991.

Apelseth, A., "Lærdom, borgarleggjering og skriftkultur.," Johnsen, E.B. and Eriksen, T. Berg, *Norsk litteraturhistorie : Sakprosa fra 1750 til 1995*. Oslo 1998: 32–51.

Arentz, F.C.H., "Om de ubestemte algebraiske Æqvationer," *Det Kongelige Norske Videnskabers Selskabs Skrifter i det 19de Aarhundrede*, vol.2, Trondhjem 1827: 87–102.

Arentz, F.C.H., "Forsøg til en med mathematisk Nøiagtighed fremsat Theorie om paralelle Linier og deres Egenskaber," *Det Kongelige Norske Videnskabers Selskabs Skrifter i det 19de Aarhundrede*, vol.2, Trondhjem 1827: 109–130.

Arvesen, O. P. and Gjærevoll, O. (eds.), *DKNVS Beretning om tohundreårsjubileet 6te til 8de mai 1960*. Trondheim, 1961.

Bauer, J. and Müller, G., "Zwischen Theologie und praktischen Wissenschaften: Der Aufklärer Joachim Georg Darjes." In: O. Breidbach und P. Ziche, *Naturwissenschaften um 1800. Wissenschaftskultur in Jena-Weimar*, Weimar 2001: 142–154.

Bauer, J., "Freimaurerei, Geheimgesellschaften und Studenten in Jena zu Beginn der zweiten Hälfte des 18. Jahrhunderts." In J. Bauer and J. Riederers, *Zwischen Gehimnis und Öffentlichkeit. Jenaer Freimauerei und studentische Geheimgesellschaften*. Jena 1991: 10–41.

Baustad, T., *Harsdorffbygningen. Trondheim Katedralskoles eldste bygning 1787–1987*. Trondheim, 1986.

Beckman, J., *Naturens Palats: Nybygnad, vetenskap och utställning vid Naturhistoriska riksmuseet 1866–1925*, Stockholm 1999.

Bennett, T., "Pedagogic Objects, Clean Eyes, and Popular Instruction: On Sensory Regimes and Museum Didactics." *Configurations*, 6–3 1998: 345–371.

Bennett, T., *The Birth of the Museum*, Oxon and New York 2005 (1995).

Berg, B.I., "Bergseminaret på Kongsberg 1757–1814," in Børresen, A.K & Kobberrød, J.T. (eds.), *Bergingeniørutdanningen i Norge gjennom 250 år*, Trondheim 2007: 13–36.

Bjelke, J.F., "Kritisk introduksjon til prisskriftets problematikk," A. Schopenhauer, *Kan menneskets frie Villie bevises af dets Selvbevidsthed?*, Oslo 1993.

Bjerke, E.,*Uavhengighet gjennom vitenskap. Naturhistorien som økonomisk og politisk redskap i opplysningstidens Danmark og Norge*. Master's thesis, University of Oslo 2008.

Bonsach-Krogh, M, "Forsøg til Besvarelse af de fremsatte Priis-Spørgsmaal om et Norsk Universitet," *Historisk-Philosophiske Samlinger* vol. 2 part 2, Christiania 1812: 1–162.

Bratberg, T.T.V., *Trondheim byleksikon*, Oslo, 2008.

Bravo, M. and Sörlin, S., *Narrating the Arctic. A Cultural History of Nordic Scientific Practices*, Canton 2002.

Bredal, T.K., "Den anden Tale, holden samme Tid, ved samme Anledning." *Skrifter*. Vol. 4. Kiøbenhavn: 1768. 27–50.

Breidbach, O. and Ziche, P., "Einführung. Naturwissen und Naturwissenchaften." In Idem, *Naturwissenschaften um 1800. Wissenschaftskultur in Jena-Weimar*. Weimar: 2001.

Brenna, B., "Halvannen tekopp av kokosnøttskall.," *Agora* 4, 2006.

Brenna, B., "Fysikoteologi, bibelsk fysikk og 'en stor og betydelig Fisk' " i *DIN* 4, 2007.

Broch, H: *Zoologiens historie i Norge til annen verdenskrig*. Oslo 1954.

Brøgger, J.,"Christian Fredrik og Videnskabselskabet," [Christian Frederik og Videnskabsselskabet] *Det Kongelige Norske Videnskabers Selskabs Forhandlinger* 1999:

Brun, J. Nordal, *Naturens Navnedag i Anledning af Skabelsens 2 Cap. 19 Vers For at lykønske Hans Høyærværdigheds Hr. Biskop GUNNERI Hiemskomst fra sin Norlandske Reise*. Tronhiem, 1770.

Brun, J. Nordal. *Det Kongelige Norske Videnskabers Selskabs Tab ved Hans Høyærværdigheds Hr. Biskops Johan Ernst Gunneri Død*. Trondheim 1773.

Brun, V., *Regnekunsten i det gamle Norge. Fra Arilds tid til Abel*. Oslo 1962.

Bryn, H: "J.E. Gunnerus og Videnskabsselskabet." In *Forhandlinger 1926–1928*. Vol. I: 47–51.

von Buch, L., *Leopold von Buchs Resa igenom Norrige åren 1806, 1807 og 1808*. Stockholm 1814.

Bugge, C, "Pettersen, Karl Johan," NBL vol. XI, Oslo 1952: 90–91.

Bugge, F.M., *Det offentlige Skolevæsens Forfatning i adskillige tydske Stater, tillige med Ideer til en Reorganisering af det offentlige Skolevæsen i Kongeriget Norge: en Indberætning afgiven til den Kgl. Norske Regjerings Departement for Kirke- og Underviisningsvæsenet, ifølge Kgl. Naadigst Resolution af 23de Juni 1836*, vol. 1–3, Christiania 1839.

Bull, F., "Arentz, Fredrich Christian Holberg," NBL vol. 1, Kristiania 1923: 223–226.

Bull, I., *Privatarkiv. Katalog over privatarkiv i Statsarkivet i Trondheim*. Vol. 2, Trondheim 1983.

Bull, I., "Foreningsdannelse i norske byer. Borgerlig offentlighet, kjønn og politisk kultur." *Heimen*, vol. 44, 2007: 311–324.

Bush, V: *Science, the endless frontier—Report to the President on a Program for Postwar Scientific Research*, Washington 1945.

Børresen, A.K. & Wale, A., *Kartleggerne. Norges geologiske undersøkelser 1858–2008*, Trondheim 2008.

Catalog over Det Norske Videnskabers Selskabs Samlinger. Første del. Bøger og Haandskrifter, Copenhagen 1808.

Christophersen, A., "Selskabets Cabinet." In *Spor. Nytt fra fortiden*, nr 1, 2003.

Clarke, E. D., Travels in Various Countries in Europe, Asia, and Africa. Part III. Vol. 10. London 1824.

Clarke, W.,"The Death of Metaphysics in Enlightened Prussia.," W. Clarke, J. Golinski and S. Schaffer. *The Sciences in Enlightened Europe*. Chicago 1999: 390–423.

Clarke, W., "The Pursuit of the Prosography of Science." In: Porter, R. (ed.). *The Cambridge History of Science*, Vol. 4. Cambridge 2003: 211–240.

Clausen, K. et al: *Med Sokrates i Rogaland. Akademi på rogalandsk i 50 år*, Stavanger 2005.

Colban, E.A., "Forsøg til en Beskrivelse over Lofodens og Vesteraalens Fogderie i Nordlands Amt, med et Situtions-Cart, *Det Kongelige Norske Videnskabers Selskabs Skrifter i det 19de Aarhundrede*, vol. 2, Trondhjem 1827: 1–86.

Collet, J.P., *Historien om Universitetet i Oslo*, Oslo 1999.

Confirmation paa Statuter for Det Kongelige Norske Videnskabers-Selskab, Christiania 1811.

Continuationscatalog over Det Kongelige Norske Videnskabers Selskabs Samlinger. Bøger og Haandskrifter, vol. 1, Trondhjem 1831.

Continuationscatalog over Det Kongelige Norske Videnskabers Selskabs Samlinger. Bøger og Haandskrifter vol. 2, Trondhjem 1848.

Continuationscatalog over Det Kongelige Norske Videnskabers Selskabs Samlinger. Bøger og Haandskrifter vol. 3, Trondhjem 1853.

Continuationscatalog over Det Kongelige Norske Videnskabers Selskabs Samlinger. Bøger og Haandskrifter vol. 4, Trondhjem 1858.

Continuations-Catalog over Det Kongelige Norske Videnskabers-Selskabs Samlinger. Bøger og Haandskrifter m.m., 1858–1862, vol. 5, Trondhjem 1863.

Cook, H. J., "Global Economies and Local Knowledge in the East Indies." In L. Schiebinger and C. Swan, *Colonical Botany. Science, Commerce, and Politics in the Early Modern World*, Philadelphia 2005: 100–118.

Cooper, A., *Inventing the Indigenous. Local Knowledge and Natural History in Early Modern Europe*. Cambridge 2007.

Daae, L., *Udvalg af Breve, hovedsagelig fra bekjendte Nordmænd til Professor N. Nyerup*. Christiania 1861.

Daae, L., *Throndhjems Stifts Geistlige Historie fra Reformationen til 1814*. Throndhjem 1863.

Dahl, G., *Questioning Religious Influence. Private Libraries of Clerics and Physicians in Norway 1650–1750*, Bergen 2007.

Dahl, O., *Norsk historieforskning i det 19. og 20. århundre*, Oslo 1990.

Dahl, O., Biskop Gunnerus's virksomhed fornemmelig som botaniker tillige med en oversigt over botanikkens tilstand i Danmark og Norge indtil hans død. [With additions:] Gunnerus's botaniseren ved Trondhjem og paa visitasreiserne & Uddrag af Gunnerus's brevveksling, særlig til belysning af hans videnskabelige sysler. *Det Kongelige Norske Videnskabers Selskabs Skrifter*. 1890–93, 1895–1900, 1902, 1906–08 og 1910, Trondhjem.

Damsholt, T., *Fædrelandskærlighed og borgerdyd. Patriotisk diskurs og militære reformer i Danmark i sidste del av 1700-tallet*, København 2000.

Daston, L. J., "The Factual Sensibility," *Isis*, Vol. 79, No. 3, 1988: 452–470.

Daston, L., "Die Kultur der wissenschaftlichen Objektivität." In: O. G. Oexle, ed., *Naturwissenschaft, Geisteswissenschaft, Kulturwissenschaft: Einheit - Gegensatz - Komplementarität*, vol. 6 of Göttinger Gespräche zur Geschichtswissenschaft, Göttingen 1998: 9–39.

Daston, L. and Sibum, H.O., "Introduction: Scientific Peronae and Their Histories," *Science in Context*, Volume 16, no 1–2, 2003: 1–8.

Det Kongelige Norske Videnskabers-Selskab af Hans Majestet naadigst sanctionerede Statuter givne i 1815, Trondheim 1829.

Devik, O., *NTH 50 år*, Oslo 1960.

Dyrvik, S. et. al., *Norsk økonomisk historie 1500–1970*, Bergen/Oslo/Tromsø 1979.

Dyrvik, S. and Feldbæk, O., *Mellom brødre. 1780–1830. Aschehougs Norgeshistorie, bind 7*. Oslo 1996.

Ekblad, F.-E., "Biskop Johan Ernst Gunnerus (1718–1773) og hans mikroskop." *Blyttia* 42 1984:

Eliasson, P., *Platsens blick. Vetenskapsakademien och den naturalhistoriska resan 1790–1840*, Umeå 1999.

Elvestrand, V., *Generalkonduktør Christopher Hammer (1720–1804) og hans manuskriptsamling. Registratur, biografi, slektshistorie. Fra Københavns Universitet, Sorø Akademi og Lederborg til Hadeland. Skråblikk på dansk-norsk opplysningstid og en selvsikker embedsmann, frimurer og odelsbonde,* Trondheim 2004.

Elvestrand, V., *Fra Københavns Universitet, Sorø Akademi og Lederborg til Hadeland. Skråblikk på dansk-norsk opplysningstid og en selvsikker embedsmann, frimurer og odelsbonde. Navneregister og korreksjoner,* Trondheim 2006.

Engelhardt, J., "Patriotism, nationalism and modernity: the patriotic societies in the Danish conglomerate state, 1769–1814." *Nations and Nationalism* 113, 2, 2007: 205–223.

Erlandsen, A., *Biographiske Efterretninger om Geistiligheden i Throndhjems Stift,* Christiania 1844–55.

Fabricius, J. C., *Reise nach Norwegen mit Bemerkungen aus der Naturhistorie und Oekonomie,* Hamburg 1779.

Falck, K., "Bergens Museum og Universitetet i Bergen," Ø. Vorren (ed.), *Museum og universitet. Jubileumsskrift til Tromsø Museum 1872–1972,* Tromsø 1972: 187–191.

Feldbæk, O. "Fædreland og Indfødsret. 1700-tallets danske identitet," Feldbæk, O. (ed.). *Fædreland og modersmål 1536–1789. Dansk identitetshistorie.* Volume 1. København 1991. 111–230

Feldbæk, O., "Aufklärung und Absolutismus. Die Kulturpolitik Friedrichs V." In: K. Bohnen and P. Øhrgaard, *Aufklärung als Problem und Aufgabe.* München 1994.

Fet, J., *Lesande bønder. Litterær kultur i norske allmugesamfunn før 1840,* Oslo 1995.

Findlen, P., *Possessing Nature. Museums, Collecting, and Scientific Culture in Early Modern Italy.* Berkeley 1994.

Forland, A. et al.: *Forskningsformidling gjennom 75 år. Selskapet til Vitenskapenes Fremme,* Bergen 2002. Also in the series: *Bergen Museums skrifter* no. 13.

Forland, A. and Haaland, A., *Universitetet i Bergens historie* vol. 1, Bergen 1996.

Fortegnelse over . . . Johan Ernst Gunneri Natural-Samling, som ved offentlig Auction bliver bortsolgt i Septembri 1774 udi hans Gaard i Tronhiem. Tronhiem 1774.

Foucault, M., *The Order of Things.* London 2002.

Forslag [til nye statutter], Trondhjem 1849.

Forster, G., *A Voyage round the World in His Britannic Majesty's Sloop Resolution, Commanded by Capt. James Cook, during the Years, 1772, 3, 4, and 5,* London 1777.

Frängsmyr, T. (ed.), *Science in Sweden. The Royal Swedish Academy of Sciences 1739–1989,* Canton MA 1989.

Garff, J., *SAK. Søren Aabye Kierkegaard. En biografi,* Oslo 2002.

Gilje, N. and Rasmussen, T., *Tankeliv i den lutherske stat. Norsk idéhistorie,* Volume 2, Oslo 2002.

Grankvist, R., "Seminarium Lapponicum Fredericianum i Trondheims-miljøet.," In Hagland, J. R. and Supphellen, S. (eds.), *Knud Leem og det samiske,* Trondheim 2003.

Gullowsen, J., *Bro mellom vitenskap og teknologi. SINTEF 1950–2000.* Trondheim 2000.

[Gunnerus, J.E.] *Dem HochEhrwürdigebn und Hochgelahrten Herrn Johann Ernst Gunnerus der Weltweisheit hochberühmtem Doktor und der philosophischen Facultät in Jena hochwerdientem*

Adjunkt . . . statten zu Seiner wholverdienten Ehrenstelle durch nachstehnende Cantate und Gedichte ihren schuldigen Glückwunsch ab, Seiner Hochehrwürden sämtliche ergebenste Zuhörer. Jena, 1755.

Gunnerus, J E. *Hans Opvækkelige Hyrde=Brev Til det Velærvædige, Høj= og Vellærde Præsteskab I Tronhjems Stift.* Tronhjem 1758. Reprint Trondheim, 1997.

Gunnerus, J E., *Johan Ernst Gunnerus erweckliched Hirten=Brief an die Wohlehrwürdige, Hoch= und Wohlgelahrte Priesterschaft im Stifte Druntheim. Von dem Verfasser selbst aus dem Dänischen ins Deutsche übersetzt und mit einigen zur Druntheimischen gelehrten Historie gehörenden Anmerkungen vermehret.* Druntheim, 1759.

[Gunnerus, J.E.], "Fortale." In: *Skrifter.* Volume 1. Kiøbenhavn 1761: 3–7.

Gunnerus, J. E., "Betragtninger over Sielens Udødelighed." In: *Skrifter.* Volume 1. Kiøbenhavn 1761: 11–70.

Gunnerus, J. E., "Betragtning over Salom. Prædik. III. 19–22." In: *Skrifter.* Volume 1. Kiøbenhavn 1761: 71–95.

Gunnerus, J.E., "Om Hav-Hesten, en Søe-Fugl." In: *Skrifter.* Volume 1. Kiøbenhavn 1761. 182–202.

Gunnerus, J.E., "Om nogle Lom-artede Fugle, (Colymbis.)." In: *Skrifter.* Volume 1. Kiøbenhavn 1761. 236–270.

Gunnerus, J.E., "Adskillige Efterretninger, fornemmelig angaaende Mineralier i Nordland og Finmarken." In: *Skrifter.* Volume 1. Kiøbenhavn 1761. 271–283.

Gunnerus, J. E., "Om Hav-Katten," *Skrifter* Vol, 2, Kiøbenhavn 1763: 270–312.

Gunnerus, J.E., " Brugden. (Sqvalus maximus)." In: *Skrifter.* Volume 3. Kiøbenhavn 1765: 33–49.

Gunnerus, J.E., "Første Tale, handlende om Nytte og Nødvendigheden af et Videnskabers Selskab in en Stat, i Særdeleshed i Norge, holdet ved Selskabets høitidelige Indvielse, paa Hans Kongelige Majestæts Høie Fødsels=Fest, den 29. Januarii 1768, i Trondhiem, ved Johan Ernst Gunnerus." in *Skrifter*, Vol. 4, Kiøbenhavn 1768: 1–26.

Gunnerus, J.E., "Videre Oplysning om Brugden (Sqvalo maximo) Samt Beviis at denne, efter al Formodning, har været den Fisk, som opslugede Propheten Jonas." In: *Skrifter.* Volume 4. Kiøbenhavn 1768: 14–37.

Gunnerus, J. E., "Første Tale, Handlende om Nytten og Nødvendigheden af et Videnskabers Selskap i en Stat, i Særdelshed i Norge." In: *Skrifter.* Volume 4. Kiøbenhavn 1768. 1–26.

[Gunnerus, J.E.], "Fortale." In: *Skrifter.* Volume 4. Kiøbenhavn 1768.

[Gunnerus, J E.] *Johan Ernst Gunnerus Mindeblade.* Trondhjem: Aktietrykkeriet, 1918.

Gustafson, L.,"I Oluf Ryghs fotspor på Veien, Ringerike," in Sandnes, B. et al (eds): *Oluf Rygh. Rapport fra et seminar på Stiklestad 13.-15. mai 1999*, Uppsala, 2000: 95–120.

Habermas, J., *The Structural Transformation of the Public Sphere. An Inquiry into a category of Bourgeois Society.* Cambridge 1989.

Hagen, A., *Gåten om Kong Raknes haug.* Oslo, 1997.

Hagland, J. R., "Vitskaplege visitasreiser i Nord-Noreg." *Nordlit* nr. 11, Tromsø 2002.

Hagland, J. R. and Supphellen, S. (eds.). *Knud Leem og det samiske.* Skrifter 2. Trondheim: Det Kongelige Norske Videnskabers Selskab, 2003.

Hammer, C., *Afhandling om Potatos, med en Deel tanker om Landhusholdningen*, Christiania 1766.

Hammer, C., *Traité boolaniques des batates accompagné des quelques reflexiones sur l'economie,* Copenhagen 1788.

Hammerstein, N., "Innovation und Tradition. Adademien und Universitäten im Heiligen Römischen Reich deutscher Nation." *Historische Zeitschrift* Volume 278 (2004): 591–623.

Haugen, E., "Construction and reconstruction in language planning," *Word* 21 (1965): 188–207.

Hanisch, T.J. and Lange, E., *Vitenskap for industrien. NTH—En høyskole i utvikling gjennom 75 år*, Oslo 1985.

Heiberg, B., Berg, A. and Sinding-Larsen, E. (eds), *Fremtid for fortiden: Fortidsvern i 125 år*, Oslo 1969.

Helsvig, K.G., *Elitisme på norsk. Det Norske Videnskaps-Akademi 1945–2007*, Oslo 2007.

Herstad, J., "De 43 Spørsmål. En arkivnær introduksjon til politiske og administrative prosesser." In: Røgeberg, K.M., *Norge i 1743. Innberetninger som svar på 43 spørsmål fra Danske Kanselli*. Volume 1. Oslo 2003.

Hestmark, G., *Vitenskap og nasjon. Waldemar C. Brøgger 1851–1905*. Oslo 1999.

Historisk Statistikk: *Befolkning* [Historical Statistics: Population] Statistics Norway.

Hjelm-Hansen, P., "En utredning om Det kongelige Norske Videnskabers Selskab, Museums-stiftelsen." *DKNVS Forhandlinger*, 1985: 3–44.

Hodacs, H. and Nyberg, K., *Naturalhistoria på resande fot*. Lund, 2007.

Holmboe, C.L., *Det norske Sprogvæsentligste Ordforraad, sammenlignet med Sanskrit og andre Sprog af same Æt. Bidrag til en norsk etymologisk Ordbog*, Wien 1852.

Holmboe, J, "Lund, Nicolai," NBL vol. VIII, Oslo 1938: 494–495.

Holmboe, J, "Norman, Johannes Musæus," NBL vol. X, Oslo 1949: 222–225.

[Slekten] Holmboe: *Stamtavle 1944 med biografiske opplysninger*, fotografier og familiedokumenter. Oslo 1944.

Horstbøl, H., "Pietism and the Politics of Cathechisms. The Case of Denmark and Norway in the Eighteenth and Nineteenth Centuries" in *Scandinavian Journal of History* 22, 2004: 143–160.

Hård, M. et. al. (eds.), *Teknologi for samfunnet. NTH i en brytningstid 1985–1995*. Trondheim, 1997.

Hård, M. and Aase, M., "'Det norska Aten'. Trondheim som lärdomsstad under 1700-talets andra hälft" in *Lychnos* 1998: 37–74.

Irgens, O., *Den Sælskabelige Stræbsomhed for Videnskabernes Vedligeholdelse og Tilvext, Som en vigtig Pligt, Forestillet i En Tale ved Tiltrædelsen som Vice=Præses I Det Kongelige Norske Videnskabers Sælskab den 12. April 1774*. Trondheim 1774.

Jakobsen, K., "Akademiene—Utvikling og oppgaver i fortid og nåtid." *Agder Vitenskapsakademi. Årbok*, Kristiansand 2003: 49–55.

Janaway, C, "Will and nature," in C. Janaway (ed.), *The Cambridge Companion to Schopenhauer*, New York 1999: 138–170.

Jørgensen, P.M. (ed), *Botanikkens historie i Norge*, Bergen 2007.

Karlsen, E., "Liturgiske bøker I Norge inntil år 1300—import og egenproduksjon," in S. Imsen (ed.) *Den kirkehistoriske utfordring*, Trondheim 2005: 147–170.

Keilhau, B.M. (ed), *Gaea Norvegica* vol. 1–3, Christiania 1838–50.

Keyser, R. & Munch, P.A., "Fortale," *Norges gamle Love indtil 1387. Første Bind. Norges Love ældre end Kong Magnus Haakonssöns Regjerings-Tiltrædelse i 1263*, Christiania 1846: II–XII

Kirkhusmo, A., *Akademi og seminar Norges Lærerhøgskole 1922–1982*, Trondheim 1983.

Klüwer, L.D., *Norske Mindesmærke aftegnede paa en Reise igjennem de Deel af det Nordenfjeldske*, Trondhjem 1823.

Koerner, L. Linneaus., *Nature and Nation*, Cambridge, Mass., 1999.

Koht, H, "Lange, Christian Christoph Andreas," NBL vol. VIII, Oslo 1938: 169–172.

Kragh, H., *Natur, Nytte og Ånd 1730–1850. Dansk naturvidenskabs historie*, bind 2. Aarhus 2005.

Kristensen, J. E. et. al (eds.), *Ideer om et universitet. Det moderne universitets idehistorie fra 1800 til i dag*. Århus 2007.

Kvaal, S., *Janus med tre ansikter. Om organiseringen av den industrielt rettede forskningen i spennet mellom stat, vitenskap og industri i Norge, 1916–1956*, Trondheim 1997.

Kvist, K., *DKNVS' medaljer—skisse av historie og problemstillinger*, manuscript 2006.

König, W., "Technical Education and industrial performance in Germany: a triumph of heterogeneity." In Fox, R., Guagnini, A. (eds): *Education, Technology and Industrial Performance in Europe 1850–1939*. Cambridge 1993: 65–88.

Lange, C. & Unger, C.R., "Forord," *Diplomatarium Norvegicum* vol. 1 part 1, Christiania 1847: V-XI.

Langlie, K.L., *"Lærde folk er irritable genus." Omorganiseringen av Det Kongelige Norske Videnskabers Selskab 1910–1926*. Master thesis, Norwegian University of Science and Technology.

Latour, B., *Science in Action. How to follow scientists and engineers through society*. Milton Keynes 1987.

Lauglo, E., *Leinstrand. Et lite stykke Norge*, vol. 1, Leinstrand 1957.

Law, J., "On the Methods of Long Distance Control: Vessels, Navigation and the Portuguese Route to India." In: Law (ed.). *Power, Action and Belief: A New Sociology of Knowledge?* London 1986: 234–263.

Lund, N., *Reise gjennem Nordlandene og Vest Finmark Sommeren 1841*, Christiania 1842.

Lysaker, T., *Fra embedskirke til folkekirke 1804–1953*, Trondheim 1987.

Lønne, H. J., "Det Kgl. Norske Videnskabers Selskab, Museet og Universitetet i Trondheim." In Ø.Vorren (ed.), *Museum og universitet. Jubileumsskrift til Tromsø Museum 1872–1972*, Tromsø, 1972: 207–214.

Mandix, I, "Biographiske Efterretninger om Justitsraad og Generalconducteur Christopher Hammer," *Det Kongelige Norske Videnskabers Selskabs Skrifter i det 19de Aarhundrede*, Vol. 1, Copenhagen 1817: 225–232.

Mansåker, D., *Det norske presteskapet i det 19. århundret*. Oslo 1954.

Markussen, I., *Til skaberens ære, statens tjeneste og vor egen nytte: pietistiske og kameralistiske idéer bag fremvæksten af en offentlig skole i landdistrikterne i 1700-tallet*. Odense 1995.

Maurseth, P., "Wedel Jarlsberg, Johan Caspar Herman," NBL vol. XVIII, Oslo 1977: 339–373.

McClellan III, J. E., *Science Reorganized. Scientific Societies in the Eighteenth Century*. New York 1985.

McClellan III, J. E., "Scientific Institutions and the Organization of Science.," R. Porter (ed.). *The Cambridge History of Science*. Vol. 4. Cambridge 2003.

Mehos, D. C., *Science displayed: Nation and Nature at the Amsterdam Zoo Artis*, Ph.D theses, Univ of Philadelphia, Dep. of History and Sociology of Science, 1997.

Michelsen, K., (ed.). *Johan Daniel Berlin 1714–1787. Universalgeniet i Trondheim*. Trondheim 1987.

Midbøe, H., *Det Kongelige Norske Videnskabers Selskabs Historie 1760–1960* vol. 1–2, Trondheim 1960.

Moe, J.: "Historien bak etableringen av Norges Tekniske Vitenskapsakademi" in A. Bjørlykke et. al. (eds), *Teknologi og samfunn*, Trondheim 2005: 43–76.

du Monceau, L. du Hamel, *Underretning om, hvorledes Træer, perenerende Urter, Frøe, og adskillige andre naturalier best kan forseendes til Søs*, Kiøbenhavn 1764.

Mordhorst, C., *Genstandsfortællinger. Fra Museum Wormianum til de moderne museer*. PhD dissertation. Roskilde 2003. Electronic version: http://hdl.handle.net/1800/634.

Mykland, K., *Trondheims historie 997–1997. Vol. 3: Fra Søgaden til Strandgaten 1800–1880*, Oslo 1997.

Nielsen, J. P., "Ishavet er vår åker." In: E.-A. Drivenes and H. D. Jølle (eds.), *Norsk polarhistorie*. Volume 2. Oslo 2004: 47–109.

Nissen, H. and Aase, M. (eds.). *Til opplysning. Universitetsbiblioteket i Trondheim 1768–1993. DKNVS Skrifter* 1, Trondheim 1993.

Njølstad, O. and Wicken, O.: *Kunnskap som våpen. Forsvarets Forskningsinstitutt 1946–1975*. Oslo 1997.

Nyerup, R., *Historisk-statistiske skildring af Tilstanden i Danmark og Norge i Ældre og nyere Tider, 2nd part of 3rd volume*, Kjøbenhavn 1805.

Nyerup, R., "Fortale," *Catalog over Det Norske Videnskabers Selskabs Samlinger. Første del. Bøger og Haandskrifter*, Copenhagen 1808: I–XXXII.

Nye statuter for det Kongelige Norske Videnskabers Selskab i Trondhjem Trondhjem 1806.

Odde, K.: "Fra teknisk mellomskole til ingeniørhøgskole." In Hovde, P. (ed): *Trondheim ingeniørhøgskole 1912–1987*, Trondheim1987: 43–106.

Ousland, K., "'Nature in League with Man': Conceptualising and Transforming the Natural World in Eighteenth-Century Scandinavia" *Environment and History*, 10, 2004: 305–25.

Pedersen, O., *Lovers of Learning. A History of the Royal Danish Academy of Sciences and Letters 1742–1992*, Copenhagen, 1992.

Petersen, T., *Karl Ditlev Rygh, 7 juni 1839 10 marts 1915* Trondheim: DKNVS skrifter, 1916.

Pomian, K., *Collectors and Curiosities. Paris and Venice, 1500–1800*, Cambridge 1990: 218–219.

Pontoppidan, E., *Erik Pontoppidans Levnetsløb. Med hans Characteristik, af Professor J. Møller. Tidsskrift for Kirke og Theologi* 1834:

Pontoppidan, E., *The Natural History of Norway: Containing, A particular and accurate Account of the Temperature of the Air, the different Soils, Waters, Vegetables, Metals, Minerals, Stones, Beasts, Birds, and Fishes; together with the Dispositions, Customs, and Manner of Living of the Inhabitants: Interspersed with Physiological Notes from eminent Writers, and Transactions of Academies*. London, 1755, 2 parts in 1 vol.

Pontoppidan, E., *Oeconomiske Balance eller Uforgribelige Overslag paa Dannemarks Naturlige og Borgerlige Formue til at giøre sine Indbyggere lyksalige, saavidt som de selv ville skiønne derpaa og benytte sig deraf*. Kiøbenhavn, 1759.

Ramberghaug, K., *Biskop Gunnerus, geistlig embetsmann eller vitenskapsmann i bispekjole?* Master's thesis, University of Trondheim 2006.

Rask, R., *Ræsonneret lappisk Sproglære efter den Sprogart, som bruges af Fjældlapperne i Porsangerfjorden i Finmarken: En Omarbejdelse af Knud Leems Lappiske Grammatica*, Copenhagen 1832.

Reinalter, H. (Ed.) "Einleitung." In: *Aufklärungsgesellschaften*, Frankfurt/Main, u. a. 1993.

Roll-Hansen, N. et. al., *Universitetet i Bergens historie, Bind II*. Bergen, 1996.

Rotblat, J., *Scientists in the Quest for Peace. A History of the Pugwash Conference*. Cambridge, Massachusetts/London1972.

Rygh, E., *Alfabetisk reigster til A. Erlandsens Efterretninger om Throndhjems og Tromsøes Stifters Geistlighed*, Christiania 1860.

Røgeberg, K. M., *Norge i 1743. Innberetninger som svar på 43 spørsmål fra Danske Kanselli*. Volume 1. Oslo 2003.

Sainovics, P. J., "Tagebuch der Reise von Wien nach Wardoe und zurück.," Littrow, C. L. P., *Hell's Reise nach Wardoe bei Lappland und seine Beobachtungen des Venus-Durchganges im Jahre 1769. Aus den aufgefundenen Tageüchern geschöpft und mit Erläuterungen begleitet*, Wien 1835.

Sakshaug, E. and Sneli, J-A.: *Trondheimsfjorden*, Trondheim 2000.

Sars, M., *Bidrag til Sødyrenes Naturhistorie*, Bergen 1829–35.

Sars, M, *Fauna littoralis Norvegica: oder Beschreibung und Abbildungen neuer oder wenig bekannten Seethiere, nebst Beobachtungen über die Organistaion, Lebensweise u. Entwicklungen deselben* vol. 1–3, Christiania 1846–77.

Schapin, S. and Schaffer, S., *Leviathan and the Air-Pump*, New Jersey 1985.

Schinnerup, P., "Plan til et norsk Universitet," *Historisk-Philosophiske Samlinger* vol. 2 part 1, Christiania 1812: 1–202.

Schlögl, Rudolf: "Die patriotisch-gemeinnützigen Gesellschaften: Organsiation, Sozialstruktur, Tätigkeitsfelder." In: Reinalter (Ed.), *Aufklärungsgesellschaften*, Frankfurt/Main, u. a. 1993: 61–81.

Schmidt, O., "Lysholm, Nicolay," NBL vol. VIII, Oslo 1938: 562–564.

Schmidt, O., *Det Kongelige Norske Videnskabers Selskab matrikkel 1760–1960*, Trondheim 1960.

Schmidt-Nielsen, S., "Karl Rygh, en merkesmann i Videnskapsselskapets historie." *DKNVS Forhandlinger*, vol. XVII, p. 4* Trondheim 1944.

Schmidt-Nielsen, S, "Halvdan Bryn," *Forhandlinger*. Vol. VI nr. 16.

Schnabel, M., "Prøve paa hvorvidt det gamle Norske Sprog endnu er til udi det Hardangerske Bonde-Maal," *Nye Samling af Det Kongelige Norske Videnskabers Selskabs Skrifter*, vol. 1, Copenhagen 1784: 297–322.

Schnapp A., *Discovery of the past*, London, 1996.

Schwach, C.N., *Throndhjems Domkirkes Historie og Beskrivelse i kort Udtog*, Trondhjem 1838.

Schwach, C.N., *Udsigt over de tre nordiske Rigers Myntvæsen fra de ældste Tider til nuværende, samt Grundrids af Heraldikken*, Trondhjem 1842.

Schwach, C.N., "Kort Udsigt over Det Kongelige Norske Videnskabers-Selskabs Historie fra dets Oprindelse til Udgangen af 1844," *Det Kongelige Norske Videnskabers-Selskabs Skrifter i det 19de Aarhundrede*, vol. 4, Trondheim 1859: 1–28.

Schwach, V., *Havet, fisken og vitenskapen. Fra fiskeriundersøkelser til havforskningsinstitutt 1860–2000*, Bergen 2000.

Schytte, E., "Adskillige Anmærkninger indsendte til Biskopen i Trondhiem." In: *Skrifter*. Volume 1. København 1761: 284–293.

Schøning, G., "Kort Beretning, om endeel Uaar og Misvæxt, særdeles i Trondhiems Stift i Norge." In: *Skrifter*. Volume 1. København 1761: 129–162.

Schøning, G., "Betænkning, om offentlige Forraads-Huses Opretning og Indretning i Norge." In: *Skrifter*. Volume 1. København 1761:163–181.

Schøning, G., *Beskrivelse over den tilforn meget prægtige og vidtberømte Dom-Kirke i Throndhjem, egentlig kaldet Christ-Kirken*, Trondhjem 1762.

Schøning, G., *Norges Riiges historie.* Vol. 1–3 Kiøbenhavn 1771–1781.

Schøning, G., "Tale over Johan Ernst Gunnerus.," H. J. Wille, *Samling af Minde-Taler, holdne i det kongelige norske Videnskabers-Selskab over adskillige af dets afdøde Medlemmer,* Kjøbenhavn 1805.

Seip, A.-L., *Demringstid. Johan Sebastian Welhaven og nasjonen,* Oslo 2007.

Selmer, L., *Opplysningsmenn i den norske kirke.* Bibliotheca Norvegiæ Sacra. Bergen 1923.

Shetelig, H., *Norske museers historie,* Oslo 1944.

Skoie, H., *Norsk forskningspolitikk i etterkrigstiden.* Oslo 2005.

Slagstad, R., *De nasjonale strateger,* Oslo 1998.

Slettstrand, K., *"Trondheimsmiljøet" og tanken om et norsk universitet ca. 1760–1811. Ballade om et nasjonalt symbol eller ektefølt behov?* Masters thesis, Trondheim 2005.

Snow, C.P., *The two cultures and the scientific revolution,* New York 1961.

Snow C. P., *The Two Cultures.* Cambridge 1998.

Sontag, O., "Albrecht von Haller on Academies and the Advancement of Science: the case of Göttingen." *Annals of Science,* 32, 1975: 379–391.

Sprauten, K., *Byen ved festningen. Fra 1536 til 1814. Oslo bys historie.* Volume 2. Oslo 2000.

Stang, G., "Samlingenes vekst." In Nissen, H. and Aase, M. (eds): *Til Opplysning. Universitetsbiblioteket i Trondheim 1768–1993* Trondheim, 1993: 131. Also published as *DKNVS Skrifter* vol. 1, 1993.

Statutes. In: *Skrifter.* Volume 4. Kiøbenhavn 1768. n.p.

Storsveen, O.A., *Norsk patriotisme før 1814.* Oslo 1997.

Strøm, H., "Fortsættelse af Metorologiske Iagttagelser paa Søndmør for de Aaringer 1767 og 1768." *Nye Samling af det Kongelige Norske Videnskabers Selskabs Skrifter.* Volume 1. Kiøbenhavn 1784: 355–372.

Stubhaug, A., *Et foranskut lyn. Niels Henrik Abel og hans tid,* Oslo 1996.

Stubhaug, A. *"Helt skal jeg ikke dø." Conrad Nicolai Schwach, hans liv og erindringer,* Oslo 2002.

Støren, W.K., "Bibliotekets ledere," H. Nissen & M. Aase (eds.), *Til opplysning. Universitetsbiblioteket i Trondheim 1768–1993,* Trondheim 1993: 19–57.

Støren, W.K., ""Ein heimstad for ånd." Bibliotekets lokaler," H. Nissen & M. Aase, (eds.), *Til opplysning. Universitetsbiblioteket i Trondheim 1768–1993,* Trondheim 1993: 64–92.

Suhm, P.F., "Nærværende 18de Seculi Character." In: *Skrifter.* Volume 1. Kiøbenhavn 1761: 96–128.

Suhm, P.F., "Anmærkninger, over Verdens Almindelige Historie." In: *Skrifter.* Volume 1. Kiøbenhavn 1761: 203–235.

Suhm, P. F., *Kammerherre og Kongelig Historiographus Peter Friderich Suhms samlede Skrifter. Tiende Deel,* Kjøbenhavn, 1793.

Suhm, P. F., *Kammerherre og Kongelig Historiographus Peter Friderich Suhms samlede Skrifter. Femtende Deel,* Kjøbenhavn, 1798.

Supphellen, S., *Den politiske bisp. Bartholomeus Deichman i norsk historie 1713–1730.* Trondheim 1989.

Supphellen, S., "Frå Johan Ernst Gunnerus til Grethe Authén Blom. Kvinners tilgjenge til Det Kongelige Norske Videskabers Selskab." In S. Supphellen (ed.), *Kongsmenn og Krossmenn. Festskrift til Grethe Authén Blom. DKNVS Skrifter 1,* 1992. Trondheim 1992.

Supphellen, S., *Innvandrernes by. Trondheim bys historie 997–1997.* Volume 2. Oslo: 1997.

Supphellen, S., "'Rational Norwegian Patriotism' in the 1780s.," *Scandinavian Journal of History*, vol. 32, no. 4. 2007: 376–387.

Svendsen, P., "Schwach, Conrad Nicolai," NBL vol. XIII, Oslo 1958: 26–30.

Svestad A., *Oldsakenes orden*, Oslo 1996.

Sylow, L, "Abels studier og hans oppdagelser," *Festskrift ved hundreaarsjubilæet for Niels Henrik Abels fødsel*, Kristiania 1902.

Sørensen, Ø., *Norsk idéhistorie vol. 3. Kampen om Norges sjel*, Oslo 2001.

Sörlin, S., "Ordering the World for Europe: Science as Intelligence and Information As Seen from the Northern Periphery.," R. Mac Leod (ed.), *Nature and Empire: Science and the Colonial Enterprise*, Osiris: Yearbook for the History of Science, vol. 15, Chicago 2001: 51–69.

Sörlin, S., "Rituals and Resources of Natural History. The North and the Arctic in Swedish Scientific Nationalism." M.Bravo and S. Sörlin. *Narrating the Arctic. A Cultural History of Nordic Scientific Practices*. Canton 2002: 73–122.

Sörlin, S., and Fagerstedt, O., *Linné och hans apostlar*. Stockholm 2004.

Sætra, G., "Kristiansand som sentrum og periferi på 1700-tallet." In M.-B. Ohman Nielsen and S. Supphellen (eds.). *Johan Ernst Gunnerus—Samtid og vitenskaper*. Kristiansand 2005: 99–118.

Thrap, D., "Gunnerus." *Luthersk Ugeskrift*. Ny Række, nr. 1 and 2, 1890: 1–6.

Tranaas, M., *Kataloger og klassifikasjonssystemer ved det Kongelige Norske Videnskabers Selskabs Bibliotek 1768–1968*, Uppsala 1971.

Trigger, B. G., *A History of Archeological thought*, Cambridge 2006.

"Tvende Skrivelser fra Selskabets Præses Hans Høihed prinds Christian Friderich av 14de og 17de Dec. 1811 med et Kongebrev om en aarlig kongelig Gave til Selskabet," *Det Kongelige Norske Videnskabers Selskabs Skrifter i det 19de Aarhundrede*, vol. 1, Copenhagen 1817: 27–32.

Utheim, J., *Oversigt over det norske civile Lægevæsens historiske Udvikling og nuværende Ordning*. Oslo, 1901. (Bilag til den kgl. Lægekommissions Indstilling).

Vedi, S.F., "Det Kongelige Norske Videnskabers Selskabs bibliotek i ny bygning." In *Nordisk tidsskrift för bok- och biblioteksväsen* vol. 66 (1979): 44–48.

Vinje, A.O., *A Norseman's View of Britain and the British*, Edinburgh 1863.

Voss, J., "Akademien und Gelehrte Gesellschaften." In: H. Reinalter (ed.). *Aufklärungsgesellschaften*. Frankfurt am Main 1993: 19–38.

Wagner, P., "En disputashandling og dens følger."*Bibliotek for Læger*, vol. 184, no 2. 1992: 145–169.

Wagner, P., "Fra Kunstkammer til moderne museum." *Nordisk museologi*, no 2, 1994: 21–30.

Wale, A., *Universitet og høgskole. Den allmennvitenskaplige høgskolen 1984–1996*. Trondheim 1997.

Wale, A., *Nyhet, nytte, framskritt. Introduksjonen av lokal elektrisitetssystem 1877–1900*. Trondheim 2004.

Walton, S.J., *Ivar Aasens kropp*, Oslo 1996.

Wegeland, H., "Forsøg til en Besvarelse af det Spørgsmaal: Hvilke ere de endnu virkende Hindringer for Jordens hensiktsmessige Dyrkning i Norge, og hvorledes kunne disse hæves?," *Det Kongelige Norske Videnskabers Selskabs Skrifter i det 19de Aarhundrede* vol. 3, Trondheim 1843: 1–141.

Wergeland, N, "Mnemosyne." Et forøg paa at besvare den af det Kongl. Selskab for Norges Vel fremsatte Opgave om et Universitet i Norge," *Historisk-Philosophiske Samlinger* vol. 1 part 1–2, Christiania 1811: 1–264.

Wille, H.J., *Samling af Minde-Taler holdne i det Kongelige Norske Videnskabers Selskab over adskillige af dets afdøde Medlemmer*, Kjøbenhavn, 1805.

Wille, N., "Mikael Heggelund Foslie," *DKNVS Skrifter 1910*, Trondheim 1911: 1–18.

Wille, N., "Ingebrigt Hagen," *DKNVS Skrifter 1917*, Trondheim 1918: 1–13.

Wille, N., "Blytt, Matthias Numsen," NBL Vol. II, Oslo 1925: 51–52.

Worm, J., *Forsøg til et Lexikon over danske, norske og islandske lærde Mænd, som ved trykte Skrifter have gjort sig bekiendte, saavelsom andre Ustuderede som noget have skrevet, hvorudi deres Fødsel, betydeligste Levnets Omstændigheder og Død ved Aarstal kortelig erindres, og deres Skrifter, saavidt mueligt, fulstændig anføres.* 3 volumes. Helsingør, 1771.

Ytreberg, N., A., *Tromsø bys historie* vol. 1, Oslo 1946.

Zaunstöck, H., "Gelehrte Gesellschaften im Jahrhundert der Aufklärung. Strukturuntersuchungen zum mitteldeutschen Raum." In: D. Döring und K. Nowak. *Gelehrte Gesellschaften im mitteldeutschen Raum (1650–1820)*. Stuttgart 2002.

Økland, F., "Sars, Michael," NBL vol. XII, Oslo 1954: 255–260.

Øverland, O. A., *Illustreret Norges Historie*, Volume 5, Kristiania, 1891.

Øverland, O.A., *Det Kgl. Selskap for Norges Vels Historie gjennem hundre Aar*, Kristiania 1909.

Øverås, A., *Frederik Moltke Bugge. Kulturarbeid og kulturstrid i 1830–40-åra*, vol. 1–2, Oslo 1949.

Øverås, A., *Ivar Aasen og Frederik Molkte Bugge—Det Kgl. Norske Videnskabers Selskab. Eit minneskrift*, Oslo 1950.

Archival Material

Bispearkivet. Bispevisitationsprotokoller. Statsarkivet i Trondheim.

DKNVS Archive. This is the archive of the Society, placed in the Special Collection of the Gunnerus library-section of the University Library of NTNU, Trondheim. All references to material in the archive can be traced by using the catalogue: M. Aase, *Universitetsbiblioteket i Trondheim. Spesialsamlingene. Katalog 16: Det kongelige Norske Videnskabers Selskabs Arkiv. Registratur*, Trondheim 1994

Gunnerus, Johan Ernst. "Tale til prinsen og prinsessen av Hessen ved deres besøk i Trondheim."

Peter Collett. Dagbok på en reise i Norge 1773. Private ownership.

Catalogues

Catalogus Librorum arqve Rerum naturalium & artificialium. Niderosiæ 1779.

Fortegnelse over forhen Hojædle og Højærværdige Hr. Doct. Johan Ernst Gunnesi Naturalie-Samling. Trondhiem 1774.

Reference Works

Biographisch-Bibliographisches Kirchenlexicon, Band XIX (2001), http://www.bautz.de/bbkl/

DBL—Dansk biografisk leksikon (Danish biographical encyclopedia) København

NBL—Norsk biografisk leksikon (Norwegain Biographical Encyclopedia) 1.st edition: Kristiania/Oslo 1922–83, 2nd edition Oslo 1999–2005.

DKNVS *Skrifter*

DKNVS *Forhandlinger*

DKNVS *Årbøker*

DKNVS *Museet Årbøker*

Norske offentlige utredninger (Norwegian official reports)

Stortingsforhandlinger (parliamentary papers)

Interviews

Kjell Eimhjellen 05.20.2008

Yngve Espmark 02.05.2008

Turid Fredagsvik 03.22.2007

Per Christian Hemmer 06.05.2008

Karsten Jacobsen 11.08.2007

Jon Lamvik 11.15.2007

Olaf I. Rønning 03.15.2007

Gunnar Sundnes 11.08.2007

Steinar Supphellen 07.26.2008

Appendices

PREPARED BY MONICA AASE, LIBRARIAN

I

Publications of The Royal Norwegian Society of Sciences and Letters

1. SKRIFTER (TRANSACTIONS)

The Society's *Skrifter (Transactions)* was first published in 1761 under the title *Det Trondhiemske Selskabs Skrifter. Første Deel. Med Kobbere*. Kiøbenhavn 1761. (The Society obtained royal approbation in 1767 and changed its name to Det Kongelige Norske Videnskabers Selskab (The Royal Norwegian Society of Sciences and Letters).

The first article in volume 1 was written by bishop and founder of the Society, Johan Ernst Gunnerus. In the same volume we also find articles by Gunnerus' co-founders of the Society: the Danish historian Peter Fr. Suhm, and the principal of *Trondheim katedralskole* (Cathedral School), Gerhard Schøning.

The series *Skrifter* has been published for almost 250 consecutive years, and is thus one of the oldest running scientific publications in the world.

2. FORHANDLINGER / ÅRBOK (PROCEEDINGS)

The Society's *Forhandlinger (Proceedings)* was started in 1926 (the first volume was published in 1929) after the Society had been divided into one academia part and one museum part. The purpose of *Forhandlinger* was to report on the activities in the academia part throughout the year, i.e. minutes from joint meetings, class and board meetings, lectures and information given at joint meetings, speeches held in remembrance of deceased members, registers of members and statutes.

In 1984 the library and museum were integrated in the Norwegian University of Sciences and Technology (NTNU). New statutes were adopted, a new form of governing was introduced and a greater emphasis was placed on disseminating knowledge and research involvement. The title, *Forhandlinger*, was changed in 2004 to *Årbok* (Annual Report). This new series not only reports on matters relevant to the academia part of the Society, but on the activities of the entire Society (see Preface of *Årbok* 2004.)

3. MEDDELELSER (ANNOUNCEMENTS).

The first issue of the *Meddelelser* series was published in 2005. *Meddelelser* is a channel for information to members and other concerned groups, containing among other things statutes and instructions to the authors.

4. DKNVS INFO.

This is a small publication of 2 pages, which contains brief information to members of The Society. It is published twice a year.

5. PRINTED REGISTERS FOR *SKRIFTER* AND *FORHANDLINGER*.

Schmidt-Nielsen, Brynjulf. *Fortegnelse over Selskabets Skrifter 1760–1910. (Det Kongelige Norske Videnskabers Selskab.* Trondhjems museum.) Trondhjem 1912. 79 s.

Flo, Olav. *Det Kongelige Norske Videnskabers Selskab. Skrifter 1911–1925.—The Royal Norwegian Society of Sciences and Letters.* "Skrifter" 1911–1925. An index. Trondheim 1977. 20 s.

Ansteinsson, John. *Det Kongelige Norske Videnskabers Selskab. Forhandlinger og skrifter 1926–1936.—Acta et Scripta Regiae Societatis Scientiarum Norvegicae 1926–1936.* Tabula auctorum et index rerum. Trondheim 1937. 51 s.

Thalberg, Knut. *Det Kongelige Norske Videnskabers Selskab. Forhandlinger og Skrifter 1947–1956.—Acta et Scripta Regiae Societatis Scientiarum Norvegicae 1947–1956.* Tabula auctorum et index rerum. Trondheim 1963. 32 s.

Thalberg, Knut. *Det Kongelige Norske Videnskabers Selskab. Forhandlinger og Skrifter 1957–1966. Acta et Scripta Regiae Societatis Scientiarum Norvegicae 1957–1966.* Tabula auctorum et index rerum. Trondheim 1969. 29 s.

Thalberg, Knut. *Kongelige Norske Videnskabers Selskab. Forhandlinger og Skrifter 1967–1976. Acta et Scripta Regiae Societatis Scientiarum Norvegicae 1967–1976.* Tabula auctorum et index rerum. Trondheim 1981. 21 s. 2005. 47 s.

Aase, Monica. *Det Kongelige Norske Videnskabers Selskab. Skrifter og Forhandlinger. Indeks 1977–2001.* Trondheim 2005. (DKNVS' s Meddelelser. 1.)

6. OTHER PUBLICATIONS.

Occasionally, the Society has also appointed teams of scientists for doing special research, assignments or investigations. Their reports have been sponsored either by the Society alone, or by the Society together with other institutions.

7. WEB-ADRESSES.

The *Skrifter* are partly scanned and available in BIBSYS, where they are alphabetically registered under the name of the author and with the relevant web-address.

II

The Archives of The Royal Norwegian Society of Sciences and Letters

The Society's collected archives from 1760 to the present days fill more the 35 meters of bookshelves. The documents are stored at the Gunnerus Library that is a part of NTNU University Library. The archives are more or less complete. New material is continuously supplied from the Society.

The archive material is divided as follows: Series published by the Society (I), Protocols (II), Correspondence and circular letters (III), Archives of matters (IV), Applications for prize awards (V) and Accounts (VI). In addition, there are private documents concerning Johan Ernst Gunnerus, in III.

Registers to the entire archives, as well as for parts of them, have been published:

Aase, Monica. *Det Kongelige Norske Videnskabers Selskabs arkiv. Registratur.* Trondheim 1994. 43 s. (Universitetsbiblioteket i Trondheim, Spesialsamlingene. Katalog 16.)

Register to incoming letters 1760–1860:

Aase, Monica. *Det Kongelige Norske Videnskabers Selskab. Brevregistrant 1760–1860.* Trondheim 1991. 243 s. (Samme serie. Katalog 14.)

This register is continued in a database: www.ntnu.no/ub/spesialsamlingene
During the years 1772–1848 the Society awarded prizes to farmers for innovations within farming. There is a register for all applications:

Aase, Monica. *Premiesøknader til Det Kongelige Norske Videnskabers Selskab 1772–1848. Landbruk, husflid, småindustri og rovdyrjakt.* Trondheim 1988. 197 s. (Samme serie. Katalog 12.)

See also: www.ntnu.no/ub/spesialsamlingene

For the correspondence between bishop Johan Ernst Gunnerus and Carl von Linné, see: Amundsen, Leiv (utg.) *Brevveksling 1761–1772. Johan Ernst Gunnerus og Carl von Linné. Utg. av Leiv Amundsen, med bistand av Rolf Nordhagen og Erling Sivertsen.* Trondheim, Universitetsforlaget, 1976. XIII, 205 s. ill.

For Johan Ernst Gunnerus' correspondence, also letters that are to be found in other institutions than NTNU Library, see:

Dahl, Ove. *Biskop Gunnerus' virksomhet fornemmelig som botaniker tilligemed en oversigt over botanikens tilstand i Danmark og Norge indtil hans død.* Trondhjem 1892–1911. I: DKNVS Skrifter 1885–1907.

Index